Targum Neofiti 1:
Genesis

THE ARAMAIC BIBLE
• THE TARGUMS •

PROJECT DIRECTOR
Martin McNamara, M.S.C.

EDITORS
Kevin Cathcart • Michael Maher, M.S.C.
Martin McNamara, M.S.C.

EDITORIAL CONSULTANTS
Daniel J. Harrington, S.J. • Bernard Grossfeld

The Aramaic Bible

Volume 1A

Targum Neofiti 1: Genesis

Translated, with Apparatus and Notes

BY

Martin McNamara, M.S.C.

A Michael Glazier Book
THE LITURGICAL PRESS
Collegeville, Minnesota

About the Translator:

Martin McNamara, M.S.C., is Professor of Sacred Scripture at the Milltown Institute of Theology and Philosophy, Dublin. He has a licentiate in Theology from the Gregorian University, Rome, and a licentiate and doctorate in Sacred Scripture from the Biblical Institute, Rome. He acquired his initial interest in the Targums from his professor Fr. Stanislas Lyonnet, S.J., of the Biblical Institute, and from his own colleague Alejandro Díez Macho, who in 1956 identified the true nature of Codex Neofiti 1. His doctoral dissertation was entitled *The New Testament and the Palestinian Targum to the Pentateuch* (1966; reprint 1978). His other publications on the Targums and Judaism include *Targum and Testament* (1972); *Palestinian Judaism and the New Testament* (1983); *Intertestamental Literature* (1983). He has a Ph.D. in early Irish biblical exegesis and has also written on Hiberno-Latin biblical literature and on biblical apocrypha in the Irish Church.

First published in 1992 by The Liturgical Press, Collegeville, Minnesota 56321.

Library of Congress Cataloging-in-Publication Data

Bible. O.T. Genesis. English. McNamara. 1992.
    Targum Neofiti 1 : Genesis / translated, with apparatus and notes
by Martin McNamara.
      p.   cm. — (The Aramaic Bible : the Targums ; v. 1A)
    "A Michael Glazier book."
    Includes bibliographical references and index.
    ISBN 0-8146-5476-2 :
    1. Bible. O.T. Genesis. Aramaic.—Targum Yerushalmi–
–Translations into English. 2. Bible. O.T. Genesis. Aramaic.—
–Targum Yerushalmi—Criticism, Textual.. I. McNamara, Martin.
II. Title. III. Series: Bible. O.T. English. Aramaic Bible.
    1987 ; v. 1A.
    BS709.2.B5 1987 vol. 1A
  [BS1233]
  221.4′2 s—dc20
  [222′.11042]
                                    91-43157
                                       CIP

Logo design by Florence Bern.
Typography by Graphic Sciences Corporation, Cedar Rapids, Iowa.
Printed in the United States of America.

TABLE OF CONTENTS

Dedicated to
MICHAEL GLAZIER,
the resource behind the Aramaic Bible Series.

EDITORS' FOREWORD

While any translation of the Scriptures may in Hebrew be called a Targum, the word is used especially for a translation of a book of the Hebrew Bible into Aramaic. Before the Christian era Aramaic had in good part replaced Hebrew in Palestine as the vernacular of the Jews. It continued as their vernacular for centuries later and remained in part as the language of the schools after Aramaic itself had been replaced as the vernacular.

Rabbinic Judaism has transmitted Targums of all books of the Hebrew Canon, with the exception of Daniel and Ezra-Nehemiah, which are themselves partly in Aramaic. We also have a translation of the Samaritan Pentateuch into the dialect of Samaritan Aramaic. From the Qumran Library we have sections of a Targum of Job and fragments of a Targum of Leviticus, chapter 16, facts which indicate that the Bible was being translated in Aramaic in pre-Christian times.

Translations of books of the Hebrew Bible into Aramaic for liturgical purposes must have begun before the Christian era, even though none of the Targums transmitted to us by Rabbinic Judaism can be shown to be that old and though some of them are demonstrably compositions from later centuries.

In recent decades there has been increasing interest among scholars and a larger public in these Targums. A noticeable lacuna, however, has been the absence of a modern English translation of this body of writing. It is in marked contrast with most other bodies of Jewish literature for which there are good modern English translations, for instance the Apocrypha and Pseudepigrapha of the Old Testament, Josephus, Philo, the Mishnah, the Babylonian Talmud and Midrashic literature, and more recently the Tosefta and Palestinian Talmud.

It is hoped that this present series will provide some remedy for this state of affairs.

The aim of the series is to translate all the traditionally-known Targums, that is those transmitted by Rabbinic Judaism, into modern English idiom, while at the same time respecting the particular and peculiar nature of what these Aramaic translations were originally intended to be. A translator's task is never an easy one. It is rendered doubly difficult when the text to be rendered is itself a translation which is at times governed by an entire set of principles.

All the translations in this series have been specially commissioned. The translators have made use of what they reckon as the best printed editions of the Aramaic Targum in question or have themselves directly consulted the manuscripts.

The translation aims at giving a faithful rendering of the Aramaic. The introduction to each Targum contains the necessary background information on the particular work.

In general, each Targum translation is accompanied by an apparatus and notes. The former is concerned mainly with such items as the variant readings in the Aramaic texts, the relation of the English translation to the original, etc. The notes give what explanations the translator thinks necessary or useful for this series.

Not all the Targums here translated are of the same kind. Targums were translated at different times, and most probably for varying purposes, and have more than one interpretative approach to the Hebrew Bible. This diversity between the Targums themselves is reflected in the translation and in the manner in which the accompanying explanatory material is presented. However, a basic unity of presentation has been maintained. Targumic deviations from the Hebrew text, whether by interpretation or paraphrase, are indicated by italics.

A point that needs to be stressed with regard to this translation of the Targums is that by reason of the state of current targumic research, to a certain extent it must be regarded as a provisional one. Despite the progress made, especially in recent decades, much work still remains to be done in the field of targumic study. Not all the Targums are as yet available in critical editions. And with regard to those that have been critically edited from known manuscripts, in the case of the Targums of some books the variants between the manuscripts themselves are such as to give rise to the question whether they have all descended from a single common original.

Details regarding these points will be found in the various introductions and critical notes.

It is recognized that a series such as this will have a broad readership. The Targums constitute a valuable source of information for students of Jewish literature, particularly those concerned with the history of interpretation, and also for students of the New Testament, especially for those interested in its relationship to its Jewish origins. The Targums also concern members of the general public who have an interest in the Jewish interpretation of the Scriptures or in the Jewish background to the New Testament. For them the Targums should be both interesting and enlightening.

By their translations, introductions and critical notes the contributors to this series have rendered an immense service to the progress of targumic studies. It is hoped that the series, provisional though it may be, will bring significantly nearer the day when the definitive translation of the Targums can be made.

Kevin Cathcart   Martin McNamara, M.S.C.   Michael Maher, M.S.C.

PREFACE

In this, the first volume in number in the Aramaic Bible Series, full credit must be given to the publisher Michael Glazier, without whose initiative and resourcefulness this project would never have been begun. Not only did he take up with enthusiasm the suggestion put to him in 1980 to publish a translation of the Palestinian Targums of the Pentateuch, but he proposed that the entire corpus be translated and published with appropriate introductions, critical apparatuses, and notes. It was an immense undertaking. Let the volumes already published and the entire corpus stand as a monument to his dedication to the publication of scholarly works.

The original plan was to publish the entire corpus of Palestinian Targums (Neofiti, Neofiti glosses, Fragment Targums, Pseudo-Jonathan) in the first five volumes of this series—one volume for each of the books of the Pentateuch. It was also planned to have Neofiti, with its apparatus and notes, on pages facing the corresponding text and notes of Pseudo-Jonathan. Detailed examination of the midrashim common to both would be in the Pseudo-Jonathan section, with reference to this in the notes to Neofiti. Such a presentation of texts and notes proved too cumbersome from the publishing point of view, principally because the space required for each of the two blocks would not correspond. It was finally decided to present each of the two (Neofiti and Pseudo-Jonathan) separately, and further, to devote a volume to each for Genesis (Volumes 1A and 1B of this series).

The introduction first of all examines the witnesses to the Palestinian Targums and then goes on to concentrate mainly on matters relating to the translation presented by Codex Neofiti. I did not believe that this was the place for a general introduction to Targums as such.

The text of Neofiti had already been translated by Michael Maher and the present writer for the *editio princeps* under the editorship of Alejandro Díez Macho (1968). I have completely revised this translation for the present work.

In this translation, as in all volumes of this series, words in italics in the translation proper denote deviation in the Targum from the Hebrew Text.

This volume contains all the material of the Palestinian Targums of Genesis, with the exception of Pseudo-Jonathan. The Apparatus contains all the marginal variants in the manuscript of Codex Neofiti 1, apart from merely orthographical and grammatical ones. The significant variants of the other Palestinian Targum texts are also given.

When it is perceived (as for Gen 4:8; 15:17; 44:18; 49:1, for instance) that the other texts contain a recension worthy of reproduction in full, this is done. In such cases mere variants would fail to do justice to the text.

The notes to Neofiti concentrate on the features and peculiarities of Neofiti's text, with the minimum of reference required for an understanding of the midrash common to Neofiti and Pseudo-Jonathan. For fuller treatment the reader is constantly referred to the notes on this latter. This concentration on the peculiarities of Neofiti will be continued in the treatment of the other four books of the Pentateuch. From this it becomes clear that in good part, at least, Neofiti represents a unified approach to the understanding and translation of the Torah.

Acknowledging once again our indebtedness to Michael Glazier for the initiation of this series, I must also express gratitude to The Liturgical Press for having agreed so generously to continue it; to Mark Twomey, managing editor, for general supervision; and particularly to John Schneider, who took over the task of editing the volumes in this series and overseeing their publication. The quality of these volumes owes much to his exceptional editorial skills.

MARTIN MCNAMARA, M.S.C.

Galway, Ireland

ABBREVIATIONS

Abod. Zar.	Abodah Zarah
Ant.	Josephus, *Jewish Antiquities*
Arak.	Arakin
ARN A	*The Fathers According to Rabbi Nathan.* Trans. J. Goldin.
ARN B	*The Fathers According to Rabbi Nathan.* Trans. A. J. Saldarini.
b.	Babylonian Talmud
B	First *Biblia Rabbinica.* Venice: Bomberg, 1517–18.
B. Bat.	Baba Bathra
Bek.	Bekhoroth
Ber.	Berakhoth
B. Mez.	Baba Mezia
B. Qam.	Baba Qamma
CCL	Corpus Christianorum, Series Latina
CD	Cairo Damascus Document (Damascus Rule)
CTg (A,B,E, etc.)	Cairo Genizah (Pal.) Tg. Manuscript
De Abr.	Philo, *De Abraham*
Deut. R.	Deuteronomy Rabbah
Erub.	Erubin
Exod. R.	Exodus Rabbah
Frg. Tg(s).	Fragment Targum(s)
Gen. R.	Genesis Rabbah

Gitt.	Gittin
Hag.	Hagigah
Hor.	Horayoth
HT	Hebrew Text
Hul.	Hullin
j.	Jerusalem (Palestinian) Talmud
Ketub.	Ketuboth
L	Frg. Tg. Leipzig MS
LAB	Pseudo-Philo's *Liber Antiquitatum Biblicarum*
Lam. R.	Lamentations Rabbah
Leq. Tob	Midrash Leqaḥ Tob
Lev. R.	Leviticus Rabbah
LXX	Septuagint
m.	Mishnah
Mak.	Makkoth
Meg.	Megillah
Mid. Agg.	Midrash Aggadah
M. Qat.	Mo'ed Qatan
N	Nürnberg Frg. Tg. MS
NAB	New American Bible
NEB	New English Bible
Ned.	Nedarim
Nf	Neofiti
Nfi	Neofiti interlinear gloss
Nfmg	Neofiti marginal gloss
Nid.	Niddah
Num. R.	Numbers Rabbah
Ohol.	Oholoth
Onq.	Onqelos
P	Paris BN Frg. Tg. MS
Pal. Tg(s)	Palestinian Targum(s)
Pes.	Pesahim
Pesh	Peshitta

Ps.-J.	Targum Pseudo-Jonathan
PRE	*Pirqe de Rabbi Eliezer*
PRK	*Pesiqta de Rab Kahana*
Qidd	Qiddushin
1 QGenApoc	The Genesis Apocryphon of Qumran Cave 1
4QTgLev	Targum of Leviticus of Qumran Cave 4
11QPsᵃPlea	A Prayer in a Psalm Scroll from Cave 11 of Qumran
Rosh. Hash.	Rosh Ha-Shanah
RSV	Revised Standard Version
Sam	Samaritan Targum
Sanh.	Sanhedrin
Shabb.	Shabbath
Sifre Deut.	Sifre to Deuteronomy
Shebu.	Shebu'oth
t.	Tosefta
Ta'an.	Ta'anith
Tanh.	Midrash Tanhuma
Tanh. B.	Midrash Tanhuma, ed. S. Buber
Tg.	Targum
V	Vatican Library Frg. Tg. MS
Vulg.	Vulgate
Yeb.	Yebamoth
Zebah.	Zebahim

Journals and Series

AJSL	American Journal of Semitic Languages and Literature
BibThB	Biblical Theology Bulletin
CBQ	The Catholic Biblical Quarterly
EJ	Encyclopaedia Judaica
EphTheolLov	Ephemerides theologicae Lovanienses
HUCA	Hebrew Union College Annual
ITQ	The Irish Theological Quarterly
JAOS	Journal of the American Oriental Society

JBL	Journal of Biblical Literature
JE	Jewish Encyclopedia
JJS	Journal of Jewish Studies
JNES	Journal of Near Eastern Studies
JNSL	Journal of Northwest Semitic Languages
JPOS	Journal of the Palestine Oriental Society
JPS	Jewish Publication Society
JQR	Jewish Quarterly Review
JSJ	Journal for the Study of Judaism
JSS	Journal of Semitic Studies
JTS	Journal of Theological Studies
MGWJ	Monatsschrift für Geschichte und Wissenschaft des Judentums
PAAJR	Proceedings of the American Academy of Jewish Research
RB	Revue Biblique
R.E.	Pauly-Wissowa, *Realencyclopädie der classischen Altertumswissenschaft*
REJ	Revue des Études Juives
RHistPhRel	Revue d'histoire et de philosophie religieuses
RHPR	Revue d'histoire et de philosophie religieuses
RSO	Rivista degli Studi orientali
RSR	Recherches de Science Religieuse
SR	Studies in Religion/Sciences Religieuses
VT	Vetus Testamentum
VTSupp	Supplement to Vetus Testamentum
ZAW	Zeitschrift für die Alttestamentliche Wissenschaft
ZeitDeutPalVer	Zeitschrift der Deutschen Palästina-Vereins
ZNW	Zeitschrift für die Neutestamentliche Wissenschaft

INTRODUCTION

I. TITLE AND CONCEPT: "PALESTINIAN TARGUMS," "TARGUM YERUSHALMI"

By the term "Palestinian Targums of the Pentateuch" is meant those Aramaic translations of the Pentateuch other than the Targum of Onqelos that have been transmitted to us by rabbinic Judaism. The designation represents that now generally followed. A little over a decade ago the title commonly used was "The Palestinian Targum to the Pentateuch." The singular form was objected to, since there appeared to be a plurality of Aramaic translations in question, not just one. The ending ("to the Pentateuch") was objected to, being regarded as a Germanicism. The traditional Jewish designation for this Aramaic translation or body of literature was *Targum Yerushalmi* (more rarely *Targum Erez Israel*), "The Yerushalmi (Jerusalem or Palestinian) Targum."

II. HISTORY OF THE TERM AND OF RESEARCH IN THE FIELD

The designation "Palestinian" or "Yerushalmi" sets off this particular Aramaic translation (or translations) against some other known Targum. The Targum in question can only be Onqelos, the official traditional Jewish Targum of Babylonian Jewry, and of Western Jewry as well from the ninth century or so onward. It was possibly at this time that the designation originated. In the ninth century, in a reply by the Jewish religious leader Gaon Sar Shalom, Onqelos is named as the author of the "official" Targum of the Pentateuch, and mention is made of other unnamed Targums regarded by him as less holy than Onqelos.[1] These are presumably Targums of the Pentateuch, those later called "Palestinian" or "Yerushalmi." The designation "Targum Yerushalmi" for this or these Aramaic renderings of the Pentateuch is found in the first half of the eleventh century in a reply to a query on the matter by Rabbi Hai Gaon (about 1038), and prob-

---

[1]Response found in *Sha'arê teshubôt*, no. 330, p. 29 of the Leipzig edition of the Gaonic responses; the Hebrew text in A. Berliner, *Onkelos*, II (Berlin, 1884), p. 172, n. 2; in German translation in Dalman, *Grammatik* (1927), p. 12, n. 2.

ably to Rabbi Jacob ben Nissim, head of the Jewish community of Kirwan in Africa.[2] The relevant part of the reply is as follows:[3]

> And regarding what you have asked about the Targum of Palestine (*Targum Yerushalmi*): by whom was it composed, and the explanations that exist in it on matters of halakoth [?;*qtnwt*, lit.: "small items"] and haggadoth, why are these added to it?
>
> We do not know who composed the Targum of Palestine (*Targum Yerushalmi*); in fact we do not even know the Targum itself and we have heard speak of it but little. But if they [i.e., the communities of Palestinian origin] possess a tradition that it was recited in the congregation from the days of the former sages such as R. Ammi and R. Asa and R. El'ai and R. Abba and R. Hananiah, the later (sages) who lived in the days of R. Asa, it is to be considered just as our Targum [i.e., Onqelos], as otherwise it would not have been recited before these princes (lit.: "columns of the world")....

These Geonim were writing from Babylon, the latter to a community believing that the Targum Yerushalmi was that used in Palestine in the fourth century by the well-known named rabbis. References to this Palestinian Targum become more frequent in writings of Western Jewry from about 1100 onward. It is referred to by Rabbi Juda ben Barzillai[4] (of Barcelona) about 1100 under the name "Targum of Palestine" (*Targum shel Erez Israel*), in numerous citations in the *Aruk* of Rabbi Nathan ben Yehiel of Rome (died 1106) under the title *Targum Yerushalmi*,[5] and likewise in citations from then on until the noted Targumic dictionary, the *Meturgeman* of Elias Levita,[6] in the mid-sixteenth century (in 1541).

The advent of printing brought early editions of Targumic material. In 1517 Felix Pratensis, a Jewish convert to Christianity, published a manuscript with portions of Targum Yerushalmi, a second edition of which was printed in 1527. This continued to be reproduced in later editions of the rabbinic Bibles, and is that now known as the Fragment Targum. Mention is made in the works of the fourteenth-century Italian kabalistic writer Menahem Recanati of a paraphrase (Targum) of the Pentateuch by Jonathan ben Uzziel, the reputed author of the Targum of the Prophets. It was apparently little known. Writing about 1540, Elias Levita says that he had heard of this work but had never seen it.[7] Writing shortly after Elias, the Italian writer Asaria de Rossi (1573–75) says that he had seen two identical copies of this paraphrase of the Pentateuch, both beginning with the words *min 'awla bera' h´*, and one bearing the title "The Targum of Jonathan ben Uzziel."[8] It is now recognized that this title, with its reference

---

[2]In Harkavy's collection of Gaonic responses, *Teshubot ha-Geonim*, 124f.; Berliner, op. cit., 57f.; see also M. McNamara, 1966A, 57f.

[3]Hebrew text in Berliner, op. cit., 173–175. Berliner takes *qtnwt* as "halakoth"; M. Ginsburger (*REJ* 42 [1901] 234), however, as smaller midrashim, such as PRE.

[4]See Dalman, 30; McNamara, 1966A, 59.

[5]*Aruk* citations in *Aruch Completum*, ed. A. Kohut (Vienna, 1878ff.); with Additamenta, ed. Krauss (Vienna, 1937). Kohut worked with inferior MSS; see below, p. 11, and n. 49.

[6]On the *Meturgeman*, see below, p. 12, and n. 55.

[7]*Meturgeman*, ed. Isny (1541); see below p. 12.

[8]In *Me'or 'enaim*, ed. Vilna, 127.

to Jonathan (in Hebrew: Yehonathan) is due to an erroneous expansion of T"Y, intended to express "Targum Yerushalmi." This form of the Palestinian Targum tradition (beginning with the words *min 'awla bera'*) is now known as "The Targum of Pseudo-Jonathan." The first printed edition of this was made already in 1591 from a MS no longer known. Another MS of the work is in the British Library, MS Add. 27031, said to be in a sixteenth-century Italian hand. It was first published in 1903.[9] Both Pseudo-Jonathan and the Fragment Targums were published in the Walton London Polyglot (1653–57) with Latin translations, extending their usefulness for scholars.[10]

A significant advance in this branch of study was made in 1930 with the publication by Paul Kahle of fragments of six manuscripts of the Palestinian Targum tradition from the Genizah of Old Cairo, the earliest of which he dated to the late seventh or early eighth century.[11] All these texts, it should be remembered, contained only portions of the true Palestinian Targum. A major advance was made when Professor José María Millás Vallicrosa and Alejandro Díez Macho came upon a new manuscript in the Vatican Library in 1949 which A. Díez Macho identified as a copy of the entire Palestinian Targum of the Pentateuch in 1956.

New interest in Palestinian Judaism and in Palestinian Aramaic of the New Testament period was engendered by the finding of the Dead Sea Scrolls from 1947 onward. The growth of interest in the Palestinian Targum, and in Palestinian Aramaic of the New Testament period, from the early sixties to the present day has been phenomenal. Interest in the Palestinian Targum tradition was helped in no small way by the contribution it was believed it could make to an understanding of the New Testament message, especially the Gospels. Paul Kahle and a number of scholars after him believed that the Aramaic of the Palestinian Targum represented the spoken Aramaic of Palestine in the New Testament era.[12] Both contentions were soon to be challenged—that of the nature of the Aramaic of the Targums by students of the history of Aramaic and of Qumran Aramaic in particular. These scholars regarded Palestinian Targumic Aramaic as at best post-200 c.e., and most probably of the fourth-fifth centuries and contemporary with that of the Palestinian Talmuds and Midrashim.[13] The dating of the Palestinian Targums and of the tradition they enshrine was also called into question, and consequently the very legitimacy of their use in New Testament studies.

The complexity of the situation was being highlighted, including the very diversity between the different manuscripts of the Palestinian Targum tradition. Scholars now began speaking of the Palestinian Targums (in the plural) of the Pentateuch.[14] In the seventies and eighties, research (particularly at the doctoral dissertation level) and publications continued apace on various aspects of the Palestinian Targum tradition.

---

[9] M. Ginsburger, *Pseudo-Jonathan nach der Londiner Handschrift (Brit. Mus. Add. 27031))* (Berlin, 1903).

[10] *Biblia Sacra Polyglotta* (London, 1653–57), vol. 4, rpt. Graz, 1964.

[11] P. Kahle, *Das palästinische Pentateuchtargum. Masoreten des Westens,* II (Stuttgart, 1930) 1*–13; 1–65.

[12] See below, p. 14.

[13] See below, pp. 14–16.

[14] See, for instance, the objections raised to the singular form and concept by J. Fitzmyer in his reviews of books bearing on the subject in *CBQ* 30 (1968), 417–28, at 420, and in *ThS* 29 (1968) 322–26, at 323.

Grammars of the different manuscripts were produced and the relation of the tradition to Jewish halakah and haggadah studied.[15] The manuscript situation continues to be explored, and critical editions of the texts are being made. In a sense, we stand at the end of one period of intense exploration and at the beginning of a new era of the study of the Palestinian Targum tradition, one in which a new assessment of the situation is called for.

III. MANUSCRIPTS OF THE PALESTINIAN TARGUMS

1. The Targum of Pseudo-Jonathan

As already mentioned, the Italian Jewish writer Asaria de Rossi noted in his work *Me'or 'Enayim* (1573–75) that he had seen two complete and identical copies of a work that can only have been the Targum of Pseudo-Jonathan.[16] Only a single manuscript of the *Targum of Pseudo-Jonathan* (sometimes referred to as *TJI*, i.e., Targum of Jerusalem I) is now known—BL Additional 27031,[17] written, it is stated, in a sixteenth-century Italian hand. This particular tradition is so distinct within the Palestinian Targum tradition that it merits examination apart. This is carried out with regard to the translation, notes, and introduction in this series by Michael Maher and Ernest G. Clarke. What is said here, outside this special paragraph, about the Palestinian Targum does not take into consideration the Pseudo-Jonathan tradition, even though what is said of the Palestinian Targum tradition in general may well hold good for it.

2. The Fragment Targums

The Palestinian Targum tradition .has been known to us since the sixteenth century through single words and briefer and longer paraphrases transmitted in various manuscripts. These texts are obviously only extracts taken from larger Targum manuscripts, and for this reason they are referred to as "Fragment Targums." The paraphrase in these fragments is not always the same or to the same words or verses, and for this reason these are now referred to as "Fragmentary Targums." The known manuscripts of these Fragmentary Targums are as follows:

i) *Paris, Bibliothèque Nationale hébr. 110*, folios 1–16 (=P); written in an unvocalized fifteenth-century Spanish cursive script.

ii) *Vatican, Ebr. 440*, folios 198–227 (=V); the end of a much larger MS (Vatican Ebr. 439–440), containing the entire Pentateuch with Tg. Onqelos, the Five Megilloth, Job, the Haftarot, and the Book of Jeremiah; written in a thirteenth-century square Ashkenazic hand and vocalized in a full Tiberian system.

---

[15]For details see below, pp. 14–16.
[16]See n. 8 above.
[17]For edition see n. 8 above.

iii) *Nürnberg, Stadtbibliothek Solger 2.2o*, folios 119–147 (=N); a thirteenth-century triple-column MS, written in a square Ashkenazic script with Tiberian vocalization. The *editio princeps* of the Frg. Tg. in the *Biblia Rabbinica* of 1517–18 was based on this Nürnberg MS and its glosses (N and Ngl).

iv) *Leipzig, Universität B.H.*, folio 1 (=L); a thirteenth/fourteenth-century Ashkenazic MS of the Pentateuch, Haftarot, Five Megilloth, etc. The layout of the pages resembles that of certain printed rabbinic Bibles in which the Hebrew text occupies the central position, flanked by a column of Onqelos and another of the commentary of Rashi. The Frg. Tg. is scattered throughout this rabbinic-type Bible in such a disorganized manner that it would seem to imply that the scribe had originally planned not to include it at all. Some of the short gloss-type passages are situated in spaces or indentations in the Onqelos column.

v) *New York, Jewish Theological Seminary (Lutzki) 605, (E.N. Adler 2587)*, folios 6, 7 (=J); probably thirteenth century;

vi) *Moscow, Günzberg 3* (copy of MS Nürnberg);

vii) *Sassoon 264*, folios 225–267, copied from the second *Biblia Rabbinica* (Venice: Bomberg, 1524–25).

The tradition in these texts is a relatively unified one, despite the differences between the Paris MS and the others, and the fact that the extant fragments do not always cover the same section of the biblical text. Fragment Targums of quite a different tradition have come down to us in two Genizah MSS as follows:

viii) *British Library Or 10794* (Gaster Collection), (Br) with Deut. 1:1–5:9) and

ix) *Cambridge University Library, T-S AS 72, 75, 76, 77*, (DD), edited, together with the preceding text, by M. Klein with other Genizah material[18] (but was already being studied by Dr. Julia A. Foster), with the text of Deut. 23:15–28:5; 32:35–33:9.

The importance of the Genizah evidence is that it shows that the Fragment Targum tradition was more widespread than scholars had suspected. It broadens our base for discussing the origins of this form of transmission.

Michael Klein[19] has made a deep study of the Fragment Targums tradition and has reduced the major texts to two families: P on the one hand and VNL on the other. Remnants of other distinct families are also J and Br. and DD. Br and DD are actually Cairo Genizah fragments and represent, as just noted, distinct forms of Fragment Targums.

Klein notes that the most enigmatic of questions concerning the Fragment Targums is that of their *raison d'être*.[20] Although a number of theories have been put forward in the last century and in this one, a satisfactory solution has not been found. One view has regarded these Frg. Tgs. as variants to Ps.-J., another as variants to Onq. We may note that the content in general is of two kinds—longer midrashim and single-word variants. The latter indicates a lexical interest in variants, and many of these single words are of the kind we find in Targum lexica (the *Aruk*, Levita's *Meturgeman*). Such con-

---

[18]M. L. Klein, 1986, 330–333; 338–341.

[19]M. L. Klein, "The Extant Sources of the Fragmentary Targum to the Pentateuch," *HUCA* 46 (1975) 115–137; idem, 1980.

[20]M. L. Klein, 1980, I, 12.

tents have much in common with the glosses of Neofiti and may have had a similar origin, which is probably the desire in preserving variant readings. A recognized feature of all the Pentateuch Targums is their synagogal-liturgical nature, and it may be that the Frg. Tgs. were also used in the synagogue liturgy as supplementary or alternate material to the base Targum being used.[21] P and J in particular display a number of features which indicate that they belong to a festival-liturgical recension, features which for the most part are missing in VNL and Br.[22]

3. Genizah Manuscripts of the Palestinian Targums

In 1930, as noted above, Paul Kahle published fragments of six Genizah manuscripts of the Palestinian Targums of the Pentateuch.[23] The Genizah fragments are found in various libraries around the world, but principally in the Cambridge University Library (Taylor-Schechter Collection), the Oxford Bodleian Library, the Leningrad Saltykov-Schedrin Library (Antonin Collection), and in the Jewish Theological Seminary of New York (the E. N. Adler Collection). They have recently been thoroughly examined by Michael Klein. In 1986, in *Genizah Manuscripts of Palestinian Targum to the Pentateuch*,[24] he published a collection of fragments from thirty-eight distinct Genizah manuscripts relating to the Palestinian Targum of the Pentateuch. These texts fall into five general categories, as follows:[25]

a) Targum proper in the order of the Bible; (b) festival-liturgical collections of synagogue readings for holy days and special Sabbaths; (c) fragment Targums, or collections of selected phrases and passages; (d) Targumic tosafoth, or additional expansive passages to the more literal Onqelos, and (e) introductory Targumic poems, recited before or during the Torah reading in the synagogue. Kahle had given the sigla A to F to six of these. Klein retains Kahle's sigla and assigns new ones in the same tradition to the others. For brevity's sake in what immediately follows, I shall refer to the sigla. I will first give a few words on each of these categories.

a) *Palestinian Targum proper*: MSS, A, B, C, D, E, H, Z; LL; NN. B, C, D are in alternating Hebrew, verse by verse; A, E, H, Z with merely Hebrew *lemmata* at beginning of all (or most) verses. B, C, E, H(?) and Z are confined to the book of Genesis; all fragments of A are from Exodus, while D, as preserved, is from Genesis, Exodus and Deuteronomy. We cannot say whether some or all of the MSS originally contained all five books of the Pentateuch.

b) *Festival-liturgical collections*: MSS, AA, BB, F, F2, HH, J, S(?), U.W(?) Y. These are booklets containing the synagogal Torah readings for festivals and for special Sabbaths preceding Festivals. This form of compilation was already known to scholars before the Genizah finds. The Cairo manuscripts present important new information. The various collections differ in content as well as in the type of readings they contain.

---

[21]Ibid., 19.
[22]Ibid., 19–24.
[23]See n. 11 above.
[24]See n. 18 above.
[25]See op. cit., xxii–29.

c) *Fragment Targums*: MSS Br (i.e., British Library Or 10794 [Gaster Collection] with Deut 1:1–5:9) and DD (i.e., Cambridge University Library, T-S AS 72, 75, 76, 77, with Deut 23:15–28:5; 32:35–33:9) already noted above under "Fragment Targum."

d) *Targumic Tosafoth*: MSS, CC, EE, FF, I, K, M, Q, R, RR.

e) *Introductory poems*: MSS, G, GG, HH, JJ, KK, MM, PP, T. Paul Kahle included MS G, with its expansion of Exod 15, in his 1930 edition of Genizah material. The present collection adds considerably to our knowledge of these expansions, which are based on the Palestinian Targum tradition.

This Genizah material in general greatly enlarges our knowledge of the Palestinian Targum tradition, taking us beyond the manuscripts from the thirteenth to the sixteenth centuries already known to a far earlier age, at least with regard to the oldest of the manuscripts. These texts also help us to bridge the gap between the earliest manuscripts and the thirteenth century. P. Kahle dated the manuscript fragments published by him as follows: MS A, late seventh or early eighth century; MS E, ca. 750–800; MSS B, C, and D, the latter half of the ninth century; MSS F and G, the tenth or eleventh century.[26] Since Genizah manuscripts contain no reference to any date or to known scribes, we must rely totally on palaeography, codicology, and on the opinion of experts for assigning a date to them, and even then one which can only be approximate. Professor Malachi Beit Arié has assigned dates as follows for the manuscripts published by Michael Klein:[27]

Very early (eighth/ninth century or earlier): A (parchment).

Early (ninth/tenth to mid-eleventh century): E (parchment), T (parchment), W (?; parchment), Y (?; even though written on paper), AA (parchment), DD (paper), HH (parchment), KK (parchment).

Ca. 1000 C.E.: B (parchment), C (Eastern; parchment), D (parchment).

Early/middle: F (parchment), CC (parchment).

Middle (mid-eleventh to late fourteenth century): MM (late eleventh century; paper), Br (paper), F2 (parchment), G (parchment), H (paper), J (paper), K (paper), M (European; parchment), Q (paper), R (paper), S (paper), X (paper), Z (paper), BB (paper), EE (paper), FF (paper), GG (paper), JJ (paper), LL (paper), MM (late eleventh century; paper), NN (paper), PP (paper), RR (paper).

Middle/late: I (after thirteenth century; paper).

Thirteenth-fourteenth century: U (Spanish; parchment).

In this dating, the Genizah material spans the eighth century, if not earlier, up to the late fourteenth, a period of six centuries. It thus takes us right up to the period that has given us the earliest Fragment Targum manuscripts.

4. Codex Neofiti 1

Codex Neofiti 1 of the Vatican Library is item number 1 in a lot of MSS that came to the Vatican Library from the Pia Domus Neophytorum in Rome. In fact, the codex bears the seal of this college on its title page, together with the name of Ludovicus

---

[26]Kahle, op. cit. (n. 11 above), 2*–3*; on reservations about Kahle's dating, see M. McNamara, 1972, p. 83, n. 21.
[27]Klein, 1986, I, xxxviif.

Canonicus Schüller, the last rector of the Domus. In 1543 Paul III founded a Domus Catechumenorum in Rome for converts from Judaism, and in 1577 Gregory XIII founded there the Pia Domus Neophytorum or, to give it its original title, the Collegium Ecclesiasticum Adolescentium Neophytorum. This was a genuine ecclesiastical college with power to grant academic degrees. Later, at the request of Cardinal Antonio Barberini, protector both of the house and college, Urban VIII, in August 1634, authorized the transfer of both to a new location in Rome, and the libraries of both were probably then united. Codex Neofiti 1 belonged to the original Collegium.[28] The last rector entered office in 1886, and during his tenure its books and manuscripts were sold to the Vatican Library.[29] The archives of the Pia Domus are now in the Vicariate of Rome and in some other Roman libraries.[30]

The codex itself was catalogued in the Vatican Library as Onqelos. Its existence was brought to the attention of Alejandro Díez Macho in 1949, who identified it for what it is—a complete copy of the Palestinian Targum of the Pentateuch—in 1956.[31]

The colophon to the MS, at the end of Deuteronomy, tells us that the transcription was completed at Rome for Maestro Egidio (written as *'yydyw*) "in the glorious (*hnhdr*) month of Adar." In keeping with an accepted Jewish practice, the date of composition is to be found in the numerical value of the Hebrew letters *h, n, h, d, r*, i.e., 5 + 50 + 5 + 4 + 200. This gives us 264, that is, the year 5264 of Jewish chronology, which corresponds to 1504 c.e.[32]

The Maestro Egidio for whom the work was written was most probably the noted humanist Giles (Egidio) of Viterbo (1469–1532), master general of the Augustinian Order between 1505 and 1517. He had a keen interest in Judaism, particularly in Kabbala, and from 1517 to 1527 had with him in Rome the Jewish scholar Elias Levita, a specialist in the Targums, who later (1542) compiled and published his noted Targumic lexicon, the *Meturgeman*.[33] It does not appear that Elias, however, had any part in the transcription of Neofiti or that he later knew of it. He does not appear to have used it for his *Meturgeman*. Furthermore, the glosses of Neofiti seem to draw on Pseudo-Jonathan, a work which Elias tells us he had heard of but had not seen.[34] Codex Neofiti 1 was apparently donated to the Pia Domus Neophytorum by one Ugo Boncampagni in 1602.[35] We know that in that year he gave eighty-two works to the Domus, among them

---

[28]On this entire question see R. Le Déaut, "Jalons pour une histoire d'un manuscrit du Targum Palestinien (Neofiti 1)," *Biblica* 48 (1967) 509–533, esp. 515f.

[29]Le Déaut, loc. cit., 526f.

[30]Le Déaut, loc. cit., 509.

[31]For accounts of the discovery and of codex itself, see A. Díez Macho, "The Palestinian Targum," in *Christian News from Israel* 13 (1962) 19–25; (also in the French edition, *Nouvelles chrétiennes d'Israël* 13 [1962] 20–25); idem, 1960, 222–245; idem, "Magister-Minister," in *Recent Progress in Biblical Scholarship*, ed. Marcel P. Hornik (Oxford, 1961) 13–53; idem, in greater detail in the *editio princeps* of the MS: *Neophyti 1. Targum palestinense. Ms de la Biblioteca Vaticana*, I: Genesis (Madrid-Barcelona, 1968) 19*–136*.

[32]On the colophon see Díez Macho, *Neophyti 1*, I, with 51*ff., discussion.

[33]A summary of Egidio's activities may be found in Díez Macho, *Neophyti 1*, I, 52*; see further Giuseppe Signorelli, *Il Cardinale Egidio da Viterbo, agostiniano, umanista, reformatore*, Biblioteca Agostiniana 16 (Florence, 1929); F. X. Martin, *The Problem of Egidio da Viterbo: A Historiographical Survey* (Louvain, 1960).

[34]On Levita, the *Meturgeman*, and Neofiti 1, see below, p. 12, and n. 56.

[35]See. R. Le Déaut, *loc. cit.* (n. 28 above), 516–518; 528–533.

two Targum texts. The first (no. 20 of the list), entitled *fogli scritti a mano dove vi è el targumio hieroslomi*, was probably a text of the Fragment Targum. The second (no. 39 of the list) was *Aparafrasi (= Una parafrasi) Caldea sopra al Pentateuco scritta a mano in carta pecora*, i.e., "A Chaldaic (Aramaic) paraphrase on the Pentateuch written by hand on sheepskin"—undoubtedly Codex Neofiti 1. Neofiti 1 and other works were bequeathed to Ugo by the renowned convert Rabbi Andrea de Monte in his will dated September 19, 1587. (He died two days later.) De Monte had been a professor at the Collegium Neophytorum and is known from other documents to have acted as official ecclesiastical censor of Jewish books. He saw anti-Christian polemic in such terms as "idols," "idolaters," etc. The censorship of precisely such words in Neofiti 1 is undoubtedly his work.[36] We can presume from this evidence that on its completion for Giles of Viterbo in 1504, the manuscript passed into his hands for censorship, and then to Ugo and the Pia Domus Neophytorum, and finally the Vatican Library.

Codex Neofiti 1 was transcribed by three chief scribes.[37] It contains the entire text of the Pentateuch, apart from about thirty verses omitted for various reasons. As stated, certain passages have been censored and in part or in whole erased. Each verse is preceded by the Hebrew *lemma*, the opening words of the verse. The text is divided into liturgical sections which, with two exceptions (Num 20:13-14; Deut 4:24-25), correspond to the *sedarim* of the Palestinian three-year cycle of readings.

A notable feature of Codex Neofiti 1 is the numerous marginal glosses (in this edition noted as Nfmg) and the occasional interlinear glosses (Nfi) it contains.[38] The indications are that all these are drawn from genuine Targum texts (whether complete or fragmentary) available to the annotators in the early sixteenth century, some of which are apparently now lost. These glosses were written by ten different hands or so, some of them identical with those of the chief scribes. The multiplicity of hands is not significant for the glosses: analysis indicates that the Targum text being excerpted from did not necessarily change with the scribe.[39] In the present edition an attempt is made to identify each of these glosses, and the results are indicated in the Apparatus. Oftentimes they agree with VNL or P, sometimes with Ps.-J. They also agree on occasion with readings of the Genizah MSS A, B, C, D. There is an altogether peculiar agreement between the glosses and the Cairo Genizah MS E,[40] unfortunately preserved only for Gen 6:18–7:15; 9:5-23; 28:17–29:17; 31:16–39:10; 41:6-26; 43:30–44:5. We shall return to the significance of all this evidence later.[41]

Although among the latest of Palestinian Targum texts to be transcribed, there is abundant evidence indicating that in Neofiti we have preserved a very good text of the Palestinian Targum, one which has been faithfully transmitted.[42]

[36]Le Déaut, *loc. cit.*, 521–523.

[37]See Díez Macho, *Neophyti 1*, I, 23*.

[38]Ibid., 24*–28*.

[39]This is particularly obvious in the glosses to Nf Gen 28:17–31:34, which are identical with the text of CTg E, although there are no less than six hands for the glosses: I, J, K, A, K, J.

[40]The correspondences also noted by Klein, 1986, II, in notes to text of E.

[41]Below, XI, 2, pp. 44–45.

[42]See below, X, XI, pp. 41–45.

5. *Targumic Tosafoth*[43]

The Targumic Tosafoth from the Cairo Genizah have been noted above. Such Tosafoth are also found outside of the Genizah. Targumic Tosafoth are expansive passages of haggadic midrash which have their source in the Palestinian Targum tradition. Some of them are preserved inserted into Onqelos manuscripts, and others have been brought together separately in booklets which probably served as supplements to Onq. They thus present evidence for the Pal. Tg. Unlike the Frg. Tgs., the Tosafoth contain expansions only and their language tends to be that of Onq., or at least in the process of being transformed from Galilean Aramaic to that of Onq.

6. *Introductory Targumic poems*[44]

Such poems from the Cairo Genizah have been noted above. These poems formed part of the synagogue liturgy before the Torah reading for festivals and special Sabbaths. They are Targumic in language, and the beginnings of the lines or strophes are often in the form of an alphabetic acrostic. They have been well known for over a century. The best known of these is that beginning *'zyl mšh*, "Go down Moses" (cf. Exod 14:16-25), the oldest text of which is in a fourth-fifth century papyrus from Egypt. Such poems are usually in separate collections but sometimes are inserted into Targumic texts in their respective places.

IV. INDIRECT TRANSMISSION: PALESTINIAN TARGUM CITATIONS

We have instanced above the main sources for our knowledge of the Palestinian Pentateuch Targums, from about 700 to 1550. Together with this we can trace the history of these Palestinian Targums through citations, using a method employed in biblical textual criticism.

It is a relatively simple matter to identify these citations from about the eleventh century onward, since they are given under the name *Targum Yerushalmi* or "The Palestinian Targum" (*Targum shel Erez Israel*). It is less easy when there are no such identifications, especially for the earlier period. However, if in a Hebrew context we find biblical citations in Aramaic which coincide with those of the Palestinian Targums, we are justified in assuming that these Targums actually existed at that time and that the citations are from them. A certain difficulty exists with regard to the ascription of such Aramaic texts to a given Rabbi, to whom we can ascribe a date, since such ascriptions can be false.

In *Genesis Rabba* 31, 8 we have an Aramaic rendering of a portion Gen 6:14 which coincides with that of the Palestinian Targums ascribed to R. Nathan (ca. 170 c.e.), and

---

[43]On the Tosafoth see A. Epstein, "Tosefta du Targoum Yerouschalmi," *REJ* 30 (1895) 44–51, with edition of texts; M. Ginsburger, "Zusätzthargumim," in *Das Fragmentumthargum*, with edition of texts (Berlin, 1899) 71–74; A. Sperber, *The Bible in Aramaic* I (Leiden, 1959) xvi–xviii, with edition of texts, pp. 354–357; M. L. Klein, "Targumic Toseftot from the Cairo Genizah," in *Salvación en la Palabra* (1986) 409–418; idem, 1986, I, xxvif.

[44]On these see M. L. Klein, 1986, xxviiif., with bibliography; idem, 1980, I, 19–23.

in *Genesis Rabba*, 70, 16 another similar one of Gen 29:17 ascribed to R. Johanan (probably from ca. 250 C.E.). And there are others besides from the earlier period.[45] Rabbi Menahem Kasher devotes chapter 17 of volume 24 of his major work, *Torah Shelemah*, to a study of the relationship between Neofiti 1 and *Genesis Rabba*.[46] He brings together fifty instances of explanations of words or of haggadoth in *Genesis Rabba* whose source he believes to be a Palestinian Targum of the kind preserved in Neofiti 1. It is very useful to collect such texts from early rabbinical sources. However, with regard to the tradition of *Genesis Rabba*, we have to bear in mind that what is in question is rather a general Jewish and rabbinic tradition, preserved both in rabbinic expository or homiletic texts such as *Genesis Rabba* and in the Palestinian Targums. Given this proviso, however, the evidence of Aramaic translations which coincide with renderings found in Palestinian Targums must be given serious consideration as witnesses for the early existence of this Aramaic version.

The evidence for citations becomes clearer from 1100 onward. We have already mentioned the *Aruk*, the dictionary compiled by R. Nathan ben Yeḥiel of Rome (died 1106). M. Kasher has noted that on 250 occasions or so the *Aruk* cites words in Neofiti not found in Ps.-J. or the Fragment Targum.[47] Solomon Speier has made a detailed study of the relationship of the *Aruk* to Neofiti 1. He lists 120 citations under the name Targum Yerushalmi found in the *Aruk*, and elsewhere attested only in Neofiti 1.[48] The number is probably greater than this; one of the defects of Speier's study is that he uses the index of Kohut's edition of the *Aruk*, in which some citations are missing.[49] This agreement of the *Aruk* with Neofiti is really impressive and leads us to the conclusion that Rabbi Nathan used a Palestinian Targum practically identical with that in Neofiti 1. This need not surprise us. Neofiti 1 was copied in Rome, where R. Nathan had lived and compiled his work.

Another work that has recently been shown to carry many Palestinian Targum citations and to be close to Neofiti 1 is *Midrash Bereshit Zuṭa*.[50] Its author was Rabbi Shemuel ben Nissin Masnut (13th cent.), who worked in Aleppo and may have been born there. He also wrote a commentary on Job called *Ma'yan gannim*, which Salomon

---

[45]See M. McNamara, 1966A, 45–57 (52–54 for R. Nathan and Johanan); also idem, 1966B, 1–15.

[46]M. Kasher, *Torah Shelemah*, vol. 24, *Targumey ha-Torah. Aramaic Versions of the Bible. A Comprehensive Study of Onkelos, Jonathan, Jerusalem Targums and the Full Jerusalem Targum of Vatican Neofiti 1* (Jerusalem, 1974) 210–224 for ch. 17: "Bereshit Rabba and Neofiti." A summary of this volume, chapter by chapter, is given by A. Díez Macho, *Neophyti 1*, V, 41*–82* (76*–80*) for ch. 17; also *Neophyti 1*, IV, 30*–35*.

[47]M. Kasher, op. cit. (vol. 17, ch. 6), 15–21; summary in A. Díez Macho, *Neophyti 1*, V, 51*–55*.

[48]S. Speier, "The Relationship between the Arukh and the Palestinian Targum, Neofiti 1," *Leshonenu* 31 (1966-67) 23–32; 189–198; 34 (1969–70), 172–179 (in Hebrew).

[49]The *Aruk* citations (together with those in Elias Levita's *Meturgeman* and in other works) are edited from printed editions and MSS by Raymondo Griño as a supplement to A. Díez Macho, ed., *Targum palaestinense in Pentateuchum*, in *Biblia Polyglotta Matritensia* (Madrid, 1977: Numeri; 1980: Exod., Lev., Deut.). See also M. Kasher, *Torah Shelemah*, vol. 24, ch. 6, pp. 1ff.; summary in A. Díez Macho, *Neophyti 1*, V, 51*.

[50]See M. Kasher, op. cit., 15ff.; in A. Díez Macho, *Neophyti*, V, 51*–53*. See also H. L. Strack and G. Stemberger, *Einleitung in Midrasch und Talmud*, 7th rev. ed. (Munich, 1982) 302f. See also A. Díez Macho, "Las citas del Targum Palestinense en el midras Bereshit Zuta," in *Mélanges bibliques et orientaux en l'honneur de M. Mathias Delcor*, ed. A. Caquot et al., Alter Orient und Altes Testament 215 (Neukirchen-Vluyn: Neukirchen Verlag, 1985) 117–126.

Buber published in 1889.[51] Mordekai ha-Kohen published Rabbi Shemuel's commentary on Genesis, under the above title, in Jerusalem in 1962,[52] and in 1973 A. Zimels[53] drew attention to the presence in it of citations from the Palestinian Targums. These citations are numerous, to at least two hundred verses of Genesis. Some of these citations are found in sources known to us, especially in Codex Neofiti 1; others are drawn from sources unknown. From his comparison of the citations with Neofiti, Zimels draws the conclusion that the author had before him a complete text of the Palestinian Targum.

There are citations under the rubric "Targum Yerushalmi" also in Jewish writers of the eleventh to the fourteenth centuries,[54] e.g., R. Hanan'el, R. Shemuel ben Meir (Rashbam), grandson of Rashi (1085–1174), R. Moshe ben Nachman (Ramban) (1194–1270), David Qimhi (Radak) (1160–1235) and others. With regard to these, however, we have to decide in each individual case whether they cite directly from Targum texts or indirectly through such works as R. Nathan's *Aruk*.

Finally, mention must be made of the *Meturgeman*, the Targumic dictionary compiled by Elias Levita and published at Isny in 1541 (with later reprints). It is also extant in the MS, Roma, Biblioteca Angelica, MS or. 84 (A 6,6), a MS finished in 1530. In a doctoral dissertation R. Griño has devoted special study to the text of the *Meturgeman* and to its relationship to Codex Neofiti 1.[55] He has also prepared a critical edition of the dictionary. He is of the opinion that Elias Levita actually makes use of Codex Neofiti 1, a contention strongly opposed by others, especially M. L. Klein.[56]

V. LANGUAGE OF THE PALESTINIAN TARGUMS

1. Aramaic

i) *History of the Aramaic language.* The Targums, that is, the Aramaic Bible, are, needless to say, written in Aramaic. Where precisely this form of the language stands in that language's long history is a matter still exercising the minds of scholars. The Aramaic language itself originated in the eleventh century B.C.E. or somewhat earlier and was used in texts from Aramaic-speaking states and statelets from the tenth century B.C.E. onward, passing through different stages of development and of status. First there was Old Aramaic (to 700 or 500 B.C.E.), followed by Imperial Aramaic (700 or 500 B.C.E.

---

[51]S. Buber, *Samuel b. R. Nissim Masnut, Ma'ajan Gannim . . . al Sefer Ijob* (Berlin, 1889; rpt. Jerusalem, 1970).

[52]Edition noted by A. Zimels, "Palestinian Targumim in Secondary Sources" (in Hebrew), *Beer-Sheva* 1 (1973) 199–203 (in Hebrew); cf. A. Díez Macho in *Neophyti 1*, V, 52*.

[53]Art. cit.

[54]On these see M. Kasher, op. cit., vol. 24; summary in A. Díez Macho, *Neophyti 1*, V, 53*–55*.

[55]See A. Díez Macho, "Neofiti I y el Meturgeman de Elías Levita," in *Neophyti 1*, II, 25*–29* (while Griño's thesis was still in progress), with Díez Macho's reflections on Griño's positions; R. Griño, "El *Meturgeman* de Elías Levita y el *Aruk* de Natán ben Yehiel como fuentes de la lexicografía targumica," *Biblica* 60 (1979) 110–117; idem, "Inportancia del *Meturgeman* de Elías Levita y del ms. Angelica 6-6 para el estudio del mismo," *Sefarad* 31 (1971) 353–361. The *Meturgeman* Pal. Tg. citations have been edited by R. Griño, op. cit., n. 49 above.

[56]R. Griño, "El Meturgeman y Neofiti 1," *Biblica* 58 (1977) 153–188; M. Klein, "Meturgeman and Neofiti 1: A rejoinder," *Biblica* 59 (1978) 267. In his reflections of Griño's position in *Neophyti 1*, II (1970) 29*, Díez Macho said that the actual state of the evidence pointed toward Elias' having known directly a text very similar to the actual Neofiti 1 as the most likely hypothesis. In the introduction to *Neophyti 1*, VI (1979; introduction finished Dec. 8, 1977), however, he states (p. 18, note) that Elias Levita knew and used MS Neofiti 1 for his *Meturgeman* (agreeing with Griño, *Biblica* 58 [1977] 153–188).

until ca. 200 B.C.E.) when chancery use in the Persian Empire ensured a great degree of uniformity in the written language. Then came the emergence of dialects such as Palmyrene and Nabataean in the first century B.C.E., accompanied by the continuation of a standard literary language. Later came the emergence of Palestinian dialects, such as Jewish Galilean, Samaritan, and Christian Palestinian Aramaic, at a time far from agreed on. Then there has been the later history of the dialects, two of which are still spoken. Until the Qumran finds, there was very little documentary evidence to go on for the history of Aramaic between the early second century B.C.E. (with the Book of Daniel) and the Aramaic sections of the Jewish and Christian documents from the third-fourth century C.E. This gap has been amply filled by the Aramaic texts from Qumran.

Going on the information available to him at the time, Franz Rosenthal in 1939 covered the history of research on the Aramaic language under the following headings:[57] (A) Old Aramaic (Altaramäisch: until the end of the eighth century B.C.E.; Reichsaramäisch; Nabatean, Palmyrenian); (B) Later Aramaic (Jungaramäisch: Jewish Palestinian—with treatment of the position of the Aramaic language at the beginnings of Christianity, Samaritan, Christian Palestinian, and the modern dialects—"Das neu-Jungaramäisch"); (C) Eastern Aramaic (Syriac, Babylonian Talmudic, Mandaic, Modern East Aramaic Dialect). His periodization would be (1) Old Aramaic; (2) Middle Aramaic, with eastern (Syriac, Mandaic, Aramaic of Talmud Babli) and western (Samaritan, Palestinian) dialects; (3) Late Aramaic, with a western (Ma'alula) and eastern (around Kurdistan, in Caucasus) branch. The Qumran finds led to a fresh consideration of the language's periodization. One initiated by Y. Kutscher (1957),[58] refined by J. Fitzmyer (1966),[59] accepted by Kutscher (1971)[60] gives the language's stages as follows: (a) Old Aramaic (925–700 B.C.E.); (b) Official Aramaic (700–200 B.C.E.); (c) Middle Aramaic, with development of dialects (200 B.C.E.–200 C.E.); (d) Later Aramaic, with western (Syro-Palestinian-Christian, Samaritan, Palestinian Jewish) and eastern branches; (e) Modern Aramaic. This division is now very widely followed, even though an authority such as Klaus Beyer prefers a different one.[61]

---

[57]F. Rosenthal, *Die aramäistische Forschung seit Th. Nöldeke's Veröffentlichungen* (1939; photomechanical rpt., Leiden: Brill, 1964).

[58]E. Y. Kutscher, "The Language of the Genesis Apocryphon. A Preliminary Study," *Scripta Hierosymitana* 4 (Jerusalem, 1957) 1–35; reproduced in E. Y. Kutscher, *Hebrew and Aramaic Studies*, ed. Z. Ben-Hayyim, A. Dotan, G. Sarfatti (Jerusalem, 1977); E. Y. Kutscher, "Aramaic," in *Encyclopaedia Judaica* 3 (Jerusalem: Keter, 1972) cols. 259–289.

[59]J. Fitzmyer, *The Genesis Apocryphon of Qumran Cave 1* (Rome, 1966), p. 90, no. 60; ed. 2 (1971), pp. 22f., no. 60.

[60]See E. Y. Kutscher, "Aramaic," in *Hebrew and Aramaic Studies*, ed Z. Ben-Hayyim et al. (1977) 90f. (earlier 1971).

[61]Klaus Beyer, *Die aramäischen Texten von Toten Meer* (Göttingen, 1984) 23–71. An updated version of pages 23–76 of Beyer's work have been translated into English by John F. Healey, *The Aramaic Language. Its Distribution and Subdivisions* (Göttingen, 1986). He classes the forms of the language that interest us as "Middle Aramaic": "In the 3rd cent. A.D. Old Aramaic merges into Middle Aramaic. There is no longer a common written language: It exists only as Eastern Middle Aramaic and Western Middle Aramaic" (Healey, p. 43). Western Middle Aramaic embraces Jewish Middle Palestinian, i.e., Galilean, Middle Judean, and Middle East Jordanian (in square script), Samaritan (in Old Hebrew script), and Christian Palestinian (in Syriac script). Galilean is the dialect of Jesus. The Galilean written language was probably developed from Jewish Old Palestinian as early as the time of Herod and not only after the Second Jewish Revolt (Healey, p. 47). Sokoloff, 1990, p. 3, n. 6, follows the old terminology in Rosenthal, regarding Jewish Palestinian Aramaic as forming the Western branch of Middle Aramaic.

ii) *Aramaic of the Palestinian Targum.* A question arising from this consideration is, Where does the Aramaic of the Palestinian Targum fit into the overall pattern? Paul Kahle[62] strongly maintained that this Aramaic represented the spoken language of Palestine in the time of Jesus. It was the language of Jesus. In this he was challenged particularly by E. Y. Kutscher.[63] A more or less general view arising from the evidence of the Qumran Aramaic texts is that the Aramaic of Qumran represents the literary Aramaic of the period prior to the destruction of the Jewish schools at the Bar Kokhba Revolt (135 C.E.), a language not far removed from the spoken tongue. Any literary text written before 135 C.E. would be presumed to have been in this language.[64] From this principle, the Palestinian Pentateuch Targums written in Galilean Aramaic are taken to be at least post-135 C.E., and are generally assumed to be some centuries later.

iii) *Contemporary studies in the Aramaic of the Palestinian Targums.* Nonetheless, the debate concerning the nature of the spoken Aramaic of first-century Palestine and the date to be assigned to the Aramaic of the Palestinian Targum(s) continued, and was even accentuated, after the identification of Codex Neofiti 1. So, too, did research into the Aramaic dialects. The need for grammars of individual Targum texts was perceived, and the production of these became the concern of scholars and university faculties during the past two decades or so. At Boston University in 1969, J. Foster presented a Ph.D. thesis entitled "The Language and Text of Codex Neofiti 1 in the Light of Other Palestinian Aramaic Sources." In 1974, at New York University, B. Barry Levy presented a Ph.D. dissertation entitled "The Language of Neofiti 1: A Descriptive and Comparative Grammar of the Palestinian Targum."[65] In this work he points to the relatively late nature of this language, a position, he notes, which has been accepted by J. Greenfield and others. While Neofiti, he remarks, may be assumed to contain some older ideas, the bulk of it dates well past the first century, and in its final form it appears to be from the Talmudic era. In 1975 Emiliano Martinez Borobio (with Professor Alejandro Díez Macho as director) defended a doctoral dissertation at the Universidad Complutense of Madrid entitled "Estudios linguisticos sobre el arameo del MS. Neofiti 1," an extract of which was published by the university that same year.

---

[62]P. Kahle, "Das zur Zeit Jesu in Palästina gesprochene Aramäisch," in *Theologische Rundschau* (1948– 49); idem, "Das Palästinische Pentateuchtargum und das zur Zeit Jesu gesprochene Aramäisch," *ZNW* 49 (1958) 100–116. On the debate see also M. McNamara, 1977, 95–138, esp. 99–115, and the bibliography in J. Fitzmyer, *A Genesis Apocryphon*, 21ff.

[63]E. Y. Kutscher, "Das zur Zeit Jesu gesprochene Aramäisch," *ZNW* 51 (1960) 46–54.

[64]See the summary in M. McNamara, art. cit. (n. 62 above), 106f. S. A. Kaufman, in *JAOS* 93 (1973) 317–327, esp. 325. In a later study, "On Methodology in the Study of the Targums and Their Chronology," *Journal for the Study of the New Testament* 23 (1985) 117–124, esp. 122f., S. A. Kaufman, while stressing that the language of the Palestinian Targum can be nothing other than the literary language of Amoraic Palestine fully contemporary with the colloquial language of the Palestinian Talmud and Midrashim, goes on to remark that since the literary language almost always reflects the colloquial speech of an earlier period, the language of the Palestinian Targum is still our best guide to the spoken dialect of first-century Galilee. Those concerned with the recovery of the language of Jesus, he notes, can take heart here.

[65]Publication promised over a number of years; see now B. Barry Levy, *Targum Neophyti 1: A Textual Study*, vol. 1: *Introduction, Genesis, Exodus*; vol. 2: *Leviticus, Numbers, Deuteronomy*, Studies in Judaism (Lanham, Md., New York, London: University Press of America, 1986, 1987). He is hopeful that his doctoral dissertation, completely revised, will appear as a supplement to this textual study. For his view of the date to be assigned to Neofiti, see op. cit., vol. 1, pp. viii–ix, 51.

Targum Neofiti 1 contains a complete Targum in its main text but presents evidence of at least three other Palestinian Targums in its numerous glosses. That the grammar of these, too, needs examination had been recognized by J. Foster in her 1969 dissertation. They were examined scientifically in 1977 by Shirley Lund and Julia Foster in *Variant Versions of Targumic Traditions within Codex Neofiti 1*.[66] In 1978 this work was the subject of a lengthy and critical review by C. Meehan,[67] who himself was working on a doctoral dissertation (Hebrew University, Jerusalem) on "Lexical Semantic Studies in the Western Aramaic Verb According to the Palestinian Targums of the Pentateuch."[68] He regarded the monograph of Lund and Foster as undoubtedly one of the most interesting and provocative works on Targum in recent years. In the course of his review he expresses his opinion that all TJII (i.e., Frg. Tg.) texts have been redacted in Galilee in the period of the Amoraim, even though there are reasons to believe that the basic substratum of TJII texts might be of a type of Judean Aramaic from the Tannaitic period (i.e., pre-200 C.E.).[69]

In 1986 another study was devoted to the Neofiti glosses, namely, Jonathan Robert Miller's "A Grammar of the Type II Marginalia within Codex Neofiti 1 with Attention to the Other Aramaic Sources" (Ph.D. thesis, Boston University, 1979, with Shirley Lund as major professor). That same year another dissertation was defended at Boston University: David M. Golomb, "A Grammar of the Aramaic in Codex Vatican Neophyti 1 (Genesis)," with Professor O. Lambdin as director. In this work Golomb restricts himself to the Book of Genesis. This thesis was later published in a revised and expanded form under the title *A Grammar of Targum Neofiti 1*.[70] In this the author goes beyond the Book of Genesis, but still restricts himself to an analysis of the single Codex Neofiti, without comparison with other texts.

In 1981 J. Lund presented a master's thesis (in Hebrew) to the Hebrew University, Jerusalem, with the title, "A Descriptive Syntax of the Non-translational Passages According to Codex Neofiti 1," and in 1983 Stephen Ellis Fassberg presented to Harvard University a Ph.D. dissertation entitled "A Grammar of the Palestinian Targum Fragments from the Cairo Geniza," made available by University Microfilms International the following year. In this thesis Fassberg, in the words of the abstract, "seeks to compare the cardinal features of the language of these fragments with those of other Palestinian Targumim and with those of other Aramaic dialects." In 1975 A. Tal (Rosenthal) published his study *The Language of the Targum of the Former Prophets and Its Position Within the Aramaic Dialects* (Tell Aviv University). This was to become a very influential work in its area of specialization. In 1986 the same scholar turned his attention to our subject in the essay "The Dialects of Jewish Palestinian Aramaic and the Palestinian Targum of the Pentateuch."[71] In his opinion, the Palestinian Targum, which is subsequent to the Bar Kokhba period and prior to the Talmudic era, displays the

---

[66]Published by Scholars Press for the Society of Biblical Literature (Aramaic Studies 2).

[67]*JSJ* 9 (1978) 97–104.

[68]See, for example, *Newsletter for Targum Studies* 1 (1974) 4.

[69]Art. cit., *JSJ*, 101f.

[70]David M. Golomb, *A Grammar of Targum Neofiti*, Harvard Semitic Monographs (Chico, Calif.: Scholars Press, 1985).

[71]*Sefarad* 46 (1986) 441–448.

characteristics of the "lost" Judean dialect of Aramaic. He believes the work deserves its old name, "Jerusalem Targum."

iv) *B. Barry Levy's textual study of Targum Neofiti 1.* The most thorough study thus far made of Targum Neofiti 1, and one deserving of special notice, is that carried out by B. Barry Levy in 1980 and 1981, and published in two volumes in 1986 and 1987. In the course of his dissertation work on the linguistic aspects of Neofiti, it became very clear to him that another dimension of the text was in greater need of analysis. While much of the text of Neofiti remains literal, it seemed obvious to him that many passages were added to it in the course of its development and were not part of the original translation, which he maintains undoubtedly differed from the present document, i.e., Neofiti as it now stands. In his view, the evidence for this claim comes from the literary layering in the text (the seams are, in many cases, still evident) and the linguistic differences evidenced in it. These passages range in size from a word or phrase to a column of text. In the later two-volume work, published in 1986 and 1987, he examines and describes what he believes is the literary development of the Neofiti 1 Targum.[72] As a fitting conclusion to this later period of research and publication, we have the new *Dictionary of Jewish Palestinian Aramaic of the Byzantine Period* (1990), edited by Professor Michael Sokoloff. It will be for contemporary and future research to sift through the information provided by all this analysis and draw from it the appropriate conclusions.

2. Greek and Latin loan words[73]

All manuscripts of the Palestinian Targum have a number of Greek and Latin loan words, particularly the former. This need not surprise us, since there are also a number of such loan words in the Palestinian Talmud and Palestinian Midrashim. After all, the Greeks were overlords of Palestine since the later fourth century, and there are some Greek loan words already in the Book of Daniel, composed around 165 B.C.E. (see Dan 3:5). The Greek loan words, and more so the Latin, may (possibly) be used as elements in assigning a date to the Targums.

The presence of these loan words in the Palestinian Targums, however, goes much deeper than this. It is not haphazard but belongs to the very nature of the work and may be due to a particular interpretative tradition. On examination it will be observed that the loan words in question tend to be for the greater part in the same verses, and as

---

[72] See op. cit. (n. 65 above). His position is summarized in the preface, vol. 1, pp. viii-ix.

[73] There is a list of Greek loan words in Frg. Tgs. in M. L. Klein, 1980, I, 252–260; for occurrences in Genizah texts, idem, *Genizah Manuscripts* II, 101–131 (in glossary); list from Neofiti with study in L. Díez Merino, "Grecismos y latinismos en el Targum Palestino (Neofiti 1)," in *Salvación en la Palabra. Targum. Derash, Berith* 347–366 (list of occurrences, 353–366); already A. Díez Macho, 1960, 230. For the larger context of Greek and the Jews, etc., see S. Lieberman, *Greek in Jewish Palestine* (New York, 1942); J. N. Sevenster, *Do you know Greek? How much Greek could the First Jewish Christians have known?* NovTestSuppl 19 (Leiden, 1968); S. Krauss, *Griechische und lateinische Lehnwörter im Talmud, Midrasch und Targum* I-II; Teil II: Wörterbuch (Berlin, 1899; rpt. Hildesheim, 1964); D. Sperber, "Greek and Latin Words in Rabbinic Literature," *Bar-Ilan Annual* 14–15 (1977) 9–60; idem, *Essays on Greek and Latin in the Mishna, Talmud and Midrashic Literature* (Jerusalem, 1982); idem, *A Dictionary of Greek and Latin Legal Terms in Rabbinic Literature* (Bar Ilan, 1984).

renderings of a particular Hebrew word. While there are exceptions, with some Pal. Tgs. having loan words where others do not have them, by and large all Targum texts (where extant) tend to have the loan words in the same verse. I regard this evidence as of such importance that I give it here in its entirety.

Since the loan words are given in transcription in Hebrew characters without vowels, it is not always certain what Greek or Latin word stands behind the Aramaic. The matter is also somewhat complicated by the fact that Greek, at least the popular language, had taken over a number of Latin words, a fact making it uncertain whether the Aramaic is borrowing directly from Latin or indirectly through a Greek borrowing.[74]

The following is a list of Greek and Latin loan words in the extant Pal. Tg. texts. The list has been made as complete as possible, but does not claim to be exhaustive. First common words are given. Toponyms follow immediately afterward.

augustus ('wgwstws), "August One" (God), CTg KK (acrostic poem) Exod 12:2.

alphabetos, "alphabet(ic)," "an acrostic poem," CTg KK Exod 12:2 (an acrostic poem).

annona (both Greek and Latin), "tax (on agricultural produce);" CTg Z Gen 49:15.

agkylê "hook," Exod 26:32, V, Nfmg; Nf, Exod 27:10, 12; 36:38; 38:10, 12, 17, 19, 28.

aêr, "air, space;" Exod 20:20, P, Nf, CTg F.; Nf Deut 4:17; 5:7.

akkoubiton (?), Greek loan word from Latin *accubitus, accubitum,* "couch,"[75] Gen 40:16, N, *qqbt[w]n;* V, *qqbṭrn;* Nfmg, *qqbṭyn.*

aktôr, "slave inspectors; slave drivers," Nfmg, Exod 14:5.

anagkê, "distress, oppression," Gen 22:14 (2x), PV, Nfmg; 38:25, CTg E, PV, Nf (and prob. CTg X); Exod 12:2 P (2x); Lev 22:27, Nf.

---

[74]See L. Hahn, "Zur Sprachenkampf im römischen Reich bis auf die Zeit Justinians," *Philologus,* Suppl. 10 (Leipzig, 1907) 677–715; R. Schmitt, "Die Sprachverhältnisse in den östlichen Provinzen des römischen Reiches," in *Aufstieg und Niedergang der römischen Welt,* ed. H. Temporini-W. Haase, vol. 29.2 (Berlin, 1983) 554–568; J. Bonner, "The Conflict of Languages in the Roman World," *The Classical Journal* 25 (1929–30) 579–592; L. Lafoscade, "Influence du latin sur le grec," in J. Psichari, *Études de philologie néo-grecque,* Bibliothèque de l'École des Hautes Études 92 (Paris, 1892) 83–158. Latin borrowings in Greek are registered in *A Greek-English Lexicon,* H. G. Liddell, R. Scott, and H. Stuart Jones, *A Supplement,* ed. E. A. Barber, with assistance of P. Mass, M. Scheller, and M. L. West (Oxford, 1968); likewise in G. W. H. Lampe (ed.), *A Patristic Greek Lexicon* (Oxford, 1961), and in the older work, E. A. Sophocles, *Greek Lexicon of the Roman and Byzantine Periods (from B.C. 146 to A.D. 1100)* (New York, n.d., but prefatory note 1887) (25–30 on "The Latin Element"); list of Latin words in Greek of NT (and period) in Walter Bauer, "Introduction to the Lexicon of the Greek New Testament," in *A Greek-English Lexicon of the New Testament,* W. F. Arndt and F. Wilbur Gingrich (Chicago and Cambridge University Presses, 1957) xv (with reference to list in F. Blass and A. Debrunner, *Grammatik d. ntl. Griechisch* [Göttingen, ed. 9, 1954 ed. 11, 1961], par. 5, 1 [Eng. trans. ed. R. W. Funk, *A Greek Grammar of the New Testament and Other Early Christian Literature* [Chicago: University of Chicago Press, 1961]); on Latin words in Greek (in papyri and elsewhere), the following works may be consulted: H. J. Mason, *Greek Terms for Roman Institutions* (Toronto, 1974); F. Viscidi, *I prestiti Latini nel Greco antico e bizantino* (Padua, 1944). For the Greek of the papyri (including loan words), see: F. Preisigke-E. Kiessling, *Wörterbuch der griechischen Papyrusurkunden,* I-IV, 1 and Supplement (Berlin, 1925–71). For Latin loan words in papyri, see S. Daris, *Il lessico latino nel greco d'Egitto* (Barcelona, 1971).

[75]The Greek or Latin word underlying the Aramaic in Gen 40:16 is not certain; *kakkabê* (Dalman); *kakkabis* (Krauss); *akkoubiton, accubitum* (Díez Macho, followed by Díez Merino, reading Aramaic *'qqwbṭwn,* "a type of bread"); see Klein, 1980, I, 256. Use of *ak(k)oubiton* is attested in Greek for the third century C.E. in the sense of "dining couch"; see Lampe, op. cit. (n. 74 above). I have failed to find evidence for use of the Greek or Latin with the meaning of "a type of bread." Sokoloff, 1990, 502, accepts the Aramaic reading as *qqbṭwn* and understands it through Greek as "fine bread (i.e., baked in a *kabbakê, kakkabos,* pot)."

apothêkê, "warehouse, storehouse," or *hypothêkê*, "pledge, mortgage," Gen 24:10, PV, Nfmg; see also *diathêkê*.

asilla, Num 13:23, Nfmg (*b'slh*; cf. Greek *asilla*, "a yoke like that of the milkman to carry buckets"—Liddel, Scott, Jones).

basis, "base," Exod 30:28, Nf; 31:9, Nf; 38:8, V, Nf; Exod 40:11, CTg D.; 40:13, Nf; Lev 8:11, Nf; Num 8:4, Nf.

bêryllion, "beryl," Exod 28:19, Nf; 39:12, Nf; see also LXX Exod 28:20.

brakai, Latin *braccae*, "breeches, short trousers," Exod 28:42, V, Nf; Exod 39:28, Nfmg; Lev 6:3, P, Nfmg.

bêlon, Latin *uelum*, "curtain," Exod 27:9, V, Nf; Exod 27:14, 15, Nf; 38:12, P, Nf; Exod 38:14, Nf; 39:12, Nfmg; Num 3:26 Nf, Nfmg. (*bêlon* in *Test. Job*, 2nd-3rd. cent.; see Lampe, s.v.).

bômos, "altar" (usually pagan), Lev 26:30, Nf; Num 33:52, V, Nf; Deut 32:13, N, Nf.

genesia, "birthday" (or "day of accession to the throne"?), Gen 40:20, Nf.

genos, "family," Gen 10:18, VN, Nf.

gerdios, "weavers," etc., Exod 28:32 Nf; 39:27, Nf.

glôssokomon, "casket," Gen 50:26, Nfmg.

gluphô, "engraver," Exod 35:33 Nfmg; Deut 7:10, P (in poem before the Ten Commandments following Deut 7:10 in MS).

diathêkê, "will and testament," Gen 24:10, P, Nf.

di-nomos/duo nomos(?), Aram. *dynwmys*, "two (bi-partate; [sic]) laws"; (thus M. Klein; usually derived from *dynamis*, "strength"), Exod 12:1, P.

diphthera, "note book" (only in colophon of CTg FF).

diplos, "double," Gen 43:12, L; Exod 16:5, Nfmg; 22:3, CTg A; Exod 22:6, 8, CTg A, Nfmg; Deut 15:18 Nfmg.

dôron, "gift," Gen 4:3, Nf; 4:4, 5, CTg B; 24:53, Nf; 25:6, Nf; 32:14, Nf, CTg C; 32:19, Nf, CTg C; 32:21, Nf; 32:22, Nf; 33:10, Nf; 43:11, Nf; 43:15, Nf, CTg D; 43:25, Nf, CTg D; 43:26, Nf, CTg E; 45:23 (2x), Nf; Num 16:15, Nfmg.

eikôn, eikonion, "figure, form," Gen 28:12, PV, Nf; Exod 12:2, CTg KK (acrostic poem); Num 34:15 (twice) Nf.

eleêson, "have mercy! save!," Exod 12:2, CTg JJ (acrostic poem).

Epicurus (?), Deut 3:14, Nf.

helkôsis (?), Aram. *glwpss*, "wound," Exod 21:25, P. The text, however, may be corrupt.

eparchia, "province, eparchy," Gen 10:2, V, Nf; 10:3, V, Nf; 10:4, V, Nf; Num 31:10, Nf; Deut 3:11, PV, Nf.

emporoi, "merchants, traders," Gen 25:3, Nf.

epitropos, "manager of an estate," Gen 39:4, Nf, VNL, CTg E; 39:5, Nf, CTg E; 39:19, P; 41:34, Nf, V; 41:40, Nf; 43:16, Nf; 44:1, 4, Nf, CTg E; 50:7, Nf.

etoimos, "ready," etc., Lev 14:53, Nfmg.

zeugos, "(a yoke, a pair) partner," Exod 39:25, Nf.

zygon, "pair, partner," Gen 1:27, PV, Nf; 2:18, PV, Nf, CTg B; 2:20, V, Nf, CTg B; 5:2, P, Nfmg; 6:19, CTg E; 7:2, 3, 9 CTg E; 35:9, PV, Nf, CTg C; Deut 32:4, Nf.

zônê, "a belt," Gen 41:44, Nf, CTg E.

thêkê, "sheath," Gen 44:18 (2x), PV, Nf; Exod 15:9, P.

thyreos, "shield," Gen 15:1, V, Nf, CTg H; Exod 13:17, P, CTg X (tosefta); Deut 33:29, PV, Nf.

idiôtês, "ordinary, profane," Gen 28:17, P, Nf; Exod 30:32, Nf; Deut 28:13, 44, Nf.

kakkabê ("a three-legged pot"?) (Dalman); *kakkabis* (Krauss); *akkoubiton,* loan word in Greek from Latin *accubitum,* with meaning "a type of bread" (A. Díez Macho, followed by L. Díez Merino)⁷⁶ (Aram. *qqbṭwn;* V. by scribal error *qqbṭrn*), Gen 40:16, N, Nfmg; cf. V.

kalamos, "a reed, pen," P in poem before Ten Commandments after Deut 7:10.

kalôs (Dalman) or *keleusai* (Krauss), Aram. root, *kls,* "praise," Gen 41:43, PV, Nf, CTg E; 49:22, P, Nf; Exod 12:2, P; 32:18, PV, Nf; Deut 32:43, V, Nf.

karchêdon (ios lithos), Aram. *krkdn',* "chalcedony" (a precious stone), Exod 28:18, V, Nf.

kastra, Latin *castra* (pl. of *castrum*), "fortress," Gen 25:16, V. Nfmg. (*kastron* attested in Greek, third century C.E.; see Lampe, op. cit., s.v.).

katella, Greek or Latin *c(k)atella;* Latin *catena;* Aram. *qṭlyn,* "a chain, necklace," Gen 49:22, PV, Nf. (*katena* attested in Greek, fourth century C.E.; see Lampe, op. cit., s.v.).

kigklis, kagellos (kankellon), Latin *cancelli,* "grating, grated barrier," Exod 27:4; V, Nf; 27:5, P. Nfmg. For occurrences in Greek, see Lampe, op. cit., s.vv.).

kassiteros, "tin," Num 31:22, V, Nf.

kedrinon, "cedar," Gen 6:14, PV, Nf.

kella, Latin *cella,* "cell, compartment," Aram. *qwly',* Num 21:29; error for *qwlry', kollarion* as in V, Nf?

kentênarion, Latin *centenarium,* a unit of weight, Exod 25:39, P, Nf; 37:24, Nf.

kênsos, Latin *census;* verb "to fine," noun "a fine," Exod 21:20, 21, 22, CTg A.

kêryx, "pronouncement," Nf 45:1, Nf; 49:22, VL; Exod 32:5, VL, Nf; Lev 10:20, PV, Nfmg.

koitôn, "room, bedroom," Gen 43:30, V, Nf, CTg D, CTg E; Num 31:50, PV, Nf; Deut 32:25, N, Nf.

kollarion, Latin *collarium,* "chains, fetters," Num 21:29, PV, Nf.

komitatos, Latin *comitatus,* "royal court," Num 12:7 (2x), PN, Nfmg.

corona, "crown," Num 31:50, PV, Nf.

kyrios, "Lord God," Exod 12:2, CTg JJ; CTg KK; Exod 14:30 CTg X; CTg T; P, in poem before Exod 14:30; Deut 34, CTg T.

lampas, "beacon, light," Exod 20:2, P, Nf, CTg F.

legeôn, Latin *legio,* Gen 15:1, PV, Nf, CTg H; Num 12:16, PV, Nf; 21:28, Nfmg; 24:24, PV, Nf. (Already in NT Greek).

liblarios, Latin *librarius,* Aram. *lblr,* "scribe," Num 12:7, LP (VN, *kyldyn*).

libyrnis, "warship," Num 24:24, V, Nf; Deut 28:68, V, Nf.

lopas, "stew pot," Num 11:8, LVP.

lybdikos, "Lybian ass," Gen 32:16, PV, Nf (cf. N), CTg C.

maniakês, "a necklace," Gen 49:22, N, Nf.

margêlis (gen. -*itidos*), Aram. *mrglyt',* Latin *margerita,* "pearl," Gen 33:19, PV, Nf;

---

⁷⁶See n. 75.

50:1, PV, Nf, CTg FF; Exod 28:20, V, Nf; Deut 33:21, PV, Nf.

mêlopemôn, "melon," Num 11:5, P, Nfmg.

moula, "mule team," Exod 14:25 (2x), PV, Nf.

nanos, "dwarf," Lev 21:20, V, Nf; P in poem.

naphtha, "naphtha," Exod 14:24, V, Nf.

nêma, "thread, string, (vocal) cord," P Deut 7:10, poem before Ten Commandments.

nêsos, "island," Gen 10:18 (error), V; 10:5, Nf; Num 34:6, VN, Nf.

nomos, "way, manner, law," Gen 19:1, Nf; 19:31, V, Nf; 23:7, Nf; 24:52, Nf; 37:10, Nf; 42:6, Nf; 43:26, Nf, CTg E; 44:14, Nf; 48:12, 22, Nf; Exod 1:8, V; 1:19, P; 12:1, P; 21:7, CTg A; Lev 18:3, Nf; 20:23, Nf; 25:39, Nf; Num 23:9, VP, Nf.

xenos, "stranger, foreigner," Gen 47:21, V, Nf; Lev 19:14, P, Nfmg; Deut 27:18, PV, Nfmg.

xiphos, "sword," Deut 33:29, PV; Exod 13:17, CTg X (tosefta).

ogmos(?), Aram. *'wmn', wmnh* "ploughed furrow," Lev 19:9, PV, Nf; Lev 23:22, CTg F.

ochlos, "mass of people," Gen 4:10, V, Nf, CTg B; 31:29, V, Nf, CTg E; 35:11, CTg C; 48:4, CTg Z; Exod 12:2, CTg KK (acrostic); 19:21, PV, Nf, CTg F; Num 21:6, PV, Nfmg; 24:24, V, Nfmg.

paidagôgos, "nurse," Num 11:12, PV, Nf.

palation, Latin *palatium*, "palace," Gen 12:15, P, VNL; 43:40, CTg C; 43:16, CTg D; 44:1, CTg D; 44:19, PV, Nf; 49:21, V; cf. Nf; 49:23, P, cf. Nf.

paragaudês, paragaudion, Latin *paragaudae*, "tunic, garment with purple border, ornamental garment," Gen 37:3, PV, Nf; 37:23, Nf, CTg D, CTg E; 37:31 (2x), 32, Nf, CTg E; 37:33, PV, Nf. 38:25(2x), PV, Nf.

parrêsia, (the Aramaic verb [*m*]*prsy'* possibly from Greek root) "publicize," Gen 38:25, PV, Nf, CTg D, CTg E; 38:26, CTg D.

patroboulos, Aram. *ptyr bwly*, "head of council, magistrate," Lev 22:27, N, Nfmg, CTg F.

patrôn, Latin *patronus*, "patron, father," Gen 45:8, P, Nfmg; (poem on Ten Commandments, inserted mistakingly in P after Deut 7:10; attested in Greek in Apocryphal *Acta Petri et Pauli*).

pelagos, "ocean, high sea," Exod 15:8, CTg W (taken as "middle" of the sea).

peribolaion, "suburb, farm, open field," Lev 25:34, PV, Nf; Num 35:2, 4, V, Nfmg; cf. Sokoloff, 1990, 445.

plateia, "street," Gen 10:11, V, Nf; 19:2, V, Nfmg.

polemarchos, "warrior, commander," Gen 36:6(7), P, N, Nf; Deut 32:42, PV, Nf.

polemos, "dispute," Exod 12:2, CTg KK (acrostic poem).

ponêria, "distress, cowardice," Num 16:1, P.

porpê, "clasp, hook, ring," Exod 35:11, V, Nf; 39:33, CTg D.

pragmateia, "business, commerce," Gen 26:16, PV, Nf; 33:18, PV, Nf.

praitôrion, Latin *praetorium*, "palace," Gen 12:15, Nf; 43:16, Nf (2x); 43:17, Nf; 43:18, Nf, CTg D; 43:19, 24, Nf; 44:14, Nf; 45:2, Nf; 45:16, Nf; 47:14, Nf; 49:21, Nf; 49:23, PV, Nf.

pronoeô, "support, provide for," Gen 30:30, CTg E; 40:12, PV, Nf, CTg E; Exod 15:13, CTg G; Deut 32:4, V, cf. Nf.

pylê, Aram. *pyly*, "gate," Gen 19:1, V, Nfmg; Exod 12:1, P (but perhaps here *pyly-phialê*, "cup, goblet"); Deut 20:11, PV, Nfmg.

pôlêtêrion, "shop," Exod 12:1, P (introductory poem).

rheda (Latin), "wagon," Exod 14:25 (2x), PN, Nf.

rododaphnê, Aram. *'rdwpny*, "oleander," Exod 15:25, V, Nfmg.

sekourion, Latin *securis*, Aram. *syqwr'*, "hatchet," Deut 19:5, V, Nf.

sêma, "sign," perhaps also "treasure," Deut 33:10, V, Nf (N, *symny'*).

sêmeion, "mark, sign," Gen 4:15, CTg B; 9:12, 13, 17, CTg E; Exod 8:5, PV, Nf; 12:13, CTg AA; Num 17:3, PV, Nf; Dt 33:19, N, Nf; Deut 34, CTg T (acrostic poem).

skynion (?), Aram. *skynh*, "eyelids, eyebrows," Deut 32:10, PV, Nf.

smaragdos, Aram. *zmrgdyn*, "emerald" or similar precious stone, Exod 28:19, V, Nf.

soudarion, Latin *sudarium*, Aram. *swdr*, Exod 34:33, PV, Nf.

spekoulatôr, Latin *speculator*, "executioner," Gen 37:33, P; 37:36, V, Nf; 39:1, CTg E, Nf; 40:1 (3x), Nf; 41:10, CTg E, Nf; 41:12, CTg E; 41:11, Nf. (Already in NT Greek).

stolê, Latin *stola*, Aram. *'stly, 'ystlyt'*, Gen 3:7, PV, Nfmg; 9:23, Nf, CTg E; 45:22 (2x), Nf; Exod 22:8, 26, CTg A; Deut 22:3, V, Nfmg; 24:13, V, Nfmg.

strata, Latin *(via) strata*, Aram. *'sṭrṭ'*, "street," Num 20:17, V, Nfmg; 21:22, P, Nfmg; Deut 1:1, PV, Nfmg, CTg Br.

taxis, tassô, "arrange, order, tie in place, hitch up a chariot," Gen 46:29, Nf, CTg D; 49:19, PV, Nf (2x); Exod 14:6, P, Nf; 28:28, Nf; 39:21, Nf; Num 1:52 (2x), Nf; 2:2, 3, 10, 17, 25, 31, 34, Nf; 3:10, Nf; 10:14, Nf; 23:10, Nf (2x); 24:1, 2, Nf.

timê, "price value," Gen 21:33, PV, Nfmg.

tolmaô, "to be bold, dare, deceive," Gen 38:26, P.

tyrannos, "tyrant, despot," Exod 12:2, CTg KK (acrostic poem).

hypopodion, Aram. *'pypwdyn, 'pypwdn*, "footstool," Exod 24:10, P (*'pydwryn*, correct), V, Nf.

phernê, "gift to bride from groom," Gen 34:12, V, Nf, CTg C; Exod 22:15(16) (2x), V, Nf, CTg A.

phialê, "cup, goblet, bowl," Gen 4:12, P, Nfmg, CTg E; Exod 12:1, P; 25:29, P, Nf; Num 4:7, PV, Nf; 7:13, PV, Nf.

phrixis, "shudder," Gen 22:10, PV, Nfmg.

chaldaios, "magician, court officer," Num 12:7, CTg VV.

chlaina, "coat," Gen 25:25, V, Nf.

cholê, "anger, rage," Gen 27:45, V, Nfmg; 44:18, P.

chrôma, "color" (of the sea), in name of precious stone, Exod 28:20, V, Nf.

ônê, "title deed," Gen 49:21, PV, Nf.

3. Toponyms in Greek and Latin[77]

Together with regular Greek and Latin loan words, we also have in the Palestinian Targums the names of peoples and countries and cities in Greek and Latin, principally in Greek. These, too, tend to be found in certain verses, particularly in the Table of Na-

---

[77]Klein, 1980, I, 256–258.

tions in Gen 10 and in the list of the border towns of the Holy Land in Num 34. They belong to a particular interpretative tradition in regard to these particular chapters. I list these Greek and Latin names here.

Africa, Aram. *'pryqy*, Gen 10:2, Nf.

Aigyptos, Aegyptus, Aram. *'ygystws* (probably error for *-yp-*), Exod 12:2, CTg KK.

Amanos (Tauros), Amanus Taurus, Num 34:7-8, V, Nf, Nfmg.

Antiochia, Antioch on the Orontes in Syria, Gen 10:18, Nf, V; Num 34:8, Nf, V.

Apameia, Apamea (=Caesarea Philippi), Num 34:11, Nf, V.

Asia, Gen 10:3, Nf, V.

Aulôn (Kilikias), lit. "a narrow place," Num 34:8, V, Nf (*'wwls*), Nfmg.

Barbaria, unidentified; in Asia Minor, Gen 10:3, Nf, V.

Batania, Batanea, Aram. *btnyn*, Deut 3:4, Nf; 32:14, Nf, V 33:22, Nf, V.

Bithynia, Aram. *wytny'*, Gen 10:2, V (*bytny'?*), cf. Nf.

Ctesiphon, Gen 10:10, Nf, PV.

Daphnê, Num 34:11, Nf, V.

Dardania, Gen 10:4, Nf, V (P *dwdny'*).

Dyoqitos (?), (*dywqts, dywqtws*), Num 34:15 (2x), Nf, V.

Ellas + Tarsus, Hellas-Tarsus in Cilicia, possibly two distinct places, Gen 10:4, Nf (Ellas and Tarsus), V.

Emesa, Gen 10:18, V.

Epikairos, town east of the Jordan, Deut 3:14, Br, V; cf. Nf.

Gabala, Gobolitis, region in Idumea, Num 24:18, Nf, P; Deut 1:2, Nf, PV; Deut 1:44, Nf, V; 2:8, Nf, V; 33:2, PV.

Genisar, Genessar, Genesareth, on the west coast of the Sea of Galilee, Deut 33:23, Nf, V.

Germania (in Asia Minor? or Germania, Germany proper, east of Rhine?), Gen 10:2, Nf, V.

Indikê (cf. LXX Esth 3:12), Aram. *hndqy*, India, Gen 2:11, Nf; 25:18, Nf, L.

Italia, southern Italy, Gen 10:4, Nf, PV; Num 24:24, Nf, PV.

Kaisareia (Philippou), Caesarea (Philippi), ([*dn* d]*qysrywn*), Gen 14:14, Nf, V; Num 34:15 (2x), Nf, V; Deut 34:1, Nf, V.

Kappadokia, Cappadocia, Gen 10:14, Nf, N (V, *qpdyq'y*); Deut 2:23 (2x), Nf, Br.

Kilikia, Cilicia, Num 34:8, Nf, PV.

Kypros, Cyprus, Gen 10:17, V.

Makedonia, Macedonia, Gen 10:2, Nf, V.

Mareôtês, Gen 10:13, V.

Mysiakê, Mysia, Aram. *mwsqy*, Gen 10:2 (N, *'nsyy'*; Nfmg *'wtyy'*; Ps.-J., *'ws'*; Onq., *mwsu'*); Nf, Mysia (*mwsy'*).

Neilos, the Nile River, Num 34:5, Nf, V.

Okeanos, occeanus, Num 34:6, PV, Nf, Nfmg.

Pêlousion, Pelusium, Aram. *pylwsyn*, Gen 10:14, V; 47:11, Nf, V; Exod 1:11, Nf, V; Num 33:3, Nf, PV.

Pentaschoinos, a town in Egypt, Gen 10:14, V.

Pentapolis, Gen 10:3, N (V, *b'nt* . . .).

Phrygia, in Asia Minor, Gen 10:2, Nf, V.

Pontos, Pontus, Gen 10:10; P; 11:2, PV; 14:9, Nf, V; Exod 12:1, P.

Romê, Roma, Aram. *rwmy, rwmh*, Exod 12:42, V; 15:18, P; Num 24:19, PV; 24: 24, P.

Saraceni, Saracens, Aram. *srqyn*, Gen 37:25, Nf, PV.

Tanis, Exod 1:11, B, V (*tnws*).

Tarsus, Gen 10:4 (*'lsṭrsws*), Nf, P (*trsws*).

Thrakê, Aram. *trqy*, Thracia, Gen 10:2, Nf, V.

Thrachôn, Aram. *ṭrkwn*, Thraconitis, Num 34:15, Nf, V; Deut 3:4, Nf, Br; 3:14, Nf, NL.

Tripolis, Gen 10:17, V.

Zephirin (Zephourion), Num 34:9, Nf, V.

Conclusions

Space and time permit no more than to open this aspect of a question which I believe merits renewed attention from different points of view, thus taking up once more topics which have been studied by scholars in the past. One such topic is the relation of the Greek loan words in the Targums to biblical interpretation as found in the Greek versions, specifically the Septuagint. P. Churgin and L. H. Brockington have already drawn attention to this matter, and more recently, principally with regard to Onqelos, J. P. Brown.[78] Brown passes by the Palestinian Targums and the various Targums of the Hagiographa for reasons of time and space and because of what he regards as "the comparatively late date of their final redaction." New Testament Greek might also conceivably be brought into such a study, taking up points earlier made by the Hebrew grammarian Paul Joüon.[79]

A matter of particular interest in assigning a date to the Palestinian Targums is the age in which the Latin loan words in question were current in Greek. The number of these Latin loan words is limited in number, less than thirty in all: *annona, augustus, accubitus, aktôr, brakai (braccae), belôn, kastra, katella (katêna), comitatus, corona, cancelli (kinglis, kankellos, -on), kella, kentenarion, kênsos, kollarion (collarium), legeôn (legio), liblarios (librarius), margaritês (if a Latin loan word), mulus, palation, paragaudês, patrôn, praitôrion (praetorium), sekourion (securis), soudarion (sudarium), spekoulatôr, strata*. At least six of these were current in the Greek of New Testament times. It remains to be determined how early the others became part of Greek vocabulary.[80]

---

[78]P. Churgin, "The Targum and the Septuagint," *American Journal of Semitic Languages* 50 (1954) 41–65; L. H. Brockington, "Septuagint and Targum," *ZAW* 66 (1954) 80–86; J. Pairman Brown, "The Septuagint as a Source of the Greek Loan-Words in the Targums," *Biblica* 70 (1989) 194–216.

[79]Paul Joüon, "Mots grecs de l'araméen d'Onkelos ou de l'hébreu de la Mishna qui se trouvent aussi dans les Evangiles," *RSR* 22 (1932) 462–469.

[80]Dr. Lucas De Coninck, Professor of Latin in the Katholieke Universiteit Leuven, Campus Kortrijk, has very kindly examined the question of these Latin loan words. On consultation with Dr. A. Wouters, Professor of Greek at the Katholieke Universiteit, he draws attention to the works of Hahn and Schmitt listed in note 74, and for the study of the Latin loan words he refers us to the works of Mason, Viscidi, Preisigke-Kiessling, and Daris included there.

VI. UNIFORMITY AND DIVERSITY IN THE PALESTINIAN TARGUMS

ANALYSIS OF ARAMAIC TEXT IN RELATION TO HEBREW[81]

A proper understanding of the Palestinian Targum tradition requires that we come to an awareness of both the diversity and unity that exists within this tradition as a whole and even within the individual Palestinian Targum manuscripts. Such an understanding is possible only after a thorough analysis of the texts from a variety of angles, such as the relation of the translation to the Hebrew Text which it purports to translate, its treatment of hapaxlegomena and rare words of the HT, the manner in which individual texts or phrases of the HT are rendered in different Pal. Tg. texts and traditions, and so forth. Some examples of what is intended are given here.

1. Calque on the HT

There are some instances in individual texts of the Pal. Tgs. in which the underlying HT is "translated" literally or through a misunderstanding, with apparently little meaning in Aramaic.[82] One such is the rendering of the HT *'t*, the sign of the accusative, as if

---

Professor De Coninck writes (Nov. 13, 1989): "I have done research in the aforementioned works, and I am coming to the following results (*Ia = first century B.C., I = first century A. D.*, etc.). 1. The *most important terms* of the list of Latin words (from *annona* to *strata*) appear to be *akkoubitos, kentênarion, korônê, moulos, paragaudês, sekourion, strata*;— *akkoubitos/n* is attested a couple of times in Greek from *III* on, and becomes common in *VI*: see G. Husson, *Le vocabulaire de la maison privée*, Paris, 1988, p. 36–7; Daris, s. v.;— *kentênarion* as *unit of weight* (for 100 librae) has been attested in Greek sources from *III* on: Viscidi, p. 30; Preisigke-Kiessling, III, p. 367 and V, p. 431; Daris, s. v.; in Latin it is attested in that sense from Vitruvius (*Ia*) on: *Thes. Ling. Lat.* III, 813, 5; *Oxf. Lat. Dict.*, p. 298. As *currency unit kentênarion* is found in Latin and Greek from *IV*: W. Kubitschek, *Pauly's Realencyclopädie der classischen Altertumswissenschaft* (= *R.E.*), III, Stuttgart, 1889, col. 1926;— *korônê* ("kind of crown") is found *V* (Liddell-Scott, p. 983); —*moulión* is found from *II* on, *moulê* from *IV* on (Daris, s. v.), but masc. *moulos* is Byzantine Greek (Viscidi, p. 38); —*paragaudês* should be "eine orientalische über das Griechische kommende Bezeichnung" and is found in Latin from *III* on (cf. Schuppe *R. E.* XVIII, 2, col. 1167; Oppermann, *Kleine Pauly*, IV, 501); perhaps by accident, in Greek it has been attested only later (see Liddell-Scott, p. 1306; Lampe, p. 1008), and never in papyri; —*sekourion* is very rare; not in papyri, once in an edict of Diocletian (*III-IV*: Liddell-Scott, p. 1589); —*strata* is found only from *VI* on (Daris, s. v.; Preisigke-Kiessling, I, 491; V, 285); the Latin equivalent was at first confined to poetry ("strata viarum," *Ia: Oxford Latin Dictionary*, s. v.) and is found in prose from *IV* only (see A. Forcellini, *Lexicon Totius Latinitatis*, IV, p. 484). —2. *Katélla* is not mentioned in any of the lexicographical works I have turned to. —3. The following loan words are attested from *II* on: *annône* (Daris, s. v.); *kastra* (Daris, s. v.); *kankellos* (Daris, s. v.); *kollarion* (Daris, s. v.; Barber, *Suppl.*, p. 86); *librarios* (Daris, s. v.; Barber, p. 93); *spekoulatôr* (Daris, s. v.). —4. From *Ia* or *I*: *augoustos* (Mason, p. 12); *aktôr* (ibid.); *brakai* (Liddell-Scott, s. v.); *bélon* (Lampe, s. v.); *kella* (Daris, s. v.); *kênsos* (Viscidi, p. 30); *legeôn* (Viscidi, p. 15; Daris, s. v.); *patrôn* (Daris, s. v.); *palation* (Liddell-Scott, s.v.); *praitôrion* (Liddell-Scott, s. v.); *soudarion* (Daris, s. v.)."

Professor De Coninck, noting that this is all he had done so far, ends with the observation: "To be completely sure, one ought to refer to the indices of the publications of Greek (mainly epigraphical and papyrological) texts found after 1965, and to consult some of the scattered articles on Greek lexicographical matter that are mentioned in *L'Annêe Philologique*. Nothing can be written definitely on the date of the Aramaic paraphrase until such work is done. Anyway, the first class of terms mentioned above will not easily be pushed aside in its entirety."

[81] Díez Macho's contention (1960, 233–236; *Neophyti 1*, I, 83*) that the HT rendered by Neofiti belongs to the fluid pre-Masoretic stage of text has not won acceptance.

[82] One has also to reckon with the possibility that individual texts or recensions of the Pal. Tg. as we now have them have been revised to bring them into conformity with the MT. This, however, is a question too great to enter into here. For a study of this nature with regard to sections of Genesis, see Maurice G. Allen's doctoral dissertation, "The

it were the conjunction *'t*, "with."[83] Aquila did likewise in the Greek of Gen 1:1 (*syn tês gês*, "with the earth"), but from a theory of translation which can hardly be presumed to have been the case for the Targumist. In Gen 39:1 Nf renders *hwrd* (*hûrad*; Hophal, "was brought down") of the HT by *hwnḥt* (from root *nḥt*), a form of the Causative stem passive which is not attested elsewhere in Neofiti or Targumic Aramaic. It is probably a calque on the Hebrew, due to the particular translator.[84] That such is so is rendered all the more probable by the fact that it is not in the translation of CTg E,[85] which has *'twḥt*, more or less the expected form. That *hwnḥt* of Nf Gen 39:1 is a calque on the HT is further indicated by the rendering in Gen 39:2 of the HT *'t*, "with," as if it were *'t*, the sign of the accusative (*yat* in Aramaic), giving a senseless translation in the context.[86]

2. Rendering of HT Pentateuch hapaxlegomena and of rare words

The manner in which these are rendered in individual texts can be instructive on the unity and diversity of the Pal. Tg. tradition. All Pal. Tg. texts render the hapax *gopher* of Gen 6:14 as *kadrinon* (*qdrynwn*), probably indicating a fixed exegetical tradition on this point.[87] This is far from being the case with regard to all such hapaxlegomena. The Hebrew word *kmr* (*nkmr rḥmyw*) of Gen 43:30 is rendered differently in Nf (*glw m'wy*), Nfmg and CTg E (*'tgllw rḥmwy*) and probably CTg D. *'t[.....rḥ]m*, probably to be read as *'tmlyy rḥm*.[88] The rare root *gw'*, "to expire, perish," of Gen 6:17; 7:21; 25:8, 17; 35:29; 49:33; Num 17:27f.; 20:3; 20:29, is generally rendered as *s'p* ("ended") in Nf (*yštyṣy*, Gen 6:17; *myt*, Num 20:3, 29); as *myt* in CTg AA, Num 20:3, PBVN Gen 20:29, and Nfmg Num 20:3, 29; as *'tngd* in Nfmg Gen 25:8, 17; 35:29, and as *'štyṣy* in CTg B, Gen 7:21.

3. Pal. Tg. translation of toledoth of HT

In Neofiti Genesis the term *toledoth* (RSV: "generations") of the MT is almost universally rendered as *yḥws twldwwt*, "pedigree of the generations" or such like (rendered

---

Palestinian Targum as Represented in Neofiti I, with Selected References to Passages of Genesis" (University of Toronto, 1972), summarized in Díez Macho, *Neophyti 1*, V, 94*f.: "N[eofiti]'s aim is to give a more literalising rendition of the Hebrew Text, sometimes more literal than O[nqelos] itself." Geoffrey J. Cowling, in his doctoral dissertation, "The Palestinian Targum: Textual and Linguistic Investigations in Codex Neofiti I and Allied Manuscripts" (University of Aberdeen, 1968), summarized in G. J. Cowling, "New Light on the New Testament: The Significance of the Palestinian Targum," in *Theological Students Fellowship Bulletin* (University of Aberdeen, 1968) propounded the view that the Pal. Tg. is not a direct translation from the Hebrew but rather from a Greek version, probably Theodotion. This thesis runs counter to the entire evidence of the Pal. Tg.; see Díez Macho, *Neophyti 1*, III, 56*–58*. The central part of Cowling's thesis was accepted by J. A. Foster in her 1969 doctoral dissertation (above, p. 14); cf. Díez Macho, op. cit., 58*–59*. She has since changed her position on this matter (personal letter of author).

[83]See David M. Golomb, *A Grammar of Neofiti*, 65, 208f.
[84]See Golomb, op. cit., 145.
[85]See S. E. Fassberg, *A Grammar of the Palestinian Targum Fragments from the Cairo Geniza* (1984) 263.
[86]See Golomb, op. cit., 65, 208f.
[87]Cf. M. McNamara, 1966A, 51f.; idem, 1966B, 5f.
[88]Thus ed. M. Klein, 1980, I, 129; II, 43.

in this translation as "genealogical pedigree"). Thus in Gen 2:4; 5:1; 6:9; 10:32; 11:10; 36:1, 9; 37:2. Exceptions to this rule are Gen 10:1, 32; 25:13, 19, with *tldwwt* (*hwn,* etc.). However, in Exodus and Numbers *toledoth* is rendered by *yḥws* alone (thus Exod 6:16, 19; 28:10; Num 1:20, 22, 24, 26, 28, 30, 32, 34, 36, 40), and in Num 3:1 with *tldwwth* alone.

4. Pal. Tg. translation of HT zr' "(human) progeny"[89]

Neofiti almost universally paraphrases the term *zr',* "seed," of the HT (when human progeny is intended) as "sons." Exceptions are Exod 33:1 (with the sing. "your son"); Gen 22:18 (with *zr'ytyk,* "your descendants"); Num 25:13 ("descendants"); Lev 20:4; Deut 30:6 ("your seeds"); and especially Deut 31:19, 21 and 34:4, with "descendants of your sons."

An almost invariable variant in Nfmg to "your sons" is "the descendants (*zr'yyt*) of your sons." It is quite obvious that we are in the presence of two distinct translation traditions. Unfortunately there are very few of the texts in question preserved in CTg or in the Frg. Tg., in fact only CTg E Gen 9:9, with "descendants of your sons."

S. Lund and J. Foster[90] use the presence of the Nfmg-type formula in Nf text at the end of Deuteronomy as evidence that the ending of Codex Neofiti 1 (Deut 29:17[18]-34:12) is not in the tradition of the central Nf text, but rather in that represented elsewhere by the marginal variants. A little further below we shall consider evidence relating to a similar situation with regard to the opening section of Nf (Gen 1:1-3:4)[91]

5. The synonyms 'wd and twb in the Pal. Tgs.

In their study of variant versions of Targumic traditions within Codex Neofiti 1, Lund and Foster[92] examine the renderings of the term *'wd* (or *'d*) ("again, yet, again") in the HT, where the term is used in the Pentateuch seventy times in sixty-seven verses. Nf as Aramaic rendering has *'wd* eleven times, *twb* forty-three times (plus one interlinear insertion of *twb* omitted in the text, Num 18:5), the conflated rendering *'d/'wd twb* three times, and other readings twelve times. Against the forty-seven uses of *twb* in the text, Nfmg has *'wd* twenty-seven times; two or three conflated Nf text readings are countered by marginal *'wd.* Four of the forty-five uses of *twb* in the text occur in a section where Nfmg were not done at all (Gen 37–38). The CTg texts employ *'wd* fourteen times (CTg B, C, E; eleven examples CTg E), *twb/twbn* (*twbn,* being a variant form of *twb*) four times (CTg D, F, two examples each). Thus the CTg tradition in this tends to agree with the Nfmg rather than with Nf.

---

[89] On this see S. Lund and J. A. Foster, *Variant Versions,* 16f., 20, 61.
[90] Op. cit., 77f., 80.
[91] Below, p. 37.
[92] Op. cit., 17, 61, 63f.; see also Meehan, loc. cit. (n. 67 above), 100.

6. The synonyms kn and kdn/kdyn in the Pal. Tgs.

Lund and Foster[93] also note that the HT Pentateuch uses *kn* ("so, thus") ninety-six times. As rendering, Nf has *kn* sixteen times, *kdyn* or *kdn* seventy-one times, other renditions nine times. Against the seventy-one text usages of *kdn/kdyn*, Nfmg gives *kn* thirty-seven times. Three additional instances fall where Nfmg were not done. All three forms are found in the CTg texts: *kn* fifteen times (CTg C, 3; CTg E, 11; CTg F, 1); *knyn* seven times (CTg C, 2; CTg D, 4; Ctg F, 11); *kdn* eight times (CTg B, 1; CTg D, 2; CTg E, 1; CTg F, 4).

7. Synonyms for rendering of HT mhr in Pal. Tgs.[94]

In the HT Pentateuch, forms of the verb *mhr* ("hurry") occur seventeen times. Nf renders almost invariably by Aphel forms of *yhy* (e.g., *'why*), i.e., sixteen times, once by a form of the verb *zrz*. The opposite is the case in Nfmg: forms of *zrz* are given against *'why*, etc., of text in thirteen of the sixteen instances. One additional occurrence of *mhr* is in a section without marginal glosses (Gen 41:32). The texts with this verb are poorly represented in CTg texts. We find *zrz* once (Gen 43:30), in CTg AA, Exod 12:33 (also in CTg AA Exod 12:21 for different word of HT, and in CTg E Gen 43:31 where HT has *wyt'pq*) and *'why* once (Lev 22:27, CTg F in an expansion, where Nf, Nfmg, PVN also have *'why*). Frg. Tgs. uses *zrz* twice (Gen 24:20, VNL; Exod 34:8, VN in corrupt text form).

8. Pal. Tg. rendering of HT terms for "young woman": n'rh, yldh, btwlh[95]

The term *na'arah* occurs in Gen 24:14, 57, 61; 34:3, 12; Deut 22:15 (2x), 16, 19, 20, 26, 28. In Neofiti it is invariably rendered by *rbyth*, with Nfmg variant in all cases except Gen 24:14, 57, *tlyth* (3 times *tlyt'*, once, Gen 24:61, *tlyyt'*). PVNL Deut 22:20 have *tlyyt'* and VN Deut 22:21 *tlyt'*. The only instance preserved in CTg is CTg C, Gen 34:12, agreeing with Nf (*rbyt'*).

The term *btwlh* (*betûlah*) occurs in Gen 24:16; Exod 22:16; Lev 21:3; Deut 22:19, and *na'arah* (written as *n'r*) *betûlah* in Deut 22:28. Nf renders as *rbyth* in Gen 24:16, otherwise as *btwlth* (Exod 22:16 *btwl'*), with *rby* (probably due to HT *n'r*) *btwlh* in Deut 22:28. Nfmg, where present (Exod 22:16 and Deut 22:19), does likewise.

The word *yldh* (*yaldah*) occurs only once in the Pentateuch, in Gen 34:4. It is rendered as *rbyth* in Nf and as *tlyt'* in Nfmg.

The conclusion from this evidence is that here again we have clear evidence of well-defined patterns of translation within the Pal. Tg. texts.

[93]Op. cit., 17, 61, 64, 67; Meehan, loc. cit., 101.
[94]Cf. Lund and Foster, op. cit., 64.
[95]Cf. Lund and Foster, op. cit., 61, 63.

9. Pentateuch Pal. Tg. treatment of "The Lord is with ..." of HT

For whatever reason, the avoidance of anthropomorphisms or otherwise, in the Targums in general such expressions as "the Lord is (*or:* I am) with you" are rendered as "the Memra of the Lord is (*or:* I, in my Memra am) at your aid." This holds true for Onqelos as well, and likewise for Ps.-J. Matters are not so clear-cut with regard to the Pal. Tgs., even though the evidence to go on is principally Gen 21:22; 26:28; 28:20; 31:5; 35:3; 39:3; 49:25; Deut 2:7. In half of these, Nf retains the HT expression. In Gen 21:22; 26:28 (RSV: "God is [was] with you"), Nf has "the Lord is (was) with you"; Nfmg, "the Memra of the Lord is (was) at your aid" (*bs'd* ...). Likewise for Gen 39:3 (RSV: "the Lord was with Joseph"), where Nf has "the Lord was with him." There is neither Nfmg or Frag. Tg., but CTg E has: "the Memra of the Lord was with him." In Gen 31:5 (RSV: "the God of my father has been with me"), Nf has "the Memra of the God of my father was at my aid" (*s'dy*), as also CTg E. In 49:25 (RSV: "... by the God of your father who will help you ..."), Nf has: "May the Memra of the God of your father be at your aid"; likewise P; there is neither VNL or CTg. Nf renders Deut 2:7 (RSV: "the Lord your God has been with you") as: "... the Lord your God was at your aid. ..."

In these texts we have evidence that in Nf the formula "... at your/my (etc.) aid" has not been so crystalized as a translation equivalent as to be introduced automatically at every occurrence of "the Lord is/was with ..." of the Hebrew text.

10. Rendering of HT Pentateuch 'bl as brm in Pal. Tg.[96]

Many of the single word texts of the Pal. Frg. Tgs. probably owe their preservation to Jewish lexical interests, specifically to the interest in synonyms. A number of these words, and others of the same nature, are found already in the *Aruk* of Rabbi Nathan (ca. 1100 C.E.). The Jewish interest in such variety of translation is probably an old one, going back to earlier rabbinic times, if not beyond. The word *'bl* ("but," "however," "in truth") occurs only twice in the HT Pentateuch (Gen 17:19; 42:21). In the exposition of Gen 42:21 ("In truth, *'bl*, we [the sons of Jacob] are guilty concerning our brother [Joseph]") in *Gen. R.* (91, 8) we have a brief comment which reads as follows: "Rabbi Abba b. Kahana [ca. 300 C.E.) said: *lšwn drwmy hw' 'bl brm*, which we may render: "*'bl* is a southern (Palestine) expression (i.e., Lydda), where it means the same as *brm*," or more probably: "... where the HT word is rendered by *brm*." In the two occurrences already noted, both Onq. and Ps.-J. render *'bl* by *bqwšṭ'*, "in truth." Neither CTg nor Frag. Tg. exists to the verses. It is to be noted that in Nf, in both occurrences, *'bl* of the HT is rendered by *brm*, the word mentioned by R. Kahana in relation to it. We may legitimately ask whether it is an indication that the translation we have in Nf represents that of third/fourth-century southern Palestine.

---

[96]See M. McNamara, 1966B, 9–10.

VII. TRANSLATION AND PARAPHRASE TECHNIQUES OF
THE PALESTINIAN PENTATEUCH TARGUMS

Within rabbinic Judaism, three sets of rules have traditionally been known for biblical interpretation and the application of the Torah to Jewish life, namely, the seven rules of Hillel, the thirteen rules (*middoth*) of Ishmael, and finally a set of thirty-three *middoth*.[97] Those who have studied the actual practice of rabbinic midrash in relation to these rules, however, find that the two do not correlate all that closely:[98] midrash seems to operate according to rules not coterminous with those formulated in the sets just referred to. In our study of rules governing the translation and paraphrase of the Palestinian Pentateuch Targum tradition, we must proceed from an analysis of the text itself, not from any pre-formed set of rules, such as those of Hillel, Ishmael, or others. When we do so, we find that there are very definite practices from which principles of translation and paraphrase can be deduced. Sometimes the actual translation may have followed principles of which the translator was quite unconscious. On many occasions, however, it seems that the translator was rendering into Aramaic according to a set pattern. What began as a practice may have in due time been raised to the status of a principle.

The laws at work in these Aramaic Pentateuch translations have been studied in some detail over the past decades, particularly by Roger Le Déaut,[99] Alejandro Díez Macho,[100] Michael Klein,[101] and Bernard Grossfeld.[102] In the list of underlying translation and paraphrase principles that follow, I draw rather heavily on M. Klein in particular.

---

[97]On these see H. L. Strack-G. Stemberger, *Einleitung in Talmud und Midrasch* (7th fully rev. ed., Munich, 1982) 25–40.

[98]See, for instance, Philip S. Alexander, "Rabbinic Hermeneutical Rules and the Problem of the Definition of Midrash," *Proceedings of the Irish Biblical Association*, no. 8 (1984) 97–115; also J. Luzarraga, "Principios hermenéuticos de exégesis biblica en el rabinismo primitivo," *Estudios Bíblicos* 30 (1971) 177–193.

[99]Cf. R. Le Déaut, "Les études targumiques: Etat de la recherche et perspective pour l'exégèse de l'Ancien Testament," *EphTheolLov* 44 (1968) 22–34; idem, "La tradition juive ancienne et l'exégèse chrétienne primitive," *RHistPhRel* 51 (1971) 31–50.

[100]A. Díez Macho, *El Targum*, 12–31; idem, in *Neophyti 1*, IV, 51*–59*; III, 47*–51*; *'al tiqrey* IV, 52*f., 56; semantic change, IV, 59*; *gematria*, III, 36*; IV, 58*, 65*; *gezerah shawah*, IV, 64*; homophony, IV, 51*; metonymy, I, 8*, 89*f.; II, 49*–51*; IV, 38*f., 42*, 53*; notarikon, III, 19*, 36*; V, 87*; divine passive, IV, 54*; *tartey mishma'*, I, 89*; IV, 52*f.; 56*f.

[101]M.L. Klein, 1986, I, xxix–xxxiv (general treatment, with illustrations from Genizah texts); idem, "Converse Translation: A Targumic Technique," *Biblica* 57 (1976) 515–537; idem, "The Translation of Anthropomorphisms and Anthropopathisms in the Targumim," *VTSupp*, Congress volume, Vienna 1980 (Leiden, 1981) 162–177; "Anthropomorphisms and Anthropopathisms in the Targumim of the Pentateuch" (Ph.D. diss., Hebrew University, Jerusalem, 1978, published Jerusalem, 1982, in Hebrew); "Associative and Complementary Translation in the Targumim," *Eretz-Israel* 16, H. M. Orlinsky volume, ed. A. Malamat and B. Levine (Jerusalem Exploration Society, 1982) 134*–140*. See also M. McNamara, 1977, 69–78 ("Characteristics of Targumic Renderings").

[102]B. Grossfeld, *An Analytic Commentary of the Targum Neofiti to Genesis: Including Full Rabbinic Parallels* (New York: Ktav, 1992), especially in the introduction in the section "Deviations in Neofiti from the Hebrew Text," under the three headings: "Syntactic expansions" (with twenty-two headings), "Interpretative translation" (with fourteen headings), and "Paraphrasis" (with fourteen headings). I wish to thank Dr. Grossfeld sincerely for having made pre-publication proofs of this work available to me.

1. The Palestinian Targums translate the HT

We should never forget that the primary intention of the Palestinian Targums seems to be to render the plain meaning of the HT into Aramaic:[103] to give the sense so that the people might understand the reading (Neh 8:8). The evidence is that by and large the translator understood his HT; how precisely remains to be determined in each case. The HT was not just a springboard for him, providing so many pegs on which to hang pet theories. It would be fair to say that what we have in the Pal. Tgs. for the most part is a more or less literal and faithful rendering of the HT, into which many additional paraphrases are inserted and interwoven. The Targumists, of course, often render differently from what translators today, given our better understanding of Hebrew, would. In the translations in this series, such "deviations" from the HT are noted by italics. That the original translator would have agreed that they were deviations is far from clear.

2. Multiple sense

Some Hebrew words have more than one meaning. Which of the meanings suits a given context can be a matter of opinion. The Pal. Tgs. often translate by retaining two or more senses for a Hebrew word. Thus, *šwp* of Gen 3:15 is rendered by "aim at" and "smite." Likewise, *b-'qb* of the same verse is translated both as "in the heel" and "in the future" (in messianic times). The point in the double rendering may have been the Targumist's desire to bring out the wealth of the HT.

3. Targumic doublets

Related to the above, or perhaps as an aspect of it, we have what Michael Klein[104] calls "targumic doublets," i.e., the use of two words to bring out the sense of a single word of the HT, e.g., *nš'* (*š't* of Gen 4:7) rendered by *šry wšbq*, "loose and forgive." Klein has made a detailed study of these in his work *Anthropomorphisms*, 145–151.

4. Stylized translation

We find in the Pal. Tgs. some fixed translation terms and formulas, sometimes differing from one Pal. Tg. tradition to another. The rendering of *zr'* ("seed") of the HT in the sense of human progeny has already been mentioned;[105] it is rendered as "sons" in Nf, as "descendance of sons" in Nfmg and other texts. Likewise, we have the rendering of HT *yldh* and *'lmh* by *rbyt'* in Nf and by *tly(y)t'* in another tradition.[106] There are

---

[103]On the relation of the Pal. Tgs. to the HT see also above note 82.
[104]M. Klein, 1986, I, xxxi; II, 4 (on Gen 4:7), with reference to the doublets in his *Anthropomorphisms*, 145–151.
[105]See above, p. 26.
[106]See above, p. 27.

many such stylized translations in the Pal. Tg., e.g., of HT's "land flowing with milk and honey" as "a land bearing good fruits, pure as milk and sweet as honey" (with slight but regular variations);[107] the regular addition of "redeemed" to the verb "bring (brought) out" of the HT: "he brought (you) out redeemed (from the land of Egypt)."

5. Associative and complementary translations

This is the name used by M. Klein[108] to describe the Targumic phenomenon of the paraphrase of some texts being colored by related biblical ones. Thus, "Remember the sabbath day" of Exod 20:8 is rendered (in CTg F) as "Beware (regarding) (*hwwn zhyryn*) the sabbath day," in Klein's view under the associative influence of Deut 5:12. Similarly, Lev 23:2 is rendered under the influence of the similar verse in Lev 19:9, and Deut 5:23(26) is rendered in some texts in association with Deut 4:7, 8. Klein further notes that this technique was expanded and consciously applied in a later period by the redactor of the Ps.-J. Targum. It is worthy of note, however, that this law seems to be less operative in Nf than in other Targums. Thus in Exod 20:8 and Deut 5:23(26) Nf follows the HT text, as indeed do P and Ps.-J.

6. Converse translation

An interpretative technique isolated by M. Klein[109] in the Genizah Pal. Tg. MSS is what he calls "converse translation," i.e., the translation says the opposite of what is in the HT. There is generally a valid midrashic or theological reason for this technique, which is not restricted to Genizah MSS. Despite the biblical text, in Pal. Tg. Gen 4:14 Cain says that it is impossible for him to hide from God. Again, despite the biblical text, in the CTg AA rendering of Exod 17:11 Israel was victorious even when Moses let down his hands. (Once again, one must note, this does not hold for Nf, which follows the biblical text.) In Deut 2:6 God tells Israel to purchase food and water from the sons of Esau. Not so in the Pal. Tg. (Nf), which renders: "You have no need to buy food from them for money because manna descends for you from heaven; and you have no need to buy water from them for money, because the well of water comes up with you...."[110] Sometimes we have not so much a converse translation as a slight variation, again for definite purposes. Thus, despite Nehemiah's campaign (Neh 13:23-27), Num 12:1 says that Moses was married to a non–Jewish Cushite. The Pal. Tg. says she was "like a Cushite in complexion"; Onq. renders "Cushite" as "beautiful"; Ps.-J. expands.

---

[107]The phrase occurs in HT Exod 3:8, 17; 13:5; 33:3; Lev 20:24; Num 13:27; 14:8; 16:14; Deut 6:3 (in VNL); 11:9; 26:9 (in CTg AA); 25:15 (in VN); 27:3 (in CTg AA); 31:20. In 3:17; Deut 27:3, "good" is omitted in Nf (added in Nfmg). In Lev 33:3; Deut 6:3; 11:9; 26:9; 31:20, Nf has "sweet and tasty," found also as a variant in a number of Nfmg and in VNL Deut 6:3; 26:15, not however in CTg AA. For similar translation techniques, see above pp. 26–27.

[108]Klein, 1986, I, xxxi.

[109]Op. cit., xxxi; loc. cit. (n. 97 above), *Biblica* 57 (1976) 515–537.

[110]See M. McNamara, 1972, 73.

7. Respect for the elders of Israel

This technique M. Klein calls "euphemistic translation."[111] The "whitewashing" translation phenomenon is present already in the LXX,[112] and possibly already in the Elohist source of the Pentateuch (cp. Gen 20:12-13 with Gen 12:19). Gen 29:17 says Leah's eyes were weak. This was rendered literally in some early Pal. Tg. texts, it would appear, a literal rendering objected to by R. Johanan in Palestine about 250 C.E.[113] Onq. renders the Hebrew term as "beautiful," Nf as "raised in prayer." According to HT Gen 29:31, 33 Leah was "hated" (*śnw'h*) by Jacob. Nf renders literally (*śny'*). CTg E, Nfmg, however, say she was "not loved in the face of her husband."[114] Examples under this heading could be multiplied but should be studied with cognizance of the variety of approaches to the problem in evidence within the Pal. Tg. tradition.

8. Derogatory translation

This is quite the opposite of the euphemistic translation just considered and describes the manner in which the Pal. Tgs. in general translate HT terms referring to idolatry or pagan worship.[115] The term "gods" (*'lhym*), when referring to pagan gods, is rendered "idols" (lit.: "errors"). Likewise, such figures as Balaam are generally referred to as "the wicked" (Pal. Tg. Num 22).

9. Updating of geographical and patronymic terms

In the Pal. Tgs. the biblical geographical and patronymic terms tend to be replaced by later forms. Together with this, later identifications of peoples connected with biblical names are given. A list of such later identifications in Greek has already been given. The fuller list of updated geographical terms in Neofiti has been studied elsewhere.[116]

10. Coins and weights[117]

i) *sheqel*. In the Pal. Tg. the Hebrew term *sheqel* is always rendered by the Aramaic term *sl'* (Gen 23:15, 16; Exod 21:32 (in CTg A); 30:13, 15, 24; 38:24, 25, 27, 29; Lev 5:15 (in VN); 27:3, 4, 5, 6, 7, 16, 25; Num 3:47, 50; 7:13 (also in PVN), 85, 86; 18:16; 31:52. This is in keeping with *j. Qidd.* I, 59d, bottom: "all shekels mentioned in the

---

[111]M. Klein, 1986, I, xxxii; see also M. McNamara, 1972, 74.

[112]Cf. D. Gooding, in *ZAW* 76 (1964) 269–280; idem, *VT* 17 (1967) 173–189; also M. McNamara, 1972, 33f.

[113]See M. McNamara, 1966A, 53f.

[114]On "hate," "love less/more," cp. Luke 14:26 with Matt 10:37.

[115]Cf. Klein, op. cit., xxxiii.

[116]On the geography of Neofiti, see McNamara, 1972, 190–205; for the larger question see also P. S. Alexander, "The Toponomy of the Targumim with Special Reference to the Table of the Nations and the Boundaries of the Holy Land" (diss. Oxford University, 1974).

[117]On this subject see the relevant entries with bibliographies in the *Encyclopaedia Judaica* (Jerusalem, 1972): "Coins and Currency" (vol. 5, 695–731, esp. 719–722); "Weights and Measures" (vol. 16, 176–329, esp. 388–390); and in the Index (vol. 1) under the relevant headings. From the older literature see Zuckermann, *Über talmudische Münzen und Gewichte* (1862); S. Krauss, *Talmudische Archäologie*, 2 (1911; rpt. 1966) 404–416; 712–720.

Pentateuch mean *sela*"; see also *b. Bek.* 50a: "every silver piece (*ksp*) mentioned in the Pentateuch without any qualification means a *sela*."

ii) HT *kkr (kikkar)*. This is a rare term in the HT; in Exod 25:39 and 37:24 rendered as *qnṭr*, "*centenarium, kentenarion,*" in Nf and P; in Exod 38:24, 25, 27, 29 Nf retains the HT *kkr*, as does Onq. throughout.

iii) *gerah* (MT). The word occurs in Exod 3:13; Lev 27:25; Num 3:47; 18:16, rendered as *m"* (*m'yn*) in Nf.

iv) *beqa'* (MT). The word occurs in Gen 24:22; Exod 38:26. In both cases it is rendered in Nf as *tb'*.

11. Targumic interpolations

The Targumic translator in both the translation and paraphrases was bound by the HT that lay before him. He had to insert traditions at the appropriate places of the text.[118] Some sections of the Pal. Tgs. are clearly recognizable as such insertions, as interpolations, since they may break both the flow of thought and even the very syntax. To illustrate by a few examples from many (inserted section in italics):

And whatever Adam called *in the language of the sanctuary* a living creature, that was its name (Nf Gen 2:19).

And he [Moses] reached the mount *over which the glory of the Shekinah of the Lord was revealed* Horeb (Nf Exod 3:1).

And when the Canaanite, the king of Arad, who dwelt in the south heard *that Aaron, the pious man for whose merit the clouds of the Glory had led forth Israel had died (lit.: had been taken up), and that Miriam the prophetess, for whose merits the well used to come up for them, had died (lit.: had been taken up),* that Israel had reached the way by which the spies used to come up (HT: the way of Atharim), he waged war on Israel and took some of them captive (Nf Num 21:1).

12. Anti-anthropomorphisms[119]

It is recognized that the Pentateuch, as indeed other books of the Hebrew scriptures, contains certain anthropomorphic ways of speaking of God that must have caused difficulties and embarrassments within the biblical period itself. It is also clear that the Targums seek to mollify such anthropomorphisms. Those who have studied the treatment of anthropomorphisms in the Targums agree that the Targumists do not delete or

---

[118]See McNamara, op. cit., 107.

[119]For modern literature on the subject see M. L. Klein, 1986, I, xxxii; idem, "The Translation of Anthropomorphisms and Anthropopathisms in the Targumim," *VT Supp*, Congress volume, Vienna 1980 (Leiden, 1981) 162–177; idem, *Anthropomorphisms and Anthropopathisms in the Targumim of the Pentateuch* (Ph.D. diss., Hebrew University, Jerusalem [in Hebrew]; published Jerusalem, 1982); D. Muñoz León, "Soluciones de los Targumim del Pentateuco a los antropomorfismos," *EstBib* 28 (1969) 263–281; Carmel McCarthy, 1989; R. Le Déaut, in *Le Targum du Pentateuque*, vol. 1, *Genèse*, 59–62.

recast them all.[120] To do so might well have proven an impossibility, given the inherent limitations of the human mind and human language in matters relating to the divine nature and activity. The approach of the Pal. Tg. to the subject can only be deduced from its usage. It would appear that, in general, anthropomorphisms tend to be avoided in the manners specified below. This has not always proved possible, and on occasion it seems that the Targumist recast one anthropomorphic expression, only to rephrase it in another equally so. Thus in Moses' prayer to God in HT Gen 18:3: "O Lord, if I have found favor in your *eyes* (*b'ynyk*), do not pass by your servant." This in Nf becomes: ". . . if I have found favor in your *face* (*b'pyk*). . . ." Bearing these translation problems in mind, I here list some of the major texts subjected to anti-anthropomorphic treatment.

i) *"in the eyes of the Lord (b'yny YHWH)."* In general, in Nf this is rendered as "before the Lord" (*qdm /mn qdm YYY*). That the change is due to the desire to remove the anthropomorphism seems clear from the fact that when the key words refer to a human person, Nf renders as "in the face of" (as it does in Gen 18:3 in a context in reality most probably to be taken as referring to God).

ii) *"the hand of the Lord."* In Nf, when there is question of rather evident anthropomorphism, this expression is changed, and indeed in a variety of ways. In Exod 7:5, Yahweh's words "when I stretch forth my hand upon Egypt" become in Nf: "when I set the plague of my punishment upon Egypt." Similarly, in Exod 9:3, "the hand of the Lord will fall with a very severe plague" becomes in Nf: "the plague of my punishment shall be upon." "Is the Lord's hand shortened?" of Num 11:23 becomes in Nf: "Is there deficiency before the Lord?" In Exod 16:3, "by the hand of the Lord" becomes in Nf: "before the Lord." The Targumist, however, sees nothing wrong in the Lord saving Israel "by a strong hand," which he leaves unchanged (Exod 13:3, 9, 14, 16; Deut 5:15; 6:21; 7:8, 19, 26; 11:2; 26:8; 34:12). And Nf renders "(the sanctuary . . .) which your hands has established" of Exod 15:17 as: ". . . your two hands have perfected it."

iii) *"the mouth of the Lord."* In Nf, in such contexts "the mouth of" is rendered "the decree of the Memra of the Lord"; when humans are in question, "decree" is still inserted, but "mouth" remains unchanged, e.g., Gen 45:21.

iv) *"the face of the Lord."* Eight occurrences of an expression in the HT which should probably be taken as referring to "seeing the face of God" caused theological difficulties to Israel's religious scribes and were vocalized as Niphal (reflexive, "to be seen/to appear before the Lord") rather than as *qal*, or as active. These, as would be expected, are also taken as reflexive in the Pal. Tg.[121]

v) *Avoiding making God the direct subject or object of actions relating to creation.*[122] This tendency is most noticeable with regard to the HT verbs "saw" and "heard" when

---

[120]Thus already L. Ginzberg, "Anthropomorphism," *The Jewish Encyclopedia*, vol. 1, 623.

[121]See Carmel McCarthy, 1981, 197–204; idem, 1989, 53f.

[122]See M. McNamara, 1972, 93–97; A. Díez Macho, *Neophyti 1*, IV, 53*f. ("El 'pasivo divino'"); D. M. Golomb, *A Grammar of Targum Neofiti*, 209. B. Barry Levy, *Targum Neophyti 1. A Textual Study*, vol. 1 (1986) 38–39, believes that the original translation of Nf did not have this passive construction ("it was revealed/heard, etc., before the Lord . . ."), which would have been introduced at a later date into the text.

these have God as subject (often also in HT having an object marked with the object particle, *'et*). In the Pal. Tg. the verb is put in the passive, followed by "before the Lord," which in turn is followed by the erstwhile object now become subject (!) but with the object particle (*yat*). Thus Gen 1:4: "God saw the light (*'et ha'or*) that (it) was good"; Nf: "It was manifest before the Lord the light (with accusative sign *yat*) that (it) was good." So also Gen 6:12; 21:17; 31:12; 31:42; Exod 2:24; 4:31; even with an angel as subject, Gen 31:12; see also Gen 4:8; 4:18; 21:5.

vi) *Actions done before God.*[123] The Targums in general, including the Pal. Tgs., frequently speak of actions being done, of events happening, "before the Lord" or "from before the Lord." While the Aramaic expression itself is not restricted to the Targums or to references to God, but is part of a broader vocabulary of reverential language, on a number of occasions its use in the Targums is for anti-anthropomorphic purposes.[124]

VIII. DIVINE NAMES IN THE PALESTINIAN TARGUMS

This is a subject closely connected with the theme of anti-anthropomorphism, as some of the terms and phrases used to describe the God of Israel have to do with avoiding or softening anthropomorphisms of the HT. Since, however, this is not always the case, it seems best to examine this theme separately. It is not always easy to determine whether the Targumist is working out of a particular theology regarding the God of Israel in his use of divine names or simply carrying a theory of translation, a translation or paraphrase technique, to its conclusion.[125]

1. Targumic translations of rare names for God

Such biblical divine names occurring mainly in the Pentateuch as El Shaddai, the Fear of Isaac, the Strong One (*'byr*) of Jacob are rendered as follows in the Pal. Tgs.:
El Shaddai (Gen 17:1; 28:3; 35:11; 43:14; 49:25; Exod 6:3; Num 24:4; 24:16): Nf, "the God of the heavens."
The Fear (paḥad) of Isaac (Gen 31:42; 31:53): Nf, "the Strong One (*tqyp'/h*) of Isaac."
The Strong One ('byr) of Jacob (Gen 49:24): Nf, "the Strong One (*tqyph'*) of Jacob."
'El 'Elyon (Gen 14:18, 19, 20, 22; Num 24:16; Deut 32:8): Nf, "the Most High God" (*'lh' 'l'h*).

2. Father in heaven[126]

This designation for God is not strongly attested in the Pal. Tgs., and what attestation there is is unevenly distributed. In all, including Ps.-J., we find thirteen occur-

---

[123]See M. McNamara, 1972, 93f.; M. L. Klein, 1979, 502–507; idem, 1981, 171; Roger Syrén, *The Blessings in the Targums*, 24–26, 202; Ribera, 1983; C. McCarthy, 1989 (to n. 34).
[124]See C. McCarthy, 1989, 50–52.
[125]See A. Díez Macho, "Las denominaciones de Dios," *Neophyti 1*, III, 70*–83*.
[126]See M. McNamara, 1972, 115–119; A. Díez Macho, *Neophyti 1*, IV, 36*f.

rences of the designation, distributed as follows: three in Ps.-J., seven in Frg. Tg., and three in Nf. The texts are as follows: Gen 21:33 (Ps.-J.); Exod 1:19 (Ps.-J., Frg. Tgs., Nf); Exod 17:11 (Frg. Tg.); Lev 27:28 (Ps.-J.); Num 20:21 (Frg. Tg.); Deut 28:32 (Ps.-J); Deut 32:6 (Frg. Tg.); Deut 33:24 (Nf). Only one of these texts (Exod 17:11, in CTg AA) is preserved in the Genizah Pal. Tg. MSS, but the designation does not occur there. In only one instance (Exod 1:19) do all the representatives carry the designation. The designation is found in three contexts: 1) prayer to the Father in heaven (Exod 1:19; Num 21:9; Gen 21:33; Deut 28:32; Exod 17:11); 2) reward before the Father in heaven (Num 23:23); 3) merciful as the Father in heaven (Lev 22:28).

3. Glory, Shekinah, Glory of the Shekinah of the Lord[127]

"The glory of the Lord" (Heb.: *kabod, kebod YHWH*) is a good biblical expression, particularly dear to the Priestly Writer, but in use by no means restricted to him. It serves a theological purpose—that of safeguarding the transcendence of God. The biblical Aramaic equivalent is *yᵉqar*, of which there are but few occurrences in the Bible (Daniel), and mainly with reference to humans ("honor"), not counting the "one like the son of man" (Dan 7:14).

The noun *shekinah* (lit.: "dwelling") does not occur in the HT. The verb from which it derives, however, i.e., *shaken*, is frequent there, in the senses of "settle down, abide, dwell." It is used of God, who is said to dwell among his people (Exod 25:8; 29:46; Num 5:3; Ezek 43:9, etc.). The tabernacle is his dwelling-place par excellence and is in Hebrew called just that—*mishken*.

In later Judaism more extensive use still was made of the term "Glory" with reference to God, especially when it was believed that the biblical text required paraphrase to safeguard divine transcendence or to avoid anthropomorphism, e.g., Exod 24:10: "And they saw the God of Israel." According to the oft-cited principle of Rabbi Judah ben Ilai, to render this literally would constitute a lie.[128] It had to be rendered: "And they say *the glory of* the God of Israel." The term "Shekinah" became equally common in later Judaism to express God's dwelling with his people.

I here study the usage of these terms principally in Codex Neofiti, the only one preserved in its fullness. In relation to the usage found there, observations are made regarding the other texts.

To begin with, it must be observed that in Neofiti the term "glory (of God)" by itself is very rarely used, and "Shekinah" alone less so. The usual formula is "the glory of the Shekinah of the Lord." The usages are as follows:

i) *The Glory of God.*[129] In a few texts in Nf, "Glory of the Lord" is a metonym for God and could be equally well expressed by the other phrase, "the Memra of the Lord," and in fact sometimes is; thus, "the *Memra of the* Lord created the two luminaries (Gen 1:16) . . . and the *Glory of the Lord* set them in the firmament" (Gen 1:17); further Nf

---

[127]See Arnold M. Goldberg, 1963; summary by A. Díez Macho, *Neophyti* 1, II, 49*–55*; D. Muñoz, 1977.

[128]Tos., *Meg.*, end; b *Kidd* 49a; see M. McNamara, 1972, 99.

[129]See M. McNamara, op. cit., 99f.

Gen 1:27; 2:2, 3. It is not easy to say whether the presence of "the Glory of the Lord" in these Nf has any special theological significance.[130]

ii) *The Shekinah of the Lord.* In Nf the term "Shekinah" occurs very rarely without being in combination with "Glory": Nf Exod 15:13: ". . . dwelling-place of the Shekinah of your holiness"; Nf Exod 15:17: "the house of your Shekinah . . . the house of your holiness"; Nf Exod 24:17: "the appearance of the Shekinah of the Lord was like a devouring fire"; Nf Num 24:6: "like the heavens which the Lord has spread out as the house of his Shekinah."

iii) *The Glory of the Shekinah of the Lord.*[131] This occurs about 101 times in all in Nf, as follows: Nf Gen, nine times; Nf Exod, thirty-seven times; Nf Lev, six times; Nf Num, eighteen times; Nf Deut, thirty-one times. The occurrences are in general not haphazard but follow regular patterns, associated with certain verbs, as follows: with the verb "dwell," forty times;[132] with "was revealed," seventeen times;[133] with the verb "lead," nine times;[134] with the verb "go up," six times;[135] with the words "is among," once (Nf Deut 6:15). There are twenty-three occurrences with other verbs or words, as follows: with "rebel against," Nf Num 14:9; with "tempt," Nf Deut 6:13; 6:16; with "to meet," Nf Exod 19:17; with "to see," Nf Exod 16:7; 33:23 ("see the Memra of the Glory of my Shekinah . . . but not . . . the face of the Glory of my Shekinah"); with "to look on," Nf Exod 3:6; with "will accompany among," Nf Exod 33:14, 16; with "will pass (by)," Nf Exod 12:23; 33:22; 34:6; with "filled," Nf Exod 40:34, 35; Num 14:21; with "was upon," Nf Exod 40:35; with "in the midst (of)," Nf Num 14:14; with "turn back," Nf Deut 23:15; with "cloud(s)," Nf Exod 19:4; Num 10:34; 14:14; Lev 23:43 ("the clouds of the Glory of my Shekinah," etc.).

4. *The Memra of the Lord*[136]

The designation for God most characteristic of all the Targums is "the Memra of the Lord." This is found 314 times in Nf and 636 times in Nfmg; in Frg. Tgs. about 99 times; in CTg text 97 times in texts published by Kahle; in Onq 178 times and 322 in Ps.-J.

---

[130]The usage, we may note, occurs in a section of Codex Neofiti (Gen 1:1–3:4) which may not belong to the tradition of the main Nf text; see S. Lund and J. A. Foster, *Variant Versions*, 72–80.

[131]For the larger study see the works noted in n. 127 above.

[132]Gen 3:24; 9:27; 28:6; 49:27; Exod 17:7; 18:5; 20:21; 25:8; 29:45, 46; 39:43; 40:35; Lev 15:31; 16:16; 26:11; Num 10:30; 11:20; 14:42; 16:3; 35:34; Deut 3:24; 4:39; 12:5, 11, 21; 14:23, 24; 16:2, 6, 11; 26:2, 15; 31:17; 32:10; 33:12, 16, 26, 27; cf. also Lev 23:43.

[133]Gen 11:5; Exod 3:1; 16:10; 19:11, 18, 20; 20:20; 24:13; 34:5; Lev 9:6, 23; Num 11:25; 12:5; 14:10; 16:19; 17:7(42); 20:6.

[134]Deut 1:30, 32; 7:21; 9:3; 20:4; 23:15; 31:3, 6, 18.

[135]Gen 17:22; 18:3, 33; 35:13; Exod 33:3, 5.

[136]For Memra in Nf, see R. Hayward, 1974; D. Muñoz, "Apendice sobre el Memra de Yahweh in Neophyti 1," in A. Díez Macho, *Neophyti 1*, III (1971), 70*–83*; on the larger question of Memra, see R. Hayward, 1981; D. Muñoz León, 1974 (summary by L. Sabourin, "The Memra of God in the Targums," in *BThB* [1976] 79– 85); also the earlier works, V. Hamp, *Der Begriff "Worte" in den aram. Bibelübersetzungen: Ein exegetischer Beitrag zum Hypostasenproblem und zur Geschichte der Logos-Spekulationen* (Munich, 1938); P. Billerbeck, in *Kommentar zum NT aus Talmud und Midrasch*, II, 303–333; G. F. Moore, 1922; M. McNamara, 1972, 101–106.

The Aramaic word *mmr'* (rarely written in original form *m'mr'* in non-Qumran texts) comes from the root *'mr*, "to say."

The term is found twice in the Qumran Targum of Job (11QtgJob XXVII, 9; XXXIII, 7, *m'mrh, m'mrk*, "his/your command") in the sense of "order," "command," and is found also, even if rarely, with this, its fundamental sense, in the Targums. In general, however, in the Targums "Memra" is used as a buffer word, introduced apparently for some theological purpose, such as to avoid anthropomorphisms, to avoid making God the direct object or subject of actions connected with creation. Its origins, development, and antiquity as used in this sense are a matter of speculation and of much study.

5. *The* Dibbera *of the Lord*[137]

In Hebrew, *dibberah* is the *nomen actionis* of the verb *dibber* ("to speak") and means "divine discourse," "revelation." The plural *dibberôt* is used for the Ten Commandments (or "Words," *debarîm*). In the earlier Tannaitic period the form generally used in Jewish sources is *dibber*, while in the later Amoraic age it is *dibbûr*. *Dibbera, debira, dibbur*(a), or however we write the words, signifies God as revealing his will to man.

In the Palestinian Pentateuch Targums this term is found on a few occasions, generally written as *dbyr'* or *dbyrh*, which, with M. Klein and others,[138] I vocalize as *Dibbera*. The occurrences are as follows: Gen 28:10, Nf, PVNL (*dbwr'*); Exod 14:30, CTg T; 19:3, Nf (*dbyr*), PVNL; 19:20, PVNL (Nf, Nfmg: Memra), CTg F; 20:2, Nf (pl. -yy'), P (*dbr'*), CTg F (*dbyrh*); 20:3, Nf, CTg F (*dbyr'*) (sing. = commandment); 33:23. Nf, Nfmg (*dbwr'*); Lev 1:1, Nf, Nfmg (in VNL: Memra); Num 7:89, Nf, Nfmg; Deut 5:21, CTg D (pl.; in Nf Memra, 3).

It is obvious that this designation for God is unstable in its attestation, and at times is found in places where a parallel Targum text sometimes has "Memra." Domingo Muñoz León believes that Targumic occurrences of the term *dibbera* are secondary, due to revision.[139] This can be doubted. The case for this term is somewhat similar to that of "Father in heaven"; irregularity in its use is not an argument against antiquity or its presence in some contexts in the Targums.

6. *The Holy Spirit*[140]

The expression "the Holy Spirit" (*rwḥ' d-qwdš'*; lit.: "spirit of holiness") occurs in Nf Gen 41:38; 42:1 (also in P); Exod 31:3 (corrected); 35:31; Num 11:17, 25, 26, 28, 29; 14:24; 24:2; 27:18—thirteen times in all. It also occurs in Nfmg Gen 31:21 and Exod 2:12 (also in PVB).

---

[137]See M. McNamara, op. cit., 108–110; D. Muñoz León, 1974, 668–679 ("Dibbera y Memra"); also A. Díez Macho, in *Neophyti 1*, IV, 75*f.

[138]M. L. Klein, 1986, II, 70, 106; D. Muñoz León, loc. cit. (n. 132).

[139]Op. cit. (1974); idem, in A. Díez Macho, *Neophyti 1*, II, 80*f.; see M. Klein, 1986, II, 70.

[140]Cf. J. P. Schäfer, 1970; idem, *Untersuchungen zur Vorstellung vom heiligen Geist in der rabbinischen Literatur* (Freiburg, 1968); résumé in A. Díez Macho, *Neophyti 1*, III, 52*–55*; idem, *Neophyti 1*, IV, 43*–47*.

In Onq. the only designation found is "the spirit of prophecy"; the use of "holy spirit" in Onq Gen 45:27 is possibly due to the influence of midrashim.[141] The designation "the Holy Spirit" is found fifteen times in Ps.-J. and "the spirit of prophecy" eleven times.

Questions such as the date to be assigned to these texts and their primary or secondary nature as used in the Pal. Tgs. need not be considered here.

7. The heavenly voice (Bath Qol)[142]

In later Judaism one manner of revelation was through the *Bath Qol*, a heavenly voice (lit.: "daughter of a voice," "an echo"). In a sense the *bath qol* was the same as the Holy Spirit, God revealing his will to man, or as continuing divine action after the Holy Spirit was believed to have ceased to be with Israel; cf. *Yoma* 9b: "after the death of the Last Prophets the Holy Spirit was taken up from Israel but the people still made use of the *bath qôl*."

In the Palestinian Targums occasional reference is made to a *bath qol* (in Aramaic: *brt ql'*), e.g., Gen 22:10 (Nf, P, VNL, "angels of above"); 27:33 (Nf); 38:25 (Nf; PVNL, CTg X, CTg FF, 38:26); Num 21:6 (Nf, PVN); Ps.-J. Deut 28:15 (Nf: "voice [*ql*] of the Memra of the Lord your God").

IX. MESSIAH, THE TORAH, PRAYER, AND GOOD DEEDS IN NEOFITI

1. The Messiah[143]

Neither Messianic times nor the person and work of the Messiah feature centrally in Targum Neofiti 1 or in any of the Pal. Tg. texts. In fact, the passages interpreted messianically are generally the same in all these texts, and the Messiah is given the title King (or the King) Messiah. The first reference occurs in Tg. Gen 3:15, where it is said that some unspecified persons (but presumably the children of the woman) will make appeasement in the end, in the day of King Messiah. Gen 49:10 is in Nf, as indeed in all the Targums, interpreted of the Messiah, and furthermore Gen 49:11-12 is paraphrased of his person and work. In the Poem of the Four Nights (Pal. Tg. Exod 12:42; Paris MS 110 Exod 15:18), the Fourth Night is that of redemption, when Moses and King Messiah will come, the latter from on high (or possibly, from Rome). In Nf, apparently inadvertently, the mention of King Messiah is omitted but should be restored to the text. According to Pal. Tg. Num 11:26, Eldad and Medad in the camp prophesied that at the very end of the days Gog and Magog would ascend on Jerusalem and would

[141]See B. Grossfeld, 1988, p. 151, n. 17 to Onq. Gen 4:17.

[142]See M. McNamara, 1972, 113f.; F. Lentzen-Deis, 1970.

[143]See S. H. Levey, *The Messiah: An Aramaic Interpretation. The Messianic Exegesis of the Targum*, Monographs of the Hebrew Union College 2 (Cincinnati/New York: Hebrew Union College-Jewish Institute of Religion, 1974); M. Pérez-Fernández, *Tradiciones mesianicas en el Targum Palestinense*, Estudios exegéticos Institución San Jerónimo 12 (Valencia/Jerusalem: Institución San Jerónimo, Casa de Santiago, 1981).

fall at the hand of King Messiah. In Pal. Tg. Num 24:8, Balaam's oracle on the star to arise out of Jacob is thus paraphrased: "Their king shall arise up from among them, and their redeemer shall be from themselves. He shall gather their captives from the provinces of their enemies and their children shall rule over many nations. He shall be stronger than Saul, who had pity on Agag, the king of the Amalekites, and the kingdom of the King Messiah shall be exalted."

2. The Torah[144]

The Law (Torah) was given through Moses. However, in the tradition enshrined in Neofiti (and the Pal. Tg. generally), the Lord created the Torah two thousand years before the world was created (Tg. Gen 2:24), a tradition based on the identification of the Torah with wisdom and a midrashic interpretation of Prov 8:22, 30. The Lord God placed the first man in the Garden of Eden to toil in the Law and to keep its commandments (Tg. Gen 2:15). The Law is the Tree of Life for all who labor in it. Anyone who observes its precepts lives and endures as the Tree of Life in the world to come. Likewise, Gehenna is established by God for the wicked, who did not observe the precepts of the Law in this world (Tg. Gen 3:24). According to Tg. Gen 3:15, the children of the woman will have victory over the serpent or be wounded by it in accord with their observance or neglect of the precepts of the Law. Similarly, with regard to the relations of Jacob and Esau, according to Tg. Gen 27:40. This concentration on the Torah, the observance of the commandments, and the rewards of this observance found in the opening section of Genesis reappears in the closing section of Deuteronomy, e.g., Tg. Deut 32:14, 29, 30, and especially 33:29: "Blessed are you, Israel! Who is like you! A people whose redemption is near from before the Lord, who is the shield of your help. . . . And your enemies shall be broken before you; and you, my people, children of Israel, shall tread on the necks of kings when you study the Law and do the commandments."

The great commandment of Deut 6:5, ". . . you shall love the Lord your God. . . ," is thus paraphrased in Nf: "And you shall live the teaching of the Law of the Lord with all your heart and all your soul and all your wealth." The "teaching (or instruction) of the Law" is a favorite expression in Nf. "A stiff-necked people" is regularly paraphrased as "a people hard at receiving instruction" (Tg. Exod 33:5). Failure or refusal to listen to God is paraphrased as failure to listen to the instruction of his Law (Tg. Lev 26:14; Deut 5:26). To "forget God" becomes "to forget the instruction of the Law of the Lord" (Tg. Deut 8:11).

3. Prayer[145]

The relatively frequent mention of prayer in Nf indicates that this was one of the concerns of the person or tradition that produced the paraphrase. Mention is made of prayer in general (with the verb *ṣly* or related words) and of petition (*bb'w*, "I beseech"—lit.: "in petition"). Any calling on God, expressed in the HT by *ṣ'q* or *qr'*, is

---

[144]On this and following sections see B. Barry Levy, *Targum Neophyti 1. A Textual Study*, vol. 1, 70–76.
[145]See M. Maher, "The Meturgemanim and Prayer," *JJS* 41 (1990) 226–246.

rendered in Nf as "praying" (*ṣly*). Thus, for instance, Nf Gen 12:8; Exod 14:15; Num 12:13; Deut 4:7; 26:7. Likewise Nf Exod 19:8; 20:24; 24:1; 32:10; Deut 3:23; 9:14, where the HT uses other words. God's reply, by listening, etc., is expressed as listening to the prayers addressed to him. Thus, Tg. Gen 17:20; Num 21:3; Deut 3:26; 9:19; 10:10; 26:7. Raising or extending the hands of the HT is paraphrased in the Tg as doing so in prayer (Tg. Gen 49:24; Exod 17:11). Exod 32:30 speaks of Moses going up to God. In Nf this becomes going up "to beg mercy from before the Lord." Reference to prayer is introduced into the paraphrase of Gen 24:63; 29:17; and 30:8.

4. Good deeds

Mention of doing the commandments already implies interest in good works. Explicit mention is often made of these. Thus, "perfect" (*tm*) of the HT, when referring to humans, is rendered as "perfect in good works." These "good deeds" to be done in obedience to the Torah can also be expressed by the term *miṣwah, miṣwoth*. "Empty" of Deut 16:16 is paraphrased in Nf as "empty (void) of every precept" (*mṣwh*) or "good work." In Tg. Gen 15:1 Abraham is worried that he might have received the reward of the precepts (*mṣwwth*; or good deeds) in this world and have no portion in the world to come. The importance of good works (*'wbdyn ṭbyn*) is evidenced by the debate on the matter between Cain and Abel on the matter in Tg. Gen 4:8. One's works (Tg. Gen 38:25), good works, in this world will be rewarded with a portion in the world to come. Neglect of good works will be punished in Gehenna (see Tg. Gen 3:22, 24; 4:8; 15:1; 38:25).

X. RELATION OF THE PALESTINIAN TARGUMS TO RABBINIC JUDAISM

The Pentateuch lay at the very heart of Jewish life and thought in the homes, the synagogues, and schools. From the time of Ezra onward it was the task of those in the succession of Ezra, priest and scribe of the Law of God given through Moses, to have it explained so that the people could understand its message. This task was carried on in particular in rabbinic Judaism as known to us through the two Talmuds and the Midrashim. The manuscripts of the Palestinian Targums of the Pentateuch have been transmitted to us by rabbinic Judaism. This is evidence that even if not an official targum, as Onqelos later was, the Palestinian Targum tradition was recognized by rabbinic Judaism as its own.

It requires little observation to note that, at least by and large, the haggadic and exegetical tradition enshrined in the Palestinian Targums coincides with that of rabbinic tradition as known to us from other sources, particularly Palestinian. The exact nature of this relationship is a matter yet to be determined, both with regard to halakah and haggadah, or non-halakic midrash.

1. The Palestinian Targums and rabbinic Halakah

The relationship of the Palestinian Targums tradition to "official" Jewish rabbinic Halakah is a matter that has exercised the mind of scholars particularly in recent decades. Certain texts have been interpreted as anti-halakic and for this reason regarded as early, and pre-Mishnaic.[146]

Some scholars, such as Michael Klein,[147] regard many of the legal interpretations in the Pal. Tgs. as reflecting the halakah of R. Ishmael as opposed to that of R. Aqiba, which later became normative, this being regarded as possibly the major reason for the eventual disappearance (suppression?) of the Pal. Tgs. and their replacement by the "halakicly-correct" Targum Onqelos.

This is a matter into which we cannot here enter. The halakah of each of the Pal. Tgs. should of course be studied in this regard to see how they differ, if at all. Such an examination might also give insights into the Targumists as translators, as it will emerge that in many cases they appear more interested in rendering the HT "neutrally" than in giving an accepted halakic rendering.

2. The Palestinian Targums and non-halakic midrash

It is quite clear that in very many instances the Palestinian Targums tradition agrees with, or is very similar to, rabbinic non-halakic midrash. The extent and nature of this relationship between Neofiti in particular and rabbinic tradition have been studied in great detail by a number of scholars, in particular Rabbi Menahem Kasher[148] and Bernard Grossfeld.[149] The notes to the translation will give some details of the relationship.

3. Palestinian Targum broader than known rabbinic tradition?

I believe it would be a mistake to work on the assumption that the Palestinian Tg. exegetical tradition did not go beyond the rabbinic as known to us from the traditional sources. To begin with, it is far from certain that present rabbinic tradition is

---

[146]A. Geiger and P. Kahle maintained that there are anti-Mishnaic texts in the Pal. Tg. and that what is anti-Mishnaic is pre-Mishnaic: A. Geiger, *Urschrift und Uebersetzungen der Bibel* (2nd ed., 1928) 451ff.; P. Kahle, *The Cairo Geniza* (1st ed., London, 1947, 122f.; 2nd ed., Oxford, 1959). See A. Díez Macho, 1960, 222–225. This principle is objected to by Ch. Albeck and others. In any event, as M. Klein (1986, I, xxxiv) notes: "the examples of identified 'early halakha' in the PTs (excluding PsJ) are still too few to serve as a means of dating the targumim relative to the *halakhic* midrashim." Among more recent studies on the topic we may note: M. Ohana, "El Targum Palestino y la halaká oficial. Estudio comparativo basado en Neofiti 1 a Exodo" (diss. University of Barcelona; cf. A. Díez Macho, *Neophyti 1*, III, 13*); D. Shofet, "Estudio de halakot de Neofiti 1 del Levitico" (diss. University of Barcelona; cf. A. Díez Macho, ibid.). On Ohana's work see A. Díez Macho, *Neophyti 1*, IV, 20*–26, 33*–35*; V, 28*–33*; see also M. Ohana, "Agneau pascale et circoncision: Le problème de la halakha prémishnaique dans le Targum palestinien," *VT* 23 (1973) 385–399.

[147]M. L. Klein, 1986, I, xxxiii; idem, in *HUCA* 50 (1979) 159–164; J. Faur, "The Targum and the Halakha," *JQR* 66 (1975) 19–26; see also M. Kasher, *Torah Shelemah*, vol. 24; ch. 8 (pp. 57–64) for the relationship of the Pal. Tgs. to Beth Hillel and Beth Shammai; also idem, *Torah Shelemah*, vol. 25, pp. 342f.: Beth Hillel follows Ps.-J. and Beth Shammai Nf.; summaries in A. Díez Macho, *Neophyti 1*, IV, 30*–35* (fol. vol. 24); *Neophyti 1*, V, 61*f. (for vol. 24, ch. 8).

[148]M. Kasher, *Torah Shelemah Neophyti 1*, V, 41*– 82*; IV, 30*–33*.

[149]B. Grossfeld, "A Commentary on the Text of a New Palestinian Targum (Codex Neofiti 1) on Genesis 1–25" (diss. Johns Hopkins University, 1968), summarized by A. Díez Macho in *Neophyti 1*, III (1971), 26*–33*; idem (in revised and expanded for all Genesis): *An Analytic Commentary of the Targum Neofiti to Genesis: Including Full Rabbinic Parallels* (New York: Ktav Publishing House, 1992).

coterminous with the earlier one, known for instance to such Fathers as Jerome.[150] In fact, we have at least one case (Nf Gen 8:6) in which Jerome notes a Jewish understanding of Gen 8:6 now preserved for us only in Nf.[151] No known rabbinic text seems to interpret Gen 3:19 of the resurrection of the body as the Pal. Tgs. do. It is also found in the apocryphal *Apocalypse of Moses*.[152] This is an area in which more work might be done.

XI. AGE AND ORIGIN OF THE PALESTINIAN PENTATEUCH TARGUMS

In this introduction we are dealing with the Pal. Tgs. as known to us through the extant sources: the entire text in Codex Neofiti, partial Cairo Genizah texts, Fragment Targums, Targumic Tosefoth, early and medieval citations. These are written texts, literature, not oral tradition. We have also seen that these texts have in general been translated from the Hebrew with no small amount of thought and art; variant traditions among them have a certain unity of translation procedures which set them off from other translations within the same tradition.[153] This again is evidence that we are here dealing with literature, not ad hoc synagogue translations.

Through the extant manuscripts and citations we can trace the history of this Targum tradition from the more recent manuscripts of the sixteenth century back to the eighth and possibly earlier. We now examine whether we can go beyond this.

1. Early written Palestinian Pentateuch Targums

From Qumran we have evidence that at least some written Targums existed in early times.[154] 11QtargJob may have originated as early as 200 B.C.E., and may have been the same as the Targum of Job known to Rabbi Gamaliel I (25–50 C.E.) and his grandson Gamaliel II (90–110 C.E.). The Qumran Job Targum is totally different from the Targum of Job transmitted by rabbinic Judaism and translated in this series. From Qumran we also have sections of a Targum (Aramaic translation) of Lev 16 (4Qtarg Lev), probably from the first century B.C.E. We do not know if it is but a portion of a Targum of all of Leviticus or of the Pentateuch or merely of Lev 16, which was of special liturgical interest. As a text it has similarities to Onq.

---

[150]For Genesis especially in his *Hebr. quaest. in libro Geneseos*. On Jerome's relation to Jewish tradition see bibliography in *S. Hieronymi Presbyteri Opera* I, 1 (CCL 72, 1959, p. xxxii; see F. Stummer, "Einige Beobachtungen über die Arbeitsweise des Hieronymus bei der Uebersetzungen des Alten Testaments aus der Hebraica Veritas," *Biblica* 10 (1929) 3–10; idem, "Beiträge zur Lexikographie der lateinischen Bibel," *Biblica* 18 (1937) 25–30; and now L. Opelt, "San Gerolamo e i suoi maestri ebrei," *Augustinianum* 28 (1988) 327–338. See especially study of the question, particularly in relation to Gen 14, by R. Hayward, "Some Observations on St. Jerome's 'Hebrew Questions on Genesis' and Rabbinic Tradition," *Proceedings of the Irish Biblical Association*, no. 13 (1990) 58–76; idem, "Saint Jerome and the Aramaic Targumim," *JSS* 32 (1987) 105–123.

[151]See below, p. 45.

[152]*Apoc. Moses* 41; ed. M. D. Johnson in J. Charlesworth, ed., *The Old Testament Pseudepigrapha* 2, 291.

[153]See above, pp. 25–28, 30–32.

[154]See M. McNamara, 1972, 62–68.

We have very strong evidence from rabbinic sources that written texts of the Targums of the Pentateuch (therefore Palestinian Targums) existed at least in the late third and early fourth centuries of our era, and there are indications that they were known there earlier still.[155]

Written Targums are legislated for in the Mishnah, *Yadaim* 4:5.

In *b. Berakoth* 8a we read of the advice given by R. Joshua ben Levi (ca. 250 C.E.) to his children on how to prepare the *parashah*, i.e., the weekly section of the Pentateuch read in the synagogue: "Even so did Joshua ben Levi say to his children: 'Complete your *parashah* together with the congregation, twice the Hebrew Text and once the Targum.'"

The same advice was given by R. Ammi (ca. 300 C.E.) to all Jews, according to the same text (*b. Berakoth* 80ab): "R. Huna ben Judah says in the name of R. Ammi: 'A man should always complete his *parashah* together with the congregation, twice the Hebrew text and once the Targum, even such verses as Ataroth and Dibon (Num 32:3), for if one completes his *parashah* together with the congregation his days will be prolonged.'" These texts are best understood if written rather than oral Targums are intended. And, in point of fact, those who examine this evidence tend to see here references to written Targums.

Some texts connected with R. Samuel bar R. Isaac clearly indicate the use of written Targums in Palestine in the early fourth century.[156] In *j. Megillah* IV, 1 (74d, top, ed., Krotoschin) we read: "R. Samuel bar R. Isaac entered a synagogue (and) saw a certain man translating while leaning against a pillar. He said to him: 'It is forbidden to you! Just as it was given in awe and reverence, thus we have to treat it with awe and reverence.'" The point being made, it would appear, is that the Targum merits the same respect as the Law itself.[157]

In *b. Berakoth* 45a we read again of R. Samuel: "R. Samuel bar R. Isaac entered the synagogue (and) saw a certain teacher interpreting the Targum from the book. He said to him: 'It is forbidden to you! Matters which are transmitted orally (should remain) oral; matters which are (transmitted) in writing (should remain) in writing.'" As Anthony D. York remarks on this passage, "Among the several interesting features of this passage, we should observe first of all that a written Targum was in use in the synagogue early in the fourth century"[158]—a point that fits in well with the evidence we have seen from R. Ammi, R. Samuel's contemporary.

2. *Likelihood of transmission to us of fourth-century Targums*

With regard to the likelihood of Palestinian Targum texts of the fourth century C.E. or earlier having been faithfully transmitted to the sixteenth, we should judge from the case of the Cairo Genizah text E Targum. This unfortunately is extant only for Genesis,

---

[155]Ibid., 83f.
[156]See Anthony D. York, "The Targum in the Synagogue and the School," *JSJ* 10 (1979) 74–86.
[157]Ibid., 75f.
[158]Ibid., 77.

and then only in fragmentary fashion: Gen 6:18–7:15; 9:5-23; 28:17–29:17; 29:17–30:2; 30:46–31:15; 31:15–31:22; 38:16–39:10; 41:6–41:26; 43:30–44:4. P. Kahle in 1930[159] dated this manuscript to 750–800 C.E. The leading present-day palaeographer, Professor Malachi Beit Arié, can be no more precise in his dating than "early," i.e., ninth/tenth to mid-eleventh century C.E.[160] The fact, however, that a text of this particular Pal. Tg., or more probably a sister copy of it, is reproduced almost verbatim in the marginal glosses of Neofiti (copied 1504) shows how an early text was faithfully transmitted.

3. Arguments linking our present Pal. Tg. texts with fourth-century Palestine or earlier

The rabbinic citations already considered,[161] when taken with the arguments for fidelity of transmission, present fairly strong grounds for seeing continuity between our present texts with fourth-century Palestine or earlier. The arguments appear strongest for an early date for the Targum of Codex Neofiti 1. To the rabbinic citations already noted we should add an extremely interesting text of Jerome. In his *Hebraicae quaestiones in Gen.* 8:6 he says: "*Post quadraginta dies aperuit Noe ostium arcae . . .* Pro ostio fenestra scripta est in hebraeo." ("*After forty days Noah opened the door of the Ark.* For 'door' in Hebrew we find written '*window.'*") The Hebrew text (*ḥlwn*) and Jerome's Vulgate rendering of it, have "window," not "door." Nor does any known translation have "door," apart from Neofiti, which Neofiti reading some scholars have regarded as a textual error.[162] Could it be that the late fourth-century scholar Jerome had access to the original of Neofiti or to a Neofiti-type text?

Much more study will be required before we can safely say that the Pal. Tg., at least of the Neofiti type, can be assigned to the fourth century, e.g., examination of the Greek and Latin loan words to ascertain when they were current; more detailed examination of the form of the Aramaic used.

XII. PALESTINIAN TARGUMS OF THE PENTATEUCH: CONCLUSION

The introduction to the Palestinian Targums which I have given above is not intended to be complete. Such a task would be too large an undertaking, and, in my opinion, less suited as an introduction to the texts being translated here. Instead of this I have concentrated on points I believe to be of importance for an understanding of our extant texts of these versions, their nature, their origins and development. It is hoped that what has been written above will help further exploration in this field of research. Despite the detailed examination of the various issues involved over the past decades, we are probably still only in the initial stages in our exploration of this rich field.

---

[159]P. Kahle, *Masoreten des Westens*, 3*.
[160]See M. L. Klein, 1986, I, xxxvii.
[161]Above, pp. 10–12.
[162]Thus Y. Komlosh, *The Bible in the Light of the Aramaic Translations*, in Hebrew (Bar Ilan, 1973) 54, n. 201, a position not accepted by A. Díez Macho, *Neophyti 1*, V, 37*.

BRIEF INTRODUCTION TO THE PALESTINIAN TARGUMS OF GENESIS

Volumes in this series, in their introductions, usually treat of the place of the particular biblical book in Jewish life: in the liturgy, schools, etc., and in the history of Jewish interpretation. The biblical book of Genesis treats of the period before the giving of the Law to Moses and is consequently of less importance for Jewish halakah. However, because it is concerned with truths and events of such importance as creation and the promises to the Fathers, Genesis has from its very composition enjoyed a central place in biblical and Jewish tradition. Its message is prolonged and interpreted in later books of the Bible. Themes from it, such as the sin of the angels or heavenly beings, are central to Jewish apocalyptic. Its story has been retold in the "Rewritten Bible," of Jubilees, the *Biblical Antiquities* of Pseudo-Philo, and of other writings. It has provided material and a jumping-off ground for many biblical Apocrypha, e.g., *The Apocalypse of Adam, The Testament of Adam, The Life of Adam and Eve (The Apocalypse of Moses), The Apocalypse of Abraham, The Testament of Abraham, The Ladder of Jacob, The Testament of Jacob, Joseph and Aseneth, The Prayer of Joseph, The Testament of Joseph, The Testament of the Twelve Patriarchs*, and many other works besides on the prediluvial (Enoch, etc.) and post-diluvial (e.g., Shem) patriarchs and personalities (e.g., Melchisedek).

This late biblical and intertestamental tradition continued to grow. Exegesis of the work and development of the traditions of Genesis flourished in rabbinic Judaism. We have a major collection of Jewish interpretations and midrash on Genesis in *Genesis Rabbah*. This Jewish tradition was transmitted to later generations down through the Middle Ages and to our own day.

The Early Church inherited and transmitted the Jewish tradition of Genesis Apocrypha. It was also in dialogue to a good extent with rabbinic tradition of the early Christian centuries. Both these traditions are to be found in works of the ecclesiastical writers of the Syriac, Greek, and Latin Churches. Together with this, of course, the Christian Church composed its own midrashic-type interpretation of Genesis and bequeathed both to the Middle Ages.

As one of the books of the Pentateuch, Genesis was part of the synagogue liturgy. Its sacred and liturgical status ensured respect for its text and its message in synagogue and school. Both these institutions were at pains that the message be understood and put before the people. To this reverence and activity the Palestinian Targums bear witness.

INDEX OF VERSES PRESERVED IN THE
FRAGMENT-TARGUMS OF GENESIS

The following list is taken from M. L. Klein, *The Fragment-Targums of the Pentateuch According to Their Extant Sources* (Rome: Biblical Institute Press, 1980), vol. I, pp. 242-244, and is reproduced by the kind permission of the publisher.

GENESIS

1:1-2	P V N	6:14	P V N L
1:3-4	P	7:10	P
1:5-6	P V N	7:11	V N L
1:7	P	7:16	P V N L
1:8	P V	8:1	P V N L
1:9-13	P	8:10/12	V N L
1:14	P V N	8:22	P V N
1:15-26	P	9:20	P V N
1:27	P V N L	10:2-3	V N
1:28-31	P	10:4	P V N
2:1-3	P	10:9-11	P V N
2:7	V N	10:12-14	V N
2:9	P V N L	10:17-18	V N
2:15	P V N L	11:1	V N
2:18	P V N L	11:2	P V N
2:20	V N L	11:4	P V N
2:22	P	11:30	P V N
2:24-25	P V N L	12:2-3	V N L
3:7-9	P V N L	12:5	P V N L
3:10	P	12:6	V N L
3:15	P V N L	12:15	P V N L
3:17	P	13:6-7	P V N L
3:18	P V N L	14:3	V N L
3:19-21	P	14:5-6	V N L
3:22	P V N L	14:9-10	P V N L
3:23	P	14:14-15	V N L
3:24	P V N L	14:17	V N L
4:7	P V N L	14:18	P V N L
4:8	P V N	14:21	V N L
4:9	P	14:23	P V N L
4:10	P V N	15:1-2	P V N L
4:13	V N L	15:7	V N L
4:16	P V N L	15:9-10	V N L
4:22	P	15:11-12	P V N L
4:26	P	15:17	P V N L
5:2	P	15:19	V N L
5:4-5	V N L	16:5	P V N L
5:24	P V N L	16:7	P V N L
6:3	P V N L	16:13	P V N L
6:6	V N L	16:17	P V N L
6:8	P V N L	18:1	P V N L
6:11	V N L	18:10	P V N L

CATALOGUE OF CAIRO GENIZAH FRAGMENTS OF
PALESTINIAN TARGUMS OF GENESIS

The following list is taken from M. L. Klein, *Genizah Manuscripts of Palestinian Targum to the Pentateuch* (Cincinnati: Hebrew Union College Press, 1986), vol. I, pp. xliv-xlvi, and is reproduced by the kind permission of the publisher.

GENESIS

2:17–3:6	MS B		37:15-33	MS E
4:4-16	MS B		38:16-26	MS D
4:8 (tosefta)	MS I		38:25, 26 (tosefta)	MS X
4:7, 8, 23 (tosefoth)	MS X		38:25, 26 (tosefta)	MS FF
5:28(?); 6:5 (*lemma only*)	MS B		38:16–39:10	MS E
6:18–7:15	MS E		40:5-18	MS E
7:17–8:9	MS B		41:6-26	MS E
9:5-23	MS E		41:32-41	MS C
15:1-4	MS H		41:43-57; 42:34–43:10	MS E
17:11(?) (tosefta)	MS EE		42:36 (tosefta)	MS X
21:6-16	MS LL		43:23–44:4	MS E
21:4-9	MS Y		43:7–44:23	MS D
21:10 (tosefta)	MS EE		44:18 (tosefta)	MS X
22:5-9	MS K		44:18	MS RR
24:3-4	MS KK		44:16-20; 47:26	MS Z
28:17–29:17	MS E		44:18 (tosefta)	MS R
29:17–30:2	MS E		44:18 (tosefta)	MS M
30:2-40	MS E		46:26–47:5; 47:29–48:10	MS D
30:40–31:15	MS E		48:11-21	MS D
31:15-34	MS E		47:28–49:17	MS Z
31:38-54	MS C		(for 47:26, see 44:16-20, MS Z)	
32:13-29; 34:9-25	MS C		49:1 (tosefta)	MS FF
35:6-15	MS C		49:18 (tosefta)	MS X
36:8-9, 24	MS D		49:18; 50:1, 16 (toseftot)	MS FF
37:19-34	MS D			

Targum Neofiti 1: Genesis

Translation

CHAPTER 1

1. *From* the beginning[1] *with wisdom*[a] *the Memra*[2] *of the Lord*[b][3] created *and perfected* the heavens and the earth. 2. And the earth was waste[4] and unformed,[c] *desolate of man*[d][5] *and beast, empty of plant cultivation and of trees*, and darkness *was spread* over the face of the abyss; and a spirit *of mercy from before the Lord* was blowing over the surface of the waters. 3. And the Memra of the Lord said: "Let there be light"; and there was light according to the decree of his *Memra.*[e] 4. And *it was manifest before the Lord that* the light[f] was good;[6] and the *Memra of the Lord*

Apparatus, Chapter 1

[a] P: "In wisdom (marg. adds "o[ther] t[ext]: from the beginning = Nf) the Lord created and perfected the heavens and the earth"; VN: "in wisdom the Lord created the heavens and the earth."

[b] Text: "in wisdom the son of the Lord (*br' dyyyy*) perfected." The text, however, in MS itself is corrected after an erasure; "and" of the original is visible before "perfected." This original reading probably was: "the Lord (or: the Memra of the Lord) created (*br'*) and perfected"; see P Nfmg: "in wisdom the Lord created" (cf. VN).

[c] P: "and the earth was waste and unformed and desolate of sons of man and empty of all cultivation and darkness was spread over the face of the deep ... " (etc. as in Nf).

[d] Lit.: "of a son of man"; PVN: "of sons of man."

[e] P: " ... and there was light by his Memra."

[f] "the light" is preceded by the sign of the accusative; also in P; cf. HT .... "God saw the light."

Notes, Chapter 1

[1] "From the beginning with wisdom": double translation of HT *br'šyt*, as "beginning" and "wisdom." For creation of the world by/in wisdom, cf. Prov 8:22; 3:19; Wis 9:9; Ps 104:24. Rabbinic tradition, identifying wisdom and the Torah, speaks of God creating the world by the Torah; "beginning" = torah, *Gen. R.* 1, 1.4: "In the beginning by means of the Torah God created...." See also Levine, 1974, 4. For commentary on Nf Gen 1:1-2, 4a, see Muñoz León, 1974A, 164–167.

[2] "the Memra of the Lord"; text of Nf has: "the son of the Lord," *br' dYYY*, (See Apparatus, note *b*), which is due most probably to a late, even sixteenth-century, correction. However, in Christian tradition from earliest times the opening word of Genesis was understood to mean "in the Son" (= Jesus, the Word); see Jerome, *Hebr. quaest.*, in Gen 1:1 (CCL 72, 3, citing *Altercation of Jason and Papiscus*; Tertullian and Hilary. The original Palestinian Targum probably read: "From the beginning in wisdom the Memra of the Lord created"; see also 2 Ezra 6:38, 43: "In the beginning (Latin trans.: From the beginning) of creation you spoke the word ... and your word perfected (i.e., carried out, completed) the work." On the possible relationship of 2 Ezra to Pal. Tg., see D. Muñoz León, 1974B, 1975, esp. 1975, 52–61; idem, 1974A (*Dios Palabra*), 162–164. On Memra and creation, D. Muñoz León, ibid. (1974A) 607–611; R. Hayward, 1974, 1981. On the use of Nf of Memra dYYY as a rendering of the HT *'lhym* and YHWH, and on the possibility of a development in this usage, see B. Barry Levy, *Targum Neophyti 1. A Textual Study* 1: Introduction, Genesis, Exodus, 1986, 41–43.

[3] "the Lord": HT: "God" (Elohim). Nf and Tgs. in general render Elohim of HT as "the Lord" (variously written in the Nf MS as YYY, YY, etc.). See note 2 to Ps.-J. (vol. 1B of this series).

[4] See note to Ps.-J. (vol. 1B in this series). See also Jer 4:23, 25; 33:10, and 2 Ezra 6:39: "and the spirit was hovering and silence and darkness embraced everything; the sound of man's voice was not yet there." On the double translation of words of HT in Tgs. see Introduction, p. 30.

[5] "desolate of man"; lit.: "of the son of man."

[6] Lit.: "and it was manifest before the Lord the light ("light" with sign of accusative) that it was good"; "it was manifest before the Lord" is a common Targumic construction to avoid making God the subject or object of actions relating to creation; HT: "and the Lord saw the light (with sign of accusative, *'t*) that it was good." Sign of accusative (*yt*) with passive construction due to slavish translation of underlying Hebrew; see on this feature Golomb, 1985, 209. See also M. McNamara, 1972, 93f.; note to Ps.-J. (vol. 1B in this series). B. Barry Levy, 1, 1986, 38–39, maintains that in the original

separated the light from the darkness. 5. And *the Memra of the Lord* called the light daytime[g7] and the darkness he called night. And there was evening and there was morning: *(in) the order[h] of the work of creation,* [8] *first* day. 6. And *the Memra of the Lord* said: "Let there be the firmament in the midst of the waters, and let it separate the *lower waters* from the *upper waters.*"[i7] And *the Lord[j] created*[9] the firmament[k] and separated the waters that were under the firmament from the waters that were above the firmament; and it was so *according to his Memra.*[m] 8. And *the Memra of the Lord* called the firmament heaven. And there was evening and there was morning: *(in) the order of the work of creation,* second day. 9. And *the Memra of the Lord* said: "Let the waters under the heavens be gathered together into one place and let the dry land appear." And it was so[m] *according to his Memra.* 10. And *the Memra of the Lord* called the dry land the earth, and *the gathering-place of* the waters he called the Seas.[n] And it was *manifest before the Lord that it was beautiful*[o] *and proper.*[10] 11. And *the Memra of the Lord* said: "Let the earth put forth[p] herbage of grass which produces seed, a fruit tree which yields fruit according to its kind, *whose shoots are from it and in it* upon the earth." And it was so *according to his Memra.*[m] 12. And the earth put forth herbage of grass which produces seed according to its[q] kind, a *fruit* tree which yields fruit, *whose shoots are from it and in it* according to its kind. *And it was manifest before the Lord that it was beautiful and proper.* 13. And there was evening and there was morning: *(in) the order of the work of creation,* third day. 14. And *the Lord[r]* said: "Let there be lights

Apparatus, Chapter 1

[g] *ymm(')* as in P, Ps.-J., Onq.
[h] P: "and there was the order ... " (etc. as in Nf), and thus in P for vv. 8, 13, 19, 23, 31.
[i] PVN: "the upper waters from the lower waters."
[j] P: "the Memra of the Lord."
[k] Nfmg: "the firmament of the heavens."
[m] P: "according to the decree of his Memra."

[n] *ymm'* = (*yammê*? error for *ymy'*? Nfmg: *ymyy'*; P: *ymy.*
[o] P: "good (and proper)."
[p] P: "make grow."
[q] Lit.: "their kind"; P: "its kind."
[r] P: "the Memra of the Lord."

Notes, Chapter 1

translation of Nf such texts were rendered literally (active verb + God + *yt* + object, a usage still visible in Nf Gen 21:17; 31:50; 39:3; 33:5; Deut 11:12). The present construction in Nf with the insertion of *gly/šmy' qdm YYY*, etc., he regards as probably a later development. He refers to Nf Exod 3:7, which contains both literal and paraphrastic translations.

[7] *ymm'*, "daytime," as opposed to night, and distinct from *ym'* ("day" of twenty-four hours); see note to Ps.-J. and detailed note by Grossfeld, *Neofiti*, note 10 to Gen 1.

[8] "the order of the work of creation"; possibly an allusion to the use of this pericope in a synagogue *ma'amadah* reading, linking a section of the Israelite people with the Temple courses of priests; cf. M *Meg* 3:6 and McNamara, 1972, 37. B. Grossfeld, however (*Neofiti*, note 11 to Gen 1) believes the insertion reflects a combination of two rabbinic stock phrases: "the works of creation" (*m'śh br'śyt*) and "the orders of creation" (*sdry br'śyt*). See also Tg. Isa 4:21.

[9] "created," HT: "made" (*'śh*); also in Frg. Tg. When the Hebrew word refers to the creation of the world (as here, in vv. 16, 25, 26; 2:2), Nf renders as "create," otherwise by "made," as noted by B. Grossfeld, op. cit. (on Gen 2:7); A. Díez Macho, *Neophyti 1*, III, 31*. See also note to Ps.-J. (vol. 1B of this series).

[10] "beautiful and proper": the regular Nf rendering of the HT: "(that it was) good" (Gen 1:10, 12, 18, 21, 25, 31; v. 4 is an exception, with no addition to HT). P has "good and proper" in all cases, again with exception of v. 4, where there is no addition to HT.

in the firmament of the heavens to separate the daytime from the night, and let them act as signs and (sacred) seasons[s] and so *that the intercalation of moons (and) months*[11] *may be consecrated by them.*[t] 15. And let them shine[u] in the firmament of the heavens to shine upon the earth." And it was so *according to his Memra.*[m] 16. And *the Memra of the Lord* created the two great lights: the greater light to rule[w] in the daytime and the lesser light to rule[w] in the night, and the *arrangement of the stars.*[12] 17. And *the Glory of the Lord*[x] set them[13] in the firmament of the heavens to shine upon the earth, 18. and to rule[u] in the daytime and in the night and to separate the light from the darkness. And *it was manifest before the Lord that it was beautiful and proper.* 19. And there was evening and there was morning: *(in) the order of the work of creation*, fourth day. 20. And *the Memra of the Lord said*: "Let the waters swarm forth a swarm of living creatures, and birds that fly[y] above the earth, across *the air of the* firmament of the heavens." 21. And *the Lord*[z] created the *two* great monsters and every living creature that creeps,[aa] which the waters swarmed forth according to their species, and every bird that flies[bb] according to its species. And *it was manifest before the Lord that it was beautiful and proper.* 22. *And the Memra of the Lord* blessed them saying: "Be strong[14] and multiply and fill the waters in the seas, and let birds multiply upon the earth."[cc] 23. And there was evening and there was morning: *(in) the order of the work of creation*, fifth day. 24. *And the Memra of the Lord* said: "Let the earth bring forth living creatures

Apparatus, Chapter 1

[s] Nf: *zmnyn*, lit.: "times"; VN: *mw'dyn*, "set times," "feasts"; P: *smnyn*, "signs," "symbols."

[t] Lit.: "to consecrate by them . . ."; P: "so that the beginnings of months and years might be consecrated by them"; VN: "and let them be as signs and sacred seasons to consecrate by them the beginnings of months and years"; Nfmg: "variant reading: the beginnings of months and years."

[u] Nf: *mnhryn*; P: "and let them be (=serve) as lights" (*lnhwryn*).

[w] P: "to render service."

[x] P: "the Memra of the Lord."

[y] read probably, with Nfmg: "and let birds fly" (but see v. 21); P: "and let birds fly swiftly across the face of the firmament of the heavens."

[z] P: "the Memra of the Lord."

[aa] P: "that crawls."

[bb] P: "that flies swiftly."

[cc] P: "on the earth."

Notes, Chapter 1

[11] "the intercalations of moons (and) months (*'bwr shryn yrḥyn*) be consecrated . . ."; HT (RSV): "let them be for signs and for seasons and for days and years." For PVN text (see Apparatus), cf. *Gen. R.* 6,1; for both Nf and Nfmg, Grossfeld (op. cit., note 24) notes the striking parallels in Pal. Talmud *Ber.* 9, 2, 13c and *Gen. R.*, loc. cit. The text of Nf, however, may be somewhat corrupt.

[12] "the arrangement of the stars"; HT: "the stars"; same rendering in Nf Deut 4:19. There are rabbinic parallels; see Grossfeld, op. cit., note 26, but note also 2 (4) Ezra 6:45: ("on the fourth day thou didst command) the arrangement of the stars" (Latin: *stellarum dispositionem*).

[13] "the Glory of the Lord set them." HT: "and God set them." Heretofore creation was said to have been by God's Memra; now in Nf mention is made of the Glory of the Lord in the creation narrative (Nf 1:17, 20, 29; also 2:3). See D. Muñoz, 1974, 164f.; idem, 1977, 40; McNamara, 1972, 99f.

[14] "Be strong"; HT: "Be fruitful," from Hebrew root *prh*. Nf almost invariably translates this Hebrew verb as "be strong." Thus Gen 1:22; 2:8; 8:17; 9:1, 7; 26:22; 35:11; 47:27; 49:22; Exod 1:7; even in causative (Hiphil): Gen 17:16, 20; 28:3; 48:4; Lev 26:9. The only exceptions are Exod 23:30 and Deut 29:17.

according to their species: cattle and creeping things and beasts of the earth according to their species." And it was so *according to his Memra.*[dd] 25. And *the Memra of the Lord created* the wild beasts of the earth according to their species,[ee] and the cattle according to their species,[ee] and all the creeping things of the earth according to their species. And *it was manifest before the Lord that it was beautiful*[ff] *and proper.* 26. And *the Lord*[gg] said: *"Let us create man*[hh] in our likeness, *similar to ourselves,*[15] and let them rule over the fishes of the sea and over the birds of the heavens, and over the cattle and over all the earth, and over every creeping thing that creeps*[ii] upon the earth." 27. And *the Memra of the Lord* created the *man*[jj] in his (own) likeness; in a likeness *from before the Lord* he created him;[kk] male and *his partner*[16] he created them. 28. And *the Glory of the Lord*[mm] blessed them, and *the Memra of the Lord* said to them: *"Be strong*[17] and multiply and fill the earth and subdue it; and rule over the fishes of the sea and over the birds of the heavens and over every wild beast that creeps upon the earth." 29. And *the Glory of the Lord*[mm] said: "Behold, I have given you all the herbs that produce seed that are on the face of all the earth and every tree[nn] that has fruit in it—seed-bearing tree—*I have given them* to you for food. 30. And to every wild beast of the earth, and to all the birds of the heavens, and to everything that creeps on the earth that has the breath of life[oo] in it, (I have given) every herb as food." And it was so *according to his Memra.* 31. And everything that he had made was *manifest before the Lord,* and behold it was very *beautiful and proper.* And there was evening and there was morning: (in) the *order of the work of creation,*[pp] sixth day.

Apparatus, Chapter 1

[dd] P: "according to the decree of his Memra"; see note *m* above.
[ee] Lit.: "its species"; P: "its kind."
[ff] P: "good (and proper)"; see note *o* above.
[gg] P: "the Memra of the Lord."
[hh] Lit.: (in Nf and P): "(let us create) a son of man" (*nbr' brnš*).
[ii] Nfmg: "crawling thing that crawls."
[jj] Nf lit.: "the son of man (*brnš'*); PVN: "created Adam" (*'dm*).

[kk] P: "created them"; VN as Nf.
[mm] P: "the Memra of the Lord."
[nn] Nf lit.: "all the trees"; P: "every tree that has fruit in it—seed-bearing tree—you shall have as food."
[oo] P: " . . . that has in the breath of life (I have given) every herb as food. And it was manifest before the Lord that it was good and proper."
[pp] P: "and there was the order of the work of creation . . . "; see note *h* above.

Notes, Chapter 1

[15]"in our likeness (*dmwt*), similar to ourselves"; HT: "in our image (*ṣlm*) and likeness" (*dmwt*). When reference is to God, Nf avoids use of the word "image" (*ṣlm*), which Hebrew term it renders by the more abstract "likeness" (*dmwt*), as in Gen 1:26, 27; 9:6. It retains *dmwt* of HT in 5:1. When the two are used in conjunction, Nf renders the second word of the pair as "similar to ourselves" (1:26; 5:3), *kd npq b—*, which corresponds to the common Hebrew Mishnaic idiom *kywṣh* b-.

[16]"partner"; *zwg*; Greek loan word: *zeugos, zygon* (found in Palestinian midrashim and Pal. Tg.); in Nf Gen 1:27; 2:18, 20; 35:9; Num 7:3; cf. Deut 32:4; in P, Gen 1:27; 2:18; 5:2; 35:9. See Introduction, p. 18.

[17]"Be strong"; HT: "Be fruitful"; see note to 1:22.

CHAPTER 2

1. And they completed[a] *the creation*[b] of the heavens [1] and the earth [2] and all their hosts. 2. And on the seventh day *the Memra of the Lord* completed[c] his work which he had created[d] and there *was sabbath and repose before him* [3] on the seventh day from all his work which he had *created.*[4d] 3. And *the Glory*[e] *of the Lord* blessed the seventh day and hallowed it because[f] on it *there was a great sabbath and repose before him* [3] from all his work which the *Glory* [5] *of the Lord*[g] had done in creation. 4. This is the genealo*gical pedigree*[6] of the heavens and of the earth [7] when they were *created.* On the day that the Lord God created[h] the heavens and the earth, 5. none of the trees[i8] that are on the surface of the field had as yet existed on the earth and

Apparatus, Chapter 2

[a] *'šlmw;* as also P.

[b] *bryyt (šmy'); so also* P (*bryyt šmy'*).

[c] P: "cherished (v[ariant] v[ersion] completed)."

[d] Nfmg: "he had done and he rested himself on the seventh day from all the work he had done" = P.

[e] Nfmg: "the Memra (of the Lord)" = P.

[f] P: "because in it he rested himself from all his work which the Memra of the Lord has created in

doing" (lit.: "created to do"); Nfmg: "he rested himself (from)."

[g] Nfmg: "the Memra of (the Lord)"; cf. P.

[h] Nfmg: "(that) the Memra of the Lord (created) the heavens."

[i] Nfmg: "(no) tree."

Notes, Chapter 2

[1]"And they completed (*'šlmw*) the creation of the heavens . . .";HT: "and there were completed (*yklw*) the heavens and the earth." Nf's *'šlmw* apparently to be taken as an Afel ("they completed"), due to *yklw* (MT: *yekullû*), the rare Pual form of *klh* (occurring only here and in Ps 72:20), being taken as a Piel and rendered as the Piel forms are in Nf Gen 2:2; 17:22; 18:33; 24:15, 19, 45; 27:30; 43:2; 49:33. A Díez Macho (*Neophyti 1*, IV, 85*) takes *'šlmw* of Nf Gen 2:1 as Perfect Peal ("were completed"), i.e., *šlmw* with prosthetic alef (cf. Dan 5:3, 4). This is less likely. Furthermore, the passive sense would require taking *bryt* ("creation") as plural. Sokoloff, 1990, 554, however, gives as the first meaning of the Afel of *šlm* "to come to an end, to be finished," instancing CTg E Gen 41:53 (Nf has *šlmwn*); CTg E Gen 29:21; Nf Deut 34:8.

[2]"creation of heavens and earth" (*bryt šmy'*), also a rabbinic expression; see B. Grossfeld, in A. Díez Macho, *Neophyti 1*, III, 30*.

[3]"there was sabbath and repose before him." HT: "and he rested"; Nf's paraphrase is made to avoid anthropomorphism. Nf's phrasing possibly influenced by Exod 31:17 and 20:11: on the seventh day God rested (*šbt*), reposed (*ynḥ*), in both of which cases Nf renders as in Gen 2:2.

[4]"created"; HT: "made." See note to 1:7.

[5]"the Glory of the Lord." HT: "God." See note to 1:17. See also Muñoz León, 1974A, 165; idem, 1977, 40.

[6]"genealogical pedigree" (*yḥws tldt*); MT: *toledot*; Nf renders MT *toledot* (RSV: "generations") with the composite *yḥws twldw(w)t* in Gen 2:4; 5:1; 6:9; 11:10; 36:1, 9; 37:2; with the simple (*t(w)ldwt* in Gen 10:1, 32; 11:27; 25:12, 13, 19, and Num 3:1; with the simple *yḥws* in Exod 6:16, 19; 28:10; Num 1:20, 22, 24, 26, 28, 30, 32, 34, 36, 40. The only text of these in PVNL is Gen 25:19 (rendered in Nf by simple *twldwt*), where the rendering is as is general in Nf Genesis: *yḥws twldt*. The sole text of these in the Genizah fragments is Gen 36:9 (CTg B, imperfectly preserved) where Aramaic rendering seems to be *twldwth* (Nf *yḥws tldt*); see M. Klein, 1986, 1, 77. The double rendering *yḥws twldwt*, confined to Nf Genesis (and also in PVNL Gen 25:19), seems to be without special significance. In this translation the double form is rendered throughout as "genealogical pedigree," *twdlwt* as "genealogy," and *yḥws* as "pedigree(s)."

[7]"the heavens and the earth." HT: "the earth and the heavens." The inversion, already in Sam. Pent. MSS, is probably due to influence of 1:1, etc., or scribal error.

[8]"trees." HT: "no bush" (*śyḥ*), as in *Gen. R.* 13,2. Same rendering in Nf Gen 21:15.

none of the herbs that are on the face of the field[9] had as yet sprouted on the earth, because the Lord God[j] had not as yet caused rain to fall, and as yet Adam[10] *had not been created* to till the *earth.* 6. But a cloud used to go up from the earth and watered all the surface of the *earth.* 7. And the Lord God *created*[12] Adam[13] (out of) dust from the ground and breathed into his nostrils[k] the breath of life, and Adam[13] became a living being *endowed with speech.*[14] 8. And the Lord God[m] had planted a garden in Eden *from the beginning*[15] and he placed there the *first* Adam[16] whom he had created. 9. And out of the ground[n] the Lord God made grow every tree that was nice to see and good to eat, and the tree of life within the middle[17] of the garden,[o] and the tree of knowledge of which *anyone who would eat would know to distinguish*[p] between good and evil. 10. And a river went out from Eden to water the garden and from there it was divided and *turned* to become four heads of *great rivers.* 11. The name of one *of them* is Pishon.[18] It is that which *surrounds and encircles* all the *land of India,*[19] from where the gold *comes.* 12. And the gold of that

---

Apparatus, Chapter 2

[j] Nfmg: "the Memra of the Lord upon."
[k] Nfmg: "into his face the breath of life."
[m] Nfmg: "the Memra of the Lord."
[n] Nfmg: "(out of) the earth."
[o] Nfmg: "(tree) of life within the garden."

[p] Nfmg: "used to know to distinguish"; PVNL: "and the tree of knowledge of which everyone who ate distinguished (VNL +: for himself) between good and evil."

Notes, Chapter 2

[9]"surface of the field" (or: "face of the field"), *b-'py br'*; HT: *śdh* (RSV: "field"). Nf renders *śdh* of the HT in three different ways: (1) most commonly be *'py br'*, "the surface (face) of the field"—thus Gen 2:5, 19, 20; 3:1, 14, 18; 4:8; Exod 1:14; Deut 11:15; 14:22, etc.; (2) *ḥql*, "field; farm; estate"—thus Gen 23:9, 13, 17, 19; 25:9, 10, 27; 37:7, 15; 47:24; 49:29, 30, 32; 50:13; Exod 8:9; 9:3, 19; 22:9; (3) *tḥwm*, "territory, boundary, border"—thus Gen 32:4; 33:19; 36:35; 41:48.

[10]"Adam," *'dm*, reproducing the HT; RSV: "(no) man". Nf generally renders *'dm* of HT, when generic, as *br nš*, "a son of man." Here Nf either reproduces the HT mechanically or takes *'dm* as a personal name; see also v. 7.

[11]"a cloud." MT: *'ed* ("mist," "cloud," RSV, etc.), occurring again only in Job 36:27, rendered as *'nn* ("cloud") in 11 QTg Job; as "cloud" also in LXX Job 36:27; also in Onq.; double translation in Ps.-J. According to *Gen. R.* 13,2 *'ed* and *'anan* are two of the five names for cloud. See also J. Luzarraga, 1973, 7ff.

[12]"created"; "made"; see note to 1:7.

[13]"Adam"; *yt 'dm*; MT: *ha-'adam*, "the man"; taken in Nf as a personal name. In v. 16 Nf retains the HT *h'dm*.

[14]"endowed with speech"; all Tgs. here add this endowment of man to the HT.

[15]"from the beginning"; *(m)qdm* of HT taken as "from the beginning" rather than as "to the east." This understanding of *qdm* as "beginning" is common: Aquila, Symmachus, Theodotion, Vulgate; see Jerome, *Hebr. quaestiones*, in Gen 2:8 (CCL 72,4). Opinion however was divided regarding the time of creation of individual items: Torah, Garden of Eden, Gehenna, etc. The Garden of Eden was not created before the creation of the world, but before Adam and on third day according to a tradition in *Gen. R.* 15, 3. See also note to Nf Gen 3:24.

[16]"the first Adam"; corresponds to the Hebrew *'adam ha-rishon*, a common rabbinic designation for Adam; cf. also 1 Cor 15:45.

[17]"within the middle"; Nf strengthens HT's "within," or "in the middle of," by a double translation.

[18]The river Pishon was identified with the Indian river Ganges in Jerome's day (cf. *Hebr. quaest.*, in Gen 2:11; CCL 72,4); see already Josephus, *Ant.*, 1, 38.

[19]"India"; HT: "Havilah"; identification known to Jerome (loc. cit.) and implicit in the identification of Pishon with the Ganges.

land is good. *From* there *comes* bdellium, and *precious stones and pearl.*[20] 13. And the name of the second river is Gihon. It is that which *surrounds and encircles* the land of Cush. 14. The name of the third river is Tigris. It is that *which surrounds and encircles* Assyria to the east. And the fourth river is the *Great*[21] *River*, the river Euphrates. 15. And the Lord God[q] took Adam and had him dwell in the garden of Eden to toil *in the Law* and to observe its *commandments.*[22] 16. And the Lord God commanded Adam,[13] saying: "From[r] all the trees of the garden you may surely eat; 17. from the tree of knowledge, however, *from which anyone who eats would know to distinguish between* good and evil, you shall not eat of it because on the day that you shall eat you shall surely die." 18. And the Lord God said, "It is not proper that man[s] should be alone; I will make[t] for him a *partner similar* to himself." 19. And from the ground[u] the Lord God *created* every beast that is on the surface of the field and all the birds of the heavens; and he brought *them* to Adam to see what[w] he would call them. And whatever Adam called a living creature *in the language of the sanctuary,*[23] that was its name.[x] 20. And *Adam* gave their names to all the cattle

---

Apparatus, Chapter 2

[q] Nfmg: "the Memra of the Lord (took) Adam and confined him in the garden to toil"; VNL: "the Memra of the Lord took Adam and made him dwell in the Garden of Eden and confined him (there) to toil in the law and observe"; P: "And the Memra of the Lord took Adam and confined him in the Garden to toil in the law and to keep its commandments"; cf. Nfmg.

[r] Nfmg: "the Memra of the Lord to Adam saying (text: keeping): From (all the trees)."

[s] Lit.: "son of man"; Nfmg: "the Memra of the Lord (said): It is not fitting that Adam be alone."

[t] CTg B: "I will create for him."

[u] Nfmg: "the Memra of the Lord (created) from the earth"; CTg B: "and Adonai God created from the earth."

[w] CTg B: "to see by what names he would call them."

[x] CTg B: "and whatever Adam called a living creature, that was its name"; Nfmg adds: "(its name) until the time of this day."

Notes, Chapter 2

[20]"pearl"; Greek loan word: *margarîtês.*

[21]For addition "great" see Gen 15:18; Deut 1:7; Jos 1:4; see also *Gen. R.* 16, 3: "greatest of all rivers."

[22]"commandments"; which commandments not specified; probably in general. Specified in *Gen. R.* 16:5 (sabbath, sacrifices); Nf Gen 3:9 speaks of a precept (not to eat from tree?).

[23]"the language of the sanctuary," lit. "language of the house of holiness," *lšn byt qdš',* i.e., Hebrew, through which, according to Nf, the world was created (Nf Gen 11:1; see also *Gen. R.* 18,4 on Gen 2:23), the language used by Abraham addressing God (Nf Gen 22:1); spoken by Jacob to the angel (Nfmg 31:11); for naming Gal-ed (Nf Gen 31:47); naming Benjamin (Nf 35:18); Moses, replying to God (Nf Exod 3:4). Elsewhere, both in Aramaic and Hebrew, Hebrew is called "the sacred language," lit. "language of holiness." See Grossfeld's note on Nf's use of the phrase in the above texts (noted in Díez Macho *Neophyti 1*, III, 31*; also in 1989, note 30 to Gen 2:19). Díez Macho notes in Nf the use of "the sanctuary" (lit. "the house of holiness," *byt qdš'*) also with other nouns, where the HT has simply "holiness," thus establishing a probability that "sanctuary" (lit. "house of holiness") in Nf may mean no more than "holiness," and "language of the sanctuary" ("of the house of holiness") another way of saying "holy" or "sacred language." For the other texts in Nf see Exod 28:43; 29:30; 35:19; 39:1; 39:41 (Nf and Nfmg), "garments of the sanctuary" (lit. "garments of the house of holiness") for "garments of holiness," "holy garments"; Lev 4:6 (mercy-seat of the sanctuary), 5:15; 8:9 (crown of the sanctuary = holy crown); 16:32 (garments of the sanctuary = holy garments), 16:33 ("for the house of the holy of holies" = "for the holy of holies"; Nfmg: "for the sanctuary of the temple," lit. "holy place of the holy of holies"); Num 35:25 ("with the oil of the sanctuary," *byt qwdšh;* = holy oil); a similar case in the Qumran Targum 4QTgLev and 4QTgLev 16:20, with *byt qdš('),* "sanctuary," "house of holiness," where Nf and Onq. have "holiness."

and to the birds of the heavens, and to all the wild beasts that are on the surface of
the field; yet for *Adam* he did not find *a partner similar* to himself. 21. And the
Lord God cast[y] a *deep* sleep[24] on *Adam*, and he fell asleep. And he took one rib of
his ribs and *placed* flesh in its stead. 22. And the Lord God perfected[z] the rib he
had taken from Adam into a woman and he took her to Adam. 23. And Adam said:
"This time, and *never again, is a woman created*[25] *from man, as this one has been
created from me*, bone from my bone and flesh from my flesh. *It is fitting* that this
one be called woman because it is from a male that this one has been *created*." 24.
For this reason shall a man *separate*[aa] *his couch*[26] *from that of* his father and *that of*
his mother and adhere to his wife. And *the two* of them will become one flesh. 25.
And both of them were naked, Adam and his wife, *and as yet*[bb] *they did not know
what shame was.*

CHAPTER 3

1. The serpent was *shrewder* than all the beasts that are on the surface of the field
which the Lord God[a] had *created*.[1] And he said to the woman: "So, *the Lord* has
said:[b] 'You may not eat of any of the trees of the garden.'" 2. And the woman said
to the serpent: "We may eat of the fruit of the trees[c2] of the garden; 3. but of the

Apparatus, Chapter 2

[y] Nfmg: "the Memra of the Lord induced a sleep";
CTg B: "and Adonai God cast a sweet sleep upon
Adam."
[z] Nfmg: "the Memra of the Lord built"; CTg B: "And
Adonai God built"; P: "and (the Lord ...) pre-
pared" (or: "adorned").

[aa] VNL: "wherefore a man shall leave the bedroom of
his father and his mother"; P: "the bedroom of his
father"; CTg B: "for this reason a man shall separate his bed from his father and from his mother."
[bb] CTg B: "... Adam and his wife and they did not
know what shame was."

Notes, Chapter 2

[24]"deep sleep." MT: *tardemah*; same rendering in Nf 15:12.
[25]"created"; HT: "taken"; in keeping with Nf's tendency to render all verbs ("create, form, make") having to do with
God's creative act by the single verb "create"; see note to 1:7.
[26]"separate his couch"; lit. "his sleeping." *mdmk'*, as CTg B. The other Pal. Tg. texts have: "his sleeping place."

Apparatus, Chapter 3

[a] Nfmg: "the Memra of the Lord."
[b] Nfmg, CTg B: "So indeed (Nf *'rwm*; Nfmg: "So
then, *lhwd 'rwm*; CTg B: "because that," *hlp 'rwm*)
the Memra of the Lord has said."

[c] Nfmg: "all the trees"; HT: "of the tree."

Notes, Chapter 3

[1]"created." HT: "made"; see note to 2:23 and 1:7.
[2]"of the trees." HT: "of the tree" (collective); Syr.: "of all the trees."

fruit of the tree[d] that is in the middle of the garden, *the Lord*[e][3] has said: 'You shall not eat of it and you shall not draw near to it, and (thus) you shall not[f][4] die.'" 4. And the serpent said to the woman: "You certainly shall not die; 5. because *it is manifest and known*[g] *before the Lord*[5] that on the day you eat of it your eyes will be opened, and that you will be like *angels before the Lord,*[6] knowing *to distinguish between* good and evil." 6. And the woman saw that the tree was good to eat and that it was a desirable to the eyes,[h] and that the tree was *suited* to have one *acquire wisdom* by it.[i] So she took of its fruits and ate and she also gave to her husband with her and he ate. 7. And the eyes of both of them were opened;[j] and they knew that they were naked and sewed fig leaves for themselves and made for themselves girdles.[k][7] 8. And they heard the sound of the *Memra of* the Lord God walking within[m] the garden at the breeze[8] of the day; and Adam and his wife hid themselves from before the Lord God[n] within *the trees* of the garden. 9. *And the Lord God*[o] *called Adam and said to him: "Behold, the whole world which I created is manifest before me; darkness and light are manifest before me. And do you reckon that the place within which you are is not manifest before me? Where is the precept*[9] *that I commanded you?"*[p] 10. And he said: "I heard the sound *of your Memra*[q] in the garden and I was afraid because I am naked, and I hid myself." 11. And he said:

Apparatus, Chapter 3

[d] CTg B: "the tree of knowledge."

[e] Nfmg: "the Memra of the Lord."

[f] CTg B: "lest you die."

[g] Nfmg: "manifest before."

[h] CTg B: "to the sight of the eyes" (i.e., eyesight).

[i] Or: "a delight to behold" (M. Klein, in translating CTg B).

[j] *w'ytpthwn*; Nfmg: *w'pthw* (with assimilation of *tau* of *'tp-*).

[k] Nfmg: "fig leaves and made for themselves robes" (*'ystlwwn*; probably Greek/Latin loan word *stolê, stola*); VNL same ending; P: "robes."

[m] Nfmg: "walking about within the garden at the height (lit.: "might") of the day; (almost verbatim as PVNL).

[n] P: "the Memra of the Lord"; Nfmg: "from the Memra of the Lord within the middle of the garden."

[o] Nfmg, P: "the Memra of the Lord"; VNL: "the Memra of the Lord God."

[p] Nfmg: "and how do you think that the place within which you are is not manifest before me (text: before him)? Where are the commandments I commanded you? = P; ending of Nf=VNL.

[q] Nfmg, P: "(the voice of) your Dibbura (Nfmg *dbrk*) I heard walking about within (P: in) the Garden."

Notes, Chapter 3

[3]"the Lord." HT: Elohim.

[4]"(you shall) not." MT: *pen*, "lest"; on Nf's rendering of HT's *pn*, see Grossfeld, *Neofiti*, note 3 to Gen 3.

[5]"manifest and known before the Lord." HT: "God knows"; paraphrase intended to avoid making God the subject of action relating to creation; cf. McNamara, 1972, 93f. and note to 1:4.

[6]"like angels before the Lord"; HT: "like God" (*Elohim*, or: "gods"), or "angels," as in Onq., Ps.-J.; cf. 2 Sam 14:17, 20. See note to Ps.-J. (vol. 1B in this series) and in Grossfeld, op. cit.

[7]R. Abba b. Kahana understood the Hebrew to imply clothes for men and women (*Gen. R.* 19,6). See note *k* in Apparatus.

[8]"breeze" (*mšb* from root *nšb*), lit. "blowing" (of the day), possibly "scorching heat"; HT: "at the *rwḥ* (i.e., wind, breeze) of the day." Rabbinic and later opinion was divided as to whether a morning or evening breeze is intended; see *Gen. R.* 19,8; M. Kasher, in Díez Macho, *Neophyti 1*, V, 78*, and B. Grossfeld, op. cit., note 9 to Gen 3.

[9]"where is the precept?"; HT: "The Lord God . . . said . . . Where are you?" (*'yykh*). Paraphrase avoids giving the impression of limitation in God's knowledge, interpreting "where" as referring to a divine precept, not to God himself.

"Who told *r* you that you were naked? Have you, perchance, eaten from the tree from which I commanded you not to eat?" 12. And Adam said: "The woman that you have *placed with me*, she gave me from the tree and I ate." 13. And the Lord God *s* said to the woman: "What is *this* you have done?" And the woman said: "The serpent deceived me and I ate." 14. And the Lord God *t* said to the serpent: "Because you have done this, you will be more accursed, *O serpent*, than all the cattle and than all the wild beasts that are on the surface of the fields. On your belly *you will crawl* and dust will be *your food*[10] all the days of your life. 15. And I will put enmity[11] between you *u* and the woman and between *your sons*[w][12] *and her sons.*[x][12] *And it will come about that when her sons*[y] *observe the Law and do the commandments they will aim at you and smite you* on your head and *kill you. But when they forsake the commandments of the Law* you will aim and *bite him* on his heel *and make him ill.*[13] *For her sons,*[z] *however, there will be a remedy,*[14] *but for you, O serpent, there will not be a remedy,*[aa] *since they are to make appeasement in the end, in the day of King Messiah.*[u]" 16. And to the woman he said: "I will greatly multiply your pains and your pregnancies.*[bb]* In pain you will bring forth children and to your husband you will turn and he will have authority over you,*[cc]* *whether to remain just*

Apparatus, Chapter 3

r Nfmg: "(who) was the cause of."

s Nfmg: "And the Memra of the Lord said."

t Nfmg: "the Memra of the Lord."

u Various Nfmg almost verbatim as P (P extra in brackets): "(enmities I will put) between the serpent and (between) the woman and between the descendants of his (P: your) sons, and the descendants of her sons. (And it shall be that when the sons of the woman) labor in [or: study] the law and keep the commandments (they shall be smiting and wounding you in your head and killing you and when) the sons of the woman refrain themselves and do not (Nfmg: so as not to) labor in the Law and keep the commandments you shall aim and bite them in their heels and wound them. However, for the sons of the woman there shall be healing but for you (Nfmg adds: O serpent) there shall be no healing. For they, one and the other are to make peace (*šwpyyt*; or: appeasement) (in the very end of the days, in the days of the King Messiah"; VNL: "and it shall be that when the sons of the

woman labor in the Law and do perform the commandments they shall be aiming at and smiting you on your head and killing you. And when the sons of the woman forsake the precepts of the Law and do not perform the commandments you shall be aiming at and biting them in their heels and making them sick. However, there will be healing (or: a remedy) for the sons of the woman, and for you, O serpent, there will be no healing. For they, one for the other, are to make peace (*špyyt*; or: appeasement) in the heel in the very end of the days, in the days of the King Messiah."

w *bnyk* (2nd per. fem. pl.).

x *bnh* (=*beneha*), for *bnyh;* cf. Golomb, p.53.

y *bnyh.*

z *bryh* (see n. 12).

aa Nf *špywtyh;* P: *šwpyyt';* VN: *špwyyt'* (root *špy?;* cf. Nf, CTg E Gen 31: 2, 5).

bb Nfmg: "your times (or: "your pregnancies) with pains will you bear."

cc Nfmg: "your safety and he will rule over you."

Notes, Chapter 3

[10]"your food"; cf. Isa 65:25 and Pal. Tg. Num 22:6, citing Pal. Tg. Gen 3:14.

[11]"enmity," *b'l dbbw;* lit. "(an) enemy"; also in Nf Num 35:21-22. The other Tg. texts have "enmity" (*db[b]w*).

[12]"your sons"; HT: "seeds"; the Pal. Tgs. generally render "seed" of HT when referring to humans as "sons." On Pal. Tg. paraphrase of Gen 3:15 see M. McNamara, 1966A, 217–222; B. Barry Levy, 1, 1986, 95–97. Note here the Targum's double, even triple, translation of certain keywords of the extremely difficult underlying HT: *šwp* ("observe, aim, smite"), *'qb* ("heel, end [of days]"). For the plural *bryh* ("her sons"; see Apparatus, note *z*), with *resh* instead of *nun* (*bnyh*), see C. Meehan in *Zeit. deut. Pal. Ver.* 96 (1980) 66; J. Levy, *Chaldäisches Wörterbuch* (1881) 111b.

[13]"make him ill . . . ," etc. For the connection between observance of the commandments and success, see Pal. Tg. Gen 27:40 (Nf, PVN), Deut 33:29 (Nf); see also biblical text Deut 28:1ff.; 30:15-18.

[14]"remedy"; cf. *Gen. R.* 20,5: "In the messianic age all will be healed except the serpent and the Gibeonite" (R. Levi).

or to sin.[15] 17. And to Adam he said: "Since you have heeded the voice of your wife and have eaten of the tree concerning which I commanded you, saying: 'You shall not eat of it,' the earth will be cursed on your account. In pain will you eat *the fruits of its harvest*[dd] all the days of your life. 18. Thorns[ee] and thistles shall it bring forth for you, and you shall eat of the herbs[ff] that are on the surface of the field." *Adam answered and said: "Pray, by the mercy (that is) before you, O Lord; let us not be reckoned as the cattle, eating the grass that is on the surface of the field. Let us stand upright, I pray, and labor; and from the labor of my hands let us eat*[16] *food from the fruits of the earth.*[gg] *Thereby shall he*[17] *distinguish the sons of man from the cattle."* 19. "You will eat[18] bread from the sweat from before your face[hh] until you return to the earth, because from it you were created; because you are dust and to dust you are to return.[19] *But from the dust you are to arise again to give an account and a reckoning of all that you have done."* 20. And the man[ii] called the name of his wife Eve[jj][20] because she was the mother of all the living. 21. And the Lord God made[kk] for Adam and for his wife *garments of glory,*[21] for[mm] the skin *of their flesh,* and he

Apparatus, Chapter 3

[dd] P: "from the fruits all the days ... "; otherwise P=Nf.
[ee] Nf=PV except in P a different word for "thorns."
[ff] P: "green herbage."
[gg] Nfmg, PVN: "from the fruits of the earth (not in P) you shall eat food now."
[hh] P: "by the sweat of your face," using MT Hebrew word for "sweat."

[ii] Using the Hebrew *h'dm*; P: Adam (*'dm*).
[jj] Nfmg: "(called the name of his wife) the serpent (*ḥwwyy'*) in that she."
[kk] P: "and the Memra of the Lord God created"= Nfmg.
[mm] P: "from"; Nfmg: "by (or: with) the skin."

Notes, Chapter 3

[15]"whether to remain just or to sin" (or: "to exonerate or convict," B. Barry Levy, 1, 1986, 97; Sokoloff, 1990, 177: "whether to be innocent or to sin"). For a similar Aramaic expression see Pal. Tg. Gen 4:7 (Nf, PVNL, Ps.-J.). According to B. Grossfeld (op. cit., note 20 to 3:16), this aggadic supplement in Gen 3:16 seems to be in direct conflict with rabbinic opinion as found in *Gen. R.* 20,7. He considers plausible the explanation offered by Bassfreund and S. Wohl (*Das palästinische Pentateuchtargum* [Zwickau, 1935] 10–11) that the Pal. Tg. and Ps.-J. at Gen 3:16 contain an erroneous transposition of an almost identical phrase occurring in Tg. Gen 4:7. However, in both cases the expression is a paraphrase added to the same Hebrew word *mšl* (*b*-, possibly a mechanical paraphrastic rendering). See note 11 to 4:7.

[16]"let us not be reckoned ..., let us stand ... eat." Note, in all texts of the midrash, the first person plur. in the verbs of Adam's words, despite the sing. "my hands." This may be due to the collectivity (i.e., mankind) intended. In Palestinian Aramaic, however, the form of the first person plur. imperfect is often used to express the first person sing. Examples in Pal. Tg. in Le Déaut, 1978 (*Genèse*) 95; see further Odeberg, 1939, II, 11, note; Dalman, 1927, 265f. (par. 61). On 3:18-19 see also B. Barry Levy, 1, 1986, 97–99.

[17]"thus shall he," i.e., God; third person impersonal; or: "one."

[18]"you shall eat ...": the speaker is God; rendering of biblical text resumes after inserted midrash.

[19]"to dust ... return." See note to Ps.-J. (vol. 1B in this series) for *Gen. R.* 20,19 on this verse and resurrection. There is reference to resurrection in all Pal. Tg. texts (Nf, P, Ps.-J.) of this verse. There is a connection between this verse and resurrection also in *Life of Adam and Eve (Apocalypse of Moses*, 41). On the question of the resurrection in Judaism, see M. McNamara, 1983A, 180–183; A. Rodriquez Carmona, 1978, 15–20, for Gen 3:19.

[20]"Eve," Nf has *Ḥwh*, with HT and P; Nfmg's text has *ḥwwyy'*. "the serpent," reflecting an interpretation attributed to R. Aha in *Gen. R.* 20,11 and 22,2 (on Gen 4:11), regarding Eve as a (or the) serpent in having seduced Adam.

[21]"garments of glory"; HT: "of skin," *'wr*; Nf's rendering reflects a tradition ascribed to R. Meir in *Gen. R.* 20,12, reading *'wr*, "light," for *'wr*, on Adam having been vested in garments of light. The tradition on Adam (or Adam and Eve) having been vested in clothes of glory (righteousness, etc.) is probably older; see *Apocalypse of Adam* (1st cent.) 20, interpreting Gen 3:7 of being naked of the righteousness with which he had been clothed. See also Ginzberg, *Legends*, V, 121f. and note 120; idem, 1900, 49f. Once again, note Targumic double rendering of Hebrew *'wr* as "glory" and "skin."

clothed them. 22. And the Lord God *nn* said: "Behold, the *first* Adam [22] *whom I have created is alone in the world as I am alone in the heavens on high. Numerous nations are to arise from him,* [23] *and from him shall arise one nation who will know to distinguish between* good and evil. *If he had observed the precept of the Law and fulfilled its commandment he would live and endure forever like the tree of life.* And now, *since he has not observed the precepts of the Law and has not fulfilled its commandment, behold we will banish him from the garden of Eden* before he stretches out his hand and takes of *the fruit* of the *tree of life* [24] and eats and lives for ever." 23. And the Lord *oo* God banished him from the garden of Eden to till *oobis* the earth from which he had been *created.* [25] 24. And he banished *Adam*; and he had made *the Glory of his Shekinah* [26] dwell *from the beginning* to the east [27] of the Garden of Eden, *between* *pp* the two cherubim. *Two thousand years* [28] *before he created the world he had created the Law; he had prepared the garden of Eden* *qq* *for the just and*

Apparatus, Chapter 3

nn P: "and the Memra of the Lord God said: Behold Adam [=Nfmg] whom I created ... good and evil. And now let us (=me) banish him from the garden ... live forever"; VNL = Nf except " ... good and evil. And now it is well that we (=I) banish him ... forever."

oo P: "And the Memra of the Lord (=Nfmg) drove him out."

oobis Nfmg: "to be tilling;" =P.

pp VNL: "above."

qq VNL: "and he banished Adam ... he created the Law and prepared Gehenna and the Garden of Eden. He prepared the Garden of Eden for the just that they might eat and enjoy themselves from the fruits of the tree because they kept the precepts of the Law in this world. For the wicked he prepared Gehenna, which is comparable to a sharp sword cutting at both edges. He prepared within it ... (etc. as in Nf). <Because the Tree of Life. Anyone who keeps it in this world will live and flourish like the Tree of Life. The Law is good for the one who labors (in it) in this world> like the fruits of the Tree of Life in (lit.: for) the world to come" (*text*

within angular brackets in N, not in V); P: "And he banished Adam and made his Shekinah dwell from the beginning above the Garden of Eden.... Before the world was created ... he established the Garden of Eden for the just that they eat and enjoy themselves ... from the fruit of its Tree because they kept the precepts of the Law in the world. For the wicked he established Gehenna, which is comparable to a sword devouring with both edges. He established within it sparks of fire and burning coals for the wicked to be avenged of them in the world to come because they did not observe the precepts of the Law in this world. Indeed the fruit of the Tree of Life is the Law. Everyone who keeps it in this world lives and endures like the Tree of Life for the world to come. The Law is good for those who labor (in it) and for those who keep the commandments like the fruits of the Tree of Life for the world to come." Nfmg carries part of the ending of this, thus: "Indeed it endures from (P: like) the Tree of Life"; for those who labor (in it) and those who keep the commandments like."

Notes, Chapter 3

[22]"the first Adam"; see note to 2:8.

[23]"from him." Corresponds to "of us" ("from us," *mmnw*) of HT ("become like one of us") and the paraphrase succeeds in avoiding the inherent anthropomorphism. See also notes 48-50 to Ps.-J. (vol. 1B in this series).

[24]For the tree of life, cf. Gen 2:9; it was identified with wisdom: Prov 3:18; 8; 11:30; 16:22; also 3:1-2; 11:30; 12:28; 30:15; 32:47; Bar 3:9–4:4; Rev 2:7; 22:2; 22:14; tree of life identified with law in Judaism; see M. Maher in *ITQ* 38 (1971) 320f.

[25]"he was created"; HT: "he was taken"; see notes to 1:7 and 2:23.

[26]On the Shekinah, see Introduction, pp. 36–37.

[27]"from the beginning to the east"; double translation of HT *mqdm* (RSV): "and to the east of their garden he placed the cherubim...."

[28]"two thousand years...." Belief in the pre-existence of Torah, Garden of Eden, Gehenna, etc., was widespread in Jewish tradition but various dates were assigned for their creation. The age of two thousand years before creation assigned to Torah was arrived at by identification of Torah and wisdom; wisdom rejoicing before God daily (lit.: day day=two days) before creation; one day = one thousand years (Ps 90:40) (a tradition associated with R. Huna, 350 C.E., and Resh Lakish, 270 C.E.). See further M. Maher, 1971, 317–320, esp. 317, n. 37.

Gehenna[29] *for the wicked. He had prepared the garden of Eden for the just that they might eat and delight themselves from the fruits of the tree, because they had kept precepts of the Law in this world and fulfilled the commandments. For the wicked he prepared Gehenna, which is comparable* to a sharp sword *devouring with both edges. He prepared within it darts of fire and burning coals for the wicked, to be avenged of them in the world to come because they did not observe the precepts of the Law in this world. For the Law is a* tree of life[30] *for everyone who toils in it and keeps the commandments: he lives and endures like* the tree of life *in the world to come. The Law is good for all who labor in it in this world like the fruit of the tree of life.*

CHAPTER 4

1. And the man[a] knew[1] Eve his wife and she conceived and bore Cain and she said: "Behold, *I have been given*[2] *a son*[b] *from before* the Lord." 2. And later she bore Abel his brother. Now, Abel was a shepherd of flocks and Cain tilled the earth. 3. And it happened in the course of time[3] that Cain brought a gift[4] from the fruits of the earth to *the name of* the Lord.[c] 4. And Abel also[d] brought (his gift) from the first-born of his flock and from the fat ones[5] among them. And the Lord[e] *received*

Notes, Chapter 3

[29]"the Garden of Eden . . . Gehenna." According to a tradition in *Gen. R.* 21,9, Gehenna was created on the second day of creation and the Garden of Eden on the third; this latter part of the tradition already in Jub 2:7. In the tradition of Tg. Cant 8:6, Gehenna was created on the last (sixth) day of creation; so also b Pes 53a on M Pes 4:4 (view of R. Jose).

[30]"the law is the tree of life"; see note to 3:22; texts in Sifre Deut 40 (end); *Lev. R.* IX, 3; XXXV, 6; Pal. Tg. (P) Exod 15:25; see M. Maher, art. cit. On 3:24, and the connection with 3:15, 19, 22 through reference to the commandments, see B. Barry Levy, 1, 1986, 101–104.

Apparatus, Chapter 4

[a] Text as in HT: *h'dm*.
[b] In text regular form *br* (*bar*); Nfmg: "*byr*" (*bîr*), a form found in Ps-J.
[c] Nfmg: "before the Lord."

[d] Text *'p*; in Nfmg the synonymous variant *lḥd*; = CTg B.
[e] Nfmg: "the Memra of the Lord."

Notes, Chapter 4

[1]"knew," Nf *ḥkm*; HT: *yd'*. When HT *yd'* denotes sexual relations, Nf tends to translate by *ḥkm*, e.g., Gen 4:1, 17, 25; 19:5, 8; 24:16; 38:26; also VNL at 19:8; PVNL at 38:26; CTg E, 38:26.

[2]"I have been given . . . from before"; HT (RSV): "I have gotten (*qnyty*) a son . . . with (the help of, *'t*) the Lord"; Nf's paraphrase avoids anthropomorphism.

[3]"course of time"; lit. "at the end of the days," =HT. On the midrash in Gen 4:3-16, see G. Vermes, "The Targumic Versions of Genesis IV 3-16," *Annual of Leeds University Oriental School* (Leiden, 1961–62) 81–114; G. Grelot, "Les Targums du Pentateuque: Etude comparative d'après Genèse IV, 3-16,"*Semitica* 9 (1959) 59–88; McNamara, 1966A, 156–160.

[4]"gift," Greek loan word: *dôron*.

[5]"fat ones," *šmynyhwn*, as in CTg B; thus also R. Jose b. T. Hanina in *Gen. R.* 25,5. Ps.-J. and Onq.: *ptymhwn*.

Abel and his offering*f* *with favor,*[6] 5. but he *did not receive* Cain and his offering*f* *with favor*; and Cain was greatly displeased and *his countenance*[7] *changed.* 6. And the Lord*g* said to Cain: "Why, I pray, are you displeased and why has your *countenance*[7] *changed?* 7. Surely, if you make your work *in this world* to be good, *you will be remitted and pardoned*[8] *in*[h] *the world to come*; but if you do not make your work *in this world* to be good, *your sin will be kept for the day of great judgment;*[9] and at the door *of your heart* your sin crouches. *Into*[i] *your hands, however, I have given the control over the evil inclination*[10] *and you shall rule it, whether to remain just or to sin."*[11] 8. And Cain said to Abel his brother:[12] *"Come!*[j] Let the

Apparatus, Chapter 4

[f] Nfmg: "gift" (Greek loan word *dôron*).

[g] Nfmg: "the Memra of the Lord"; = CTg B.

[h] Nfmg: "for" = CTg B.

[i] Nfmg: "between your hand(s)"

[j] Verse 8: CTg B: "and Cain answered his brother Abel and said: Come and let the two of us go out into the open field. And when the two of them had gone out into the open field Cain answered and said to Abel: I see that the world has been created by (or: in) mercy and it is guided (= governed) by (or: in) mercy. Why (*mn bgll mh*) was your offering received favorably from you and mine was not received favorably from me? Abel answering said to Cain: What matters it that the world has been created in mercy, and that it is governed by mercy; surely (*brm*) it is (also) governed by the fruits of good works. Because my deeds were better than yours my offering was received from me favorably and from you (your offering) was not received favorably. And the two of them were disputing in the open field. And Cain rose up against his brother Abel and killed him"; P: " ... and it came to pass when the two of them went out to the open field Cain answered and said to Abel: There is no judgment and there is no judge and there is no other world. Nor is there any giving of good reward to the just nor is retribution demanded from the wicked. And the world was not created in mercy nor is it governed by (or: in) mercy. Why (*mn bgll m'*) has your offering been favorably received from you and (mine) has not been received from me? Abel answering said to Cain: There is judgment and there is a judge and there is another world and there is good reward for the just and retribution is exacted of the wicked. And the world was created in mercy and is governed by mercy. Because the fruits of my deeds were better than yours, my offering was received favorably from me and (yours) was not favorably received from you. And the two of them quarreled in the open field and Cain rose up against Abel his brother and killed him"; V=P with minor variants, except that after "the world ... is governed by mercy" V adds: "However (*brm*) by the fruits of good works is it governed";—CTg X (*Tosafoth*, Gen 4:7,8): "*Tosefta. Why if you improve*. Why, if you improve your deeds it will be par(doned) you). (Cain answered and said to his brother Abel:) There is no judgment and there is no judge and there is no world outside this one. Abel answered (and said:) There is judge(ment and there is) a judge and there is another world for the giving of retribution for evil and for good. At that moment (lit.: hour) <Cain> considered in his heart what he might do to him but failed to find (anything). After this (his) wrath subsided (or: was removed; or: he loathed his wrath) and he said to Abel: Let there, I pray, be no (quarreling) between me and you. Separate from me and take the flock as your portion. Abel said to him: My desire is (in) a true division. (After) Abel had gone to his flock and had departed from Cain, Cain considered in his heart and said: What have I done? The summer (month will pass) and I will have no (lit.: there will be no) milk to drink (lit.: to eat) and no wool to wear. He rose up and ran after him and overtook him and said (to him: This is now) a trustworthy division. Take for yourself half the flock and half of the land and I (lit.: we) will take half of the flock and half of the land. Abel said to him: Do what you desire. And that moment (lit.: at that time) they made the division. Abel said to him: This is an even division, which is (done) in fairness (lit.: in truth). Abel went on his way. Cain (then) sought to graze his portion of the flock. He found he could not graze the flock and (thereby) give up working the land. He went to Abel and said: There is another (division) fairer than this. You take the flock as your portion and I (lit.: we) will take the land as my portion. Abel agreed (lit.: said in his heart) to do Cain's desire. Cain, however, was bearing a grudge against Abel from before this, because Abel's (twin) sister was Cain's wife and she was not as beautiful in appearance as Cain's (twin) sister who was Abel's wife. When Cain remembered what was in his heart, Cain said: Now I have found the occasion (lit.: time; = opportunity) for my grudge

two of us go out into the open field." And when the two of them had gone out into the open field, *Cain answered and said to Abel: "I perceive that the world was not created by mercy and that it is not being conducted according to the fruits of good words, and that there is favoritism in judgment. Why was your offering received favorably and my offering was not received favorably from me?" Abel answered and said to Cain: "I perceive that the world was created by mercy and that it is being conducted according to the fruits of good words. And because my works were better than yours, my offering was received from me favorably and yours was not received favorably from you." Cain answered and said to Abel: "There is no judgment, and there is*

Apparatus, Chapter 4

(?; reading uncertain). He ran after him and said to him: Get out from my land which I have taken as my portion. Abel found no place to go out to and he (i.e., Cain) did not know with what (or: in what place) he would strike him. He turned here and there until he saw two birds fighting and one arose against the other and struck it in the mouth and the blood spurted out until it died. Cain learned from it and did the same to Abel his brother. And when he saw that he had died (lit.: and he saw and behold he was dead and) he feared that his father would demand Abel from him and he did not know what to do. He raised his eyes and saw the bird that had killed its fellow putting its mouth to the ground, digging (a hole) and burying its dead neighbor, and putting earth over it. At that moment (lit.: hour) Cain did the same with Abel, so that (his father) might not find him."

Notes, Chapter 4

[6]"received with favor." HT: "had regard for, looked at" (*š'h*); a common idiom in Nf and Pal. Tg.

[7]"countenance (changed)"; lit. "splendor/countenance of his/your face (changed)"; HT: "his/your face fell." The same Aramaic expression renders different Hebrew words in Deut 34:7.

[8]"remitted and pardoned"; Aramaic *šry wšbq*. Compare NT expressions in John 20:23; Matt 16:19; 18:18. See discussion in Z. W. Falk, "Binding and Loosing," *JJS* 25 (1974) 92–100; Vermes, art. cit., *Annual of Leeds University Oriental School* (Leiden) 107–109; Strack and Billerbeck, *Kommentar*, I, 637; II, 585. For rabbinic parallels see Grossfeld, *Neofiti*, note 10 to Gen 4.

[9]"a day of great judgment." This expression, originating in apocalyptic, is very common in rabbinic writings; see M. McNamara, 1968, 135f.; idem, 1983A, 188–192.

[10]"the evil inclination." A typically rabbinic concept and expression, found already in 11QPsaplea, line 15: "neither let pain nor the evil inclination take possession of my bones" (cf. M. McNamara, 1983B, 159, 184).

[11]"whether to remain just or to sin (*byn lymzky wbyn lmḥṭy*); already in Nf Gen 3:16 (with *lmzkh*). In both cases it occurs as an additional paraphrase on the Hebrew *mšl b-*, "to rule over, have power over." See note to Ps.-J. (vol. 1B in this series). The origin of the paraphrase was facilitated by the difficulty of the HT. For midrash in Ps.-J., see Gerard J. Kuiper, "Targum Pseudo-Jonathan: A Study of Genesis 4:7–10:16," *Augustinianum* 10 (1970) 533–570. For a textual study of Nf Gen 4:7, see B. Barry Levy, 1, 1986, 105–106.

[12]The developed midrash in this verse has been transmitted in a variety of texts: Nf, PVN, Ps.-J., CTg B, as tosafoth in CTg I, FF and X. The differences between the various texts seem at times to be redactional. The midrash has been studied from a variety of angles: literary, redactional, regarding the Sitz-im-Leben (adversaries intended), etc. To literature noted at 4:7 add: S. Isenberg, "An Anti-Sadducees Polemic in the Palestinian Targum Tradition," HTR 63 (1970) 433–444; R. Le Déaut, "Traditions targumiques dans le corpus paulinien?" *Biblica* 42 (1961) 28–44; A. Marmorstein, "Einige vorläufige Bemerkungen zu den neuendeckten Fragmenten des Jerusalemischen (palästinischen) Targums," *ZAW* 49 (1931) 232–242; J. Ramón Diaz, "Dos notas sobre el Targum Palestinense," *Sefarad* 19 (1959) 133–136; M. McNamara, 1966A, 156–160; A. J. Braver, "The Debate Between a Sadducee and Pharisee in the Mouths of Cain and Abel," *Beth Mikra* 44 (1971) 583–585 (in Hebrew); J. M. Bassler, "Cain and Abel in the Palestinian Targums. A Brief Note on an Old Controversy," *JSJ* 17 (1986) 56–64; B. D. Chilton, "A Comparative Study of Synoptic Development: The Dispute Between Cain and Abel in the Palestinian Targums and the Beelzebul Controversy in the Gospels," *JBL* 101 (1982) 553–562; B. Barry Levy, 1, 1986, 107–109 (textual analysis). See also Grossfeld, *Neofiti*, note 16 to chapter.

no judge and there is no other world. There is no giving of good reward[13] *to the just
nor is vengeance exacted of the wicked."* Abel answered and said to Cain: "There is
judgment, and there is a judge, and there is another world. And there is giving of
good reward to the just and vengeance is exacted of the wicked in the world to come."
Concerning this matter the two of them were disputing in the open field. And Cain
rose up against Abel his brother and killed him. 9. And the Lord said to Cain:[k]
"Where is Abel your brother?" And he said: "I do not know. Am I my brother's
keeper?" 10. And he said: "What is this that you have done? The voice of the blood
of the righteous multitudes[14] *that were to arise from Abel* your brother is crying
against you before me from the earth. 11. And now, Cain, *you will be* cursed from
the earth that opened its mouth to receive the blood of your brother from your
hands. 12. When you till the earth[m] it will no longer yield the fruits *of the harvest* to
you. You, *Cain,* shall be an exile and a wanderer on the earth."[n] 13. And Cain said
before the Lord: "My *debts* are too numerous to bear;[o] *before you, however, there is
power to remit and pardon.*[p][15] 14. Behold, you banish me this day from the face of
the earth, yet from before you *it is not possible for me* to hide.[q][16] And Cain shall be
an exile and a wanderer on the earth,[r] and anyone who meets him will kill him."
15. And the Lord[s] swore to him: "Anyone who kills Cain, *(judgment) will be suspended for him for seven generations."*[17] And the Lord placed a sign on Cain so that
anyone who might meet[t] him would not kill him. 16. And Cain went out from before the Lord and dwelt in the land, *an exile and a wanderer,* to the east of Eden.[u]

Apparatus, Chapter 4

[k] Nfmg: "the Memra of the Lord (said) to Cain" = P,
CTg B.

[m] CTg B (lit.): "till within the land."

[n] CTg B (lit.): "a wanderer within the land."

[o] CTg B: " ... to carry and there are ways before you
to remit and pardon."

[p] Nfmg: "to pardon me" = VNL.

[q] CTg B: "from before you, O Lord, it is not possible
for a son of man (=anyone)."

[r] CTg B: "within the land and anyone who finds
him."

[s] Nfmg, CTg B: "the Memra of the Lord."

[t] CTg B: "find him."

[u] CTg B and VNL: "of the Garden of Eden."

Notes, Chapter 4

[13]C. Meehan (*JSJ* 9, 1978, 104) renders: "a good reward should not be given to the righteous nor should the wicked be
punished. ... A good reward should be given. ... ," etc.

[14]"multitudes"; Greek loan word: *ochlos*; HT: "the blood (lit. "bloods") of your brother; rabbinic parallels in Grossfeld,
op. cit., note 17.

[15]"remit and pardon"; see note to 4:7.

[16]"(from your face) it is not possible for one to hide." HT: "from your face I shall be hidden"; converse translation (cf.
Introduction, p. 31) to avoid attributing limitation to God.

[17]"Judgment will be suspended for seven generations"; these generations are spelled out in CTg X (see Apparatus to
4:23). Clemency was shown Cain for seven generations, at which time Lamech accidently killed him; Grossfeld, op. cit.,
note 23 to verse refers to *Gen. R.* 22:4; *Tanh* (A) Bereshit XI (p. 225) and the following appropriate rabbinic sources. T.B.
Sanh 37b; PRK, *swbh,* p. 160A; cf. also *Tanh* (B) Bereshit XXV, p. 19; *Lev. R.* X, 5, pp. 204f.; *Deut R.* VIII, 1, p. 114. *Mid.
Agg.* ad hoc.

Now before he killed Abel, the earth used to produce before him[w] *like the fruits of the garden of Eden; after he had sinned, however, and killed Abel it changed to produce before him*[x] *thorns and thistles.* 17. And Cain knew his wife and she conceived and bore Enoch. And he built a city and called the name of the city according to the name of his son, Enoch. 18. And to Enoch was born Irad, and Irad begot Mehujael, and Mehujael begot Methushael, and Methushael begot Lamech. 19. And Lamech took two wives; the name of one *of them* was Adah and the name of the second was Zillah. 20. And Adah bore Jabel; he was the father of tent dwellers and cattle owners.[y] 21. And the name of his brother was Jubal; he was the father of all who play the harp and the flute.[z] 22. And Zillah: she also bore Tubal-cain, *a craftsman in every art* of bronze and iron. And the sister of Tubal-cain was Naamah, the inventor of dirges and songs. 23. And Lamech said to his *two* wives, Adah and Zillah: "Listen to my voice, wives of Lamech; attend to the words *of my mouth.* For I have not killed a man so that I should be killed because of him[aa] and I have not destroyed a young man so that my descendants should be destroyed after me. 24. If Cain, *who killed Abel, had (judgment) suspended for him for seven generations, it is but right*[18] *that for Lamech, his grandson, who did not kill (judgment) be suspended: for seventy-seven generations it will be suspended for him."* 25. And Adam knew his

Apparatus, Chapter 4

[w] CTg B and P and VNL: "for him fruits like the fruits of the Garden of Eden. . . . "

[x] P: "for him."

[y] Nfmg: "father of all who dwell in tents and owners of herds."

[z] Nfmg: "and who play the harp and little flute."

[aa] Nfmg: "that we (=I) should be killed in his stead and my descendants should perish"; CTg X (continuation of CTg X, note *j* to v. 7 above): "*Tosefta. And Lamech said.* And Lamech said to his wives: Enter with me to the bedchamber so that I may raise up progeny (lit.: seed) from you because Henoch has ascended to above and Tubal-cain lies ill (and) will now be gathered to his people. The wives refused and said to him: We do not wish to become pregnant and to give birth, to have (the child) devoured. He answered them: Adah and Zillah, hear my voice; wives of Lamech, listen to my words. If this is so, come in with me to the court of justice. Both of them went with him to Adam. Lamech conversed with him and told him what had happened to him with them [i.e., the wives] and how (*kd*) they had refused to listen to him (lit.: receive from him). The two of them answered and said (. . . *text lost* . . .) We do not wish (. . . .). Lamech pleaded and said: I have not slain a man (that I should bear guilt on his account) nor have I wounded a young man that my progeny should be wiped out because of him. Be(cause for seven generations punishment is to be ex)acted for Cain, that is Cain, Enoch, Irad, Mehuyael, Methusael, Lamech, Tubal-(cain). Behold, will it not be seventy-seven times (for Lamech)? Adam said to him: What the Merciful One has said (is): Therefore anyone who kills Cain for seven generations shall retribution be exacted of him. At that moment (lit.: time) he ordered the wives of Lamech to obey him (lit.: receive from him). The wives said (to Adam that they would take an example) from him [i.e., Adam] in this matter, separating from him just as you [i.e., Adam] separated from Eve your wife. At that moment Adam was astounded at their words in this argument and he said in his heart: It is only right that I should (return to Eve and continue to have children)" (*restoration in part uncertain; see M. Klein, following Gen. R. 23:5*).

Notes, Chapter 4

[18]"it is but right," *bdyn hw'*; a frequently used expression in the Mekilta and elsewhere, with the sense "it is logical to infer," "it only makes sense," and the like; see B. Barry Levy, 1, 1986, 113.

wife again and she bore a son and called his name Seth: "Because *the Lord* has appointed for me another *son* in the place of Abel; for Cain killed him." 26. And to Seth there was also born a son[bb] and he called his name Enosh. Then the[cc] *sons of man* began to make idols for themselves and to surname them by the name of *the Memra of the Lord*.[19]

CHAPTER 5

1. This is the book of the genealo*gical pedigree*[1] of Adam. The day *the Lord* created Adam, he *created*[2] him in a likeness *from before* the Lord.[3] 2. Male and female[a4] he created them; and he blessed them and called their name Adam the day he created them. 3. And Adam lived one hundred and thirty years and begot (a son) in his likeness, *similar to himself*,[5] and called his name Seth. 4. And *all* the days *of the life*[6] of Adam after he had begotten Seth were [b]eight hundred years; and

Apparatus, Chapter 4

[bb] Text of Nf: *br*; Nfmg: *byr*.
[cc] Nfmg, P: "in his days, behold then (P adds: "the sons of man") began to serve in a foreign cult and to call them (Nfmg: "it") by the name of the Memra of the Lord."

Notes, Chapter 4

[19]"began to make idols . . . to surname them"; HT: "men began (*hwhl*) to call on the name of YHWH" (cf. RSV). Nf and the Pal. Tgs. give a double interpretation to the HT *hwhl*, first as if from *yhl*, "to begin," and then as if from *hll*, "to profane," i.e., to profane the name of God by idolatry and giving the divine name to idols. This exegesis finds extensive support in the Midrashim, e.g., *Gen. R.* 23,7; *Tanhuma B*, Noah 24; texts in Grossfeld, *Neofiti*, note 34 to Gen 4. There is a detailed study of the text and of the rabbinic interpretation of Gen 1–11 by S. Fraade, *Enosh and His Generation; Pre-Israelite Hero and History in Postbiblical Interpretction*, SBL Monograph 30 (Chico, Calif.: Scholars Press, 1984; ("Rabbinic Interpretations: Rabbinic Targumim," 111–119).

Apparatus, Chapter 5

[a] Nfmg: "and his partner" = P.   [b-b] = VNL.

Notes, Chapter 5

[1]"genealogical pedigree"; see note to 2:4.
[2]"he created"; HT: "he made." See note to 1:7.
[3]"a likeness from before the Lord"; HT: "in the likeness of God." See note to 1:26.
[4]"male and female = HT, as in Nf Gen 6:19; 7:3, 16; elsewhere Nf renders "female" of HT as "partner/mate"; Gen 1:27; 7:9, CTg E has "partner" (7:3, 9, 16) and Frg. Tg. also (1:27; 5:2).
[5]"(in his likeness), similar to himself." HT: "(in his own likeness), after his image." See note to 1:26.
[6]"of the life"; addition to HT in Gen 5:4, 8, 11, 14, 20, 23, 27; perhaps through influence of Gen 25:7; 47:8, 9, 28. Pesh also adds but in 5:4 only. See Grossfeld, *Neofiti*, Gen 5, note 4.

in those years[7] he begot sons and daughters.[b] 5. And all the days of the life of Adam were nine hundred and thirty years, [c]and *he died and was gathered*[8] *from the midst of the world.*[c] 6. And Seth lived a hundred and five years and begot Enosh. 7. And Seth lived after he had begotten Enosh eight hundred and seven years, and *in those years he begot* sons and daughters. 8. And all the days *of the life* of Seth were nine hundred and twelve years, and he died *and was gathered from the midst of the world.* 9. And Enosh lived ninety years and begot Kenan. 10. And Enosh lived after he had begotten Kenan eight hundred and fifteen years, and *in those years* he begot sons and daughters. 11. And all the days *of the life* of Enosh were nine hundred and five years, and he died *and was gathered from the midst of the world.* 12. And Kenan lived seventy years and begot Mahalalel. 13. And Kenan lived after he had begotten Mahalalel eight hundred and forty years, and *in those years* he begot sons and daughters. 14. And all the days *of the life* of Kenan were nine hundred and ten years, and he died *and was gathered from the midst of the world.* 15. Mahalalel lived sixty-five years and begot Jared. 16. And Mahalalel lived after he had begotten Jared eight hundred and thirty years, and *in those years* he begot sons and daughters. 17. And all the days of the life of Mahalalel were eight hundred and ninety-five years, and he died *and was gathered from the midst of the world.* 18. And Jared lived a hundred and sixty-two years and begot Enoch. 19. And Jared lived after he had begotten Enoch eight hundred years, and *in those years* he begot sons and daughters. 20. And all the days *of the life* of Jared were nine hundred and sixty-two years, and he died *and was gathered from the midst of the world.* 21. And Enoch lived sixty-five years and begot Methuselah. 22. And Enoch *served in truth before the Lord* after he had begotten Methuselah for three hundred years, and *during these years* he begot sons and daughters. 23. And all the days *of the life* of Enoch were three hundred and sixty-five years.[d] 24. And Enoch *served in truth*[9] *before the Lord* and *it is not known where he is,*[e][10] because *he was withdrawn*[11] *by a*

Apparatus, Chapter 5

[c-c] = VNL.

[d] Nfmg adds: "and he died and was gathered from the midst of the world."

[e] Nfmg: "and behold, he is not" = VNL; P: "and Henoch served in truth before the Lord and we do not know what happened to him in the end (=end of him) because he was led (away) from before the Lord." Cf. VNf: "by a *memar* ('command') from before the Lord."

Notes, Chapter 5

[7](etc.) "in these years"; addition to HT in ch. 5, possibly to specify that he begot only during the years immediately preceding.

[8]"he was gathered from the midst of the world." HT: "and he died." This addition is found in Nf Gen 5:5, 8, 11, 14, 17, 20, 27, 31 and 9:29 may have been influenced by Gen 25:8, 17, 35, 29; 19:33.

[9]"served in truth before the Lord"; HT: "walked with God." See note 6 to Ps.-J. (vol. 1B in this series). See also Nf Gen 6:9.

[10]"and it is not known where he is." HT: w'ynnw; RSV: "and he was not." See note to Ps.-J. (vol. 1B in this series).

[11]"he was withdrawn ('tngd) by a word (or command) from before the Lord." See note 8 to Ps.-J. (vol. 1B in this series) 'tngd of Nf (from ngd, "to draw") can be used in the sense of "to die," as in Ps.-J., Gen 25:8 (of Abraham; Nf "to cease to exist"), 49:33. However, in view of preceding "was not found," in Nf Gen 5:24 there appears to be a reference to Enoch's translation or ascension, although Grossfeld, *Neofiti*, Gen 5, note on verse, thinks otherwise. See F. Luciani, "La sorte di Enoch in un ambigo passo targumico," *Bibbia e Oriente* 22 (1980) 125–158; also K. Luke, "The Patriarchal Enoch," *Indian Theological Studies* 23 (1986) 125–153 (discussion of the Targums, 149f.).

command[12] *from before the Lord.* 25. And Methuselah lived a hundred and eighty<-seven> years and begot Lamech. 26. And Methuselah lived after he had begotten Lamech seven hundred and eighty-two years, and *in those years* he begot sons and daughters. 27. And all the days *of the life* of Methuselah were nine hundred and sixty-nine years and he died and *was gathered from the midst of the world.* 28. And Lamech lived a hundred and eighty-two years and begot a son. 29. And he called his name Noah, saying: "This one will console us from our *evil* deeds and from *the robbery* of our hands, from the earth which has been cursed *by a command from before the Lord.* 30. And Lamech lived after he had begotten Noah five hundred and ninety-five years, and *in those years* he begot sons and daughters. 31. And all the days of Lamech were seven hundred and seventy-seven years, and he died *and was gathered from the midst of the world.* 32. And Noah was five hundred years and Noah begot Shem, Ham and Japheth.

CHAPTER 6

1. And it came to pass that the *sons of man*[1] began to multiply on the face of the earth and *female* daughters were born to them. 2. And the sons of the *judges*[a2] saw that the daughters *of the sons of man*[3] were beautiful *in appearance*[4] and they took wives[5] for themselves from among whomsoever they chose. 3. And the Lord[b] said:

Notes, Chapter 5

[12]"by a word (*mmr*) from before the Lord"; HT: "the Lord took him"; *mmr:* "word" or "command." See note to Ps.-J. (vol. 1B in this series).

Apparatus, Chapter 6

[a] Nfmg: "of the kings" (*mlkyy'*); corr. to "angels" (*ml'k-*).
[b] Nfmg and VNL: "the Memra of the Lord"; P: "and the Memra of the Lord said: The generations that are to arise after the generation of the flood will not be judged. The decree of judgment (= verdict) of the generation of the Flood is sealed, to be destroyed and blotted out in a complete stroke. So, have I not given my spirit in the sons of men so that they might perform good works and since they are flesh, their deeds are evil? Behold, I have given them the span of a hundred and twenty years so that they might perform repentance and have not done it"; VNL: "and the Memra of the Lord said: The generations that are to arise after the generations of the Flood will not be judged to be de-stroyed and blotted out, a complete eradication (lit.: stroke). Lo, have I not given my spirit in the sons of man because they are flesh and their deeds (are) good deeds? Behold I have given them the span of a hundred and twenty years (in the hope that) perhaps they might perform repentance, but they have not done (it)." Nfmg: "after the judgment of the generations of the flood. The judgment of the generations of the Flood is sealed to be destroyed and blotted out (by) a complete destruction (lit.: stroke, blow). Have I not given my spirit in the sons of man so that they might perform good works? Since they are flesh (they perform) evil deeds (or: "flesh of evil deeds"). Behold I have given you (read: them) a span of a hundred and twenty years that they might do."

Notes, Chapter 6

[1]"sons of man"; HT: *h'dm* (RSV: "men").
[2]"sons of the judges," *bny dyyny'* (Grossfeld: "of the nobles"); HT: "sons of Elohim" (*h'lhym*). Nf's identification is the same as that of R. Simeon b. Yohai (in *Gen. R.* 26,5), who cites Aramaic words as in Nf. Further rabbinic parallels to Nf in Grossfeld, *Neofiti*, note 1 to Gen 6. *Elohim* of MT also translated as "judges" in Nf Exod 22:7.

"None of the generations[6] *yet to arise will be judged according to the order of the judgment of the generation of the flood. Behold, the order of the judgment of the generation of the flood has been sealed before him: to be destroyed and blotted out from the midst of the world. Behold, I have* put my spirit[7] *in the sons of man* because they are flesh *and their deeds are evil.*[8] *Behold, I have given the span of* one hundred and twenty years *(in the hope that) perhaps they might do repentance, but they have not done so."* 4. There were *giants*[c] on the earth in those days and also later when the sons of the *judges*[9] went in to the daughters *of the sons of man* and they bore children to them. These are the giants that (were there) from the beginning of the world,[d] *giants of distinguished names.* 5. And *it was manifest before* the Lord[10] that the wickedness[e] of *the sons of man* had increased upon the earth and that every inclination of the thought of[f] their heart *meditated* only[11] on evil all the day. 6. And *there was regret before* the Lord[12] that he had created Adam[g] on the earth, and he got *impatient* and *was quieted*[13] in his heart. 7. And the Lord said:[h] "I will blot out

Apparatus, Chapter 6

[c] Nfmg: "there were warriors dwelling on the earth in those days, and also afterward, after the sons of the angels had joined (in wedlock with) the daughters of the sons (of man)."

[d] Nfmg: "these are the warriors that were there from eternity" (lit.: "from the day of the world").

[e] Nfmg: "the sins (lit.: debts)."

[f] Nfmg: "the good thought meditated."

[g] In text *'dm*: "Adam" (same word as HT); Nfmg: "the son of man"; VNL: "and there was regret before the Memra of the Lord that he had made man (*'ynš'*) on the earth and he said (=spoke) and debated (reading *'dyyn* as = *'dyyny*, Ps-J.) with his heart."

[h] Nfmg: "the Memra of the Lord (said): I will blot out the son of man whom I have created."

Notes, Chapter 6

[3]"daughters of the sons of man"; HT: ". . . of the sons of *h'dm*" (RSV: "of men").

[4]"beautiful in appearance"; HT: "(that they were) good." Nf's addition possibly to stress that the goodness was merely external; see Grossfeld, ibid., note 2.

[5]"wives"; Aramaic text has *'nšy'*, which may be expanded as *'nšyn*. This may conceivably be an error or intended to stand for *nšn*, "women," "wives." However, it ordinarily means "men," "husbands." Grossfeld explains it as (1) either the subject of the verbal clause: "and men took for themselves . . . ," or (2) as the object: "and they took for themselves men/males . . . ," implying homosexuality, of which the Generation of the Flood is accused in rabbinic sources (*Gen. R.* 26,5; *Tanh.* (B) 33, p. 24; or (3) an error for *nšn*, "women, wives."

[6]"none of the generations," etc. See note 6 to Ps.-J. (vol. 1B in this series); also B. Barry Levy, 1, 1986, 115.

[7]"my spirit." See note 8 to Ps.-J. (vol. 1B in this series).

[8]"their deeds are evil." See note 9 to Ps.-J. (vol. 1B in this series).

[9]"Sons of the judges"; See note to 6:2.

[10]"it was manifest before the Lord (that)"; HT: "And the Lord saw (that)." See note to 1:4.

[11]"only," correction *lhzy* of text to *lhd*.

[12]"there was regret before the Lord"; HT: "*wynhm Y*; RSV: "the Lord was sorry." The paraphrase avoids anthropomorphism. When the subject of the verb *nhm*, in the sense of "to regret," is God, Nf paraphrases as in 6:6: "there was regret before"; thus Gen 6:7; Exod 32:12, 14; Nf translates otherwise when the subject of the verb is not God (Exod 13:17), or when it means "to console," "be consoled" (Gen 5:29; 24:67; 38:12; 50:21) or "take pity on" (Deut 32:36).

[13]"got impatient and was quieted" (*'ryq w'tpyys*); double translation of HT: *wyt'sb*; RSV: "it grieved him (to his heart)." Nf's *'ryq* ("to pour out," "empty") probably an error; corrected by some to *'dyyn*, "debated" (with Ps.-J.). L and N of Frg. Tg. and the *Meturgeman* (cf. M. Klein, *Biblica* 56 [1975] 245) have *'dyyn* (= *'dyyn*?). V is unclear, possibly reading *'dyṣ* (=?); see Klein, 1980, II, 93, note 17. Others amend to *'dyq* (common confusion of *resh* and *daleth*), "examined himself." See further Grossfeld, *Neofiti*, note 10 to Gen 6.

Adam whom I have created from the face of the earth, from *the sons of man* to the beast, the creeping things and the birds of the heavens, because *there has been regret before* me that I *created*[14] them." 8. And Noah, *since there was not a righteous man*[15] *in his generation,*[i] found grace *and mercy*[16] *before* the Lord. 9. This is the genealog*ical pedigree*[17] of Noah: Noah was a just man. He was perfect *in good works*[18] in his generations;[j] Noah *served before the Lord in truth.* 10. And Noah begot three sons—Shem, Ham, and Japheth. 11. And *the inhabitants* of the earth had corrupted *their works* before *the Lord,*[k] and the earth was filled with deeds of violence *and with robbers.* 12. And the earth *was manifest before the Lord*[19] and behold it had become corrupted, because all flesh had corrupted its way upon the earth. 13. And *the Lord*[m] said to Noah: "*The outcry* of all flesh *has come up* before me,[20] because the earth has become filled with violent men *and robberies* before them. Behold I am going to destroy both themselves and the earth.[21] 14. Make an ark (of) *timbers of cedar;*[n][22] you will make the ark *as* having compartments, and plaster it inside and outside with asphalt. 15. *According to this plan* will you make it:[o] the length of the ark will be three hundred cubits, fifty cubits its breadth, and

---

Apparatus, Chapter 6

[i] Nfi: "in that generation"; PVNL: "and Noah, since he was just in his generation found grace and mercy."

[j] Nfmg: "in his generation."

[k] Nfmg: "and the earth was corrupted before (the Lord)."

[m] Nfmg: "the Memra of the Lord."

[n] *dqdrynyn*; PVNL: *dqdrynwn*.

[o] Nfmg: "and this shall be the size (of the ark) which you shall make."

Notes, Chapter 6

[14]"created"; HT: "made"; see note to 1:7.

[15]"Since there was not a righteous man (*'l dl' hwh ṣdyq*) in his generation" is a more probable rendering than: "Since he was not just"; cf. v. 9.—unless *l'* is an intrusion; cf. PVNL: "Since he was just"—*'l dhwh ṣdyq*, see also note 16 to Ps.-J. (vol. 1B in this series); also B. Barry Levy 1, 1986, 117, who renders: "since there was no righteous man in that generation".

[16]"grace and mercy (*ḥn wḥsd*) before . . ."; HT: "grace (*ḥn*) in the eyes of." When *ḥn* is found alone in the HT, Nf almost invariably adds *w-ḥsd*, to give us the better known formula, as here in 6:8. Thus also: Nf Gen 18:3; 19:19; 30:27; 32:6; 33:8, 10, 15; 34:11; 39:4, 21; 47:25, 29; 50:4; Exod 32:5; 33:12, 13, 16, 17; 34:9; Num 11:15; Deut 24:1. The only exceptions are Exod 3:21; 11:3; 12:36; Num 11:11.

[17]"genealogical pedigree"; see note to 2:4.

[18]"perfect in good works." HT: "perfect," *tmym*. When the HT uses "perfect" (*tm, tmym*) with regard to persons, Nf renders as: "perfect in good works," and as "perfect without blemish" when used of sacrificial animals. Thus for persons in Gen 6:9; 17:1 (HT: *tmym*); Gen 25:27 (*tm*). The same holds for *šlm* ("whole") of the HT. Thus of persons, Nf Gen 33:18; 34:21. (The same word *šlm*, in reference to the iniquity of the Amorites of Gen 15:16, is rendered as a verb in Nf.) The word *tmym* is used in reference to sacrificial animals in Exod 12:5; 29:1; Lev passim; Num passim; Deut 18:13; 32:4. See also note 18 to Ps.-J. (vol. 1B in this series).

[19]Lit. "and it was manifest before the Lord the earth"—"the earth" preceded by the sign of the accusative. HT: "and God saw the earth" (with sign of accusative). See note to Gen 1:4.

[20]"before me"; correcting text which reads "before him."

[21]"and the earth" (preceded by sign of accusative); thus also LXX (*tēn gēn*). HT *'t* (either sign of accusative or = "with") here generally rendered as: "with (the earth)."

[22]"timbers of cedar"; "cedar," Greek loan word: *kedrinos*. The Aramaic words found in Nf are cited in *Gen. R.* 31,8 (as words of R. Nathan). See McNamara, 1966A, 51f; 1966B, 5f.

thirty cubits *the measure of* its height. 16. You shall make a window[23] for the ark; and you shall bring it to completion *to the distance* of one cubit from above, and you shall put the door of the ark at the side. You will make it *with stories*: a ground story, a second, and a third one. 17. And behold, I am bringing the flood of waters upon the earth to destroy from under the heavens all flesh[p] in which there is the breath of life; everything that is on the earth will be blotted out. 18. And I will establish my covenant with you and you shall enter the ark: you and your wife and the wives of your sons. 19. You will cause to enter the ark with you, to survive with you, from all living creatures, from all flesh, two from each (species); they shall be male and female;[q] 20. from the birds of the air according to their species, and from the cattle according to their species, and from every creeping thing[r] of the earth according to its species, two of each shall go in to you[s] so as to survive. 21. And, as for you, take to yourself of all the food[t] that can be eaten, and gather (it) to you so that it may serve you and them as food." 22. And Noah did all that *the Lord*[u] had commanded him. Thus he did.

CHAPTER 7

1. And the Lord[a] said to Noah: "Go into the ark, you and *the men of*[1] your house, because I have seen that you are righteous[2] before me in this generation. 2. You shall take with you seven pairs of all clean animals, *male and female*[b3] and two of all the animals that are not clean, *male and female*;[b] 3. also seven pairs of the

Apparatus, Chapter 6

[p] Nfmg: "on the earth and the spirit."
[q] Nfmg adds: "and its mate" = CTg E.
[r] Nfmg: "every creeping thing (different word; *rmšh*, cf. HT) of the earth, according to their species" = CTg E.

[s] Tg E: "to the ark"; Nfmg: "they shall go in with you."
[t] CTg E and Nfmg: "food"; a different word.
[u] CTg E, Nfmg: "the Memra of the Lord, thus he did."

Notes, Chapter 6

[23]"a window"; lit. "place of light." See note 25 to Ps.-J. (vol. 1B in this series).

Apparatus, Chapter 7

[a] CTg E and Nfmg: "the Memra of the Lord."

[b] CTg E and Nfmg: "and his mate."

Notes, Chapter 7

[1]"men of (your house)"; HT: "house." See Ps.-J. note 1 (vol. 1B in this series).
[2]"righteous"; as in HT. See Gen 6:8 and note 16 of Ps.-J. (vol. 1B in this series).
[3]"male and female"; HT: lit. "man and his wife"; CTg E: "male and its partner," or Nfmg.

birds of the heaven, male and female,[b] to keep *progeny*[4] alive on the face of the[c] earth. 4. For, *behold*, after seven days[d] I am *going to make* rain fall on the earth for forty days and forty nights, and I will blot out from the face of the earth all its *creatures* which I have *created.*"[5] 5. And Noah did everything[e] that the Lord[f] commanded him. 6. And Noah was six hundred years old when the flood—the waters—came upon the earth. 7. And Noah and his sons, his wife and his sons' wives with him, entered the ark from[6] the waters of the flood. 8. Of the animals that are clean, and of the animals that are not clean, and of the birds and of everything that creeps[g] upon the earth, 9. two pairs entered into the ark with Noah,[h] male and *its mate,*[7] as *the Lord*[i] had commanded Noah. 10. And *at the end of*[8] the seven days[j] *of the mourning of Methusaleh*[9] the waters of the flood came upon the earth. 11. And *at the end*[10] of six hundred years of the life of Noah, in the second month, on the seventeenth day of the month, *on that very day,*[11] all the springs[k] of the great abyss were rent and the apertures[m] of the heavens were opened. 12. And the rain fell upon the earth forty days and forty nights. 13. And on[n] *the very same*

Apparatus, Chapter 7

[c] CTg E and Nfmg: "of all the."

[d] CTg E and Nfmg: "in a few days, seven, I am going to make rainfall."

[e] CTg E: "according to (everything)"; *kkl*, as HT; (correct Nf to CTg E); Nfmg: "in all."

[f] Nfmg: "the Memra of the Lord."

[g] CTg E and Nfmg: "that creeps" (another word, *rmš*); cf. HT and 6:20, note *r* in App.

[h] CTg E and Nfmg: "to Noah."

[i] CTg E and Nfmg: "the Memra of the Lord."

[j] In v. 10: Nf = P; CTg E: "and it came to pass at the end of a few days that the waters of the flood came (lit.: were, happened) upon the earth."

[k] CTg E and Nfmg: "sources" (another word).

[m] CTg E and Nfmg: "windows."

[n] Lit.: "time"; CTg E and Nfmg: "according to the time" (correcting CTg E slightly).

Notes, Chapter 7

[4] "progeny"; lit. "sons" (*bnyn*); HT: "seed."

[5] "created"; HT: "made." See note to 1:7.

[6] "from"; lit. "from before."

[7] "male and its mate"; HT: "male and female." See note to 5:2 and 1:27.

[8] "at the end of . . ."; HT: *lšb't hymym* (RSV: "after the seven days"). Nf gives a more precise dating.

[9] "of the mourning of Methusaleh." A seven days' mourning for Methusaleh is mentioned in *Gen. R.* 32,7 (on this verse), 3,6; t. *Sota* 10:3; b. *Sanh.* 108b and other rabbinic sources. See Grossfeld, *Neofiti*, Gen 7 note 8. This tradition is based on the chronology of Gen 5:25-28; 7:11. Methusaleh died at 969 years or in the six hundredth year of Noah's life, the same year in which the Flood began: he must have been dead before the Flood, otherwise his righteousness would have prevented it.

[10] "at the end of six hundred years"; HT: "in the six hundredth year. . . ." Nf again makes the date precise. See also 8:13; HT: "in the six hundred and first year"; Nf: "and at the end of six hundred and one years." It was debated among Rabbis whether at the Flood Noah was starting or had completed his six hundredth year. Invoking Gen 9:29, R. Judah concluded that the year of the Flood was to be omitted from the counting. See Grossfeld, op. cit., note 11 to Gen 8:13. It may be that Nf's insertion of "at the end of" in 7:11 and 8:13 may have to do with this exegetical problem.

[11] "On the very day"; lit. "as the time of this day" (*hyk zmn ywm' hdyn*); HT: *bywm hzh*, (RSV: "on that day"). See note to 7:13.

day, [12] Noah and Shem, Ham and Japheth, the sons of Noah, and the wife of Noah, and the three wives of his sons with them, went into the ark, 14. they and every beast according to its species, and all the cattle according to their species, and every creeping thing that creeps [o] upon the earth according to its species, and all the birds according to their species, and everything that flies and everything that hovers. [p] 15. They went into the ark *with* Noah, two pairs of all flesh in which there is the breath [q] of life. 16. And they that went in, male and female, [r] from all flesh, went in as the Lord had commanded him; [s] and the Lord *protected him in his good mercies.* [13] 17. And for forty days the flood was upon the earth; and the waters increased and bore the ark and it rose high [t] above the earth. 18. And the waters grew strong and increased greatly upon the earth and the ark moved on the surface of the waters. 19. And the waters grew so strong upon the surface of the earth that all the high mountains that are under all the heavens were covered. 20. The waters increased fifteen cubits higher and covered the mountains. 21. And *an end came* [14] to all flesh [u] that creeps upon the earth: birds, cattle, *all* wild beasts, all creeping things that creep [w] upon the earth and all *the sons of man.* 22. Everything that had the breath of life in its nostrils, from among whatsoever was on the dry land, died. 23. And he blotted out all *the creatures* [x] that were on the face of the earth, from *the sons of man* to beasts, the creeping things [y] and the birds of the heavens; they were blotted out from the earth and Noah alone was left, and whoever was with him in the ark. 24. And the waters swelled strong above the earth for one hundred and fifty days.

Apparatus, Chapter 7

[o] CTg E and Nfmg: "(every) creeping thing that creeps (using another word; *rmš*; see note *g* to 7:8.

[p] CTg E and Nfmg: "(and every) bird that hovers."

[q] CTg E: "spirit."

[r] Nfmg: "and those that went in, male and his mate from."

[s] Nfmg: "as the Memra of the Lord had commanded and the Memra of the Lord spared (*ḥs*; a different word from Nf) and protected him." PVNL: "and the Memra of the Lord spared (*ḥs*) them."

[t] CTg D: "it was lifted above (or: suspended)."

[u] CTg D: "and all flesh was blotted out"; Nfmg: "and he caused to melt away."

[w] Nfmg: "and in every reptile that creeps (*šrṣh dšrṣ*) upon the earth and in all"; different Aramaic words; the text has *rḥš' drḥš.*

[x] CTg D (B): "everything that stood upright"; or "all the beings."

[y] Nfmg: "creeping things" (another word: *rmš*); cf. HT and note *g* above to 7:8.

Notes, Chapter 7

[12] "on the very same day" (*bzmn ywm' hdyn*); HT: *b'ṣm hywm hzh*; lit. "in the bone (or essence) of this day"; "this selfsame day," "exactly at this day." Nf uses the word "time" (*zmn*) to translate *'ṣm* of the HT phrase but in slightly different ways: "on (or: at) the time of (*bzmn*) this day" (Gen 7:13; 17:23, 26; Exod 12:17; Deut 32:48); "as the time of (*hyk zmn*) this day" (Exod 12:41, 51; Lev 23:21, 28, 30—written as *hkzmn* in all three occurrences). Nfmg, where present (Gen 7:13, 23, 26; Exod 12:17; Lev 23:21; Deut 32:48), has "as the time (*hyk zmn*) (of this day)," and so also VN Deut 32:48; a different rendering: Nf, Nfmg, PVN, Lev 23:29 and Nf, Nfmg Lev 23:14. Ps.-J. and Onq. usually agree in translating the HT as *bkrn ywm' hdyn*: "at the hour/essence of this day," unless *krn* is a Greek loan word (*chronos*); see M. Kasher, *Torah Shelemah*, vol. 24, ch. 5, p. 227; summary in A. Díez Macho, *Neophyti 1*, V, 50f.

[13] "protected him in his good mercies"; HT: "and the Lord shut him in." For rabbinic parallels, see Grossfeld, note 15 to Gen 7.

[14] "and an end came to"; HT: ". . . died," *wygw'.*

CHAPTER 8

1. And *in his good mercies the Lord*[a] remembered[1] Noah,[b] *and his sons,*[2] and all the wild beasts and all the cattle that were with him in the ark; and *the Lord* made a spirit *of mercy*[3] to pass over the earth and the waters came to rest.[c] 2. And the springs of the abyss and the apertures of the heavens were closed up, and the *flood* rain was withheld *beneath* the heavens.[d] 3. And the waters receded continuously above the earth; and at the end of one hundred and fifty days the waters had diminished. 4. And in the seventh month, on the seventeenth day of the month, the ark came to rest on the mountains of *Kardun.*[e][4] 5. And the waters went on diminishing until the tenth *month.* In the tenth (month), on the first of the month, the tops of the mountains were revealed.[f] 6. And at the end of forty days Noah opened *the door*[g][5] of the ark which he had made. 7. And he sent out the raven, and it went out[h] *and returned*, went out and returned, until the waters had dried up above the earth. 8. And he sent out the dove from beside him to see if the waters had subsided from above the face of the earth. 9. And the dove did not find a resting place for the sole of its foot and returned to him to the ark, because the waters *were* upon the face of all the earth. And he stretched out his hand and took hold of it and brought it inside the ark to himself. 10. And he *began*[6] again to *count* seven more days, and he sent forth the dove from the ark again. 11. And the dove *returned* at eventime, and lo, on its beak a *cut-off*[7] olive leaf.[i] And Noah knew that the waters

Apparatus, Chapter 8

[a] Nfmg: "the Memra of the Lord."
[b] PVNL: "he remembered in his good mercies that are with him Noah and all the wild beasts"; CTg D: "Noah and all the wild beasts ... "
[c] Nfmg: "were quieted."
[d] Nfmg: "and the sources of the abyss and the windows of the heavens were closed and all the rain of the heavens."
[e] CTg D: "Kardu"; Nfmg: "*Qwwrdwm.*"

[f] CTg D and Nfmg: "on the first day of the month the tops of the mountains were [= could be] seen."
[g] CTg D and Nfmg: "the window."
[h] CTg D and Nfmg: "(it went and returned), went and returned until the time that."
[i] Nfmg: "a (freshly) picked olive leaf in its beak"; another Nfmg adds to "beak," "which it had brought from the mount of Olives."

Notes, Chapter 8

[1] "The Lord remembered in his good mercies"; HT: "God remembered"; when "remembering" of the HT is predicated of God and not explicitly connected with the covenant, Nf adds: "in his (your) good mercies" or "mercy." Thus Gen 8:1; 19:29; 30:22; Exod 2:24; 32:13; Deut 9:27. In Lev 26:42, where there is mention of God remembering the covenant, Nf adds "with mercy," and Nfmg does so once. See also note to Gen 21:1.

[2] "and his sons"; not in HT, added possibly through the influence of other texts, e.g., 7:7; 8:18; 9:1, 8.

[3] "a spirit of mercy"; or "a merciful wind." A similar addition of "mercy" in Nf Gen 1:2.

[4] Kardun, Nf text apparently, Kadrun (*kdrwn*), with transposition signs on the two letters *d* and *r*. See note to Ps.-J. (vol. 1B in this series).

[5] "the door"; Nf's reading here is unique, supported by Jerome, *Hebr. quaest.* in Gen 8:6 (CCL 72,10): *aperuit Noe ostium arcae*; see Introduction, p. 45. There is no need to correct Nf to *hrk'* of Nfmg, as Komlosh, 1973, 54, note 201, suggests, a suggestion not accepted as probable by Díez Macho (*Neophyti 1*, V, 37f.

[6] "began"; cf. Grossfeld, *Neofiti*, note 10 to verse. See note 11 to 6 to Ps.-J. (vol. 1B in this series).

[7] "cut off"; *qtym*; also in *Aruk.* See also note to Ps.-J. (vol. 1B in this series).

had subsided from above the earth. 12. And again Noah began *to count* seven more days, and he sent out the dove and it returned no more to him. 13. And *at the end of* six hundred and one years, on the first[j] *month*, on the first of the month, the waters were dried up from above the earth. And Noah removed the covering of the ark and looked, and behold, the surface of the earth had dried up. 14. And in the second[k] month, on the twenty-seventh of the month, the earth had become dry. 15. And *the Lord* spoke with Noah, saying: 16. "Go out from the ark, you, and your wife and your sons, and your sons' wives with you. 17. Take out with you every living thing that is with you from all flesh: the birds, the animals, and every creeping thing that creeps[m] upon the earth. Let them reproduce[n] on the earth and *grow strong* and multiply[o] upon the earth." 18. And Noah went out, and with him his sons and his wife and his sons' wives. 19. And all the beasts, every creeping thing, all the birds *and* everything that creeps upon the earth according to their families went forth from the ark. 20. And Noah built an altar *to the name of the Memra* of the Lord; and he took some of all the clean animals and of all the clean birds and *set* holocausts *in order on top of* the altar. 21. And the Lord[p] *received the offering of Noah favorably*, and the Lord said *in the thought of* his heart:[q] "I will never again curse the earth on account *of the son of man*, because the inclination of the heart *of the sons of man, their heart, is meditating* evil from their youth and I shall never again blot out all life as I have done.[r] 22. From now onward, for all the days of the earth, seed times and harvests, cold and heat, winter and summer, daytime and night, will not cease.[s]"

CHAPTER 9

1. And *the Lord*[a] blessed Noah and his sons and said to them: *"Grow strong*[1] and multiply and fill the earth. 2. And let the fear of you and the dread of you[b] be upon every beast of the earth and on every bird of the heavens: I have given them into your hands with whatsoever creeps[c] upon the earth and with all the fishes of the

Apparatus, Chapter 8

[j] Nfmg 1°: "in Nisan"; Nfmg 2°: "in Tishri."
[k] Nfmg: "of Marcheswan"?
[m] Nfmg: "creeping things that creep" (a different word, *rmš*; cf. HT, and above note to 7:8.
[n] Nfmg: "let them swim."
[o] Nfmg: "and let them increase and be multiplied."

[p] Nfmg: "the Memra of the Lord."
[q] Nfmg +: "good" ("heart").
[r] Nfmg: "which I have created."
[s] Nfmg: "and heat, and summer and winter and day and night shall not cease."

Apparatus, Chapter 9

[a] Nfmg: "the Memra of the Lord."
[b] Nfmg: "the dread of you and the fear of you."

[c] Nfmg: "that creeps" (a different word, *rmš*, as in 7:8, etc.).

Notes, Chapter 9

[1]"grow strong"; HT: *prw* (RSV: "increase"), rendering as in Nf 1:22, 28, etc. See note to 1:21.

great[2] sea. 3. Everything that moves, that has *the breath of life in it,*[d] you shall have as food. I give them all to you in the same manner as (I have given you) the green herbs. 4. Only flesh, the blood, with the soul you shall not eat. 5. For I will demand your life blood:[e] of every beast I will demand it; *of the son of man* and from the brothers *of the son of man* I will demand the life of the *son of man.*[f3] 6. *Whoever sheds the blood of a son of* man,[3] by the hands of *a son of man*[3] shall his blood be shed;[g] because in a likeness *from before the Lord*[4] *he created*[5] Adam.[h6] 7. As for you, *grow strong*[1] and multiply and reproduce[i] on the earth and multiply *within it.*"[j] 8. And the Lord[k] said to Noah and to his sons with him, saying: 9. "And as for me, behold, I establish my covenant with you and with your sons after you,"[m] 10. and (with)[7] every living being that is with you,[n] the birds and the cattle and with any wild beasts of the earth with you,[o] from all that come out from the ark, to every living being of the earth. 11. And I will establish my covenant with you, and never again[p] shall all flesh be blotted out by the waters of the flood, and there shall never again[p] be a flood to destroy the earth. 12. *And the Lord*[q] said: "This is the sign[8] of the covenant which I place[9] between *my Memra*[r] and you, and every living being that is with you, for the generations of *the earth.*[s10] 13. I *shall place* my bow

Apparatus, Chapter 9

[d] Nfmg: "everything that creeps (*rmš*, as in 7:8), with life for you."

[e] Nfmg CTg E: "your blood of (or: from) your souls"; for close relationships of Nfmg and CTg E, see above Introduction, pp. 9, 44–45.

[f] Nfmg: "I will demand; of the wild beasts I will demand it; of the sons of man, of man and his brothers, I will demand it"; almost = CTg E.

[g] Nf text lit.: "shall be shed his blood"; HT lit.: "his blood shall be shed." Nfmg and CTg E lit.: "his blood shall be shed because."

[h] Nfmg and CTg E: "the son of man (*brnš'*) for *'dm*.

[i] Nfmg and CTg E: "swarm."

[j] Nfmg and CTg E: "in it."

[k] Nfmg and CTg E: "the Memra of the Lord."

[m] Nfmg and CTg E: "and the descendants of your sons after you" (in both texts with sign of the accusative, taking *'t* of HT as sign of accusative rather than as "with").

[n] Nfmg and CTg E: "that there is with you, in the birds (and the cattle)."

[o] Nfmg: "that there is with you from all."

[p] Nfmg and CTg E: "never more."

[q] Nfmg and CTg E: "the Memra of the Lord."

[r] Nfmg and CTg E: "which I am giving between my Memra" (correcting last word slightly).

[s] Nfmg and CTg E: "which is alive which there is with you for eternal generations."

Notes, Chapter 9

[2]"great sea"; see note to Ps.-J. (vol. 1B in this series); for rabbinic parallels, see Grossfeld, op. cit., ch. 9, n. 1.

[3]"son of man" =a man, a human being.

[4]"in a likeness (*dmw*) from before the Lord"; HT. See note to 1:26 above.

[5]"created"; HT: "made"; see note to 1:7 above.

[6]Nf has *'dm* (HT: *h'dm*, "man"), which word generally in Nf is to be taken as a proper name, *Adam*. When Nf understands the Hebrew *'dm* as "man," it generally renders as "son of man." The retention of *'dm* in the present case may be a slip; see Nfmg: "a (the) son of man."

[7]"and (with) every"; for "with" Nf (and CTg E) have *yt*, the sign of the accusative, taking *'t* of the HT (here = "with") as the sign of the accusative.

[8]"sign"—*symn*; a Greek loan word (*semeion*).

[9]"place"—*mšwy* (*šwy*); HT: *ytn* (*ntn*)—"give." When this Hebrew verb is seen to denote "placing," "setting," Nf renders by the verb *šwy*, "place," "set" (cf. Gen 1:17; 3:12; 15:10; 18:8; 30:35, 40; 32:17; 39:20; 40:3, 13, 21; 41:10; 42:30; 45:2; cf. also Deut 28:34. See Grossfeld, *Neofiti*, n. 27 to Gen 7.

[10]"of the earth" (*'r''*); HT: "of the future (*'wlm*); Nf takes the Hebrew word in its later sense of "earth"; cf. Eccl 3:11; Dan 12:7; cf. Nfmg and CTg E: "eternal (in) generations."

in the cloud and it will be a covenant-sign between *my Memra* and the earth. 14. And when the *clouds are spread*[t] over the earth, the bow will be seen in the cloud. 15. And I will recall my covenant[u] between *my Memra* and you, and every living soul in all[w] flesh; and never again will there be waters of a flood to destroy[x] all flesh. 16. And the bow will be seen in the cloud and I will see it, recalling the eternal covenant[y] between *the Memra of the Lord* and every living[z] soul in all the flesh that is[aa] upon the earth." 17. And *the Lord*[bb] said to Noah: "This is the sign of the covenant which I have established between *my Memra* and all flesh that is[cc] upon the earth." 18. And the sons of Noah who came out[dd] of the ark were Shem, Ham, and Japheth. And Ham was the father of *the Canaanites*. 19. These three, they are the sons of Noah. And from these[dd] the whole earth *was filled*. 20. And Noah, a *just*[11] man,[dd] began to *till*[dd] the earth,[12] and he planted[ee] a vineyard. 21. And he drank some of the wine[ff] and became drunk[gg] and uncovered himself within his tent.[hh] 22. And Ham, the father of *the Canaanites*, saw his father's nakedness, and told his two brothers in the *market place*. 23. Then Shem and Japheth took his mantle[13] and placed (it)[ii] over both their shoulders. They walked backward and covered their father's nakedness, and *turned* their faces backward and did not see their father's nakedness. 24. And Noah awoke from[jj] his wine and came to know what his youngest son had done to him. 25. And he said: "Cursed be Canaan; he shall be for his brothers an *enslaved* servant." 26. And he said: "Blessed be the Lord, the God of Shem, and let Canaan be for them an *enslaved* servant. 27. May *the Lord*[kk] enlarge *the borders* of Japheth, and may *the Glory of his Shekinah*[14]

Apparatus, Chapter 9

[t] Nfmg and CTg E: "(when) my cloud shall spread over."

[u] Nfmg and CTg E: "which there is."

[w] Nfmg and CTg E: "which is alive in (or: for) all."

[x] Nfmg and CTg E: "never more waters, as a flood to destroy."

[y] Nfmg and CTg E: "and I shall recall the (eternal) covenant."

[z] Nfmg and CTg E: "(creature) that lives."

[aa] Nfmg and CTg E: "that there is."

[bb] Nfmg and CTg E: "the Memra of the Lord."

[cc] Nfmg and CTg E: "that there is."

[dd] Nfmg and CTg E identical in vv. 18–21, as elsewhere in minor lexical variants (in v. 20 definite form *gbr'* for Nf. *gbr*; in 21 *rbh*).

[ee] Nfmg and CTg E add: "for himself."

[ff] Nfmg: "wine" (different word).

[gg] Nfmg: "and he was relaxed," *rbh* = CTg E for Nf's *rwwh*, "become drunk."

[hh] Nfmg: "Yeru[shalmi]: He stretched himself out in the midst of the tents of the Syrians and he was despised in the m(idst of the tents)."

[ii] Nfmg and CTg E and "it."

[jj] Nfmg: "(from) the taste of."

[kk] Nfmg: "(may) the Memra of the Lord (enlarge) the bor(der)."

Notes, Chapter 9

[11] "Noah, a just man"; see to Gen 6:8 and note 16 to that verse in Ps.-J. The addition of "just" here in Nf may be to compensate for the incident about to be narrated.

[12] "Noah a just man began to till the earth"; HT: "Noah began to be a man of the ground."

[13] "mantle"—Greek loan word: *stolê*.

[14] "may the Glory of his Shekinah dwell"; HT: "let him (i.e., Japheth) dwell" (*yškn*). Nf took the subject of the verb to be the Lord, not Japheth; same interpretation in *Gen. R.* 36,8. On the use of "Glory of Shekinah," see Introduction, pp. 36–37.

dwell in the midst of the tents of Shem, and let Canaan be for them an *enslaved servant.*" *ᵐᵐ* 28. And Noah lived after the flood three hundred and fifty years. 29. And all the days of the *life of Noah* were nine hundred and fifty years; and he died and *was gathered from the midst of the world.*

CHAPTER 10

1. These are the genealogies *ᵃ* of the sons of Noah: Shem, Ham, and Japheth. [1] And sons were born to them after the deluge. 2. And the sons of Japheth: *ᵇ* Gomer, Magog, Madai, *ᶜ* Javan, Tubal, Meshech, and Tiras. *And the name of their provinces:* *ᵈ²* *Phrygia, Germania, Media, Macedonia, Bithynia, Mysia, and Thracia.* *ᵉ* 3. And the sons of Gomer: *ᶠ* Ashkenaz, Riphath, and Togorma. *And the name of their provinces:* *ᵍ* *Asia,* *ʰ* *Barkewi,* *ⁱ* *and Barbaria.* 4. And the sons of Javan: *ʲ* Elisha, Tarshish, Kittim, and Dodanim. *And the name of their provinces: Hellas, Tarsis,* *ᵏ*

Apparatus, Chapter 9

ᵐᵐ Nfmg 1°: "and when his sons become proselytes (or "sojourn among the Jews") let them dwell in the schools of Shem"; Nfmg 2°: and let (Canaan be enslaved to them)."

Apparatus, Chapter 10

ᵃ Nfmg: "the genealogical pedigrees" (*yḥws tlwwdtyh*).

ᵇ VN: "and the sons of Japheth and Gomer. And the name of their provinces Phrygia (*'pryqy*) and Germania and Media and Macedonia (*mwqdwny'*) and Bithynia (*wytny*) and Thracia." (The word *'pryqy* is to be understood as "Phrygia" rather than as "Africa").

ᶜ Nfmg: "and the Medes (*ḥmd'y*), and the Macedonians (*mqdwny'ḥ*), and Bithynia (*wytynyy'*), and Mysia (*mwsyy'* corr. seemingly to "Asia") and Thracia."

ᵈ In Aramaic: *'prkywthwn*; Greek loan word *eparcheia*; cf. Acts 23:34.

ᵉ text *'pryqy*; see *b* above.

ᶠ Nfmg: "And Bithynia (*wytynyyh*) and Asia (?; *w'wtyyh*) and Thracia."

ᵍ VN: "and the sons of Gomer. And the name of their provinces Asia (*'sy'*) and Barkewi (*prkwy*) and Barbaria."

ʰ Nfmg: "Asia," written differently (*'syyh*).

ⁱ correcting *brbwy* of Nf text; Nfmg: "and Barkewi" (*wprkwwy*).

ʲ VN: "and the sons of Javan, Elisha; and the name of their provinces Elastarsus (as one word) Italy and Dardania"; P: "Tarsus (*ṭrsws*), Italy (Italy/ Italia) and Dardania."

ᵏ Nfmg: "Elas-tarsus"; see VN.

Notes, Chapter 10

[1] The identification of the proper names in this chapter is almost always the same in Nf and Ps.-J. For these see notes to Ps.-J. (vol. 1B in this series); for charts with equivalents in rabbinic texts (*Gen. R.* 37; Tg. Chron; *j. Meg* 1 11, 71b; b. *Yoma* 10a, see Grossfeld, *Neofiti*, notes to Gen 10. For a textual study and a literary history of 10:2-32, see B. Barry Levy, 1, 1986, 121–122. Noting the transfer from Hebrew to their Targumic equivalents in vv. 10, 11, 17 and 18 of the names of various parts of Mesopotamia and Syria, he surmises that this may suggest a Syrian and Mesopotamian provenance for either the writing or editing of the text of Neofiti, or at least more familiarity with these places than others in the chapter.

[2] "provinces"; Greek loan word: *eparcheia*; cf. Acts 23:34.

Italy,[m] *and Dardania.*[n] 5. From these were spread abroad the islands[o] of the nations in their lands: each according to his language, according to their families, in their nations. 6. And the sons of Ham: Cush, Misrayim, Put, and Canaan.[p3] 7. And the sons of Cush: Seba, Havilah, Sabta, Raamah, and Sabteca.[4] And the sons of Raamah: Sheba and Deda.[q] 8. And Cush begot Nimrud. He began to be a giant on the earth. 9. He was a giant[r] *in sin*[s5] before the Lord, wherefore[t] is it said: "Like Nimrod, *a giant in sin* before the Lord."[u] 10. And the beginning of his kingdom[w] was Babel,[x] *Edessa,*[y] Nisibis, and *Ctesiphon* in the land of *Babel.*[z6] 11. From that land the Assyrian came out[aa] and built Nineveh, city streets[7] and *Adiabene,*[8] 12. and *Talsar*[9] between Nineveh and *Adiabene:*[bb] that is the big city.[cc] 13. And Misrayim begot the Lydians,[dd] the Anamim, the Lehabim, the Naphtuhin,[ee] 14. the Pathrusin,[ff] and the Casluhin, whence came the Philistines and the *Cappa-*

Apparatus, Chapter 10

[m] In text: "Italia" (*'ṭly'*); Nfmg: "Ilathia" (*'lṭy'*).

[n] Nf: *drdny*; Nfmg: "Dardariah"; *drdryy'.*

[o] *nṣy* (with samech); Nfmg: "the great ones" (from *nṣy* with sin).

[p] Nfmg and: "and the name of their provinces Arabia, Egypt, Allihroq (*'lyyhrq*) and Canaan"; cf. Ps.-J. (vol. 1B in this series).

[q] Nfmg adds: "and the name of their provinces, the Sinirites, the Indians, the Semarae, the Libyans and the Zingites. And the sons of the Mauritanus: Zemargad and Mazag"; cf. Ps.-J.

[r] Nfmg: "in sin and in rebellion before the Lord on the earth."

[s] VNP: "He was mighty (P: mighty strong) at the hunt (*ṣyd'*) [and] in sin before the Lord; he used to catch (*ṣwd*) men by their tongue (=speech) and say to them: Depart from the laws of Shem and adhere to the laws of Nimrod. Wherefore it is said: Like Nimrod mighty in the hunt, mighty in sin before the Lord."

[t] *bgyn kdyn,* as also in PVN; Nfmg: (*bgyn*) *kn.*

[u] Nfmg: "from the day the world was created there was none mighty in sin like Nimrod nor <in> rebellion <before> the Lord"; see Ps.-J.

[w] VN: "and the beginning <of his kingdom was Babel, Edessa>, Nisibis and Ctesiphon in the land of Babel" (text within brackets missing in V); P: "Haran and Nisibis and Ctesiphon in the land of Pontus."

[x] Nf text: *bkl,* for *bbl.*

[y] Nf text: *hdm,* for *hds.*

[z] Nfmg: "of Pontus" = P.

[aa] VN= Nf in v. 11; P: "from that counsel went forth the Assyrian" (marg. gloss in P: "Abraham").

[bb] Nfmg has minor variants, including a variant reading *hdyyp* instead of *hdyp* for "Adiabene," one found in Talmud Yerushalmi.

[cc] Nf v. 12 = VN.

[dd] VN: "and Misrayim begot the Lydians and the Mareothians (*mrywṭ'y*) and the Pentapolitaneans (*b'nṭpwlṭ'y*) and the Lustaneans."

[ee] Nfmg: "the Lybians and the Mareothites and the Pentopolitaneans and the Sickenites" (with some variation of text).

[ff] VN: "and the Pelusites and the Pentasekinites, whence come forth the Philistines and the Cappadocians"; Nfmg: "and the Pelusites and the Pentasekinites."

Notes, Chapter 10

[3] "Cush, . . . Canaan"; identification absent from Nf: added in Nfmg.

[4] "sons of Cush"; identifications absent from Nf; present in Nfmg, from Ps.-J.

[5] "a giant in sin"; (HT: "a might hunter"); part of an extensive tradition; rabbinic sources in Grossfeld, *Neofiti*, note 4 to this chapter. See also *Gen. R.* 37,2; 23,7.

[6] "Edessa Nisibis, Ctesiphon and Babel." Same identifications in *Gen. R.* 37,4.

[7] "city-street." Greek or Latin loan word: *plateia/platea*; cf. Matt 6:5; 12:19, Acts 5:15; Rev 11:8, 21:21.

[8] "Adiabene"; cf. *Gen. R.* 37,2 (where we find the same identification).

[9] "Talsar"; same identification in *Gen. R.* 37,4.

docians.[10] 15. And Canaan begot Sidon, as first-born, and Heth; 16. the Jebusites, the Amorites, the Girgashites, 17. the Hivvites,[gg] the Arkites, the *Orthosites,*[hh][11] 18. the Arwidites,[ii] the Zemarites, and the *Antiochenes.*[jj][12] And afterward the families of the Canaanites were divided. 19. And the territory of the Canaanites was from Sidon in the direction of Gerara as far as Gaza in the direction of Sodom and Gomorrah, Admah and Zeboim, as far as *Callirrhoe.*[13] 20. These are the sons of Ham according to their families, according to their languages, in their lands, in their nations. 21. And (children) were also born to Shem: he is the father of all the sons of the *Hebrews,*[kk] the elder brother of Japheth. 22. The sons of Shem: Elam, Asshur, Arpachshad, Lud, and Aram. 23. And the sons of Aram: Uz, Hul, Gether, and Mash. 24. And Arpachshad begot Shelah. And Shelah begot Eber. 25. And two sons were born to Eber. The name of one of them was Peleg, for in his days *the inhabitants* of the earth were divided.[mm] And his brother's name was Joktan. 26. Joktan begot Almodad, Sheleph, Hazar Maveth, Jerah, 27. Hadoram, Uzal, Diklah, 28. Obal, Abimael, Sheba, 29. Ophir, Havilah, and Jobab.[nn] All these were sons of Joktan. 30. And their dwelling-places were from Meshah in the direction *of the Sepharites,*[oo] *the mountains*[pp] of the east.[14] 31. These are the sons of Shem according to their families, according to their languages, in their lands, in their nations. 32. These are the families of the sons of Noah according to their genealogies in their nations. And from these the nations were separated abroad on the earth after the flood.

Apparatus, Chapter 10

[gg] VN: "and the Tripolitanians and the Arkites and the Cypriots (*kprws'y*)."

[hh] Nfmg: "the Arkites and the Sinnites."

[ii] VN: "And the Antardians and the Emesans and the Antiocheans. Afterwards the islands (*nysy*, Greek *nêsos*; correct to *gnysy*: "families") of the nations separated." For "Arwidites," Nfmg has variant: "Lutasites."

[jj] Nfmg: "the Hamasites and the Antiochenes."

[kk] Nfmg: "of Abar Nahara" (=beyond the Euphrates).

[mm] Nfmg: "the earth was divided."

[nn] In text: "Joktan."

[oo] Nfmg: "Sepharwites" (*sprwwyy*); cf. 2 Kgs 17:24.

[pp] Nfmg: "to the mountain of."

Notes, Chapter 10

[10]"Cappadocia"; HT: Caphtorim; same identification in Onq., Ps.-J.; Pesh, LXX, Vulg., Symm., Philo.

[11]"Orthosites"; HT: "Sinites"; cf. *Gen. R.* 37,6.

[12]"Antiochenes"; HT: Hamath; cf. *Gen. R.* 37,6.

[13]"Callirhoe"; HT: Lesha; cf. *Gen. R.* 37,6; *j. Meg* 1:11, 71b, bottom.

[14]"mountains of the East"; HT: mountain (RSV: "hill country) of the East." Same Aramaic rendering as in Nf in *Gen. R.* 37,8 (cf. Num 23:7); sing. in other Tgs. and versions.

CHAPTER 11

1. Now, all *the inhabitants*^a of the earth[1] had one language[2] and one speech.^b And *they used to*[3] *converse*^c *in the language of the sanctuary by which the world was created*[4] *in the beginning.* 2. And^d when they *caused their hearts to move away*^e[5] (from the Lord), they found a valley in the *land of* Babel^f[6] and settled there. 3. And they said to one another: "Come, let us make bricks and heat *them in a furnace.*" And they had bricks for stones and had asphalt for mortar. 4. And they said: "Come, let us build ourselves a city and a tower, with its top *reaching toward* the heavens; and let us make ourselves *an idol on top of it*[7] *and let us put in its hand a sword to make war against him before*^g we are scattered abroad upon the face of all the earth." 5. And *the Glory of the Shekinah of* the Lord *was revealed*[8] to see^h the city and the tower which the sons of man had built. 6. And the Lordⁱ said: "Behold, one people and all of them have one language and behold, now they have begun to act, *and, now*, nothing they plan to do will be held back from them. 7. Come, *now*,

Apparatus, Chapter 11

^a VN: "and all the inhabitants of the earth had one language and one speech and one counsel because they used to converse in the holy language, in which the world was created from the beginning"; Nfmg: "and all the earth."

^b Nfmg +: "and one counsel" =VN.

^c Nfmg: "and speaking in one counsel they arose to rebel."

^d PVN: "And when they caused their hearts to move away from following (lit.: from after) the Memra of the one who spoke (lit.: said) and the world came into being, they found a valley (P: a level place) in the land of Pontus and settled there."

^e Nfmg: "in their journeyings from the east" (or: "from the beginning").

^f Nfmg: "of Pontus" = PVN.

^g PVN: "and they said (P: and each to his neighbor): Come now let us build ourselves a city with a tower and its top reaching toward heaven and let us make for ourselves within (it) a temple (lit.: a place of kneeling or of worship) at its top. And let us put a sword in the hand of the idol, perhaps it might make war (lit.: arrange battle lines) against him (=God) before we are scattered from upon the earth" (VN: "scattered upon the face of all the earth").

^h Nfmg: "and it was manifest before the Lord to see."

ⁱ Nfmg: "the Memra of the Lord."

Notes, Chapter 11

[1] "inhabitants of the earth"; HT: "all the earth"; "inhabitants of"; syntactic expansion as in Nf 6:11; 10:25; 11:9; 18:25; 41:57; 47:13.

[2] "one language and one speech"; HT (RSV): "one language and few words." All Aramaic versions (including Peshitta) render as Nf; cf. C. Peters, 1935, 9.

[3] "They used to ..."; for translation see Golomb, 1985, 197.

[4] "by which the world was created"; or "since by it the world. . . ." On the traditions, see notes to Ps.-J. (vol. 1B in this series) and Grossfeld, *Neofiti*, note 3 to Gen 11.

[5] "they caused their hearts to move away," *'s'w;* or "they removed their minds (from God)"; HT: *bns'm mqdm*, "in their journeying (=when they journeyed) from the East." Nf takes "journeying" in the moral sense and understands *qdm* (East or Early) as a name for God. Cf. *Gen. R.* 38:7, with same verb: "R. Leazar b. R. Simeon interpreted: They betook themselves away from the Ancient (*qdmwn*, Kadmon) of the world, saying, We refuse to accept either him or his divinity."

[6] "Babel"; MT: *shinar;* same identification in Nf Gen 10:10; 14:9.

[7] For rabbinic parallels to the midrash, see Grossfeld, op. cit., note 8 to Gen 11; also notes in Ps.-J. (vol. 1B in this series). "Let us make ourselves an idol on top ..."; HT: "Let us make a name (*šm*) for ourselves. . . ." Nf reads HT *šm* (MT: *sem*, a name) as *šam*, "there" ("on top ...").—"toward the heavens," lit. "to the height of"; see Nf Gen 28:2.

[8] The HT (RSV) has: "And the Lord came down to see the city and the tower"; Nf avoids the anthropomorphism; see Introduction, pp. 33–35, 37.

and I will be revealed[j]9 and there we shall confound their tongues so that one will not give heed[k] to the language of the other." [m] 8. And the Lord[n] scattered them abroad from there over the face of all the earth, and they *were held back*[o] from building the city. 9. For this reason he called its name Babel, for *thus* did the Lord[p] confound the tongues of all *the inhabitants of* the earth, and from there the Lord[q] scattered them abroad upon the face of all the earth. 10. This is the genealog*ical pedigree* of Shem: Shem was a hundred years when he begot Arpachshad two years after the deluge. 11. And Shem lived after he had begotten Arpachshad five hundred years, and during *these years* he begot sons and daughters. 12. And Arpachshad lived thirty-five years and begot Shelah. 13. And Arpachshad lived after he had begotten Shelah four hundred and thirty years, and *during these years* he begot sons and daughters. 14. And Shelah lived thirty years and begot Eber. 15. And Shelah lived after he had begotten Eber four hundred and three years, *and during those years* he begot sons and daughters. 16. And Eber lived thirty-four years and begot Peleg. 17. And Eber lived after he had begotten Peleg four hundred and thirty years, and *during those years* he begot sons and daughters. 18. And Peleg lived thirty years and begot Reu. 19. And Peleg lived after he had begotten Reu two hundred and nine years, and *during those years* he begot sons and daughters. 20. And Reu lived thirty-two years and begot Serug. 21. And Reu lived after he had begotten Serug two hundred and seven years, and *during these years* he begot sons and daughters. 22. And Serug lived thirty years and begot Nahor. 23. And Serug lived after he had begotten Nahor two hundred years, *and during those years* he begot sons and daughters. 24. And Nahor lived twenty-nine years and begot Terah. 25. And Nahor lived after he had begotten Terah one hundred and nineteen years, *and during those years* he begot sons and daughters. 26. And Terah lived seventy years and begot Abraham, [10] Nahor, and Haran. 27. This is the genealogy of Terah: Terah begot Abram, Nahor, and Haran. And Haran begot Lot. 28. And Haran died *during the lifetime* of Terah his father in the land of his birth, in the *furnace of fire*[11] of the Chaldeans. 29. And Abram and Nahor took wives for themselves. The name of [r]<the wife of Abram was Sarai, the name>[r] of the wife of Nahor was Milcah, the daughter of Haran, the father of Milcah and the father of Iscah. 30.

Apparatus, Chapter 11

[j] Nfi: "and we will be revealed"; Nfmg: "and you (or she) will be revealed and we will confound."

[k] Nfmg: "so that one (lit.: a son [*byr*] of man) was not able to."

[m] Nfmg: "the language of his companions."

[n] Nfmg: "the Memra of the Lord."

[o] Nfmg: "and they left off."

[p] Nfmg: "the Memra of the Lord the language of all the earth."

[q] Nfmg: "the Memra of the Lord."

[r-r] Missing in text: in mg.

Notes, Chapter 11

[9]"will be revealed"; paraphrase mitigates the anthropomorphism of the HT (RSV): "let us go down." 11:11. Also 11: 13, 15, 17, 19, 21, 23, 25; "during these years"; see note to 5:4.

[10]"Abraham"; thus MS, for "Abram."

[11]"furnace of fire (of the Chaldeans)"; HT: "Ur (of the Chaldeans)." For this well-known legend on Abram, see notes to Ps.-J. (vol. 1B in this series). The legend is an old one, already in Pseudo-Philo, *LAB* 6,16, and Jerome, *Hebr. quaest.*, in Gen 11:28 (CCL 72,15); see also Grossfeld, op. cit., Gen 11 note 15.

And Sarai was barren; she had no children. 31. And Terah took Abram his son and Lot, his grandson, and Sarai his daughter-in-law, his son Abram's wife, and went forth with them from *the furnace of the fire* of the Chaldeans, [12] to go to the land of Canaan; and they arrived at Haran and dwelt there. 32. And the days *of the life* of Terah were (two) hundred and five years; and Terah died in Haran.

CHAPTER 12

1. And the Lord[a] said to Abraham: "Go from your country and your kindred and from your father's house to the land which I will show you. 2. And I will *appoint* you[1] *to become* a great nation and I will bless you and I will make your name powerful and *you will be* blessings.[b2] 3. And I will bless whoever blesses you and whoever curses you *shall be cursed.*[c3] And in *your merit*[4] all the families of the earth shall be blessed." 4. And Abram went as the Lord[d] had spoken with him, and Lot went with him. And Abram was seventy-five years *at the time* he went forth from Haran. 5. And Abram took Sarai his wife and Lot, his brother's son, and all their wealth which they had acquired and the souls *they had converted.*[5] And he went

Notes, Chapter 11

[12]"from the furnace of the fire of the Chaldeans"; HT: "from Ur of the Chaldeans"; Nf, here as elsewhere (Gen 11:28, 31; 15:7), translates the place name Ur as "furnace of the fire."

Apparatus, Chapter 12

[a] Nfmg: "the Memra of the Lord."
[b] Nfmg: "And Abraham will be many blessings" = VNL.
[c] Nfmg: "(the one) who blesses you like Aaron the priest, and (the one) who curses you I will curse,

like Balaam the Wicked" (lit.: " . . . of the wicked"); cf. Ps.-J.
[d] Nfmg: "the Memra of the Lord."

Notes, Chapter 12

[1]Nf and Frg. Tg.: "I will appoint you"; HT and other versions: "I will make you."
[2]"and you will be blessings"; HT: *whyh lbrkh* (RSV): "and you shall be a blessing"; lit. "and you, be (imperat.) a blessing"; or: "he was (or: shall be) a blessing"; cf. Nfmg, VNL: "and Abraham will be many blessings." Nf renders HT "blessing" (sing.) as plural, as it does in Gen 27:12 (possibly also 27:41); otherwise in Gen 27:36, where a single blessing is clearly intended. B. Barry Levy (1, 1986, 125) renders 12:2 as: "you will be a blesser."
[3]"shall be cursed"; softening HT's "I will curse"; cf. Nf Gen 3:14; 4:11.
[4]"in your merit" (*b-zkwt-k*): HT: "by (in) you." The Aramaic *zkw(t)* means "merit," but *bzkwt(-k)*, "in (or: by) (your) merit" may also be rendered, "for your sake"; cf. Onq. *bdylk*, "for your sake," "because of you." See *Gen. R.* 39,12 on "in you shall be blessed": "the rains for your sake (*bzkwk*; lit. "for your merit"); the dews for your sake (*bzkwtk*)." See also below, note to 12:13.
[5]"they had converted"; same interpretation in *Gen. R.* 39,14; HT: "they had made." See also Nf Gen 21:31 and note to verse.

forth to go to the land of Canaan, and they came to the land of Canaan. 6. And Abram passed on to the place of Shechem, to *the Plain of the Vision.*[6] And as yet the Canaanites had been dwelling in the land. 7. And the Memra of the Lord was revealed to Abram and said to him: "To your sons[e] I will give this land." And he built there an altar to the name of the Memra of the Lord,[h] who was revealed to him. 8. And from there he went up to the mountain, to the east of Bethel, and spread his tent with Bethel to *the west* and Ai to the east. And he built an altar there to *the name of*[f] *the Memra of* the Lord and he *worshiped and prayed*[7] there in the name *of the Memra* of the Lord. 9. And Abram moved on, going gradually to the south. 10. And there was a famine in the land, and Abram went down to Egypt to dwell there, because the famine was severe in the land. 11. And when he drew near to enter Egypt he said to Sarai his wife: "Behold, now, I know you are a woman of beautiful appearance. 12. And it will happen that when the Egyptians see you they will say: 'She is his wife.' And they will kill me but they will let you live. 13. Say, I pray, *that* you are my sister, so that it may go well with me[g] because of you[8] and that my life may be spared for your *sake*." 14. And it happened when Abram entered into Egypt, the Egyptians saw that his wife was very beautiful. 15. And the nobles of Pharaoh saw her and praised her before Pharaoh. And the woman was taken[h] to the *palace*[i][9] of Pharaoh. 16. And because of her[j] he treated Abram well. And he had sheep, oxen, he-asses, menservants, maidservants, she-asses, and camels. 17. And the Lord[k] *unleashed great* plagues against Pharaoh and

Apparatus, Chapter 12

[e] Nfmg: "to the descendants of your sons."

[f] Nfmg: "before the Lord."

[g] Nfmg: "to have it go well with me for your sake and that my life might be spared because of you."

[h] In text: "was remembered."

[i] *plṭyryn*: Latin/Greek loan word (*praitôrion*); Nfmg *plṭyn*: Latin/Greek loan word, *palation*, "palace"=PVNL.

[j] Nfmg: "he treated (Abraham) well for her sake" (or "merits"; *bzkwwth*), and there was."

[k] Nfmg: "the Memra of the Lord."

Notes, Chapter 12

[6]"the Plain of the Vision"; HT: "Oak (*'lwn*) of Moreh"; Hebrew *'lwn* also rendered as "Plain/Valley" in Vulg.; Onq., Ps.-J.; also in *Gen. R.* 41,8; same rendering in Nf Gen 13:18; 14:13; 18.1. In Gen 35:8 Heb. *'lwn* rendered in Nf as *blwṭh*; cf. *Gen. R.* 15,1. The Hebrew place name Moreh (*mwrh*) appears to have been understood by the Targumists as connected with *mr'h*, "vision," or *r'h*, "to see." See F. Stummer, "Convallis Mambre und verwandtes," *JPOS* 12 (1932), 6–12; M. Delcor, "Quelques . . . ," 108ff.

[7]"worshiped and prayed"; HT: "called on (the name of Yahweh)"; same paraphrase in Nf Gen 13:4; 16:13; 21:33; 26:25; 33:20. Hebrew translated by "he prayed" alone in Gen 13:4; 33:20; Exod 17:15; 34:5.

[8]"because of you" (*bgllk*; HT: *b'bwrk*); "for your sake" (*bzkwwtk*, or: "for your merits"; HT: *bgllk*)." See above, note to 12:3. The preposition *bgll* exists already in biblical Hebrew in the sense of "because" (Gen 12:13, the present text), of Sarai; in Gen 30:27, of Jacob; in Gen 39:5, of Joseph; in Deut 13:7, of the people; in Deut 15:10, of an action; in Deut 18:12, of abominable practices. In all cases in Genesis Nf renders as *bzkwt-*, "for the merit(s) of . . ." (or simply: "because of"; see note to 12:3), whereas in the texts of Deut in Nf the word *bgll*, as in the HT, is used. The difference may be due to varying translation practice, no difference having been perceived between the two terms. However, the different translations may also have originated in the belief that one should use *bzkwt* when speaking of the Fathers (or in the case of Gen 12:13 of the Mothers), with implicit reference to their merits.

[9]"palace" (*plṭyryn*); Latin, or Greek through Latin, loan word: *praetorium, praitôrion*; the Latin term is already found as a loan word in the Greek NT; Matt 27:27; John 18:28, 33; 19:9; Phil 1:13; Acts 23:35.

against *the men of* his house[m] on account of Sarai, the wife of Abram. 18. And Pharaoh called Abram and said to him: "What is this you have done to me? Why, *I pray*, did you not tell[n] me that she was your wife? 19. Why[o] did you say: 'She is my sister,' so that I took her to myself as wife? And now, behold your wife; take her and go." 20. And Pharaoh commanded the *leading men*[p][10] concerning her and they sent him away and his wife and all that he had.

CHAPTER 13

1. And Abram went up from Egypt, he and his wife and all that he had, and Lot with him, toward the south. 2. And Abram was very rich in cattle, in silver, and in gold.[a] 3. And he went on his journeyings from the south to Bethel, to the place where he *had* earlier[b] *spread* his tent, between Bethel and Ai, 4. to the place of the altar which he had earlier built there, and there Abram prayed[c][1] in the name of *the Memra of* the Lord. 5. And Lot, who went with[d] Abram, also had sheep and oxen and tents. 6. And the land did not have room for[2] (both of) them to dwell together because their wealth[e] was plentiful, and they were not able to dwell together. 7. And there were *disputes*[f] between the herdsmen of Abram's cattle and the herdsmen of

Apparatus, Chapter 12

[m] Nfmg: "And upon the men of the house of Pharaoh because of."
[n] Nfmg: "did you (not) show me."

[o] Nfmg and "now" (or: "I pray").
[p] Nfmg adds *w^{c}1* = "and concerning" or "and he entered."

Notes, Chapter 12

[10]"leading men"; HT: "men" (*'nšym*), possibly going on the rabbinic notion that *'yš* (sing. of *'nšym*) denotes a great man, not an ordinary one.

Apparatus, Chapter 13

[a] Nfmg: "in flocks, silver and gold."
[b] Nfmg: "from the beginning."
[c] Nfmg: "to the place of the altar where he had prayed from the beginning, and he worshiped and prayed."
[d] Nfmg: "who was leading on for the merits of (or: "because of") of Abraham"; cf. Ps.-J.
[e] Nfmg: "the property"; cf. PVNL.
[f] Nf v. 7 = VNL, with following variants: "stock" for "cattle" of Nf; "come to (the pastures)" for "reached," (commanded by) "Abram the just ... do

not go ... as yet they have authority in the land"; P= Nf, NVL except: "And there was wrangling ... stock ... reached the pastures ... but let them graze and pasture in outside field(s); also the herdsmen of Abram the just would tie up (lit.: muzzle) their bridles, and they would not extend (? or: "were not extended," *'ytrbw*) either to the Canaanites or to the Perizzites, who until then (or: "since until then," *d'l kn*) were dwelling in the land."

Notes, Chapter 13

[1]"prayed"; HT: "called on the (name of Yahweh)"; see note to 12:8.
[2]"did not have room for"; Aramaic *'šn*. For a note on the Aramaic word, see Grossfeld, *Neofiti*, Gen 13, note 3.

Lot's cattle. *Abram's herdsmen muzzled their cattle*[3] *until they reached the pastures and Lot's herdsmen did not muzzle their cattle but allowed them to graze freely and they roamed about. Besides, Abram's herdsmen had been commanded by their master Abram, saying: "Do not turn aside*[g] to the Canaanites or the Perizzites. These were still dwelling in the land." 8. And Abram said to Lot: "Let there not, I pray, be disputes[h] between me and you, between my herdsmen and your herdsmen, because we[i] are *as* kinsmen. 9. Is not all the land before you? Separate yourself, I pray, from me. If you (go) <to the *north*>[j] I (will go) to the south; if you (go) to the south I (will go) to the north." 10. And Lot lifted up his eyes and saw all *the plain of* the Jordan, that it[k] was all irrigated, before the Lord had *blotted out* Sodom and Gomorrah, like a garden of the Lord *for trees,*[m] like the land of Egypt[n] *for fruits,*[o][4] as you come to Zoar. 11. And Lot chose for himself all *the plain* of the Jordan. And Lot moved toward the east and they separated one from the other. 12. Abram dwelt in the land of Canaan and Lot dwelt in the cities *of the plain,* and *he spread his tent* as far as Sodom. 13. And the people of Sodom were evil, *one toward the other,* and were very guilty *before* the Lord *of revealing their nakedness and of the shedding of blood*[p] *and of foreign worship.*[5] 14. And the *Memra* of the Lord said to Abram after Lot had separated from him: "Lift up your eyes, I pray, and look from the place where you are, to the north, to the south, to the east and to the *west,* 15. because all the land which you see I will give to you and to your *sons*[q] forever. 16. And I will make your *sons* like the dust of the earth, because just as it is *impossible*[6] *that anyone* number the dust[r] of the earth, likewise is it *impossible* that your sons be numbered.[s] 17. Arise, walk in the land,[t] in its length and in its breadth, for I will give it to you." 18. So Abram *spread his tent* and came[u] and dwelt in the *Plain of the Vision,*[7] that is, in Hebron, and he built an altar there *in the name of the Memra of the Lord.*[w]

Apparatus, Chapter 13

[g] Nfmg: "(Abram) the just saying: You shall not go (*tkwn*)."

[h] Nfmg: "let there (not) be, I pray, wrangling between me."

[i] Text of Nf: "I am."

[j] Missing in text.

[k] Nfmg: " ... and behold it was ..."

[m] Nfmg: "a place of irrigation before the Memra of the Lord had destroyed <...> for trees."

[n] Nfmg: "and like the land of Egypt as you came."

[o] Nfmg: "for produce."

[p] Nfmg: + "innocent."

[q] Nfmg: "and to the descendants of your sons after you I will give the land."

[r] Nfmg: "for if a man could count the dust."

[s] Nfmg: "likewise the descendants of your sons (cannot) be counted."

[t] Nfmg: "journey in the land."

[u] Nfmg: "and Abram journeyed and came."

[w] Nfmg: "before the Lord."

Notes, Chapter 13

[3]Nf's Aggadic paraphrase also in Ps.-J.; see also *Gen. R.* 40,5.

[4]"for trees ... for fruits"; additions in Nf; see *Sifre, Deut* 38 (on Deut 11:10).

[5]Or: "sexual sin, murder, idolatry." On these central sins in Judaism, with regard to Sodom, see *Gen. R.* 40,7; Tos, *Sanh.* 13:8; *Sanh.* 109a.

[6]"as it is impossible"; HT: "if a man can."

[7]"Plain of Vision"; HT: "Oak or Moreh." See note to 12:6.

CHAPTER 14

1. In the days of Amraphel, king of Shinar,*ᵃ¹* Arioch, king of Ellasar,*ᵇ¹* Chedorlaomer, king of Elam, and Tidal, king of the nations, 2. drew up battle lines with Bera, king of Sodom, and with Birsha, king of Gomorrah, Shinab, king of Admah, Shemeber, king of Zeboim, and with the king of *the city*ᶜ *that swallowed up* its inhabitants,² that is, Zoar. 3. All these *kings* had become united with each other*ᵈ³* in the valley of *Orchards,*⁴ that is, the Sea of Salt. 4. Twelve years they had served *before* Chedorlaomer and in *the thirteenth* year⁵ they rebelled *against him.* 5. In the fourteenth year Chedorlaomer came and the kings that were with him and they killed the *giants*⁶ in Ashtarta of Karnaim and *the noblest who were among them*⁷ *and the Ematanaeans*ᵉ *who were dwelling* within the city,*ᶠ⁸* 6. and the

---

Apparatus, Chapter 14

ᵃ Nfmg, Nfi: "of Babel."
ᵇ Nfmg: "of Pontus."
ᶜ Nfmg: "of the fortress."
ᵈ Nfmg: "all these had become united with one another" (omits "kings"); VNL: "all these had become united with one another in the plain of Orchards"; for "Orchards," Nf writes *prdysy'*; Nfmg with VNL, Ps.-J. has *prdsyy'*.

ᵉ "nobles," in Nf, VNL, *zywtny (h)*; "Emataneans," *'(y)mtny(h)*.
ᶠ VNL: "and they killed the Giants in Ashtaroth Karnaim and the noblest who were among them and the Ematheans those who were dwelling of the sons of (*bny*) of the city," but read probably: "dwelling in the city."

Notes, Chapter 14

¹In Nf names left in Hebrew without identification; identified below in v. 8.
²"the city that swallowed up (*bl't*) its inhabitants" (as in *Gen. R.* 41,5), taking the place name Bela (*bl'* = "swallow") as a verb. So also with regard to this name in Nf Gen 14:2, 8; the same in Jerome, *Hebr. quaest.* on verse. On Jerome here, see S. Klein, "Targumische Elemente in der Deutung biblischen Ortsnamen bei Hieronymus," *MGWJ* 83 (1939) 137; and for Gen 14, esp. Robert Hayward, "Some Observations on St. Jerome's 'Hebrew Questions on Genesis' and Rabbinic Tradition," *Proceedings of the Irish Biblical Association*, no. 13 (1990) 58–76.
³"had become allies to each other" (*'tḥbrw*; also in Ps.-J.); HT: *ḥbrw*, "they joined forces." Nf probably takes it that the preceding five kings are intended; in *Gen. R.* it is the earlier four, and they fell into the hands of Abraham.
⁴"Valley of the Orchards" (or: "Groves"); see note 14 to Ps.-J. (vol. 1B in this series).
⁵"in the thirteenth year" (*btlt 'sry snyn*); HT has: *wslš 'srh snh*, "in/for thirteen years (they rebelled)" (RSV: "but in the thirteenth year they rebelled"), with variant *wb(slš)*, "and in the (thirteenth year)," a variant underlying Sam, 1QGenAp, Ps.-J. The Nfmg *tlt*, "thir(teen)" follows the HT. The question of the length of the rebellion (one or thirteen years) is connected with the exact reading.
⁶"giants," as in Ps.-J., LXX, *Gen. R.* 26,7; HT: Rephaim.
⁷"the noblest of them"; see note 18 to Ps.-J. (vol. 1B in this series). The Aramaic rendering, as in Nf, is cited verbatim in *Gen. R.* 41,6, in a gloss on the HT.
⁸"who were dwelling within the city." HT: "in Shaveh-Kiriathaim." Nf takes *qrytym* of the HT as a common noun, "city" or "cities," and apparently leaves Shaveh untranslated.

Horites *who dwelt*[g] on the mountain of *Gabla*[9] as far as *the border* of Paran[h10] which *is near* the desert. 7. And they turned back and entered the *Spring of Judgment,*[11] that is, *Rekem,*[12] and subdued all the *territory*[13] *of* the Amalekites and also the Amorites who dwelt in *En-Gedi of the Palm Trees.*[14] 8. And the king of Sodom, the king of Gomorrah, the king of Admah, the king of Zeboim, and the king of *the city that swallowed up its inhabitants,*[i15] that is, Zoar, went out and set battle lines against them[j] in the valley *of the Orchards,*[16] 9. against Chedorlaomer, king of Elam, Tidal, king of the nations, Amraphel, *king of Babylon,*[17] and Arioch, king of *Pontus;*[k18] four kings *gave battle* to five and *they overcame them.* 10. And in the valley of *the Orchards*[m16] there were many *wells* full of bitumen, and as the kings of Sodom and Gomorrah fled they fell in there and those who were left[n] fled to the mountains. 11. And they took all the wealth of Sodom and Gomorrah and all their provisions and went their way. 12. And they took Lot—Abram's nephew— and his wealth[o] and went their way; and he was dwelling in Sodom. 13. And a fugitive came and informed Abram the Hebrew; he was dwelling in the *Valley of the Vi-*

Apparatus, Chapter 14

[g] Nfmg: "the Horanites those who dwelt"; very probably from VNL: "And the Horanites those who dwelt on the mountain of Gabla to El-paran, to the plain of Hazoza which is near to the wilderness."

[h] Nfmg: "Hazoza which is near"; = VNL.

[i] Nfmg: "the fortress which swallowed up its inhabitants."

[j] Nfmg: "with them."

[k] Nfmg: "of Ellasar"; VNL: "and Amraphel the king of Pontus and Arioch the king of Ellasar, four kings gave battle to five"; P: "four kings against five gave battle."

[m] P: "of the Orchards"; VNL in v. 10 = Nf.

[n] Nfmg: "within them and what was left."

[o] Nfmg: "the property of his brother's son."

Notes, Chapter 14

[9]"on the Mountain of Gabla"; HT: "in their Mount Seir." The identification of Seir with Gabla, Gebal, Gobolitis is early; see note to Ps.-J. (vol. 1B in this series) and Grossfeld, *Neofiti*, Gen 14 note 8.

[10]"as far as the border of Paran" (*'d dgbwl' dp'rn*); HT: *'d 'yl p'rn*, "to El-Paran." The reason for Nf's rendering is unclear. LXX and Syr render as "terebinth of Paran," apparently reading or understanding *'yl* as *'ylwn* (see to 12:6). Vulg., Onq., Ps.-J., rendering as "plain," also seem to have read or understood as *'ylwn*. Nfmg, VNL render Paran as "Hazoza" (="Vision"), which is there rendering of "(Oak of; in Tg.: "Plain of") Moreh" of 12:6. See note to that verse.

[11]"Spring of Judgment"; HT: "En-Mispath," probably, as Pesh., taking place names as common names; see Ps.-J. (vol. 1B in this series).

[12]"Rekem"; HT: Kadesh; see note to Ps.-J. (vol. 1B in this series). See also McNamara, 1972, 199f.

[13]"territory (of the Amalakites)," *thwmhwn . . .*; HT: *śdh*; Nf's translation is in keeping with the practice governing its rendering of this HT word; see note to 2:5.

[14]"Ain-gedi of the Palm Trees"; HT: Hazazan-tamar. This identification also in 2 Chr 20:2; Onq., Ps.-J., Pesh., and *Gen. R.* 41,7.

[15]"Valley of the Orchards"; see note to 14:3.

[16]"the City that swallowed up . . ."; see note to 14:2. For Jerome's similar understanding of the text, see R. Hayward, art. cit., in note to 14:2 above.

[17]"King of Babylon"; HT: "king of Shinar"; see note to 10:10.

[18]"Pontus"; HT: Ellasar; same identification in Symmachus and Vulg. On Pontus, see Grossfeld, op. cit., Gen. 14 note 15.

sion of Mamre[19] the Amorite, the brother of Eshcol, the brother of Aner. These were allies of Abram. 14. And when Abram heard that *Lot, his brother's son*, had been taken captive, he armed *his young men[p] (who had) been reared[20] in his* house, *three hundred and ten*[21] (of them), and followed after *them* as far as *Caesarea*. 15. And he and *his captains[q]* divided their forces against them by night and slew them and pursued them to Hoba, which is *north* of Damascus.[r] 16. And he returned all the wealth; and Lot, his *brother's* son, and his wealth also he returned as well as the women[s] and the people. 17. And the king of Sodom came out to meet him, after he had returned from slaying Chedorlaomer[t] and the kings who were with him, in the Valley *of the Orchards,[t]* that is, the valley of the king. 18. And Melchisedech,[u] king of *Jerusalem—he is Shem the Great*[22]—brought out bread and wine, for he was the priest *who ministered in the high priesthood*[w][23] *before* the most High God. 19. And

Apparatus, Chapter 14

[p] Nf = VNL, with the following variants: "retainers (lit.: "those who recline") of his house ... three hundred and eighteen ... as far as Dan of Caesarea"; Nfmg: "those born in his house, and they did not desire to go with him and he chose from among them Eleazar who was...." There are further unconnected Nfmg, e.g.: "eight" (of "eighteen," cf. HT); "Dan of Caesarea," cf. VNL.

[q] Nfmg: "and his servants."

[r] VNL: "and he pursued them as far as Enwata (= the Springs) north of Damascus"; Nfmg: "Aynwata ("the Springs") of Damascus."

[s] Nfmg: "(all) the property and also Lot, his brother's son, and the property he restored and also the women."

[t] VNL: "and the kings who were with him in the Valley of Hazoza, that is, the place (lit.: house) of the Valley of the King"; Nfmg: "to the Valley of Hazoza, that is"; = VNL.

[u] VNL: "and Melchi Sedek, the king of Jerusalem, he was Shem the Great, he was a priest to God the Most High"; P: "and Melchi Sedek, the king of Jerusalem—who was Shem the Great—was a priest of the Most High; he brought out food and wine, and he was standing and serving in the high priesthood before God the Most High (God)."

[w] Nfmg: "(ministered) to God the Most High."

Notes, Chapter 14

[19]"Valley of the Vision of Mamre"; HT: "by the Oaks (*'lwny*...) of Mamre the Amorite," Mamre here, unlike in other texts, being a person. The Hebrew phrase "Oaks of Mamre" is elsewhere (Gen 12:6; 13:18; 18:1; Deut 11:30) rendered by Nf as "the Valley of Vision" simply. Here in 14:13, apparently under the influence of these texts, Nf translates in like manner, leaving, however, Mamre untranslated.

[20]"reared"; as in 17:12 for HT "born in."

[21]"three hundred and ten"; HT: "three hundred and eighteen"; see Nfmg (no. *p*) to word.

[22]"Melchizedek ... he is Shem the Great." The identification with Shem is facilitated by the biblical chronology of Gen 11:10-26 (Hebrew text), which gives 290 years from the birth of Shem's first son to the birth of Abram and says Shem lived five hundred years after the birth of his first son. In Nf and Pal. Tg., Shem was also in contact with Isaac (Nf Gen 24:62) and Rebekah (Nf Gen 25:22). The identification is also in rabbinic sources; see Grossfeld, op. cit., Gen 14 note 26. Jerome (*Hebr. quaest.* in Gen 14:18-19, CCL 72,29) tells us that the Hebrews say that Melchizedek was Shem the Great, and reckoning his lifespan they show that he lived to Isaac's time, and they say that all the firstborn of Noah, until Aaron, exercised the priesthood and were priests. The identification of Melchizedek and Shem was also known to Ephrem. On the same views in Jerome, see Hayward, art. cit., in note to 14:2 above.

[23]"high priesthood"; that Melchizedek was believed to have been a "high priest" may be implied in *Gen. R.* 46,5: arguing that Abraham was a high priest from Ps 110:4 ("thou art a priest according to the order of Melchizedek"). Melchizedek is also called a high priest in the Roman Canon (*summus sacerdos tuus Melch.*); see R. Le Déaut, "Le titre *Summus Sacerdos* donné a Melchisedech est-il d'origine juive?" *RSR* 50 (1962) 222–229. See also M. Kasher, *Torah*

he blessed him and said: "Blessed is *Abram* before[x] the most High God who *by his Memra* created the heavens and the earth; 20. and blessed is the most High God who *crushed*[y][24] your enemies *before* you." And he gave him a tithe of everything. 21. And the king of Sodom said to Abram: "Give me the persons and take the wealth[z] for yourself." 22. But Abram said to the king of Sodom: "Behold, I have lifted up my hand[aa] *in an oath before* the Lord, the most High God, who *by his Memra* created the heavens and the earth: 23. not even a thread of a shoelace[bb] will I take of anything belonging to you,[cc] lest *you boast* and say: 'I have enriched Abram.' 24. I need not be considered; only what the young men have eaten and the portions of the men who went with me, Aner and Eshcol and Mamre; they will take their portions."[dd]

CHAPTER 15

1. After these things,[a] *after all the kingdoms*[b] *of the earth*[c] *had gathered together*[1] *and had drawn up battle-lines against Abram*[d] *and had fallen before him, and*[e] *he*

Apparatus, Chapter 14

[x] Nfmg: "to God the Most High."
[y] Nfmg: "(who) handed over, your enemies."
[z] VNL: "and the property take for yourself"; Nfmg: "and the property."
[aa] Nfmg: "I have raised the palm of my hand."
[bb] VNL: "even a thread or a sandal strap, nor shall I

take anything that is yours; that you may not boast and say: I have enriched Abram"; Nfmg: "of my sandal if."
[cc] Nfmg: "of what you have, so that you will not take vain glory, saying I."
[dd] Nfmg: "one part of the whole."

Notes, Chapter 14

Shelemah, vol. 35 (=*Aramaic Versions of the Bible*, vol. 2), Jerusalem, 1983, 170–185, who maintains that the designation is late. Likewise A. O. H. Okamoto in doctoral dissertation, summary in A. Díez Macho, *Neophyti 1*, II, 74-76.
[24]"crushed." HT (RSV): "delivered" (*mgn*; hapax in the Pentateuch).

Apparatus, Chapter 15

[a] PVNL: "After these things, after all the kings of the earth and (P + all) the rulers of the provinces had gathered together and had drawn up battle lines against (P: with) Abram (V: Abraham) the just and they had fallen before him and had killed four kings (P: kingdoms) from among them and had brought back nine encampments, Abram the just thought in his heart and said: Woe, now, is me. Per-

haps I have received the reward of the precepts (P: my precepts) in this world and there is no portion for me in the world to come."
[b] PVNL: "all the kings of"; Nfmg: "(every) king."
[c] Nfmg and PVNL: "and all the rulers of the provinces" (or "cities").
[d] Nfmg, PVNL: "(Abraham) the just."
[e] Nfmg: "he killed" (without "and").

Notes, Chapter 15

[1]This developed aggadic supplement is found in all Pal. Tg. texts (Nf, Frg. Tgs., CTg H, Ps.-J.) and in *Gen. R.* 44. Gen 15:1 is the beginning of a *sidra* (i.e., a biblical passage appointed as a synagogue reading), and R. Le Déaut has noted that some of the longer Pal. Tg. paraphrases correspond to the beginnings of such *sedarim*: thus Tg Gen 22:1 (Ps.-J.); Gen 28:10 (Nf, Ps.-J.); Gen 44:18 (Nf, CTg D, FF); Gen 49:1 (Nf, Ps.-J.); Exod 20:1 (Nf, Ps.-J.); Lev 1:1 (Nf, Ps.-J.); Lev 22:26 (Nf, Ps.-J.), etc. See Le Déaut, 1978, 167; also M. Klein, 1986, 10; likewise note 6 to Ps.-J. (vol. 1B in this series). There is a detailed textual examination of the Nf text in B. Barry Levy, 1, 1986, 130–135. He believes that we can trace (at least) three stages in the development of the present form of the midrash found in Nf.

*had killed four kings from among them and had brought back nine encampments,
Abram thought in his heart and said: "Woe, now, is me! Perhaps I have received[f] the
reward of the precepts[g] in this world and there is no portion for me in the world to
come. Or perhaps the brothers or relatives[h] of those killed, who fell before me, will go
and will be in their fortresses and in their cities and many legions[2] will become allied
with them[i] and they will come against me and kill me. Or perhaps[j] there were a few
meritorious deeds in my hand the first time they fell before me and they stood in my
favor, or perhaps no meritorious deed will be found in my hand the second time and
the name of the heavens will be profaned in me." For this reason there was a word of*
prophecy from before the Lord upon Abram *the just* saying: "Do not fear, Abram,
for although many legions are allied[k] and come against you to kill (you), my Memra
will be a shield for you; *and it will be a protection for you in this world. And although I delivered up your enemies before you in this world, the reward of your good
works is prepared for you before me in the world to come." 2. And Abram said:[m] "I
beseech[3] by the mercies that are before you, O Lord;[n] many things have you given to*

Apparatus, Chapter 15

[f] Expressed in Nf and VNL by Ithp: *'ytqblt*: ("to be
received"; "to be made the recipient of"), in P and
Nfmg by the regular form *qblyt*.

[g] Nfmg and P: "my precepts" (or: "good deeds").

[h] "or relatives," Nf; "and relatives," PVNL.

[i] Nfmg: "strong (?) and they join with them"; VNL:
" ... of those killed and they join with them many
legions ... "; P: "and they join with them many
legions."

[j] Nfmg, PVNL: "or perhaps he found (P: there was
found) merit for me the first time that they fell before me (Nfmg = VNL), or perhaps that merit will
not be found for me the second time and the
(Nfmg: in the) name of Heaven will be profaned in
me"; P: " ... it will not be found in me the second
time. And a word came from before the Lord with
Abraham the just saying: Fear not Abraham. ... "

[k] Nfmg, P: "the brothers and relatives of those slain
should go and (P + many) legions be joined with
them and they come against you (Nfmg: against
me), my Memra is a covering <shield> (Nf. corrected by VNL; P: "my Memra will assure you")
for you in this world and a shield upon you all the
days. But your reward and your good works are
prepared for you (Nfmg + before me; lit.: "before
him") for the world to come"; VNL: "even if they

gather together and many legions come against
you, my Memra (is) (as) a shield spread out
(*mymry prys trys*; CTg H, *trys lk*, "shield you") for
you in this world and protects you (*mgyn'lk*) every
day for (or: in) the world to come, and even though
I have delivered up your enemies before you in this
world, the reward of your good works is prepared
for you before me in the world to come."

[m] VNL: "And Abraham said: I beseech, (by) the mercies before you, O Lord God, many blessings have
you given me and many are there before you to
give me. But what are these to me, since I go from
the midst of the world without (*bl'* thus L; VN *dl'*)
children and Eliezer, the son of my house(hold), by
whose hand wonders were worked for me in
Damascus, he is hoping in himself to inherit, to be
my heir"; P: Abraham said: O Lord God,
<many> are what you have given me and many
things are there before you to give me. However,
what benefit do I have since I go from the midst of
the world without children, and Eliezer, the son of
my house(hold), at whose hand (= through whom)
you worked wonders for me in Damascus, will finally be my heir."

[n] Nfmg: "(O) Memra of the Lord, many blessings
have you given"; cf. VNL.

Notes, Chapter 15

[2] "legions"; Latin loan word: *legiones*, already in the Greek of the NT (Matt 26:53; Mark 5:9, 15; Luke 8:53).

[3] "I beseech by the mercies that are before you, (O Lord)"; Nf's introductory phrase normally inserted whenever in the
HT God is addressed directly in petition. HT: "O Lord God." See also 15:8 and Grossfeld, *Neofiti*, note 2 to Gen 18.

me and many things[o] *there are before you, to give me, but I am going from the world without*[p] *sons, and Eliezer, the son of my household,*[4] *by whose hand wonders were worked*[q] *for me in Damascus, will be*[r] *my heir."* 3. And Abraham said: "Behold you did not give me *sons,*[s] and behold a son of my house will be my heir." 4. And behold a word of *prophecy*[5] *from before* the Lord was upon *Abram* saying: "This one will not be your heir, but only he who comes from your own bowels will be your heir." 5. And he brought him outside and said: "Look, *now,* at the heavens, and count the stars if you are able to count them." And he said to him: "Thus shall be the descendants of your sons." 6. And *Abram* believed *in the name of the Memra of* the Lord and it was reckoned to him as righteousness. 7. And he said to him: "I am the Lord who brought you out of the *furnace of fire* of the Chaldaeans[6] to give you this land to inherit it." 8. And he said:[t] "*I beseech by the mercies that are before you,*[3] how, I pray, will I *know*[this] that I shall inherit it?" 9. And he said to him: "*Sacrifice*[u] *before* me a heifer, three years old, a goat, three years old, and a ram, three years old, a turtle dove and the young of a pigeon."[w][7] 10. And he sacrificed before him[x] all these things, and he divided them in the middle[y] and he placed each piece opposite the other, but the birds he did not divide. 11. And *the birds* came down[z] upon the pieces and *the merit of* Abram[8] *removed*[9] them. *When* the bird of

Apparatus, Chapter 15

[o] Nfmg: "and many things there are before you to give me, but" = VNL.

[p] Nf text *bl'*, as PL; Nfmg, *dl'*, as VN.

[q] Nfmg: "you worked"= P.

[r] Nfmg: "hopes in himself (lit.: in myself) he will inherit" (i.e., he hopes to be my heir).

[s] Nfmg: "the seed of sons."

[t] Nf text, both Hebrew lemma and Aramaic translation, has "he said to him," but "to him" deleted in both cases.

[this] correct text with Nfi.

[u] Lit.: "offer," Nfmg, "bring me a heifer."

[w] VNL: "a turtle dove, and the young of a pigeon"; see note 7 to verse.

[x] Nfmg: "and he sacrificed to him."

[y] Nfmg and VNL: "into pieces and set each of the pieces before its counterpart."

[z] PVNL: "And when the bird of prey (pheasant or peacock, VNL) came down, it did not draw near the pieces. And what is this bird of prey? This is the unclean bird. And what is this unclean bird? They are the kingdoms of the earth. And it shall be that when they scheme counsel(s) (VNL: scheme evil counsels) against the children of Israel the merits of the righteous Abram (P: of Abraham) makes them void"; Nfmg: "and the nations, which are comparable to the unclean bird, came down to plunder the possessions of Israel and the righteousness of Abraham protected them"; = Ps.-J. with exception of a few words.

Notes, Chapter 15

[4]"Eliezer, the son of my household" (*br byty*); HT: "Eliezer of Damascus" (*bn mšq byty*). Same paraphrase of HT is *Gen. R.* 44,9 (R. Shimeon b. Lakish in the name of Bar Kappara); also ibid., "Eliezer of Damascus by whose assistance (*š'l ydw*; cf. Nf) I pursued the kings as far as Damascus"; also *Gen R.* 43,2 on Gen 14:14, where Abram's 318 men are taken as Eliezer alone: "the numerical value of Eliezer's name being 318."

[5]"word of prophecy . . ."; HT: "the word of the Lord."

[6]"furnace of fire of the Chaldaeans"; HT: "Ur of the Chaldaeans"; see note to 11:28.

[7]"and the young of a pigeon"; lit. "a chick (*gwzl*), the young of a pigeon (*br ywn*)." HT: "*gwzl* (RSV: "a young pigeon"). In the gloss on *gwzl* of the HT, *Gen. R.* 44,14 uses an Aramaic paraphrase as found in Nf.

[8]"the merits of Abraham," mentioned twice: as removing the birds of prey and as being instrumental in delivering Israel; see also *Gen. R.* 44,16. For detailed textual analysis of 15:11, see B. Barry Levy, 1, 1986, 136–139.

[9]"removed"; lit. "caused to cease" (*'šbt*); HT *wyšb*, from root *nšb* (occurs only here in Pentateuch), "drove away"; PVNL at end of midrash renders as "cancel" (*btl*). For further information on translation, see Grossfeld, op. cit., Gen 15 note 17 with reference to Geiger, 457f.

prey came down he *hovered over the pieces. What is this bird of prey? This is the im-pure bird of prey. This is the impure bird. These are*[aa] *the kingdoms of the earth; when they plot evil counsel against the house of Israel, in the merits of their father Abram they find delivery.* 22. *The sun was*[bb] *at the time to set and*[cc] *a pleasant*[dd] sleep[10] fell upon Abram; and behold *Abram saw four kingdoms*[ee][11] *rising against him: DREAD: that is Babylon; DARKNESS: that is Media; GREAT: that is Greece; FELL UPON HIM: this <is Edom, the wicked which will fall and will not rise again>.*[ff][13] 13. And he said to Abram: "Know of a surety that the descendants *of your sons* will be strangers *and sojourners*[gg][12] in a land that is not theirs; and they will enslave them and afflict them for four hundred years. 14. I, however, will *be avenged* of the nations that will *enslave* them. After that they will go out with great riches.[hh] 15. And *you shall be gathered*[ii][13] to your fathers in peace and you shall be buried at a good old age. 16. And the fourth generation will return here, because the *sins of* the Amorites are not as yet complete." 17. And behold the sun set[jj] and there was darkness, and behold Abram *looked while seats were being arranged and*

Apparatus, Chapter 15

[aa] Nfmg: "these are the four kingdoms that are to en-slave the children of Abram and the righteousness of Abram the just will save them."

[bb] Nfmg: "and the sun was nigh to setting when a deep sleep was cast upon Abram and behold four kingdoms arose to enslave his sons: DREAD: this is Babel; DARKNESS: this is Media; GREAT: this is Greece; FELL UPON HIM this is < ..... >" (words erased, but cf. Ps.-J. = "that is Edom"; for entire gloss see Ps.-J.); PVNL: "and the sun went to set and a deep sweet sleep fell upon Abram. And Abram saw the four kingdoms that were to arise to enslave his sons. (P +: DREAD, DARKNESS, GREAT, FELL UPON HIM) DREAD that is Babel; DARKNESS, that is Media; GREAT, that is Greece; FELL UPON HIM, that is Edom (P +: "the wicked"). She is the fourth kingdom which is destined to fall and there will be no rising for her for all ages."

[cc] Nfmg: "went to set" = PVNL.

[dd] Nfmg: "deep."

[ee] Nfmg: "the kingdoms which were to arise to en-slave his sons: DREAD, DARKNESS" = P.

[ff] words erased by censor; apparently those within brackets. Nfmg (to end of verse?): "and after that the kingship will return to the people of the house of Israel."

[gg] Nfmg: "they will be sojourners."

[hh] Nfmg: "the nations that enslave them I will judge. And after this they will come out with great possessions."

[ii] Nfmg: "you shall enter."

[jj] PVNL: "And (P + behold) the sun went to set and there was darkness and behold Abram saw while seats were being arranged and thrones erected. And behold, Gehenna which was prepared for the wicked in (or: "for") the world to come like an oven. Sparks of fire surrounded it and flames of

Notes, Chapter 15

[10]"pleasant sleep"; see also at 2:21. For a textual analysis of 15:12, see B. Barry Levy, 1, 1986, 139–140.

[11]"four kingdoms"; same interpretation *in Gen. R.* 44,17.

[12]"strangers (*gywryn*) and sojourners (*twtbyn*)," a double translation of the HT *gr*, due most probably to the occurrence of the word in combination with *twšb* (RSV: "sojourner") elsewhere (Gen 23:4; Lev 25:35, 47). The HT *gr* in 15:13 is a collective rendered in Nf as plural; RSV: "sojourners." The usual rendering of the HT *gr* in Nf is, as here, *gywr* (Gen 23:4 is an exception, with rendering *dyr*, "resident"), which in this rendering is generally translated as "stranger." See also note to Gen 23:3.

[13]"will be gathered"; HT: "will come." Nf renders as at 5:5; 9:29; cf. HT 25:8, 17; 35:29; 49:33; Deut 32:50 (the right-eous gathered to their people by death).

thrones were erected. And behold, Gehenna[14] *which is like a furnace, like* an oven *surrounded by sparks of fire, by flames of fire,*[kk] *into the midst of which the wicked fall, because the wicked rebelled against the Law in their lives in this world. But the just,*[mm] *because they observed it, have been rescued from the affliction. All was thus shown to Abram when he* passed between these parts. 18. <On that day>[nn] the Lord[oo] established a covenant with Abram saying: "To your *sons*[pp] I will give this land, from the Nile of Egypt to the Great River, the river Euphrates, 19. the *Salmites,*[15] the Kenizzites and the *Orientals*; 20. the Hittites, the Perizzites and the *Giants*; 21. the Amorites, the Canaanites, the Girgashites and the Jebusites."

CHAPTER 16

1. And Sarai, Abram's wife, bore no children and she had an Egyptian maid whose name was Hagar. 2. And Sarai said to Abram: "Behold, I pray; the Lord[a] has prevented me from bearing.[b] Go in, I pray, to my maid; perhaps[c] I also may get

Apparatus, Chapter 15

fire, into the midst of which the wicked will fall (P: fell), because they rebelled against the Law during their lifetimes (VNL = in this world), but the just, because they will have observed (P: "because they observed") it, will be delivered from the affliction (VNL = from it). Thus was it shown (P: all was thus made seen) to Abram (VNL: Abraham) as he passed between these places"; Nfmg 1°: "and the sun went to disappear and it became dark, and behold, Abram saw that seats were placed and thrones were erected, and (he saw) Gehenna which is likened to a furnace that is prepared for the wicked in the world to come because they did not occupy themselves with the study of the Law in this world and did not observe the commandments. All that Abram saw when Abram passed between these pieces"; Nfmg 2°: "and the sun sank and it became dark. Abram was (seeing) and behold he (saw) Gehenna which was burning like a furnace, with sparks of fire and glowing coals of

fire with smoke arising, and the wicked cast into it because during their lives they had rebelled against the teaching of the Law in this world and had not fulfilled the precepts. But the just were delivered from the judgment (= chastisement) because they had served (+?: the Law) during their lives in this world and had fulfilled the commandments, and for their merits the flame of fire is to be let loose at the end of the days from the throne of Glory. Every kingdom will be burned and dissolved (cf. Ps.-J. Num 11:26). These great visions Abram saw at the time he passed between these pieces."

[kk] Nfmg: "of fire and within it the wicked who renounced the Law."

[mm] Nfmg: "and the just who fulfilled the Law were delivered from the tribulation. All this.... "

[nn] Missing in text; supplied in Nfi.

[oo] Nfmg: "the Memra of the Lord."

[pp] Nfmg: "the descendants of your son(s)."

Notes, Chapter 15

[14]"behold Gehenna." According to *Gen. R.* 44,21, God at that time showed Abraham four things: Gehenna, the (foreign) kingdoms, revelation, and the Temple. See also note to Ps.-J. (vol. 1B in this series). For a textual analysis of 15:17, see B. Barry Levy, 1, 1986, 140–142.

[15]"the Salmites"; HT: Kenites. See note to Ps.-J. (vol. 1B in this series); also Grossfeld, *Neofiti*, Gen 15 note 31. One view (of Rabbi) in *Gen. R.* identifies the Kennizites of the same verse as the Shalamites (or Salmites).

Apparatus, Chapter 16

[a] Nfmg: "the Memra of the Lord."
[b] Thus Nfi; in text: "from speaking."

[c] Nfmg: "Join yourself, I pray, to my handmaid; perhaps."

children *d* through her." And Abram listened to the voice of Sarai. 3. And Sarai the wife of Abram took Hagar the Egyptian, her maid, after Abram had dwelt ten years *of days* [1] in the land of Canaan, and she gave him to Abram her husband as wife. 4. And he went in *e* to Hagar and she conceived. And when she saw that she had conceived the honor of her mistress *f* was of little value in her sight. 5. And Sarai said *g* to Abram; "My judgment and my humiliation, my insult and the beginning of my affliction, are delivered into your hand. *h* I forsook my country, the house of my birth, and the house of my father and I have come *i* *with you with faith.* *j* *I went in with you before the kings* *k* *of the earth, before Pharaoh king of Egypt and before Abimelech king of Gerar* *m* *and I said: 'He is my brother,' so that* *n* *they might not kill you. And when I saw that I did not bear* *o* *I took Hagar the Egyptian,* my maid, and gave her to you *as wife, and I said: 'She will bear children and I will rear (them). Perhaps I too will get children through her.'* But when she saw that she had conceived *my honor* was of little value in her sight. And *now* let the Lord *be revealed* *p* and let

Apparatus, Chapter 16

d Nfmg: "she will bear children and I also will rear (them)"; see Nf v. 5.

e Nfmg: "and joined himself to."

f Nfmg: "and despised her mistress."

g PVNL: "and Sarai said to Abram: My judgments and my humiliation have been delivered into your hand. I forsook (P: I forgot) my country and the house of my birth (P: my birthplace) and the house of my father and I came (?; or: "brought myself," *w'tyt ly*) with you; in the faith (or: "trust") of heaven (i.e., God) (P: + "upon you") I went in with you before all the kings (P: before the kingdoms of the earth), before Pharaoh the king of Egypt, and before Abimelech the king of the Philistines and I said (VNL: + "concerning you"): He is my brother, so that they would not (P: lest they) kill you. And now I have seen that I am not becoming pregnant and (P: and now that I saw that I do not bear children) and I have taken Hagar the Egyptian my handmaid and have given her to you as wife (VNL: and I said: She will give birth and I will rear: perhaps I too will acquire children through her). And when she saw that she had become pregnant, my honor became of little value (P: was despised) in her sight. And now let the Lord be revealed and let him judge between me and you (VNL:+ "and let

mercy be fulfilled upon [or: concerning] me and you) and let him (or: may he) spread peace between me and you (P: upon me and you) and let the world be filled (P: may the earth be restrained/consumed) from me and you, and we will not need the sons of Hagar the Egyptian, the slave girl, who belongs to the children of the sons of the people who threw (P: cast) you into the furnace of fire (P +: of the Chaldeans)."

h Lit.: "is delivered"; Nfmg: "are delivered into my (read: your) hand. I forsook"= VNL.

i The text seems corrupt; lit.: "I have come (*'tyt*) it/ him" (= accusative); or possibly, through defective writing as: "I have brought it/him." For "it" (*yth*) Nfmg has: *'ly*= "to me"; or "me" (accusative) = PVNL, where meaning is also problematical.

j Nfmg: "in the faith of heaven I entered";= VL.

k Nfmg: "the king of."

m Nfmg: "the king of the Philistines"; cf. VNL ("the king of . . .) and P.

n Nfmg: "in order that."

o Nfmg: "And now that I saw that I do not bear" = P.

p Nfmg: "and she saw (corr. text which lit. reads: "was of little value") that she had conceived and my honor became of little value in her sight and there is (read "let there be") revealed" = PVNL.

Notes, Chapter 16

[1] "year of days"; HT: "year." The addition "of days" is a peculiarity of Nf rendering; also in Gen 29:18, 20, 22; 41:1; Exod 21:2; 23:10; Lev 19:23; 25:3 (twice), 21; Deut 14:28; 15:1, 12, 18; 31:10. M. Kasher (*Torah Shelemah*, vol. 24, 65–71—summary in A. Díez Macho, *Neophyti 1*, V, 62*f.) believes that by the addition "of days" a (solar) year of 365 days is intended.

him judge[2] between me and you, *and let him spread his peace*[q3] *between me and you,*[r] *and let the earth be filled from us and we will not need the son*[s] *of Hagar the Egyptian, who belongs to the children of the sons of the people who gave you into the furnace of fire of the Chaldeans."*[4] 6. And Abram said to Sarai: "Behold your maid is in your hand.[t] Do to her whatever seems good[u] in your sight."[w5] And Sarai afflicted her and she fled from before her.[x] 7. And the angel of the Lord met her at the spring of water in the desert at the spring, on the way to *Haluzah.*[y6] 8. And he said: "Hagar, maid of Sarai, where are you coming from and where are you going? *And where did you find a house like the house of Abram your master?"* And she said: "I am fleeing from before my mistress Sarai." 9. And the angel of the Lord said to her: "Return to your mistress and humble yourself under her hand."[z] 10. And the angel of the Lord said to her: "I will surely multiply your sons so that they cannot be numbered for multitude." 11. And the angel of the Lord said to her: "Behold you are with child and you will bear a son and you will call his name[aa] Ishmael, because your afflictions[7] *have been heard before* the Lord.[bb] 12. And *he shall be like a*

Apparatus, Chapter 16

[q] Nfmg: "between me and you his peace and let (the earth) be filled."

[r] Nfmg: "upon me and you and let the world be filled from me and you and (we will) not (need)"; cf. VNL.

[s] Nfmg: "who cast"= P.

[t] Nfmg: "your handmaid has been delivered into your hand."

[u] Nfmg: "do to her what is good and right before you and (Sarah) afflicted."

[w] Nfmg: "in your eyes."

[x] Nfmg: "before him."

[y] Nfmg: "in the way of Haluzah" = PVNL.

[z] Nfmg: "her authority."

[aa] Nfmg: "and you shall bear a son (*byr*) and you shall call his name" (lexical variants, including *byr*, "son").

[bb] HT: "The Lord has heard (= given heed to) your afflictions"; in Nf "your afflictions" preceded by the sign of the accusative; Nfmg: "the Memra of the Lord has heard."

Notes, Chapter 16

[2]"let the Lord be revealed and let him judge"; HT: "May the Lord judge." For a detailed textual examination of Nf 16:5, see B. Barry Levy, 1, 1986, 142–147.

[3]"spread his peace" (or: "... peace," *wyprwš šlmh*); thus also P (*šlmyh*, "his peace"); VNL (*šlm'*, "peace"), reading *šlmh*, as if with initial *shin*. B. Barry Levy (op. cit.) suggests that we read as with initial *sin*, *šlmh*, "garment;" "May the Lord spread a garment between us," with the connotation of marital relations, as in Ruth 3:9; Deut 27:20. This gives better meaning in the present context.

[4]"furnace of fire of the Chaldeans"; see 11:28. A tradition that Hagar the Egyptian was a descendant of the people of Ur appears to be unknown to rabbinic sources. See Grossfeld, *Neofiti*, Gen 16 note 6.

[5]For Pal. Tgs. Gen 16:5-7 and Gal 4:25a, etc., see M. G. Steinhauser, in *Biblica* 70 (1989), 234-240; also R. Le Déaut, "Traditions targumiques dans le corpus paulinien?" *Biblica* 42 (1961) esp. 37–43.

[6]"Haluza." HT: "Shur." The name Shur occurs in HT Gen 16:7; 20:1; 25:18; Exod 15:22; always identified as Haluza in Nf and Frg. Tg.; in Onq. as Hagra; in Ps.-J. as Haluza, except in Gen 20:1, where we have Hagra. In *Gen. R.* 45,7 Shur is identified as Haluza, with use of the very same words as in Nf (*b'rh' dhlws'*); see McNamara, 1972, 195; Grossfeld, op. cit., Gen 16 note 9.

[7]"your afflictions (*preceded by sign of the accusative*) have been heard before the Lord"; HT: "the Lord has heard your affliction" (*preceded by sign of accusative*). Passive construction to avoid making God the direct subject of the verb, with retention of the sign of the accusative from the HT. See note to Nf Gen 1:4 and Golomb, 1985, 209.

wild ass *among*^{cc} *the sons of man*; his hands *shall rule*⁸ over all and the hands of all shall *rule over* him; and he shall dwell before all *the nations.*"^{dd} 13. And she *prayed*^{ee} in the name of the *Memra of the* Lord who *was revealed* to her:⁹ "You are^{ff} the God who sustains^{gg} *all ages*"; for she said: *"Behold also now he has been revealed* to me *after he has been revealed to my mistress Sarai."* 14. Therefore the well was called: The well *beside which the One who sustains all ages*¹⁰ *was revealed.*^{hh} Behold it is between *Rekem*¹¹ and *Haluzah.*¹² 15. And Hagar bore a sonⁱⁱ to Abram. And Abram called the name of his son whom Hagar bore him, Ishmael. 16. And Abram was eighty-six years when Hagar bore Ishmael to Abram.

CHAPTER 17

1. When Abram was ninety-nine years, *the Memra of* the Lord was revealed to Abram and said to him: "I am the God *of the heavens.*¹ *Serve* before me *in truth*² and be perfect *in good work.*³ 2. And I will set my covenant between me and you and I will *make* you very, very *powerful."*^{a4} 3. And Abram prostrated himself upon^b

---

Apparatus, Chapter 16

^{cc} Nfmg: "he will be like a wild ass among the sons of men."

^{dd} Nfmg: "his brothers."

^{ee} PVNL: "and Hagar gave praise and prayed in the name of the Memra of the Lord who was revealed to her (P = : and to Sarah her mistress) and she said: Blessed are you, O God, sustainer of all ages (P: living, [or: sustaining] for ever), and have seen my tribulations, because she said: Also to me you

have been revealed just after you have been revealed to Sarah my mistress."

^{ff} Nfmg: "And she said: You are."

^{gg} Nfmg: "(sustainer, or living) over (all ages)."

^{hh} Nfmg: "above which was revealed the glory of the Shekinah of the Lord. Behold it is between."

ⁱⁱ In text Hebrew work *bn* (for regular Aramaic *br*); Nfmg: *byr* ("son") (variant writing).

Notes, Chapter 16

⁸"shall rule." HT: "shall be against"; see *Gen. R.* 45,9.

⁹"who was revealed to her." HT: "who spoke to her."

¹⁰"... sustains all ages." HT: "you (are) El Roi" (*'l r'y*).

¹¹"Rekem." HT: Kadesh. Rekem=Petra; see 14:7 and note to Ps.-J. (vol. 1B in this series).

¹²"Haluza." HT: "Bered," a name occurring only here in the HT. Haluza identification of Shur of HT in Gen 16:17; 20:1; Exod 15:22.

Apparatus, Chapter 17

^a Nfmg: "I will multiply."

^b Nfmg: "Abram bowed down in prayer upon."

Notes, Chapter 17

¹"God of the heavens." HT: "El Shaddai." Same rendering of this divine name throughout in Nf.

²"serve before me in truth." HT: "walk before me"; see note to 5:22.

³"perfect in good work." HT: "perfect" (RSV: "blameless"). See note to 6:9.

⁴"I will make you very powerful" (or: "strong"); HT: "I will multiply." Thus Nf only; other Tgs. as HT.

his face and the *Memra of the Lord* spoke with him saying: 4. "And as for me, behold my covenant with you and you shall become *an assembly* of a congregation of *just*[c] nations.[5] 5. And your name will no longer[d] be called Abram, but your name will be Abraham, because I have set you as *an assembly* of a congregation of *just*[e] nations.[5] 6. And I will *make* you very, very *powerful* and I will make nations of you; kings[f] *who rule nations*[6] will come forth from your *loins.* 7. And I will establish my covenant between me and you, and your *sons*[g] after you throughout their generations, as an eternal covenant, to be *in my Memra* a God[h] for you[i] and for your *sons*[j] after you. 8. And I will give to you and to your *sons* after you the land of your sojournings, all the land of Canaan, as an everlasting inheritance. And I will be for them *in my Memra*[k] a *redeemer* God." 9. And *the Lord*[m] said to Abram: "And as for you: You shall observe my covenant, you and your *sons*[n] after you in their generations. 10. This is the covenant which you shall observe between men and you, and between your *sons* after *you*: to circumcise every male among you. 11. And you shall circumcise the flesh of your foreskin and it will be a covenant-sign between my *Memra* and you. 12. And he that is eight days old among you shall be circumcised;[o] every male throughout your generations: *he that is reared in*[p][7] your houses and those bought with your money from any gentile that is not from among your *sons*. 13. Both he that is reared in[q] *your* houses and those that are bought with your money shall be circumcised; and my covenant will be in your flesh as an everlasting covenant. 14. And any uncircumcised male[r] who will not have circumcised (the flesh of his foreskin),[s] this person will be cut off from the midst of his people; he has broken my covenant."[8] 15. And the Lord[t] said to Abraham: "Your wife Sarai, you shall not call her name Sarai, but Sarah will be her name. 16. And I have

Apparatus, Chapter 17

[c] Nfmg: "numerous."

[d] Nfmg: "(no) more."

[e] Nfmg: "numerous (nations) I have made"; cf. note *c* above.

[f] omitted in text; added from Nfmg.

[g] Nfmg: "and between you and the descendants of your sons."

[h] Nfmg: "my Memra."

[i] in text singular; in Nfmg plural.

[j] Nfmg: "for the descendants of your sons"; a very frequent variant.

[k] Nfmg: "and his Memra will be for you."

[m] Nfmg: "the Memra of the Lord."

[n] Nfmg: "between my Memra and you and between the descendants of your sons."

[o] Nfmg: "Circumcise" (imper. pl.).

[p] Nfmg: "those that are raised in/of."

[q] Nfmg: "those that are raised in (your) houses shall surely be circumcised."

[r] Nfmg: "and every male son of the nations" (i.e., gentiles).

[s] Text erased by censor, as also corresponding marginal variant.

[t] Nfmg: "the Memra of the Lord."

Notes, Chapter 17

[5]"assembly of a congregation of just nations"; HT: "multitude of nations."

[6]"kings who rule nations"; HT: "kings." Nf renders "kings of peoples" of 17:16 in like manner.

[7]"reared in." HT: "born in" (*ylyd*). See Gen 14:14.

[8]"broken ('*ps*; root *pys*) my covenant." HT: "broken" (*hpr*). Similar rendering in Nf Lev 26:15; Num 15:31; Deut 31:16, 20. Different rendering (referring to breaking a vow) in Nf Num 30:9, 13, 14, 16.

blessed her,^{u} and I have also given you a son from her; and I have blessed her and she will become nations; and kings^w *who rule* nations will arise from her." 17. And Abraham prostrated himself^x upon his face and *was astonished* and said in his heart: "*Is it possible* for me, a man of a hundred years, to beget^y sons? And *is it possible* for Sarah, a woman who is ninety years, to bear?"^{z} 18. And Abraham said *before the Lord*: "Oh, that Ishmael might live before you!" 19. And *the Lord* said *to Abraham*: "But, *behold* your wife Sarah will bear you a son and you will call his name Isaac; and I will establish my covenant with him as an everlasting covenant, and with his sons after him. 20. And I have heard *the voice of your prayer*^{9} concerning Ishmael. Behold^{aa} I have blessed him and made him powerful and multiplied him exceedingly. He will beget^{bb} twelve chiefs and I will make him a great inheritance.^{cc} 21. But I will establish my covenant with Isaac whom Sarah will bear you at this time^{dd} next year." 22. When he had finished speaking with him, the *Glory of the Shekinah of the Lord* went up from Abraham. 23. And Abraham took his son Ishmael and all *those reared in*^{7} his house^{ee} and all those bought with money, and every male among the men of the house of Abraham; and he circumcised the^{ff} flesh of their foreskins that very day according as *the Lord* had^{gg} spoken with him. 24. And Abraham was ninety-nine years when he circumcised$^{hh\,10}$ the flesh of his foreskin. 25. And his son Ishmael was thirteen years when he circumcised$^{hh\,10}$ the flesh of his foreskin. 26. That *same* day^{11} Abraham circumcised *the flesh of his foreskin* and his son^{12} Ishmael.^{ii} 27. <And all the men>^{jj} of his house, all *those reared in*$^{kk\,7}$ *his house,* those bought with money from a gentile, were circumcised with him.

Apparatus, Chapter 17

^{u} Nfmg: "and he was blessed," but corr. to: "and I will bless"?

^{w} Nfmg: "and I will give you a son from her and I will bless you and she will become numerous peoples and kings."

^{x} VNL: "and Abraham fell upon his face and was astonished"; P: "and was astonished"; Nfmg: "and (Abraham) fell (upon his face)"= VNL.

^{y} Nfmg: "shall Abraham a hundred years old beget."

^{z} Nfmg: "shall she bear?"

^{aa} Nfmg: "as regards Ishmael I have heard your voice; behold."

^{bb} Nfmg: "you shall beget."

^{cc} Nfmg: "a (great) nation."

^{dd} Nfmg: "according to (this) time."

^{ee} Nfmg: "those raised in his house."

^{ff} Nfmg: "and they circumcised."

^{gg} Nfmg: "the Memra of the Lord."

^{hh} Nfmg: "at the time he circumcised."

^{ii} Nfmg: "Abraham and Ishmael was (= were) circumcised."

^{jj} Missing in text, supplied in Nfmg.

^{kk} Nfmg: "and those raised in."

Notes, Chapter 17

^{9}"the voice of your prayer." HT: "(I have heard) you." When "heard," "heard your voice" of HT concerns God's relations to humans, Nf paraphrases by introducing reference to prayer or the voice of prayer: Gen 17:20; 21:17; 30:17, 22; Deut 3:26; 9:19; 10:10; 26:7.

^{10}"when he circumcised" (*bmgzr lyh*; lit. "in the circumcising to him," or: "when he was circumcised"?); HT: *bhlmlw*; MT: *behimmolô*; Niphal, passive: "when he was circumcised," as RSV; of reflexive? Note that in v. 24 Sam has *'t* (the sign of the accusative?) before "flesh," which would indicate an active sense, as in Nf.

^{11}"that same day"; lit. "at the time of that day." See note to 7:13.

^{12}"Abraham . . . circumcised . . . his foreskin and his son Ishmael." HT: "Abraham was circumcised (*nmwl*, Niphal, passive) and his son Ishmael."

CHAPTER 18

1. Three angels[a] were sent to our father Abraham at the time he circumcised the flesh of his foreskin.[1] The three of them were sent for three things, because it is impossible for one angel from on high that he be sent[b] for more than one thing.[c] The first angel was sent[d] to announce to our father Abraham that Sarah would bear him Isaac;[e] and the second angel was sent to deliver Lot from the destruction; and the third angel was sent to destroy Sodom and Gomorrah, Admah and Zeboim. And the Memra of the Lord was revealed[f] to Abraham in the plain of the Vision,[2] as he was sitting at the door of his tent in the strength of the day, warming himself, because of the blood of[g] his circumcision, in the heat of the day. 2. And he lifted up his eyes and saw, and behold, three *angels in the likeness of* men[3] standing beside him.[h] And he saw and he ran from the door of the tent to meet them, and saluted them[4]*

Apparatus, Chapter 18

[a] VNL: "three angels were sent to our father Abraham and the three of them were sent for three things because it is not possible for one of the angels on high that he be sent for more than one thing. The first angel was sent to announce to our father Abraham that, behold, Sarah would bear Isaac. The second angel was sent to deliver Lot from the destruction. The third angel was sent to destroy Sodom, Gomorrah, Admah, and Zeboim. For this reason there was a word of prophecy from before the Lord to Abram (*sic*) the just, and the Memra of the Lord was revealed to him in the plain of Hazoza as he was seated at the door of his tent, warming himself (= recovering) from his circumcision at the strength of the day." The same in P, with variants: "At the time Abraham circumcised the flesh of his foreskin; and the three (lit.: the three of them) angels were sent .... angels on high to be sent ... Zeboim: these angels were sent to Abraham our father. The Memra of the Lord

was revealed to him in the Plain of the Vision (*ḥyzww'*) ... from his circumcision in (lit.: according to) the heat (variant reading P: the strength of) the day."
[b] Nfmg: "to be sent"; = P.
[c] Nfmg: "one thing"; inverted order of Aramaic words, as in VNLP.
[d] Nfi: lexical variant; = VNLP.
[e] Nfmg: "that behold, Sarah would bear Isaac"; = VNL; compare P.
[f] Nfmg: "for this reason there was a word of prophecy from before the Lord to Abraham the just"= VNL.
[g] Nfmg: "his circumcision at the strength of the day= VNL.
[h] Nfmg: "standing before him: one of them went to announce to Sarah that she would bear a male son, and one of them went to destroy Sodom, and one of them went to deliver Lot from destruction."

Notes, Chapter 18

[1] For rabbinic parallels to this midrash (also in Frg. Tg.), see Grossfeld, *Neofiti*, Gen 18, note 1. "One angel (not for more than one thing)"; thus *Gen. R.* 50,2 (on Gen 19:11). That the three men were angels also in Josephus (*Ant.* I, 11, 2, no. 197) and Philo (*De Abr.* xxiii, no. 110). A textual analysis of the midrash in B. Barry Levy, 1, 1986, 150–151.

[2] "the Plain of Vision"; see 12:6 (HT: "the Oak of Moreh"); 13:8 (HT: "the Oaks of Mamre"); 14:13 (HT: "the Oaks of Mamre the Amorite").

[3] "three angels in the likeness of men." HT: "three men."

[4] saluted them (lit. "inquired about their welfare," *s'l bšlmhwn*) according to the custom of the land"); this is Nf's rendering of the Hebrew *(w)yštḥw 'rṣh* of the HT ("bowed himself down to the earth"), here and in Gen 19:1; 33:3; 37:10; 42:6; 43:26, and sometimes elsewhere (23:7); also Nfmg Gen 48:12; VNL 19:1. When *wyštḥw* is not followed by *'rṣh* ("to the ground"), Nf generally renders as *s'l bšlm(hwn)*, without the additional "according to the custom of the country" (Gen 23:7 is an exception). It may be that Nf understood *'rṣ* ("ground") of this phrase as "land," "country." When the verb *yštḥw* is used in the sense of "worship," "praise (God)," Nf renders accordingly, e.g., Gen 24:26, 48, 52; 47:31 (in all these cases worshiping God); 43:28 (a human person). Special cases in Nf's rendering of the verb are Gen 22:5; 27:29. See further Grossfeld, *Neofiti*, Gen 18, note 5. See also D. M. Golomb, "The Targumic Renderings of the Verb *lehištaḥawôt*: A

after the custom[5] *of the land.* 3. And he said: "*I beseech before you*, O Lord,[6] if now I have found grace *and favor* in your sight,[i] let not *the Glory*[j] *of your Shekinah go up*[7] from your servant. 4. *I* will fetch, now, a little water; wash[k] your feet, and *refresh* yourselves under the tree. 5. And I will fetch *a little food* that you may strengthen your hearts, and after that you can pass on; because for this reason you have passed[m] by near your servant *at the time of repast.*" And they say: "Do just as you have spoken." 6. And Abraham hurried *and*[n] went to the tent, to Sarah, and he said: "Hurry[o] and take three seahs of fine flour, spread it and make *unleavened* bread.[p] 7. And Abraham ran to the *cattle-yard* and took a calf, tender and good, and gave it to his boy-servant, who hurried to prepare it. 8. Then he took curds and milk and the calf which he had prepared, and placed it before them; and he stood beside them under the tree and *they were giving the impression of* eating *and drinking.*[8] 9. And they said to him: "Where is your wife Sarah?"; and he said: "Behold she is in the tent." 10. And he said: "I will surely return[q] to you at this hour, and behold,[r] your wife Sarah will have a *male* son." And Sarah was listening at the door of the tent and *Ishmael*[9] *was standing* behind her[10] *listening.* 11. Now Abraham and Sarah had grown old, had advanced in days; the way of woman *had been withheld*[11] from being with Sarah. 12. And Sarah wondered in her *heart* saying:[s] "After I have *grown old, is it possible for me to return to the days of my youth and to have pregnancies;*[12] and my husband *Abraham* has grown old." 13. And the

Apparatus, Chapter 18

[i] Nfmg: "before you."

[j] Nfmg: "I beseech, let (not) the Glory (of . . .) pass by."

[k] Nfmg: "a little water and let them wash."

[m] Nfmg: "(for) this have you passed by, to justify (or: declare innocent) your servant."

[n] Nfmg: "hastened."

[o] Nfmg: "hasten."

[p] Nfmg: "(knead) them and make cakes."

[q] VNL: "and he said: I will surely return to you at this time (at) which you are (now) standing and, behold, Sarah your wife will have a male child. And Sarah was listening at the door of the tent; she was listening and Ishmael was standing behind her"; P: "and Ishmael was standing behind it (or: him)."

[r] Nfmg: "I will surely return to you at this time/period and, behold, a son (*byr*)"; cf. VNL.

[s] VNL: "And Sarah laughed in her heart (= herself) saying: After I have grown old, is it possible to return to the days of my youth so that I have a pregnancy, and Abraham has grown old."

Notes, Chapter 18

Targumic Translation Convention," in *Working with No Data. Semitic and Egyptian Studies Presented to Thomas O. Lambdin*, ed. D. M. Golomb (Winona Lake, Ind.: Eisenbrauns, 1987) 105–118.

[5] "custom"; Greek loan word: *nomos*.

[6] "I beseech before you, O Lord." HT: "O Lord." For addition see to 15:2; 19:3; "by the mercies" seems to have been omitted inadvertently before "O Lord."

[7] "glory of your Shekinah go up;" HT: "do not pass by"; cf. Introduction, p. 37.

[8] "they seemed to be eating and drinking." HT: "they ate"; see 18:2: "angels in the likeness of men."

[9] "Ishmael was standing behind her." Paraphrase due to the Targumist having understood HT's *whw'* (vocalize as *wehi'* = "she") (was) behind him" as "he (vocalizing *wehû*), i.e., Ishmael (was) behind (her, or: him)." Thus also Ps.-J., Frg. Tg. and *Gen. R.* 48,10.

[10] "behind her" (*btrh, batarah*), or possibly, with HT, VNL, and *Gen. R.* 48,16: "behind him" (*batareh*).

[11] "had been withheld" (*'tmn'*); HT: *ḥdl*; RSV: "It has ceased to be."

[12] "pregnancies" (*'dwyyn*) rather than "menstrual periods" (Golomb, 1985, 104); VNL: sing., *'ydwy*; cf. Gen 3:16, *'dwnwk.* HT: *'dnh*; RSV: "pleasure."

Lord[t] said to Abraham: "Now, Sarah has laughed,[u] saying: 'Will I truly bear a child, now that I am old?' 14. *Is it possible* that[w] anything be *hidden before* the Lord?[13] At (this) time I will return to you, at this hour, and Sarah will have a *male son.*"[x] 15. But Sarah denied saying: "I did not laugh,"[y] because she was afraid. And he said to her: "No, but you did laugh."[y] 16. And the men arose from there and looked attentively in the direction of Sodom,[z] and Abraham went with them to accompany them. 17. And the Lord said[aa] *through his Memra*: "Am I to hide from *my friend*[14] Abraham what I am going to do? *Since the city of Sodom is among the gifts I have given him,*[15] *it is right that I*[bb] *should not overthrow it until I inform him.* 18. And Abraham will surely become a great and powerful nation and *in his merits*[16] all the nations of the earth shall be blessed. 19. Because *it is manifest before me*[cc][17] that he will charge his sons and *the men of* his house after him that they observe the way of the Lord by doing justice and right,[dd] so that *the Memra of* the Lord may bring upon Abraham what he spoke with him." 20. And the Lord[ee] said: "The plaint *of the people of*[ff] Sodom and Gomorrah is surely great, and their sin has increased greatly. 21. I will now *be revealed*[18] and I will see[ffbis] if according to the plaint that has *ascended* before me they have *performed the destruction. They are worthy of total destruction.*[19] *And if they seek*[20] *to do repentance and if they hope*

Apparatus, Chapter 18

[t] Nfmg: "the Memra of the Lord."

[u] Nfmg: "has denied."

[w] Nfmg: "that there be deficiency (before the Lord)? At this time I will return"; for first part see Nf and Nfmg, Num 11:23.

[x] Nfmg: "a son" (*byr*).

[y] Nfmg: "you have laughed" (a different Aramaic word).

[z] VNL: "and they gazed (Afel) in the direction (*'l 'py*) of Sodom"; Nfmg: "and they gazed towards (*klqbl*) Sodom."

[aa] P and VNL the same as P for v. 17.

[bb] Nfmg: "that we should overthrow"=VNLP.

[cc] Nfmg: "I know."

[dd] Nfmg: "judgment and justice."

[ee] Nfmg: "the Memra of the Lord."

[ff] Nfmg: "the plaint of Sodom."

[ffbis] PVNL: "I will be revealed and see whether in accordance with the plaint of the people of Sodom and Gomorrah <which> has come up before me,

Notes, Chapter 18

[13]"Is it possible that anything is hidden (*dytks'*) before the Lord." HT: "Is anything too hard (*hypl'*) for the Lord?" Same rendering of this Hebrew word in Nf Deut 17:8 (also in VNL); 30:11. Different rendering of Hebrew in Nf Deut 28:59 (*'tprš*).

[14]"Ab. my friend"; cf. Isa 41:8.

[15]"the gifts I have given him"; see *Gen. R.* 49,2; also note to Ps.-J. (vol. 1B in this series).

[16]"in his merits" (lit. "in the merits," *bzkwwt'*); cf. Nfmg, "in his merits"; see note to 12:3. HT: "in him."

[17]"manifest before me." HT: "I have known (=chosen) him."

[18]"I will be revealed and see." Nf avoids anthropomorphism of HT: "I will go down and see."

[19]"they have performed the destruction . . . total destruction"; Aramaic: *klyyh 'bdw gmyr' 'ynwn ḥyybyn.* HT: *'šw klh (w'm l' 'd'h)*; RSV: "they have done altogether (and if not I will know)." *klh* of the HT is problematic and variously rendered or emended, e.g., as "destruction," "at all" (vocalizing as *kullah*). Nf can also be variously understood, depending on the punctuation and the syntactical position of *gmyr'* and how it is understood, e.g., as "entirely" or as "destruction" (in this sense a synonym of *klyyh*). Thus: "they have performed the destruction (*klyyh*) completely (*gmyr'*); or: "they have performed the destruction (*klyyh*). They are worthy of total destruction (*gmyr'*)." The latter understanding seems best and is in agreement with *Gen. R.* 49,6, where as a gloss on *'šw klh* we have: *klyyh hn ḥyybyn*, "they must be completely destroyed," agreeing verbatim with Nf's *gmyr' 'ynwn ḥybbyn.* See further on text Grossfeld, op. cit., Gen 18 note 33.

[20]"and if they seek . . . ," a paraphrase based on the elliptic HT: "and if not, I will know."

in their souls that their evil works are not manifest before me—behold they are before me, as if I did not know." 22. And the men turned away from there and went to Sodom, and Abraham was still standing, *beseeching mercy* from before[gg] the Lord. 23. And Abraham approached and said: "Will you *in anger*[21] blot out the innocent with the guilty? 24. Perhaps there are fifty innocent men in the midst of the city. Will you *in anger*[21] blot (them) out *and not remit and pardon*[22] *the sins*[hh] of the place because of fifty innocent men who are in the midst of it?[ii] 25. Far be it from before you to do such a thing: to kill[jj] the innocent with the guilty, so that *the judgment of* the innocent be like *the judgment* of the guilty. Far be it from before you *to do such a thing*. Will the Judge *of the judges*[kk] *of all the inhabitants* of the earth not do justice?"[mm] 26. And the Lord[nn] said: "If in Sodom I find fifty innocent in the midst of the city, *I will remit and pardon*[22] all *the guilty* of the place because of them."[oo] 27. And Abraham answered and said: "Behold, now, I have begun to speak *before the Lord*, though I be dust and ashes. 28. Perhaps five of the fifty innocent will be lacking. Will you blot out[pp] all the city because of five?" And he said: "I will not blot it[qq] out if I find[rr] forty-five there." 29. And he spoke with him again and said: "What if forty are found there?" And he said: "I will not *blot (it)* out on account of forty innocent." 30. And he said: "Let not, I pray, the anger of *the Lord*, grow strong, and I will speak: What if thirty are found there?" And he said: "I will not *blot (it) out* if I find[ss] thirty there." 31. And he said: "Behold now I have begun to speak *before the Lord*: "Perhaps twenty are found there." And he said: "I will not blot[tt] (it) out on account of twenty innocent." 32. And he said: "Let not the anger of the Lord, I pray, grow strong and I will speak again this time. Perhaps ten are found there." And he said: "I will not destroy on account of ten."[uu] 33. And *the Glory of the Shekinah*[23] *of the Lord went up* when it had finished speaking with Abraham. And Abraham returned to his place.

Apparatus, Chapter 18

they have performed [missing in P] the destruction completely. They are guilty. They imagine in their souls (= they delude themselves) that perhaps their evil deeds are not manifest before me. And if they seek to do repentance (P +: and to turn back from their evil deeds), behold they are before me (P: before him) as if I did not know."
[gg] Nfmg: "in prayer before."
[hh] Nfmg: "(pardon) the place because."
[ii] Nfmg: "just who are in the midst of it."
[jj] Nfmg: "to blot out."
[kk] Nfmg: "the judge that judges all."

[mm] Nfmg: "this order of judgment."
[nn] Nfmg: "the Memra of the Lord (said): If there be found."
[oo] Nfmg: "I will remit and pardon the city for their merits" (i.e., their sakes).
[pp] Nfmg: "will you destroy."
[qq] Nfmg: "I will not destroy"; Nfi: "it will not be blotted out."
[rr] Nfmg: "if there be found."
[ss] Nfi: "if they find" (i.e., "if there be found").
[tt] Nfmg: "I will not destroy because of."
[uu] Nfmg: "I will not destroy if ten be found there."

Notes, Chapter 18

[21]"in anger"; likewise Onq., Ps.-J., *Gen. R.* 49,8. HT: *'p*, taken as "anger" rather than as here intended, an interjection, "even."

[22]"remit and pardon," *šry wšbq*. See note to 4:7.

[23]"the Glory of the Shekinah ... went up." HT: "the Lord went (his way)."

CHAPTER 19

1. And the two angels went into *a* Sodom in the evening and Lot was seated at the gate *b* of Sodom; and Lot saw them and ran out to meet them and saluted them *according to the custom of the land.* [1] 2. And he said: "I beseech you, my lords, come as far as the house of your servant, I pray, and pass the night and wash your feet; *c* and you can arise early in the morning and go on your way." *d* And they say to him: "No, but we will pass the night in the square *of the city."* *e* [2] 3. And he pressed them greatly; and they turned aside to him and entered into *f* his house. And he made them a meal and baked unleavened bread; and they ate. 4. They had not yet slept *g* when the *people* of the city—*the people* of Sodom—surrounded his house from their young to their old, all the people *from one side.* 5. And they called to Lot and said to him: "Where are these men who have come to you tonight? Bring them out to us that we may know them." 6. And <Lot> went out to them, *outside,* *h* and bolted the door behind him. 7. And he said: *i* "I pray, my brothers, do not do evil. 8. Behold, I pray, I have two daughters who know not man; *j* I will bring them out to you now, and do to them what appears good *k* in your sight; only do nothing to these men because for this have *m* they come—*to pass the night* in the shade of my roof." 9. And they say: "Move off!" And they say: "One comes to sojourn *amongst us* and, behold, he seeks *to be judge of our judgments!* [3] Now are we to do to you greater evil than to them." And they pressed hard against the man, against Lot, and

Apparatus, Chapter 19

a VNL: "and the two angels came to Sodom in the evening and Lot was seated at the gate (*pyly*: Greek loan word, *pylos*) of Sodom; and he saw them and ran and enquired about their welfare (= saluted them) and bowed down to the ground upon his face"; Nfmg: "and they came"; = VNL).

b Nfmg: "at the gate (*pyle*) of"; = VNL.

c VNL: "and wash your feet and bathe (an erroneous reading?) in the morning and you shall go to your tents in peace. And they said: No, for we shall spend the night in the city street (*plṭywt*, a Greek loan word, *plateia*)"; Nfmg: "pass the night and wash."

d Nfmg: "in the morning you shall go in peace to your tents."

e Nfmg: "we shall pass the night in the city street (*plṭywt*)";= VNL.

f Nfmg: "and he made a meal for them and they appeared as if they were eating and as if they were drinking"; PVNL: "and they appeared as if they were eating and as if they were drinking"; = Nfmg (a minor variant in P).

g Nfmg: "and they had (not) lain down."

h Nfmg +: "from the doors."

i VNL: "And Lot said to them: Wait here a little while until we (= I) beseech mercy from before the Lord"; a misplaced paraphrase (from v. 18) on the Heb. text of v. 7.

j VNL: "who have not known intercourse with man"; cf. Nfmg: "there are who know not intercourse with man."

k Nfmg: "(good) and proper before you; only to (these) men."

m Nfmg: "nothing evil at all, for because of this."

Notes, Chapter 19

[1]"according to the custom of the land." HT: *(w)yšthw 'pym 'rṣh*; RSV: "bowed himself with his face to the earth." See note to 18:2. See Apparatus for variants.

[2]"in the square of the city." HT: "in the square."

[3]"judge of our judgments." HT (RSV): "to play the judge."

they drew near to break the door. 10. But the men stretched out their hands and brought Lot into them to the house, and they bolted the door. 11. And the men who were at the door of the house they smote with blindness,[n4] from those of them *of tender years*[5] to their *old*;[6] and they labored to find the door *of the house and did not find the door.* 12. And the men said to Lot: "Right now, what have you here?[o] Your son-in-law and your sons and your daughters and all whatsoever you have in the city, take from the place; 13. for we are going to destroy this place because their plaint has increased before the Lord and he[p] has sent us to blot it out."[q] 14. And Lot went out and spoke with his sons-in-law, given in marriage to his daughters, and said: "Arise, go forth from this place because the Lord[r] is going to destroy the city." And it was as if he jested in the sight of his sons-in-law. 15. And at the time of the rise of the *morning* dawn[s] the angels *laid hold of* Lot, saying: "Arise, take your wife and your two daughters who are present,[t] lest you be blotted out because of the sins of the city." 16. And as they delayed, the men took hold of his hands, and of the hands of his two daughters, in compassion before the Lord upon him; and they took him out and set him down outside the city. 17. And when they had taken them outside he said: "Save your life; do not look behind you and do not stand (anywhere) in the entire *plain*,[7] save yourself[u] on the mountain that you may not come to an end." 18. And Lot said to them: *"Wait*, I pray,[w] *a little while until I*[x] *beseech mercy*[8] *from before the Lord.* 19. Behold, I pray,[y] your servant has found grace *and favor* before you[z] and you have increased your favor which you have done with me, prolonging my life; but I cannot save myself on the mountain, lest the evil overtake me and I die. 20. Behold, I pray, this city is near to flee there; it is *near.*[aa]

Apparatus, Chapter 19

[n] Thus Nf with *Aruk* (s.v. *sdr*); rendering a rare word for "blindness" of the HT (found only in Gen 19:11 and twice in 2 Kgs 6:18). P: *bḥbrbry'*, "blindness, groping in the dark"; variant readings (with same meaning?) in V (*bḥbryyh*), N (*bḥrbryh*), L (*bḥbrbryh*); Nfmg: "with confusion (in burning, *bḥrbyy'*—unless corrupt) from their young men to."
[o] Nfmg: "(what) still have you here? Sons-in-law."
[p] Nfi +: "the Lord"; Nfmg: "the Memra of the Lord."
[q] Nfmg: "to destroy (it)."
[r] Nfmg: "the Name of the Lord."

[s] Lit.: "the column of the dawn"; so also PVNL.
[t] Nfmg: "those who are found with you that they may not be made an end of because of the sins (lit.: debts) of the city."
[u] Nfmg: "flee."
[w] PVNL in v. 18 = Nf, with variants: "wait a little while," P; "wait here a little while," VNL; Nfmg here= VNL.
[x] Lit.: "we" (in all texts).
[y] Nfmg: "I beseech."
[z] Nfmg: "in your eyes."
[aa] Nfmg: "it is little."

Notes, Chapter 19

[4]"with blindness," *b-sydwryh*; "presumably = *siddurayya*, meaning "blindness," cf. Job 10:22; Golomb, 1985, 119. HT: *snwrym* (MT: *sanwerîm*; elsewhere in HT only in 2 Kgs 6:18. See Apparatus, note *n*.
[5]"tender years," *dqyqyhwn*. HT: "small."
[6]"old"; HT: "great."
[7]"plain"; HT: *kkr* (*kikkar*); RSV: "valley."
[8]"until I beseech mercy. . . ." Added in order to complete HT, "O no, my lords."

Let me be saved there, I pray. Is it not small? And my life will be preserved." 21. And he said to him: "Behold, I have accepted you in this matter also, not to over- throw the city (of) which *bb* you have spoken. 22. Make haste; *cc* save yourself there, because I cannot do anything until the time you enter there." For this reason he called the name of the city Zoar. 23. And the sun *went down* over the earth as Lot entered *Zoar.* 24. And the Memra of the Lord made sulphur and fire come down upon Sodom and Gomorrah *from before* the Lord, from the heavens. *dd* 25. And he overthrew these cities and all the *plain* and all the inhabitants of the cities, and the plants of the earth. 26. And *because* the wife of *Lot was from the daughters of Sodomites* she looked back to see what would be the end of her father's house, *ee* and behold, she stands as a pillar of salt until *the time the dead are brought to life.* *ff* 9 27. And Abraham went early in the morning to the place where he had stood *and prayed* there before *gg* the Lord. 28. And he looked attentively in the direction of Sodom and *in the direction of Gomorrah,* and in the direction of the land *of the plain.* He saw, and behold, the fumes *hh* of the land went up like *the fumes of* the smoke of a furnace. 29. And when *the Lord* blotted out *ii* the cities of *the plain, the Lord jj in his good mercies* remembered [10] Abraham and sent Lot forth from the midst of the overthrow when he overthrew the cities in which Lot dwelt. [11] 30. And Lot went up from *Zoar* and he dwelt in a cave, *kk* he and his two daughters with him, because he was afraid to dwell in *Zoar.* And he dwelt in a cave, he and his two daughters. 31. And the elder said to the younger: "Our father is old and there is no man in the land to come in to us according to the way of all *mm* the earth. 32. Come

Apparatus, Chapter 19

bb Nfmg: "according as."

cc Nfmg: "hurry."

dd PVNL: "the Memra of the Lord made rains of good pleasure come down on the people of Sodom and Gomorrah so that (VNL: perchance) they might perform repentance from their evil deeds but they did not. And when they saw the rain come down they said: Perchance our evil deeds are not manifest before him (VNL: before me), and he began (lit.: turned) to rain down on them sulphur and fire from before the Lord from the heavens."

ee PVNL: "And Lot's wife because she was of the daughters of the people of Sodom (VNL: because Lot's wife was from the sons of the sons of the peo- ple of Sodom) ... until the time that the dead will arise (VNL: until the time that there comes the viv-

ification, that the dead will arise)"; Nfmg: "And the wife of Lot because she was of the people of Sodom looked to see what would be the end of her father's house."

ff Nfmg: "the vivification of."

gg Nfmg: "where (she stood) in prayer before."

hh Nfmg: "smoke."

ii Nfmg: "at the time the Memra of the Lord de- stroyed."

jj Nfmg: "the Memra of the Lord."

kk In HT, Tg. Onq., Ps.-J.: "on the mountain."

mm VNL: "and there is no man in the land to join (= have intercourse) with us according to the custom (= *nomos,* Greek loan word) of all the earth"; Nfmg: "and ... custom of all"; = VNL.

Notes, Chapter 19

9"until the time the dead be brought to life." Reference to the resurrection in the verse also in PVNL. On formula see A. Rodriguez Carmona, *Targum y resurrección,* 1978, 26, 29, 167.

10"in his good mercies remembered"; see note to 8:1.

11"in which Lot dwelt," *dy šr' bhwn.* There may be a reflection of this Aramaic text in *Gen. R.* 51,6.

and let us make our father drink wine and we will have intercourse with him,[nn] and we will raise up *sons*[oo] from our father." 33. And they gave wine to their father to drink that night, and the elder went in[pp] and had intercourse with her father and he did not know either when she *lay down* or when she got up. 34. And the following *day* the elder said to the younger: "Behold, during the evening I had intercourse with my father; let us give him wine to drink also tonight and go in, you, and have intercourse with him, and we will raise up *sons* from our father." 35. And that night also they gave wine to their father to drink and the younger, rising up, had intercourse with him,[qq] and he did not know either when she *lay down* or when she got up. 36. And the two daughters of Lot conceived from their father. 37. And the elder bore a son and called his name Moab. He is the father, the father of *the Moabites* unto the time of this day. 38. And the lesser also bore a son[rr] and called his name Son of my People.[12] He is the father of the Ammonites until *the time of* this day.

CHAPTER 20

1. And Abraham journeyed from there to the land of the south, and dwelt between *Rekem*[1] and *Haluzah,*[2] and he sojourned at Gerar. 2. And Abraham said *concerning* his wife Sarah: "She is my sister." And Abimelech the king of Gerar[a] sent and took Sarah. 3. And *the Memra of the Lord was revealed* to Abimelech in a dream at night and said to him: "Behold, you are to die on account of the woman whom you have taken, for she is married." 4. And Abimelech had not approached[b] her, and he said: "I *beseech, by the mercy*[3] *before you, O Lord*; shall an innocent

Apparatus, Chapter 19

[nn] Nfmg: "let us join" (= have intercourse).
[oo] Nfmg: "seed of sons."
[pp] Nfmg: "And (the elder) came."

[qq] Nfmg: "she joined with."
[rr] In text *br*; Nfmg: *byr.*

Notes, Chapter 19

[12]"son of my people," *br 'my* (*bar 'Ammi*).

Apparatus, Chapter 20

[a] VN: "king of Arad"; L: "at Arad," possibly intended for v. 1, Nfmg: "of Arar (*sic*) and led away."

[b] Nfmg: "joined."

Notes, Chapter 20

[1]"Rekem." HT: Kadesh. See note to 14:7.
[2]P: "Haluza." HT: "Shur." See note to 16:17.
[3]"I beseech by the mercies. . . ." Prefaced to HT: "O Lord." See note to 15:2; also 18:13; 24:42.

people *be killed in justice?*[4] 5. Did he not say to me: 'She is my sister'; and she said: 'He is my brother.' I did this in the integrity of my heart and in the *uprightness*[5] of my hands." 6. And *the Memra of the Lord* said to him in a dream: "It is also *manifest*[c] *before me*[6] that you did this in the integrity of your heart, and I have also restrained you[d] from sinning *before* me; for this reason I did not give you *the authority*[7] to approach her.[e] 7. And now, return the wife of the man, for he is a prophet and he will pray for you and you will live; but if you do not return her, know that you will surely die, *Abimelech*, and all that are his." 8. And Abimelech arose early in the morning and called all his *rulers*[f8] and spoke these words in their hearing; and the men were very much afraid. 9. And Abimelech called Abraham and said to him: "What have you done to us? And what have I sinned[g] against you that you have brought upon me and my kingdom great sins? Deeds *that are not proper* to be done, you have done with me." 10. And Abimelech said to Abraham: "What had you in mind that you did this thing?" 11. And Abraham said: "Because I said: 'There is no fear of *the Lord* at all to be found in this place and they will kill me on account of Sarah my wife.' 12. And yet, of a truth she is my sister; she is the daughter of my father but not the daughter of my mother, and she became my wife. 13. And when *the nations tried*[9] to lead me astray *after their idols* and *the Memra of the Lord took me*[h10] from the house of my father, I said to her: 'This is your favor that you shall do me: in every place where we shall enter, say, I pray, concerning me: He is my brother.'" 14. And Abimelech took sheep and oxen, man-servants and maid-servants and gave (them) to Abraham and he showed him[i] Sarah his wife. 15. And Abimelech said: "Behold my land before you; dwell where it appears good to you." 16. And he said[j] to Sarah: "Behold I have given a thousand *selas*[k] of silver[11]

Apparatus, Chapter 20

[c] Nfmg: "I know."

[d] Nfmg: "(you did) this: I also withheld."

[e] Nfmg: "from sinning before me; therefore did I not permit you to join."

[f] Nfmg: "his servants."

[g] Nfmg: "what is this you have done to us and what have we sinned?"

[h] text: "him."

[i] Nfmg: "and he returned (*ḥzr*) to him," text of Nf: "showed" (*ḥwy*) probably to be amended accordingly.

[j] Text: "she said."

[k] Text: lit.: "a thousand of selas"; Nfi: "(a thousand) selas" (see note to text); Nfmg: "zuzim of shekels."

Notes, Chapter 20

[4] "killed in justice." HT: "will you slay... ?"

[5] "integrity, uprightness" (*tmymwt, qšyṭwt*). HT: *tm, nqyn*; RSV: "integrity, innocence."

[6] "... manifest before me." HT: "I know."

[7] "the power (or: authority)," *ršw*; HT, lit. "I did not give you"; RSV: "I kept you from."

[8] "rulers." HT: "servants"; cf. Nfmg.

[9] "the nations tried..."; a midrash occasioned by difficulties in the HT (in RSV): "and when God caused me to wander (*ht'w 'lhym*) from my father's house," with verb in the plural (*ht 'w*) after the Hebrew for God, which (*'lhym*) is plural in form. The interpretation in Nf is the same as that of R. Hanan in *Gen. R.* 51,1.

[10] "... the Lord took me"; new verb is necessary in Nf, since the principal verb of HT is interpreted as "leading astray."

[11] "a thousand silver *selas*" (Nf lit. "a thousand of selas of silver"; Nfi: "[a thousand] selas"). HT: "a thousand of silver." When the material involved is silver, Nf (and other Tgs.) understand that shekels (in Tg.=selas) are intended; otherwise in Nf when the material is gold; see 24:22 and note thereto. On *sela*, see Introduction, pp. 32–33.

to your brother; behold, *that silver*[12] *is given to you as a gift on account of your having been hidden even one night* from the eyes of *the just one* and from all who were with you, and you have been justified above all. *But were I to give all*[m] *that I have I would not be worthy—that Abraham the just should know that I have not known you."*[n] 17. And Abraham prayed *before the Lord,* and *the Lord* cured Abimelech and his wife and his handmaids and they bore children. 18. Because the Lord[o] had indeed locked up[p] completely every *opening*[q] *of* the womb[13] in the house of Abimelech, on account of Sarah, Abraham's wife.

CHAPTER 21

1. And the Lord *remembered* Sarah *in his good mercies*[1] as he had said, [a]*and the Lord worked* signs *for Sarah as he had spoken.*[a] 2. And Sarah conceived and bore

Apparatus, Chapter 20

[m] Nfmg: "the just Abraham one night and above all that is with me (cf. VNL) and above all I have been justified. Behold these (*'lyn*; read: *'ylw,* "if") I had given"; VNL: "And to Sarah he said: Behold I have given a thousand selas of silver to your brother. Behold, I have given it to you as a gift for the reason that you were concealed from the eyes of Abraham your husband even for one night, and from all that was with me (read: "with you"? or: "for all that you were with me"?), since above everyone you have been vindicated. Behold, even if I had given all that I had, I would not be worthy. And the(se) words are justified; Abraham the just knows (or: may Abraham the just know) that I did not know you (carnally)"; P: "And to Sarah he said: Behold I

have given (text: given you) a thousand selas of silver to your brother. Behold that money I give to you as a gift for the reason that you were concealed from the eyes of Abraham the just your husband (even) for one night with all that is with you and with (*yt*, the sign of the accusative; a calque on the HT, *'t,* here with meaning of "with") all you are justified. Behold, had I given all that I have I would not have been (found) worthy. And the(se) words are justified, and may Abraham the just realize that I have not known you."

[n] Nfi: "(that) I have (not) drawn near to you."

[o] Nfmg: "the Memra of the Lord."

[p] VNL "locked up"; sole gloss on v. in VNL; = Nf.

[q] Nfmg: "(every) membrane (of the womb)."

Notes, Chapter 20

[12]"behold that silver. . . ." HT: "behold it is a covering (*kswt*) of the eyes to all . . . ," which might be taken to imply a form of bribery on Abimelech's part and reflect unfavorably on Sarah. Nf, through interpretation of *ksy*= "to hide," paraphrases in favor of Sarah's honor and integrity. See also B. Barry Levy, 1, 1986, 158–159.

[13]"(every) opening of the womb" (or: "every birth-opening"), *b'd pty yldh*; HT: *b'd kl rḥm. b'd* in Nf is probably an intrusion from the HT or a Hebrew gloss; cf. Golomb, 1985, 24. This translation of Nf (of this and similar expressions of the HT) is found also in Nf Exod 13:2, 12, 15; 34:19; Num 3:12; 8:16; 12:12; 18:15.

Apparatus, Chapter 21

[a-a] VNL verbatim as Nf.

Notes, Chapter 21

[1]"The Lord remembered . . . in his good mercies." HT: "The Lord visited Sarah"; see note to 8:1. The word "visited" (*pqd*) of the HT is translated in Nf as "remembered in his good mercies," also in Gen 50:24,25; Exod 4:31; 13:19. In Exod 3:16 Nf renders as "the Lord shall surely remember you," while Nfmg has: "I remembered you in my (corr. from: "his") good mercies."

Abraham a son *[b]* at *the time of* his old age, at the time of which *the Lord*[2] had spoken. 3. And Abraham called the name of his son who was born to him, whom Sarah bore to him, Isaac. 4. And Abraham circumcised Isaac his son when he was eight days old, as the Lord *[c]* had commanded him. 5. And Abraham *was* a hundred years old *at the time that*[d3] Isaac his son was born to him. 6. And Sarah said: "*A great joy has been* made for me *from before the Lord*: *[e4]* everyone who hears (of it) will *rejoice with me.*"*[f]* 7. And she said: "*Oh! who will go and relate in the house of Nahor, brother of* Abraham:[5] 'Sarah suckles sons,' because *she has* borne *him* a son *at the time* of his old age"?*[g]* 8. And the child grew and was weaned;*[h]* and Abraham made a great feast on the day that Isaac[6] was weaned.*[i]* 9. And Sarah saw the son of Hagar, the Egyptian, whom she had borne to Abraham, *doing improper actions,[j7]* <such as jesting in *a foreign cult*>.*[k8]* 10. And she said to Abraham: "Cast out this slave woman and her son, because the son of this slave woman shall not inherit with my son, with Isaac." 11. And the thing seemed very bad in the sight of

---

Apparatus, Chapter 21

[b] Nfmg: "a son (*byr*, text *br*) of old age at the time that the Memra of the Lord spoke with him."

[c] Nfmg: "the Memra of the Lord."

[d] Nfi: "when."

[e] Nfmg: "great joy (lit.: "great for me joy) has the Lord made for me."

[f] Nfmg: "great joy has the Memra of the Lord made for me. Every one who hears my voice rejoices with me" (lit.: "to me"); ending repeated in slightly different words: "and will rejoice with me."

[g] Nfmg: "and she said: How trustworthy were the (good) tidings of him who announced to my master Abraham from the beginning and said: Sarah is to give suck to sons; because I have borne him a son for old age"; cf. VNL: "and she said: What were the (good) tidings that he announced (= were announced) to my master Abraham from the beginning. She is (destined) to give suck, because I have borne a child for her old age."

[h] Nfmg: "and he weaned."

[i] Nfmg: "that he weaned (Isaac)." In text of Nf at end of v. 8, after "Isaac was weaned," there is erroneously inserted from v. 9: "the son of Hagar the Egyptian who had borne to Abraham doing deeds that were not fitting such as jesting in a foreign cult." To this text we have the Nfmg: "(not fitting) to be done, jesting" (= PVNL).

[j] Nfmg: "bad (actions) which it was not."

[k] Ending missing here in Nf; supplied from end of Nf v. 8, where it is wrongly inserted; see n. *i* above. PVNL: "And Sarah saw the son of Hagar the Egyptian, who had borne to Abraham doing bad actions which are not fitting to be done, (such as) jesting in a foreign cult."

Notes, Chapter 21

[2]"the Lord." HT: "God"; see note to 1:1.

[3]"at the time that." HT: "in the being born (*bhwld*) (to him Isaac)"—"Isaac" preceded by the sign of the accusative, even though the verb is passive. Same phenomenon in HT Gen 21:8; 4:18 (Niphal of *yld*), 17:25, in all of which cases Nf imitates the Hebrew, with the passive and the sign of the accusative; see Golomb, 1985, 209.

[4]"a great joy ... from before the Lord." HT (RSV): "God has made laughter for me."

[5]"... who will go and relate to the house of Abraham...." HT: "who would have said to Abraham." Paraphrase may be intended to avoid contradiction with 17:19, where Abraham is explicitly told by God of the birth of a son to Sarah and himself.

[6]"that Isaac was weaned"—"Isaac" preceded by the sign of the accusative as in HT. See note to 21:5. For displacement at end of 21:8 in Nf, see Apparatus.

[7]"doing improper actions." HT (RSV): "playing."

[8]"jesting in a foreign cult," or: "entertaining himself with idolatry." For rabbinic parallels see *Gen. R.* 53,11; further, Grossfeld, *Neofiti*, Gen 21 note 8. For possible relationship of the Pal. Tg. tradition with Gal. 4:29-30, see R. Le Déaut, *Biblica* 42 (1061) 37–43.

Abraham on account of Ishmael his son. 12. And *the Lord* said to Abraham: "Let it not seem bad in your sight concerning the boy and your slave woman. Whatsoever Sarah says to you listen to her voice, because through Isaac shall there be named for you the seed *of sons.*[m][9] 13. And I will also make the son of the slave woman to be *a great*[10] nation, because he is your *son.*" 14. And Abraham arose early in the morning and took bread and[n] a skin of water and gave it to Hagar, placing it upon her shoulder, together with the boy, and sent her forth. And she went and wandered in the desert of Beersheba. 15. And the water in the skin[o] was finished and[p] she cast away the boy under one of the *trees,*[11] 16. and went and sat down opposite[q] *it* at about the distance of a bowshot, because she said: "I will not see the death of the child." And she sat down opposite it and she lifted up[r] her voice and cried. 17. And the voice[s] of the boy *was* heard <before> *the Lord;*[12] and the Angel of *the Lord* called to Hagar from the heavens and said to her: "What is the matter, Hagar? Fear not, because *the Lord* has heard the voice *of the prayer* of[13] the boy[t] in the place in which he is. 18. Arise, raise up[u] the boy and take him by the hand, because I will make him a great nation." 19. And *the Lord*[w] opened her eyes and she saw a well of water; and she went and filled the water-skin[x] and gave the boy to drink. 20. And *the Lord* was with the boy[y] and he grew big and dwelt in the desert and was of those *expert* in the bowshot.[z] 21. And he dwelt in the desert of Paran and his mother took him a wife from the land of Egypt. 22. And in that *hour* Abimelech and Phicol, the commander of his army, said to Abraham, saying: "*The Lord* is with you[aa] in all

Apparatus, Chapter 21

[m] Nfmg: "righteous (sons)."

[n] Nfmg: "food and a water-skin and he gave it to Hagar. He placed (it) upon."

[o] Nfmg: "of his water-skin," *qrbtyh = qrwtyh*; so also = *qrnt* of N; VL have = *rwqbt*(?)' (an erroneous writing?); otherwise VNL = Nf.

[p] Nfmg: "and it was ended."

[q] Nfmg: "and put."

[r] Nfmg: "and she raised."

[s] Nfmg: "the Memra of the Lord (has heard) the voice."

[t] Nfmg: "the Memra of the Lord (has heard) the voice of the child."

[u] Nfmg: "take."

[w] Nfmg: "the Memra of the Lord."

[x] Nfmg: "the water-skin" (*qrbt' = qrwwt'*; see *o* above).

[y] Nfmg: "the Memra of the Lord (was) at the aid of the child."

[z] Nfmg: "a master at the bow."

[aa] Nfmg: "the Memra of the Lord is at your aid."

Notes, Chapter 21

[9]"seed of sons." HT: "seeds," a word which Nf, when it refers to humans, generally translates as "descendants"; see Introduction, p. 26, and note to 7:3.

[10]"great nation." HT: "nation"; see v. 18 below.

[11]"trees." HT: "bushes," *syhm*. Nf renders as "trees" as in 2:5.

[12]"the voice (*preceded by sign of accusative*) was heard <before> the Lord . . . ," *wšmy' YYY yt qlyh*; HT: "and God heard the voice of the boy." Nf text, unlike other such cases, does not contain *qdm*, "before," which A. Díez Macho believes should be introduced. Thus emended, the paraphrase would avoid the anthropomorphism of the HT. B. Barry Levy (1, 1986, 160 and 39), however, believes that in all likelihood the literal rendering, without *qdm* ("before") and the passive, represents the earliest translation of Nf (as in Nf Gen 31:30; 39:3; 33:5; Deut 11:2). Note also Nf's literal translation of the same Hebrew text later in this verse.

[13]"the voice of the prayer of." HT: "the voice of the boy." See note to 17:20.

whatsoever you do. 23. And now, swear to me by *the name of the Lord,* [14] here, that you will not deceive me, nor my *son,* nor *the son of my son;* [15] according to the kindness I have done with you, you will do with me and with the land in which you sojourn." [bb] 24. And Abraham said: "*Behold* I swear and *I will fulfill the oath.*" [16] 25. And Abraham reproached Abimelech concerning a well of water which the servants of Abimelech had robbed. [cc] 26. And Abimelech said: "I do not know who did this thing; and you did not even tell it to me, and I have heard it only today." [dd] 27. And Abraham took sheep and oxen and gave them to Abimelech and the two of them made a covenant. 28. And Abraham set aside seven lambs of the flock. 29. And Abimelech said to Abraham: "What are these seven lambs which you have set aside?" 30. And he said: "Because you will take from my hand these seven lambs so that they may be a witness to me that I have dug this well." 31. Because of this he called the name of that place Beersheba, because there the two of them made a covenant. 32. And having *made the covenant* in Beersheba, Abimelech and Phicol, the commander of his armies, arose and returned to *their* country, to the Philistines. 33. And *Abraham* planted *an orchard* [17] in Beersheba [ee] and *within it gave food to the*

Apparatus, Chapter 21

[bb] Nfmg: "and now swear to me in an oath by the name of the Memra of the Lord here, that you will not deceive me, my son, nor my grandson according to the kindness of truth (read: "and the truth") which (I have done)."

[cc] Nfmg: "which your servants digged."

[dd] Nfmg: "and neither have you told me and I (corr. from "you") have not known it until this day (lit.: "until the time of this day")."

[ee] VNL: "and Abraham planted an orchard in Beersheba (thus NL; V has: "the Well of the Seven," or " ... of Sheba") and established within it food and drink at (or: "for"; lit.: "and for/at") the borders (?, *lthwmyy'*; or: "for the neighbors"?; see Nfmg: *lthwmyy'*, with *he*). And they used to eat and drink and seek to give him the price (Greek loan word *timê*) of what they had eaten and drunk and he was not willing to accept (it) from them. And our father Abraham used to say to them: (It was) from him who spoke and the world came into being by his Memra (or: command). Pray before your Father who is in heaven, since it is from his bounty you have eaten and drunk. And they used not move from their places until he had made them proselytes and taught them the way of the world. And Abraham gave thanks and prayed there in the name of the Memra of the Lord, the God of the world"; P: "And Abraham planted an orchard in Beersheba and brought within it food and drink for the uncircumcised. And it was that when they had eaten and drunk, they used to seek to give him the price (Greek loan word *timê*) of what they had

Notes, Chapter 21

[14]"by the name of the Lord." HT: "by God."

[15]"my son ... son of my son." HT: *nyny wnkdy*, rare words, in the Pentateuch used only here; RSV: "my offspring, my posterity."

[16]"I swear ('*štb'*) ... I will fulfill ('*qyym*) the oath." HT simply: "I will swear" ('*šb'*; root *šb'*). Nf renders the Hebrew *šb'* by two different Aramaic ones: *qyym* and *šb'*. When the Hebrew *sb'* refers to God, it is translated in Nf as *qyym*, "fulfill" (but also with possible meaning "swear"): thus here, Gen 22:16; 24:7; 26:3; 50:24; Exod 13:5, 11; 32:13; 33:1; Num 32:10, 11. When the Hebrew verb *šb'* refers to man, Nf uses the same Aramaic word *šb'*. Thus, Gen 21:23; 24:3, 9, 37; cf. Lev 19:12; Num 5:19, 21; by *qyym* only (of man), cf. Gen 21:31; Num 11:12; 14:16. The Hebrew word gets a dual translation, by *qyym* and *šb'*, in Gen 21:24 and Deut 6:13. See further Grossfeld, op. cit., Gen 21 note 20.

[17]"an orchard," or: "pleasure garden," "enclosure"; *prds*, a Persian loan word. Also in Nf and Pal. Tg. Gen 14:10. HT: *'šl*, variously interpreted in rabbinic writings as *prds* (that of Pal. Tg.), as an inn (*pwndq*), a court of law. In *Gen. R.* 54,6 we find the tradition of Abraham's hospitality given as in Nf and Pal. Tg. but connected with the understanding of *'šl* as "inn."

passersby.[18] *And it came about that while eating and drinking they would seek to give him the price of what they had eaten and drunk and he would say to them: "You are eating from him who said and the world was." And they would not move from there until he would convert them, and would teach them to give praise to the Lord*[ff] *of the world. And he worshiped and prayed in the name of the Memra of the Lord,* God of the world. 34. And Abraham sojourned in the land of the Philistines many days.

CHAPTER 22

1. And it happened after these things that *the Lord*[a] tempted Abraham *with the tenth temptation,*[1] and said to him: "Abraham!" *Abraham answered in the language of the sanctuary*[2] *and Abraham said to him*: "HERE I AM."[b] 2. And he said: "Take,

Apparatus, Chapter 21

eaten and drunk, our father Abraham used to say to them: Pray before your Father of the heavens (read: "who is in heaven") from whose bounty you have eaten and from whose bounty you have drunk. And they would not move from there until he had made proselytes and taught them the way of the world. And Abraham worshiped and prayed there in the name of the Memra of the Lord God of the worlds"; Nfmg: "in the Well of the Seven and established within it eating and drinking for the passers-by and for the neighbors (?;

thwmyy', with *he*; see above VNL). And after they had eaten and drunk they used to seek to give him the price (Greek loan word *timê*) of what they had eaten and drunk. Our father Abraham answered and said to them: Pray before your Father who is in heaven from whose bounty you have eaten, and from whose goods you have drunk. They used not move from there he had made proselytes of them in the name of the Memra of the Lord, the God of the world."
[ff] Nfmg: "to him who created."

Notes, Chapter 21

[18]On the midrash concerning Abraham, see note to Ps.-J. (vol. 1B in this series); also B. Barry Levy, 1, 1986, 160f. On Abraham's hospitality and reception of guests, see already *The Testament of Abraham*, Recension A, 1 and 4. Abraham's interest in converting people is also mentioned in Nf Gen 12:5 and in rabbinic sources.

Apparatus, Chapter 22

[a] Nfmg: "the Memra of the Lord."
[b] VNL: "and it happened ... (etc.= Nf) ... and said to him: "Abraham, Abraham, and he answered: Be-

hold. Here I am." In Nf Abraham's reply is in Hebrew; in VNL in Aramaic.

Notes, Chapter 22

[1]This verse represents the beginning of a seder, i.e., a biblical text appointed as a synagogue reading. Such verses often carry expansive paraphrases. See the note to Gen 15:1 and R. Le Déaut, 1978, 1967; "with the tenth temptation." According to rabbinic tradition, God tempted Abraham with ten tests, of which this was the last; see Grossfeld, *Neofiti*, Gen 22 note 1, with rabbinic references. Another of the temptations was Abraham's having been cast into the furnace of fire of (Ur of) the Chaldaeans, mentioned in Nf Gen 11:28; 11:31; 16:5.
[2]"in the language of the sanctuary," i.e., Hebrew (in Nf Abraham's reply, "Here I am" being in the Hebrew of the HT). See note to Gen 2:19 (Ps.-J.) and 11:1; also Grossfeld, op. cit., Gen 2 note 30; A. Shinan, "The Language of the Sanctuary in the Aramaic Translations of the Torah," *Beth Miqra* 21 (1976) 472-474 (in Hebrew).

I pray, your son, your only son Isaac, whom you love, and go to the country of *Mount* Moriah[c3] and offer him there as a burnt offering on one of the mountains which I will say to you." 3. And Abraham arose early in the morning and prepared his ass, and took his two young men with him and his son Isaac; and he cut wood[d] for a burnt offering and rose up, and went to the place which the Lord[e] said to him. 4. On the third day Abraham raised his eyes and saw the place from afar. 5. <And> Abraham <said>[f] to his young men:[g] "Wait here with the ass and I and the boy will[h] arrive there, and *we will pray*[4] and return to you." 6. And Abraham took the wood of the burnt offering and placed them upon his son Isaac; and took in his hand the fire and the knife and they went, the two of them together, *with a perfect heart.*[i5] 7. And Isaac spoke to his father Abraham and said: "Father!" And he said "HERE I AM, MY SON." And he said: "Behold the fire and the wood; but where is the lamb for the burnt offering?" 8. And Abraham said:[j] "*From before the Lord*[k] *has he prepared for himself* a lamb the burnt offering; *otherwise you will be the lamb of the burnt offering.*"[6] And the two of them went together *with a perfect heart.*[m5] 9. And they came to the place which *the Lord* had said to him, and Abraham built the altar there, and arranged the wood and bound his son Isaac and placed him upon the altar above the wood. 10. And Abraham stretched out his hand[n] and took the knife to slaughter his son *Isaac. Isaac answered and said to his*

Apparatus, Chapter 22

[c] VNL: "Mount Moriah"; = Nf; Nfmg +: "where the temple was to be built."
[d] Nfmg: "and divided."
[e] Nfmg: "the Memra of the Lord."
[f] Missing in text.
[g] Nfmg: "his two boy-servants."
[h] Nfmg: "the young lad."
[i] Nfmg: "with a heart at ease."
[j] VNL: "and Abraham said: The Memra of the Lord will prepare for himself (text: "for me") the lamb, and if not you will be the lamb for the burnt offering, my son. And the two of them walked together with a heart at ease"; P: "And Abraham said: From before the Lord a lamb has been prepared for the burnt offering, my son; and if not you are the lamb. And the two of them walked together with a perfect heart, Abraham to slaughter and Isaac his son to be slaughtered."
[k] Nfmg: "the Memra of the Lord will prepare the lamb for himself"; = VNL.
[m] Nfmg: "a heart at ease"; = VNL.
[n] PVNL: "and Abraham stretched out his hand and took the knife to slaughter his son Isaac. Isaac answered and said to his father Abraham: Father, tie my hands well, lest, in the hour of my distress I (lit.: "we") confound you, and your offering be found unfit and I (lit.: "we") be thrust down to the pit of destruction in (lit.: "for") the world to come. The eyes of Abraham were scanning the eyes of Isaac and the eyes of Isaac were scanning the angels

Notes, Chapter 22

[3]"Mount Moriah." HT: "Moriah." See 2 Chr 3:4.
[4]"(arrive there) and we will pray." HT: *nšthw*; RSV: "and worship." For Nf's translation of this HT verb in certain contexts, see the note to 18:2. When the action is done directly to God, Nf paraphrases in a variety of ways: "pray," as here (22:5), "gave thanks and glorified," Gen 24:26, 48. In 24:52, in keeping with the presence of *'rsh* in the HT, we have: "gave thanks and glorified according to the custom of the land." See note to 24:52, also to 23:12 and 48:12.
[5]"with a perfect heart." Addition to HT's "went together." See also Pal. Tg. Exod 19:8, Deut 6:4. The Aramaic phrase seems to mean "with complete, undivided, devotion to God," the opposite of a divided heart; see Nf Gen 22:14. See McNamara, 1972, 121f. and note to Ps.-J. (vol. 1B in this series).
[6]"otherwise you will be . . . burnt offering"; an addition to the HT, and verbatim as the Hebrew paraphrase of the HT in *Gen. R.* 56,4.

father Abraham:[7] *"Father, tie me well lest*[o] *I kick*[p] *you and your offering be rendered unfit and we be thrust down into the pit of destruction in the world to come." The eyes of Abraham were on the eyes of Isaac and the eyes of Isaac were scanning the angels on high.*[g] *Abraham did not see them. In that hour a Bath Qol*[8] *came forth from the heavens and said: "Come, see two singular persons who are in my world; one slaughters and the other is being slaughtered. The one who slaughters does not*[r] *hesitate and he who is being slaughtered stretches out his neck."* 11. And the angel of the Lord called to him from the heavens and said: "Abraham, Abraham."[s] And he said: "HERE I AM." 12. And he said: "Do not stretch out your hand against the boy[t] and do nothing to him, because now I know that you fear *before the Lord* and that you have not withheld your son, your only son, from me." 13. And Abraham raised his eyes and saw, and behold a ram <entangled>[u] in *the tree*[9] by his horns. And Abraham went and took the ram and offered it as a burnt offering in place[w] of his son. 14. And Abraham *worshiped and prayed*[x][10] in the name *of the Memra of*

Apparatus, Chapter 22

on high. Isaac was seeing them, (P +: and) Abraham did not see them. At that time (lit.: "hour") the angels on high (P: a *bath qal*) came out and said to one another: Come, see two unique righteous ones who are in (VNL: within) the world. The one slaughters and the other is being slaughtered. The one who slaughters does not hesitate (P: "has no pity") and the one who is being slaughtered stretches out his neck."

[o] Nfmg: "in the hour of my distress I (lit.: "we") move convulsively and I (lit.: "we") confound you and our offering be found unfit and I (lit.: "we") be made guilty from you in the hands of heaven. The eyes of Isaac."

[p] The form of the verb in first person pl. ("we").

[q] Nfmg: "Isaac saw them"= PVNL.

[r] Nfmg: "righteous ones in (lit.: "to," "for") the world; one slaughters and the other is being slaughtered. The one who slaughters has no pity; the one who is being slaughtered"; = P.

[s] PVNL: "And the angel of the Lord called to him from heaven and said: Abraham, Abraham. Abraham answered in the language of the sanctuary and said: HERE I AM" (in Hebrew); Nfmg: "Abraham answered in the language of the sanctuary and said";= PVNL.

[t] Nfmg: "against the young lad."

[u] Missing in text; supplied from Nfmg.

[w] Nfmg: "instead of."

[x] VNL = Nf, with following variants: "and said: You are the Lord, who sees and is not seen. I beseech by the mercy (that is) before you Lord ... the time that you said.... I immediately arose early in the morning and put your command into practice and fulfilled the command of your mouth. And now, I beseech (by) the mercies that are before you Lord God: when the sons of Isaac enter the hour of distress, remember in their favor the binding of Isaac their father and forgive and remit their debts and redeem them from every distress. For the generations that are to arise after him will say: On the mountain of the sanctuary of the Lord Abraham offered his son Isaac, and on this mountain, which is the sanctuary, there was revealed to him the Glory of the Shekinah of the Lord"; P = VNL save: "and Abraham worshiped and prayed there ... and said: You, O Lord God, are he ... in the hour that you said: Offer Isaac your son before me (text: him). Immediately I arose early in the morning and put your command into practice and kept your decree ... forgive and remit their debts and save them from every tribulation. Indeed those future

---

Notes, Chapter 22

[7]See notes 22-33 and 44 to Ps.-J. (vol. 1B in this series) (also B. Barry Levy, 1, 1986, 163f.) for this midrash.

[8]"Bath Qol"; see Introduction, p. 39.

[9]"(entangled) in the tree"; HT (RSV): "caught in a thicket" (*b-sbk*). Same rendering in Onq. and Ps.-J. See note 39 to Ps.-J. (vol. 1B in this series) and B. Barry Levy, 1, 1986, 164–166.

[10]"Ab. worshiped and prayed." HT: "Ab. called the name of that place. . . ." See note 40 to Ps.-J. (vol. 1B in this series).

the Lord and said: "I beseech by the mercy*ʸ* that is before you O Lord:—*everything is manifest and known before you*—that there was no division in my heart the first time*ᶻ* that you said to me to offer*ᵃᵃ* my son Isaac, to make him dust and ashes before you;*ᵇᵇ* but I immediately arose early in the morning and diligently put your words into practice with gladness and fulfilled your decree.*ᶜᶜ* And now, when*ᵈᵈ* his sons are in the hour of distress you shall remember the Binding of their father Isaac, and listen to the voice of their supplication, and answer them and deliver them from all distress, so that the generations to arise after him may say: 'On the mountain of the sanctuary of the Lord Abraham sacrificed his son Isaac, and on this mountain *the glory of the Shekinah of* the Lord *was revealed to him.'*" 15. And the angel of the Lord called from the heavens to Abraham a second time. 16. And he said: "*In the name of his Memra* I have sworn,"[11] says the Lord, "because you have done this thing and have not withheld your son, only son, 17. I will certainly bless you and multiply *your sons* as the stars of the heavens and as the sand that is upon the sea shore. And *your sons*[12] will inherit the *cities* of their enemies. 18. And because you listened to the voice of his *Memra,*[13] in your *descendants* will all the nations of the earth be blessed." 19. And Abraham returned*ᵉᵉ* to his young men and they arose and went together to Beersheba; and Abraham dwelt in Beersheba.*ᶠᶠ* 20. And it came to pass after these things that it was related to Abraham saying: "Behold, Milcah also has borne children to your brother Nahor: 21. Uz his firstborn, his brother Buz and Kemuel, the father of Aram, 22. Chesed, Hazo, Pildash, Jidlaph, and Bethuel." 23. And Bethuel begot Rebekah. These eight Milcah bore to Nahor, the brother of Abraham. 24. And his concubine,*ᵍᵍ* whose name was Reumah, she also bore Tebah, Gaham, Tahash, and Maacah.

Apparatus, Chapter 22

generations that are to arise, will say: On the Mount of the Sanctuary of the Lord Abraham offered his son Isaac and upon this Mount was the glory of the Shekinah of the Lord revealed to him."

ʸ Nfmg: "You are the Lord who sees and is not seen; everything"= PVNL.

ᶻ Nfmg: "in the hour that you said"= P.

ᵃᵃ Nfmg: "Offer"= P.

ᵇᵇ Nfmg: "your son before him and in number (?; read: "immediately") I arose early"; cp. P.

ᶜᶜ Nfmg: "your commandment and kept your decree"= P.

ᵈᵈ Nfmg: "I beseech by the mercies before you, O Lord God. When the sons of Isaac enter into the hour of their distress, remember in their favor (lit.: for them) the binding of Isaac their father, and forgive and remit their debts and save them from every tribulation. Indeed those future generations that are to arise will say: On the Mount of the Sanctuary of the Lord Abraham offered"; = P almost verbatim.

ᵉᵉ Nfmg: "went back."

ᶠᶠ Nfmg: "and they walked together to the Well of Seven" ("the Beer of Sheba").

ᵍᵍ Nfmg and PVNL: "concubine" (another word).

Notes, Chapter 22

[11]"in the name of his Memra I have sworn." HT: "by myself I have sworn."

[12]"your sons." HT: "your seed."

[13]"voice of his Memra." HT: "my voice."

CHAPTER 23

1. And the life of Sarah was one hundred and twenty-seven years: the years of the life of Sarah. 2. And Sarah died in the *city of the Four Patriarchs,*[1] which is[a] Hebron, in the land of Canaan; and Abraham came to mourn Sarah and to weep over her.[b] 3. And Abraham arose from beside his dead and spoke with the sons of Heth, saying: 4. "I am *a resident* and a sojourner[2] with you. Give me a burial-possession among you so that I may bury my dead from before me." 5. And the sons of the *Hittite* answered Abraham, saying to him: 6. "Listen to us,[3] our master; you are a prince[c] *from before the Lord*[4] among us; in the best place of our graves bury[d] your dead.[5] <None of us will WITHHOLD FROM YOU[6] his grave (or hinder you) from burying your dead>."[e] 7. And Abraham arose and *saluted them according to the custom of the land*[7] of the sons of Heth.[f] 8. And he spoke with them saying: "If it *pleases* you that I bury my dead from before me, listen to me and entreat for me Ephron,[g] the son of Zohar. 9. And let him *sell* me the cave *of*

Apparatus, Chapter 23

[a] VNL: "and Sarah died in the city of the warriors, that is, Hebron, in the land of Canaan"; Nfmg: "of the men (corr. to: "of the warriors"), that is"; cf. VNL.

[b] Nfmg: "and to mourn her."

[c] Nfmg: "behold you are a lord and ruler."

[d] Nfmg: "in a good grave bury."

[e] This portion of Nf is missing at v. 6 but is found at the end of v. 11; vv. 6b–11 are repeated after v. 11. Some words of the texts are left in Hebrew, untranslated.

[f] Nfmg: "and he gave thanks and praised the people of the land before the sons of Heth."

[g] Nfmg 1°: "plead for her (*'ly*') to Ephron"; Nfmg 2°: "plead for me."

Notes, Chapter 23

[1] "City of the Four Patriarchs." MT: "*Qiryath-'Arba*," "The City of the Four." According to a Jewish tradition, it was the burial place of the four patriarchs Adam, Abraham, Isaac, and Jacob (*Gen. R.* 58,4; Jerome, *Hebr. quaest.* in Gen. 23:2, CCL 72,28).

[2] "a resident and a sojourner" (*dyr wtwtb*). HT: *gr wtwšb* (RSV: "stranger and sojourner"). The same combination occurs again in Lev 25:35, 47, where Nf renders as *gywr wtwtb*; *gr* alone occurs more often in the HT and is generally rendered in Nf as *gywr'*, "stranger," "alien," "proselyte." In Gen 15:13 *gr* alone is taken as a collective and rendered as "strangers (*gywryn*) and sojourners." The unique rendering of *gr* as *dyyr*, "resident," in 23:3 is also in Onq., and in *Gen. R.* 58,6 the Hebrew *gr* of this verse is explained through the Aramaic *dyyr*.

[3] "listen to us," *qbl mnn*, lit. "accept from us," a verb used commonly in this sense in Nf, whether in translation or free paraphrase (e.g., Gen 38:26). HT: "hear (*šm'*) us."

[4] "a prince from before the Lord." HT: "a prince of God."

[5] The Aramaic Targum of this section is given twice in Nf, the last part of v. 6 and vv. 7-11 following on the first translation of v. 11. There are but minor differences between the two texts, and Nfmg appear to both texts.

[6] "withhold from you." This is omitted in the first occurrence; it is in the second but in Hebrew (untranslated), with translation in the margin.

[7] "saluted . . . custom of the land"; HT: "bowed (*yšthw*) to the people of the land (*l'm h'rṣ*), the sons of Heth." On the translation, see note to 18:2 and note the rendering of Nfmg (in Apparatus); see also note to 22:5 and Nf 24:26, 48. In this particular instance Nf omits the translation of HT "to the people of the land." This may be through inadvertence or due to the difficulty of including it in this particular instance. B. Barry Levy (1, 1986, 167f.), however, thinks that the regular Nf idiomatic translation may be a later, secondary development and that the earlier form of the translation was more literal.

Kephelah[8] which is at the end of his field; for full money let him sell it to me among you as a burial-possession." 10. And Ephron *was dwelling* in the midst of the sons[h] of Heth; and Ephron the Hittite answered Abraham, *in the hearing* of[9] the sons of Heth, for all who were entering the gate of the city, saying: 11. "No, my lord, listen to me;[i] I give you the field, and I will give you the cave that is in it. Before the sons of the people I give it to you; bury your dead."[j] 12. And Abraham bowed down before the people of the land. 13. <And he spoke with Ephron>[k] *in the hearing* of[9] the people of the land, saying: "But if only you would listen to me. Behold, I give you the money for the field, receive (it) from me[m] and I will bury[n] my dead there." 14. And Ephron answered Abraham, saying to him: 15. "My lord, listen to me;[o] land of four hundred *selas*[10] of silver, what is that between me and you? Count (it) and[p] bury your dead." 16. And Abraham listened to Ephron; and Abraham weighed the money of which he had spoken *in the hearing* of[9] the sons of Heth: four hundred *selas*[10] of silver, current *in every place;*[q] *accepted in all commerce.*[11] 17. And the field of Ephron, which is in *Kephelah,*[12] which is before Mamre—the field and the cave that is in it and every tree that is on the face of the field in all the territory *round* about—was constituted 18. the possession of Abraham in the presence of the sons of Heth, for all who entered the gate of his city. 19. <And afterwards>[r] Abraham buried Sarah his wife in the cave of the field of Kephelah[13] which is before Mamre, that is Hebron in the land of Canaan.

Apparatus, Chapter 23

[h] Nfmg: "in the territory of the sons of."

[i] Nfmg +: "I beseech."

[j] Thus v. 11 repeated; v. 11 first time reads: "No, my lord; listen to me. I give you the field and I will give you the cave that is in it; bury your dead. Before < ... > I give it to you. Bury your dead"; Nfmg 1°: "before the sons of the people I will give it to you; go bury"; Nfmg 2°: "before the sons of my people I will give it to you. Go bury."

[k] Missing in text.

[m] Nfmg: "to do me this favor; receive it from me."

[n] Same form as first per. pl.: ("we will bury"); Nfmg: "and I will bury" (in usual form).

[o] Nfmg: "I beseech, listen."

[p] Nfmg: "between me and you what is it and bury your dead."

[q] VNL: "four hundred selas of silver, current for every money-changer's table (Latin loan word *patera*) and acceptable in all commerce" (Greek loan word *pragmateia* in Nf and PVNL); P: "current in every money-changer's table and acceptable <in> commerce"; Nfmg: "for every money-changer's table and acceptable for all"; cf. VNL.

[r] Missing in text.

Notes, Chapter 23

[8]"(the Cave of) Kephelah," *m'rt kpylh*. HT: *mkplh* (Machpelah), a proper name in Gen 23:9, 17, 19; 25:9; 49:30; 50:13. Machpelah, the proper name, is rendered as *kpylh* in Nf (23:17, "which is in Kpylh"). In some texts it appears that Nf has taken the HT to mean "double," "the Double Cave"; cf. Vulg., *spelunca duplex.*

[9]"in the hearing of ..."; as RSV; HT lit. "in the ears of."

[10]"selas"; HT: "shekels"; see Introduction, pp. 32–33, and *Gen. R.* 58,7 (on Gen 23:15): shekel in the Pentateuch means sela (view of R. Hanina).

[11]"current in every place, accepted in all commerce"; see note 8 to Ps.-J. (vol. 1B in this series); "commerce," Greek loan word *pragmateia*, also in *Gen. R.* 58:7.

[12]"which is in Kephelah." HT: "in Machpelah."

[13]"the cave (*bm'rty*) of the field of Kephelah," with slight correction of the text.

20. And the field and the cave that is in it was constituted the burial-property *s* of Abraham from the sons of Heth.

CHAPTER 24

1. And Abraham had grown old and advanced in days; and the *Memra of* the Lord had blessed Abraham in everything. 2. And Abraham said to his servant, the oldest of his house, who *was in possession* *a1* of all that he had: *b* "Place, I pray, your hand under my thigh, 3. and I will make you swear in *the name of the Memra* of the Lord, the God of the heavens, he is the God *who rules over* the earth, *c* that you will not take a wife for my son from the daughters of the Canaanites, among whom I dwell, 4. but will go to my country and to my kindred and you shall take a wife for my son, for Isaac." 5. And the servant said to him: "What if the woman is not willing to come after me to this land? Shall I then make your son return to the land from where you went forth?" 6. And <Abraham> *d* said to him: "Take care that you do not make my son return there. 7. The Lord, the God of the heavens, who led me from the house of my father and from the land of my kindred, and who spoke to me and who made a covenant *e* with me saying: 'To *your sons* I will give this land'; he will send the angel of *mercy* before you and you will take a wife for my son from there. 8. And if the woman is not willing to come after you, you are freed from this my oath, but my son you will not make return there." 9. And the servant placed his hand underneath the (sign of) *the covenant* *f2* of Abraham his master and

Apparatus, Chapter 23

s Nfmg: "which (is) in the field, which is in all the territory round about ... which is in front of <Mamre> as a burial possession."

Apparatus, Chapter 24

a VNL: "and Abraham said to his servant, the ruler of his house, the one who had control of all that was his: Put, I pray, your hand under the thigh of my covenant"; Nfmg: "ruler" (correcting *ṭlyš'* to *šlyṭ'*) = VNL.
b Nfmg: "who had control of all that he had"; cf. VNL.

c Nfmg: "God of the land."
d Missing in text.
e Nfmg +: "with an oath."
f Taking the Aramaic *qyym* (generally = "covenant") in this sense; cf. also VNL at v. 2: "thigh of the covenant"; see 49:29 and also note to v. 9.

Notes, Chapter 24

1"was in possession of," *dtpys*. HT: *hmwšl* (root *mšl*), lit. "ruled." In Nf this Hebrew verb is generally rendered by *šlṭ* (Gen 1:18; 4:7; 37:8; 45:8, 26; Deut 15:6) and also in VNL, Nfmg in Gen 24:2. It is rendered by *ršw* in Nf 3:16; Exod 21:8. See also Nf Gen 4:7 (with double translation) and note to verse.
2"underneath the (sign of) the covenant," *thwt qyymh*, taking *qyymh* (lit. "covenant") here as "sign of the covenant." HT: "under my thigh." Same rendering of this phrase in Nf (and also CTg D) in Gen 47:29. "Place hand under the thigh" (in oath-taking) occurs in Gen 24:2, 9; 47:29. Nf renders literally in 24:2. In 24:2 VNL renders: "under thee thigh of my covenant"; see Apparatus. The place of circumcision is intended, as implied in *Gen. R.* 59,11.

swore to him[g] concerning this matter. 10. And the servant took with him ten camels from the camels of his master, and all the best things *of the testament of*[h] his master;[3] and he arose and went to *the land* (of) Naharaim,[4] to the city of Nahor. 11. And he made the camels lie down outside the city, by the well of water at eventime, *at the hour* in which the women who draw water go forth. 12. And he said: "O Lord, God of my master Abraham, I pray, prepare it for me, I pray, before me this day and do favor[i] with my master Abraham. 13. And behold, *I stand* placed[5] beside the source of water, and the daughters of the people *of the land* are coming out[j] to draw water. 14. And let it be thus: the girl to whom I shall say: 'Lower, I pray, your jar that I may drink,' and who will say: 'Drink, and I will make your camels drink,' she is the one you appointed for your servant for Isaac, and in this shall I know that you have done favor[k] with my master." 15. And it happened that before he had finished speaking, behold, Rebekah—who was born to Bethuel, the daughter of Milcah, the wife of Nahor, the brother of Abraham—came out with a jar on her shoulder. 16. And Rebekah was very beautiful in appearance, a virgin; no man had known her; and she went down to the spring and she filled her jar and came up. 17. And the servant ran to meet her and said: "I pray, give me to drink[m] from your jar." 18. And she said: "Drink, my lord"; and she hastened to lower her jar over his hand and gave him to drink. 19. And when she finished giving him to drink she said: "I will fill also for your camels, until *the time*[n] they have finished drinking." 20. And she hastened to empty her jar[o] within *the feeding trough* and

Apparatus, Chapter 24

[g] Nfmg: "and he promised him by an oath concerning."

[h] VNL: "and the servant took ten camels from the camels of his master and went, and all the best (things) of the storehouse (*apothêkê*, Greek loan word) of his master with him (lit.: "in his hand"), and he arose and went to Ar(am) which is beside the Euphrates of the two rivers (or, lit.: "of Naharaim") to the city of Nahor"; P: "and all the best (things) of the storehouse (*apothêkê*; variant reading "covenant," *dywtyqy*)"; Nfmg: "storehouse" (*apothêkê*). Note two traditions regarding the exact Greek loan word: *apothêkê*: Nf, PVNL,

Nfmg, Ps.-J., *Aruk* edition, Elias Levita's *Meturgeman*; *diathêkê*, P, variant; *Gen. R.* 59,11 (citation), *Aruk* MS.

[i] Nfmg: "and do favor and truth."

[j] Nfmg: "(of the people) of the city, that go out."

[k] Nfmg +: "and truth."

[m] Nfmg: "water from your jar."

[n] Nfmg: "I will give drink until."

[o] Nfmg: "and hastened and lowered her jar"; VNL: "and she hastened and lowered her trough (read:? bucket) within the drinking-place and ran once more to the well to fill, and filled and gave to drink to all the camels."

Notes, Chapter 24

[3]"of the testament (*dyytyq'*) of his master"; HT: "of his master." The Greek loan word *diathêkê* also in (a manuscript) *Aruk* citation of verse and in *Gen. R.* 59,11. Other Pal. Tg. texts, instead of *diathêkê*, have the Greek loan word *apothêkê*, "storehouse." See McNamara, 1966A (*NT and Pal. Tg.*) 56, and 1966B (*RSO* 41, 1966) 10.

[4]"the land (of) Naharain." MT: "Aram Naharaim." See also VNL in Apparatus.

[5]"I stand placed." HT: "*nṣb* (*niṣṣab*). This double rendering of this same Hebrew word also in Nf Gen 24:43; Exod 17:9; Num 22:31; and Deut 29:9. Elsewhere Nf renders by one or other of the two Aramaic words; see Grossfeld, *Neofiti*, Gen. 24 note 12; B. Barry Levy, 2, 1987, 126f. (note to Num 22:31).

ran again[p] to the well to fill; and she filled[q] for all his camels. 21. And the man *drank* and observed her silently to see whether the Lord had made his way prosper or not. 22. And when the camels had finished the man took a ring of gold, a *teba*[6] its weight, and two bracelets for her hand,[7] ten (*selas*) of gold[8] was their weight. 23. And he said: "Whose daughter are you? Tell me,[r] I pray. Have you at home, perchance, a place for us to pass the night?"[s] 24. And she said to him: "I am the daughter of Bethuel, the son of Milcah, whom she bore to Nahor." 25. And she said to him: "We have abundant straw and fodder with us, and also a place to pass the night." 26. And the man bowed down and *gave thanks and glorified*[9] *the name of the Lord.*[t] 27. And he said: "Blessed be the Lord, the God of my master Abraham, who has not forsaken favor and truth with my master. As for me, the Lord[u] led me on the road to the house of my master's brethren." 28. And the maiden ran to the house of the *brethren* of her mother's *master* and told all these things. 29. And Rebekah had a brother and his name was Laban; and Laban ran to the man outside at the spring. 30. And when he saw the ring and the bracelets on his sister's arms, and when he heard the words of Rebekah, his sister, saying: "Thus did the man speak with me," he came to the man; and behold he was standing by the camels beside the spring.[w] 31. And he said to him: "Come in, blessed of the Lord. Why, I pray, are you standing outside? *Behold*, I have cleansed[x] the house of *foreign worship*[10] and (there is) room for the camels." 32. And the man went into the house; and he[y] loosed[z] the camels,[aa] and gave straw and fodder to the camels and water to wash his feet and the feet of the men who were with him. 33. And they set before him to eat, but he said: "I will not eat until I speak[bb] my words." And he

Apparatus, Chapter 24

[p] Nfmg: "once more" = VNL.
[q] Nfmg: "and she gave to drink" = VNL.
[r] Nfmg: "show me."
[s] Nfmg: "as a stall" (or: "as a resting-place").
[t] Nfmg: "before the Lord."
[u] Nfmg: "the Memra of the Lord."
[w] Nfmg +: "of water."
[x] Nfmg: "and I have cleansed the house; I have cleansed (it?) for (worship?). I have set it in order from three harsh services that stood within it: from

foreign worship, from the revealing of nakedness and from the shedding of innocent blood; and I have arranged a place for the camels."
[y] I.e., Laban.
[z] Nfi +: "the muzzles of."
[aa] Nfmg: "the muzzles of the camels which were muzzled during the travel so that they would not eat of what was stolen."
[bb] Nfmg: "until there be spoken."

Notes, Chapter 24

[6]"*teba*" HT: *beqa'*, i.e., a half-shekel; in Pentateuch only here and in Exod 38:26.

[7]"for her hand" (sing.); HT: "for her hands" (plur.).

[8]"ten (selas?) of gold." *mn 'srh ddhb*. Nf here reproduces the ambiguity of the HT: *'srh zhb*, lit. "ten of gold," generally understood to be shekels of gold. The material intended is sometimes omitted after *'srh* and is supplied by translators and expositors. The same ambiguous words, *'srh zhb*, occur again in Num 7 (thirteen times) and is generally understood and rendered as "ten shekels of gold." Nf, however, paraphrases as: "its weight: ten selas of silver was its make and it was of gold" (Nf Num 7:14, 26, 32, 38, 44, 50, 56, 62, 68, 74, 80; cf. also 84, 86). See also Grossfeld, *Neofiti*, Gen 24 note 18; B. Barry Levy, 2, 1987, 70 (note to Nf Num 7:14).

[9]"gave thanks and glorified the name of the Lord." HT: "worshiped (*ysthw*) the Lord"; see note to 22:5.

[10]"cleansed ... of foreign worship." HT: "I have prepared the house."

said: "Speak."^{cc} 34. And he said: "I am the servant of Abraham. 35. And the Lord has^{dd} blessed my master abundantly and he has grown powerful, and he has given him sheep and oxen and silver and gold and men-servants and maid-servants and camels and he-asses. 36. And Sarah, the wife of my master, bore a son^{ee} to my master after *he had grown old,*^{ff} and he has given him all that he has. 37. And my master made me swear saying: 'You shall not take a wife for my son from the daughters of the Canaanites, in whose land I dwell. 38. But you shall go to the house of^{gg} my father and to my kindred, and you shall take a wife for my son, *for Isaac.*' 39. And I said to my master: 'What if the woman will not come after me?'^{hh} 40. And he said to me: '<The Lord>^{ii} before whom *I have served in truth*[11] shall send his angel *before you,*[12] and will make your journey prosper and you shall take a wife for my son from my kindred and from the house of my father. 41. Then you will be free from my oath when you come^{jj} to my kindred; and if they do not give her to you, you are free from my oath.' 42. And I came this day to the spring and I said:^{kk} *'I beseech, by the mercy that is before you,*[13] O Lord, God of my master Abraham; if there is good pleasure before you to make prosper my road on which I walk, 43. behold *I will stand* placed[14] by the spring of water, and behold the maiden who comes out to fill her jar, and when I say to her: 'Give me a little water from your jar to drink'; 44. she says to me: 'Drink, you; and I will also fill for your camels,' she^{mm} is the wife which the Lord has appointed for my master's son.' 45. I had not finished speaking with my heart when, behold, Rebekah came out with her jar on her shoulder, and lowered it to the spring^{nn} and filled (her jar); and I said to her: 'Give me to drink, I pray.' 46. And she hurried^{oo} and lowered her jar from above her (shoulder) and said: 'Drink, and I will also give your camels to drink.' And I drank and she gave the camels to drink also. 47. And I asked her and said *to her*: 'Whose daughter are you?' And she said: 'The daughter of Bethuel, the son of Nahor, whom Milcah bore him'; and I placed the ring on her nose and the bracelets on her arms. 48. And I

Apparatus, Chapter 24

^{cc} Nfmg: "(until) I speak my words; and he (Laban) said to him: Speak." (For "I speak" the form used is that of first per. pl.)

^{dd} Nfmg: "the Memra of the Lord."

^{ee} In text regular for: *br*; Nfmg: *byr.*

^{ff} Nfmg: "after she had grown old."

^{gg} Nfmg: "(but) go."

^{hh} Nfmg: "the maiden is not prepared to come after me."

^{ii} Missing in text; Nfmg: "the Memra of the Lord."

^{jj} Nfmg: "you enter into."

^{kk} Nfmg: "this (day) by the spring of water and said."

^{mm} Nfmg: "and I will also give your camels to drink; she."

^{nn} Nfmg: "to the waters."

^{oo} Nfmg: "and she hastened."

Notes, Chapter 24

[11]"whom I have served in truth." HT: "the Lord before whom (or: before whose face) I have walked."

[12]"before you." HT: "with you."

[13]"I beseech, by the mercy that is before you." Additional paraphrase, introducing direct discourse of God. See note to 15:2; also 18:3; 20:4.

[14]"stand placed." See note to 24:13.

bowed down and *gave thanks and glorified*[15] *the name of* the Lord, and *prayed before* the God of my master Abraham who led me in the way of truth to[pp] take the daughter of my master's brethren for his son. 49. And now, if *it is in your good pleasure*[16] *to* do favor and goodness[qq][17] with my master, tell me; and if not, tell me and I will turn aside to[rr] the right or to the left." 50. And Laban and Bethuel answered and said: "From *before* the Lord has the thing gone forth; we can speak with you neither good nor evil.[ss] 51. Behold, Rebekah is before you; take her and go, and let her be wife to my[tt] master's son as the Lord has spoken."[uu] 52. And when the servant of Abraham heard their words *he gave thanks and glorified*[18] *the name of* the Lord,[ww] *according to the custom of the land.* 53. And the servant took out objects of silver and objects of gold and clothes, and gave them to Rebekah; and *a gift* he gave to her brothers and to her mother. 54. And they ate and drank, he and the men who were with him, and they passed the night there>. And they arose in the morning and said: "Send me to my master." 55. And her brother and her mother said: "Let the maiden remain with us *two* days or ten *days,*[xx][19] and after that she can go." 56. But he said to them: "Detain me not, now that the Lord has prospered my journey. Send me forth and I will go to my master." 57. And they said: "Let us call the maiden and ask her own mouth." 58. And they called Rebekah and said to her: "Will you go with this man?" And she said: "I will go." 59. And they sent forth Rebekah their sister and her nurse,[yy] and the servant of Abraham and his men.[zz] 60. And they blessed Rebekah and said to her:[a] *"Truly, until now*[20] you were our sister, *but from now onward, you go and cleave to him, to the pious man; and from*

Apparatus, Chapter 24

[pp] or "fidelity."

[qq] Nfmg: "and now if you do favor and truth."

[rr] Nfmg: "show (me) and I will turn aside unto."

[ss] Nfmg: "the thing has been determined, I cannot speak with you good or good."

[tt] HT: "your (master's son)."

[uu] Nfmg: "the Memra of the Lord has spoken."

[ww] Nfmg: "before the Lord."

[xx] Nfmg: "a complete year or ten months (of) days"; perhaps an error for: "the days of a complete year or ten months"; cf. Ps.-J.

[yy] Nfmg: "and the maiden and teacher (or: "nurse," *paidagôgos*, Greek loan word) and Eleazar the servant."

[zz] Nfmg: "the men who were there."

[a] P: "and they blessed Rebekah and said to her: Our sister, you are parting from us and going to cling to righteous men and you are a righteous woman, from you shall arise thousands and myriads of holy angels and the descendants of your sons shall inherit the gates of their enemies"; Nfmg: "they said to her: Until now you have been our sister; now you go to be joined to that righteous man. May there be good pleasure (= may God grant) that from you there come forth thousands and myriads of righteous multitudes."

Notes, Chapter 24

[15]"gave thanks and glorified." HT: "worshiped" (*'šthwh*). See v. 26 above and note to 22:5.

[16]"if it in your good pleasure." HT (RSV): "if you will deal loyally and truly with my master."

[17]"favor and goodness," *ḥsd wṭbw*. See detailed note in Grossfeld, op. cit., Gen. 24 note 31.

[18]"gave thanks and glorified." HT (RSV): "bowed himself (*ysthw*) to the earth before the Lord." See v. 48 and notes to 18:3 and 22:5.

[19]"two days or ten days." HT: "days (*ymym*, or dual: two days) or ten." See also note 33 to Ps.-J. (vol. 1B in this series).

[20]"truly until now. . . ." HT: "our sister, be the mother of ten thousands and may your seed possess . . . ," etc. See also *Gen. R.* 60,13.

you there will arise thousands and myriads;^b and *your sons* will inherit *the cities* of their enemies." 61. And Rebekah and her maiden rose up and mounted on camels and went after the man. And the servant took Rebekah and went.^c 62. And Isaac was coming *from the sanctuary of Shem*[21] *the Great*, to *the well over which was revealed*[22] *the One who sustains every age.*^d And he was dwelling in the land of the South. 63. And Isaac had gone out *to pray*[23] in the open field at *evening time*;[24] and he raised his eyes and saw and behold, camels were coming. 64. And Rebekah raised her eyes and saw Isaac and *she let herself down* from the camel. 65. And she said to the servant: "Who is that man who is coming in^e the open field toward us?" And the servant said: "It is my master." And she took her veil and covered herself^f with it. 66. And the servant told Isaac everything that he had done. 67. And Isaac <brought her> into the tent of *Sarah* his mother; and he took Rebekah and she became his wife; and he loved her and Isaac was consoled[25] after^g Sarah his mother had died.

CHAPTER 25

1. And Abraham took another wife and her name was Keturah.^a 2. And she bore him Zimran, and Jokshan, and Medan and Midian, and Ishabak and Shuah. 3. And Jokshan begot Sheba and Dedan. And the sons of Dedan were *merchants and trad-*

Apparatus, Chapter 24

^b Nfmg: "and myriads of righteous angels and the descendants of your sons shall inherit the cities of (their) enemies"; cf. P.

^c Nfmg: "and they went."

^d PVNL: "and Isaac was coming from the school of Shem the Great to the well over which the glory of the Shekinah of the Lord was revealed"; VNL continues: "and he dwelt in the land of the South"; P continues: "and he dwelt between Hagra and Haluza"; Nfmg: "over which the glory of the

Shekinah of the Lord was revealed and he" = PVNL.

^e Nfmg: "is walking" (or "leading").

^f PVNL: "and she took a veil and veiled herself with it"; Nfmg 1°: "wrapped herself" = PVNL; Nfmg 2°: "and wrapped herself in it" = Ps.-J.

^g Nfmg: "after the death of Sarah."

Notes, Chapter 24

[21] "from the sanctuary (*byt mqdš*) of Shem." Very probably an error for "from the school house (*byt mdrš*) of Shem," as in other texts of the midrash (see also Nf 25:22). The Jewish tradition of Shem living into the time of Abraham and Isaac is found in Nf Gen 14:18 (Shem=Melchisedek) and 25:22. See also Grossfeld, *Neofiti*, Gen 24 note 40 and note 37 to Ps.-J. (vol. 1B in this series).

[22] "the well over which was revealed. . . ." MT: "Beer-la-roi"; see also 16:14; 25:11 for the same paraphrase.

[23] "to pray." HT: "to meditate," which according to rabbinic theology is to pray; see *Gen. R.* 60,14; other parallels in Grossfeld, *Neofiti*, Gen. 24 note 42, and note 40 to Ps.-J. (vol. 1B in this series).

[24] "evening time"; lit. "evening times." HT: *lpnt 'rb*. The same rendering of the same Hebrew words in Nf Deut 23:12; see also Nf Exod 14:27, "times of the morning"; HT: *lpnt bqr*.

[25] "was consoled," *w-'nḥm* (Ithp. with assimilation of *tau*?; HT: *w-ynḥm*).

Apparatus, Chapter 25

^a PVNL and Nfmg 1° +: "she is Hagar who was bound to him from the beginning"; Nfmg 2°: "she is Hagar who was tied (*qṭyr'*) to him from the start."

ers and heads of peoples.[b1] 4. And the sons of Midian were Ephah and Epher and Hanoch and Abida and Eldaah. All these were the sons of Keturah. 5. And Abraham gave all that he had to Isaac. 6. And to the sons of the concubines which Abraham had, Abraham gave a gift[2] and he sent them away from his son Isaac, while he was still alive, eastward[c] to the land of the east. 7. <And these are the days of> the years of the life which Abraham lived: one hundred and seventy-five years. 8. And Abraham ended[3] (his days)[d] and died at a good[e] old age, old and satisfied, and he was gathered to his people. 9. And Isaac and Ishmael, his sons, buried him in the cave Kephela in the field of Ephron, son of Zohar, the Hittite which is in front of Mamre, 10. the field of which Abraham had taken possession from the sons of Heth. There were Abraham and Sarah his wife buried. 11. And after Abraham had died,[f] the Lord blessed his son Isaac. And Isaac dwelt at the well at *which was revealed the One who sustains all ages.*[g4] 12. And this is the genealogy of Ishmael, the son of Abraham which Hagar, the Egyptian, the bond-woman of Sarah, bore to Abraham. 13. And these are the names of the sons of Ishmael, by their names, according to their genealogies: Nebaioth the firstborn of Ishmael and Kedar and Adbeel and Mibsam, 14. and Mishma and Dumah and Massa, 15. and Hadad and Tema, Jetur, Naphish and Kedemah. 16. These are the sons of Ishmael and these are their names according to their villages and encampments,[h] twelve chiefs according to their peoples.[h] 17. And these are the years of the life of Ishmael, a hundred and thirty-seven years; and he ended (his days)[5] and died and was gath-

Apparatus, Chapter 25

[b] VNL: "and Jokshan begot Sheba and Dedan. And the sons of Dedan were traders and craftsmen (*'wmnyn*) and heads of people"; HT (RSV) "Asshurim, Letushim and Leummim" (names of tribes); cf. Jerome, *Hebr. quaest. in Gen* 25,3 (CCL 72,31; PL 23,1026): "Asurim ... merchants (*negotiatores*), Latusim ... brass and iron metal beaters (*aeris ferrique metalla cudentes*), Laomim ... tribal chiefs (*phylarchous*), that is princes of many tribes and peoples." The best reading is probably that of VNL: "craftsmen, merchants." Nf and *Aruk 'mwpryn* (Ps.-J. *'mpwryn*) is a Greek loan word, *emporoi*; Nfmg: "encampments and dwellers in tents and in plains" = Onq. See also note to v.
[c] Nfmg: "to the border of."
[d] Nfmg: "and died" (lit.: "and stretched himself"); cf. Onq. + Ps.-J.
[e] "good"; by correcting text slightly; cf. Ps.-J. and Onq.; Nfmg: "in complete (health?)" or "in peace."
[f] Nfmg: "at the death of (Abraham)."
[g] Nfmg: "besides which the glory of the Shekinah of the Lord (was revealed) to him," cf. Gen 24:62, Nf and Nfmg.
[h] VNL = Nf in v. 16, except "fortresses" (Latin loan word *castra*) for "encampments" (with Nfmg, Ps.-J.).

Notes, Chapter 25

[1] "merchants, traders, and heads of peoples," *tgryn w'mwpryn wr'šy 'wmyn*. HT: *'šwrym, lṭwšym, l'wmym*; RSV: "Asshurim, Letushim, Leummim." The Aramaic translation of this text is cited in *Gen. R.* 61,5 (R. Shmuel bar Nachman) as *tgryn w'npryn wr'šy 'wmyn*; see McNamara, 1966A, 54ff.; *RSO* 41 (1966), 8f. A paraphrastic rendering of the text also known to Jerome (*Hebr. quaest.* on Gen 25:1-6), rendering "Asurim" as *negotiatores* (=traders?) and "Latusim" as *aeris ferrique metalla cudentes* (bronze- and metal-beaters), or as *malleatores*. Modern translators are not at one in the exact rendering of the first two words of the Pal. Tg.: "merchants, traders" (M. Klein); "traders, merchants" (Grossfeld).

[2] "a gift"; Greek loan word: *dôron*.

[3] "ended his days," *s'p*. HT: *w-ygw'* (root *gw'*), rendered in like manner in Nf Gen 7:21; 25:17; 35:29; 49:33; Num 17:27, 28; 20:29.

[4] "at which was revealed ... all ages." MT: "Beer-la-hai-roi." See 16:14.

[5] "ended his days"; see to v. 8.

ered to his people. 18. And they dwelt from *India* to *Haluzah,*[6] which is opposite Egypt, as you go toward Assyria. And he dwelt opposite all his brothers.[i] 19. And this is the genealogy of Isaac,[j] the son of Abraham. Abraham begot Isaac. 20. And Isaac was forty years when he took as wife Rebekah, the daughter of Bethuel the Aramaean from Paddan,[7] the sister of Laban the Aramaean. 21. And Isaac *prayed before* the Lord[k] concerning Rebekah his wife because she was barren; and the Lord answered him and Rebekah his wife conceived. 22. And the children pushed one another in her womb and she said: "If such is the *tribulation*[m] *of children,*[8] why, now, do I have children?" And she went *to the school of Shem the Great*[g][9] to beseech *mercy from before* the Lord. 23. And the Lord said to her: "Two peoples are in your womb, and two *kingdoms* from your womb will be separated; and one *kingdom* will be stronger than the other *kingdom*, and the greater will serve *before* the smaller."[n] 24. And her days were completed to bring forth, and behold there were twins within her womb. 25. And the first came forth red, all of him, like a purple cloak of hair; and they called his name <Esau.[o] 26. And afterward his brother came forth and his hand holding Esau's heel; and they called his name> Jacob. And Isaac was sixty years at the time he begot them. 27. And the boys grew[p] and Esau was a man[q] knowing the hunt, a man of the fields, and Jacob was a man per-

Apparatus, Chapter 25

[i] VNL = Nf. in v. 18, except "Assyrians" for "Assyria" (with Nfmg).

[j] VNL, Nfmg: "this is the genealogical pedigree of Isaac."

[k] Nfmg 1°: "on the Mount of worship, the place where his father bound him, on behalf of his wife"; cf. Ps.-J.; Nfmg 2°: "and the Memra of the Lord heard the voice of his prayer and (Rebekah ...) conceived."

[m] Nfmg 1°: "if the pains of childbirth are such, why should I be with child? And she went to the school of Shem the Great, beseeching and praying before the Lord"; Nfmg 2°: "(why) am I alive to have children? And she went to seek mercy from before the Lord in the school house of Shem the Great" ("of" expressed by post-biblical Hebrew word *shel*; otherwise = VNL); P: "and the children pushed one another in her womb and she said: If the pains of childbirth are like this, why, I pray, have I children. And she went to the school of Shem the Great to seek mercy from before the Lord."

[n] Nfmg: "because of the (impending) end of the kingdom of Esau, and afterwards Jacob (shall come), whose kingdom shall not be destroyed and shall not cease from him for all ages. For this reason he called his name Jacob."

[o] In v. 25 VNL = Nf; word "Esau" of 25, and 26a, omitted through homoioteleuton in Nf.

[p] Nfmg: "and the young men grew and Esau was a man of bronze thighs (cf. Ps.-J.), and he was a man of bronze thighs because he had bronze in his left thigh, likened to a sword which served him as the distinctive sign of a robber lord; (Greek loan word *lêstês*). He went out to rob the passers-by (lit.: "those who passed and returned"), and thus, in fact, did his father bless him saying: And you shall live by your sword. Jacob was a man perfect in good work, seated and serving at the school of Shem and of Eber, seeking instruction from before the Lord;" cf. Ps.-J.

[q] Nfmg: "a mighty man; he was a deceiver, and he used to test some of his hunt with his mouth; but

Notes, Chapter 25

[6]"India (*hndyn*) to Haluza." HT: "Havilah to Shur." On this identification of Havilah (identified as *hndyqy*, India) in Nf Gen 2:11 (see note to that verse); on the identification of Shur see note to 16:7.

[7]"Paddan" (Nf text *bdn*; elsewhere *pdn*); MT: Paddan-aram." Elsewhere Nf reproduces the full form of the HT place name; likewise in Nf 48:8 (even though HT has merely *pdn*).

[8]"if such is the tribulation of children why ... ," i.e., if such is the pain of being pregnant with children; paraphrasing the elliptical HT: "if (it is) thus, why this I?" Nf's paraphrase is in keeping with Jewish tradition as found in *Gen. R.* 63,6.

[9]"to the school (*lbyt mdrš*) of Shem the Great" (see 24:26 and 14:18, for the "school" or "academy" of Shem). HT: "to inquire (*ldrš*) of the Lord."

fect *in good work*; he dwelt in the *schoolhouses*. 28. And Isaac loved Esau because he used to eat from his hunt, but Rebekah loved Jacob. 29. And Jacob had cooked a dish of lentils and Esau came from the open field and was weary. 30. And Esau said to Jacob: "Give me to eat, I pray, from this red dish because I am weary"; because of this his name was called Edom. 31. And Jacob said: "Sell me, now, your birthright." 32. And Esau said: "Behold, I go to die and of what use is my birthright to me?" 33. And Jacob said: "Swear to me this day";*r* and he swore*s* to him and sold his birthright to Jacob. 34. And Jacob gave bread and a dish of lentils to Esau and he ate and drank and rose and went his way;*t* and Esau despised his birthright, *and <made denial>*u *concerning the vivification*w[10] *of the dead and denied*x *the life of the world to come.*

CHAPTER 26

1. And there was a famine in the land besides the first famine that occurred in the days of Abraham. And Isaac went to Abimelech, the king of[1] the Philistines, to Gerarah.[2] 2. And the Lord*a was revealed* to him and said: "Do not go down to

Apparatus, Chapter 25

Rebekah loved Jacob because he was meek (lit.: "meekness") and examined the teaching of the Law in the school"; probably originally a paraphrase of v. 28.
r Nfmg: "swear to me by an oath (to)day."
s Nfmg: "and he swore" (a different word).
t P: "And Jacob gave food and a dish of lentels to Esau and he ate and drank; (text continues with

PVNL) and he arose and went and Esau (missing in VNL) despised his birthright and blasphemed concerning his portion of (P: for) the world to come and denied the vivification of the dead."
u "made denial" added from Nfmg.
w Nfmg: "and denied the vivification of the dead."
x Nfmg: "and he blasphemed concerning the life of the world (to come)."

Notes, Chapter 25

[10]"made denial concerning the vivification . . ."; additional to the HT "he despised his birthright"; see Grossfeld, *Neofiti*, Gen. 25 note 21.

Apparatus, Chapter 26

a Nfmg: "the glory of the Shekinah of the Lord."

Notes, Chapter 26

[1]"king of . . . ," *mlk'hwn*, for usual *mlkhwn*; alef used to represent vocal shewa?; cf. Golomb, 1985, 51.
[2]"Gerarah"; Nf retains the Hebrew *he locale* of "Gerar," with final *-h*, or the accusative of direction, while at the same time prefixing the preposition "to" (*lamed*). Nf may have misunderstood the original purpose of the *he locale*. We have other examples of the retention of the accusative of direction in Nf in Gen 26:2 ("to Egypt," *l-mṣrymh*); 31:26; 33:17 (possibly; "to Sukkothah"); 35:6 ("Luzah," without initial preposition *lamed*); 37:25 ("Gileadah"); 46:28 ("Goshenah").

Egypt;[3] dwell in the land which I will say to you. 3. Stay in this land and I, *in my Memra,*[b] will be with you and I will bless you; because to you and to *your sons*[c] I will give all these lands and I will fulfill the oath which I swore to Abraham your father. 4. And I will multiply you[d] like the stars of the heavens and I will give to your sons[e] all these lands; and in *your merit*[4] will all the nations[f] of the earth be blessed, 5. because of the fact that Abraham listened to the voice *of my Memra* and kept my charge, my precepts[g] and my covenant, and *the ordinances* of my judgments."[h][5] 6. And Isaac dwelt[6] at Gerar. 7. And the people of the place asked about his wife and he said: "She is my sister"; because he was afraid to say she was his wife, lest the people of[i] the land should kill him[7] on account of Rebekah, because she was very beautiful.[8] 8. And it happened that, having passed many days there, Abimelech, the king of the Philistines, watched attentively[j] by the window[9] and saw, and behold[k] Isaac was playing with Rebekah, his wife. 9. And Abimelech called Isaac and said: "Truly, she is your wife; and how have you said: 'She is my sister?'" And Isaac said to him: "Because I said: 'Let me not die'[m] because of her.'" 10. And Abimelech said: "What is this you have done to us? Behold, for very little[10] one *of the young men*[11] could have had intercourse with your wife and you would have brought *great sins*[n][12] upon us." 11. And Abimelech commanded all the people, saying: "Whoever draws near[o] this man and his wife shall certainly be killed." 12. And Isaac sowed in

Apparatus, Chapter 26

[b] text: "in the Memra."

[c] Nfmg: "and to the descendants of your sons."

[d] Nfmg: "the descendants of your sons."

[e] Nfmg: "to the descendants of your sons."

[f] Nfmg: "in the descendants of your sons all the nations."

[g] Nfmg: "my commandments."

[h] Nfmg: "and the instruction of my Law."

[i] Nfmg: "his sons" (or: "the sons of the").

[j] VNL: "watched."

[k] Nfmg: "by the window and saw (*ḥm'*; Nf: *ḥz'*), and behold."

[m] Nfmg: "be killed because of."

[n] VNL for v. 10 = Nf, but with: "a great sin" (lit.: "debt"); Nfmg: "a great sin" = VNL; P: "behold for very little one of the young men could have used (= have intercourse with) your wife."

[o] Nfmg: "anyone who draws near."

Notes, Chapter 26

[3]"to Egypt" (*mṣrymh*, with *he locale*); see note to 26:1.

[4]"in your merit"; HT: "in your seed"; see note to 12:3. In Nf 12:5 and 28:14 "in you" of HT is rendered by "in your merit."

[5]"ordinances of my judgments" (*sdry dyyny*); HT (RSV): "my laws" (*twrty*); sole occurrence of "my laws" (*twrty*) in Genesis. Nf renders the Hebrew word (in plur.) in the same fashion in Exod 16:28.

[6]"dwelt" (*šry*). The HT: *yšb* can mean "to dwell" or "to sit." Unlike other Tgs., Nf renders by *šry* when the former is meant; by *ytb* when the HT is understood as meaning "to sit."

[7]"lest they kill him"; HT: "lest they kill me."

[8]"very beautiful"; HT: "beautiful"; addition of "very" perhaps through the influence of 24:16.

[9]"by (*'l*) the window"; HT: *b'd*, which here is best understood as "from" (RSV: "out of"); elsewhere it generally means "on behalf of," and the Tgs. render it by *'l*.

[10]"for very little"; HT: *km'ṭ* (RSV: "only"); this is the sole occurrence of the word in the Pentateuch.

[11]"one of the young men"; HT: "one of the people."

[12]"great sins"; HT: *'šm* (RSV: "guilt"); only here and in Num 5:7-8 (where in 5:7 Nf retains the Hebrew word and in 5:8 renders as "guilt"), in the sense of "guilt," "compensation," "satisfaction for injury." Elsewhere in the Bible *'šm* means "guilt offering," and Nf retains the Hebrew word.

that land and gathered in that year a hundredfold *in grain.*[13] And the Lord[p] *protected and* blessed him. 13. And the man became powerful and went on growing powerful until such time as he was very powerful. 14. And he had possessions in sheep and possessions in oxen and an enlarged retinue.[q] And the Philistines were jealous of him. 15. And all the wells that the servants of his father had dug, they sealed them up and filled them with earth. 16. And Abimelech said to Isaac: "Go away[r] from us; you are more powerful than we by far." 17. And Isaac went away from there and encamped in the valley of Gerar and dwelt there. 18. And Isaac returned to dig the wells of water that they had dug in the days of Abraham his father, and which the Philistines had sealed up after Abraham had died.[s] And he called them by the names with which his father had called[t] them. 19. And the servants of Isaac dug in the valley and they found there a well of spring water.[14] 20. And the shepherds of Gerar quarreled with the shepherds of Isaac saying: "The waters are ours." And he called the name of the well Esek, because they quarreled with him. 21. And they dug another well and they also quarreled about it.[u] And he called its name Sitnah. 22. And he went away from[w] there and dug another well and they did not quarrel about it;[x] and he called its name Rehoboth and said: "Because now the Lord has made room for us and we have made ourselves *strong* in the land."[y] 23. And he went up to Beersheba.[z] 24. And the Lord[aa] *was revealed* to him that night and said: "<I>[bb] am the God of Abraham your father. Fear not,[cc] I am with you and I will bless you and multiply your *sons* for the *merits* of Abraham, my servant."[dd] 25. And he built there an altar and *prayed*[ee] in the name of the *Memra* of the Lord and spread his tent there. And the servants of Isaac dug a well there. 26. And Abimelech came[ff] to him from Gerar with *a company* of his friends[gg][15]

Apparatus, Chapter 26

[p] Nfmg: "the Memra of the Lord."
[q] Nfmg: "and flocks and many servants."
[r] Nfmg: "go from."
[s] Nfmg: "after the death of (our) father."
[t] Nfmg: "with which he called them."
[u] Nfmg: "and they disputed likewise about it."
[w] Nfmg: "and he moved from."
[x] Nfmg: "and otherwise they did not dispute."
[y] Nfmg: "the Memra of the Lord (has made room for) us and we have increased."

[z] Nfmg: "the Well of Sheba."
[aa] Nfmg: "the Memra of the Lord."
[bb] Missing in text.
[cc] Nfmg: "Fear (not), my Memra is at your aid and I will bless you and increase the descendants of your sons."
[dd] Nfmg: "your father."
[ee] Nfmg: "and worshiped."
[ff] Nfmg: "went."
[gg] Nfmg: "his companions."

Notes, Chapter 26

[13]"(a hundredfold) in grain"; addition to the HT: "a hundred measures" (*š'rym*, with *shin*). Nf may be giving a double translation of the Hebrew consonants *s'rym*: (1) =measures (with *shin*); (2) *s'rym=śe'orim*, with *sin*, "barley," or grain in general. See Jerome, *Hebr. quaest.*, in Gen 26:12 (CCL 72,32): *inuenit in anno illo centuplum hordei*, "a hundredfold of barley."

[14]"spring water" (water of a source); HT: "living (=running) water"; same rendering of Hebrew words in Nf Lev 14:5, 16; 15:13; Num 19:17.

[15]"a company of his friends"; HT (RSV): "Ahuzzath his adviser." Nf takes the proper name as a common noun. Thus also Tg. Onq. R. Nehemiah in *Gen. R.* 64,9 on this verse cites an Aramaic text identical with Nf. See also Jerome, *Hebr.*

and Phicol the commander of his army. 27. And Isaac said to them: "Why have you come to me if you hate me and have sent me away from you?" 28. And they said: "We have truly seen that the Lord was with you [hh] and we have said: 'Let there be now, we pray, an oath between us and you and we will establish [16] a covenant with you, 29. that you will do us no evil, just as we do not draw near you and as we have done [ii] good things [jj] to you and have sent you away in peace. You are *from now* the blessed of the Lord.'" 30. And he made a feast [kk] and they ate and drank. 31. And they arose in the morning and swore, [mm] each man with his brother; [nn] and Isaac sent them away and they went from him in peace. 32. And it happened on that day that the servants of Isaac came and told him concerning the well which they had dug and they said to him: "We have found water." 33. And he called it Shibah; because of this, the name which *he called the well* is Beersheba [oo] to *the time of* this day. 34. And Esau was forty years old when he took as wife Judith, the daughter of Beeri the Hittite and <Basemath the daughter of Elon the Hittite>. [pp] 35. And they were *obstinate and overbearing of spirit* [qq][17] *and acted licentiously* [18] *in idol worship; and they did not receive instruction, either from* Isaac *or* from Rebekah. [rr]

Apparatus, Chapter 26

[hh] Nfmg: "the Memra of the Lord at your aid."

[ii] Nfmg: "that he has done."

[jj] Nfmg: "a good (thing) and have s(ent)."

[kk] Nfi: "feasts."

[mm] Nfmg: "and they swore by an oath."

[nn] Nfmg: "his companion."

[oo] Nfmg: "wherefore they called the name of the city the Well of Sheba."

[pp] Missing in text.

[qq] or: "despairing"?. (See note 17.) PVNL: "and they were rebellious and exasperating(?), worshiping in a foreign cult. And they would not receive instruction either from Isaac or Rebekah"; Nfmg: "and they were rebellious and would not receive"; = PVNL.

[rr] Nfmg: "and they embittered the lives of Isaac and Rebekah."

Notes, Chapter 26

quaest. in 26:26: *Pro Ochozath pronubo* (Och. the best man at a wedding) *in hebraeo habet* **collegium amicorum** *eius . . . amicorum turba* ("a group, a company of friends"); see also Vulg.: "Ochozath his friend."

[16]"we will establish"; HT lit. "we will cut" or "let us cut" (cf. Tg. Onq., Ps.-J.). Nf translates this Hebrew phrase in like manner throughout: Gen 15:18; 26:28; 31:44; Exod 23:32; 24:8; 34:10, 27; Deut 4:23; 5:2; 7:2; 9:9; 28:69; 29:13, 24.

[17]"obstinate and overbearing in spirit," *mpḥn rwḥ*; HT: *mrt rwḥ*, "rebellious in spirit (for Isaac and Rebekah)." RSV: "they made life bitter (for Isaac and Rebekah)." Nf actually gives a double rendering of the root *mrt* of the HT. The word translated by "overbearing (in spirit)" is but a tentative rendering of the Aramaic *mpḥn (rwḥ)*, from the root *npḥ*, "inflate." Other renderings given are "despairing," "such as quench the spirit"; this latter rendering is that of A. Díez Macho ("extinguidoras del espiritu"); see 1 Thess 5:19 and A. Díez Macho, in *Mélanges E. Tisserant*, I, Studi e Testi 231 (Città del Vaticano, 1964) 183. P has *mpḥt*, VNL *'pḥt*, which M. Klein renders as "exasperating." Sokoloff, 1990, 355, renders Nf as "causing distress".

[18]"acted licentiously," *mgḥkn*. Nf uses the verb *gḥk* usually as a translation of HT *ṣḥq*, a term with a variety of meanings, e.g., "to laugh," "play." Here in Nf probably "playing" in a sexual sense is intended; cf. also Nf Gen 22:9. See B. Barry Levy, 1, 1986, 177f. Sokoloff, 1990, 126, understands it here as "bowing down in idolatry" (as also in Nf Exod 32:6 and Frg. Tg. Gen 21:9).

CHAPTER 27

1. And it came about that Isaac grew old and his eyes were dim so that he could not see; and he called Esau, his older son, and said to him: "My son!" And he said to him: "Here *a* I am." 2. And he said: "Behold, I pray, I have grown old; I do not know the days of my death. *b* 3. And now, I pray, take your arms, *c* your quiver and your bow and go out into the open field and hunt game for me. 4. And make for me dishes such as I like and bring them to me and I will eat, so that my soul may bless you before I die." 5. And Rebekah was listening when Isaac spoke with Esau, his son. Esau went out into the open field to hunt game to take back. 6. And Rebekah said to Jacob: "Behold, I heard *the voice of* your father speaking with Esau your brother saying: 7. 'Bring me game and make me dishes and I will eat and bless you *d* before the Lord, before I die.' *e* 8. And now, my son, hear my voice *f* and *go where* I command you. 9. Go, I pray, to the flock and bring[1] me *g* from there two good kids and I will make of them dishes for your father just as he likes. 10. And you will bring them to your father and he will eat so that he may bless you *before the Lord* before he dies." 11. And Jacob said to Rebekah his mother: "Behold, Esau, my brother, is a hairy man and I am a man of smooth skin. 12. Perchance my father will feel me and I will be in his face as one who mocks him, and I will bring upon myself *curses* and not *h blessings.*" 13. And his mother said to him: "Let these your curses be upon me, my son. Only listen to my voice and go and bring *i* them to me." 14. And he went and took and brought to his mother and his mother made dishes just as his father liked. 15. And Rebekah took the best garments of Esau, her older son, that were *j* in the house and clothed Jacob, the younger son. 16. And the skin of the kid goat she clothed over his hands and over the smooth part of his neck; 17. and she gave the dishes and the bread which she had made *k* into the hand of Jacob her son. 18. And he came *m* to his father and said: "Father!" And he said: "HERE I AM.[2] Who are you, my son?" 19. And Jacob said to his father: "I am Esau your

Apparatus, Chapter 27

a P: "and it came about that Isaac grew old and his eyes were dim so that he could not see; and the holy spirit was taken up (or: removed) from upon him so that Jacob might receive the order of the blessings. And he called Esau his elder son and said to him: My son. And he said to him: Behold, here I am"; cf. Ps.-J.; Nfmg: "Esau answered and said: Behold (here I am)."

b Nfmg: "I know not the day of my death."

c Nfmg: "and now, fetch, I pray, your arms."

d Nfmg: "dishes and we (prob. = "I") will bless you."

e Nfmg: "We are (prob. = "I am") dying."

f Nfmg: "in (or: "for") what I."

g Nfmg: "and take."

h Nfmg: "instead of."

i Nfmg: "and take (them)."

j Lit.: "was"; Nfmg: "(most) desirable (garments) that were with her in the house."

k Nfmg: "the food that she had made."

m Nfmg: "and he entered."

Notes, Chapter 27

[1]"bring"; HT: "take."

[2]"Here I am," *hnny*, the HT term left in Hebrew, untranslated, without, however, any explicit reference being made to "the language of the sanctuary." While Jacob speaks here in Hebrew to Esau, the same HT term on the lips of Esau in 27:1 is translated into Aramaic (*h' 'nh*).

firstborn. I have done as you have spoken to me. I pray sit up and eat of my[n] game so that your soul will bless me." 20. And Isaac said to his son: "How, now, have you found so quickly,[o] my son?" And he said: "Because the Lord your God *prepared* it before me."[3] 21. And Isaac said to Jacob: "Draw near me, I pray, that I may feel[p] you, my son, to see if you are this my son Esau or not." 22. And Jacob drew near Isaac his father and he touched him and said: "*Behold,*[q] the voice is the voice of Jacob but *the touch[r] of* his hand is *the touch of* the hands of Esau." 23. And he did not recognize him because his hands were as the hands of Esau his brother, hairy; and he blessed him. 24. And he said: "Are you really my son Esau?" And he said: "I am." 25. And he said: "Bring (it) near[s] to me that I may eat of my son's game, so that my soul may bless you." And he brought (it) to him and he ate; and he brought him wine and he drank. 26. And his father Isaac said to him: "Draw near, I pray, and kiss me, my son." 27. And he drew near *to him* and kissed him; and he smelled the smell of his garments and blessed him and said: "*See,*[t] the smell of my son is as the smell *of incense*[u][4] *of choice perfumes*[w] *which will be offered upon the altar on the mountain of the sanctuary, that is, the mountain which he who lives and endures for all ages*[5] *has blessed.* 28. And may *the Lord* give you of *the good* of the dew that *descends* from the heavens *(and of) the choicest, and of the good of* the earth, and plenty of grain and wine[6] *and oil.*[7] 29. Let nations serve *before you*[8]—*all the sons*

Apparatus, Chapter 27

[n] Nfmg: "(seat) yourself and eat of."

[o] Nfmg: "(how) is it that you have found so readily?"

[p] Nfmg: "that I may touch (you)."

[q] Nfmg: "when the voice of Jacob is heard in prayer, Esau had no power to harm him and when he is lax in the words of the Law, the hands of Esau rule over him."

[r] VNL: "the feeling of the hands (is) the feeling of the hands of Esau."

[s] Nfmg: "draw near (or: bring it near) to me, I pray, that I may eat of."

[t] Nfmg: "come and see."

[u] Nfmg: "as the smell of the garden planted in the field of Eden which the Lord has blessed."

[w] P: "and he drew near and kissed him; and he smelled the smell of his garments and blessed him and said: See, I pray, the smell of my son (is) (P and VNL) as the smell of incense of choice perfumes which are (yet) to be offered upon the altar (VNL: "which they are to offer") on the mountain of the sanctuary (P +: "of the Lord") which the One who lives and endures has blessed"; Nfmg: "choice perfumes which are to be offered on the mountain of the sanctuary which the Memra of the Lord has blessed"; cf. VNL.

Notes, Chapter 27

[3]"before me," with HT; in text "before himself."

[4]"smell of incense." The midrash referring this verse to the Temple is also in *Gen. R.* 65,23. For the form of the midrash in Nfmg (note *u*), with reference to the Garden of Eden, see *Gen. R.* 65,22.

[5]"he who endures for all ages"; see Nf paraphrase of MT "Beer-la-hai-roi" in Gen 16:14; 24:62; 25:11. For the midrash of 27:27 see B. Barry Levy, 1, 1986, 179f.

[6]HT (RSV): "May God give you of the dew of heaven and of the fatness of the earth, and plenty of grain and wine." Nf's paraphrase is partly an explanatory midrash and may also have intended to balance both parts of the verse; "the choicest of" is not in the HT or other Tgs. of the verse; in Nf it may be slightly displaced, having originally come a little later, e.g., "of the choicest good."

[7]"oil"; not in HT; added under the influence of rather common biblical expression: "corn, new wine, and oil."

[8]The identification by Nf (and other Pal. Tgs.) of the persons involved with the sons of Esau, Ishmael, Keturah, and Laban is found also in Jewish midrashic sources, even though the exact identification is not always as in Nf, e.g., *Gen. R.* 66,4. There is a chart for rabbinic identification of groups mentioned in v. 29 in Grossfeld, *Neofiti*, note 18 to Gen 27. See also B. Barry Levy, 1, 1986, 180–182.

of Esau;[x] let *kingdoms*[y] *be enslaved to you— all the sons of Ishmael; be master and ruler*[9] over your brethren—*all the sons of Keturah*; and let them *advance and salute you*— all the sons *of Laban, who is* your mother's *brother*. Whoever[z] curses you[aa] let him be cursed, *like Balaam*[10] *the son of Beor*; and whoever blesses you[bb] let him be blessed, *like Moses the prophet, the scribe of Israel.*" 30. And when Isaac had finished blessing Jacob and Jacob had just come out from the face of Isaac his father, his brother Esau came in from the hunt. 31. And he also made dishes and brought (them) to his father and said to his father: "Arise, father, and eat from your son's game so that your soul may bless me." 32. And Isaac his father said to him: "Who are you?" And he said: "I am your firstborn son Esau." 33. And Isaac was frightened with a very great fright and said: "Who, I pray, is the one who hunted game and brought (it) to me and I ate of it all before you came to me? And I blessed him." *And*[cc] *a Bath Qol went forth from the heavens and said:*[11] "He will also be blessed." 34. When Esau heard the words of his father he made a great cry, *exceedingly* strong[12] and bitter, and he said to his father: "Bless me, also me, father." 35. And he said: "Your brother came with *great cunning*[13] and took your blessing." 36. And he said: "Behold, has his name not *rightly*[14] been called[15] Jacob? *Behold*, he has supplanted me these two times. He has taken my birthright and behold, now he has taken my blessing." And he said: "Have you not[16] a blessing left for me?"[dd] 37.

Apparatus, Chapter 27

[x] In v. 29 PVNL = Nf, save for minimal differences, found also in Nfmg.

[y] Nfmg: "all the (kingdoms)"; = PVNL.

[z] Nfmg: "those who curse you, let them be cursed like Balaam"; cf. Ps.-J.

[aa] Nfmg + "Jacob my son" = PVNL.

[bb] Nfmg: "and those who bless you will be blessed like Aaron the priest."

[cc] Nfmg: "and he will be blessed," i.e., omits intervening paraphrase of Nf.

[dd] Nfmg: "has there (not) been left a blessing for Esau?"

Notes, Chapter 27

[9]"master and ruler"; a rather common combination in Nf; here (and in 27:37) renders *gbyr* (RSV: "lord") of the HT.

[10]"(cursed) like Balaam"; not in HT; the same understanding of the text is found in rabbinic sources, e.g., *Gen. R.* 66,4; see Grossfeld, loc. cit., in chart to verse.

[11]In HT Isaac says: "I have blessed him and he shall surely be blessed." On the voice from heaven (lit. *brt qwl*, "daughter of a voice," "echo"), see Introduction (p. 39) and note 142 to text. The *Bath Qol* is also mentioned in Nf Gen 22:10; 38:27. The heavenly voice is introduced here very probably in view of the solemnity and abiding nature of the blessing given by Isaac to Jacob, indicating that Isaac's words "He will also be blessed" are uttered under divine inspiration or movement. In *Leq. Tob* on verse (Hebrew text of which is in Grossfeld) it is the Shekinah who utters the words "He will also be blessed." A comment (by R. Levi) on the verse in *Gen. R.* 67, 3 seems to imply that the Holy One blessed be He (i.e., God) made Isaac speak the words of blessing ("Let him indeed be blessed") on Jacob and according to a general principle: "when a person is righteous the Holy One blessed be He puts those (organs, e.g., mouth) over which a person is normally master out of his power"; cf. John 11:51f.

[12]"exceeding strong"; HT: "strong"; note also double rendering in Nf.

[13]"great cunning"; lit. "plenitude of wisdom"; a euphemistic rendering of HT's "cunning."

[14]"not rightly"; lit. "(not) of a truth." HT: "did he not call his name."

[15]"was called"; passive for HT, which is active in form but passive in sense.

[16]"have (you) not," *hl'*, rendering literally *hl'* (*ha-lô'*) of HT.

And Isaac answered *ee* and said to Esau: "Behold, a *master and ruler*[17] I have set him *ff* over you, and all his brothers I have set before him *gg* as slaves, and with grain and wine I have sustained him. And *from now*, what can I do for you, my son?" 38. And Esau said to his father: "Have you (but) one blessing father? Bless me, also me, father." And Esau raised *hh* his voice and wept. 39. And his father Isaac answered and said to him: "Behold, far from *the good of* the land shall your dwelling be, and far from *the good of* the dew that *falls* from the heavens above. 40. And by your sword shall you live,*ii* and *before* your brother*jj* shall you serve and be *subjected.*[18] *And when the sons of Jacob study the Law and keep the commandments,*kk* they will place the yoke of their burden*mm* upon your neck. And when the sons of Jacob abandon the commandments and withhold themselves from studying the Law,*nn* you will rule over him and shall break the yoke of servitude from off your neck.*"[19] 41. And Esau *oo* hated Jacob*pp* on account of the blessing with which his father *qq* had blessed him. And Esau said *rr* in his heart:[20] *"I am not going to do as Cain did, who killed Abel*ss* during the lifetime of his father and who turned*tt* and begot Seth and called*

Apparatus, Chapter 27

ee Nfmg: "replied."

ff Nfmg: "I have given (= set)."

gg Nfmg: "I have given (= set) as slaves to him."

hh VL: "and Esau lifted up his voice and wept"; Nfmg: "and (Esau) lifted up"; = VL.

ii PVNL: "and by your weapons shall you live and before your brothers (P +: "the Jews") shall you be enslaved (P: "shall you serve"); (P: and it shall be that) when the sons of Jacob labor in the Law and keep the commandments, the yoke of (P +: their) bondage shall be placed (P: given) upon your neck; and when the sons of Jacob withhold themselves so as not to labor (P: "from laboring") in the law, and so as not to keep (P: "from keeping") the commandments, behold, then, you shall break the yoke of their bondage from off your neck."

jj Nfmg: "the Jews shall you be enslaved"; = P.

kk Nfmg: "and keep the commandment."

mm Nfmg: "(yoke of) bondage upon the necks (read: your neck) and when the sons of Jacob withhold themselves so as not to labor in the law, and not to keep the commandments, behold, then you shall break the

yoke of their bondage from off your neck" = VNL; Nfmg: "your weapons": = PVNL.

nn Nfmg: "in the Law, and when the sons of Jacob forsake the commandments of the Law."

oo P: "and Esau harbored hatred for Jacob on account of the blessing with which his father had blessed him. And Esau said in the thoughts of his heart: As for me, I am not going to do as Cain did who killed his brother Abel during the lifetime of his father, and turned and begot Seth, and called his name according to the name of his brother. I, however, will wait until what time the days of the mourning for my father draw nigh and I will kill Jacob my brother and I (lit.: "we") will be called a killer and an heir."

pp Nfmg: "and Esau harbored hatred for Jacob"; = P.

qq Nfmg: "his father Isaac."

rr Nfmg: "(said): I am not."

ss Nfmg: "Abel his brother whom he killed in the lifetime of his father."

tt Nfmg and Nfi combined: "and his father went back" (*hdr*, Nf: *ḥzr*).

Notes, Chapter 27

[17]"master and ruler"; see note to 27:29; HT: "lord."

[18]"serve and be subjected"; double rendering of HT "serve."

[19]With this midrash on the conditions laid down for Jacob's supremacy, compare Nf (and Pal. Tg.) paraphrase of Gen 3:15. The point made in this paraphrase of v. 48 is that the supremacy of Jacob over Esau is not absolute but is linked to Jacob's (=Israel's) fidelity to the Law. There is a similar paraphrase in *Gen. R.* 67,7. On the similarity of Nf 3:15 and Nf Gen 27:40 (and of the differences between them), see B. Barry Levy, 1, 1986, 183–186.

[20]This midrash on Esau's designs on Jacob links Esau's thoughts and plans with the death of his father. A similar midrash in *Lev. R.* XXVII,11 is given (in Hebrew) in Grossfeld, *Neofiti*, note 33 to Gen 27. For a textual study and on the relation of the text to Nf Gen 4:24, see B. Barry Levy, 1, 1986, 186f.

his name according to his own name.[uu] *Behold, I will wait until what time* the days of the mourning of my father draw nigh; and I will kill Jacob my brother and *I will be called a killer and an heir."*[21] 42. And the words of Esau her older son were related to Rebekah and she sent and called Jacob her younger son and said to him: "Behold, Esau your brother *has designs*[22] *on* you, to kill you. 43. And now, my son, hear my voice and arise; *go*[ww][23] to Laban my brother, to Haran. 44. And you shall dwell with him[xx] a few days until the time that *the fury* of your brother has appeased,[24] 45. until the might of the anger of your brother turns from you[yy] and he forgets what you have done; and I will send and take[zz] you from there. Why now, I pray, should I be bereaved of both of you in one day?" 46. And Rebekah said to Isaac: "I am weary of life because of the daughters of the *Hittites.* If Jacob takes a wife from among the daughters of *the Hittites*[a] such as these, from among the daughters of the people of the land, why *I pray*, should I live?"

CHAPTER 28

1. And Isaac called Jacob and blessed him and commanded him saying to him: "Do not take a wife from the daughters of the Canaanites. 2. Arise and go to Paddan-aram, to the house of Bethuel, your mother's father, and take for yourself a wife from there from the daughters of Laban, your mother's brother. 3. And may the God *of the heavens*[1] bless you and make you *strong*[2] and multiply you; and may

Apparatus, Chapter 27

[uu] Nfmg 1°: "(according to the name) of the one killed. For I will wait until the time that (the days . . . .) draw near"; Nfmg 2°: "other books (= a variant reading): of Abel. But I will hold back until the time the days of the mourning of the death of my father arrives and, then, I will kill Jacob my brother and I will be found to be a murderer and an heir."

[ww] Nfmg: "flee"; cf. Ps.-J.
[xx] Nfmg: "and you shall reside with him (a few) days."
[yy] VNL, Nfmg: "(until) the time that the wrath of your brother turns (from you)."
[zz] lit.: "lead"; Nfmg: "and I will take."
[a] Nfmg: "of Heth."

Notes, Chapter 27

[21]"a killer and an heir"; also in *Gen. R.* 67,8 on verse; not in HT. The designations seem to depend on words of Elijah's hostile attack on Ahab (1 Kgs 21:19). In Nf it appears that Esau wants to acquire this title for himself, to become as Ahab.

[22]"has designs," paraphrasing HT *mtnhm (mitnahem)*, which in the ordinary meaning of the word ("consoles himself") is difficult in the present context. Note RSV rendering: "comforts himself by planning."

[23]"go" (perhaps due to 28:5). HT: "flee," *brh*, which Hebrew word is generally rendered as "flee" in Nf. See B. Grossfeld, "The Relationship Between the Biblical Hebrew *brh* and *nws* and Their Corresponding Aramaic Equivalents in the Targum— *'rq, 'zl, 'pk*: A Preliminary Study in Aramaic-Hebrew Lexicography," *ZAW* 91 (1979) 106–123, esp. 112.

[24]"appeased"; HT: *šwb*, lit. "return"; RSV: "turn away."

Notes, Chapter 28

[1]"God of the heavens"; Nf's constant rendering of HT: "El Shaddai": Gen 17:1; 28:3; 35:11; 43:14; 49:25; Exod 6:3; Num 24:4, 16. See Introduction, p. 35.

[2]"make you strong"; HT: "make you fruitful." Nf constantly renders "make fruitful" by "make strong"; see Gen 1:22 (with note); 8:17; 9:1; 28:3; 35:11; 47:27.

you become an assembly of a *congregation, just*[a] nations.[3] 4. And may he give to you the blessing of Abraham, to you and to *your children* with you, so that you inherit the land of your sojournings which *the Lord*[b] gave to Abraham." 5. And Isaac sent forth Jacob and he went to Paddan-aram to Laban, the son of Bethuel the Aramean, the brother of Rebekah, the mother of Jacob and Esau. 6. And Esau saw that Isaac had blessed Jacob and sent him to Paddan-aram to take to himself a wife from there when he blessed him and gave him command saying: "Do not take a wife from the daughters of the Canaanites," 7. and that Jacob had listened to his father and to his mother and had gone to Paddan-aram. 8. And when Esau saw that the daughters of the Canaanites were evil in the sight of Isaac his father, 9. Esau went to Ishmael and took to himself a wife, besides the wife he had, Mahalath, the daughter of Ishmael, Abraham's son, the sister of Nebaioth. 10. *Five miracles were worked for our father Jacob*[c] *the time that he went forth from Beersheba to go to Haran.*[4] *The first miracle: the hours of the day were shortened,*[d] *and the sun set before time because the Dibbera*[e] *desired to speak with him. And the second miracle:*[f] *the stones which our father Jacob took*[g] *and placed under his head-pillow, when he arose*[h] *in the morning he found all of them had become one stone. This is the stone which he erected as a pillar and he poured oil over the upper part of it. And the third*[i] *miracle: when our father Jacob raised his feet to go to Haran the earth shrank before him and he was found dwelling in Haran.*[j] *And the fourth miracle: the stone which all the pastors had come together to roll away*[k] *from over the mouth of the well and could not, when our father Jacob came he raised it*[m] *with one hand*[n] *and gave to drink to the flock of Laban, his mother's brother. And the fifth: when our father Jacob raised*[o] *the stone from above the mouth of the well, the well overflowed and*

Apparatus, Chapter 28

[a] Nfmg: "numerous."

[b] Nfmg: "the Memra of the Lord made."

[c] PVNL in v. 10 = Nf, apart from variants noted here.

[d] Nf as in VNL, P: "were quickened," or: "made firm" (*'ytqypw*); possibly an error for *'tqṣrw* of NL Nf.

[e] *dbyr'*; PVNL: "Dibbura" (*dbwr'*).

[f] VNL: "The second sign: when our father Jacob set out (lit.: "lifted his feet") from Beersheba to go to Haran, the earth shrank before him and he was found dwelling (correction *yhyb*: "being given," to *ytyb*) in

Haran" = third miracle of Nf and P.

[g] VNL +: "in the evening."

[h] VNL: "when he stood up."

[i] The second miracle in VNL; see note *f* above.

[j] Nfmg 1° and 2°: "(and he was found) in Haran in (missing in P) a short time" (lit.: "a small hour").

[k] Nfmg, P: "to remove."

[m] Nfmg, P: "he removed."

[n] Nfmg, P: "with one of his hands."

[o] Nfmg, P: "removed."

Notes, Chapter 28

[3]"assembly of a congregation of just nations"; a favorite phrase in Nf in translation of *qhl* of the HT; here HT: *lqhl 'mym*; RSV: "a company of peoples." See also Nf Gen 17:7; 25:11; 48:4; 49:6.

[4]This verse is the beginning of a *seder (sidra)*, i.e., a passage appointed as a synagogue liturgical reading. As observed earlier (see note to Gen 15:1), the beginnings of such passages tend to have expansive paraphrase. The present elaborate midrash of Nf (and Pal. Tgs.) on the five miracles worked for Jacob as he fled from Beersheba to Haran is also found in rabbinic sources, although not all five of them are listed in any single one of these (apart from the Pal. Tgs.). Thus in *Gen. R.* 68,10 (with miracle 1) and 68,11 (with miracle 2). For a detailed textual study of the midrash in Nf, see B. Barry Levy, 1, 1986, 187–192. Four of the five events in question are mentioned in the Bible, although not as of a miraculous nature; cf. Josh 10:12-14; comparison of Gen 28:11 and 28:18; juxtaposition of Jacob's departure and arrival in Gen 29:1; Gen 29:4-10. There is no biblical text for the fifth miracle, referred to again in Nf Gen 31:22.

came up to its mouth, and was overflowing for twenty years—all the days that he dwelt[p] in Haran. These are the five miracles that were worked with[q] our father Jacob the time he went out from Beersheba[r] to go to Haran. 11. And *he prayed*[s5] in the place, and he spent the night[t] there because the sun had *set*[6] *on him* there. And he took from the stones[u] of the place and set them under his *head*-pillow[7] and *he slept* in that place. 12. And he dreamed,[w] and behold, a ladder was fixed on the earth and its head reached *to the height of*[8] the heavens; and behold, the angels *that had accompanied him from the house of his father* ascended *to bear good tidings to the angels on high, saying:*[x] *"Come and see the pious man*[y] *whose image*[z] *is engraved*[aa] *in the throne of Glory,*[bb] *whom you desired to see."*[cc][9] And behold, the angels[dd] *from before the Lord* ascended and descended[10] *and observed him.* 13. And behold, the Lord[ee] stood beside him and said: "I am the Lord, the God of Abraham your father and the God of Isaac. The land on which *you are sleeping,* I will give it to you and to *your sons.*[ff] 14. And *your sons*[gg] will be as the dust of the earth, and you will *have power* to the west and to the north and to the south and to the east; and in *your merits* will all the families of the earth be blessed and in the *descendants* of *your*

Apparatus, Chapter 28

[p] Nfmg, P: "resided."

[q] Nfmg, P: "for (our father)."

[r] Nfmg, P: "the well of Sheba."

[s] In v. 11 P = Nf, with variants noted below; Nfmg: "and he reached the sanctuary and passed the night there because the sun had set. And he took four stones from the stones of that holy place and he placed them as a pillow and they were made into a single stone. At that time he knew that he was to take four wives and that four camps were to go forth from them and that they would be one people. And he lay down in that place."

[t] Nfmg, P: "and stayed overnight" (Afel in both).

[u] P: "from the rocks."

[w] In v. 12 PVNL = Nf, with variants noted below.

[x] P lacks: "saying."

[y] "the man," in Nf with sign of accusative; the sign lacking in Nfi, PVNL; VNL: "(see) Jacob the pious man."

[z] Greek loan word: *eikôn,* or rather its diminutive, *eikonion.*

[aa] "engraved" lacking in VNL.

[bb] Orthographical variants of Nfmg are almost identical with PVNL.

[cc] Nfmg, P: "to gaze upon."

[dd] P: "holy (angels)."

[ee] Nfmg: "an angel of mercy from before the Lord stood placed beside him."

[ff] Nfmg: "and to the descendants of your sons after you."

[gg] Nfmg: "the descendants of your sons."

Notes, Chapter 28

[5]"he prayed"; HT: "he chanced on" (RSV: "he came"); the same understanding of the Hebrew verb also in *Gen. R.* 68,9 and in other rabbinic sources.

[6]"sun had set," lit. "had sunk"; HT: "had come." Same rendering by Nf in Gen 15:12. In *Gen. R.* 68,10 a cognate Hebrew word with Aramaic one of Nf used to paraphrase "came" of HT.

[7]"head-pillow." Only Nf notes explicitly that it was a "head" pillow.

[8]"the heights of," or: "in the direction of," "toward." The same words used at v. 17 and Gen 11:11 (tower of Babel); HT: "reached to the heavens."

[9]On this midrash and its bearing on the NT, see E. G. Clarke, "Jacob's Dream at Bethel as Interpreted in the Targums and the New Testament," *SR* 4 (1974–75) 367–377. See also B. Barry Levy, 1, 1986, 192f.

[10]"angels . . . ascended"; HT: "the angels of God were ascending and descending on it" (or: "on him"; Hebrew: *bô*). Rabbinic opinion was divided as to whether the angels ascended and descended on the ladder or on Jacob; see *Gen. R.* 68,12,13 and other Jewish sources (cited in Hebrew in Grossfeld, *Neofiti,* note 16 on Gen 28).

sons.[hh] 15. And behold, I *in my Memra* am with you and shall keep you wherever[ii] you go; and I will make you return to this land, because *my Memra* shall not forsake you until I have done what I spoke to you." 16. And Jacob awoke from his sleep[jj] and said: "*Behold, truly, the glory of the Shekinah*[11] *of the Lord—it dwells* in this place and *I*, I did not know it." 17. And he was afraid[kk] and said: "How awe-inspiring is this place. This *place* is not[mm] *an ordinary place,*[12] but *a place designated before the Lord;*[13] *and this gate is the gate of prayer designated*[14] toward heaven." 18. And Jacob arose early in the morning and he took the stone he had placed as his *head-pillow*[nn] and set[oo] it as a pillar and poured oil on top of it. 19. And he called the name of that place Bethel, but[pp] Luz was the name of the city first.[qq] 20. And <Jacob>[rr] made a vow, saying: "If *the Lord*[ss] *is at my aid,*[15] and protects me on the road[tt] on which I journey[uu] and gives me bread[ww] to eat and clothes to clothe myself, 21. and (if) I return in peace[xx] to the house of my father, and (if) the Lord is for me a *redeeming* God,[yy][16] 22. (then) this stone which I set[zz]

Apparatus, Chapter 28

[hh] "families of the earth and in the descendants of your sons after you."

[ii] Nfmg: "and I will guard you in all that."

[jj] Nfmg: "(from his) agreeable (sleep)."

[kk] Verse 17 extant in P; Tg. Gen 28:17b–31:32 in CTg E; variants noted below.

[mm] Omitted through homoioteleuton; Nfmg 1°: "this is not a profane place but rather the place of the sanctuary of the Lord; and this temple corresponds to the gate of the sanctuary which is in heaven"; Nfmg 2°: "and this place is no common (Greek loan word, *idiôtês*) place, but rather is it a place set aside as a house of prayer and this gate which corresponds to (or: is directed toward) (the height)"; Nfmg 2° = CTg E; P: "and he was afraid and said: How awe-inspiring is this place. This place is not a common place but rather it corresponds to the house of prayer and this

gate a gate corresponding to (or: directed toward) the height of heaven."

[nn] Nfmg: "under the basis of" (*yswdy*) = CTg E; ("the basis of his head" = his head-pillow).

[oo] Nfmg: "and erected it" = CTg E.

[pp] CTg E: "however"; cf. Nfmg.

[qq] Nfmg: "from the beginning"; = CTg E.

[rr] Missing in text.

[ss] Nfmg: "the Memra of the Lord."

[tt] CTg E: "this road."

[uu] CTg E: "I go."

[ww] Nfi: "food" = CTg E.

[xx] Nfmg: "and brings me back in peace."

[yy] Nfmg: "the Memra of the Lord is at my aid as a Redeemer God" = CTg E.

[zz] Nfmg: "(which) I erected" = CTg E.

Notes, Chapter 28

[11] "glory of the Shekinah of the Lord"; HT: "surely the Lord." On the Shekinah, see Introduction, pp. 36–37, esp. 37.

[12] "not an ordinary place"; HT: "Behold, this." The paraphrase of Nf is intended to emphasize the awesomeness of the place.

[13] "a place designated before the Lord"; HT: "the house of God" (*beth Elohim*).

[14] "this gate is the gate of prayer designated ..."; HT: "is the gate of heaven."

[15] "at may aid"; HT: "with me." So also 31:5; 35:3. On Nf's translation of this HT text, see Introduction, p. 28.

[16] "as a redeeming God," or: "redeemer God" (*l-'l'h pryq*); HT: "as God." This paraphrase of HT: "as God" found elsewhere in Nf: Gen 17:8; Exod 6:7 (*pryq*); 29:45 (*pryq*); and as (*l-'l'h*) *prwq* in Lev 11:45; 22:33; 25:38; 26:12, 45; Num 15:41; Deut 26:17; 29:12.

as a pillar will be *a sanctuary*[17] *to the name of the Lord,*[a] *and I will separate*[b] *a tithe* of all of which you will give me, *for your name.*"

CHAPTER 29

1. And Jacob continued on his journey and went to the land[a] of the sons of the east. 2. And he saw and behold, there was a well in the field, and behold there were three flocks of sheep lying down beside it, because out of that well they used to water the flocks. And there was a great stone over the mouth of the well. 3. And when all the flocks were gathered there, they used to roll away the stone from above the mouth of the well and water the sheep and put back the stone to its place over the mouth of the well. 4. And <Jacob>[b] said to them: "My brothers, from where are you?" And they said: "We are from Haran." 5. And he said to them: "Do you know[1] Laban, the son of Nahor?" And they said: "We know him."[c] 6. And he said to them: "Is it well with him?" And they said: "It is well; and behold Rachel his daughter comes with[d] the flock." 7. And he said: "Behold, it is still high day;[2] it is not time to gather[e] the cattle together; water the sheep and go pasture them." 8.

Apparatus, Chapter 28

[a] "to the name of the Lord" not in CTg E.

[b] Lit.: "(it will separate) them"; Nfmg: "it" = CTg E.

Notes, Chapter 28

[17]"a sanctuary"; lit. "house of holiness"; HT: "a house of God." The holy place in Bethel is again identified as a temple or the Temple.

Apparatus, Chapter 29

[a] *l'r'' bny* . . . : lit.: "to the land the sons of . . ."; Nfmg, CTg E: *l'r'*, "to the land of . . ." In ch. 29 there are numerous agreements between Nfmg and CTg E, some too small to note.

[b] Missing in text; in CTg E.

[c] Verse 5 missing in Nf text; added in mg.

[d] Nfmg: "from."

[e] VNL: "it is not time to gather" (with orthographic variants from Nf, some as in Nfmg); Nfmg: "now the day is at (its) strength; there is not time to gather the flocks; water the sheep and go, pasture (them)" = CTg E.

Notes, Chapter 29

[1]"Do you know," *ḥkymyn*; HT: *(h-yd'tm.* Nf uses two different words in rendering *yd'* ("to know") of the HT, i.e., *yd'* and *ḥkm*. B. Grossfeld notes (Grossfeld, *Neofiti*, note 1 on Gen 29) that Nf's use of the root *ḥkm* for the Hebrew *yd'* is exclusively employed in cases where the Hebrew term implies more than just "knowing," as in the case of sexual knowledge (with reference to Gen 4:1, 17, 25; 19:5, 8; 38:26; Num 31:17, 18, 35) as well as in cases where "acquaintance" with somebody or something is involved, e.g., Exod 1:8; Deut 34:6.

[2]"high (day)," *tly*; HT: "big," i.e., "long." This translation is found only in Nf among the Pal. Tg. texts.

And they said: "We cannot until *the time* all the flocks are gathered together and they roll the stone from above the mouth of the well. Then we may water[f] the sheep." 9. He was still speaking with them when Rachel came with her father's sheep,[g] because she was a shepherdess.[h] 10. And when Jacob saw Rachel, the daughter of Laban, his mother's brother, and the sheep of Laban, his mother's brother, Jacob drew near and rolled[i] the stone from above the mouth of the well, and watered the sheep of Laban, his mother's brother. 11. And Jacob kissed Rachel, and raising[j] his voice he cried aloud. 12. And Jacob told Rachel that he was her father's brother, and that he was the son of Rebekah; and she ran to tell it to her father. 13. And when Laban heard the news of Jacob, his sister's son, he ran to meet him and embraced[k] him and kissed him, and brought him into the house; and he told Laban all these things. 14. And Laban said to him: "Certainly you are *as my blood-relation.*"[m][3] And he dwelt with him a month *of days.*" 15. And Laban said to Jacob: "*Behold*, you are my brother.[o] *It is not possible* that you serve *before* me for nothing.[4] Tell me,[p] now, I pray, what will your wages be?" 16. And Laban had two daughters; the name of the older was Leah and the name of the younger was Rachel. 17. And the eyes[q] of Leah were *raised in prayer,*[5] *begging that she be married to the just Jacob*; and Rachel was nice in figure[r] and beautiful in appearance. 18. And Jacob loved Rachel and said: "I will serve *before* you[s] seven years[t] for Rachel,

Apparatus, Chapter 29

[f] Nfmg: "and they (may) water" = CTg E.

[g] Nfmg: "which her father had"; = CTg E.

[h] Nfmg +: "of sheep"; = CTg E.

[i] "rolled," with Nfmg and CTg E; text: "revealed."

[j] Nfmg: "and lifting up" (lit.: "and he lifted up"); same rare form in CTg E.

[k] Nfmg: "and threw his arms around"; = CTg E.

[m] Lit.: "flesh relation"; CTg E: "indeed, you are my relation and my blood"; Nfmg: "my blood (lit.: flesh) relations" (fem.), omitting: "certainly, as."

[n] Nfmg: "and he resided beside him a month of days" = CTg E.

[o] Nfmg: "in truth you are my brother and there is not"; cf. P: "and Laban said to Jacob: Behold of a truth, you are my brother. It is not good that you serve before me . . . ," etc., as in Nf.

[p] Nfmg: "that you serve beside me for nothing; show me"; = CTg E.

[q] CTg E, PVNL: "and the eyes of Leah were tender because she used to weep and pray that she should not end up (lit.: "go up," "go away") in the lot of the wicked Esau; and Rachel was beautiful (CTg E; VNL: "pretty") in appearance and beautiful in countenance."

[r] Nfmg: "tender because she used to weep and pray that she should not end up (lit.: "go up," "go away") in the lot of the wicked Esau; but Rachel."

[s] Nfmg: "that I serve beside you"; = CTg E.

[t] Nfmg +: "of days" = CTg E.

Notes, Chapter 29

[3] "as my blood relation"; HT: "she is my bone and my flesh." Nf's use of "as" is intended to remove the metaphor.

[4] "it is not possible . . . for nothing"; HT (RSV): "should you serve me for nothing?" As elsewhere (e.g., Gen 18:14), Nf's paraphrase removes the question.

[5] "eyes of Leah . . . raised in prayer"; HT (RSV): "Leah's eyes were weak." To translate the HT literally (as RSV does) was considered disparaging to the ancestors of Israel, and for this reason the text tended to be paraphrased to avoid this lack of respect. See the variants in the Apparatus; also McNamara, 1966A, 53f.; 1966B, 7. Further texts in Grossfeld, *Neofiti*, note 7 to Gen 29.

your younger daughter." 19. And Laban said: *"* "It is more proper to give her to you *in marriage*" than to *give* her to any other man. *ˣ* Dwell with me." *ʸ* 20. And Jacob served for Rachel seven years, *ᶻ* and they were in his face as but a few days because of the love *with which he loved* her. *ᵃᵃ* 21. And Jacob said to Laban: "Give me my wife because *ᵇᵇ* the days *of my service*⁶ are completed and I will go in to *ᶜᶜ* her." 22. And Laban gathered together all the people of the place and made a feast. *ᵈᵈ* *Laban answered and said*⁷ *to them: "Behold, this pious man has dwelt among us seven years. *ᵉᵉ* Our wells have not diminished; our watering troughs*ᶠᶠ* have multiplied and now, what counsel do you give me that we may make him dwell amongst us here seven more years?"*ᵍᵍ* And they gave him deceptive counsel: to marry him*ʰʰ* to Leah instead of Rachel.* 23. And it came to pass that in the evening he took his daughter Leah and brought her *ⁱⁱ* to him; and he went in *ʲʲ* to her. 24. And Laban gave Zilpah, his maid, to Leah, his daughter, as her maid. 25. And behold, in the morning there was Leah. And he said to Laban: "What is this that you have done to me?" *ᵏᵏ* Did I not serve you for Rachel? And why, now, have you deceived me?" *ᵐᵐ* 26. And Laban said: *"It is not*ⁿⁿ* proper* to act thus *in our land*, to give the younger before the older.

Apparatus, Chapter 29

ᵘ CTg E, v. 19: "And Laban said: It is better for me to give her to you than to give her to another man. Dwell beside me."

ʷ Nfmg: "better for me to give her"; cf. CTg E.

ˣ Nfmg: "to give (her) to (another) man"; cf. CTg E.

ʸ Nfmg: "(dwell) beside me"; = CTg E.

ᶻ Nfmg +: "of days"; = CTg E.

ᵃᵃ CTg E: "because of the extent that he loved her"; Nfmg: "because of the extent that he" = CTg E.

ᵇᵇ Missing in text of Nf; supplied in Nfi.

ᶜᶜ Nfmg: "and I will be joined"; = CTg E.

ᵈᵈ P, CTg E: "And Laban gathered together all the people of the place and made a feast. Laban answered and said to the people (CTg E +: of the place): Behold this man has dwelt among us seven years of days; our springs have been blessed and our flocks of sheep have multiplied; and, now, give me counsel as to what we should do for him so that he dwell beside us (P +: yet) seven further years. And the people of the place stood up (correct P: saw) and gave him deceptive counsel and they married him to (P: "and they married off") Leah instead of Rachel"; VNL: "and Laban gathered all the people of the place and Laban made a feast. Laban answered and said to

them: These seven years I have this righteous man (lit.: "this righteous man has"). Since he came to us our troughs have not been wanting (water) and our springs have multiplied. And now, come, give me counsel that we might force him (to remain) with us yet another seven years. And they gave him deceptive counsel, to give him in marriage to Leah instead of Rachel."

ᵉᵉ Nfmg: "this man has dwelt among us seven years. And the people of the earth (read: "the place") arose and gave"; = CTg E, P.

ᶠᶠ Nfmg: "in troughs"; cf. VNL.

ᵍᵍ Nfmg: "Give counsel that he dwelt among us here yet."

ʰʰ Nfmg: "deceptive (counsel) and they married him (to Leah)"; = CTg E.

ⁱⁱ Nfmg: "and he brought (her) in"; = CTg E.

ʲʲ Nfmg: "and he was joined"; = CTg E.

ᵏᵏ Nfmg: "to us."

ᵐᵐ Nfmg: "beside (i.e., with) you and why, now, have you lied to me?"; cf. CTg E.

ⁿⁿ Nfmg: "it is not done so in our place: to give"; cf. CTg E.

Notes, Chapter 29

⁶"my service"; HT: "my days" = "my time."

⁷"Laban answered and said. . . ." This haggadic development on Laban's plan for deception is found also in Jewish midrashic literature, e.g., *Gen. R.* 70,19. Laban's reply echoes Jacob's retort in Gen 31:38-39.

27. Finish the seven *days of this feast*[oo][8] and *I will* also *give you* this one for the service you will render for yet <seven>[pp] other years." 28. And Jacob did so. And he finished the seven *days of this (nuptial) feast;*[qq] and Laban gave him Rachel his daughter as wife. 29. And Laban gave to his daughter Rachel, Bilhah the maid,[9] as her maid. 30. And he also went in to Rachel,[rr] and he also loved Rachel more than Leah. And he served with him yet again seven other[ss] years. 31. And *it was manifest before*[10] the Lord that[tt] Leah was hated, and he *decided in his Memra to give her*[11] *children.*[12] And Rachel was barren. 32. And Leah conceived and bore a son and called his name Reuben, because she said: "Because my affliction is *manifest before* the Lord; because surely now, my husband will love me." 33. And she conceived yet again and bore a son and said: "Since it *has been heard*[uu] *before*[13] the Lord that I am hated, he has also given me this one."[ww] And she called his name Simeon. 34. And she conceived again and bore a son[xx] and said: "Now, this time, my husband will *be joined*[14] to me because I have borne him three sons." For this

---

Apparatus, Chapter 29

[oo] VNL, CTg E: "finish the seven days of the (nuptial) feast of Leah and I will give you." In Nfmg various variants corresponding in part with VNL, CTg E.

[pp] "seven" missing in text; Nfmg: "you shall serve beside me yet seven"; = CTg E.

[qq] CTg E: "and he finished the seven days of the (nuptial) feast of Leah"; Nfmg: "the seven days of this one"; Nfi (to "this" of Nt text): "(feast) of Leah," = CTg E.

[rr] Nfmg: "and he was joined" (= had intercourse) likewise with Rachel"; = CTg E.

[ss] Nfmg: "beside him still seven"; = CTg E.

[tt] Nfmg: "that Leah was not loved in the sight of her husband and he said"; = CTg E.

[uu] Nfmg: "manifest"; = CTg E.

[ww] Nfmg: "I was not loved in the sight of my husband and he gave me also this one"; = CTg E.

[xx] In text *br*; in Nfmg and CTg E: *byr*.

Notes, Chapter 29

[8]"the seven days of this feast"; HT lit. "the week of this" is a text requiring expansion and one variously expanded: RSV: "the week of this one." It was the bridal week (NAB) lasting seven days (cf. Judg 14:12). In some later translations it is often expanded as in Nf, e.g., "the seven days' feast" (NEB); and already in the Vulg.: *imple ebdomadem dierum huius copulae.*

[9]"the maid"; perhaps an error for "his maid"; cf. CTg E; HT: "his maid."

[10]"it was manifest before . . ."; HT: "God saw." Nf's paraphrase avoids anthropomorphism. See Introduction, pp. 34–35.

[11]"to give her," correcting text of Nf: "to give me."

[12]"he decided . . . to give her children." Nf's paraphrase avoids anthropomorphism; HT: "and he (i.e., God) opened her womb."

[13]"it has been heard before . . ."; avoids the anthropomorphism of the HT: "the Lord heard." See Introduction, pp. 34f.

[14]"my husband will make himself available (*yzdmn*, from root *zmn*) to me"; HT: "will join himself" (*ylwh*, from the root *lwh*). B. Grossfeld has noted that the Aramaic *zmn* in the Tgs. is used to translate principally the Hebrew roots *y'd*, *qrh*, *qdš*, terms having the connotation of "preparing oneself," "availing oneself" ("to be available"), "meeting someone," never in the sense of "to be joined." Even though in the present text it translates a Hebrew word meaning "to be joined" (in a sexual sense), it should not be translated as "to be joined" but should be regarded as a euphemism for the Hebrew term and rendered by a different word or group of words, e.g., "meet with," "make himself available." It should be noted that the Aramaic root *zmn* is used frequently in the Pal. Tgs., especially in Nfmg, in the sexual sense as a rendering of the HT's "to join" (as in Gen 29:34), "to use" ("make use of").

reason his name was called Levi. 35. And she conceived again and bore a son and said: "This time*ʸʸ we* will praise and *glorify*ᶻᶻ *before*[15] the Lord." For this reason she called his name Judah. And she ceased from bearing.

CHAPTER 30

1. When Rachel saw that she did not bear sons to Jacob, Rachel was jealous of her sister and said to Jacob: "Give me sons; otherwise I die."ᵃ 2. And Jacob's anger grew strong against Rachel and he said: "*Is it from me*[7] *the fruit, offspring of the womb comes?*ᵇ *Behold, I and you will go*[2] *and we will beseech before the Lord* who <has withheld>ᶜ from you the fruit, the offspring, of the womb."[3] 3. And she said: "Behold, my maid Bilhah. Enter toᵈ her and she will conceive, and *I will rear;*[4] *perhaps* even I will have children *through her.*" 4. And she gave himᵉ Bilhah her maid as wife; and Jacob went inᶠ to her. 5. And Bilhah conceived and bore Jacob a son.ᵍ 6. And Rachel said: "*The Lord*ʰ has judged me and has also heard my voice and

Apparatus, Chapter 29

ʸʸ Nfmg: "now, this (time)"; = CTg E.   ᶻᶻ CTg E: "I will praise and we (= I) will glorify."

Notes, Chapter 29

[15]"praise and glorify before . . ."; HT: "praise (the Lord)." Nf, as often, has a double translation of the Hebrew.

Apparatus, Chapter 30

ᵃ Nfmg: "I am reckoned as of the dead" (sing.; CTg E pl.); = CTg E.
ᵇ Nfmg: "that we (= I) should withhold them. Come, I and you, and we will go and beseech mercy from before."
ᶜ Missing in text; present in Nfi.
ᵈ Nfmg: "My maid Bilhah; be joined (= have intercourse)"; = CTg E.

ᵉ Nfmg: "and she gave [another verb] him"; = CTg E.
ᶠ Nfmg: "and he joined"; = CTg E.
ᵍ In text *br*; Nfmg: *byr*; = CTg E; Nfi +: "male."
ʰ Nfmg: "the Memra of the Lord (has judged me?) in (or: by) his good deeds and he has likewise heard"; = CTg E (in both Nfmg and CTg E for "his [good deeds]" read "my [good deeds])"?

Notes, Chapter 30

[1]"Is it from me . . . comes?"; HT: "Am I in the place of God?" Nf's paraphrase tones down the HT somewhat.
[2]"Behold I and you will go . . . ; . . . the offspring of the womb"; HT: "(Am I in the place of God, who has withheld from you the fruit of the womb?" Nf's additional paraphrase helps take from the directness of the HT.
[3]"the fruit, the offspring, of the womb," *pry wwld m'yy*'; HT: "fruit of the womb." The same rendering is found in Nf for the other occurrences of the Hebrew phrase: Deut 7:13; 28:4, 11, 18, 53; 30:9. See also B. Barry Levy, 1, 1986, 196f.
[4]"I will raise him"; HT: "she will give birth on my knees."

given me a son";[i] because of this she called his name Dan. 7. And Bilhah, Rachel's maid, conceived again[j] and bore Jacob a second son.[k] 8. And Rachel said: "*I was also heard*[5] *in the prayer that I prayed*[m] *before the Lord that he give me sons as he gave* to my sister."[n] And she called his name Naphtali. 9. When Leah saw that she had ceased from[o] bearing, she took Zilpah her maid and gave her to Jacob as wife. 10. And Zilpah, Leah's maid, bore Jacob a son.[i] 11. And Leah said: "*Good luck*[p] *has come which will cut off the foundation*[q] *of the nations.*"[6] And she called his name Gad. 12. And Zilpah, Leah's maid, bore a second son to Jacob. 13. And Leah said: "The daughters *of Israel will praise me with great praises in the syna-gogues.*"[q bis][7] And she called his name Asher. 14. And Reuben went in the days of the cutting of the wheat and found mandrakes in the field, and brought them to Leah his mother. And Rachel said to Leah: "Give me, I pray, of your son's man-drakes." 15. And she said to her: "Is *this* a small thing that you have taken my hus-band? And you *seek* to take[r] my son's mandrakes? And Rachel said: "For this rea-son he will have intercourse with[s] you[8] this night in recompense for your son's mandrakes." 16. And Jacob came from the field in the evening;[t] and Leah went out to meet him and she said *to him*: "You shall come in[u] to me for I have hired you with my son's mandrakes." And he had intercourse with[w] her that night. 17. And

---

Apparatus, Chapter 30

[i] Nfmg: "son (*byr*); for this reason she called."

[j] Nfmg: "once more"; = CTg E.

[k] text: *br*; Nfmg and CTg E: *byr*.

[m] In Nfmg and CTg E minor variants from Nf almost identical with one another.

[n] Nfmg: "that he gave to Leah my sister and also"; = CTg E.

[o] Lit.: (with MT): "stood ("came to stand") from"; in Nfmg a different verb: "ceased from"; = CTg E.

[p] Nfmg: "good fate"; v. 11 in PVN; variants below.

[q] Correcting text: *mštwrhwn* (or possibly *mštwdhwn*) to *mštythwn*; VN; *mštwyyhwn*, "foundations"; P: "camps" (*mšryyt'*). CTg E: "and Leah said: Good luck has come and she called his name Gad."

[q bis] Nfmg: "the praises (with) which the daughters of Is-rael will praise me in the schools, and she called"; = CTg E.

[r] Nfmg: "(take) also"; = CTg E.

[s] Lit.: "use"; VN: "of an oath he will be joined [= VN] with you this night in recompense for the man-drakes"; CTg E: ". . . of an oath he will use you this night in recompense the mandrakes of your son."

[t] Nfmg: "at eventime"; = CTg E.

[u] Nfmg: "(and she said): you shall join yourself to me"; = CTg E.

[w] Lit.: "he used her"; Nfmg: "and he joined himself with her that night"; = CTg E.

Notes, Chapter 30

[5]"I was also heard. . . ." A paraphrase of a difficult, somewhat harsh HT passage, one possibly felt as derogatory of the ancestors of Israel. In the RSV it reads: "With mighty wrestlings I have wrestled with my sister, and I have prevailed." Nf's paraphrase is also in Onq., on which see B. Grossfeld, 1988, 109; Aberbach, 1969, esp. 20.

[6]"good luck . . . foundations of the people"; HT: "good fortune." The same understanding of the HT is found in *Gen. R.* 71,9.

[7]"The daughters of Israel . . . in the synagogues"; HT: "Happy am I. The daughters call me happy."

[8]"he will have intercourse with me," lit. "he will use (make use of) me"; HT: "he will lie with me." "Lie with" is HT's common expression for sexual intercourse, which, when used in this sense, Nf translates by *šmš*, "use," "make use of" (probably as a Hebrew rabbinic expression, "use the (marital) bed." See also A. Shinan and Y. Zakovitch, *The Story of the Mandrakes. Genesis 30:14–18 in the Bible, the Old Versions and the Ancient Jewish Literature*, Research Projects of the Institute of Jewish Studies, Monograph Series 8 (Jerusalem: Hebrew University, 1985).

the Lord[x] heard *the voice of the prayer of* Leah[9] and she conceived and bore to Jacob a fifth son.[y] 18. And Leah said: "*The Lord has given me*[z] my wages because I have given my maid to my master." And she called his name Issachar. 19. And Leah conceived again[aa] and bore a sixth son to Jacob. 20. And Leah said: "The Lord has[bb] presented me these *good presents.*[10] This time my husband will *make presents to me because*[cc] I have borne him six[dd] sons." And she called his name Zebulun. 21. And after (this)[ee] she bore a female daughter[11] and called her name Dinah. 22. *Four keys*[12] *there are*[ff] *which are given into the hand of*[gg] *the Lord, the master of all worlds, and he does not hand over them either to angel or to Seraph:*[hh] *the key of rain and the key of provision*[ii] *and the key of the sepulchres and the key of barrenness.* *<The key of rain>, for*[jj] *thus does the Scripture explain and say:*[13] *"The Lord will open for you the good treasure from the heavens." The key of provision, for thus does the Scripture explain and say:*[13] *"You open your hand and satisfy all living things in whom there is good pleasure." The key of the sepulchres, for thus does the Scripture explain and say:*[13] *"Behold, I will open your graves and will lead you from your graves, my people." The key of barrenness, for thus does the Scripture explain and*

Apparatus, Chapter 30

[x] Nfmg: "the Memra of the Lord"; = CTg E.

[y] text: *br*; Nfmg: *byr*, = CTg E.

[z] Nfmg: "behold the Memra of the Lord has given me."

[aa] Nfmg: "once more"; = CTg E.

[bb] Nfmg: "the Memra of the Lord"; = CTg E.

[cc] Nfmg: "now at this time, my husband will be joined with me because"; = CTg E.

[dd] "six:" identical lexical variant in Nfmg, CTg E.

[ee] "after this": identical minor variant in Nfmg and CTg E.

[ff] The additional midrash of v. 22 is in PVN, with vari-

ants noted below; VN is nearest to Nf. The midrash not in CTg E, which renders HT thus: "And the Memra of the Lord in his good mercies remembered Rachel and the Memra of the Lord heard the voice of her prayer and he promised (lit.: said) in his Memra to give her children" (almost identical with Nf).

[gg] P: "Four keys (there are) in the hand of."

[hh] Nfmg: "(Seraph) or to a troupe (of angels); the key of rain"; = VN.

[ii] P: "sustenance."

[jj] Text: ". . . and the key of barrenness. And thus . . . "; emendation from PVN, Nfmg, Nfi.

Notes, Chapter 30

[9]"the Lord heard the voice of the prayer of Leah"; HT: "the Lord listened to (or: heard) Leah." This is one of the few texts in Nf with the construction: active verb + God +*yt* + object, instead of the more commonly used passive construction ("it was heard, etc., before the Lord"). See Introduction, pp. 34f., note to Nf Gen 1:4, and B. Barry Levy, 1, 1986, 38f.

[10]"good presents" (*zbydyn ṭbyn*); HT: *zbd ṭwb*, "good portion."

[11]"female daughters"; HT: "daughters." Nf occasionally adds "male" to "son(s)" and "female" to "daughter(s)." The addition in this instance may have been due to an opinion known in rabbinic circles that the child in Leah's womb was only transformed into a female after Leah's prayer for Rachel; see Grossfeld, *Neofiti*, note 21 to Gen 30.

[12]The midrash in this verse on the four keys (the key or rain, of sustenance or provision, of the grave and of barrenness) is built on biblical key texts: Deut 28:12; Ps 145:16; Ezek 37:12; Gen 30:22, respectively. Rabbinic tradition, e.g., *Gen. R.* 73,4 (on Gen 30:22) knows of a midrash on three keys (of burial, rain, the womb, with the texts of Ezek 37:12; Deut 28:12; Gen 30:22), noting that "some add a key of sustenance too," with reference to Ps 145:16. B. Barry Levy, 1, 1986, 199–201, believes that the midrash occurring in Nf after the translation of the key proof texts was not original to Nf, but is translated from a Hebrew text and added later.

say: [13] *"The Lord in his good mercies* [14] remembered Rachel and *the Lord heard the voice*[kk] of the prayer of Rachel and said*[mm]* in his Memra to give her sons."*[nn]* [15] 23. And she conceived and bore a son and said: *"The Lord* gathered in*[oo]* my shame." 24. And she called his name Joseph saying: "The Lord*[pp]* has added another*[qq]* son to me." 25. And when Rachel bore Joseph, Jacob said to Laban: "Send me away, I pray, and I will go to my place and to my country. 26. Give me my wives and my sons, for whom I have served *before* you [16] and I will go because you know the service which I have rendered *before* you." *[rr]* 27. And Laban said to him: "If, now, I have found grace *and favor* in your sight, *[ss]* I have found out by divination*[tt]* that the Lord*[uu]* has blessed me *for your merit."* [17] 28. And he said: "Determine,*[ww]* now, your wage before me*[xx]* and I will give (it)." 29. And he said to him: "You know how I have served*[yy]* before you, and what your cattle were*[zz]* *before me* and (how) *they have grown strong and numerous.* [18] 30. Because the few *cattle* which you had before me have grown strong *and numerous*, and the Lord*[a]* has blessed you *for my merits* and now, what *can I do?*[b] *I am also obliged to provide for my sons and the men of my house."* [19] 31. And he said: "What will I give you?" And Jacob said: "Do not give*[c]* me anything (at all). If you do this thing for me I will continue to feed your flock and guard it.*[d]* 32. I will pass through all your flock this day. I will separate

Apparatus, Chapter 30

[kk] Nfmg: "the Memra of the Lord (listened to) the voices of her prayer"; cf. CTg E.

[mm] I.e., "promised"; VN +: "in his Memra."

[nn] P: "of the fruit of the womb"; Nfmg +: "because there are four keys which are given neither to angel nor to Seraph: the keys of rain, the keys of sustenance, the keys of the grave, and the keys of barrenness."

[oo] Nfmg: "the Memra of the Lord had gathered"; = CTg E.

[pp] Nfmg: "the Memra of the Lord."

[qq] Nfi, CTg E: "another" (an identical lexical variant).

[rr] Nfmg: "beside you"; CTg E: "with you."

[ss] Nfmg: "before you"; = CTg E.

[tt] Nfmg, PVN, CTg E: "I have discovered through augury."

[uu] Nfmg: "the Memra of the Lord"; = CTg E.

[ww] Nfmg: "specify"; = CTg E.

[xx] Nfmg: "beside ("to," '*lwy*) him"; CTg E: "beside ("to," '*ly*) me."

[yy] Lit.: "you know which"; cf. HT; Nfmg: "(you are) aware of my (CTg E: the) service which I have served"; = CTg E.

[zz] Nfmg: "how (lit.: what) your flocks are pasturing before (= under) me"; = CTg E (with "before him").

[a] Nfmg: "the Memra of the Lord."

[b] Nfmg: "and now what can I do?"; minor but identical variants in Nfmg and CTg E.

[c] In text: "(do not) do," under influence of 31b. CTg E: "give"; Nfmg: "you will (not) give me anything at all of the flock"; CTg E: "anything."

[d] Nfmg: "I will guard them"; CTg E: "I will guard you."

Notes, Chapter 30

[13]"(Scripture) explains (*mprš*) and says," *kn ktb' wmprš w'mr* (lit.: "and explains and says"). B. Barry Levy (1986, 199) notes that *mprš* may mean "translated" (with reference to Neh 8:8 as interpreted in *b. Ned* 37b). Sokoloff, 1990, 451, understands through *prš*, "specify": "For scripture specifically says" (with reference to Gen 35:9, etc.).

[14]"in his good mercies." HT: "the Lord remembered." On this addition of Nf, see notes to Gen 8:1 and 21:1; also Grossfeld, *Neofiti*, note 23 to Gen 30.

[15]"said (=decreed, promised) in his Memra to give her sons"; avoids the anthropomorphism of the HT: "and opened her womb."

[16]"served before you"; HT: "served you." Nf commonly uses "before" in the translation of this Hebrew verb, when the service spoken of is rendered to humans, e.g., Gen 25:23; 27:40; 29:15; 30:26 (twice), 29; 31:6, 41.

[17]"for your merit"; HT: "on your account" (*bgllk*); see note to 12:3 and 12:13.

[18]". . . grow strong and numerous"; HT: "how they have fared with me"; see following verse. See also note to 1:22.

[19]"I am obliged . . . house." Nf's paraphrase spells out the HT's "when will I provide (lit. "do") for my house also."

from there every white-spotted and speckled[e] lamb[20] and every reddish lamb among the lambs, and the speckled and white-spotted among the goats; (this) will be my wage. 33. And *my merits shall testify* for me *this day* and (the day) of tomorrow, when you enter[f] *to account*[21] my wages before you. Everything that is not white-spotted and speckled[g] among the goats and reddish among the lambs shall be with me[h] (as) a stolen animal." 34. And Laban said: "Behold, it is good.[i] Oh that it be according to your words."[j] 35. And that day he separated the *white-spotted* and speckled he-goats, and all the white-spotted and speckled she-goats, and all that had *anything* of white and all the reddish among the lambs and placed them in the hands of his sons.[k] 36. And he put a distance of three days' *journey* between himself and[m] Jacob; and Jacob tended[n] the flocks of Laban that were left behind.[n] 37. And Jacob took rods of fresh-green poplar[o] and of almond and of the plane-tree, and peeled white streaks in them from off the white *skin* that is upon the rods. 38. And he placed the rods he had peeled[p] in the troughs of the watering-pools[q] into which the sheep[r] entered[s] to drink <in front of the sheep;[r] and (since) they used to mate when they entered to drink>,[t] 39. the sheep mated near the rods and the sheep bore white-spotted, speckled and striped (young). 40. And Jacob separated the lambs,[u] and he put the sheep[r] facing the *white-spotted ones* and all the reddish of the sheep[r] of Laban. <And he made flocks for himself and did not mix them with the flocks of Laban.>[w] 41. And every time early-born[x] sheep were mating,[y] Jacob set the rods before the sheep[r] in the watering-troughs to have them mate

Apparatus, Chapter 30

[e] For v. 32b minor variants from Nf in Nfmg and CTg E. The text also in VN, agreeing with Nf, with some variants.

[f] Nfmg: "I enter"; = CTg E.

[g] minor identical variants, as in *e* above, in Nfmg and CTg E.

[h] Nfmg: "beside me"; = CTg E.

[i] Nfmg: "I have spoken well: would that."

[j] Nfmg: "according to your word" (a different term); = CTg E.

[k] Nfmg: "in the hands of his sons"; = CTg E.

[m] Nfmg: "of days between his sons and between."

[n] Minor identical variants in Nfmg and CTg E.

[o] Nfmg: "of a white flower."

[p] Nfmg: "pared off"; = CTg E.

[q] Correcting text slightly, with VN, Nfmg, and CTg E.

[r] The Aramaic word *'nh ('n')* could also be rendered "flock(s)."

[s] Nfmg: "came." Cf. Ps.-J.

[t] Missing in text: in slightly different form in CTg E and Ps.-J.

[u] In Aramaic *'mry'*; "sheep" is also a possible rendering.

[w] Missing in text: supplied according to Ps.-J. CTg E ends: ". . . and he did not set them against the flock of Laban."

[x] Nfmg: "later-born."

[y] Nfmg: "at every mating"; = CTg E.

Notes, Chapter 30

[20]"(every) white-spotted and speckled lamb," *(kl) 'mr qrḥ wnmr;* HT: *(kl) śh nqd wṭlw';* RSV: "every speckled and spotted sheep."

[21]"when you enter to account," *lmqblh;* the HT is difficult: "when you will come (=will go?) over my wages"; RSV: ". . . to look into my wages."

among the rods.[z] 42. But before the later-born of the sheep[r] he used not set them; and *he had numerous flocks*, the *later-born*[22] were for Laban and the *early-born* for Jacob. 43. And the man became very, very[aa] powerful and he had many flocks and maidservants and menservants and camels and he-asses.

CHAPTER 31

1. And he heard the words of the sons of Laban saying: "Jacob has taken everything belonging to our father,[a] and from what belongs to our father *he has acquired all these riches.*"[b1] 2. And Jacob saw Laban's countenance,[2] and behold, it was not *friendly* toward him,[c] not like yesterday and not like earlier. 3. And the Lord[d] said to Jacob: "Return to the country of your fathers and to your *kindred* and I, *in my Memra*, will be with you."[e] 4. And Jacob sent and called Rachel and Leah to the field, beside his flock. 5. And he said to them: "I see your father's countenance, and behold it is not *friendly*[3] toward me,[f] not like yesterday and not like earlier, but the *Memra of* the God of my father[g] has been *at my aid.*[h4] 6. And you know[i] that I

Apparatus, Chapter 30

[z] Nfmg: "water troughs to have them mating among the rods"; = CTg E. (A number of minor but identical variants from Nf in Nfmg and CTg E.)

[aa] *lḥd' lḥd'*; Nfmg, CTg E: *ḥd' lḥd'*.

Notes, Chapter 30

[22]"the later-born," *lqyšy'*. HT: *'ṭp*. The meaning of the Hebrew root, occurring only twice in the Pentateuch (in Gen 30:42), was debated among the Rabbis. Resh Lakish held it meant "later-born" (as in Nf), while R. Yohanan believed it meant "earlier-born"; see *Gen. R.* 73,9.

Apparatus, Chapter 31

[a] Nfmg: "that belongs to our father and from what (= CTg E) belongs to our father he has seized"; CTg E: "... he has made all this glory."

[b] Nfmg: "this glory" (cf. HT); = CTg E.

[c] Nfmg: "the same toward him"; = CTg E.

[d] Nfmg: "the Memra of the Lord"; = CTg E.

[e] Nfmg: "at your aid"; = CTg E.

[f] Nfmg: "they (were not) the same toward me"; = CTg E.

[g] Nfmg: "and the God of my father (= CTg E) his Memra has been."

[h] Nfmg: "beside me."

[i] Nfmg: "are aware"; = CTg E.

Notes, Chapter 31

[1]"acquired all these riches"; HT: "made all this *kbd*" (="glory"); RSV: "... wealth."

[2]"countenance," *sbr 'pwy*, lit. "the brightness (splendor) of (his) face"; Nf's regular rendering of HT *pnym*, esp. after the verb "to see," e.g., Gen 31:2, 5; 32:21; 33:10; 43:3; 44:23, 26; 48:11. The phrase also occurs occasionally in Nf with other verbs.

[3]"friendly"; added in Nf; HT: "it was not toward him."

[4]"at my aid"; HT: "with me"; see to 28:20, etc.; see Introduction, p. 28, and notes to 28:20.

served *before* your father with all my strength. 7. And your father cheated me and changed my wages ten[j] times, but *the Lord* did not give him the *power*[5] *to* do me evil.[k] 8. If he said thus: 'The white-spotted[m] will be your wages'; all the flocks bore <white-spotted young; and if he said thus:>[n] 'The *speckled* will be your wages,' all the flocks bore *speckled* (young). 9. And *the Lord*[o] has *emptied*[6] the riches of your father and has given (them)[p] to me. 10. And in the *hour* that the flocks mated,[q] I raised my eyes and saw in a dream and, behold, the he-goats[r] that mounted the flock were white-spotted, speckled and striped. 11. And the angel of *the Lord* said to me in a dream: 'Jacob.' And I said: 'Here I am.'[s] 12. And he said: 'Raise, I pray, your eyes and see all the he-goats[t] that mount the flock are white-spotted, speckled and striped; because all whatsoever Laban has done to you[u] *is revealed before me.*[7] 13. I am the God *who was revealed*[w] to you at Bethel,[8] where you anointed a pillar and where you made a vow to me.[x] Now arise; go forth from this land and return to the land of your *kindred*.'" 14. And Rachel and Leah answered and said to him: "Have we *still* a portion and an inheritance in the house of our father? 15. Were we not considered by him as strangers because he sold us and has even eaten the money[y] of *our sale*? 16. All the property[z] that *the Lord*[aa] has taken[9] from our father belongs to us and to our children;[bb] and now do what[bb bis] *the Lord*[aa] has com-

Apparatus, Chapter 31

[j] Nfmg and CTg E: "and your father has lied to me and (Nfmg + your father) has altered my wages already ten times"; PVN: "altered (VN + my wages)."

[k] Nfmg: "the Memra of the Lord has restrained him from doing me harm"; = CTg E.

[m] Identical orthographic variant in Nfmg and CTg E.

[n] Missing in the text: in CTg E.

[o] PVN: "the Memra of the Lord has emptied"; Nfmg and CTg E: "the Memra of the Lord."

[p] In Nfmg and CTg E.

[q] In Nfmg and CTg E an identical variant: as in 30:41 above.

[r] Nfmg: "in a vision and behold, the he-goats (CTg E: male-goats) that come up"; = CTg E.

[s] VN, Nfmg, CTg E: "and Jacob answered in the language of the sanctuary (Nfmg: in the holy tongue) and said: [in Hebrew] *HERE I AM*."

[t] Nfmg: "male-goats" (or: "rams"); = CTg E.

[u] Nfmg and CTg E: "before him all that Laban (*d'yt llbn*) has done (Nfmg: is to do) to you."

[w] Identical lexical variants in Nfmg and CTg E.

[x] Nfmg: "an explicit vow" (lit.: "the distinct expression of a vow"); = CTg E.

[y] VN, Nfmg, CTg E: "and he also wants to take the money of our marriage contract (*ketuba*)"; P: "because he sold us and he also wants to take the money of our virginity and our marriage contracts (*ketuba*)"; Nfmg 2°: "our purchase money."

[z] Nfmg: "the riches"; = CTg E.

[aa] Nfmg: "the Memra of the Lord"; = CTg E.

[bb] Minor variants identical in Nfmg and CTg E.

[bb bis] Nfmg: "all (that)"; = CTg E.

Notes, Chapter 31

[5] "the power," *ršw*; or: "authority"; HT: "God did not give you to harm me."

[6] "emptied"; HT, root *nṣl*; RSV: "taken away"; the same rendering of the Hebrew root occurs in Nf Exod 3:22; 12:36, not however in Gen 31:15, where in the same context as here, Nf renders *nṣl* by "has taken (out)."

[7] "all whatever . . . is revealed before me" (with the sign of the accusative before "all"); HT: "I saw all . . ."; Nf's usual method of avoiding anthropomorphism; see Introduction, pp. 34–35.

[8] "who was revealed to you at Bethel"; HT: "I am the God Bethel," *h'l byt'l*.

[9] "has taken"; HT with root *nṣl*; see note 6 to v. 9.

manded you." 17. And Jacob arose and set his sons and his wives[cc] on camels. 18. And <he took>[dd] his cattle, and all his wealth[ee] which he had acquired—his riches *and* his possessions which he had acquired in Paddan-aram—to go[ff] to Isaac his father, to the land of Canaan. 19. And Laban had gone to shear[bb] the sheep, and Rachel stole the *images*[10] belonging to her father.[gg] 20. And Jacob *outwitted*[11] Laban the Aramaean[bb] because he did not tell him he was fleeing.[bb] 21. And he fled with all that was his. And he arose and crossed the river (and) set his face to the mountain of Gileadah.[hh] *22. And it happened that[ii] when the shepherds of Laban went to water the sheep from the well, they were not able. And they waited two and three days, hoping[jj] that perchance it would overflow; but it did not overflow.*[12] Then[kk] it was told to Laban on the third day that Jacob had fled. 23. And he took his brothers with him and pursued after him, *a traveling distance of* seven days,[13] and overtook him on the mountain of Gileadah. 24. And *the Lord[mm] was revealed*[14] to Laban the Aramaean[nn] in a dream at night and said to him: "Take care for yourself. You shall not[nn] speak with Jacob good or[nn] evil." 25. And Laban overtook Jacob. And Jacob had spread his tent on the mountain; and Laban *made* his broth-

---

Apparatus, Chapter 31

[cc] Nfmg: "and carried his men (i.e., people) (and sons)"; cf. Samar, LXX; CTg E: "and carried his sons and women."

[dd] Missing in text: in CTg E.

[ee] Nfmg, CTg E: "(CTg E only; and he took all his riches and all) the treasure which he had laid by, the riches of possessions which he had laid aside in Paddan (-aram) to enter to Isaac"; VN: "the treasure."

[ff] Nfmg: "to enter"; = CTg E.

[gg] Nfmg: "and the images of idols which his father had"; = CTg E.

[hh] Nfmg: "because he had seen in the holy spirit that liberation would be effected there for Israel in the days of Jephthah, who was from Gilead" ("liberation," *šyzbwt'*, by correcting *šhbyt'* of text; possibly: "resting," *šbwt'*).

[ii] N: "and it happened when the shepherds gathered together seeking to water the sheep, they were not able; and they waited two or three days (hoping) perchance the well would overflow but it did not overflow; and then they told Laban on the third day that Jacob had fled"; P as Nf except some variants noted below; Nfmg: "Jacob there near the well, and they did not find water and waited three days for it to overflow, but it did not overflow and then it was related on the third day that the pious Jacob had gone, for whose merit(s) the waters had flowed over for twenty years."

[jj] P: "expecting that perchance the well might overflow."

[kk] Nfmg: "and it was told Laban," etc. (as Nf).

[mm] Nfmg: "the Memra of the Lord"; = CTg E.

[nn] Minor identical variants in Nfmg and CTg E.

Notes, Chapter 31

[10] "images"; HT: *trpym*; RSV: "household gods."

[11] "outwitted"; lit. "stole the wits/mind/knowledge of"; HT: "stole the heart (=mind) of."

[12] This haggadic supplement refers back to the fifth miracle of Pal. Tg. Gen 28:10.

[13] "traveling distance of (seven days)"; HT: "distance of." Nf also elsewhere adds "traveling" to "distance." In the present case, however, the addition may be connected with a particular understanding of HT's "seven days' journey," namely, that Laban overtook Jacob on that very day; hence, the distance that Jacob had traveled in seven days Laban covered in one single day; cf. *Gen. R.* 74,6.

[14] "Gileadah," as HT but with final *he*; probably a *he locale*; see note to 26:1, 2; also 33:17; 37:6.

ers *encamp* on the mountain of Gileadah.[15] 26. And Laban said to Jacob: "What have you done? You have deceived me <and have taken my daughters like prisoners *that flee from the edge of the sword*>.[oo] 27. <Why, *now*, have you fled in secret and deceived me and *my daughters*>[oo][16] and have not told me? *Had you but told me* I would have sent you forth in joy, with songs, with timbrels, and with harps. 28. Nor did you permit me to kiss my sons and my daughters. Now, you have acted foolishly (in) what you have done. 29. *I have with me strength and numerous multitudes*[pp] to do you evil, but the God of your father said to me, during the evening, saying: 'Take care not to speak with Jacob, either good or evil.' 30. And now, you have gone away because you have greatly desired[qq] the house of your father.[17] But why[rr] did you steal my *gods*[18] <.......>.[ss] 31. And Jacob answered and said to Laban: "Because I was afraid, because you said: 'Do not take your daughters from me illegitimately.' 32. He with whom you find <your gods, *shall not live*>.[tt] In the presence of our brothers see for yourself what I have with me[uu] and take it." And Jacob did not know that Rachel had stolen them. 33. And Laban went into the tent of Jacob and into the tent of Leah and into the tent of the two *concubines*,[19] and did not find them. And he went out of the tent of Leah and went into the tent of Rachel. 34. And Rachel had taken <*the images*>[ww] and had put them in the camel's saddle and had sat on them. And Laban examined all the tent and did not find (them). 35. And she said to her father: "Let it not appear evil in the sight of my lord[xx] that I cannot stand up before you, because the way of women is upon me." And *Laban* examined *all the tent* and did not find the *images*. 36. <And the anger of Jacob was enkindled>[yy] and he quarreled with Laban. And Jacob an-

---

Apparatus, Chapter 31

[oo] Missing in Nf; supplied in Nfmg, which = CTg E.

[pp] VN: "I have strength and (a numerous) host."

[qq] Nfmg: "you have surely been called in (or: "have had to retire") to the house of."

[rr] Nfmg, CTg E +: "now" (or: "I pray").

[ss] Lit.: "my fears," word following (with six consonants) erased by Christian censor as in vv. 32, 34; Nfmg + CTg E: "statues of my idols."

[tt] These or similar words (of about nine consonants) erased by censors. CTg E v. 32: "with whom you find my [sic] idols shall not live. Before our brothers

<see> what is beside you [sic] and take it for yourself . . ."; Nfmg: "(the statues—[erased by censor] of your idols."

[uu] Nfmg: "of what is beside me of what is yours."

[ww] Word erased by censor; Nfmg: "the images [erased] of the idols and she put them" [here wrong word erased]; = CTg E: "the images of the idols and set (them) under the saddle" (= Nfmg); CTg E breaks off here.

[xx] Nfmg: "Let not the anger of my Lord be enkindled."

[yy] Missing in text; supplied from Nfmg.

Notes, Chapter 31

[15]"the Lord was revealed"; HT: "God came"; the same in Nf Gen 20:3.

[16]"and my daughters." Thus, following A. Díez Macho's reconstruction, which B. Barry Levy (1986, 203) considers problematic.

[17]This section of the Neofiti 1 MS has been censored by a Christian censor to remove what appeared to be anti-Christian references. On this censorship, see Introduction, p. 9.

[18]"gods," *dhlty*; lit. "my (objects of) fear."

[19]"concubines"; HT: "maids." Nf gives them their true status; same rendering in 32:23; 33:1. The rendering of Tg. Onq. and of Ps.-J. is the same as that of Nf; see Grossfeld, 1988, 113 (on Onq. Gen 31:33).

swered and said to Laban: "What is my sin *and* what is my offense that you have pursued after me? 37. Now that you have examined all my objects, what have you found of all the objects of your house? [zz] Put them here in front of my brothers and your brothers so that they may judge between the two of us. 38. These twenty years I am with you; your ewes and your she-goats were not without young and the male lambs[a] of your flock I did not eat. 39. *What was killed* I did not bring to you.[b] *Every one of them that fled from the numbers I made good.* From me you demanded it. What *the thieves* stole in the daytime, and what *the wild beasts killed* during the night, *I made good*. 40. During the daytime the heat devoured me and the frost[c] at night, and my sleep fled from my eyes. 41. I am these twenty years in your house; I served *before* you[d] fourteen years for your two daughters and six years for your flock, and ten times have you changed[e] my wages. 42. Were not the God of my father, the God of Abraham and the *Strong One* of Isaac, with me, you would surely have sent me away now empty(-handed). My sorrows and the labor of my hands[f] *are manifest before the Lord,*[20] and last night[g][21] he admonished (you)." 43. And Laban answered and said to Jacob: "The daughters are my daughters, and the sons are my sons, and the flocks are my flocks,[h] and all that you see is mine. And what can I do to these daughters of mine this day, and to the sons they have borne? 44. And now, *come* let us make a covenant, I and you, and it will be a *sign*[i] between me and you." 45. And Jacob took a stone and set it up as a pillar. 46. And Jacob said to his brethren: "Gather stones."[j] And they took stones and made a heap; and they ate there upon the heap of stones. 47. And Laban called it: *Igar Sahaduta* and Laban

Apparatus, Chapter 31

[zz] Nfmg: "your instruments of war (probably error for: "household objects); place (them), I pray, between my brothers and your brothers and let them judge."

[a] CTg C, (which begins here): "the males" (or: "rams"); Nfmg: "the reward (of your male lambs)."

[b] VN, CTg C, in v. 39 = Nf, also P except endings: ". . . I made good: the wages of my day's labor and the watchfulness of my eyes at night."

[c] In text: *qls'*; Nfmg: "and the frost (*qrws'*; regular form) at night."

[d] Nfmg: "beside you."

[e] Nfmg: "you have altered" (some variant at v. 6 above).

[f] Nfmg: "and the uprightness of my hands is manifest."

[g] Lit.: "(last) evening"; Nfmg: "he admonished him last night (lit.: "evening"); CTg C: "he admonished you."

[h] Nfmg: "these women are my daughters: and these sons are reckoned as my sons, since they have been born from my daughters; and the flock is from my flock."

[i] Nfmg: "as a witness"; as CTg C.

[j] Nfmg: "to his sons whom he called in the language of the sanctuary his brothers"; CTg C: "to his sons whom he called his brothers."

Notes, Chapter 31

[20]"my sorrows are manifest before the Lord" (with the sign of the accusative before "sorrows"); HT: "God saw. . . ." On this method for avoiding anthropomorphisms, see Introduction, pp. 34–35.

[21]"last night," *b-rms'* (rendering HT's *'ms*), as in Gen 19:34; 31:29, 42. *b-rms'*, lit. "in the evening," "this (last) evening."

called it *in the language of the sanctuary,* [22] GAL ED. 48. And Laban said: "This heap of stones is a witness between me and you this day." Because of this he called its name Gilead; 49. And *Zapit,* [k] because he said: "*Let* the Lord *be revealed* [23] and let him *judge* between me and you when we are removed one from the other. 50. If you ill-treat my daughters, and if you take wives besides my daughters, although no one is with us, see, *the Lord* [m] is witness between me and you." 51. And Laban said to Jacob: "Behold this heap and *this* pillar which I have set up between me and you. 52. This heap is a witness, and *this* pillar is a witness, that *I will not pass over* and take this heap to you, <and that you will not pass over this heap to me> [n] or this pillar to do harm. [o] 53. The God of Abraham and the God of Nahor judge between us—the God of their fathers." And Jacob swore by the *Strong One* of [24] his father Isaac. 54. And Jacob offered *sacrifices* on the mountain and called his brethren to eat bread; [p] and they ate bread [p] and they spent the night on the mountain.

CHAPTER 32

1. And Laban arose early in the morning and kissed his sons and his daughters and blessed them. And Laban went and returned to his place. 2. And Jacob went on his journey and angels *from before the Lord* [a][1] overtook him. 3. And Jacob said when he saw them: *"Perhaps they are messengers from Laban,* [2] *my mother's*

Apparatus, Chapter 31

[k] CTg C: "And Zapita because he said: May the Memra of the Lord watch out (*yṣpy*) and judge in."
[m] Nfmg, CTg C: "the Memra of the Lord."

[n] Omitted in text; in CTg C.
[o] Nfmg: "for evil."
[p] Nfmg: "food"; CTg C breaks off at v. 54a.

Notes, Chapter 31

[22]"Let the Lord be revealed"; HT: "May he (i.e., God) keep watch."
[23]"the language of the sanctuary," i.e., Hebrew. See also Nf Gen 2:19; 11:1; 22:1; 45:12.
[24]"the Strong One of . . ."; HT: "the Fear of. . . ." See Introduction, p. 35.

Apparatus, Chapter 32

[a] Nfmg: "the angels of the Lord."

Notes, Chapter 32

[1]"angels from before the Lord"; HT: "angels of God."
[2]The haggadic development, with Jacob's inner reflections, in this verse is similar to what we find in certain rabbinic sources. Texts in Grossfeld, *Neofiti,* note 2 to Gen 32. See also B. Barry Levy, 1, 1986, 205f.

brother, who has returned to pursue after me; or the hosts of Esau, my brother, who comes to meet me, or hosts of angels from before the Lord come to deliver me from the hands of both of them." Because of this[b] he called the name of that place Mahanaim. 4. And Jacob sent envoys before him to Esau his brother to the land of *Gabla,*[3] *to the territory*[c] *of the Edomites.*[4] 5. And Jacob commanded them, saying: "Thus shall you speak to my master, to Esau: 'Thus says your servant Jacob: I have sojourned with Laban and *I have tarried* until now.[d] 6. And I have oxen and he-asses and menservants and maidservants, and I have sent to relate[e] (it) to my master, so that I may find grace *and kindness*[5] in your sight.'"[f] 7. And the *spies*[6] returned to Jacob, saying: "We reached[g] as far as your brother, to Esau, and *behold he* is coming to meet you and four hundred men, *generals,*[h7] with him." 8. And Jacob was very much afraid and in distress; and he divided the people that were with him, the sheep and the oxen and the camels into two camps. 9. And he said: "If Esau comes to one camp and kills it, the camp that remains will be saved." 10. And Jacob said: "O God of Abraham my father, and God of Isaac my father, O Lord,[i] (you) who have said to me: 'Return to your land and to your *kindred* and I will do you good';[j] 11. *behold,* I am little *and I am not worthy* of all the favors and of all

Apparatus, Chapter 32

[b] PVN, Nfmg: "(PVN: And Jacob said) when he saw them: Perhaps they are (the, P, Nfmg) camps of (VN: from) my brother Esau coming against me (PVN: to wage war against me) to kill me, or perchance the camps of (Nfmg: Laban), my mother's brother, coming after me to kill me, or perchance (the P) camps of (PVN: holy angels from before) the Lord (VN: who are) coming to save me (P + from their hands; VN: from the hands of both of them). For this reason (PVN: he called the name of that place Menahem)."

[c] Nfi: "adjoining (the Edomites)"; or: "boundary," "limits."
[d] Nfmg: "I have delayed coming until now."
[e] Nfmg: "to tell (lit.: "show") it."
[f] Nfmg: "before you."
[g] Nfmg: "we came."
[h] Greek loan word: *polemarchos* (cf. Nfmg, Gen 33:1 below); also in PVN.
[i] Nfmg: "the Memra of the Lord."
[j] Nfmg: "and we (= I?) will do good with you."

Notes, Chapter 32

[3]"Gabla"; HT: "Seir." Nf's constant identification of HT Seir; see McNamara, 1972, 194.

[4]"territory of the Edomites"; HT: "field (*śdh*) of Edom." As noted to Gen 2:5, Nf renders HT's *śdh* by "territory," "boundary," "limits" in Gen 14:7; 32:4; 33:19; 36:35; 41:48; 47:24.

[5]"grace and kindness," *ḥn wḥsd*; HT: *ḥn* (RSV: "favor"). As remarked in the note to 6:8, to express divine favor the HT uses both the simple *ḥn* and the composite *ḥn wḥsd*, the latter being the more frequently used in later times. When the HT has the simple *ḥn*, Nf almost universally paraphrases by the composite *ḥn wḥsd*; thus: 6:8; 18:3; 19:19; 30:27; 32:6; 33:8, 10, 15; 34:11; 39:4, 21; 47:25, 29; 50:4; Exod 32:5; 33:12, 13, 16, 17; 34:9; Num 11:15; Deut 24:1. The only exceptions are Exod 3:21; 11:3; 12:36; Num 11:11.

[6]"spies"; HT: "messengers."

[7]"generals" ("four hundred men generals"); HT: "four hundred men," *'yš*, a term often taken in the Tgs. as denoting more than an ordinary man (see note to 12:20). The identification of the men as generals is in keeping with one of the rabbinic views on who these particular men were. *Gen. R.* 75,12 has: "R. Samuel b. Nahman said: Four hundred kings wearing crowns were with him; others say: Four hundred prefects were with him. R. Jannai said: Four hundred generals were with him."

the truth that you have done with your servant, because with my staff I crossed this Jordan and now *behold*, I have become two camps.[k] 12. Save me, I pray, *from the hands* of Esau, because I fear him, lest he come and kill me *and blot out* the mother[m] with the sons. 13. And you have said: 'I will surely do you good, and I will make *your sons* like the sand of the sea which cannot be counted for multitude.'" 14. And he passed that night there; and he took from what he had brought in his hands a gift[n] for Esau his brother: 15. two hundred she-goats, twenty he-goats; two hundred ewes and twenty rams; 16. thirty milch-camels and their young; forty cows and ten bulls; twenty she-asses and ten Libyan asses.[o] 17. And he put then in the hand of his servants, each flock separately. And he said to his servants: "Pass before me and place (some distance) between one flock and the other." 18. And he gave command to the first saying: "When my brother Esau meets you and asks you, saying: 'From (whom) do you come, and where are you going, and to whom do these that precede you belong?' 19. you shall say: 'To your servant, to Jacob; it is a gift and has been sent to my master, to Esau, and behold, moreover he is behind us.'" 20. And he commanded also the second and the third, and also the one who walked after[p] the flocks saying: "According to this word shall you speak with Esau *the time* you *meet* him. 21. And you shall say: 'Behold, Jacob also comes after us.'" Because he said: "I shall appease his face[q] with the gift that goes before me, and after that I will see his countenance;[8] perhaps he will receive me favorably."[r] 22. And the gift passed on before him, and he spent that night in the camp. 23. And he arose that night and took his two wives and his two *concubines*[s][9] and his eleven sons and crossed the ford of the Jabbokah. 24. And he took them and made (them) cross the stream and made all he had go across. 25. And Jacob was left alone; and *the angel Sariel wrestled*[t] with him *in the appearance of* a man[10] and he embraced him until *the time* the dawn arose.[u] 26. When he saw that he could not prevail against him, he touched the hollow of his thigh and the hollow of Jacob's thigh be-

---

Apparatus, Chapter 32

[k] Nfmg: "very large (camps)."

[m] Nfmg: "the mothers."

[n] Greek loan word *dôron*; also in CTg C.

[o] Nf: *lwwdqyn*; CTg C: *lwbdqyn*; P: *lwbdykym*; VN: *lwydyn dqyn* (!)

[p] Nfmg: "also all those who walked after"; = CTg C.

[q] Nfmg: "(his) countenance"; = CTg C.

[r] Lit.: "accept me the face"; Nfmg: "receive his countenance"; = CTg C.

[s] Nfmg: "his maidservants"; = CTg C.

[t] Nfmg: "struggled"; CTg C: "and an angel wrestled with him in the form of a man until the rise of the column of the dawn."

[u] Nfmg: "until the rise of dawn" (a different word).

Notes, Chapter 32

[8]"his countenance"; see note to 31:2.

[9]"concubines"; HT: "maids." The same rendering in Nf 31:33.

[10]"the angel Sariel . . . appearance of a man"; HT: "a man wrestled with him." The identification of the "man" as an angel is found in Jewish sources; the identification with Sariel, however, only in Nf. See further, Ginzberg, *Legends*, V, pp. 305–310; Grossfeld, *Neofiti*, note 28 to Gen 32.

came *benumbed*[w][11] in his wrestling[x] with him. 27. And he said: "Let me go because the rise of the dawn[12] has arrived,[y] *and because the time of the angels on high to praise*[z][13] *has arrived, and I am a chief of those who praise.*"[aa] And he said: "I will not let you go unless you bless me." 28. And he said to him: "What is your name?" And he said: "Jacob." 29. And he said: "Your name shall no longer be called[bb] Jacob but Israel, because you have claimed superiority with *angels from before the Lord*[14] and with men[cc] and you have prevailed against them." 30. And Jacob asked and said: "Tell me your name I pray"; and he said: "Why, now, do you ask my name?" And he blessed him there. 31. And Jacob called the name of the place Peniel because: "I have seen *angels from before the Lord* face to face and my life has been spared." 32. And the sun shone for him when he crossed Peniel and he was limping on account of his thigh. 33. Because of this, until *the time of this day,* the sons of Israel do not eat the sinew of the hip which is above the hollow of the thigh because he touched the hollow of Jacob's thigh on the sinew of the hip.

CHAPTER 33

1. And <Jacob>[a] lifted up his eyes and saw and behold, Esau was coming and with him four hundred men *on foot.*[b] And he divided the children between Leah

Apparatus, Chapter 32

[w] *yqht* (VN, *wqh't*) (from *qhy*) a rare word used to translate a rare Hebrew term in all Pal. Tg. texts (corr. *qtt* of P); lit.: "to be blunt (and loose)"; cf. Pal. Tg. (VN), Gen 33:4.

[x] Text: *'tpgšwt'*; VN: "in his wrestling"; another term, *bšdrwtyh*; correct Nfmg (*bstd/r/wt'*) accordingly; CTg C as Nf.

[y] VN, CTg C, Nfmg: "because the column of dawn has arisen."

[z] Nfmg: "to send"; VN, CTg C as Nf.

[aa] Nfmg: "of the messengers"; CTg C as Nf.

[bb] Nfmg: "(no) longer be said."

[cc] Nfmg: "in the form of men"; = CTg C: "with holy angels from before the Lord in the form of men."

Notes, Chapter 32

[11]"was benumbed," *w-qht*, from *qhy*; rendered thus following Jerome A. Lund, "On the Interpretation of the Palestinian Targumic Reading *wqht* in Gen 32:25," *JBL* 105 (1986) 99–103. Modern translations generally render as "was dislocated," "became disjointed."

[12]"dawn," *'mwd dšr'*, lit. "the column of the morning." ". . . of the dawn" (also in Hebrew: *'mwd hšr*). HT: *šr*. Nf renders *šr* ("dawn") throughout in like manner: Gen 19:15; 32:25, 27.

[13]"time to praise. . . ." The same reason for the angel's departure is given in *Gen. R.* 78,2 and in other rabbinic texts. In Pal. Tgs. this angel is presented as the chief of the angels of praise.

[14]"with angels from before the Lord"; HT: "with *'lhym*" (=with God, or with divine beings).

Apparatus, Chapter 33

[a] Missing in text; in Nfi.

[b] Nfmg: "(men), war leaders" (or: "generals") (*pwlymkyn*; read *pwlmrkyn*; see Nf Gen 32:7).

and Rachel and the two *concubines*.[c1] 2. And he placed the concubines and their sons to the front and Leah and her sons <and Rachel and Joseph behind>.[d] 3. And he passed in front of them and saluted them *according to the custom of the land*,[e2] seven times until *the time that* he drew near to his brother. 4. And Esau ran to meet him and embraced him and fell on his neck and kissed him and wept.[f] 5. And he lifted up his eyes and saw the women and the little ones and said: "Who are these with you?" And he said: "Children with whom the Lord favored me."[g] 6. And the concubines drew near, they and their sons and *saluted*[3] him.[h] 7. And Leah and her sons also drew near and *saluted*[3] him; <and after that Joseph and Rachel drew near and they saluted him>.[i] 8. And he said: "What does all this host that I have met (mean) for you?"[4] And he said: "To find grace *and favor*[5] in your sight."[j] 9. And Esau said: "I have plenty, my brother; keep for yourself *all that is yours.*" 10. And Jacob said: "No, I pray; if, I pray, I have found grace *and favor in your sight,*[k] let my gift be received from me, because for this reason have I seen your countenance[m] as one sees the countenance *of angels from before the Lord*[6] and you have showed yourself kindly disposed. 11. Receive, I pray, my goodwill gift that I have brought you, because *the Lord* has favored me[n] and because I have everything." And he pressed him and he took (it). 12. And he said: "Let us move, *I pray*, and *let us proceed* and I will go before you." 13. And he said to him: "My master knows[o] that the children are tender[p] and that I have sheep and cows that give suck[q] *before* me. If they are overdriven[r] for one day, all the flock will die. 14. Let my lord pass, I

Apparatus, Chapter 33

[c] Nfmg: "maidservants"; see Gen 32:23 above.
[d] Missing in text.
[e] Nfmg: "he prostrated himself upon the ground."
[f] Nfmg, PVN add: ("and kissed him; P: "and both of them wept"; cf. *Gen. R.* 78, 9). Esau wept because his teeth had grown blunt (corr. Nfmg) (VN: + as [text: "in"] wax) and Jacob wept because of the tenderness of his neck."
[g] Nfmg: "the Memra of the Lord had consideration for and protected."
[h] Nfmg: "the maidservants drew near, they and their sons, and bowed down."
[i] Missing in the text.

[j] Nfmg: "before my lord."
[k] Nfmg: "before you, and receive the gift" (*dôron*).
[m] Nfmg: "from my (text: his) hands, because for this reason have I (or: you) reconciled your countenance."
[n] Nfmg: "the Memra of the Lord has had consideration of me."
[o] Nfi: "is aware."
[p] Nfmg, PV: "(that the children) are delicate" (Ptc. peal; in Nf Ptc. pail).
[q] Nfmg: "going up."
[r] Nfmg: "(if) I overdrive."

Notes, Chapter 33

[1]"concubines"; HT: "maids." The same rendering in Nf 31:33 and 32:23.
[2]"saluted according to the custom . . ."; see note to Gen 18:2. HT (RSV): "bowing himself to the ground."
[3]"saluted them"; HT: "bowed down"; see note to 18:2.
[4]"What . . . (mean) for you?"; lit. "who for you. . . ," rendering HT literally.
[5]"grace and favor in your sight"; HT: "grace (*ḥn*) in your eyes"; "grace and favor"; *ḥn wḥsd*; HT: *ḥn*. See note to 6:8 and 32:6.
[6]"of angels from before the Lord"; (RSV): "like seeing the face of God."

pray, before his servant and I will lead them *leisurely,*[s7] according to the pace of the beasts of labor which are *in my hand* and according to the pace of the children, until *the time that* I go[t] to my master at *Gabla.*"[u8] 15. And Esau said: "Let me, I pray, leave[w] with you some of the people that are with me." But he said: "Why, now? Let me find[x] grace *and favor* in the sight of my lord.""[y] 16. And Esau returned that day on his way to *Gabla.*[8] 17. And Jacob moved to Succothah[9] and built a house for himself, and for the cattle he made booths. For this reason he called the name of the place Succothah. 18. And Jacob came, perfect *in good work,*[10] to the *fortress* of Shechem which is[z] in the land of Canaan, on coming from Paddan-aram; and he camped before[aa] the city. 19. And he bought the territory of the area[11] where he spread his tent from the sons of Hamor, the father of Shechem, for a hundred *pearls.*[bb12] 20. And he erected an altar there, and he *prayed*[cc] *there in the name of the Lord,*[dd13] the God of Israel.

Apparatus, Chapter 33

[s] *lhwny* as in Ps.-J., *Aruk* (s.v. *hn*), Levita, *Meturgeman; Gen. R.* 78, 14.

[t] Nfmg: "we (= I) enter."

[u] Nfmg: "let my lord, I pray, go ahead before his servant and receive his portion and the reward of the great blessing (with) which my father blessed him in this world, and I by myself will lead the sons of the captivity to the instruction of the law which is before me, and to the hope in its (or: his) righteousness (or: by his merits) until the time the captivities are ended and I enter to my master to wage war in Gebula."

[w] Nfmg: "let me set up" (same Aramaic word used to render the Hebrew in Nf Gen. 30:38; 43:9; 47:2; Exod 10:20).

[x] Nfmg: "let us (= let me?) find," (*nškhh*).

[y] Nfmg: "before my lord."

[z] Nfmg: "the city of Shechem which is in the land."

[aa] Nfmg: "opposite."

[bb] PVN: "(for a hundred) pearls" (in Nf, PVN: *margarites* [*margĕlis*], a Greek loan word).

[cc] Nfmg: "worshiped."

[dd] Nfmg: "the Memra of the Lord."

Notes, Chapter 33

[7]"leisurely," *lhwny*; HT: *l'ty*, "slowly." Precisely this same Aramaic word, found only in Nf as the rendering of HT 33:14, is cited in *Gen. R.* 78,14 in explanation of the Hebrew. See McNamara, 1966B, 12.

[8]"Gabla"; Nf's rendering of HT "Seir"; see McNamara, 1972, 194.

[9]"to Sukkothah." Nf retains the Hebrew final *he locale*, adding the preposition "to." See note to 26:1, 2; also 31:23; 35:6.

[10]"perfect (*šlm*) in good works"; HT: *šlm*, in the sense of "safely." The rendering here is in keeping with Nf's translation technique of qualifying *šlm* (as also *tm, tmym*) when referring to persons with the words "good works"; thus Gen 6:9; 15:16; 17:1; 25:27; 33:18; 34:21; Deut 18:13. In this instance (33:18) Nf's rendering is not in order, since *šlm* does not have a moral connotation.

[11]"territory of the area," *thwmh dhql'*; HT: *hlqt hśdh*; RSV: "the piece of land." Nf uses three different words to render *śdh* of the HT (see note to 2:5), two of which (*thwmh, hql'*) it uses here to translate the HT composite expression.

[12]"pearls," *mrglyyn*, Greek loan word *margarêtês* or *margêlis*; HT: *qśyth*, a word of unknown meaning, rendered in RSV as: "pieces of money." The exact meaning of the Hebrew term was discussed by the Rabbis. One identification proposed was "precious stones"; see *Gen. R.* 79,7. This same text of *Gen. R.* tells us that about 200 C.E. R. Hiyya the Elder and R. Simeon b. Halafta forgot the translation of several words of the HT and went to an Arab market town (probably the Aramaic Nabatean-speaking Hegra in Northern Arabia) to relearn them. One of the difficult Hebrew words was *qśyta* of Gen 33:19, and the Aramaic term mentioned as translating it was *kesitta*, which may mean either "diamonds" of "sheep." See *Gen. R.* 79,7, with translator's note in the Soncino translation.

[13]"in the name of the Lord . . ."; HT (RSV): "(he erected an altar) and called it El-Elohe-Israel" (=the God, the God of Israel). In Nf's paraphrase "call" of the HT is interpreted as praying.

CHAPTER 34

1. And Dinah, the daughter of Leah, whom she had borne*ᵃ* to Jacob, went out *to let herself be seen* with the daughters *of the people* of the land.[1] 2. And Shechem, the son of Hamor*ᵇ* the Hivite, the master of the land, saw her and took her and abused[2] her*ᶜ* and disgraced her. 3. And his soul found delight in Dinah, Jacob's daughter; and he was enamored of the maiden*ᵈ* and he spoke *words of peace*ᵉ[3] with the heart of the maiden. 4. And Shechem said to Hamor, his father, saying: "Take this maiden*ᵈ* (for me) as wife." 5. And Jacob heard that he had defiled Dinah, his daughter; and his sons were with the cattle*ᶠ* in the field, and Jacob remained silent*ᵍ* until the time they came. 6. And Hamor, the father of Shechem, went out to Jacob to speak with him. 7. And the sons of Jacob entered from the field when they heard (of it); and the men were very angry and they were very much offended because he had done*ʰ* an abomination in Israel in having intercourse with*ⁱ* the daughter of Jacob, for it was *not proper*[4] that such a thing be done. 8. And Hamor spoke with them saying: "The soul of Shechem, my son, found delight in your daughter. I pray, give her in marriage to him as wife,*ʲ* 9. and mingle[5] with us; give us*ᵏ* your daughter and take our daughters for yourselves. 10. And you shall dwell with us and the land will be before you. Dwell*ᵐ* and *trade in it* and take possession of it." 11. And Shechem said to his father and brothers: "I have found*ⁿ* grace *and favor* in your sight, and what you will say to me I will give. 12. Make very great for me the *dowry* and the *marriage contract*ᵒ[6] and I will give just*ᵖ* as you say to me, but give me the

Apparatus, Chapter 34

ᵃ Nfmg: "the daughter of Leah who was born."
ᵇ Nfi: "of the nations of the world" (i.e., Gentiles).
ᶜ Nfmg: "and joined (sexually) with her."
ᵈ Nfmg: "the girl."
ᵉ Nfmg: "of peace to the heart of the girl."
ᶠ Nfmg: "herds."
ᵍ Nfmg: "he abandoned."
ʰ Nfmg: "there had been done."
ⁱ Nfmg: "in joining (sexually) with."
ʲ Nfmg: "give her to him, I pray, as wife."

ᵏ Nfmg: "You shall give" (another word); = CTg C.
ᵐ Nfmg: "Reside in it"; CTg C: "reside and trade in it."
ⁿ Nfmg: "we (= I) have found," or "let us (= me) find."
ᵒ PVN: "(make very great for me) the dowry and the marriage contract" (*ketuba*, as in Nf); "dowry" in Nf *prn*; in VN *pwrn*: in CTg C: *pryn*; = Greek loan word *pherne*.
ᵖ Nfmg: "all (that you say)."

Notes, Chapter 34

[1]"(the daughters of the land) to be seen with"; HT: "to look at," *r'h b-*. See Ginzberg, *Legends*, V, pp. 313f., and comment of B. Barry Levy, 1, 1986, 209.
[2]"abused," lit. "used"; HT: "lay with." See note to 30:15.
[3]"words of peace"; not in HT.
[4]"it was not proper." HT: "thus it was not done." Nf translates passive of "to do" with the negative in similar fashion elsewhere (Gen 20:9; 29:26; Lev 4:2, 13, 22, 27; 5:17).
[5]"mingle"; HT: "intermarry."
[6]"dowry and marriage contract"; HT (RSV): "marriage present and gift"; "dowry," Greek loan word *pherne*; also used here in the LXX.

maiden[d] as wife." 13. And the sons of Jacob answered Shechem and Hamor his father in the *vastness of their wisdom,*[7] and they spoke[q] (thus), because he had violated[r] Dinah their sister. 14. And they said to them: "We cannot do this thing—to give[s] in marriage our sister to a man who has <a foreskin>[t] because he is a disgrace[u] to us. 15. But we will *become mingled*[8] with you if you become like us, circumcising every male of you. 16. And we will give our daughters to you, and your daughters we will take to ourselves, and we will dwell with you and *all of us* will become one people. 17. And if you will not listen to us by becoming circumcised, we will take our daughter and go." 18. And their words were pleasing[w] in the sight of Hamor and in the sight of Shechem, the son of Hamor. 19. And the young man[x] did not delay to do the deed because his soul found delight in the daughter of Jacob; and he was the most honored of all *the men of* the house of his father. 20. And Hamor came, and Shechem and his son, to the gate of their city and spoke with the men of their city,[y] saying: 21. "These men are perfect *in good work*[9] with us, and let them dwell in the land and trade in it; and the land— behold, it is broad *in its territory*—lies before them. We will take their daughters to us as wives and we will give our daughters to them. 22. But only on this condition will the men *mingle*[10] with us, to dwell with us, to become one nation: that we circumcise[z] every male as they are circumcised. 23. Their possessions and their wealth[aa] and all their cattle, are they not ours? Only *let us mingle*[10] with them and they will dwell with us." 24. And every one going out the gate of his city listened to Hamor and Shechem, his son; and they circumcised every male, everyone going out the gate of his city. 25. And it happened that on the third day, when they were sore *from their circumcision,*[11] two sons of Jacob, Simeon and Levi, brothers of Dinah, took each man his sword, and entered the city in all safety and killed every male. 26. And they killed Hamor and Shechem, his son, with the edge of the sword and took Dinah from the house of Shechem and went out. 27. The sons of Jacob went in upon the slain and plundered the city because they had defiled their sister.[bb] 28. They took their sheep and their oxen, <and their he-asses>,[cc] and what was in the

Apparatus, Chapter 34

[q] Nfmg: "he spoke."
[r] Nfmg: "they had violated"; = CTg E.
[s] Nfmg: "to give" (another word, that in CTg C).
[t] Missing in text, and glosses; in CTg C.
[u] Nfmg: "an abomination"; = CTg C.
[w] Nfmg: "looked good."
[x] Nfmg: "boy"; = CTg C.
[y] Nfmg: "the people of the city"; CTg C: "the wise men of their city."
[z] Nfmg: "when he circumcises."
[aa] Nfmg: "the herds (or: riches) and their possessions"; CTg C: "their wealth and their possessions."
[bb] Nfmg: "they had defiled Dinah."
[cc] Missing in the text.

Notes, Chapter 34

[7]"in the vastness of their wisdom"; HT: "with guile." The same translation occurs again in Nf, in the only other occurrence of the word in the Pentateuch (Gen 27:35).

[8]"we will become mingled"; HT: *n'wt*; RSV: "we will consent"; a word found only in Gen 34:15, 22, 23, and rendered in like manner in Nf in all occurrences.

[9]"perfect in good work"; HT: "perfect." The translation is in accord with Nf practice. See note to 33:18.

[10]"mingle"; see note to 34:15.

[11]"sore from their circumcision"; HT: "when they were sore."

city and what was in the field; 29. and all their *wealth*[12] and all their little ones and their wives and all that was in the houses they took captive and made (their) spoil. 30. And Jacob said to Simeon and Levi: "You have done evil to me, *making my name*[dd] *evil* before the inhabitants of the land, among the Canaanites and the Perizzites. I am a people few in number and they will be gathered <against me and will kill me>[ee] and *will blot out (both) me* and *the men* of my house."[ff] 31. And *the two sons*[13] of Jacob,[gg] Simeon and Levi, answered[hh] and said *to Jacob, their father: "It is not fitting that they should say*[ii] *in their congregations and in their schools:*[jj] <'*Uncircumcised*>[kk] *have defiled virgins*[mm][14] *and servers* <*of idols*>[nn] *the daughter*[oo] *of Jacob.' But it is fitting that they should say in the congregations*[pp] *of Israel and in their schoolhouse:*[qq] '*Uncircumcised were slain on account of a virgin* <*and servers of idols*>[rr] *because they defiled*[ss] *Dinah, the daughter of Jacob'*; so *that after all this Shechem,*[tt] *the son of Hamor, might not become proud in his soul and exalted in his heart and say: 'Like a woman who has not a son of man, avenging humiliation,* thus was it done to *Dinah* our sister: like a lost woman, *a prostitute.'"*[uu]

Apparatus, Chapter 34

[dd] Nfmg: "my reputation" (*ṭby* = *ṭyby*); cf. Ps.-J.

[ee] Missing in text: supplied from Nfmg.

[ff] Nfmg: "and they shall kill and destroy the mothers with the children."

[gg] PVNL as Nf, with variants as below.

[hh] VNL: "the two sons of Jacob answered together, and said to Israel"; P: "Simeon and Levi answered and said to Jacob."

[ii] Nfmg: "that it be said"; = VNL.

[jj] Nfmg: "in their school houses"; = PVNL.

[kk] Erased by censor; in PVNL.

[mm] P: "uncircumcised defiled (*s'ybw*) virginity" (*btwln*). VNL: "uncircumcised defiled virginity" (*btwlt'*); Nfmg: "*s' (s'ybw* = defiled?; or: *sepher 'aḥer*= variant readings) "virgins with regard to virginity" (*btwln lbtwlt'*). *j. Nid.* 49a bot. speaks of: "a *betulah* (virgin) as to virginity (*lbtwlyn*)," i.e., a virgin with regard to the hymen as opposed to menstruation (lit.: "*bloods*"). See Jastrow, I, 200.

[nn] Erased by censor; in PVNL.

[oo] Nfmg: "they have violated the daughter of."

[pp] Nfmg: "that it should be said in congregations of"; = VNL.

[qq] Nfmg: "in the (school) houses"; = P.

[rr] Erased by censors; in PVNL.

[ss] Nfi: "they have defiled Dinah"; Nfmg: "because of the daughters of Jacob and not only (this) but lest."

[tt] Nfmg: "after this it is not fitting for Shechem"; P: "from now it is not fitting for Shechem."

[uu] Nfmg 1°: "(like a) lost woman, a prostitute who has no avenger, has it been done to my sister Dinah. Because of this have we done this thing"; Nfmg 2°: "(who has no) avenger of blood nor avenger of humiliation, thus did it happen to Dinah, the daughter of Jacob. And he said: Like a whoring woman and a prostitute he has reckoned our sister"; cf. VNL: "like a woman who has no man to avenge her humiliation, thus was it done to Dinah the daughter of Jacob, and they say: Like a whoring woman and a prostitute have they reckoned our sister"; P almost identical.

Notes, Chapter 34

[12]"wealth," *mmwn*; HT: *ḥyl*, "might," etc.

[13]"The two sons . . . humiliation." This elaborate aggadic supplement in Nf Gen 34: 31, which is also present in the Frg. Tgs. and in a shorter form in Ps.-J., "finds no reflection in any known rabbinic literature" (Grossfeld, *Neofiti*, note 24 to Gen 34). For a textual study of the midrash, see B. Barry Levy, 1, 1986, 210–212.

[14]"defiled virgins." R. Le Déaut, 1978, 321, note 14 (with reference to S. Lieberman, *Hellenism*, 167, and G. Vermes, *Jesus the Jew*, 219) draws attention to a Nfmg which clarifies this expression: "virgins with regard to virginity," i.e., with regard to the hymen, as opposed to menstruation, this being the formula of *j. Nid.* I, 49a. See Apparatus, note *mm*.

CHAPTER 35

1. And *the Lord*[a] said to Jacob: "Arise, go up to Bethel and dwell there and *build*[b] an altar there *to the name of the Memra*[1] *of the Lord*, who was revealed[c] to you when you fled[d] from before Esau your brother." 2. And Jacob said to *the men of* his house[2] and to everyone that was with him: "Remove the foreign *worship from among*[3] you; and purify yourselves and wash your garments.[e] 3. And let us arise and go to Bethel and *I will build* an altar there *to the name of the Lord*[4] who answered me in the *hour*[f] of my affliction and[g] *was at my aid*[5] on the journey on which I went." 4. And they gave to Jacob all the foreign *worship*[6] that was in their hands,[h] and the rings that were on their ears;[i] and Jacob hid them under the oak[j][7] which *is near* Shechem. 5. And they journeyed on, and the fear of *the Lord*[k] was upon the villages that were around them and they did not pursue the sons of Jacob. 6. And Jacob entered[m] Luzah[8] which is in the land of Canaan—that is, Bethel—he and all the people that were with him. 7. And he built an altar there and called[n] the place where *the Lord was revealed to him* Beth-El,[9] because there the Lord had been revealed to him when he fled from before *Esau*, his brother. 8. And Deborah, the

Apparatus, Chapter 35

[a] Nfmg: "the Memra of the Lord."

[b] Nfmg: "and you shall make."

[c] Nfmg: "to God who was revealed."

[d] Nfmg: "at the time you fled from."

[e] Nfmg: "which were with him. Remove the images of (*word erased by censor*) the idols which are among you and purify yourselves and wash your garments."

[f] Nfmg: "the altar to God who answered me in the hour of."

[g] Nfmg +: "his Memra."

[h] Nfmg: "the images of (*word erased by censor*) the idols which were in his hands."

[i] Nfmg: "which were on their ears."

[j] Nfmg: "which was opposite Shechem."

[k] Nfmg: "the sons of Israel (journeyed on) and (the fear of the Lord) was."

[m] Nfmg: "and (Jacob) came."

[n] CTg E: "... and he called the name of the place El Beth-El, because there were the angels revealed to him when he was fleeing from before Esau his brother"; Nfmg: "and he worshiped and prayed there in the name of the Memra of the Lord God who was revealed to him in Bethel because there was revealed to him there the glory of the Shekinah of the Lord the time that he fled before Esau."

Notes, Chapter 35

[1] "in the name of the Memra ..."; HT: "to the God who appeared to him."

[2] "the men of his house"; HT: "his house (hold)." The addition of "men," etc., is a translation technique of Nf in the rendering of "house" when humans are intended, e.g., Gen 7:1; 12:17; 18:19; 34:19; 35:2; 41:51; 45:8; 46:27; 47:12; 50:4, 22.

[3] "foreign worship from among you"; HT: "the foreign gods which are in your midst." Nf uses "foreign worship" in general for Ht's "foreign gods" (Gen 35:2, 4; Deut 31:16; 32:12).

[4] "to the name of the Lord"; HT: "to God."

[5] "was at my aid"; HT: "was with me." On this paraphrase see note to 28:20 and Introduction, p. 28.

[6] "foreign worship." See note to v. 3.

[7] "oak"; HT: "terebinth." Nf renders the Hebrew words for "terebinth" (*'lh*) and "oak" (*'lwn*) by the same term "oak" (*'lwn*). See note in Grossfeld, *Neofiti*, note 8 to Gen 25.

[8] "Luzah"; HT: "Luzah" = Luz, with *he locale*. On the *he locale*, see note to Gen 26:1, 2; also 33:17.

[9] "where the Lord was revealed to him Bethel"; HT: "he called the place El Bethel because God revealed himself to him."

nurse*º* of Rebekah, died and she was buried*ᵖ* under the oak; [10] and he called the name of the oak "Weeping." [11] 9. *O God of eternityᵍ—may his name be blessed for ever and forever and ever* [12]—*your meekness and your rectitude, and your justice and your strength and your glory, will not pass for ever and ever.ʳ You have taught us to bless the bridegroom and the bride from Adam and his consorts.ˢ And again you have taught us to visit those who are ill from our father Abraham, the righteous one, when you were revealed to him in the Valley of the Vision* [13] *while he was stillᵗ suffering from circumcision. And you taught us to console the mourners from our father Jacob*

Apparatus, Chapter 35

º Nfmg: "the foster-mother"; = VNL; similar word in CTg C.

ᵖ VNL +: "below Bethel"; CTg C +: "beneath Bethel under the oak"; VNL v. 8 almost = Nf.

ᵍ VNL: "God of eternity, may his name be blessed for eternal ages, you have taught us to bless the bridegroom and the bride from Adam and his partner, since thus does the Scripture clearly state: And the Memra of the Lord said to them: Grow strong and multiply and fill the earth and subdue it. You taught us to visit those who are ill from our father Abraham, the righteous, when you were revealed to him in the Valley of the Vision. And you further taught us to bless those who mourn from our father, the righteous Jacob, when you were revealed to him when he came from Paddan-aram, as the way of the world (= death) had encountered Deborah, the foster-mother of Rebekah, his mother, and Rachel died beside him on the way and our father Jacob sat there crying aloud, lamenting, mourning and weeping. And you, master of every age, O Lord, in the measure of your good mercies were revealed to him and consoled him, and blessed him with the blessing of those who mourn over his mother. Wherefore does the Scripture clearly state and say: The Memra of the Lord was revealed to Jacob a second time on his return from Paddan-aram and blessed him"; P: "The God of eternity, may his name be praised for everlasting ages and for all generations. From the primeval example (Greek loan word: *dogma*) you have taught your forbearance for eternal generations. Your forbearance, your righteousness, your grandeur, your rectitude, your power and your glory do not cease from all generations. You have taught us fitting commandments and beautiful statutes" (etc., as in VNL, but with the Scripture citations in Hebrew. CTg C is close to P, again with biblical texts left in Hebrew: "God of eternity, may his name be blessed for all ages from the day of eternity. You have taught your forbearance to endless generations, since your rectitude, your righteousness, your grandeur, your majesty, your power and your glory do not cease for ever and ever. You have taught us seemly commandments, etc."

ʳ Nfmg: "You have taught us fitting commandments and beautiful statutes, you have taught us to bless, etc."

ˢ Nfmg: "because thus does the Scripture clearly state: And the Memra of the Lord blessed them and the Memra of the Lord said to them: Be strong and multiply and fill the earth and subdue it. And again you have taught us (to visit)"; cf. VNL.

ᵗ Nfmg: "and you commanded him to circumcise his foreskin ... you blessed him over his mother, because thus does the Scripture clearly state and say"; = VNL.

Notes, Chapter 35

[10]"the Oak," as in the HT (*'lwn*). See note to v. 4.

[11]"he called the name of the Oak Weeping"; HT: "he called its name 'The Oak of Weeping.'" Nf probably to be corrected accordingly.

[12]This is the beginning of a *sidra* (*seder*), i.e., a biblical passage appointed as a synagogue reading. The beginning of these tends to have an expansive paraphrase. See note to Gen 15:1. The paraphrase to 35:9 is found in whole or in part in Nf, Nfmg, Frg. Tgs., CTg. C, Ps.-J. This midrash is on God as model for certain works of mercy and human consideration: blessing the bridegroom and bride, visiting the sick, consoling the mourners, with supporting Bible texts, respectively: Gen 1:28; 17:1, 9-14 and 18:1; Gen 35:9, i.e., the present text which it introduces. See also M. Klein, 1986, II, 26f; Grossfeld, *Neofiti*, note 12 to Gen 35. There is a detailed analysis of the text in B. Barry Levy, 1, 1986, 212-219.

[13]"a second time"; HT: "again."

the righteous one. The way of the world[14] *overtook Deborah, the foster mother of Rebekah his mother. And Rachel died beside him on his journey; and he sat down crying aloud and he wept and lamented and wailed and was dejected. But you in your good mercies were revealed to him and blessed him; (with) the blessing*[u] *of the mourners you blessed him and consoled him. For thus the Scripture explains and says: And the Lord was revealed* to Jacob a *second time*[15] when he came[w] from Paddan-aram and blessed him. 10. <And *the Lord* said to him: "Your name is Jacob; your name shall no longer be called Jacob, because Israel shall be your name." And he called his name Israel.>[11] And *the Lord*[x] said to him: "I am the God *of the heavens.*[16] *Be strong* and multiply. A nation, and an assembly *of a congregation* of *just* nations, shall arise from you, and kings *who rule nations shall* come forth from your loins. 12. And the land that I gave to Abraham and to Isaac, I will give it to you; and to your sons after you I will give the land." 13. And *the Glory of the Shekinah*[y] *of the Lord* went up[17] from above him in the place[z] in which it spoke with him. 14. <And Jacob erected a pillar in the place in which he had spoken with him[aa]>, a pillar of stone; and he poured *libations* upon it and poured oil upon it. 15. And Jacob called the name of the place where *the Lord*[bb] had spoken with him Bethel. 16. And they moved from Bethel, and it was *the time of the harvest*[cc][18] of the land,[dd] to come to Ephrath. And Rachel brought forth and had difficulty in bringing forth. 17. And when she had difficulty in bringing forth, the midwife said to her: "Do not fear; because this one is a son."[ee] 18. And when she gave forth her soul—because she died—she called him:[19] the son[ff] of my sor-

Apparatus, Chapter 35

[u] Nfmg: "You blessed him with the blessing of him who mourns and consoled him. For thus does the Scripture clearly state and say that he was revealed. And again you have taught us to bury the dead from our master Moses, whom the Lord, the Lord of ages—may his name be blessed for ages—buried."

[w] Nfmg: "the Memra of the Lord a second time when he came"; cf. VNL, CTg C.

[x] Nfmg: "the Memra of the Lord"; = CTg C. The verse is omitted in Nf text but is supplied in margin.

[y] Nfi: "the Shekinah of the Glory."

[z] Nfmg: "from beside him, the Glory of the Shekinah of the Lord (went up) in the place"; = CTg C.

[aa] Missing in the text: in CTg C.

[bb] Nfmg: "the Memra of the Lord"; CTg C ends at v. 15a.

[cc] *'swn 'llth.*

[dd] VNL: "and it was (the) time (of) the *kibra* (a good stretch) of the land to go in to Ephratah and Rachel was in childbirth, and she had difficulty in giving birth"—retaining *kibrah*, the obscure word of the Hebrew text; cf. Gen 48:7; Nfmg: "the *kibra* of the land to go in"; = VNL.

[ee] Nfmg: "a male son" (*byr*).

[ff] Nfmg: "a son" (*byr*); v. 18b in PVNL; = Nf.

Notes, Chapter 35

[14]"the way of the world"; a euphemism for death; cf. Jos 23:14; 1 Kgs 2:2.

[15]"Plain of the Vision." See Nf Gen 18:1; also 12:6; 13:18; 14:13; McNamara, 1972, 198.

[16]"God of the heavens"; HT: "El Shaddai." Regular translation of Nf; see Introduction, p. 35.

[17]"Glory of the Shekinah went up"; HT: "God went up." On Nf's translation see Introduction p. 37.

[18]"the time of the harvest"; HT: "and there was still a *kibrah* (?="stretch") of land." Ps.-J. as Nf. See also *Gen. R.* 82,7, linking the HT word with *kbr* ("already") and *bar* ("corn"): "The corn was already grown and the rainy season had passed . . . but the hot season had not yet come." VNL and Nfmg retain the Hebrew word *kibrat* (. . .).

[19]"he called him"; HT: "she called him." This text of Nf may be intentional, since Rachel is presumed dead. However, it could also be an error, as immediately afterward we read: "but his father called him."

row; but his father called him, *in the language of the sanctuary,*[20] Benjamin. 19. And Rachel died and was buried on the way of Ephrath, that is, Bethlehem.[gg] 20. And Jacob erected a pillar above her grave; this is the pillar of the grave of Rachel until *the time of* this day. 21. And Israel journeyed and spread his tent *further*[hh] from the Tower of the Flock. 22. And when Israel dwelt in that land Reuben went[ii] and lay with Bilhah[21] <the concubine of his father>;[jj] and Israel heard (of it). And the sons of Jacob were twelve. 23. The sons of Leah: Reuben, the firstborn of Jacob, Simeon, Levi, Judah, Issachar, and Zebulun. 24. The sons of Rachel: Joseph and Benjamin. 25. The sons of Bilhah, the maid of <Rachel: Dan and Naphtali; 26. the sons of Zilpah, the maid of>[kk] Leah: Gad and Asher. These are the sons of Jacob that were born to him in Paddan-aram. 27. And Jacob came to his father Isaac at Memre, the city of the *giants,* that is, Hebron, where Abraham and Isaac had sojourned. 28. And the days[mm] of Isaac were one hundred and eighty years. 29. And Isaac ended his days and died[nn] and was gathered to his people, old and satisfied in days. And his sons Esau and Jacob buried him.

CHAPTER 36

1. And this is the genealog*ical pedigree*[1] of Esau, that is, Edom. 2. Esau took his wives from the daughters of the *Canaanites:*[2] Adah, the daughter of Elon the Hittite, Oholibamah, the daughter of Annah, daughter of Zibeon the Hivite, 3. and

Apparatus, Chapter 35

[gg] Nfmg +: "of Judah."
[hh] Nfmg: "at the far side of"; cf. Ps.-J.
[ii] In VL the text. "Reuben went in concubine of his father" in Hebrew only, followed in Hebrew, by rubric: "It is not translated." This is in accord with M. *Meg.* 4:10. In Nf, it is translated except for "lay with Bilhah," which is in Hebrew. In Nfmg: text in Hebrew without translation. See note 21.

[jj] Missing in text: supplied in Nfi, in Hebrew.
[kk] Missing in text.
[mm] Nfmg: "the days of the life of."
[nn] Nfmg: "he died," lit.: "he stretched himself," as in Ps.-J.; cf. Nfmg. Gen 25:8, 17.

Notes, Chapter 35

[20]"in the language of the sanctuary," i.e., Hebrew. See note to Gen 2:19; also 11:1; 22:1.

[21]"and lay (*wyškb*) (with) <Bilhah>," "lay" being the Hebrew word left untranslated; the word rendered as "with" is really in Nf the sign of the accusative (*yt*), which mistranslates the Hebrew *'t*, which may be the preposition "with" or the sign of the accusative—in this case the former. Also in Nf, part of the text is omitted or left without translation. The explanation of all this lies in the fact that this section of the HT on Reuben's sinful behavior was one of the passages to be read out in Hebrew but not translated into Aramaic. On these see McNamara, 1966A, 46f.; M. Klein, "Not to Be Translated in Public—*l' mtrgm bṣybwr',*" *JJS* 39 (1988), 80–91; 82–84 for Gen 35:22.

Notes, Chapter 36

[1]"genealogical pedigree"; HT: *tldwt.* See note to Gen 2:4.
[2]"Canaanites"; HT: "of Canaan."

Basemath, Ishmael's daughter, sister of Nebaioth. 4. And Adah bore to Esau Eliphaz; and Basemath bore Reuel. 5. And Oholibamah bore Jeush, Jalam, and Korah. These are the sons of Esau who were born to him in the land of Canaan. 6. And Esau took his wives and his sons, and his daughters and all the persons of his household, his wealth[a] and all his cattle and all his property,[b] which he had acquired[c] in the land of Canaan, and he went from before his brother Jacob to *another* land. 7. For their wealth[d] was too great for them to dwell together; and the land of their sojournings could not have room for[e] them because of their cattle. 8. And Esau dwelt in the mountain of Gabla; Esau is Edom. 9. This is the <genealogical>[ebis] *pedigree*[3] of Esau, father of the *Edomites,*[4] in the mountain of *Gabla.*[5] 10. These are the names of the sons of Esau: Eliphaz, the son of Adah, the wife of Esau. This is Reuel, daughter of Basemath, the wife of Esau. 11. The sons of Eliphaz were Teman, Omar, Zepho, Gathem, and Kenaz, 12. Timna was a concubine[f] of Eliphaz, son of Esau, and she bore Amalek to Eliphaz. And these are the sons of Adah, wife of Esau. 13. And these are the sons of Reyek: Nahath, Zerah, Shammah, and Mizzah. <These are the sons of Basemath, wife of Esau>.[g] 14. These were the sons of Oholibamah, the daughter of Anah, the daughter of Zibeon, wife of Esau: she bore to Esau Jeush, Jalam, and Korah. 15. These are the chiefs of the sons of Esau. The sons of Eliphaz the firstborn of Esau: the chief Teman, the chief Omar, the chief Zepho, the chief Kena, 16. the chief Korah, the chief Gatam, the chief Amalek. These are the chiefs of Eliphaz in the land of the Edomites. These are the sons of Adah. 17. And these are the sons of Reuel, the son of Esau: the chief Nahat, the chief Zerah, the chief Shammah, the chief Mizzah; these are the chiefs of Reuel in the land of the *Edomites.*[4] They are the sons of Basemath, Esau's wife. 18. And these are the sons of Oholibamah, wife of Esau: the chief Jeush, the chief Jalam, the chief Korah. These are the chiefs (born) of Oholibamah, the daughter of Anah, Esau's wife. 19. These are the sons of Esau—that is, Edom— and these are their chiefs. 20. These are the sons of Seir, the *Hauranite,*[6] the inhabitants of the land: Lotan, Shobal, Zibeon, Anah, 21. Dishon, Ezer, and Dishan.

Apparatus, Chapter 36

[a] Nfmg: "his riches."
[b] Nfmg: "his possessions."
[c] Nfmg: "he had saved up."
[d] Nfmg: "their possessions were (too) great."
[e] *shn* = *hsn*; Nfmg: "(could not) support."

[ebis] Written above the line and added in different spelling in Nfmg.
[f] Nfmg: "concubine" (*plqy*, another word).
[g] Missing in the text.

Notes, Chapter 36

[3]"genealogical pedigree"; HT: *tldwt.* See v. 1 and note to 2:4.
[4]"Edomites"; HT: "of Edom."
[5]"Gabla"; HT: "Seir." The constant identification of Nf; see McNamara, 1972, 194.
[6]"Hauranite"; HT: *hhry;* RSV: "the Horite." Same identification in Deut 2:12,22. In all these cases the identification is in Nf only; Onq. and Frg. Tgs. have "Horites." The "Hauranites" of Nf are apparently the residents of Hauranitis or Auranitis = Hauran of Ezek 17:16, 18. See McNamara, 1972, 195.

These are the chiefs of the *Hauranites* <the sons of *Gabla*> [h] in the land of *Gabla*. [i] < .... 30. ......> according to their chieftains in the land of Gabla. 31. And these are the kings who reigned in the land of the *Edomites* [4] before any king ruled over the sons of Israel. 32. Bela the son of Beor reigned in Edom, and the name of his city was Dinhabah. 33. And Bela died and Jacob <son of Zerah of Bozrah> reigned *after* him. 35. And Husham died, and Hadad the son of Bedad, who *killed the Midianites* [7] in *the territory of the Moabites*, reigned after him, and the name of his city was Avith. 36. And Hadad died, and Samlah of Masrekah reigned *after* him. 37. And Samlah died and Shaul of *Mesopotamia* [8] reigned *after* him. 38. And Shaul died and Baal-hanan the son of Achbor reigned *after* him. 39. And Baal-hanan the son of Achbor died and Hadar reigned *after* him, and the name of his city was Pau; and his wife's name was Mehetabel, the daughter *of a maker of hunting-nets,* [9] *who worked with his hunting spear all the days of his life; and he grew rich and acquired wealth, and he knew what is silver and what is gold.* 40. These are the names of the chiefs of Esau, according to their families, their places, according to their names: the chief Timna, the chief Alvah, the chief Jetheth, 41. <the chief Oholibamah, the chief Elah, the chief Pinon>, [j] 42. the chief Kena, the chief Teman, the chief Mibzar, 43. the chief Magdiel, the chief Iram. These are the chiefs *of the Edomites*—that is, Esau, father of *the* Edom*ites*—according to their dwellings in the lands in which *they dwelt.*

Apparatus, Chapter 36

[h] Missing in the text. Nfmg: "the sons of Gabla in the land of the Edomites."

[i] Vv. 22-30 omitted in the text by homoioteleuton.
[j] Missing in text.

Notes, Chapter 36

[7] "killed the Midianites . . . territory of (*thwmyyhwn*) the Moabites"; HT: "defeated Midian in the country (*śdh*, lit. "field") of Moab." Nf employs the Aramaic word *thwm'*, "territory," "border," "boundary" as one of the terms to render *śdh* of the HT; see note to 2:5. For the rendering of 33:19, see note to that verse.

[8] "Mesopotamia," lit. "between the Rivers"; HT: "from Rehoboth-of-the-River," "Rehoboth" being from a root meaning "broad."

[9] "daughter of a maker of hunting nets . . . what is gold?"; HT: "daughter of Matred, daughter of Mezahab." Matred is interpreted as "maker of hunting nets," as if from root *trd*, "to hunt," "to chase," and Mezahab as if from *mah*, "what?" and *zahab*, "gold." The same paraphrase is found in the Frg. Tgs. and in Ps.-J. The understanding of the names in *Gen. R.* (83,4) is almost identical with Nf's paraphrase: "*The daughter of Mezahab.* They were net-makers (*trwdym*), and when they became wealthy they used to say: 'What (is) gold and what (is) silver?'" See also B. Barry Levy, 1, 1986, 221–222.

CHAPTER 37

1. And Jacob dwelt in the land of his fathers' sojournings, in the land of Canaan.
2. This is the genealog*ical pedigree*[1] of Jacob. Joseph, when he was seventeen years old, was tending the flock with his brothers; he was a youth *brought up*[2] with the sons of Bilhah, and with the sons of Zilpah, his father's wives. And Joseph brought the bad rumor[3] of *his brothers*[4] to his father. 3. And Israel was enamored of Joseph more than all his sons, because he was the son of his old age; and he made him an *embroidered ornamented garment.*[a][5] 4. And his brothers saw that their father loved him more than all his brothers, and they hated him and could not speak *words* of peace with him. 5. And Joseph had a dream, and he told (it) to his brothers and they hated him still more. 6. And he said to them: "Hear, I pray, this dream which I dreamed. 7. Behold, we were binding sheaves[b][6] in the midst of the field, and behold my sheaf arose and also stood upright, and behold your sheaves *gathered around* and *saluted*[7] my sheaf." 8. And his brothers said to him: "Are you indeed going to reign over us? Or are you indeed to have dominion over us?" And they hated him yet more because of his dreams and because of his words. 9. And he dreamed again *a second time,*[8] and he related it to his brothers, and said: "Behold I have again dreamed, and behold the sun and the moon and eleven stars *saluted* me." 10. And he related it to his father and to his brothers; and his father rebuked

Apparatus, Chapter 37

[a] "an embroidered ornamented garment," *prgwd mṣyyr*; loan word: Latin, *paragauda*; Greek, *paragaudês*.

[b] "binding sheaves": also in PVNL.

Notes, Chapter 37

[1] "genealogical pedigree"; HT: *tldwt*. See note to 2:4.

[2] "brought up with"; not in HT.

[3] "the bad rumor of his brothers," or: ". . . concerning his brothers," *ṭbhwn (=ṭybhwn) d'hwy byš*; *ṭyb*, as in Onq. = "rumor, (evil) report." Nf's paraphrase renders an awkward HT construction: "their report (=the report about them), the evil one." B. Grossfeld (*Neofiti*, note 3 to Gen 37) understands *ṭb* of Nf as "nature," and the entire clause as: "the evil nature of his brothers." See also Grossfeld, 1988, 126 on Onq., where the same Aramaic word as Nf is used; see also Sokoloff, 1990, 219. *ṭb, ṭybh*, "nature," "character." On the Targumic presentation of Joseph, see M. Niehoff, "The Figure of Joseph in the Targums," *JJS* 39 (1988) 234-250; V. Monsarrat, "L'Histoire de Joseph dans le Targum Palestinien," *Foi et Vie* 86 (1986) 17-23.

[5] "(embroidered) ornamented garment," *prgwd (mṣyyr)*; HT: *ktnt psym*; RSV: "a long robe with sleeves." There is mention of this garment in HT Gen 37:3, 23, 32 (cf. also 2 Sam 13:18, 19). Nf, and Pal. Tgs. generally, render *ktnt* ("robe") of the HT with the loan word (Greek *paragaudês*; Latin *paragaudae*; probably ultimately a term of Oriental origin; see Introduction, note 80), "a tunic or garment with purple border," and render HT *pssym* by *mṣyyr*, "embroidered."

[6] "binding sheaves," *kwrkwwn/mkwrkyn*. This rendering of Nf is found as a Pal. Tg. citation in the *Aruk* and is cited by medieval commentaries. David J. Martin comments on this, and such like medieval Pal. Tg. citations found in Nf, that Neofiti must be the *Targum Yerushalmi* or *Targum Erez Israel* known to these writers. See D. J. Martin, "New Directions in Biblical Scholarship. Targum Yerushalmi to the Pentateuch," *Tradition* 13–14 (1973), 201–220; 203 for Gen 37:7. See also above, Introduction, pp. 10–12.

[7] "saluted," lit. "inquired about the welfare of"; HT: "bowed down." See note to 18:2.

[8] "a second time"; HT: "another dream."

him, and said to him: "What is this dream that you have dreamed? Shall I, and your mother and brothers truly come to salute you *according to the custom of the land*?"[9] 11. And his brothers were jealous of him, but his father was keeping note of the matter. 12. And now his brothers went to tend their father's flock at Shechem. 13. And Israel said to Joseph: "Are not your brothers tending (their flocks) in Shechem? *Come*, and I will send you to them." And he said to him: "Here I am." 14. And he said: "Go, I pray, and see how your brothers are, and how the flock is, and bring me word." And he sent him from the plain of Hebron, and he came to Shechem. 15. And *an angel in the appearance of* a man[10] met him[c]—for behold he was lost in the field—and the man asked him saying: "What are you looking for." 16. And he said: "I am looking for my brothers. Tell me,[d] I pray, where they are tending (their flocks)." 17. And the man said: "They moved on from here, for I heard *them* say: 'Let us go to Dothan.'" And Joseph went after his brothers and he met them in Dothan. 18. And they saw him afar off, and before he came near to them they conspired against him to kill him. 19. And they said one to another: "Behold, here comes the lord of these[e] dreams. 20. And, now, come and let us kill him, and let us throw him into one of the pits and we will say: 'An evil beast devoured him'; and we will see, what will be *the end* of his dreams." 21. And Reuben heard it and he delivered him out of their hands and said: "Let us not *kill* him, *and let us not become guilty of his life*."[f][11] 22. And Reuben said to them: "Do not shed *innocent* blood;[12] throw him into this pit which is in the desert and do not extend the hand[g] *of murderers* against him"—that he might rescue him from their hands to restore him[h] to his father. 23. And it happened when Joseph came to his brothers, they stripped him of the *embroidered ornamented garment*[i] which was on him. 24. And they took him and cast him into the pit; but the pit was empty, there was no water in it. 25. And they sat down to eat bread; and they lifted up their eyes and saw, and behold a caravan of *Saracens*[j][13] coming from Gileadah,[14] with their camels laden

Apparatus, Chapter 37

[c] Gen 37:15-34 in CTg E.
[d] CTg E: "show me."
[e] CTg E: "the master of the evil dreams."
[f] CTg E: "let us not become guilty"; CTg D: "guilty of his blood."
[g] CTg D and E: "a hand."

[h] CTg D, E: "they stripped Joseph of the (or "his") garment (*prgwdh*), the embroidered garment."
[i] *prgwd' mṣyyrh*.
[j] PVNL: "a caravan of Saracens"; in Nf "of Saracens" repeated.

Notes, Chapter 37

[9]"salute . . . according to the custom of the land"; HT (RSV): "bow ourselves to the ground." See note to 18:2. The mechanical nature of Nf's paraphrase is well illustrated in the rendering of 37:7 and 10.

[10]"an angel in the appearance of a man"; HT: "a man." Nf's paraphrase is in keeping with rabbinic tradition; cf. *Gen. R.* 84,14 (on Gen 37:15) and 75,4 (on Gen 32:4): Joseph was met by three angels.

[11]"kill him and become guilty of his life"; HT lit.: "let us not strike (=kill) a life." In Deut 19:6, 11 Nf renders the same Hebrew words in identical fashion.

[12]"innocent blood"; HT: "blood."

[13]"Saracens." Nf's text repeats the word (*d-srqyn d-srq'yn*); HT: "Ishmaelites"; the same identification occurs in Nf throughout (Gen 37:25, 27; 39:1). See McNamara, 1972, 200; Grossfeld, *Neofiti*, note 17 to Gen 37. There is mention of a Saracen in *Gen. R.* 48,9 (on Gen 18:2).

[14]"Gileadah"; HT: "Gilead" (without any final *he locale*). Possibly Nf's Aramaic form of the place had a final -*a*. See note to 26:1, 2. In 31:47, however, Nf has form "Gilead."

with *wax*, balm,[15] and resin, on the way to bring (it) down to Egypt. 26. And Reuben said to his brothers: What *wealth*[k][16] will we have if we kill our brother and conceal his blood? 27. Come, let us sell him to the *Saracens*, and let us not *extend our hands*[m][17] against him because he is our brother, a blood *relation*";[18] and his brothers listened to him. 28. And some Midianite men, traders, passed by; and they lifted up and took Joseph out of the pit, and they sold Joseph to the *Saracens* for twenty *selas*[n][19] of silver; and they *brought* Joseph to Egypt. 29. And Reuben returned to the pit, and behold, Joseph was not within the pit and he rent his clothes. 30. And he returned to his brothers and said: "The boy is not and *I do not know*[20] where to go." 31. And they took the *ornamented garment*[o] of *Joseph* and they killed a young he-goat and dipped the *ornamented garment* in the blood. 32. And they sent the *embroidered ornamented garment*[p] of *Joseph* and brought it to their father and said: "This we have found. Examine, we pray, whether it is the *ornamented garment* of your son or not." 33. And he recognized it and said: *"This is* the *ornamented garment*[q] of my son; an evil beast has devoured him. Joseph has surely been killed."[r] 34. And Jacob rent his garments and put on sackcloth *in their stead* and mourned for his son many days. 35. And all his sons and daughters rose up to console him; but he refused to be comforted and said: "No, I shall go down to my

Apparatus, Chapter 37

[k] CTg D, E: "what benefit is there to us if we kill."
[m] CTg E: "the hand of murderers."
[n] CTg D, CTg E: "twenty Zuzim," "twenty *meahs.*"
[o] Nf: *prgwd'*; CTg D, E: "the linen garment" (*ktnt'*).
[p] In all texts, *prgwd'*.
[q] Nf, CTg E: *prgwd'*; CTg D: *ktwntyh.*
[r] CTg E: "And he recognized it and said: This is the garment (*prgwdh*) of my son; a wild beast has not devoured him, nor has my son been surely killed" (CTg E ends here); CTg D: "He recognized it and said: This here is the linen garment (*ktntyh*) of my son Joseph. Joseph my son has not surely been killed, nor has an evil beast devoured him; but rather, an evil woman, who is comparable to a wild beast is standing up opposite him. However, I trust in the Lord, the Lord of all ages, that he will save him from the hands of the woman and will show me the countenance of Joseph my son in peace while I am still alive"; VNL: "And he recognized (. . . as Nf . . . .); . . . it devoured my son Joseph. However, I see in the holy Spirit one like (as it were) an evil woman standing opposite him"; P: "He recognized it <. . .> . . . my son has not been surely killed. Besides, I see in the holy Spirit an evil woman standing opposite him, the wife of Potiphar, the ruler of Pharaoh, the chief of the executioners (Latin loan word: *speculator*; also in Greek, *spekoulatôr*) and she is comparable to a wild beast. Besides I trust in the Lord of all the world to save him from sexual offenses and to show me the face of Joseph my son in peace while I am still alive."

Notes, Chapter 37

[15]"balm," *ltwm*; Akkadian, *ladinnu*; Greek *lêdon, lêdanon (ladanon)*; Latin *ladanum.*
[16]"their wealth" (or "profit, *mmwn, mamôn*), will we have?"; HT: "what profit (*bṣ'*) is it."
[17]"extend our hands"; HT: "let not our hand be."
[18]"blood relation"; HT: "our (own) flesh."
[19]"shekels," *sl'*; HT: "pieces of silver," *ksp.* The identification in Nf is according to the principle in *Bekh* 50a: "every silver piece (*ksp*) mentioned in the Pentateuch without any qualification means a *sela'*; see also Introduction, pp. 32f.
[20]"I do not know"; HT: "and I, where (shall) I come" (=go). In its paraphrase Nf, here as elsewhere, removes the question.

son to Sheol." And his father wept for him. 36. And the Midianites sold him to the *Egyptians*, to Potiphar, an *officer*[21] of Pharaoh, the captain of the *executioners.*[s][22]

CHAPTER 38

1. And it happened in that *hour* that Judah went down from his brothers and turned aside to an Adullamite man whose name was Hirah. 2. And there Judah saw the daughter of a Canaanite whose name was Shua; and he took her to wife and went in to her. 3. And she conceived and bore a son and she called[1] his name Er. 4. And she conceived again and bore a son and called his name Onan. 5. Yet again she bore a son and called his name Shelah. And it happened that she ceased[a][2] (from bearing) *after* she had borne him. 6. And Judah took a wife for Er, his firstborn,

Apparatus, Chapter 37

[s] Latin loan word: *speculator* (also in Greek); VNL: "Potiphar, Pharaoh's ruler, chief of executioners."

Notes, Chapter 37

[21]"officer"; HT: "eunuch." Apart from Tg. Isa 56:3f. (where the literal translation is inevitable), the Tgs. never render this term of the HT literally. Nf translates as *šlyt*, "officer," "ruler"; other Tgs. as *rb*, "magnate," etc.

[22]"executioner"; a Latin-through-Greek loan word: *speculator/spekoulatôr*; HT: "stewards," "guards." Nf renders in the same manner throughout.

Apparatus, Chapter 38

[a] Nf, P: "as she paused"; VNL = Nf.

Notes, Chapter 38

[1]"she called"; HT: "he called." We find the same rendering as Nf in Ps.-J., with Sam. Pent.; feminine also in *Gen. R.* 85,4.

[2]"paused," etc., *psqt*; HT: "He was in Chezib when she bore him." Nf renders the place name Chezib as if it were a verb, as do also Ps.-J., Pesh., Vulg. (*quo nato parere ultra cessavit*). The Hebrew verb in question, however, i.e., *kzb*, generally means "to tell a lie," and thus did Aquila render (as given by Jerome, *Hebr. quaest.* in Gen 38:5): . . . *ut mentiretur a partu (postquam genuit eum).* Jerome, in the same place, takes the Hebrew verb *kzb* to mean "cease," "stop": *stetit partus eius,* and refers to Hab 3:17, where, he says, *kzb (mentiretur opus oliuae)* must mean "cease." *Gen. R.* 85,4 glosses the Hebrew word in 38:5, as Nf does, i.e. *psqt*, "she ceased." B. Grossfeld, *Neofiti,* note 3 to Gen 38, notes that Isenberg (*Studies,* p. 17) believes that the fundamental meaning of *kzb* is "to cheat, to lie," but also refers to the meaning "to fail" in Isa 5:11, which text he believes has influenced Nf's present rendering. Grossfeld himself adds support from Tg. Isa 5:11; 58:11; Tg. Jer 13:1, where the Hebrew *kzb* is rendered by *psq*.

and her name was Tamar. 7. And Er, the firstborn of Judah, *did evil deeds*[3] *before the Lord, and he died by a decree from before the Lord.*[4] 8. And Judah said to Onan: "Go in to your brother's wife and marry her, and raise up the seed *of sons* to *the name* of your brother."[5] 9. And Onan knew that the *sons would not be called by his name*;[6] and when he went in to his brother's wife he destroyed *his works*[7] upon the ground, so as not *to raise up sons*[8] to *the name* of his brother. 10. And what he did was displeasing *before* <the Lord>,[b] and *he* also *died by a decree*[9] *from before the Lord*. 11. And Judah said to Tamar, his daughter-in-law: "Remain a widow in your father's house until the time my son Shelah grows up"—for he said: "Lest he die like his brothers." And Tamar went and dwelt in her father's house. 12. And many days went by[c] and the daughter of Shua, the wife of Judah, died; and when Judah was comforted he went up to Timnah, to the sheep-shearers, he and his friend Hirah the Adullamite. 13. And it was related to Tamar saying: "Behold, your father-in-law is coming up to Timnah to shear the sheep." 14. And she took off her widow's garments, and covered herself with a veil and wrapped herself up in it, and sat down *at the crossroads*[10] which is on the way to Timnah; because she saw that Shelah had grown up and she had not been given to him as wife. 15. And *Judah* saw her, and Judah thought her to be a harlot, because her face *was* covered[d] *in the house of Judah, and Judah had not known her.*[11] 16. So he turned aside to her at the road and said: "Allow me, I pray, that I go in to you"; for he did not know that she was his daughter-in-law. And she said: "What will you give me that you may come in to me?"[e] 17. And he said: *"Behold* I will send you a kid-goat from the flock."

Apparatus, Chapter 38

[b] Missing in text.

[c] Lit.: "and the days become many"; cf. HT.

[d] VNL: "because she had veiled her face."

[e] In Nf "that you may come in to me" twice in text; first time after "his daughter-in-law"; CTg D and E begin here imperfectly: "behold my coming (or: my corpse?) is here. Let me (form of 1st pl.) join sexually with you . . . and she said: What will you give me to join sexually with me?"; CTg D as Nf.

Notes, Chapter 38

[3] "did evil deeds"; HT: "did evil."

[4] "he died by a decree from before the Lord"; HT: "and the Lord slew him." Nf paraphrases in such a manner as to avoid attributing this action to God.

[5] "sons to the name of your brother"; HT: "raise up seed (=offspring) to. . . ."

[6] "sons would not be called by his name"; HT: "that the seed (=offspring) would not be his."

[7] "his works"; added in Nf (and Ps.-J.) to supply a direct object lacking in the HT, which has: "he destroyed to the (=on the) ground." "His works" of Nf = "his seed."

[8] "to raise up sons . . ."; HT: "to give seed (=offspring) to his brother."

[9] "died by a decree"; HT: "he (i.e., Yahweh) killed him also"; see v. 7.

[10] "at the crossroads"; HT: "at Enaim" (place name, lit. "the eyes"). Pesh renders as Nf; so also Vulg. (*in bivio itineris*) and Jerome, *Hebr. quaest*, in Gen 38:14: (Enaim is not the name of a place but the meaning is): *sedit in biuio, siue in compito* (i.e., crossroads) (CCL 72,46). A similar understanding is found in rabbinic texts; see Grossfeld, *Neofiti*, note 14 to Gen 38.

[11] "in the house of Judah and Judah had not known her"; an explanatory paraphrase beyond the HT.

And she said: "Will you give me a pledge until *the time* you send it?" 18. And he said: "What pledge shall I give you?" And she said: "Your *signet-ring*, the cord of your seal, and the staff that is in your hand." And he gave them to her, and he went in to her and she conceived by him. 19. And she arose and went away, and took off her veil[f] and put on the garments of her widowhood. 20. And Judah sent the kid-goat by the hand of his friend[g] the Adullamite, to receive the pledge from the hand of the woman, but he did not find her. 21. And he asked the people of the place saying: "Where is the harlot[h] *who sat at the crossroads*[12] in the road?" And they said: "There is no harlot woman here." 22. And he returned to Judah and said: "I have not found her, and even the people of the place said: 'There is no harlot woman here.'" 23. And Judah said: "Let her take it as her own, lest we become the object of mockery. Behold, I have sent this kid, and behold now, I have not found her." 24. And it happened about three months later that it was related to Judah, saying: "Tamar, your daughter-in-law, has played the harlot. And behold she is with child because of harlotry." And Judah said: "Bring her out and let her be burned." 25. *And Tamar went out*[13] *to be burned by fire*[i] *and she asked for the three witnesses, but*

Apparatus, Chapter 38

[f] VNL: "her veil" (same word as Nf, CTg D + E).

[g] CTg D, E: "his companion."

[h] CTg D: "the woman, the harlot."

[i] CTg E, P: "And Tamar was going out to be burnt by fire; (P+: and) she sought the three witnesses but could not find them. She raised her eyes on high and said: I beseech by the mercies that are before you, O Lord God, answer me in the hour of my affliction (P: in this hour which is the hour of my affliction) and I will raise up to you three righteous ones in the Valley of Dura—Hananiah, Mishael, and Azariah. At that hour the Lord beckoned to (P: the Holy one, Blessed be He, summoned) Michael the angel and said to him: Go down, give them to her. When she saw them her eyes shone and she cast them under the feet of the judges and said: The man to whom these belong, from him am I with child. But even if I am to be burnt, I will not reveal him. However, the witness that is between me and him will put in his heart to recognize them to whom these belong—the signet ring, the cloak, and the staff"; CTg D, VNL: "And Tamar was going out to be burnt. She sought the three witnesses but could not find them. She raised her eyes on high and said: (VNL +: I beg from before you, O Lord). You are the Lord (VNL: You are the God) who answers (D +: the prayer of) the afflicted in the hour of their affliction. Answer me in this hour (VNL +: which is the hour of my affliction) and I will raise up to you three righteous ones from (VNL: in) the Valley of Dura—Hananiah, Mishael, and Azariah. At that hour the Lord beckoned to Michael and said to him (VNL: the Memra of the Lord heard the voice of her prayer and said to Michael): Go down, give them to her. Her eyes were lit up when she saw them. She took them and cast them before the feet of the judges and said: The man to whom these belong—it is from him that I am with child. Even though I were burnt, I am not going to reveal (VL: defame) him. However, I trust in the master of all ages, the Lord (VNL +: who is witness between me and

Notes, Chapter 38

[12]"who sat at the crossroads"; HT: "at Enaim"; see note to v. 14.

[13]This lengthy midrash is found in essentially the same form in Nf, Frg. Tgs., and in a somewhat briefer form in Ps.-J. and in CTg D and E. It is also preserved in Targumic Tosafoth. The Genizah texts, including tosafoth, have been edited by M. Klein, 1986 (*Genizah Manuscripts*), I, 88–99; with notes in II, 31–33. Genizah tosafoth also in M. Klein, "Targumic Toseftot from the Cairo Genizah," in *Salvación en la Palabra ... En memoria ... A. Díez Macho* (Madrid, 1986) 409–418. Related rabbinic and NT texts are brought together by B. Grossfeld, *Neofiti*, note 21 to Gen 38. See also R. Bloch, 1955B ("Notes sur l'utilisation ...") and McNamara, 1966A, 138–142; B. Barry Levy, 1, 1986, 225–231 (for a textual analysis).

did not find them. She lifted up her eyes on high and said: "I beseech by the mercies from before you, O Lord, you are he who answers the afflicted in the hour of their affliction; answer me in this hour, which is the hour of my distress. O God who answers the distressed, enlighten my eyes and give me the three witnesses and I promise you three just men in the valley of Dura:[14] *Hananiah, Mishael, and Azariah. When they go down into the burning fire they will sanctify your holy name." And immediately the Lord heard the voice of her supplication, and he said to Michael: "Go down and give her his three witnesses." And her eyes were enlightened and she saw them and she gave them into the hands of the judges and said:* "By the very man to whom those things belong am I with child. *But although I may be burned I will not make him known. And the witness that is between me and him will put in his heart to see them in this hour, and will deliver me from this great judgment." Judah immediately stood upon his feet and said: "I beg of you brothers, and men of my father's house, listen to me: It is better for me to burn in this world, with extinguishable fire, that I may*[j] *not be burned in the world to come whose fire is inextinguishable. It is better for me to blush in this world that is a passing world, that I may*[j] *not blush before my just fathers in the world to come. And listen to me, my brothers and house of my father: In the measure in which a man measures it shall be measured to him, whether it be a good measure or a bad measure. Blessed is every man who reveals his works. Inasmuch as I took the ornamented garment of my brother Joseph and dipped it in blood of the kid-goat and I said to Jacob*: 'Examine, examine I pray *whether this is the ornamented garment of your son or not.' And (as for) me it is now said to me*: 'To whom this *signet-ring* and cord and staff belong, *by him am I with child.' Tamar, my daughter-in-law, is innocent;*[15] *by me she is with child. Far from her—from Tamar, my daughter-in-law—to conceive sons of harlotry." But a Bath Qol came forth from heaven and said: "They are both just; from before the Lord the thing has come about."* 26. And Judah acknowledged (them)[k] and said: "*Tamar, my daughter-in-*

Apparatus, Chapter 38

him) that he will put in the heart of the man to whom these belong to recognize them: this signet ring, the cloak, and the staff."

[j] In Aramaic the same form as "we may (not)."

[k] CTg E + : "when Judah saw them he said in his heart: It is better for me that I (*same form as*: "we") be confounded in this world than I (*same form as*: "we") be confounded in the world to come. It is better for me to burn in extinguishable fire in this world than that I (*same form as*: "we") burn in the inextinguishable fire (lit.: "fire that devours fire") in the world to come. And Judah recognized them and said: Tamar is innocent because I did not give her to Shelah my son. And he did not know her again"; CTg D, P: "And when Judah saw the three witnesses he arose to his feet (D +: and cried aloud) and said: Listen to me (lit.: accept from me) my brothers and men of my father's house (P: I beseech you my brothers

---

Notes, Chapter 38

[14]"three just men in the Valley of Dura . . ."; cf. Dan 1:6; 3:14-27. The reference assumes that Hananiah, Mishael, and Azariah were descended from Judah and Tamar. M. Klein, 1986, II, 31 refers in this connection to *Ber. R.* pp. 1211, 1213 (=*Midrash Bereshit Rabba*, ed. J. Theodor and Ch. Albeck, Jerusalem, 1965).

[15]"Tamar is innocent"; HT: "she is more righteous than I" (*mny*). All the Pal. Tg. texts tone down Judah's profession of guilt and in different ways; see chart in Grossfeld, *Neofiti*, note 22 to Gen 38.

law, is innocent; for this reason [16] I did not give her to Shelah, my son." And he did not know her again. 27. And it happened in the *hour* that she bore that there were twins in her womb. 28. And when she was giving birth *a child* [17] put forth his hand and the midwife took (it) and tied a crimson thread *m* on his hand saying: "This came out first." 29. And it happened when he drew back his hand, behold his brother came out and she said: "How *strong you are, and how strong you will be my son.*" *n* [18] And she called his name Perez. 30. And after this his brother, on whose hand was the crimson thread, *m* came out and his name was called Zerah.

Apparatus, Chapter 38

and men of my father's house, accept this word from me): In what measure a man measures (P + : in this world), in that measure is it measured to him (P: do they measure to him in heaven), whether it be good measure or bad measure. And blessed is every man whose works are manifest (lit.: "they make manifest; VNL: "who reveals his works"; P: "who has good works"). It is better for me (P corrupt) to be ashamed in this world than to be confounded in the world to come. It is better for me to burn in extinguishable fire than to burn in inextinguishable fire (lit.: "fire devouring fire"). Because I took the cloak of Joseph my brother and dipped it in the blood of the kid-goat and sent it (P: "oppressed": or emending: "deceived"; "cast it") to my father and said to him: Look now. Is this the cloak of your son Joseph or not? — measure (corresponding to) measure and legal decision corresponding to legal decision. Tamar my daughter is innocent. From me is she with child." CTg D breaks off here. P continues: "Far be it from her, from Tamar my daughter-in-law. She is not with children of fornication, because I did not give her to Shelah my son. A voice (lit.: daughter of a voice, a *Bath Qol*) came out from heaven and said: Both of you are innocent. From before me did this thing occur. And he did not know her again." VNL as above as far as:

"who reveals his works." Text continues thus: "Because I took the embroidered cloak (*prgwdh*) of Joseph my brother and dipped it in the blood of the kid-goat and offered it before the feet of my father and said to him: See, now; is this the embroidered cloak (*hprgwdh*, with prefixed Hebrew definite article!) of your son or not?—measure corresponding to measure and (legal) decisions corresponding to (legal) decisions. It is better for me to be ashamed in this world than to be ashamed in the world to come; it is better for me to burn in extinguishable fire than to burn in inextinguishable fire (lit.: "fire devouring fire"). Tamar, my daughter-in-law, is innocent in judgment. From me is she with child. Far be it from her, Tamar, my daughter-in-law. She is not bearing children of prostitution. Because I did not give her in marriage to Shelah my son. A voice (lit.: "daughter of voice," *Bath Qol*) came forth from heaven and said: Both of you are innocent in judgment. From before the Lord has this thing occurred. And he did not know her again."

m In Nf *zhwr zyhwryh* (*zyhwr*, with -*he*), in CTg E; *zyhwry* (with heth).

n CTg E: "how strong you are, and again you will seek to be strong."

Notes, Chapter 38

[16]"for this reason (I did not give)," or possibly: "because (I did not give)," *bgyn kk*, rendering HT *'l kn* (RSV: "in as much as." The combination *bgyn kk* occurs only here in Nf; elsewhere Nf renders the HT *'l kn* by *bgyn kdn*; cf. Golomb, 1985, 40. Possibly in Nf *bgyn kk* has the same meaning as *bgyn kdn*. CTg FF has: *'ry 'l kn* (I did not give her), which Klein, 1986, I, 92, renders as: "for this reason I did not give"; CTg E has: *mn bgyn kn* "[this is] because I did not give" (Klein, 1986, I, 98).

[17]"a child." Nf adds a subject to the HT: "one (or: he) put out a hand."

[18]"how strong you are . . . my son"; HT: "What a breach you have made for yourself." Nf may possibly contain a reference to the Messiah who would descend from Perez, as noted in *Gen. R.* 85,14.

CHAPTER 39

1. And Joseph was taken down *a* to Egypt, and Potiphar, *an officer* [1] of Pharaoh, captain of the *executioners,* [2] an Egyptian man, bought him from the hands of *the Saracens* who had taken him down *b* there. 2. And the Lord was (with) *c* [3] Joseph and he became a man prospering *in good work;* [4] and he became a *(magnate) and a ruler* [5] in the house *d* of his Egyptian master. 3. And his master saw that the Lord was with him, *e* and that whatever he did, the Lord *f* caused to prosper in his hands. 4. And Joseph found grace *and favor* [6] in his sight, and he waited upon him and he appointed him *administrator* *g* [7] over his house. *h* He delivered all that was his under his *authority.* *i* [8] 5. And it happened that from the time *j* that he appointed him *administrator* [7] over his house and over all that he had, the Lord *f* blessed the house of the Egyptian for *the merit* [9] of Joseph; and the blessing of the Lord was upon all that he had in his house and on the face of the field. 6. And he left all that he had *under the authority* [8] of Joseph; and he had no concern for anything after him except the bread *k* which he ate. And Joseph was handsome of form, *m* beautiful in appearance. *n* 7. And it happened after these things that the wife of his master lifted up her eyes to Joseph and said to him: "Lie with me." 8. And he refused, and said

---

Apparatus, Chapter 39

a hwnḥt, a unique Hufal form, under influence of HT; CTg E *'twḥt*, Ithp form.
b *'whtw* of text = *'ḥytw* of CTg E.
c In text *yt*, the sign of the accusative; a slavish reproduction of *'t* of HT (which here = "with"); CTg E: "and the Memra of the Lord was at the aid of Joseph."
d CTg E: "and he was a man prospering and he was placed in the house of his Egyptian master"; cf. HT.
e CTg E: "the Memra of the Lord was at his aid."
f CTg E: "the Memra of the Lord."
g In Nf. CTg E = VNL Greek loan word *epitropos*; VNL: "and he appointed him administrator."
h CTg E: "over the men of his house."
i CTg E: "between his hands."
j CTg E: "from the hour."
k CTg E: "the food."
m Lit.: "in his form."
n Correcting text slightly in accord with CTg E.

Notes, Chapter 39

[1]"an officer"; HT: "a eunuch"; see note to 37:36.

[2]"executioners," Greek loan word, as noted at 37:36; HT: "stewards," "guards."

[3]"(was) with," *yt*, rendering *'t* (in Hebrew = "with," or simply the sign of the accusative) as the sign of the accusative, contrary to the context.

[4]"prospering in good works"; HT: "prospering"; the addition in line with Nf's paraphrase of "perfect," etc.; see note to 6:9.

[5]"a magnate and a ruler," *rb wšlyṭ*; an addition to the HT. The combination occurs often in Nf and can be variously rendered, e.g., "captains and officers."

[6]"grace and favor," *ḥn wḥsd*; Nf's almost invariable expansion of HT *ḥn*; see note to 6:8 and 32:6.

[7]"administrator"; Greek loan word *epitropos*; an addition to the HT.

[8]"delivered ... under his authority"; HT: "gave into his hand."

[9]"the merit of"; HT: "because of" (*bgll*). See notes to 12:3,13.

to his master's wife: "Behold, my master has no concern for (anything) *after* me;[o][10] <and all that he has in his house, and all>[p] that is his, he has delivered *into my authority.*[i8] 9. There is no captain *or officer*[11] in this house outside of me, and he has not kept back[q] anything from me except yourself, for you are his wife. How can I do this great evil, and sin[r] *before* my God?"[12] 10. And it happened that although she spoke with Joseph day *after* day, he did not listen to her, to have intercourse with her *in this world*, so as not to be *with*[13] her *in the world to come.*[s][14] 11. And on one of those days he entered within the house *to reckon his accounts,*[15] and there was no one of the people of his house there in the house. 12. And she caught him by his clothe*s* saying: "Have intercourse[16] with me."[17] But he left his clothe*s with her* and fled and went out into the market-place. 13. <And when she saw that he left his garment (with her) in her hand and went out into the market-place>.[t] 14. <She called>[t] to the men of the house and spoke to them saying: "Behold he has brought to me a Hebrew man to make fun of us. He came in to me to have intercourse with me,[u] and I cried out in a loud voice. 15. And when he heard that I raised my voice and cried out, he left his clothes with me and fled and went out into the market-place."[w] 16. And she kept his clothes *in her hand*[x][18] until *the time that* her husband came to his house. 17. And she spoke to him these words saying: "<The Hebrew servant whom you brought to us to jest with me, came in to me.

Apparatus, Chapter 39

[o] CTg E: "behold my master does not know anything besides me. Everything that is in his house he has handed over between my hands."

[p] Omitted in text of Nf.

[q] CTg E: "withheld."

[r] Lit.: "and I sin"; CTg E: "and we (= I) become guilty of it before the Lord."

[s] CTg E, P: "to unite sexually" (P: "to sleep) with her in

this world, (CTg E + sufficient) so as not to be a partner with her in Gehenna in the world to come." CTg E breaks off before the end of v. 10.

[t] Missing in text.

[u] Nfmg: "to unite sexually with me."

[w] Nfmg: "outside."

[x] Nfmg: "beside her."

Notes, Chapter 39

[10]"had no concern for anything after him"; lit. "and he used not know anything after him." M. Klein (1986, I, 100) renders: "and he did not check after him at all"; HT: "and he did not know anything with him." Grossfeld, 1988, 132, renders Onq., which is almost identical with Nf, as: "and he had no concern for anything with him there."

[11]"captain and officer," *rb wšlyṭ*; cf. v. 2; HT: "great one" (or: "greater").

[12]"sin before my God"; HT: "sin to God." Addition of "my" not attested outside of Nf.

[13]"with her"; HT: *'ṣlh*, which term ordinarily means "beside (her)."

[14]"in this world . . . in the world to come"; additions in Nf, and in Pal. Tgs., to HT. This paraphrase is very similar to the comment on the verse in *Gen. R.* 87,6: "*to lie by her.* in this world. *and to be with her*—so that he should not be with her in the Gehenna in the world to come."

[15]"to reckon his accounts"; HT: "to do his works." The rabbis discussed the meaning of this Hebrew phrase, with special interest in what precise work Joseph was doing. One view was that it was sexual intercourse; another (as in Nf) was that it was to do his master's accounts; thus *Gen. R.* 87,7.

[16]"have intercourse with"; lit. "use"; HT: "lie with." Nf renders the Hebrew in the usual manner, when this is seen as denoting intercourse. See Gen 30:15, etc.

[17]"with me"; HT: *'sly*. See to v. 10.

[18]"in (her) hand"; HT: *'ṣlh*. See to v. 10.

18. And when I raised[y] my voice and cried out he left his clothes *in my hand*[18] and fled into the market-place." 19. And when her master heard the words which his wife spoke to him saying: "According to these things your servant did to me," his anger grew strong. 20. And Joseph's master took him and placed him in the prison, *in* the place where the prisoners of the king were imprisoned. And he was there in the prison. 21. And the Lord was with Joseph and he placed *grace and* favor upon him and made him find grace in the sight of the captain of the prison.[z] 22. And the captain of the prison placed all the prisoners who were in the prison *under the authority of* Joseph;[aa] and whatever was done there, it was he who did it. 23. And the captain of the prison was not concerned about anything[bb] at all after him,[19] because the Lord was with him; and all that he did the Lord made prosper *in his hands.*

CHAPTER 40

1. And it happened after these things that the *chief* cup-bearer and the *chief*[1] baker of the king of Egypt fell foul of their master, the king of Egypt. 2. And Pharaoh became angry with his two *officers,*[2] with the chief cup-bearer and the chief baker. 3. And he put them in custody in the house of the captain of the *executioners,*[3] in the place where Joseph was imprisoned. 4. And the captain of the *executioners*[3] appointed Joseph over them and he ministered to them. And they spent (some) days in custody. 5. And they both dreamed a dream—the *chief*[1] cup-bearer and the *chief* baker of the king of Egypt who were imprisoned in the prison— each man a dream in one night, each dream with its own interpretation. 6. And Joseph came to them in the morning[a] and saw them, and behold their *faces* were *troubled.*[b]

Apparatus, Chapter 39

[y] In text *'rymt*: written differently (*'r'ymt*) in Nfmg, PVNL.
[z] Nfmg: "the Memra of the Lord (was) at the aid of Joseph and he inclined (its) kindness toward him and put kindness in the sight of the prison officer."

[aa] Nfmg: "in the hands of Joseph."
[bb] Nfmg: "nothing (that was) in his hand, because the Memra of the Lord was at his aid; and all that he did the Memra of the Lord made prosper."

Notes, Chapter 39

[19]"was not concerned ... after him." See note to v. 6.

Apparatus, Chapter 40

[a] Nfmg: "about morning time."

[b] Nfmg: "excited"; = CTg E.

Notes, Chapter 40

[1]"chief ..."; addition to HT: "the butler ... the baker."
[2]"(his) officers," *šlyṭwy*; HT: "eunuchs"; see to 37:36.
[3]"executioners"; a Latin-through-Greek loan word; see to 39:1; HT: "stewards," "guards."

7. And he asked the *officers*[c2] who were with him in prison in his master's house saying: "For what reason are your faces troubled today?"[d] 8. And they said to him: "We have dreamed a dream and there is no interpretation for it."[e] And Joseph said to them: "Are not interpretations from *before the Lord*?[f4] Relate them to me I pray." 9. And the chief cup-bearer told his dream to Joseph and said to him: "In my dream, behold there was a vine before me.[g] 10. And on the vine there were three branches. And it bloomed; it sent out blossoms, the clusters ripened and *became* grapes. 11. And Pharaoh's cup was in my hand and I took the grapes and pressed them into Pharaoh's cup, and I placed the cup in the palm of Pharaoh's *hand*." 12. And Joseph said to him: "This is its interpretation:[h] The three branches[5] are the three *fathers of the world:*[i] *namely; Abraham, Isaac, and Jacob, the sons of whose sons are to be enslaved in the slavery of the land of Egypt*[j] *and are to be delivered by the hands of three faithful leaders:*[k] *Moses, Aaron, and Miriam, who are to be likened to the clusters of grapes. And as regards what you said: 'I took the grapes*[m] *and pressed them into Pharaoh's cup and I placed the cup in the hands of Pharaoh,' this is the cup of retribution*[n] *which Pharaoh is to drink in the end. And you, chief cupbearer,*[o] *(your) reward*[p] *shall not be lost, because you have dreamed this good dream." But Joseph did not say the interpretation of the dream. And*[q] *Joseph interpreted as seemed good in his sight.* And Joseph said to him: "This is its interpretation;[r] the three branches are three days. 13. *At the end of* three days[6] Pharaoh will lift up your

Apparatus, Chapter 40

[c] Nfmg: "the officer."
[d] Nfmg: "excited"; CTg E = Nf.
[e] CTg E: "we have no one who would interpret it."
[f] CTg E: "interpretations before the Lord."
[g] Nfmg, CTg E: "planted before me" (Nfmg: "before him").
[h] Nfmg: "This is the interpretation of the dream"; cf. PVNL, CTg E.
[i] CTg E, P: "fathers of the world, from whose (sons)"; Nfmg: "they are the three from whose"; VNL as Nf.
[j] CTg E, P, VNL: "to be enslaved in the land of Egypt."
[k] Nfmg: "righteous, faithful (leaders)."
[m] P: "clusters of grapes. And as to your having pressed them into Pharaoh's cup and having placed the cup in the palm of Pharaoh's hand, this is the bowl

(Greek loan word: *phialê*) of wrath that Pharaoh is destined to finally drink. And you also, chief cupbearer, (will) receive a good reward for that you have dreamt."
[n] Nfmg: "the bowl (*plyty*) of wrath that Pharaoh is destined to finally drink. You also, chief cup-bearer"; = CTg E; cf. P.
[o] Nfmg: "chief cup-bearer (that) you took them"; = CTg E.
[p] VNL: "your rewards"; Nfmg: "receive a good reward for the dream that you dreamed"; = CTg E; cf. P: "receive a good reward (for the fact) that you dreamed."
[q] CTg E, P, VNL +: "afterward."
[r] CTg E, P +: "of the dream."

Notes, Chapter 40

[4]"from before the Lord"; HT: ". . . belong to God."
[5]This interpretation of "the tree branches" is found also in rabbinic sources, e.g., *Gen. R.* 88,5 on this verse: "*three branches*—Moses, Aaron and Miriam; *its blossom shot forth*—the redemption of Israel blossomed." For a detailed analysis of 40:12-13, see B. Barry Levy, 1, 1986, 233–236.
[6]"at the end of (three days)"; HT (RSV): "within (three days)."

head and he will restore[s] you to your service;[t] and you will place the cup in the *palm of* Pharaoh's hand according to the previous *procedure,*[u] when you were cup-bearer[w] to him. 14. But remember me when it is well with you, and do me, I pray, favor *and goodness,*[x7] and remember me to Pharaoh[y] and deliver me from this *prison.* 15. For I was indeed stolen from the land of the Hebrews, and here also[z] I have done nothing that they should have put me in *prison.*"[8] 16. And the chief baker saw that he had interpreted well, and he said to Joseph: "I was also in my dream, and behold there were three baskets of *white bread*[aa9] upon my head, 17. and in the uppermost basket there were all kinds of edibles[bb] for Pharaoh, the work of a baker, and a bird was eating them out of the basket from above my head." 18. And Joseph answered and said:[cc] "This is the interpretation[dd] *of the dream.*[10] The three baskets are the *three hard*[ee] *enslavements which Israel is to serve in the land of Egypt, with clay and bricks and with all sorts of work on*[ff] *the face of the field. And Pharaoh*[gg] *is to decree evil decrees against Israel, and he will throw their sons into the river.*[hh] *But Pharaoh will perish and his forces will be blotted out, and the sons of*

Apparatus, Chapter 40

[s] Nfmg: "and will return you."

[t] CTg E: "to your place."

[u] Nfmg: "(place the) cup of Pharaoh in my (read: his) hand according to the (previous) procedure"; = CTg E.

[w] Nfmg: "you gave him to drink"; = CTg E.

[x] Nfmg: "and truth"; CTg E damaged.

[y] Nfmg: "before Pharaoh."

[z] Nfmg and CTg E have identical minor variants.

[aa] VNL: "and behold upon my head three baskets of fine coal-baked bread" (VL, *ryp't'* [N, *drypt'*] *qqbtwn*); Nfmg: "fine bread" (*qqbtyn*); = VNL. See note 9.

[bb] Nfmg, CTg E: "in the uppermost basket all kinds of food for Pharaoh"; (agreement between Nfmg and CTg E also on many minor lexical variants).

[cc] Verse 18 is in PVNL; 18a in CTg E: "Joseph answered and said: This is the interpretation of the dream: the three baskets (are) the three harsh servitudes which the Israelites are destined (to serve)"; = P. CTg E breaks off at 18a and resumes at 41:43.

[dd] Nfmg: "interpretation"; a different form of the word, that of P.

[ee] Nfmg: "harsh" = CTg E; P (VNL; = Nf).

[ff] Nfmg: "of the face of."

[gg] Nfmg: "(Pharaoh), that is, Pharaoh king of Egypt, (will) decree evil decrees"; Nfi: "will decree (lit.: be decreeing) decrees"; = VNL.

[hh] Nfmg: "into the river but the end of Pharaoh (is that) he will perish"; cf. P: "into the river but the end of Pharaoh and his servants."

Notes, Chapter 40

[7]"favor and goodness," *ḥn wḥsd*; HT: *ḥn*; Nf's constant paraphrase; see note to 6:8 and 32:6.

[8]"this prison"; HT: "this house."

[9]"white bread," *dpyt' nqyt'*; HT: *ḥry*, RSV: "white bread." Ps.-J. also has *d-pyt'*. A. Díez Macho suggests reading *rypt'* in Nf. This is the reading of VNL (VL, *ryp't'*; N, *drypt'*), which add *qqbt(w)n* (V, *qqbtrn*). Some scholars wish to derive the Aramaic *qqbtwn* (or in corrected form *'qqbwn* (or -*yn*) from the Greek *kakkabê* or *kakkabos*, "a pot" (thus, "fine bread, baked in a pot"); others from the Latin *accubitum*, through Greek *akkoubiton*, "reclining" (i.e., "fine bread used at the meals of the upper class". See Introduction, p. 17, and note 75. Nf's *dpyt'* can be retained and understood as *d-pyt'*; *pyt'*, "bread"; see Sokoloff, 1990, 433. The translation in text and apparatus follows Sokoloff, 1990, in interpreting *qqbtw(y)n* as "fine bread" and *rypt'* as "coal-baked bread" (Sokoloff, 1990, 523).

[10]"B. Grossfeld (Grossfeld, *Neofiti*, note 17 to Gen 40) notes that this lengthy haggadic supplement, also present in the various Pal. Tgs. and in Ps.-J. in abbreviated form, is not reflected exactly as here in rabbinic literature. The closest parallel is in *Gen. R.* 88,6.

Israel will come forth redeemed with head uncovered.[11] *But you, chief baker, will receive an evil recompense,*[ii] *because you have dreamed this dream." And Joseph did not say the interpretation of the dream,*[jj] *and Joseph explained to him what seemed* <good> *in his sight. And Joseph said to him*: "This is its interpretation: the three baskets are three days. 19. *At the end of* three days Pharaoh will lift up your head from above you and *he will hang*[kk] you on a *gibbet;*[mm][12] and the birds will eat the flesh from off *your head.*" 20. And it happened on the third day, the birthday[nn] of Pharaoh,[13] that he made a feast for all his *officers,* and he lifted up the head of the chief cup-bearer and he lifted up the head of the chief baker among his *officers.*[oo] 21. And he restored the chief cup-bearer to his *services*[pp] and he placed the cup in the palm of *the hand of* Pharaoh. 22. And he *hanged* the chief baker as Joseph had interpreted to them. 23. *Joseph forsook*[14] *the favor that is from above and the favor that is from below, and the favor which had accompanied*[qq] *him from his father's house, and he trusted in the chief cup-bearer, in flesh*[rr] *that passes,*[ss] *in flesh that tastes the cup of death.*[15] *And he did not remember the Scripture, for it is written in the book of the Law of the Lord,*[tt] *which is like the book of the Wars: 'Cursed be the*

Apparatus, Chapter 40

[ii] P: "an evil reward since this dream is an evil dream."

[jj] Nfmg: "(of the dream) Joseph did (not) say to him. After this Joseph interpreted to him what was not good in his sight, and he answered him and said: This is the interpretation of the dream: the three baskets are three days"; cf. VNL.

[kk] Or: "crucify you on a cross."

[mm] Nfmg: "tree"; cf. Ps.-J.

[nn] Greek loan word *genesia.*

[oo] Nfmg: "among his servants"; cf. Ps.-J.

[pp] Nfmg: "to his place."

[qq] Nfmg: "that had accompanied him in mercy from"; v. 23 in PVNL; variants below.

[rr] Nfmg: "and in flesh"; = PVNL.

[ss] Nfmg: "that passes and that tastes the cup of death."

[tt] PVNL: "the Scripture, because it is written and clearly stated: Cursed be the man."

Notes, Chapter 40

[11]"with head uncovered," *bryš gly.* For a possible relation of this phrase to *parrhêsia* in the NT, see McNamara, 1966A, 176f.

[12]"hang you on a gibbet," *yṣlb 'l ṣlybh*; HT: ". . . on an *'ṣ,*" i.e., on a tree or timber pale. The Hebrew word *'ṣ* is used in the sense of "gallows" or "stake" here and in Deut 21:22, 23. *'ṣ* in the sense of "tree" is normally translated by *'yln'* in Nf (e.g., Gen 1:29; 2:16, 17; 3:1 and ch. 3 passim; 6:14; 18:4, 8; 22:7, 9, 17). In 40:19 both verb and noun ("hang, gibbet") have the root *ṣlb*; in Nf Deut 21:22, however, we have the noun *qysh*: "you shall hang (*tṣlbwn*) him upon a tree" (*qysh*), although in both Deut 21:22 and 23 the verb used is *ṣlb.* The verb *ṣlb* can mean "hang," "impale," or "crucify," and the noun *ṣlybh* either "stake" or "cross." For the midrash in Nf Gen 40:18-19, see B. Barry Levy, 1, 1986, 236–240.

[13]"the birthday (of Pharaoh)"; a Greek loan word: *genesia*; cf. Mark 6:21; Matt 14:16. For a discussion on the meaning of this word (whether "birthday" or "anniversary of accession to the throne"), see Schürer, I (rev. G. Vermes, F. Millar, eds.), 1973, note 26 to pp. 346–348.

[14]This long midrashic development, present also in Frg. Tgs. and in shorter form in Ps.-J., is also reflected in rabbinic sources (texts given in Grossfeld, *Neofiti,* note 23 to Gen 40), e.g., *Gen. R.* 89,3 on Gen 41:1.

[15]"the flesh that tastes the cup of death." On this see R. Le Déaut, "Goûter le calice de la mort," *Biblica* 43 (1962) 82–86 and S. Speier's reply, "Das Kosten des Todeskelches im Targum," *VT* 13 (1963) 344–345. See also B. Barry Levy, 1, 1986, 240–242.

son of man who trusts in flesh and who places his trust in flesh.'[uu] Wherefore the chief cup-bearer did not remember Joseph, and he forgot him *until the appointed time*[16] *to be redeemed had arrived.*

CHAPTER 41

1. And it happened at the end of two days that Pharaoh dreamed. And behold, he was standing on *the bank of*[1] the river. 2. And behold, there came up from the river seven cows, pleasant to see, fat of flesh, and they fed among the reeds.[a] 3. And behold, seven other cows came up from the river after them, evil to see, thin of flesh, and they stood beside the (other) cows on the bank of the river. 4. And the cows[2] that were ugly to see and thin[b] of flesh ate the seven cows that were pleasant to see and fat of flesh. And Pharaoh awoke. 5. And he fell asleep and dreamed a second time and behold seven ears[c] of corn growing on one stalk, fat and good. 6. And behold, seven ears, thin and *burned*[3] by the east *wind,*[4] grew after[d] them. 7. And the seven thin ears devoured the seven fat and full ones. And Pharaoh awoke, and be-

Apparatus, Chapter 40

[uu] Nfmg: "and makes flesh his trust. And blessed is the man who trusts in the name of the Memra of the Lord, and makes the Memra of the Lord his trust; because of this"; = P.

Notes, Chapter 40

[16]"until the appointed time"; an addition to the HT. The same idea is found in *Gen. R.* 88,7 on the verse which lists the unlikely divine interventions in Israel's history, from Abraham and Sarah until the final unification of the human race (citing Zech 3:9).

Apparatus, Chapter 41

[a] VNL: "they were feeding among the papyri"; Nfmg, Nfi: (with slight corrections) "among the papyri."
[b] Nfmg: "and tender."
[c] Nfmg: "full ears."

[d] Nfmg: "of the east come up after"; CTg E: "came up after" (opening words of text). There are no glosses in Nf between Gen 41:7 and 43:26.

Notes, Chapter 41

[1]"on the bank of"; an addition to HT in Nf.
[2]"cows," *twryn*, actually the masc. form; HT has the feminine *prwt*. Both the Hebrew fem. and the Aramaic masc. may in fact refer to the species in general (cf. Gen 32:16). The HT speaks of forty *prwt* (fem. plur.) and ten *pryn* (masc. plur.), which Nf (and CTg C) renders as: forty female *twryn*. See Grossfeld, *Neofiti*, note 2 to Gen 41.
[3]"burned"; HT: "blighted."
[4]"wind"; added in Nf; implicit in HT.

hold, it was a dream. 8. And it happened in the morning that the spirit *of Pharaoh* was troubled; and he sent and called all the magicians of the *Egyptians,*[5] and all *their* wise men; and Pharaoh related his dreams[e] to them, but there was no one who could interpret them to Pharaoh. 9. And the chief cup-bearer spoke to Pharaoh saying: "I remember my sins today. 10 Pharaoh was angry with his *officers*[6] and (he) placed me[f] in prison in the house of the captain of the *executioners,*[g7] me and the chief baker. 11. And we dreamed a dream on one night, I and he, each of us dreamed a dream with its own interpretation. 12. And a young Hebrew was there with us,[g] a servant of the captain of the *executioners,*[h7] and we told him[i] and he interpreted our dream for us, he interpreted to each man according to his dreams.[j] 13. And it happened that it came to pass just as he had interpreted to us; he restored me to my service,[k] but he *hanged* him *on a gibbet.*"[m8] 14. And Pharaoh sent and called Joseph, and they brought him quickly from the *prison.*[n9] He shaved himself, *washed*[10] his clothes[o] and went in to Pharaoh. 15. And Pharaoh said:[p] "I dreamed a dream and there is no one[q] to interpret it, and I have heard about you thus: You hear the dream to interpret it." 16. And Joseph answered Pharaoh saying: "Not I; *from before the Lord,* will answer be made[11] (concerning) the welfare of Pharaoh."[r] 17. And Pharaoh spoke to Joseph: "In my dream behold, I was standing on the bank of the river. 18. And behold, there came up from the river seven cows, fat of flesh and pleasant in form,[s] and they fed among the rushes. 19. And behold, seven other cows came up after them, very lean and evil to see, thin[sbis] of flesh, and I had never seen (cows) as bad as them in all the land of Egypt. 20. And the thin[s bis] and the bad cows ate up the first seven fat cows. 21. Although they entered

Apparatus, Chapter 41

[e] CTg E: "his dream."

[f] CTg E: "them."

[g] CTg E: "beside us" (= with us).

[h] Latin, *speculator*; Greek, *spekoulatôr.*

[i] CTg E: "we told (i.e., narrated) before him."

[j] CTg E: "each man according to the interpretation of the (or: his) dream we had dreamed."

[k] CTg E: "my place."

[m] or: "crucified him on a cross."

[n] CTg E: "and they drew him from the pit."

[o] CTg E: "he shaved his beard and changed his clothes."

[p] CTg E +: "to Joseph."

[q] CTg E: "I have no one."

[r] CTg E: "the Memra of the Lord will answer (= provide for?) Pharaoh's welfare" ("the Memra of" interlineated).

[s] CTg E: "pleasant to see."

[sbis] *ḥsy*; CTg E: "small" (*dqyq*).

Notes, Chapter 41

[5]"of the Egyptians ... their"; HT: "of Egypt ... its."

[6]"his officers"; HT: "his servants."

[7]"executioners"; a Latin-through-Greek loan word; see to 37:36. HT: "stewards," "guards."

[8]"on a gibbet," *ṣlyb'*; an addition in Nf to HT; on the word see note to 40:19.

[9]"prison"; HT (RSV): "dungeon," lit. "pit."

[10]"he washed"; HT: "he changed."

[11]"Not I; from before the Lord ... will answer be made"; HT: God will answer." "Not I"; lit. "except for me," rendering HT *bl 'dy* literally (as also in Nf Gen 14:24; 41:44). The passive, "will answer be made," is followed by the sign of the accusative (*-yt*). See Introduction, pp. 34f. B. Barry Levy, 1, 1986, 242, considers the passive verb secondary here in Nf.

into their inwards,[t] one did not know they entered into their inwards,[t] for their appearance was as *lean*[u][12] as it was before.[w] And I awoke. 22. And I saw in my dream, and behold, seven ears coming out of one stalk full and good. 23. And behold, seven ears, withered[x] and thin, and burned[y] with the east wind, sprouted after them. 24. And they devoured the seven good ears. And I told it to the magicians and there was no one *to interpret*[13] it to me." 25. And Joseph said to Pharaoh: "The dream of Pharaoh is one; what *the Lord*[14] is to do has been related[z] to Pharaoh. 26. The seven good cows are seven years and the seven good ears are seven years; the dream is one. 27. And the seven thin[s][bis] and bad cows that come up after them are seven years, and the seven thin ears, *burned* by the east *wind,*[15] are seven years of hunger. 28. That is the matter which I said to Pharaoh: 'What *the Lord*[14] is to do had been *related to Pharaoh.'*[16] 29. And behold, seven years of hunger are coming, and all the abundance will be forgotten in the land of Egypt; for the famine will blot out the land. 31. And the abundance will not be known in the land by reason of that famine which will (come) after; for it will be very severe. 32. And the fact that the dream has been related twice to Pharaoh (means) that the thing has been determined from before *the Lord,*[17] and that there is a hurry *from before the Lord*[aa] to do it. 33. And now, let Pharaoh *appoint*[18] an understanding and wise man and set him[bb] over the land of Egypt. 34. Let Pharaoh *charge a man,*[19] and let him appoint *administrators*[20] in *all* the land *of Egypt,*[21] and let them take a fifth *of the produce*[22] of the land of Egypt, during the seven years of plenty.[cc] 35. And let them gather all the provisions of those *seven*[23] good years that are coming, and let them

Apparatus, Chapter 41

[t] CTg E: "within them."

[u] CTg E: "bad" ("sickly").

[w] CTg E: "from the beginning."

[x] CTg E: "shrunken."

[y] CTg E: "blasted."

[z] CTg E: "what the Memra of the Lord is to do he has shown to Pharaoh."

[aa] CTg C: "the Memra (of the Lord)."

[bb] CTg C: "I have appointed him lord and ruler."

[cc] VNL: "Let Pharaoh act and appoint him administrator (*epitropos*) over the land and let him set aside (lit.: divide) a fifth part of (lit.: in) the land of Egypt during the seven years of plenty"; cf. CTg C: "and let Pharaoh act and appoint a man . . . years of plenty."

Notes, Chapter 41

[12]"lean"; HT: "bad."

[13]"to interpret"; HT: "to tell."

[14]"The Lord"; HT: "God."

[15]"burned east wind"; see v. 6.

[16]"related to"; HT: "has been shown."

[17]"from before the Lord"; HT: "from God."

[18]"appoint"; HT: *yr'*; RSV: "select."

[19]"charge a man"; HT: "let him make" (i.e., take steps; RSV: "proceed").

[20]"administrators"; Greek loan word *epitropos*; HT: "officials," "overseers."

[21]"all . . . of Egypt"; addition to HT in Nf.

[22]"of the produce"; addition to HT in Nf. HT: "divide the land into five parts," or: "take a fifth (of the land)."

[23]"seven"; an addition to HT in Nf.

gather all the provisions of those *seven*[23] good years that are coming, and let them gather corn under the *authority* of[24] the Pharaoh as provisions in the cities, and let them conserve them. 36. And the provisions will be *a good remembrance*[25] for the land for the seven years of famine which will be in Egypt, that the land may not be blotted out by the famine." 37. And the thing seemed good in the sight of Pharaoh and in the sight of all his *officers.*[26] 38. And Pharaoh said to his *officers:*[dd][26] "Where will we find a man like this upon whom there *dwells a holy* spirit from *before the Lord.*"[27] 39. And Pharaoh said to Joseph: "Since *the Lord* has caused you to know all this, there is no one as understanding and wise as you. 40. You will be *appointed administrator*[ee][28] over my house,[ff] and *by the decrees of* your mouth[gg] all my people will be *provided for.*[29] Only (as regards) the throne *of my kingdom*[30] will I be greater than you." 41. And Pharaoh said to Joseph: "See that I have appointed you *master and ruler*[31] of all the land of Egypt." 42. And Pharaoh took the ring from his hand and he put it on the hands of Joseph; and he dressed him in garments of linen and he put a golden necklace about his neck. 43. And he made him ride in his second chariot and they acclaimed[32] before him:[hh] *"Long live*[33] *the father of the king who is master in wisdom, although small in beauty and tender in years."*[ii] And he appointed him *master and ruler*[34] over all the land of Egypt. 44.

Apparatus, Chapter 41

[dd] CTg C: "to all his officers."

[ee] Greek loan word: *epitropos.*

[ff] CTg C: "over my palace" (Greek or Latin loan word: *palation, palatium*).

[gg] CTg C: "the command of your mouth."

[hh] CTg E +: "saying."

[ii] CTg E: "great in wisdom but tender in years"; = PVNL.

Notes, Chapter 41

[24]"the authority of"; HT: "the hand of."

[25]"a good remembrance"; HT: "as a reserve."

[26]"his officers"; HT: "his servants."

[27]"dwells a holy spirit from before the Lord"; HT: "the spirit of God is in him." Ps.-J. has: "spirit of prophecy."

[28]"administrator," Greek loan word *epitropos*; added to HT in Nf.

[29]"be provided for"; HT (RSV): "shall order itself."

[30]"... of my kingdom"; HT: "only the throne will I make greater than you."

[31]"master and ruler," *rb wšlyt*; a common combination in Nf; here added to HT.

[32]"acclaimed," *mqlsyn*; HT: "and they called out." The Aramaic verb *qls* can mean "call out," "praise," "tramp," or "stamp." In Nf Exod 32:18 it is probably to be rendered as "praise" (although "tramp" and "stamp" are also possible); in Deut 32:43, in parallelism with "praise," it is probably to be translated as "acclaim." M. Klein (1986, II, 39) regards it as a Greek loan word (*kalôs, kaleusai*); see also A. A. Bevan, "The Aramaic Root *qls*," in *Orientalische Studien: Theodor Nöldeke zum siebzigsten Geburtstag*, ed. Carl Bezold (Giessen, 1906) 581f.; Sokoloff, 1990, 494f.

[33]"long live ... tender in years." A double paraphrase of HT "Abrek," which word is apparently a cry of homage, but of uncertain derivation (most probably Egyptian) and meaning. Nf first paraphrases as "Father (*'ab*) of the king," *rek* being regarded in b. *Baba Bathra* 4a as meaning "royalty." This is the sole paraphrase in Tg. Onq. *Abrek* is next paraphrased in Nf, Frg. Tgs., and Ps.-J. as if from *'ab*, "father," and Hebrew *rak*, i.e., "tender." This second paraphrase is found in a number of rabbinic texts and is particularly close to *Gen. R.* 90,3: "*Abrek*, which means father (*'ab*) in wisdom, though tender (*rak*) in years." The final element (*rk*) gets a double interpretation in Nf: "small" and "tender." See also B. Barry Levy, 1, 1986, 243f.

[34]"master and ruler"; added to HT in Nf, as in v. 41, etc.

And Pharaoh said to Joseph: "I am Pharaoh; without you no one will *stretch forth*[ij][35] his hand *to tie his cincture,*[kk][36] nor his foot to *mount a horse* in all the land of Egypt." 45. And Pharaoh called the name of Joseph *"The man to whom hidden things are revealed."*[37] And he gave him as wife Asenath,[mm] the daughter of Potiphera, *master of Tanis.*[nn][38] And Joseph went out into *all*[39] the land of Egypt. 46. And Joseph was thirty years old when[oo] he stood before Pharaoh the king of Egypt. And Joseph went out from before Pharaoh, and he went through all the land of Egypt. 47. And the land produced in the seven years of plenty, and *the granaries were filled.*[pp][40] 48. And he gathered all the provisions of the seven years that were in the land of Egypt and he put the provisions in the cities; the provisions of the *territory*[41] round about the city he placed within it.[qq] 49. And Joseph gathered corn like the sand of the sea in great quantities until *the time that* he *was withheld*[42] from counting because there was no *sum total*[43] *for such a quantity.*[rr] 50. And to Joseph two sons were born, before the year of the famine came, whom Asenath, the daughter of Potiphera, *master of Tanis*, bore him. 51. And Joseph called the name of the firstborn Manasseh, because *"the Lord*[ss] made me forget all my labor, and all *the men of*[44] my father's house." 52. And the name of the second he called Ephraim, because *"the Lord* has strengthened me in the land of my affliction."[tt] 53.

Apparatus, Chapter 41

[ij] CTg E: "raise."

[kk] Greek loan word: *zonê*.

[mm] CTg E retains the Hebrew form of the sign of the accusative before "Asenath."

[nn] P: "master of Tanis" (= Nf).

[oo] CTg E: "at the time that."

[pp] CTg E: "years of plenty, abundance of grain for the granaries."

[qq] CTg E: "the provisions of the estates of the city that were round about it, he put within it."

[rr] CTg E: "until the time that he ceased to count because there was no sum total."

[ss] CTg E: "because he said: Because the Memra of the Lord made me forget."

[tt] CTg E: "because he said: "because the Memra of the Lord has strengthened me in the land of my affliction."

Notes, Chapter 41

[35] "stretch out"; HT: "lift up."

[36] "tie his cincture, mount his horse"; HT: "hand and foot."

[37] "the man to whom hidden things are revealed"; a paraphrase of HT proper name "Zaphenath-Paneah"; cf. Onq. and Ps.-J. There is a similar interpretation of the HT in *Gen. R.* 94,4: "R. Johanan said: The name connotes: He reveals things that are hidden (Hebrew: *zephunoth*) and easily declares them." Other interpretations of the name are also given in the same passage.

[38] "master of Tanis"; HT: "priest of On." "Tanis" renders "Pithom" in Nf Exod 1:11 and "Zoan" in Nf Num 13:22.

[39] "all"; addition to HT in Nf.

[40] "the granaries were filled"; HT (RSV): "abundantly."

[41] "territory, *thwmh*; HT: "field(s)," *śdh*; the same rendering as in 36:35 and elsewhere in Nf; see note to 2:5.

[42] "was withheld," *'tmn'*; HT: *ḥdl*, "ceased." Nf consistently (10 cases out of 11) translates *ḥdl* of the HT in the same manner (Gen 11:8; 18:11, etc.). See Grossfeld, *Neofiti*, note 37 to Gen 41.

[43] "there was no sum total . . . quantity"; HT: "there is no number."

[44] "the men of"; an addition to HT in Nf.

And the seven years of plenty that were in Egypt ^{uu} were completed. 54. And the seven years of famine began to come as Joseph had said. And there was famine in all the countries, but in all the land of Egypt there was bread. ^{ww} 55. And all the land of Egypt was hungry, and the people cried out *before* Pharaoh[45] for bread. ^{ww} And Pharaoh said to all the Egyptians: "Go to Joseph; whatever he says to you, do." 56. And since there was famine over all the face of the earth, Joseph opened all *the granaries*[46] in which there was <grain> and *he sold* (it) to Egypt. And the famine grew severe in the land of Egypt. 57. And all *the inhabitants of*[47] the earth entered into Egypt to buy *corn*[47] from Joseph, because the famine was growing strong in all the earth.

CHAPTER 42

1. And Jacob saw *in the holy spirit*[1] that corn *was being sold*[2] in Egypt, and Jacob said to his sons: "Why *now* do you look *sated between the famines?*"^a[3] 2. And he said: "Behold, I have heard that there is corn *being sold*[2] in Egypt. Go down there and buy for us from there, that we may live and not die." 3. And ten brothers of Joseph went down to buy born in Egypt. 4. But Jacob did not send Benjamin, the brother of Joseph, with his brothers, because he said: "Lest any *calamity*[4] befall him." 5. And the sons of Israel entered to buy among those (others) who entered, because there was a famine in the land of Canaan. 6. Joseph was the ruler of the land, and he sold to all the people of the land. And the brothers of Joseph came,

Apparatus, Chapter 41

^{uu} CTg E: "that were in the land of Egypt."   ^{ww} CTg E: "food."

Notes, Chapter 41

[45]"before Pharaoh"; HT: "to Pharaoh."
[46]"all the granaries"; HT: "everything."
[47]"the inhabitants of; corn"; both are additions to HT in Nf.

Apparatus, Chapter 42

^a Verse 1 in P = Nf verbatim.

Notes, Chapter 42

[1]"(Jacob saw) in the holy spirit"; HT: "Jacob saw." This is the only text in Nf where Jacob is said to have had the holy spirit. Nf Gen 42:1 is in agreement with a number of rabbinic midrashic statements, given in Hebrew in Grossfeld, *Neofiti*, note 1 to Gen 42. According to *Gen. R.* 91,6 (on Gen 42:1), the holy spirit departed from Jacob the day Joseph was stolen, and (presumably) was not with him at the Gen 42:1 stage of his life. Jacob would have foreseen the future only imperfectly. On the holy Spirit in Nf, see Introduction, pp. 38–39.
[2]"being sold"; addition in Nf.
[3]"sated between the famines" (or: "among the hungry"); an addition in Nf; cf. *Gen. R.* 91,2.
[4]"calamity" (*sql*); HT: "plague" (*'swn*). The same translation by Nf is found in the other occurrences of the word (42:38; 44:29; Exod 21:22; 21:23). Ps.-J. renders differently.

and they saluted him *according to the custom of the land.*[5] 7. And Joseph saw his brothers, and he recognized them, and *he showed himself hostile*[6] to them, and he spoke harsh *words* to them, and he said to them: "Where did you come from?" And they said: "From the land of Canaan to buy provisions." 8. And Joseph recognized his brothers, but they did not recognize him. 9. And Joseph remembered the dreams he had dreamed about them, and he said to them: "You are spies. You have come to see the *entrances*[b7] of the land." 10. And they said to him: "<No>,[c] my lord; but your servants have come to buy provisions. 11. All of us are the sons of one man; we are trustworthy; your servants are not spies." 12. And he said to them: "Surely you have come to see the *entrances*[b7] of the land." 13. And they said to him: "We your servants are twelve brothers, the sons of one man, in the land of Canaan, and behold the youngest is with our father today; and one of us, *since he went out*[8] *from among us, we do not know what has been his end.*"[d] 14. And Joseph said to them: "Behold the *word*[9] which I spoke to you saying: 'You are spies.' 15. By this you will be tested: by the life *of the head*[10] of Pharaoh, you shall not go out from here unless your youngest brother comes here. 16. *Send one of you*, and let him bring your brother, and you shall *remain in prison* and your words will be tested <to see> if *you are truthful*. If not, by the life *of the head*[10] of Pharaoh you are spies." 17. And he put them in prison for three days. 18. And on the third day Joseph said to them: "Do this and you will live: for I fear *before the Lord.*[11] 19. If you are trustworthy, let one *of you, another* brother[12] of yours, remain confined in your prison, and (the rest of) you go, (and) carry *provisions of grain*[13] (because) your houses are hungry. 20. And you shall bring your youngest brother to me so that your words may be confirmed, and you shall not die." And they did so. 21. And the brothers said to one another: "Surely[14] we are guilty *of the blood*[15] of our

Apparatus, Chapter 42

[b] Nf text, *m'lly'*, as *Aruk* Pal. Tg. citation; Elias Levita, *Meturgeman, m'l'l'*; = "weak points of entry"? See note 7.

[c] Missing in text.
[d] P: "another, we do not know what has been his end."

Notes, Chapter 42

[5] "saluted according to the custom of the land"; HT: "bowed to the ground"; the regular Nf paraphrase; see note to 18:2.
[6] "he showed himself hostile"; HT: "he concealed his identity."
[7] "entrances, *m'lly'*; HT: *'rwt (h-'rs)*, "the nakedness of (*pudenda*) (of the land)," i.e., the vulnerable, exposed places. Jastrow (817b) understands *m'll* as "evil deed," and the similar *m'l'l'* as "that which is to be explored," "weak points." See Apparatus.
[8] "since he went out . . . his end"; an addition in Nf (and Ps.-J.) to HT (RSV): "and one is no more."
[9] "word"; addition in Nf.
[10] "life of the head"; HT: "(by) the life of . . ."; = "I swear by Pharaoh."
[11] "fear before the Lord"; HT: "fear God."
[12] "one of you, another brother"; HT: "one of your brothers."
[13] "provisions of grain"; HT: "rations."
[14] "surely" (*brm*), rendering *'bl* of HT in agreement with R. Kahana's view in *Gen. R.* 91,8. See McNamara, 1966B, 9, for the significance of the rendering; see Introduction, p. 28.
[15] "of the blood"; addition in Nf.

brother, whom we saw in the distress of his soul when he *moved convulsively before*[16] us, and we did not listen. Therefore this *great* affliction has come upon us." 22. And Reuben answered them saying:[e] "Did I not say to you: 'Do not sin against the boy,' and you did not listen. And behold now his blood is being sought." 23. And they did not know that <Joseph was listening to them because>[c] *Manasseh was standing*[17] between them *as* interpreter.[f] 24. And he turned aside from them and wept. And he returned to them and spoke with them. And he took Simeon from among them and bound him before them. 25. And Joseph gave command to fill their receptacles with corn, and to return the money of each in his sack, and to give them provisions for the road. And it was done so for them. 26. And they loaded their wheat on their asses and they went from there. 27. And one *of them* opened his sack to give fodder to his ass at the resting house, and he saw the money which was in the mouth of his bag. 28. And he said to his brothers: "My money has been returned and behold, it is in the mouth of my bag." And their heart *was agitated*[18] and they trembled one *before*[19] the other saying: "What is this that *the Lord* has done to us?" 29. And they came to their father Jacob, to the land of Canaan, and they related to him all that had happened to them saying: 30. "The man, the master of the land, spoke harsh *words*[20] to us and considered us to be spying the land. 31. And we said to him: 'We are trustworthy. We are not spies. 32. We are twelve brothers, the sons of our father; one *of us, since he went out*[21] *from among us, we do not know what has been his end.* And the youngest is with our father this day in the land of Canaan.' 33. And the man, the master of the land, said to us: 'By this I will know that you are trustworthy: keep one *of you* with me, and take (grain) for the hunger of your households and go. 34. And bring your youngest brother to me, so that I may know that you are not spies,[g] that you are trustworthy. I will give you your brother, and you will take *possession* of the land.'"[h] 35. And as they were emptying their sacks, behold the money-bag of each one was in his sack. And when they and their father saw their money-bags they were afraid. 36. And

Apparatus, Chapter 42

[e] In text: "Do not sin" follows; repeated here erroneously.
[f] PVNL: "and they did not know that Joseph understood (lit.: was listening (VNL: was knowing in) the language of the sanctuary, because Manasseh was standing (VNL: dwelling) among them as an interpreter." In Nf, PVNL the Aramaic term for "interpreter" is: *turgeman*; in Ps.-J.: *meturgeman*.
[g] CTg E resumes here; continues to 43:7.
[h] CTg E: "and you shall make do with it" (or: "him").

Notes, Chapter 42

[16] "moved compulsively before"; HT (RSV): "when he sought"; with Nf compare *Gen. R.* 91,8.
[17] "Manasseh was standing"; an addition in Nf (and Ps.-J.). That Manasseh was the interpreter is in agreement with *Gen. R.* 91,8. (The section within angular brackets is Díez Macho's restoration, and is considered possible by B. Barry Levy, 1, 1986, 246, as is also the version offered by Ps.-J. and the Frg. Tg.; for which see Apparatus.)
[18] "agitated" (or: "was frightened"); HT: "it went out," i.e., "sank."
[19] "before"; HT: "to (one another)."
[20] "words"; an addition in Nf.
[21] "Since he went out ...";see to v. 13 above.

Jacob their father said to them:[i] "You have bereaved me of Joseph; *since I sent him to you to Dothan I do not <know> what has been his end*;[22] and *<now> you seek* to take Benjamin. *And you want*[23] me *to raise up twelve tribes*."[24] 37. And Reuben said to his father saying: "Kill my two sons if I do not bring him to you. Put him in my hands,[j] and I will bring him back to you." 38. And he said: "My son will not go down with you, for his brother is dead, and he alone is left. And if any calamity should befall him on the journey on which you are to go, you would bring down my old age with sorrow to Sheol."

CHAPTER 43

1. And the famine was severe in the land. 2. And when they had finished eating the corn which they had brought from Egypt, their father said to them: "Go again; buy us some little sustenance." 3. And Judah said to him, saying: "*Behold* the man warned us solemnly, saying: 'You shall not see my countenance if your brother is not[a] with you.' 4. If you are *willing* to send our brother with us, we will go down and buy you sustenance.[b] 5. But if you do not send him we will not go down, be-

Apparatus, Chapter 42

[i] CTg E: "and Jacob their father said to them: You have bereaved me of Joseph. I do not know what has been his end since the hour that he went with (lit.: beside) you to Dothan; and Simeon—from the hour (= time) he went down with you to Egypt—I do not know what has been (. . .) the end of him and (*with Hebrew sign of accusative as in HT*) Benjamin you (now) seek to take. And they (reckon) on me to raise up twelve tribes"; VNL: "And Jacob their father said to them: You have bereaved me of Joseph. From the hour that I sent him to you I do not know what has been the end of him; and Simeon, from the hour that he went down with you to Egypt, I do not know what

has been the end of him. And (now) you seek to take Benjamin. They (reckon on me) to raise up twelve tribes"; P: "and Jacob their father said to them: You have bereaved me of Joseph. When he went down to you to Dothan, I do not know what has been the end of him. I said concerning him: A wild beast has devoured him. And Simeon, from (lit.: "in") the hour that he went down to Egypt (lit.: Egyptian) (because of) famine, I do not know what has been the end of him. I said: The ruler of the land has imprisoned him. And (now) you want to take Benjamin and you reckon on me to raise up twelve tribes."

[j] CTg E: "place him between my hands."

Notes, Chapter 42

[22]"Since I sent him, . . . his end"; HT: "Joseph is not"; a similar paraphrase to that of vv. 13 and 32.

[23]"and you want . . . twelve tribes"; a paraphrase not in HT, but in Pal. Tg. texts, including Ctg E and in a Targumic Tosefta. CTg X, ed. Klein, 1986, I, 118f. Notes in Klein, 1986, II, 40. M. Klein compares the rendering here with that at Gen 5:24 and expresses the belief that the non-literal interpretation on Joseph reflects the fact that Joseph and Enoch had not really died but continued their existence elsewhere; see M. Klein, in *Biblica* 57 (1976) 519–521; and Klein, 1986, II, 40; Sperber, *The Bible in Aramaic II*, 1959, 355; Grossfeld, *Neofiti*, note 22 to Gen 42. On the text see also B. Barry Levy, 1, 1986, 246.

[24]"raise up twelve tribes"; HT (RSV): "all this has come upon me."

Apparatus, Chapter 43

[a] CTg E: "does not come."

[b] CTg E: "buy ourselves a little sustenance."

cause the man said to us: 'You will not see my countenance if your brother is not with you.'" 6. And Israel said: "Why*c* did you do evil to me by telling*d* the man: 'Behold, now, you have*e* a brother'?" 7. And they said: "The man questioned us carefully about ourselves and about our kindred saying: 'Is your father still alive?*f* Have you a*g* brother?' And we informed him according to these words." And Judah said: "Could we have known that he would say: 'Bring down your brother'?" 8. And Judah said to Israel his father: "Send the boy with me, and we will arise and go, so that we may live and not die, neither we nor you nor our little ones. 9. I will be surety for him;*h of me*[1] you may require him. If I do not bring him back to you and place him <before you>,*i let me be removed from your salutation*[2] for ever.*j* 10. For if we had not been delayed, surely we would have already returned *and come*[3] twice." 11. And Israel their father said to them: "If *you have* so *determined,*[4] do this. Take some of the *best*[5] of the land in your receptacles, and bring as a gift a little balm and a little honey, *wax,*[k] *oil*[6] of pistachios and of almonds. 12. And take double*m* the money in your hand, and bring back in your hand the money that was returned in the mouth of your bags. Perhaps there was a mistake. 13. And take your brother, and *go,* and return to the man. 14. And may the God *of the heavens*[7] grant you mercy before the *ruler;*[8] and may he send back to you your other brother and Benjamin. And I, as I have been bereaved of *Joseph my son,*[n] *will not be further* bereaved of Benjamin."[9] 15. And the men took this gift, and they took double the money in their hands, and Benjamin; and they arose and went down to Egypt and

Apparatus, Chapter 43

c CTg E: "why I pray."

d CTg E: "by showing the man."

e CTg E: "you have yet."

f Lit.: "surviving"; CTg E: "alive" (another word).

g CTg E: "another."

h CTg E: "I am the one to go surety for him; from my hand you may require him."

i Missing in text; is in CTg E.

j Lit.: "all the days"; CTg E: "let us (= I) be removed from your salutation all days" (= for ever); PVNL:

"let me (VNL: "us") be removed from the salutation of my father all the days."

k CTg D: "wax and gum mastich, oil of pistachios."

m VN: "double" (same as Nf).

n PVNL: "and I as I have not been bereaved of Joseph my son, thus I shall not again be bereaved, neither of Simeon nor of Benjamin"; CTg D: "(and may El Shaddai) grant (you mercy before) the man (the ruler) of the land . . . And I, as I have been bereaved of Joseph my son, may I not again be bereaved either of Simeon or of Benjamin."

Notes, Chapter 43

[1]"of me"; HT: "from my hand"; cf. 31:39 above.

[2]"let me (lit.: let us) be removed . . . salutation"; HT (RSV): "let me bear the blame."

[3]"and come"; addition in Nf.

[4]"you have . . . determined"; addition in Nf.

[5]"best"; HT: "choice fruits"; cf. Vulg.: *de optimis.*

[6]"oil"; an addition to HT in Nf.

[7]"God of the heavens"; Nf's standard rendering of HT: "El Shaddai." See Introduction, p. 35.

[8]"the ruler"; HT: "the man."

[9]"as I have . . . Benjamin"; HT: "as I am bereaved (RSV: "If I am bereaved of my children"), I am bereaved." The paraphrase is essentially the same in Nf, Frg. Tgs. CTg D, Ps.-J., and in *Gen. R.* 92,3, but with significant differences, e.g.: "Just as I have *not* been bereaved . . . ," in Nf. Frg. Tgs.; ". . . as I have been bereaved . . ." in the other texts. For details see Grossfeld, *Neofiti*, note 10 to Gen 43; B. Barry Levy, 1, 1986, 247.

stood before Joseph. 16. When Joseph <saw>[o] Benjamin with them, he said to him who *had been appointed administrator*[p][10] over his house: "Bring the men into *the palace*[q][11] and slaughter some animals and prepare (them), because the men will eat with me *at mealtime.*"[12] 17. And the man did as Joseph said, and the man brought the men into Joseph's palace. 18. And the men were afraid because they were brought into *Joseph's palace,* and they said: "(It is) because of the affair of the money that was replaced in our bags[r] at first that we have been brought in, so that he *may lord it* over[13] us, and *seek occasion*[s][14] against us, and take us as slaves, and our asses." 19. And they approached the man *who had been appointed*[15] over Joseph's *palace,*[t] and they spoke to him at the door *of the palace.* 20. And they said: "We beseech, my lord; we came down earlier to buy provisions. 21. And it happened that we went into the resting house and opened our bags, and behold the money of each man was in the mouth of his bag, our money in its (full) weight; and we have returned it in our hand. 22. And we brought other money down in our hands to buy provisions. We do not know who placed the money in our bags." 23. And he said: "Peace be with you; do not fear. Your God and the God of your fathers[16] gave you hidden *treasures*[17] in your bags.[u] I received your money." And he brought Simeon to them. 24. And the man brought the men into the palace of Joseph, and he gave them water and they washed their feet, and he gave fodder to their asses. 25. And they prepared the present *for the time that* Joseph should come[w] *at mealtime,*[18] because they had heard that they would eat there. 26. And Joseph came into the house, and they brought[x] him into *the palace*[19] the present they had in their hands, and they saluted[y] him *according to*[z] the custom of the

Apparatus, Chapter 43

[o] Missing in text.

[p] *epitropos.*

[q] *palation,* Greek loan word; CTg D: "who had been appointed over his palace (*palation*): Bring the men into the palace ..."

[r] CTg D: "in the mouth of our bags."

[s] CTg D: "and to be overbearing" (or: "exalted").

[t] P: "who had been appointed administrator (*epitropos*) over the house of (Joseph)."

[u] CTg D: "in the mouth of your bags."

[w] CTg D: "and they brought in the gift for the entry of Joseph"; CTg E: "and they prepared the present for the entry of Joseph at the hour of midday (*thrh*)."

[x] CTg E: "and they brought into him the gift that they had brought (lit.: that was in their hands) to the house"; Nfmg: "to the house"; = CTg E; Nf variants recommence at 43:26.

[y] Identical minor (lexical) variant in Nfmg and CTg E.

[z] In text: "in"; CTg E: "according to."

Notes, Chapter 43

[10]"had been appointed administrator" (*epitropos*); HT: "steward of his house"; see Gen 39:4.

[11]"palace"; HT: "house." Latin loan word through Greek: *praitôrion, praetorium.*

[12]"mealtime"; HT: "at noon."

[13]"to lord it over" or "make himself lord," i.e., overpower; HT: "seek occasion against."

[14]"seek occasion"; HT: "fall upon."

[15]"had been appointed ..."; see v. 16 and 39:4.

[16]"your fathers" (plur.); HT: "your father" (sing.).

[17]"treasure," *symn* (plur.); HT: "treasure" (sing.).

[18]"mealtime"; HT: "noon."

[19]"palace"; see vv. 6, 16.

land.[20] 27. And he saluted them[aa] and said: "Is your father well—the aged man of whom you spoke?" Is he still[y] *alive*?" 28. And they said: "Your servant, our father, is well. *Behold* he is *alive.*"[bb] And they bowed down, and *gave thanks and praise.*[21] 29. And he lifted up his eyes and saw Benjamin his brother, the son of his mother, and he said: "Is this your young brother of whom you spoke[y] to me?" And he said: "May pity be upon you, my son, *from before the Lord.*"[cc][22] 30. And Joseph made haste[dd] because his emotions were *moved*[ee][23] for his brother, and he wanted to cry. And he went into his bedroom[ff][24] and cried there. 31. And he washed[gg] his face and came out. And he controlled himself,[hh] and said: "Set food."[ii] 32. And they set (it) for him by himself, and for them by themselves, and for the Egyptians who ate with him by themselves, for the Egyptians could not eat bread[jj] with the Hebrews,[kk] because it is an abomination for *the Egyptians.*[25] 33. And he *made them lie down*[mm][26] before him, the older according to his seniority,[kk] and the younger according to his youth. And the men were amazed, one before the other.[kk] 34. And he took[kk] portions from his table and *divided* (them) *amongst them,*[27] and he made the portion of Benjamin five times greater than the portion of all of them.[kk] And they drank and became drunk[kk] with him.

Apparatus, Chapter 43

[aa] Lit.: "and he inquired of them about (their welfare)"; CTg E: "and he inquired of them words of peace (or: welfare)"; Nfmg: "words of peace (or welfare)"; = CTg E.

[bb] CTg D, E, Nfmg: "behold he is still alive" (with minor variants).

[cc] CTg E, Nfmg: "the Memra of the Lord will have pity on you."

[dd] CTg E: "hurried."

[ee] Nfmg: "his love was moved"; = CTg E.

[ff] Greek loan word: *koitôn* in all Pal. Tg. texts: Nf, CTg D, CTg E, and VNL.

[gg] Correcting text from *šgg*, "to do wrong inadvertently," to *šzg* with CTg D, CTg E, VNL, Nfmg.

[hh] Nfmg, CTg D: "and delayed"; CTg E as Nf.

[ii] Lit.: "bread"; Nfmg: "food"; = CTg E.

[jj] CTg E, Nfmg: "food."

[kk] Identical lexical variants in Nfmg and CTg E.

[mm] Nfmg: "and they sat down before him"; =CTg E.

Notes, Chapter 43

[20]"saluted . . . of the land"; Nf's customary translation of the HT expression; see note to 18:2.

[21]"gave thanks and praise"; HT (RSV): "and made obeisance."

[22]"may pity be upon you . . . from before the Lord"; HT: "may God be gracious to you."

[23]"his emotions were moved"; lit. "his insides unfolded"; HT: "his compassion warmed up.

[24]"his bedroom"; a Greek loan word: *choitôn*; (also in Deut 32:25). HT: "into the chamber."

[25]"the Egyptians"; HT: "Egypt."

[26]"he made them lie down"; HT: "and they sat down."

[27]"divided amongst them," addition to HT.

CHAPTER 44

1. And he commanded the one *a* who had been *appointed administrator* *b1* over *c* his house *d* saying: "Fill the bags of the men with provisions, as much as they can carry, *e* and put the money of each in the mouth of his bag. 2. And you shall put my cup, the silver cup, in the mouth of the bag of the youngest, together with his purchase money." And he did according to the word *f* which Joseph spoke. 3. And the morning shone, *g* and the men were sent away, they and their asses. 4. And they went forth, and had not put the city far behind *h* when Joseph said to the one who *was administrator* *i* over his house: *j* "Arise, and pursue after the men. And overtake them and say to them: 'Why, now, have you repayed evil for *k* good? *2* 5. Is it not in this my lord drinks, *m* and he surely divines *n* by it? You have done evil in what you have done.'" 6. And when he overtook them he spoke these words with them. 7. And they said to him: "Why, *now*, does my lord speak these words? <Far from your servants to do such things.> *o* 8. Behold, the money which we found in the mouth of our bags, we brought it back to you *earlier* *3* from the land of Canaan. Just how could we have stolen silver and gold from the house of your master? 9. With whomever of your servants it is found, let him be *put to death*, *4* and let us also be slaves to my master." 10. And he said: "Also now let it be according to your words. He with whom it is found shall be my slave and you shall be innocent." 11. And every man hurried and lowered *p* his bag to the ground, and each man opened his bag. 12. And he searched, *q* beginning with the oldest and ending with the youngest; and the

Apparatus, Chapter 44

a Nfmg: "the one"; cf. CTg E; CTg D: "the man."
b In Nf and CTg E, Greek loan word: *epitropos*.
c Nfmg: "over the men of"; = CTg E.
d CTg D: "his palace" (*palation*).
e Identical lexical variant in Nfmg 1° and CTg E: Nfmg 2° = "(they can) bear."
f An identical synonym in Nfmg and CTg E.
g Nfmg: "in the morning (?; correcting *hyspr'* of text to *bsprh*, as in CTg E) in splendor"; (*bnwgh'*), (gloss possibly not for here).
h Nf as HT; CTg D, E: "and they went forth from the city"; CTg E continues: "and had not gone far"; Nfmg: "gone far"; = CTg E.
i *epitropos*; CTg E: "the one who had been appointed

administrator" (*epitropos*); Nfmg: "to the one who had been appointed officer (*mmny*)" (possibly error through dittogrophy and Nfmg text; = CTg E.
j Nfmg: "(in charge) of the men." Another Nfmg adds: "the men of" to "over."
k identical lexical variant in Nfi and CTg E. CTg E ends here.
m Nfmg1°: "drank"; Nfmg2°: "from which my lord drank."
n Nfmg VNL: "he used to make auguries by it."
o Missing in text.
p Nfmg: "and they hastened and lowered."
q VNL: "and he searched"; = Nf.

Notes, Chapter 44

1 "appointed administrator" (*epitropos*); HT: "the steward"; cf. 39:4, etc.
2 "evil for good"; lit. "bad things for good things" (plur.); HT: sing. The LXX adds at the end of v. 4: "Why have you stolen my silver cup?" Compare Vg; see RSV.
3 "earlier"; addition in Nf.
4 "be put to death" (passive); HT: "he shall die."

cup was found in Benjamin's bag.[r] 13. And they rent their garments, and every man[s] placed (his load) upon his ass and they returned to the city. 14. And Judah and his brothers came *to the palace*[15] of Joseph, and he was (by) now there,[u] and they saluted him *according to the custom of the land.*[6] 15. And Joseph said to them: "What deed is this you have done? Do you not know[w] that a *lord and ruler*[x7] like me can indeed divine?"[y] 16. And Judah said: "What shall we say to my master?[z] What shall we speak and how shall we justify ourselves? *From before the Lord*[8] the guilt[9] of your servants has been found. Behold we and he are slaves to my master,[aa] both we and he in whose hand the cup was found." 17. And he said: "Far be it from me to do this. The man in whose hand the cup has been found, he will be my slave. But you, go in peace to your father." 18. And Judah approached him, *raging in words*[10] *and contrite in tongue.*[bb] He *roared like a lion* and said: "I beseech, my lord, let your servant now speak a word;[cc] and, *my lord*, let not your anger be enkindled against your servant. *Did you not say to us from the first time that we came*[dd] *to you: 'From before the Lord I fear'? And now your judgments have turned to become*[ee] *like to the judgments of Pharaoh, your master."* And he said: "Behold now, our lord, the first time we came, you said to us: 'From before the Lord I fear'; and now you

Apparatus, Chapter 44

[r] Nfmg: "in the mouth of the bag"; = CTg D.

[s] Nfmg: "and every man loaded."

[t] *plṭryn; praitôrion* (Greek), *praetorium* (Latin).

[u] Nfmg: "and he was still to be found (lit.: "given" or "giving"; corr. to "dwelling"?) there and they prostrated themselves upon the ground before him"; ending = CTg D (which is fragmentary).

[w] Nfmg: "are you not aware?"

[x] CTg D: "a man like me can make auguries"; P: "that he makes auguries."

[y] Nfmg: "a man like me has power to divine."

[z] CTg D: "(and Judah said: What) shall we speak and how shall we be acquitted?"

[aa] CTg D: "servants enslaved to our master."

[bb] CTg D; P: "(and Judah approached) and said: I beseech"; VNL: "and Judah approached like a lion and said: I beseech. . . ."

[cc] CTg D, P, VNL: "in the hearing of."

[dd] CTg D, VNL: "we went down."

[ee] P: "now, however, your judgments are like the judgments of Pharaoh your master. However, I am as honorable as you are and my father is as honorable as Pharaoh your master by whom you swear. I swear by the life of the head of Pharaoh your master. Because were I to unsheath the sword from (its) scabbard [Greek loan word: *thêkê*], I would not return it to (its) sheath until I had filled all the land of Egypt with dead and until I (*same form as* "we") had made all

Notes, Chapter 44

[5]"to the palace"; (Latin through Greek loan word: *praitôrion, praetorium*); HT: "to the house."

[6]"saluted . . . custom of the land"; HT (RSV): "fell before him to the ground"; Nf's paraphrase is made under the influence of the similar HT expression with the verb *hšthwh*; here, however, the Hebrew verb is *npl*; cf. note to 18:2.

[7]"lord and ruler" (*rb wšlyt*); HT: "a man (*'yš*) (like me)." See notes to Nf Gen 12:20; 32:7.

[8]"from before the Lord . . . has been found"; HT: "God has found"; paraphrase is intended to avoid the anthropomorphism.

[9]"the guilt" in Nf plur.; in HT singular.

[10]"raging in words . . . rulers in the land of Canaan." This lengthy midrash on Judah's rage is found in the Frg. Tg. (PVNL), in CTg D, in Targumic Tosafoth from the Cairo Genizah (CTg X, FF, Z, R) (ed. M. Klein, 1986, I, 132–143), briefly in Ps.-J.; and in a scattered form in *Gen. R.* and *Tanhuma* (B) (texts of both in Hebrew in Grossfeld, *Neofiti*, note 11 to Gen 44). For a detailed discussion and literary analyses of the midrash, see G. Vermes, 1961 (*Scripture and Tradition*) 11–25; also B. Barry Levy, 1, 1986, 248–259 (for 44:18–19). See also L. G. Pautasso, "Gen. 44:18—A Case for the Textual Relevance of the Targumic Tosefta," *Henoch* 10 (1988) 205–218; E. M. Martinez Borobio, "El midras de Neofiti Gen. 44,18. Dos versiones diferentes de una hagada," *Estudios Biblicos* 35 (1976) 79–86.

say: 'Of Pharaoh I am afraid.' Perhaps it has not been said to you, and perhaps it has not been heard by you, what my two brothers Simeon and Levi did in the fortress of Shechem, that they entered into it and killed every male in it, because within it they defiled our sister Dinah, who is not of the number of the tribes and who has not portion and inheritance in the division of the land. How much more for the sake of

Apparatus, Chapter 44

the land of Egypt bereft of human beings (lit.: "sons of man"). I would begin with you and would finish with Pharaoh your master. Has it not been heard by you, or has it not been told you what my two brothers Simeon and Levi did in the city of Shechem, within which they entered in all safety (cf. Pal. Tg. Gen 34:25) and killed in it all males at the edge of the sword, because they had violated Dinah our sister? How much more so (on account of) tender (*dq'*) Benjamin who is counted with us in the division of the land with the tribes, and receives portion and inheritance in the division of the land? And I, in my strength, am harsher (i.e., stronger) than the two of them, (I) who have gone surety for the boy with my father saying: If I do not bring him back to you and set him before you, let me (*same form as*: "let us") be guilty and banned from inquiring about the welfare of my father all days. Has it not been heard by you and has it not been told you that we are kings and rulers, like you, in the land Canaan?"; VNL: "your judgments (= ways) have turned to become like the judgments of Pharaoh your master by whom you swear. For I am as honorable as you, and my father is an honorable as your master Pharaoh by whom you swear. Do I not swear by the life of the head of my father? And I do not tell a lie, that if I draw my sword from within (its) sheath I will not return it to (its) sheath until I (*same form as* "we") make all the land of Egypt bereft of inhabitants. I shall begin with you and I shall finish with Pharaoh your master I shall stop, even if it means acting against the will of my father. Or perhaps it has not been heard by you, or narrated to you, what his (*read*: my) two brothers Simeon and Levi did, who entered the city of Shechem, which was dwelling in tranquility, and slew every male at the edge of the sword because they defiled Dinah their sister who was not numbered with us in the tribes, and who does not receive part or inheritance with us in the division of the land? How much more (for) Benjamin our brother (who is) numbered with us in the tribes and receives part and inheritance with us in the division of the land. And I, in my strength, am harsher than they (lit.: theirs), (I) who have gone surety for the boy from my father's hands, and have said to him: If I do not take him back to you and set him before you, I (*same form as*: "we") will be guilty to you and removed from your welfare all days. Or perhaps it has not been here or told to you that we are kings and *rulers* like you in the land of

Canaan?"; CTg D: "And Judah drew near him and said: I beseech you, my master. Let your servant, I pray, speak, a word in the hearing of my master, and let not your anger grow strong against your servant. Is it not (a fact) that from the first time that we went down to you, that you said to us: I fear before the Lord? And now your judgments (= ways) have turned to become like the judgments of Pharaoh your master <*text broken . . .*> . . . Has it not been heard by you, and has it not been told you what my two brothers Simeon and Levi did (. . . text broken) . . . and killed every male at the edge of the sword because they had defiled Dinah our sister who was not counted with us from the tribes, and was not to receive share and inheritance with us in the division of the land? How much more (for) Benjamin who is counted with us from the tribes and receives share and inheritance with us in the division of the land. And I in my strength, am harsher than both of them. If I draw my sword I shall not return it to its sheath (*thêke*) until I have killed all the Egyptians. I begin with you and end with Pharaoh. And again, (more over since) I have gone surety for the boy from my father's hands saying to him: Unless I bring him to you, and set him before you, let me (*same form as*: "let us") be in sin to my father (and removed from) inquiring (of his welfare) all days. For just as your master Pharaoh is lord and ruler in the land of Egypt, (and you) his second-in-command, so is my father lord and ruler in the land of Canaan"; Nfmg: "And he said: I beseech our master. Behold, the first time that we came you said to us: I fear before the Lord. But now you have said: Before Pharaoh I fear. Perhaps it has not been said to you, or perhaps it has not been heard by you, what Simeon and Levi, my two brothers, did in the city of Shechem, how they entered within it and killed in it every male because they had defiled within it our sister Dinah, who is not from the number of the tribes and has neither portion nor inheritance in the division of the land? How much the more because of Benjamin our brother, since he is of the number of the tribes and has portion and inheritance in the division? And as regards me, my strength is stronger than the strength of Simeon and Levi. On an oath, if I draw my sword from (its) sheath (*thêke*) I will not put it back within it until the time I have slain every Egyptian. With you I begin and with Pharaoh your master I finish."

Benjamin, our brother, who is of the number of the tribes and who has portion and inheritance in the division of the land? As for me, my strength is greater than the strength of Simeon and Levi. By an oath, if I draw my sword from the scabbard I will not return it within it until I have killed all the Egyptians.[ff] I will begin with you and I will finish[gg] with Pharaoh your master. Because I am as honorable as you, and my father as (honorable as) Pharaoh your master. Since what you confirm by[hh] oath, you swear by him. I swear to you by the life of the head of my father, as you swear by the life of the head of Pharaoh your master, that if I draw my sword from within the scabbard I will not return it to its scabbard until the time all the land of Egypt is filled with the slain. I will not return it to its scabbard until the time that we make all the land of Egypt desolate of inhabitants. With you I will begin, and with Pharaoh your master, in whom you swear, I will end. For the sake of doing it, I will do it despite the unwillingness of my father. Has it not been heard by you, and has it not been told to you, what my two brothers Simeon and Levi did, in the fortress of Shechem, which was in peace, and they entered within it and they killed every male at the edge of the sword because they defiled our sister Dinah, who was not reckoned with us from the tribes and who will not receive inheritance with us? How much more[ii] so since I am harsher than they? And how much more so since my strength is harsher then theirs, and since I have gone bail for the child before my father, and I have said to him these words: 'If I do not bring him to you and place him before you, let me be far from the salutation of my father all days?' Or perhaps it has not been heard by you, or it has not been told to you, that we are kings and rulers like you in the land of Canaan? As you and Pharaoh your master are rulers in the land of Egypt, so I and Jacob my father are rulers in the land of Canaan.[jj] 19. And when[kk] the be-

Apparatus, Chapter 44

[ff] Nfmg1°: "until the time we (= I) have made all the land of Egypt a desolation"; = PVNL; Nfmg2°: "until the time that they fill all the land of Egypt with slain," cf. PVNL; Nfmg 3°: "(until) we (= I) fill all the land," cf. P.

[gg] "I will finish" (*msyym*) (a verb used rarely in this sense). Nfmg: "and with Pharaoh your master I will finish (*msyym*). Has it not been heard." Correct to *msyyp*?, Sokoloff, 1990, 374.

[hh] A hopelessly corrupt text; see parallel in other Pal. Tg. texts cited.

[ii] Nfmg: "and she was not numbered with us; (was) not in the division with us, a portion or inheritance in the division of the land. How much more so."

[jj] There are a number of other minor variants to the ending of the verse in Nfmg. The variants and the text itself give evidence of the composite nature of Nf v. 18.

[kk] VNL: "when the beloved and noble Joseph saw that the fury (lit.: might) of his brother Judah had mounted, and that the hairs of his chest (lit.: "heart," as in Nf) had come out, and that they had torn his gar-

ment, at that hour Joseph nodded to Manasseh his firstborn and stamped with his shoe, and the whole palace (*palation*) (NL +: of Joseph) trembled. At that hour Judah said: If he were not a rib from my father's house, he would not be fit to have done this (lit.: "that it be done thus"). Then Judah began to be gentle in his words and said: My master asked his servants, saying: Do you have a father or a brother?"; P: "When Joseph saw that the anger (*cholê, Greek loan word*) of his brother Judah had mounted, and that the hairs of his chest (lit.: heart) had come out, and that they had torn his garment, at that time Joseph nodded to Manasseh his son, and struck with his foot within the palace (*palation*); and they (all?) trembled. Judah thought in his heart and said: This strength is from the house of my father. For this reason he began to grow gentle in his words and said: My master asked his servants, saying: Do you have a father or a brother"?; CTg D: (incomplete) ". . . this . . . to speak words of peace before his brothers; since my master asked his servants saying: Do you have a father or a brother?"

loved and noble Joseph[11] *saw*[mm] *that the fury of his brother Judah had mounted, and when he also saw that hairs had come forth from his chest, and that they had rent their garments, at that hour Joseph was agitated and he trembled*[nn] *before Judah. And Joseph beckoned to his son Manasseh. He stamped with his foot on the palace, and all the palace was shaken.*[oo] *Judah answered and said: "Here is a confirmation that this strength is from the house of my father, and this strength is <so> great because it is from the rib of my father. If not, would he be able to do such a thing?" Then Judah began to be modest*[pp] *in his words and spoke modest words:* "My lord asked his servants saying: 'Have you a father or a brother?' 20. And we said to my lord: 'We have our father, an aged man, and a*[qq] *child the son of his old age, a young lad; and his brother is dead, and he alone remains to his mother, and his father loves him.' 21. And you said to your servants: 'Bring him down to me and I will set eyes upon him.'*[rr] *22. And we said to my lord: 'The boy cannot forsake his father. If the boy*[12] *forsakes his father,*[ss] *he will die.' 23. And you said to your servants: 'If your youngest brother does not come down with you, you will not see <my> countenance*[13] *(again).' 24. And we went up to your servant my father*[tt] *and related to him the words of my lord.*[uu] *25. And my father*[tt] *said: 'Return, buy us some provisions.' 26. And we said: 'We cannot go down; if our youngest brother comes down*[ww] *with us <we will go down>;*[xx] *because we will not be able to see the countenance of the man if our youngest brother is not with us.' 27. <And>*[xx] *my father <said>*[xx] *to us: 'You know*[yy] *that Rachel*[14] *my wife bore me two sons. 28. And one of them went away from me and I said: 'Surely he had been killed.*[15] *And I as yet have not seen him. 29. And if you take this one also from me,*[16] *and if any calamity*[17] *befall him, you will make my old age descend in sorrow to Sheol.' 30.*

Apparatus, Chapter 44

[mm] Nfmg: "when Joseph saw that. . . . had mounted he beckoned to Manasseh."

[nn] Nfmg: "before him and Joseph trembled."

[oo] Nfmg: "and he shook it. Joseph thought in his heart and said: this is the strength . . . . For this reason"; cf. P.

[pp] Nfmg: "humble in words."

[qq] Nfmg: "and he has in his old age a little one."

[rr] VNL: "the favor of my eye is on him."

[ss] CTg D +: "one brief hour."

[tt] Nfmg: "our father."

[uu] Nfmg: "our lord."

[ww] Nfmg: "is."

[xx] Missing in text.

[yy] Nfmg: "are aware."

Notes, Chapter 44

[11]"and when the beloved . . . Joseph . . . in modest words." This lengthy midrash on Joseph's response to Judah's rage is found in the Frg. Tgs., partly in CTg D, Z, and is paralleled in *Gen. R.* 93, 8. For a detailed discussion of the midrash, see Vermes, 1961, 18–25.

[12]"the boy" (*ṭly'*); addition in Nf to HT.

[13]"countenance," lit. "expression of (my) face"; *sbr 'pwy*; HT: "my face." In 31:2 the same Aramaic expression translates the same Hebrew word: "face of Laban." See note to 31:2.

[14]"Rachel"; an addition in Nf to HT.

[15]"he has been killed"; HT: "has been torn to pieces."

[16]"from me"; HT, lit. "from my face."

[17]"calamity" (*sqwl*); HT: "plague"; See note to 42:4.

And, now, when I enter to your servant, my father,[u] and the boy is not with us,[zz] since his life is *as beloved*[18] to him as his own, 31. it will happen when he sees that the boy is not *with us* he will die;[a] and your servants will make the old age of your servant our father go down in sorrow to Sheol. 32. For your servant went surety for the boy before my father saying: 'If I do not bring him back to you[b] *let me be*[c] removed *from the salutation*[19] of my father for ever.' 33. And now, I pray, let your servant remain in place of the boy as slave to my lord, and let the boy go up with his brothers. 34. For how now can I go up to my father if the boy is not with me? May I not see the evil which will overtake my father.

CHAPTER 45

1. And Joseph could not *endure*[1] all *that were standing* beside him and he cried aloud and said: "Make every man[a] go out from beside me." And no man stood beside him when Joseph made himself known[b] to his brothers. 2. And he gave forth[c] his voice in weeping, and the Egyptians heard it, and it was heard *in the palace*[d2] of Pharaoh. 3. And Joseph said to his brothers: "I am Joseph. Is my father still alive?" And his brothers could not answer him because they were confounded before him. 4. And Joseph said to his brothers: "Draw near to me, I pray." And they drew near and he said: "I am Joseph, your brother, whom you sold[e] to Egypt. 5. And now do not be *angered*,[3] and let it not seem evil in your sight, that you sold me here; be-

Apparatus, Chapter 44

[zz] Nfmg: "with me since the life of the boy is so dear."
[a] Nfmg: "with me (*text*: with him) that I die."

[b] Nfmg: "and I place him before you."
[c] Form used same as for 1st per. pl. ("Let us be").

Notes, Chapter 44

[18]"beloved ... as his own"; HT: "his life is bound up with his own."
[19]"far from the salutation ..."; HT (RSV): "let me bear the blame." See 43:9.

Apparatus, Chapter 45

[a] Nfmg: "(all) the men."
[b] Nfmg: "made him known" (a different word).
[c] Nfmg: "and he raised."
[d] *plṭwryn*: A Latin loan word, through Greek *praitôrion*; Latin *praetorium*; Nfmg: "his voice (was heard) in the palace" (*palation*).
[e] Nfi: "who was sold."

Notes, Chapter 45

[1]"endure (*lmswbr*) all ..."; HT: "to restrain himself (before) (*lht'pq*). The same Hebrew word is translated by *'zdrz*, "controlled himself," in Nf Gen 43:31.
[2]"in the palace," loan word *praitôrion/praetorium*; HT: "the house."
[3]"angered"; HT: "saddened."

cause *the Lord* sent me before you to save.[f]4 6. Because[g] the famine has been in the land these two years, and for yet five years[h] they will neither *sow*[5] nor harvest. 7. And *the Lord*[i] sent me before you to set you *a remnant*[6] in the land for you and keep you alive for a *great deliverance.*[7] 8. And now, you have not sent me[j] hither but *the Lord.*[i] And he has set (me) as father to Pharaoh and as master[k] to all *the men of*[8] his house, and as ruler[m] in all the land of Egypt. 9. Hurry and *go out*[n]9 to my father and say to him: 'Thus said your son Joseph: *The Lord*[o] has set me as master to all *the Egyptians:*[p]10 go down to him and do not *delay.*[11] 10. And you will dwell in the land of Goshen and you will be near to me, you and your sons and your son's sons, and your sheep and your oxen and all that is yours. 11. And I will maintain[q] you there, because there still (remain) five years of famine,[r] lest you and the *men* of your house be *blotted out.'*[12] 12. And behold, your eyes have seen, and the eyes of <my>[s] brother Benjamin, that *in the language of the sanctuary*[13] <my> mouth[t] speaks with you. And you shall tell my father of all my glory in Egypt and of all that you have seen. And you shall hurry to bring my father down hither." 14. And *he threw himself*[14] upon the neck of his brother Benjamin and wept; and Benjamin wept upon his neck. 15. And he kissed all his brothers and wept[u] *before* them;[15] and after this his brothers spoke with him. 16. And the report was heard in *the palace*[w]16 of Pharaoh saying: "The brothers of Joseph have come, and it is

Apparatus, Chapter 45

[f] Nfmg: "so as to keep alive numerous multitudes the Memra of the Lord sent me."
[g] Nfmg +: "already."
[h] Nfi: "another (five years) (they) will not."
[i] Nfmg: "the Memra of the Lord."
[j] in text: "him."
[k] P: "and as a protector (loan word: Greek *patrôn*: Latin *patronus*) to all the men of his house"; Nfmg (probably to this word: "as a protector" (*patrôn*).
[m] Nfmg: "and lord."
[n] Nfmg: "hasten and go up."

[o] Nfmg: "the Memra of the Lord."
[p] Nfmg: "Egypt."
[q] Nfmg: "and I will provide for."
[r] Nfmg +: "that is in the land."
[s] Text: "his brother"; Nfmg: "of Benjamin my brother."
[t] Text: "his mouth"; Nfmg: "as in the interpreter (*turgeman*) of my mouth."
[u] Nfmg: "and they embraced one another and he wept."
[w] *praitôrion-praetorium*; Nfmg: "palace" (*palation*).

Notes, Chapter 45

[4] "to save"; HT: "to preserve life."
[5] "sow"; HT: "plough."
[6] "a remnant"; lit. "salvation"; "refuge"; HT: "remnant."
[7] "great deliverance" (pl. *pylṭn rbrbn*); HT: sing. *plyṭh gdlh*; cf. Gen 32:9, where *plyṭh* is rendered by *l-šyzbh*, "salvation," "remnant."
[8] "men of"; addition to HT, as regularly in Nf.
[9] "go out"; HT: "go up."
[10] "Egyptians"; HT: "Egypt."
[11] "delay"; HT: "stand still."
[12] "be blotted out"; HT: "become impoverished."
[13] "in the language of the sanctuary," i.e., Hebrew; an addition to HT; see note to 2:19, and Grossfeld, *Neofiti*, note 11 to Gen 45, for midrashim on this text, e.g., *Gen. R.* 93,6. The use of Hebrew in this instance is natural.
[14] "and he threw himself"; lit. "and he lowered himself"; HT: "and he fell."
[15] "before them"; HT: "upon them."
[16] "the palace"; Greek-Latin loan word as frequently before; HT: "the house."

good^x in the sight of^y Pharaoh and in the sight^y of his servants."^{y} 17. And Pharaoh said to Joseph: "Say to your brothers: 'Do this: Load your beasts and go, ascend to the land of Canaan. 18. And you shall take your father and *the men of*^{17} your houses, and you shall come to me; and I will give you the best of the land of Egypt, and you shall eat of *the best*^{18} of the land.' 19. And you^z are commanded (to say to your brothers): 'This shall you do: take for yourselves from the land of Egypt wagons for your little ones and for your wives, and you shall put your father aboard and come. 20. And let not your eyes take your instruments *of war*^{19} into consideration, because the best of all the land of Egypt will be yours.'" 21. And the sons of Israel did thus and Joseph gave them wagons, according to *the decree of*^{20} the mouth^{aa} of Pharaoh, and he gave them provisions for the journey. 22. And to all of them—to every man—he gave *a robe*^{bb} *and a garment*;^{21} but to Benjamin he gave three hundred *selas*^{22} of silver^{cc} and five *robes and their garments.*^{dd} 23. And to his father he sent *as a gift*$^{ee\,23}$ ten he-asses laden with the best things of Egypt, and ten she-asses laden with grain and bread and food for his father on the road.^{ff} 24. And he sent forth his brothers, and they went, and he said to them: "Do not quarrel on the way." 25. And they went up from Egypt and came^{gg} to the land of Canaan to Jacob their father. 26. And they related to him saying: "Joseph is still living and he is ruler in all the land of Egypt." But his heart was *undecided,*$^{hh\,24}$ because he did not believe them. 27. And they spoke with him all the words that Joseph had spo-

Apparatus, Chapter 45

^{x} Nfmg: "(and that) his words (are good)."

^{y} Lit.: "in the face of"; Nfmg 1°: "in the eyes of (Pharaoh)"; Nfmg 2°: "and in the face of all his rulers."

^{z} Nfmg: "Joseph commanded: You are commanded to say to your brothers: Take for yourselves from the land of Egypt traveling carriages (*sidnin*; possibly adaptation of Latin *essedum*) drawn by cows"; cf. Ps.-J.

^{aa} Nfmg: "the command (*memar*)"; cf. Ps.-J.

^{bb} Greek loan word: *stolê*; Nfmg: "a garment and robes."

^{cc} Nfmg: "(three) hundred zuzim."

^{dd} Nfmg: "five garments and their robes" (*stolê*).

^{ee} Greek loan word: *dôron*.

^{ff} Nfmg: "provisions for the road."

^{gg} Nfmg: "they entered."

^{hh} Lit.: "was divided" (*'tplg*); VNL: "his heart was divided" (*'plg*). In Nfmg same variant; *'plg*.

Notes, Chapter 45

^{17}"the men of"; addition to HT; see v. 8, etc.

^{18}"the best"; HT: "the fat of."

^{19}"instruments of war"; HT: "vessels," "instruments."

^{20}"the decree of"; addition to HT's: "the mouth of."

^{21}"a robe and a garment"; "robe," Greek-Latin loan word: *stole/stola*; HT: "changes of clothing."

^{22}"selas (=shekels) of silver"; HT: "silver," identified as "shekels" in accord with the principle given in note to 37:28; see also 20:16; 23:16.

^{23}"as a gift" (Greek loan word: *dôron*); an addition to HT in Nf.

^{24}"undecided" ("was divided"); HT: "went numb."

ken with them, and he saw the wagons that Joseph had sent to transport *ii* him, and the spirit of Jacob, their father, *was set to rest.*^{*jj*25} 28. And Israel said: *kk* "Many *good things and consolations have I expected to see, but this*^{*mm*} *I did not expect:*[26] *that* Joseph my son should still *live*. I will go^{*nn*} now and see^{*nn*} him before I die." *nn*

CHAPTER 46

1. And Israel set out on his journey with all that was his, and came to Beersheba, and offered sacrifices to the God of his father Isaac. 2. And *the Lord* said to Israel in a vision of the night *a* and said: "Jacob, Jacob." And he said: *b* "HERE I AM." *c1* 3. And he said: "I am the God of your father; do not be afraid to go down into Egypt, because I will make you a large people there. 4. I will go down with you into Egypt and I, *in my Memra,* [2] will also bring you up; and Joseph will place his hand upon your eyes." *d* 5. And Jacob arose from Beersheba; *e* and the sons of Israel carried *f* Jacob their father and their little ones and their wives on the wagons that Pharaoh had sent to carry him. *g* 6. And they took their possessions, *h* and their

Apparatus, Chapter 45

ii Nfmg: "to carry."
jj Nfmg: "was set at rest."
kk PVNL with identical texts, almost verbatim as Nf, but with "I" "go" "see" having a as 1st per. pl. imperf.; Nfmg: "good things and many consolations have I expected to see, but this consolation I had not

hoped to see (again), and since my son Joseph still lives I will go."
mm Lit.: "and for this"; Nfi: "and this," as in PVNL.
nn Nfmg: "I will go, I will see, I die," with same form as 1st per. pl., as in PVNL.

Notes, Chapter 45

[25]"was set to rest"; HT: "and it lived."
[26]"(many) good things . . . expect." An expansive paraphrase of "many" of the HT.

Apparatus, Chapter 46

a Nfmg: "the Memra of the Lord (said) to Israel in a vision of the night."
b Nfmg: "Jacob answered in the language of the sanctuary and said."
c "Here I am" is in Hebrew.
d Nfmg: "the favor of your eyes" or "your gracious eyes"; cf. Gen 44 Appar. *rr* in Nf above.

e Nfmg: "the well of Sheba" (or "of swearing").
f Nfmg: "the sons of Israel took."
g Nfmg: "to bear."
h Nfmg: "their property."

Notes, Chapter 46

[1]"*Here I am,*" left in Hebrew, untranslated.
[2]"In my Memra"; inserted as usual in Nf and the Pal. Tg.

wealth which they had acquired*i* in the land of Canaan, and came to Egypt, Jacob
and all *his sons* with him, 7. his sons and *all* his sons' <sons> with him, his
daughters and the daughters of his *daughters,*[3] and all his issue they brought *down*[j][4]
to Egypt with him. 8. And these are the names of the sons of Israel, who entered
into Egypt:*k* Jacob and his sons. The firstborn of Jacob, Reuben. 9. And the sons of
Reuben: Hanoch, Pallu, Hezron, and Carmi. 10. And the sons of Simeon: Jemuel,
Jamin, Ohad, Jachin, Zohar, and Shaul, the son of the Canaanite woman. 11. And
the sons of Levi: Gershon, Kohath, and Merari. 12. And the sons of Judah: Er,
Onan, Shelah, Perez, and Zerah. <And Er and Onan died in the land of Canaan.
And the sons of Perez were*m* Hezron and Hamul. 13. And the sons of Issachar:
Tola, Puvah, Iob, and Shimron. 14. And the sons of Zebulun: Sered, Elon, and
Jahleel. 15. These are the sons of Leah, which she bore to Jacob in Paddan-aram to-
gether with his daughter Dinah; all the persons between sons and daughters: thirty-
three. 16. And the sons of Gad: Ziphion, Haggi, Shuni, Ezboh, Eri, Arodi, and
Areli. 17. And the sons of Asher: Imnah, Ishvah, Ishvi, Beriah, with Serah their sis-
ter. And the sons of Beriah: Heber and Malchiel. 18. These are the sons of Zilpah,
whom Laban gave to his daughter Leah and she bore to Jacob: sixteen persons. 19.
The sons of Rachel, Jacob's wife: Joseph and Benjamin. 20. And to Joseph were
born in the land of Egypt Manasseh and Ephraim, whom Asenath, the daughter of
Potiphera, *master* of On,*n* bore him. 21. And the sons of Benjamin: Bela, Becher,
Ashbel, Gera, Naaman, Ehi, Rosh, Muppim, and Ard. 22. These are the sons of
Rachel *whom she bore*[o][5] to Jacob: all the persons fourteen. 23. And the sons of
Dan: Hushim. 24. And the sons of Naphtali: Jahzeel, Guni, Jezer, and Shellem. 25.
These are the sons of Bilhah, whom Laban gave to his daughter Rachel; she bore
these to Jacob; all the persons: seven *persons.*[6] 26. All the persons that entered with
Jacob into Egypt, who had gone forth from *his loins*—not including the wives of
the sons of Jacob—all the persons: sixty-six. 27. And the sons of Joseph, who were
born*p* to him in Egypt: two persons. All the persons *of the men* of the house[7] of

Apparatus, Chapter 46

[i] Nfmg: "the good they had amassed."
[j] Nfi: "they went down"; Nfmg: "he brought in."
[k] Nfmg: "and those who entered Egypt."
[m] Omitted in text.

[n] Nfmg: "Tanis"; cf. Ps.-J.
[o] Nfmg: "these are the sons of Rachel which were
born"; cf. HT.
[p] Nfmg: "who were born"; cf. HT.

Notes, Chapter 46

[3]"they brought down"; HT: "he brought."
[4]"of his daughters"; HT: "of his sons."
[5]"whom she bore"; HT: "who were born."
[6]"all the person seven persons"; HT: "every person! seven."
[7]"all the persons (lit. "souls") of the men of the house"; HT: "every person of the house"; the addition of "men" is regular in Nf.

Jacob who entered Egypt: seventy. 28. And he sent Judah before him to ^{q} Joseph, *to prepare for him a site for his dwelling-place*[8] in Goshenah;^{r9} and they entered^s into the land of Goshen. 29. And Joseph harnessed *his chariots* and went out to meet^t his father Israel to Goshen; and he *saw him*[10] and fell upon his neck and wept upon his neck again.^{u} 30. And Israel said to Joseph:^{w} "Even if I die,^{x} this time[11] *I would not die* after I have seen your countenance,[12] because now^y you are alive." 31. And Joseph said to his brothers and to *the men of*[13] his father's house: "I will go up *now* and tell Pharaoh, and I will say to him: 'My brothers and *the men of*[13] my father's house, who were in the land of Canaan, have come to me. 32. And the men tend flocks because they are *owners*[14] of cattle, and they have brought their sheep^z and their oxen and all that belongs to them.' 33. And when Pharaoh calls you and says: 'What is your occupation?' 34. you shall say: 'Your servants are *owners* of cattle^{aa} from *their* youth^{bb} until now, both we and <our fathers>,'^{cc} so that you may dwell in the land of Goshen; because all that tend flocks are an abomination to the Egyptians.'"

Apparatus, Chapter 46

^{q} Nfmg: "with this gift (*dôron*) to."
^{r} Nfmg: "to prepare for him a school house in Goshen"; PVNL in v. 28a = Nf, but with: "to Goshen."
^{s} Nfmg: "to Goshen and they came to the land."
^{t} Nfmg: "his chariots and went up to meet."
^{u} Nfmg: "a second time."
^{w} P: "and Israel said to Joseph: Were I to die this time, (it would be) as if I did not die after I have seen your countenance, because you are still alive."

^{x} Nfmg: "(if) I were to die this time, it would be for me as if I did not die after I have seen"; cf. P.
^{y} Nfmg: "(you are) still (alive)"; = P.
^{z} Nfmg: "they are men, owners of herds, and sheep."
^{aa} Nfmg: "they were men, owners of herds."
^{bb} Nfmg: "your youth" (corr. to: "our youth"; cf. HT).
^{cc} Missing in text.

Notes, Chapter 46

[8]"to prepare for him a site for his dwelling-place; HT: "to show (the way)." The Frg. Tgs., CTg D, and Ps.-J. paraphrase as Nf. Here the additional paraphrase is apparently intended to provide an object for the HT's "to show." See also Grossfeld, *Neofiti*, note 7 on Gen 46:28. In *Gen. R.* 95,3 "to show" of HT is understood as "to prepare" (a place to teach the Law). A text nearer still to Nf is in the Vatican Codex of *Gen. R.*: "to prepare a dwelling-place for him" (text in Grossfeld, loc. cit.). The expression occurs also elsewhere in Nf; Deut 1:33; Num 10:33; Exod 33:14. See McNamara, "'To prepare a place for you.' A Targumic Expression and John 14:2f," *Milltown Studies* 3 (1979) 100–108; also McNamara, 1983A, 239–241.
[9]"Goshenah," retaining the *he locale* of the HT.
[10]"and he saw him"; HT (RSV): "he presented him to him.."
[11]"even if I die this time (Grossfeld: I wish not to die), I would not die"; HT: "let me die this time." There is a similar paraphrase in Tg. Onq. and Ps.-J.
[12]"your countenance," *sbr 'pyk*; HT: "your face"; Nf renders as elsewhere (31:2; 44:23). See note to 31:2.
[13]"the men of"; added in Nf.
[14]"owners (of cattle)"; HT: "men of"; Nf intends to bring out the meaning of the HT.

CHAPTER 47

1. And Joseph went and told Pharaoh and said: "My father and my brothers, and their sheep and their oxen and all that belongs to them, have come from the land of Canaan; and behold, *they are*[1] in the land of Goshen." 2. And he took some <of his brothers>, five men, and set them before Pharaoh. 3. And Pharaoh said to his brothers: "What is your occupation?" And they said to Pharaoh: "Tenders of flocks are they[a] your servants—both *they*[a2] and our fathers." 4. And they said to Pharaoh: "We have come in to sojourn in the land; for there is no pasture for the flocks belonging to your servants, because the famine is *very*[3] severe[b] and they *languished*[4] in the land of Canaan; and now, we pray, let your servants dwell in the land of Goshen." 5. And Pharaoh said to Joseph: "Your father and your brothers have come to you. 6. The land of Egypt lies before you. Settle your father and your brothers in the best *place*[5] of the land.[c] Let them dwell in the land of Goshen. And if you know that there be among them warriors, valiant men, you shall place them as masters of *our*[6] flocks,[d] over *all*[6] that belongs to me." 7. And Joseph brought[e] Jacob his father and placed him before Pharaoh, and Jacob blessed Pharaoh. 8. And Pharaoh said to Jacob: "How many *are* the days of the years of your life?" 9. And Jacob said to Pharaoh: "The days of the years of my sojourn are one hundred and thirty years; few and evil have the days of the years of my life been, and I have not overtaken the days of the years of the lives of my fathers in the days of their sojournings." 10. And Jacob blessed Pharaoh, and went out from before Pharaoh.[f] 11. And Joseph settled his father and his brothers, and all the men of his house; <and he gave them an inheritance in the land of Egypt, in the best *place*[g5] of the land, in the land of *Pelusium*[h7] according as Pharaoh had commanded him. 12.

Apparatus, Chapter 47

[a] I.e., "we"; cf. HT.
[b] Nfmg: "(because) there is a famine."
[c] Nfmg: "in the best choice place of the land."
[d] Nfmg: "herds."
[e] Nfmg: "brought it."
[f] Nfmg: "and he said: Let the good pleasure before the Lord be that the waters of the Nile (*Nilus*) be raised and let them irrigate all the land of Egypt; and may the hunger pass away in your day(s). And Jacob went out from Pharaoh."
[g] Nfmg: "in the best choice place."
[h] Nfmg, VNL: "of Pelusium."

Notes, Chapter 47

[1] "they are" (*yhybyn*), lit. "are given"; not in HT, a feature of the language of Nf.
[2] "both they"; HT: "we."
[3] "very"; an addition in Nf; not in HT.
[4] "languished"; an addition in Nf; from influence of v. 13.
[5] "the best place" (*bbyt špr*); HT: "in the best of."
[6] "our ... all"; additions to HT in Nf.
[7] "*Pelusium*"; HT: "Rameses"; Nf's usual identification (also in Exod 12:37; Num 33:3; also in Nf Num 33:5, possibly by scribal error.

<And Joseph provided[i] his father and his brothers and all *the men of*[8] his father's house>[j] with bread[k] according to their dependents. 13. And there was no bread[m] in all the land; because the famine was very severe and *the inhabitants*[9] in the land of Egypt and in the land of Canaan languished before the famine. 14. And Joseph gathered[n] together all the money that was found in the land of Egypt, and in the land of Canaan, in exchange for the wheat[o] which they <bought>,[p] and Joseph brought the money into the *palace*[q][10] of Pharaoh. 15. And the money of the land of Egypt and of the land of Canaan *was spent,*[r][11] and all the Egyptians came to Joseph saying: "Give us bread,[s] for why should we die before you, for the money is spent?" 16. And Joseph said: "Bring your cattle[t] and I will give you according to your cattle[u] if the money is spent." 17. And *all the Egyptians* brought (them) to *Joseph saying: "Give us bread."*[12] And Joseph gave them *provisions* in exchange for horses, for the sheep, for (their) possessions in herds of oxen,[w] and for the he-asses, and he led them with bread[x] in exchange for all their cattle that year. 18. And that year ended[y] and they came to him the second year and said to him: "We will not *lie*[13] to my master, but[z] the money is spent; and *the sheep*[14] and the cattle belong to my master, and there does not remain back from my master except alone our bodies and our land.[aa] 19. Why should we die before you,[bb] both we and our land? Purchase[cc] us and our land for bread[dd] and we and our land will be slaves to Phar-

---

Apparatus, Chapter 47

[i] Nfmg: "sustained."

[j] Missing in text; added in Nfmg.

[k] Nfmg: "of his father with food according to."

[m] Nfmg: "food."

[n] Nfmg: "and (Joseph) collected."

[o] Nfmg: "for the purchases."

[p] Missing in text.

[q] *praitôrion, praetorium*; Nfmg: "palace" (*palation*).

[r] Nfmg, VNL: "was exhausted."

[s] Nfmg: "give us food, for why should we die."

[t] Nfmg: "give your herds."

[u] Nfmg: "your herds."

[w] Nfmg: "and for property in sheep and for property in oxen."

[x] Nfmg: "and Joseph sustained them with bread and with (= and in exchange for) all their herds."

[y] Nfmg: "and (that year) went by."

[z] Aramaic *'rwm 'lhn,* (here rendering MT *bilti 'im*) generally to be rendered "except," "but rather."

[aa] Nfmg: "and the holdings of cattle are with our master and nothing is left before our master except their (= our) bodies and our land."

[bb] Nfi: "in your sight" (lit.: "eyes"); Nfmg: "in your presence."

[cc] Nfi: "buy."

[dd] Nfmg: "for food."

Notes, Chapter 47

[8]"the men of"; the addition is usual in Nf in such contexts.

[9]"the inhabitants"; an addition in keeping with Nf's translation technique.

[10]"the palace"; Latin-Greek loan word: *praetôrion, praetorium*; HT: "the house."

[11]"is spent," *šlm*; HT: ("has ceased") (*'ps*); the same translation by Nf in 47:16; the only other occurrence of the word in the Pentateuch.

[12]"all the Egyptians . . . bread"; HT in v. 17a has: "they brought their cattle to Joseph," which was not translated in Nf. Nf's text may have been intended as an introduction to v. 17b, but is more probably an erroneous text due to the influence of v. 15.

[13]". . . not lie to"; HT: "not hide from."

[14]"sheep and cattle"; no "and" in HT (RSV): "herds of cattle."

aoh; and give us seed that we may live and not die and our land will not perish."
20. And Joseph *bought* for Pharaoh all the land of the Egyptians;[ee] because the
Egyptians, each one sold his field because the famine was severe upon them. And
the land became Pharaoh's. 21. And, as for the people[ff] that slandered with evil
tongue, *Joseph* displaced them and *exiled them,*[15] *and changed them from one city*
to another and from one end of the territories *of the Egyptians* to the other. *And the
people who were in the city he settled in the provinces; and the people of the provinces
he settled in the cities, from one end of Egypt to the other, so that the Egyptians
would not taunt the brothers of Joseph and say to them: "Homeless strangers."*[gg] 22.
Only the land of the priests he did not *buy*, because the priests had a *portion* from
Pharaoh and they ate their *portion* which Pharaoh gave them. Because of this they
did not sell their land. 23. <And Joseph said to the people: "Behold I have *bought*
you this day, (you) and your land for Pharaoh. *Take* seed and sow the land>.[hh] 24.
And *at the time of*[16] the harvest you will bring one fifth to Pharaoh, and the four
parts will be[ii] for yourselves, to sow your *territories,*[17] and as your provisions, and
the *sustenance of*[jj][18] your houses, and as provisions for your young ones." 25. And
they said: "You have sustained our life. We shall find grace *and favor*[19] in the sight
of my master[kk] and we shall be slaves of Pharaoh." 26. And Joseph set as
statute[mm][20] until this day over the land of the Egyptians: "For Pharaoh one fifth."
Only the land of the priests, theirs alone, did not become Pharaoh's. 27. And Israel
dwelt in the land of Egypt, in the land of Goshen, and they acquired an inheritance
in it and *grew strong* and increased[nn] greatly. 28. And Jacob lived in the land of

Apparatus, Chapter 47

[ee] Nfmg: "the land of Egypt."

[ff] Nfmg 1°: "and as for the people, he moved them
from one city to another so that they would not call
his brothers displaced persons, and castabouts (reading *gylwly'* of Nf as *glwl'y* of VNL). Wherefore from
one end of the territory of Egypt to the other"; Nfmg
2°: "and the people who dwelt in the provinces he removed to the cities, and the people who dwelt in the
cities he removed to the provinces, so that they
should not taunt the sons of Jacob and say to them:

strangers (Greek: *xenos*) and castabouts." Nfmg 2°
= VNL verbatim.

[gg] Greek loan word: *xenos*.

[hh] Missing in text; supplied from Nfmg.

[ii] Nfmg: "for you to sow in the field" (reading *bara'* for
bira').

[jj] Nfmg: "as provision."

[kk] Nfmg: "in the sight of our master."

[mm] Nf text: "as a sign"; Nfmg: "as a statute."

[nn] Nfmg: "and they increased and were multiplied."

Notes, Chapter 47

[15] The midrashic paraphrase is intended to explain Joseph's mass transportation of population, i.e., so that the Egyptians would not call his brothers "homeless strangers." The midrash exists also in rabbinic sources; texts in Hebrew in
Grossfeld, *Neofiti*, note 15 to Gen 47. There is an analysis of Nf's text in B. Barry Levy, 1, 1986, 262-264.

[16] "the time of"; an addition to HT in Nf.

[17] "territories"; HT: "field" (*śdh*); in keeping with Nf's translation principle noted at 32:4 for other translations of *śdh*
by Nf, see note to 2:5 and 32:4 (translation by *'py br'*), and 23:9 (translation by *ḥql*).

[18] "sustenance of"; an addition in Nf.

[19] "grace and favor," *ḥn wḥsd*; HT: *ḥn*; Nf's general translation of the HT word; see note to 6:8 and 32:6.

[20] "or a statute" (*l-symn*); HT: "law" (*ḥq*); Nf's translation of *ḥq* here is unique; it is not paralleled in Nf elsewhere or in
other Tg. texts.

Egypt seventeen years; and the days of *the life of*[21] Jacob,[oo] the years of his life, were a hundred and forty-seven years. 29. And the days drew near for Israel to die and he called his son Joseph and said to him: "If, I pray, I have found grace *and favor*[19] in your sight, put, I pray, your hand under *the sign of* my *covenant,*[pp][22] and you shall do with me grace *and goodness.*[qq] Do not, I pray, bury me in Egypt. 30. When *I am gathered*[23] to my fathers, you shall take me from Egypt and bury me in their graves." And he said: "*Behold,*[24] I will do according to your words." 31. And he said: "Swear to me."[rr] And he swore to him. And Israel *praised and glorified*[25] upon the head of the bed.

CHAPTER 48

1. And it happened after these things that it was said to Joseph: "Behold, your father is ill." And he took[a] with him his two sons Manasseh and Ephraim. 2. And it was told to Jacob and he said: "Behold, your son Joseph comes to you." And Israel summoned his strength[b] and sat up *on the head*[1] of his bed. 3. And Jacob said to Joseph: "The God *of the heavens*[2] was revealed to me at Luz in the land of Canaan and blessed me. 4. And he said to me: <Behold, I will make you *powerful* and will

Apparatus, Chapter 47

[oo] Nfmg: "the days of Jacob."
[pp] Also in CTg D; see note.
[qq] Nfmg: "and truth."
[rr] Nfmg: "swear to me by an oath. And he swore to him by an oath. And he praised (the Lord) and as soon as

the Glory of the Shekinah of the Lord was revealed, Israel bowed down"; VN: "and Israel glorified (the Lord) upon the head of his bed."

Notes, Chapter 47

[21]"the life of"; an addition in Nf.
[22]"sign of my covenant," lit. "my covenant," *qyymy,* as in 24:9. HT: "thigh." The (sign of the) covenant was circumcision.
[23]"I am gathered to"; HT: "I lie down with," i.e., die; the same rendering in Nf Deut 31:16; cf. Gen 49:33, where HT has "to be gathered," and where Nf retains the HT.
[24]"behold"; an addition to HT.
[25]"and praised and glorified"; HT: "and bowed down" (*wyšthw*).

Apparatus, Chapter 48

[a] Nfmg: "is ill. And he brought."

[b] Nfmg: "and (Israel) made an effort."

Notes, Chapter 48

[1]"on the head of . . ."; HT: "in bed."
[2]"God of the heaven"; as elsewhere, this is Nf's translation of HT: "El Shaddai."

multiply[c] you; and *you will become* an assembly of a *congregation of holy* nations;[3] and I will give this land to your sons[d] after you as an eternal inheritance. 5. And, now, your two sons that were born to you in the land of Egypt before my coming[e] to you, they shall be (called) by *my name*; Ephraim and Manasseh, like Reuben and Simeon, will be (called) by *my name.*[4] 6. And your offspring that you begot after them shall be (called) by *your name;*[4] and they shall be called according to the name of their brothers in their possessions.[f] 7. And when I came from Paddan of Aram, Rachel died in my presence[g] in the land of Canaan on the way, *at the time of the harvest*[h5] of (the) land, at the entrance to Ephrath. And I buried her there on the road of Ephrath, that is, Bethlehem."[i] 8. And Israel saw the sons of Joseph and said: "Who are these?"[j] 9. And Joseph said to his father: "They are my sons whom *the Lord*[k] gave me here." And he said: "Bring them,[m] I pray, to me that I may bless them." 10. And the eyes of Israel *were dim*[6] with age and he was not[n] able to see; and he brought them near to him, and he embraced them and kissed[o] them. 11. And Israel said to Joseph:[p] "Your *countenance*[7] I did not expect to see, and behold *the Lord*[q] has made me see your sons also." 12. And Joseph brought them out *after he had blessed* them,[r8] and *they*[9] prostrated themselves *before him*[10] on the

Apparatus, Chapter 48

[c] Nfmg: "and I will multiply you and make you an assembly."

[d] Nfmg: "the descendants of your sons."

[e] Nfmg: "our coming in."

[f] Nfmg: "the name of their brother they will take in inheritance."

[g] Nfmg: "from Paddan-aram Rachel (died) beside me."

[h] Nf: "time of the harvest" (*'šwn 'llt'*), taking HT *'wd* ("still") as meaning "time," and the obscure Hebrew *kibrah* (= stretch?; a good stretch?) as "harvest." Same understanding in Nf Gen 35:16. Nfmg in both cases restores obscure Hebrew word. Nfmg: "at the time, the exact time (reading *'swn* as *'šwn*) a *kibrah* of the land to enter Ephrath"; cf. Nfmg Gen 36:16.

[i] Nfmg: "of Judah."

[j] Nfmg: "from where have these been begotten?"

[k] Nfmg: "the Memra of the Lord."

[m] Nfmg: "bring them near."

[n] Nfmg: "hardened with old age (and he was) not."

[o] Nfmg: "and he embraced."

[p] CTg D: "and Israel said to Joseph: I had not hoped to see (text: to be seen) your countenance and behold, the Memra of the Lord has shown me also the descendants of your sons."

[q] Nfmg: "the Memra of the Lord (has shown me) also the descendants of your sons"; = CTg D.

[r] CTg D: "Joseph brought them out from his knees and they prostrated. . . ."

Notes, Chapter 48

[3]"assembly . . . holy nations"; HT: *qhl 'mym*: "an assembly of nations." A favorite phrase in Nf in the translation of these and some related Hebrew words; cf. Gen 17:4; 28:3; 35:11 and note to 17:4.

[4]"by (my/your) name" (*b-šmy/k*); HT: "for me, for you."

[5]"at the time of the harvest"; HT: *b'wd kbrt 'rṣ*. The same Hebrew phrase and Nf translation as in Gen 35:16. See note there.

[6]"were dim" (*khwn*); HT: "become heavy"; Nf uses the same verb as for Isaac in 27:1 (where HT also has *khn*).

[7]"your countenance," *sbr 'pyk*; Nf's regular rendering of HT *pnym*, "face," especially with the verb "to see." See note to 31:2.

[8]"after he had blessed them" (*mn dbrk*); HT: "from his knees" (*m'm brkyw*). Nf either misunderstands the Hebrew or wishes to avoid a misunderstanding (indecent exposure); cf. Grossfeld, *Neofiti*, note 13 to Gen 48. See also B. Barry Levy, 1, 1986, 265.

[9]"they (prostrated)"; HT: "he (prostrated)."

[10]"before him"; HT: "to his face."

ground.[s] 13. And Joseph took the two of them, Ephraim on his right to the left of Israel, and Manasseh on his left to the right of Israel, and he drew near to him.[t] 14. And Israel stretched out his right hand, and *stretched* (it) *out*[11] and placed it[u] on the head of Ephraim, who was the younger, and the left hand upon the head of Manasseh, *crossing*[12] his hands,[w] because Manasseh was the firstborn. 15. And he blessed Joseph and said: "*The Lord,*[x] before whom my fathers Abraham and Isaac walked *in truth,*[13] *the Lord*[y] who has *led* me[14] from *my youth*[15] until this day, 16. the angel who has redeemed me[z] from all *tribulation,*[aa][16] may he bless the boys and let my name be called in them and the names of my fathers, Abraham and Isaac. And may *they multiply*[bb][17] in the land *like the fishes multiply in the waters.*"[cc] 17. And Joseph saw that his father had placed his right hand upon the head of Ephraim and this did *not appear good in his sight,*[dd][18] and he raised the hand of his father to change[ee] it from upon the head of Ephraim to the head of Manasseh. 18. And Joseph said to his father: "Not thus, my father, because this is the firstborn; place your right hand upon his head." 19. And his father refused and said: "I know, my son, I know; he also[ff] will become a nation and he also[ff] will be powerful, but his younger brother will be more powerful then he and *his sons*[gg] *will rule* nations."[hh][19] 20. And he blessed them that day, saying: "*By your merit*[20] shall Israel[ii] be blessed saying: 'May *the Lord* make you like Ephraim and like Manasseh.'" And he gave

Apparatus, Chapter 48

[s] Nfmg: "from his knees and they saluted according to the custom of the land."

[t] Nfmg: "and he brought them near to him."

[u] CTg D: "stretched out his right hand and put it. . . ."

[w] VN: "he interchanged his hands"; CTg D = Nf.

[x] Nfmg: "the Memra of the Lord (before whom my fathers) walked."

[y] Nfmg: "the Memra of the Lord who led."

[z] CTg D: "the angel (. . . *letters missing*) that rescued me from all evil."

[aa] Nfmg: "evil"; = CTg D.

[bb] CTg D: "may they grow strong and multiply within the land."

[cc] Nfmg: "like fishes multiply in the sea."

[dd] CTg D: "and it was displeasing before him"; Nfmg: "displeasing."

[ee] CTg D + Nfmg: "to alter."

[ff] CTg D: "he too."

[gg] CTg D: "the descendants of his sons."

[hh] Nfmg: "and of his sons seventy sages will sit in the Grand Sanhedrin according to the number of the worlds" (or: "of the young men"?).

[ii] CTg D: "by you let each man bless his neighbor in Israel, saying."

Notes, Chapter 48

[11]"and stretched (it) out"; repetition not in HT.

[12]"crossing"; lit. "changing," *šlḥp*; see also *Aruk.* HT *śkl* (only here, with this sense in HT). VN, Ps.-J. render by Aramaic *prq.* The medieval Jewish commentators R. Hananel, R. Alfasi and Rashbam cite as from the Palestinian Targum the word found in Nf. This is a further indication of the use of a Neofiti-type Pal. Tg. in the Middle Ages. On this see D. J. Martin (art. cit., note to 37:7) *Tradition* 13–14 (1973) 203; also Grossfeld, *Neofiti,* note 16 to Gen 48.

[13]"in truth"; addition to HT.

[14]"(from) my youth"; HT: *m'wdy*; RSV: "all my life long."

[15]"led me"; HT: "shepherded me"; "pastured me."

[16]"tribulation"; HT: "evil."

[17]"may they multiply . . . in the waters"; HT: "and may they multiply in the midst of the earth"; a paraphrase also reflected in some rabbinic texts (given in Hebrew in Grossfeld, *Neofiti,* note 20 to Gen 48).

[18]"this did not appear good in his sight"; HT: "was evil in his eyes."

[19]"his son will rule nations"; HT: "and his seed will become a multitude of nations."

[20]"by your merit"; HT: "by (in) you."

<him> *the blessing*[21] *of* Manasseh.[jj] 21. And Israel said to Joseph: "Behold, I die; but the Lord will be with you and make you return to the land of your fathers.[kk] 22. And I[mm] give you[nn] *a portion more than your brothers:*[22] *the garment of the first*[oo] *Adam, which Abraham, my father's father, took from the hands of evil Nimrod and gave to Isaac, my father; and Isaac, my father, gave it to Esau, my brother; and I took it from the hands of Esau, not with my sword and my bow,*[23] *but by my merits and by my good works, which are better for me than* my sword and my bow. And now, I give you *a part more* than your brothers: Shechem, which I took *from the hands of the Amorites, by my merits and my good works, which are better for me than* my sword and my bow."

Apparatus, Chapter 48

[jj] CTg D: "and he placed the order of Ephraim's blessing before Manasseh."

[kk] CTg D: "and Israel said to Joseph: Behold I am now dying (lit.: "being gathered") and may the Memra of the Lord be at your aid and make (you) return." (CTg D breaks off here.)

[mm] P: "and I give you a portion more than your brothers: the garment of the first man (or: first Adam) that was given to Abraham, and he gave it to Isaac my father, and Isaac my father gave it to Esau, and I have not taken it from him either with my sword or with my bow but rather by my righteousness and my good works"; VNL: "and I have given you a portion more than your brothers: the garment of Adam the First (or: the first man). Abraham your father's father took it from the hands of the wicked Nimrod and gave it to my father Isaac, and my father Isaac gave it to Esau. And I took it from the hands of Esau, neither with my sword or my bow, but rather by my righteousness and my good works."

[nn] "you," sing. in text; Nfmg 1°: "to you (plur.) a portion more than your brothers, which I took by my righteousness and my good works from the hands of the Amorites, since these (or: which) were better to me than my sword and my bow"; Nfmg 2°: "to you (sing.) <...> your brothers <...> (2 separate glosses) from the hands of the Amorites by my righteousness and my good works since they (or: and they) were better."

[oo] In Nf text: lit.: "the first Adam; Abraham took it"; Nfmg: "the first, that Abraham took from the hands of Nimrod and gave them to Isaac, and Isaac gave them to Esau who walked in the way (Greek loan word: *nomos*) of the Amorites (*ending of lines illegible*) by my strength . . . (great) deeds that are pure . . . between swords and more than my bow."

Notes, Chapter 48

[21]"he gave (lit. "set") (him) the blessing of . . ."; HT: "he put (set) Ephraim before (=ahead of) Manasseh."

[22]"a portion more . . . better for me than." This is an elaborate paraphrase of the HT: "And I give to you one *shechem* (RSV: one mountain slope; lit. "shoulder") rather than to your brothers, which I took from the hand of the Amorite with my sword and bow." The interpretative paraphrase is also in *Gen. R.* 97,6 under the name of R. Judah. "R. Judah maintained: the *portion* (*shechem*) means the birthright and the raiment of Adam *which I took . . . of the Amorite*, viz. Esau, *with my sword and . . . bow*—with pious and noble deeds." According to various midrashic texts, the "garments of Adam" were made by God himself (Gen 3:21), were indestructible and possessed miraculous powers, such as success at the hunt; Nimrod (Gen 10:9, and *PRE* 241, Esau [Gen 25:27; 27:15]). Summary in Klein, 1986, II, 51; also Ginzberg, *Legends*. See B. Barry Levy, 1, 1986, 266–268, for an analysis of the text of Nf.

[23]"not by my sword or bow"; an example of converse translation; see Introduction, p. 31. J. Heinemann, *Aggadah and Its Development* (Jerusalem, 1974) 154; M. L. Klein, *Biblica* 57 (1976) 525–527.

CHAPTER 49

1. And Jacob called his sons and said to them:[a][1] "Gather together[2] and I will tell[b] you *the concealed secrets, the hidden ends, the giving of the rewards of the just, and the punishment of the wicked, and what the happiness of Eden is." The twelve tribes gathered together[c] and surrounded the bed of gold on which our father Jacob*

Apparatus, Chapter 49

[a] P (v. 1): "and Jacob called his sons and said to them: Gather together and I will show you what is to come upon you: the giving of reward to the righteous, the retribution that is to come to the wicked, at the time they are gathered together at the end of the days. <They were hoping> that he would reveal to them all that was destined to come at the final end (i.e., in the days) of the Messiah (lit.: in the end of the heels of the Messiah = the Footsteps of the Messiah). As soon as it was revealed to him, it was hidden from him. And Jacob arose and blessed them, each according to the measure of his blessing he blessed them"; VNL: "and Jacob called his sons and said to them: Gather together and I will relate to you the hidden determined ends, the concealed secrets, the giving of the reward of the righteous and the retribution of the

wicked and what the delights of Eden are. The twelve tribes of Jacob were gathered together surrounding the bed of gold within which our father Jacob lay, requesting that he relate to them the determined end of the blessing and the consolation. As soon as the secret was revealed to him, it was hidden from him (or: as soon as it was revealed to him, the secret was hidden from him); as soon as the door was opened to him, it was closed from him. Our father Jacob turned and blessed his sons, each in accord with his good works he blessed them."

[b] Nfmg: "and I will relate to you the hidden signs (or: miraculous events), the guarded mysteries, the giving of (reward)."

[c] Nfmg: "the twelve tribes gathered together surrounding the bed of (gold)."

Notes, Chapter 49

[1] This lengthy paraphrase of Jacob's blessing on the tribes, together with the introduction to it, is found in the various Pal. Tg. texts: Nf, Frg. Tg., CTg Z, Ps.-J.; and in the Targumic Tosefta from the Cairo Genizah, CTg FF, for vv. 1 and 18. A long history of composition seems to lie behind the present Pal. Tg. paraphrase; some of it is apparently very old and underlying Tg. Onq. The bulk of the paraphrase, however, as it now stands, seems to be no earlier than the Pal. Tgs. in general. The interpretative tradition enshrined in Pal. Tg. for Gen 49 should be studied in connection with the Jewish understanding of this very important text in other Jewish works such as the *Testaments of the Twelve Patriarchs* and Qumran texts on the patriarchal blessings. The closest parallels, however, seem to be with the Jewish tradition transmitted in rabbinic sources. These at times are extremely close, occasionally to the extent of almost verbal identity. It is not easy, however, to determine where the dependence really lies—whether the Pal. Tg. draws on rabbinic tradition or vice versa. It may well be that both are but different formulations of the same interpretative tradition. For a detailed study of these chapters, see R. Syrén, *The Blessings in the Targums. A Study of the Targumic Interpretation of Genesis 49 and Deuteronomy 33* (Abo, 1986), with special treatment of the theological ideas in the paraphrase: Memra and Shekinta; messianic expectations; eschatology; ethical teaching; relationship to rabbinic doctrine; parallels to the Targumic expositions; Y. Komlosh, "Ha-Aggadah betargumê birkat ya'akob," *Annual of Bar-Ilan University: Studies in Judaica and the Humanities I, Pinkhos Churgin Memorial Volume*, ed. H. Z. Hirschberg and P. Artzl (Jerusalem, 1963) 198ff. For the text of Onqelos, in these chapters closer than usual to the Pal. Tg. tradition, see Grossfeld, 1988, 158–173; Grossfeld and Aberbach, 1982, 280–311. There is a detailed analysis, mainly textual, of Nf Gen 49 in B. Barry Levy, 1, 1986, 268–306.

[2] "Gather together . . . the concealed secrets . . . he blessed them." HT: "Gather together that I may tell you what shall befall you in the days to come." The long paraphrase is almost identical in Nf and N. The opening section ("Gather together . . . he blessed them") shows dependence on apocalyptic texts, e.g., Dan 2:18, 28, 30, 47f.; also 2 Baruch 81:4; compare also Tg. Isa 24:16. This is seen in such terms and expressions as: "hidden mysteries" (*rzyy'*), "determined ends" (*qṣyy'*); the rewards of the righteous; the punishment of the wicked; the happiness (*šlwwth*, or: "security"—Syrén, 120; "tranquility"—Klein, 1986, I, 162); "revealed to him, concealed from him."

was lying *daftere the end was revealed*[3] *to him and thatf the determined end of the blessing and the consolation*[4] *might be communicated to them. As soon as the end was revealed to him, the mystery was hidden from him.d They hopedg that he would relate to them the determined end of the redemption and the consolation. As soon as the mystery was revealed to him, it was hidden from him and as soon as the door was opened to him, it was closed from him.*[5] *Our father Jacob answered and blessed them; each according to his good works he blessed them. 2. After the twelve tribesh*[6]

Apparatus, Chapter 49

d-d This section ("after the end ... from him") in Nf seems interpolated.

e or: "as soon as."

f Nfmg: "he (they) asked that he relate to them the determined end of the blessing and the consolation, and it was hidden from him, and as soon as (or: since) it was hidden from him he blessed them in accord with (their) good works."

g Nfmg: "upon him. They were hoping that he would relate to them all that would occur, that would happen to them at the end of the days. As soon as (or: since) it was revealed to him, the mystery was hidden from him. He turned and blessed them, each according to the interpretation (? *mptr*) of his blessing he blessed them."

h In PVN v. 2 as in Nf with variants as noted here.

Notes, Chapter 49

[3]"the golden bed ... after the end was revealed." It is to be borne in mind that parts of the paraphrase of 49:1 in Nf are very obscure, possibly corrupt, and almost defy punctuation and translation. The obscurity may be due to the combination of diverse traditions, especially concerning the revelation and non-revelation to Jacob. Syrén (p. 120) translates the section rendered "the golden bed ... was lying.... was revealed," as follows: "... was lying. After the end had been revealed to him, so that he would tell them about the end with bliss and consolation—after the end was revealed to him, the secret was concealed from him. They expected him to tell them about the end with redemption and consolation, (but) after the secret had been revealed to him, it was concealed from him. ...." The fact that the mystery of messianic redemption, expressed in different ways (consolation, redemption), was withheld from Jacob is stated more than once in the Targumic paraphrase. That Jacob was prevented by God from carrying out his desire of revealing the messianic message is also noted in rabbinic sources, e.g., *Gen. R.* 98(99),3: "He (i.e., Jacob) was going to reveal the end (*hqṣ*), but it was concealed from him"; also in *b. Pes* 56a.

[4]"the determined end (*qṣ*) of the blessing and the consolation." On the eschatology of this section, see Syrén, 119–121. Le Déaut, 163, 274, followed by Syrén, 122, and Grossfeld, *Neofiti*, note 1, has remarked that the eschatological teaching on the determined end (*qṣ*) being hidden is to be compared with that of the Qumran pesher of Habakkuk (1QpHab VII on Hab 2:3; "*For still the vision awaits its time and hastens to the end (qṣ), it will not lie.* The explanation is that this determined fixed end (*qṣ*) will be of long duration, and it will exceed all that the prophets have said; for the mysteries of God (*rzy 'l*) will be marvelous. *If it delays wait for it; for it will surely come and not delay* (Hab 2:3b). The explanation of this refers to the men of truth ... when the final end is delayed for them; for all the times arrive in their due season in accord and with what he has decreed about them and in the mysteries of his prudence."

[5]"as soon as (or: "after") the door was opened to (or: "for") him, it was closed (*'trd*) from him." Thus also Syrén, 120. Grossfeld renders: "and as the gate opened to him, he was banished from it" (Grossfeld, *Neofiti*, note 1 to Gen 49), taking *'trd* as if from *trd* I, "banish," instead of from *trd* II, "close," as Jastrow and others do, and as the present context seems to require. See also B. Barry Levy, 1, 1986, 270f.

[6]"After the twelve tribes ... one Lord"; HT: "Assemble and hear, O sons of Jacob, and hearken to Israel your father." Practically nothing of the HT is translated in Nf's paraphrase (or in the Pal. Tgs.), which is really a continuation, or part repetition, of the paraphrase on v. 1. This is probably due to the similarity of the opening words in the biblical text of vv. 1 and 2. In Nf and the Pal. Tgs., Jacob's blessing on the tribes proper is introduced by an examination on his part of his sons' fidelity to the God of Israel. The response to this examination by Jacob is the recitation of the *Shema'*, Israel's profession of faith, by the tribes. (The same midrash occurs in Nf Deut 6:4 as an introduction to the *Shema'*, which is again represented as Israel's response to Israel [= Jacob's] inquiry.) Ishmael, the sons of Keturah and Esau are presented as examples of infidelity. In Nf (and the Pal. Tgs.) Gen 50:1 these are presented as present at the burial of Jacob. In Nf (and the Pal. Tg.) the *Shema'* is given in Aramaic. Jacob responds by reciting the later rabbinic counterpart of the confessional (Grossfeld), *Neofiti*, note 2 to Gen 49), given also in Aramaic in Nf but containing the Hebrew loan word *kbwdh*, "the glory of his. ...." However, this particular Hebrew word is probably an interpolation in Nf. It is absent from P and from VNL, the text of which is otherwise here very close to that of Nf. In the paraphrase the *Shema'* ("Hear, O Israel") is made to fit in nicely, "Israel" in this context being the dying Jacob.

of Jacob had gathered together and surrounded^i the bed of gold on which our father Jacob lay, they were hoping that he would reveal to them^j the order of the blessings, but it was hidden from him. Our father Jacob answered and said to them: "From Abraham, my father's father, arose the blemished^k Ishmael and all^m the sons of Keturah. And from Isaac, my father, arose the blemished^n Esau, my brother. And I fear lest there should be among you one^o whose heart is divided^{6a} against his brothers to go and worship before foreign idols." The twelve sons of Jacob answered^p together and said: "Hear us, O Israel, our father; the Lord our God is one Lord."^{q} Jacob answered and said: "Blessed be his name; may the glory of his kingdom be for ever and ever. 3. Reuben,^{7} my firstborn are you; my strength and the beginning of my *sorrow*. You were destined^r to take three portions more than your brothers. The birthright was yours;^{s} and the kingdom and the high priesthood were destined for you. Because you have sinned,^{t} Reuben, my son, the birthright has been given to Joseph, my son, and the kingdom to Judah, and the high priesthood to the tribe of Levi. 4. I will compare you,^{8} my son Reuben, to a small garden into which entered

Apparatus, Chapter 49

^{i} In P (erroneously): "and it was revealed."

^{j} P: "reveal to them the determined end of this redemption and it was hidden. . . ."

^{k} Lit.: Nf, VN: "the blemish of Ishmael"; P: "the blemish in Ishmael."

^{m} P: "and the sons of."

^{n} Lit.: "the blemish Esau."

^{o} P: "one who adheres to the sons of his brother to worship."

^{p} VN: "all of them answered together"; P: "the twelve tribes of Jacob answered with one heart: Hear, O Israel, the Lord our God is one Lord."

^{q} VN: "is one Lord. Let his name be blessed for ever and ever."

^{r} Nfmg: "It was destined for you, Reuben, my son to take"; = VN.

^{s} PVN: "your brothers; the birthright and the kingdom"; almost identical with Nfmg.

^{t} P: "because you incurred debt" (= sinned).

Notes, Chapter 49

^{6a}"heart divided"; see already in Nf Gen 22:14; "perfect heart" in Nf Gen 22:8 (see note to verse); cf. *Sifre Deut.* 32, on Deut 6:5: "*with all your heart*: that means with all the heart in you, lest your heart be divided regarding the Lord." Nf's paraphrase agrees with *Gen. R.* 98,3 on 49:2: "Eleazar b. Ahaway said: From here Israel received the privilege of reciting the Shema. When the patriarch Jacob was departing from the world, he called his twelve sons and said to them: 'Is the God of Israel in heaven your father? Maybe in your hearts you wish to break away from the Holy One blessed be He?' 'Hear, O Israel (Deut 6:4), our father,' they replied. He too (i.e., Jacob) thereupon made utterance with his lips saying: 'Blessed be the name of his glorious kingdom for ever and ever.'" See also Nf Deut 6:4.

^{7}"Reuben . . . of Levi"; HT: "Reuben, you are my first-born; my might and the first fruits of my strength, pre-eminent in pride and pre-eminent in power." The paraphrase of Nf (and Pal. Tgs.) is here almost identical with the understanding of the verse in *Gen. R.* 98,4 (presented as one of the opinions of Rabbi): "The birthright should have been yours, priesthood yours, and royalty yours. Now that you have sinned, however, the birthright has been given to Joseph, and the royalty to Judah."

^{8}"I will compare you . . . remitted you"; HT (RSV): "Unstable (*pḥz*) as water, you shall not have pre-eminence, because you went up to your father's bed; then you defiled it, when you went up to my couch." In the Tg., while Reuben is regarded as having sinned in the affair of Bilhah, his father's secondary wife or concubine (Gen 35:22), pardon is promised if he repents. He is excused on the grounds of human frailty and lack of premeditation. This particular paraphrase found in Nf and the Pal. Tgs. is not attested in rabbinic sources. Yet, also among the rabbis the need to exculpate Reuben was strongly felt, both by reason of his being one of the patriarchs and because of his role at Mount Ebel (Deut 27:20) on precisely his own sinful action. One way of exculpating him was by reading *pḥz* ("unstable") of the HT backward and as an abbreviation (*notarikon*) for three Hebrew verbs: *z*: "you shuddered"; *ḥ*: "you trembled"; *p*: "the sin has flown from your head." Thus R. Eleazar of Modiim in *Gen. R.* 98,4—a text to be compared with the Nf paraphrase. See further Syrén, 129f., and Grossfeld, *Neofiti*, note 5 to Gen 49. In Nf the second part of the verse is left in Hebrew, untranslated, in keeping with certain rabbinic rules; see McNamara, 1966A, 46f.; M. L. Klein, art. cit. (note to Gen 35:19), *JJS* 29 (1988) 80–91, esp. 82–84.

overflowing streams of water[u] *which you were not able to endure, and you were crushed before them, my son; so have you been crushed, Reuben, my son, by your wisdom and from your good works.*[w] *The sin you have committed, do not commit any more, my son, and what you sinned will be forgiven and remitted you. BECAUSE*[x] *YOU WENT UP TO YOUR FATHER'S BED; THEN YOU DEFILED GOING UP ON MY BED.* 5. Simeon and Levi[9] are *twin* brothers, *masters*[y] *of sharp arms, waging war*[10] *from their youth. In the land of their enemies they have wrought the victories of their combats.* 6. *In their assemblies,*[z] *in their counsels, my soul*[11] *has* not *delighted; when they assembled, against the fortress of Shechem, to destroy it they did not have consideration for* my honor, because in their anger they killed *kings*[aa][12] and according to their desires *they broke down the walls of their enemies.*[13] 7. Accursed[14] *was the city of*[bb] *Shechem when Simeon and Levi went within it*[cc] *to destroy it, in their anger; because their anger is strong*[dd] *and the fear of them*[15] *is*

Apparatus, Chapter 49

[u] VN: "overflowing streams."

[w] VN: "Reuben my son by your good works"; Nfmg: "by your good works, you shall not return (to sin again)."

[x] The words "BECAUSE ... MY BED" left untranslated, in Hebrew; likewise in VN; cf. Gen 35:22.

[y] VN: "men, masters. . . ."

[z] VN lacks "in the assemblies."

[aa] VN: "they killed kings with rulers and in their desire they sold Joseph their brother who was comparable to an ox"; Nfmg: "they sold Joseph their brother who was like an ox."

[bb] or: "fortress"; P = "city"; Nfmg: "accursed were the masters of Shechem."

[cc] P: "when they rose up against it."

[dd] Nfmg, VN: "in their anger because it was strong and in their passion because it was harsh."

Notes, Chapter 49

[9]"Simeon and Levi . . . twin (*tlymyn*) brothers"; HT (RSV): "Simeon and Levi are brothers." All Pal. Tg. texts describe the brothers as *tlymyn* (rendered here as "twin"), the exact meaning of which is uncertain: (1) "bold" (J. Levy, *Chaldäisches Wörterbuch*, II, 540, deriving it from the Greek *toleros; cf. Aruk*); (2) "twins" (M. Jastrow, *Dictionary*, II, 1672a.s.v.*tlm'*, with reference to Akkadian *talimu*, and note: "alike in character" for Tg. Gen 49:5; likewise Sokoloff, 1990, 582); (3) "like furrows" (D. Rieder, *Sinai* 30, 1965, 11); see Grossfeld, *Neofiti*, note 6 to Gen 49. The HT word for twins, i.e., *t'wmym* (Gen 38:27) is rendered in the Pal. Tg. texts by cognate Aramaic *twmyyn* (Nf) or *tywmyn* (Ps.-J.).

[10]"waging war . . . victories of their combats," paraphrasing the very difficult HT word *mkrtyhm*. For rabbinic parallels to Nf, see Syren, 130; Grossfeld, op. cit., note 7.

[11]". . . my soul . . . of their enemies"; HT (RSV): "O my soul, come not into their council; O my spirit (*kbdy*, "my glory:, "my honor"?) be not joined to their company." "In their council" has a double translation: "in their assemblies" and "in their councils." Nf links the latter part of the HT text with the destruction of Shechem, an understanding also found in rabbinic texts, e.g., *Gen. R.* 98,5.

[12]"they killed kings"; HT: "they killed men" (lit. "man," collective). Nf's paraphrase is in accord with a view found in rabbinic texts that in Shechem they slew Shechem and Hamor, the royalty of the city; cf. Gen 34:2: "Shechem ben Hamor, the prince of the land."

[13]"they broke down the walls of their enemies"; HT: "they uprooted (RSV: "hamstrung") oxen" (lit. "an ox," *šwr*, collective). Since Gen 34:28 makes no mention of Simeon and Levi injuring oxen, all the Tgs. (Onq., Ps.-J., Pal. Tg.) and most ancient versions (Vulg., Pesh., Sym.) read as *šur*, "wall(s)." *Gen. R.* 98,6 understands likewise.

[14]"accursed . . . in their anger"; HT: "cursed be their anger." The Pal. Tg. transfers the curse from the anger of Simeon and Levi to the city of Shechem, apparently out of respect for the elders of the nation. So too does *Gen. R.* 98,5. The HT also has: "(cursed be) their wrath," which Nf avoids translating.

[15]"the fear of them"; HT: "their wrath." Nf's rendering is unique, found in no other Pal. Tg. text where we have *ḥymt(hwn)*, "(their) anger."

harsh," *said our father Jacob.* *"If Simeon and Levi dwell together, there is no nation nor king that can stand against them. I will divide*[16] *the inheritance*[ee] *of Simeon in the midst of the house of Jacob and I will multiply the inheritance of Levi in the midst of the tribe(s) of the sons of* Israel. 8. Judah, you[ff] will your brothers[gg] praise, *and by your name shall all the Jews*[17] *be called Jews.*[hh] Your hands *will avenge you* of your enemies; *all* the sons of your father *shall advance to salute* you. 9. *I shall compare you,* Judah,[ii] to a lion's *whelp; you saved my son Joseph from his murderers.*[18] *From the judgment*[jj] *of Tamar,*[19] *my son, you are innocent;*[kk] *you will rest and dwell in the midst of battle,*[20] like the lion and like the lioness, *and there is no nation nor kingdom*[21] that shall stand *against you.* 10. *Kings*[mm] shall not cease from among *those of the house of* Judah[22] and neither (shall) *scribes*[nn] teaching the

Apparatus, Chapter 49

[ee] Nfmg, PVN: "(I will distribute) the (P +: sons of the) tribe of Simeon as scholars teaching the Law (P: as scribes and teachers of the Law) in the congregation of Jacob and I will scatter the (P +: sons of the) tribe of Levi in the schoolhouses of the sons of Israel."

[ff] Nfmg, P: "Judah, all your brothers will praise (or: confess) you, according to your name."

[gg] PVN: "all your brothers"

[hh] Text: "all Yehudim called Yehudain"; P: "all Jews (*Yehudae*) will be called Jews (*Yehudain*); VN: "all will be called Jews" (*Yehudae*).

[ii] VN +: "my son."

[jj] P: "in the matter of the judgment of Tamar (of) whom you said: (She is) more innocent than I am. You will repose and rest in the midst of battle like the lioness; there is no kingdom to stand up before you."

[kk] Nfmg: "rescued."

[mm] In v. 10 VN verbatim as Nf save "scholars" for "scribes"; Nfmg: "there shall (not) cease either kings or rulers from"; cf. P.

[nn] VN: "scholars"; P: "until the time that King Messiah (lit.: "the king of the Messiah; or: who is the Messiah") comes who is destined to arise from those of the house of Judah."

Notes, Chapter 49

[16]"I will divide . . . sons of Israel"; HT: "I will divide them in Jacob and scatter them in Israel." Nf's paraphrase adds a reason for this, in keeping with an understanding we find in rabbinic tradition; texts given in Grossfeld, op. cit., note 16.

[17]"Judah . . . called Jews." This addition to the HT is in accord with the Jewish interpretative tradition preserved in rabbinic sources, e.g., *Gen. R.* 98,6: "R. Simeon ben Yohai said: *All your brethren will be called by your name.* A man does not say: I am a Reubenite or a Simeonite, but I am a Yehudi (Jew)."

[18]"you saved my son from his murderers," a paraphrase of HT: "From the prey, my son, you have gone up." The reference is to Judah's position in the sale of Joseph (Gen 37:26f.).

[19]"From the judgment of Tamar . . ."; probably a second interpretation of "prey" of the HT. There is a similar double interpretation in *Gen. R.* 98,7: "*From the tearing* (or: *prey*) *my son, you are gone up,* you went up from the tearing of my son, and were thereby exalted; you went up from the tearing (=destruction) of Tamar and were thereby exalted." On double translations in Tg. Gen 49, see Syrén, 17–19.

[20]"you will rest and dwell in the midst of battle"; HT (RSV): "he stooped down and couched as a lion." *Gen. R.* 98,7 also interprets the text of defeat of enemies.

[21]"and there is no nation or kingdom . . ."; HT: "and like a lioness; who dares rouse him up?" Nf translates Num 24:9 in an identical manner.

[22]"kings shall not cease . . . of Judah"; HT: "the sceptre shall not depart from Judah." Nf's interpretation of "sceptre" is the natural one, found also in *Gen. R.* 98,8: "*The sceptre.* This refers to the throne of kingship." As usual, Nf paraphrase the more abstract "Judah," "house of Judah" by explicit mention of the people involved: "those of." For studies of this important section of Tg. Gen 49:8-12, esp. 10-12, see Syrén, esp. 102–112; B. Grossfeld, 1988, notes to vv. 8-12, pp. 161–166; Aberbach and Grossfeld, 1982, 284–292; Aberbach and Grossfeld, 1976, notes 13-34, pp. 10–30.

Law from *his son' sons*[23] until *the time King Messiah shall come,*[24] *to whom the kingship belongs; to him shall all the kingdoms[oo] be subject.* 11. *How beautiful[pp] is King Messiah*[25] *who is to arise from among those of the house of Judah. He girds his loins and goes forth to battle against[qq] those that hate him; and he kills kings with rulers,*[26] *and makes the mountains red*[27] *from the blood of their slain and makes the valleys white from the fat of their warriors.[rr] His garments are rolled[ss] in blood; he is like a presser of grapes.* 12. *How beautiful[tt] are the eyes of King Messiah; more than pure wine, lest he see with them the revealing of nakedness or the shedding of innocent blood.*[28] His teeth are purer than milk, *lest he eat with them things that are*

Apparatus, Chapter 49

[oo] Nfmg: "the nations."
[pp] In v. 11 VN = Nf with few variants as noted below; likewise P, which begins: "He girds."
[qq] A different Aramaic word in PVN, Nfmg.
[rr] In text: "men"; "warriors" in PVN.
[ss] P: "made clear"; probably erroneously.

[tt] V: "how beautiful to behold"; otherwise V in v. 12 = Nf; Nfmg: "(How) beautiful is King Messiah who is to arise from those of the house of Judah. His eyes are more tender (read: purer) than pure wine lest the revealing of nakedness be seen by them, and lest they see the shedding of (innocent) blood by them."

Notes, Chapter 49

[23]"scribes teaching the law from his sons"; HT: "nor the mace (or: staff; *mḥqq*) from between his feet." The Hebrew *mḥqq* is understood in the paraphrase through the root *ḥq*, "statute," "law," as meaning "an instructor in (or: teacher of) the Law," i.e., scribe in the richer sense. Nf, and all Tgs., translate *mḥqq* in the same way in the other occurrence of the word in Deut 33:21 ("Moses the scribe of Israel") and in Num 21:18. We have a similar interpretation in rabbinic sources, e.g., *Sanh* 5a: *mḥqq*, the descendant of Hillel who teaches the Torah in public; see further the observations and references of Syrén, Grossfeld, Aberbach and Grossfeld in works indicated in preceding note. This interpretation of *mḥqq* is a very old one, found already in the Qumran Damascus Document (CD VI, 7). See further, G. Vermes, 1961, 49–55. Syrén (55) notes that the Targums in Gen 49:10 do not identify the "scribes" with any specific persons; rather, the institution of the scribes and teachers is indicated by them.

[24]"until the time king Messiah comes . . . the Kingship"; HT: *'d ky yb' šylh*; which could be understood at its face value in later Judaism in different ways, e.g., "until Shiloh comes," or: "until he comes to Shilo," or: "until he comes to whom it belongs" (*shelo*). The original reading and meaning of the text are quite uncertain. In the paraphrase Shilo is first interpreted as a person, i.e., King Messiah, and then through later Hebrew *shelo*, "whose it is," i.e., "the Messiah to whom kingship belongs." The direct messianic interpretation is found in all the Tgs. (Onq., Pal. Tgs., Ps.-J.), and already in 4Qpatr: "until the Messiah of justice, the sprout of David, comes; for to him and to his seed has been given the covenant of kingship." See further Syrén, 56–58; Grossfeld, *Neofiti*, note 27 to Gen 49; also the works referred to in previous note. The messianic interpretation of Shiloh has also been constant in rabbinic Judaism, e.g., *Gen. R.* 98,8: "*Shilo.* This alludes to the Royal Messiah." Further texts in Syrén, 131; Grossfeld, *Neofiti*, note 47; etc.

[25]On vv. 11-12 and the theology they contain, their relationship to the text of the Bible, to Jewish pseudepigraphical and apocryphal literature, and the Qumran *Genesis Apocryphon*, see Syrén, 102–111. The paraphrase of these verses is practically identical in all Pal. Tg. texts and in Ps.-J. See also B. Barry Levy, 1, 1986, 283–287.

[26]"How beautiful . . . kings with rulers"; HT: "binding his foal to the vine, and his ass's colt to the choice vine."

[27]"He makes the mountains red . . . presser of grapes"; HT (RSV): "He washes his garments in wine and his vesture in the blood of grapes." The Pal. Tg. paraphrase is but loosely connected with the biblical text. It presents a picture of a warring Messiah, in a paraphrase linking Gen 49:11b and Isa 63 and found also in the NT Apoc 19:11-16. See further McNamara, 1966A, 23–33; Syrén, 105. There are no known texts in rabbinic literature reflecting the Pal. Tg. paraphrase of v. 11. This particular paraphrase is believed to be very old and probably pre-Christian; see Syrén, 107.

[28]"How beautiful . . . innocent blood"; HT (RSV): "His eyes shall be red with wine." This paraphrase is in all Pal. Tg. texts and in Ps.-J. "but appears to have no parallel in the midrash and Talmud" (Grossfeld, *Neofiti*, note 32 to Gen 49).

stolen or robbed.[uu] The mountains will become red from his vines and the vats from wine; and the hills will become white from the abundance of grain and flocks of sheep. 13. And Zebulun will dwell by the coasts of the *Great* Sea,[29] and *he shall rule over the ports*[30] *of* ships; *and his territory shall reach as far as* Sidon. 14. Issachar (is) *a strong tribe,*[31] lying between two *territories.*[ww] 15. And he saw *from the beginning*[xx32] that it was good, and the land *of Israel that its fruits were* rich; and he bends his shoulders *for the study of the Law, and his brothers bring him* up tribute.[yy] 16. *From those of the house of* Dan[33] *shall redemption*[zz] *arise, and a judge. Together,*[a] *all* the tribes[b] *of the sons of* Israel *shall obey him.* 17. This[c] shall be *the redeemer who is to arise from the house of Dan; he will be strong, exalted above all nations.*[d] *He will be compared to the* serpent *that lies on the ground,*[e] and *to a venomous serpent that lies in wait at the crossroads,* that bites the horses in the heels and *out of fear of it* the rider *turns around and* falls backward. *He is Samson bar Manoah, the dread of whom is upon his enemies and the fear of whom is upon those*

Apparatus, Chapter 49

[uu] Nfmg: "so that he might not eat by them either what is stolen or robbed."

[ww] Nfmg, PVN: "(P: Issachar a strong tribe) and his territory passes between (PVN +: the two boundaries)."

[xx] PVN, Nfmg; PVN: "and he saw the sanctuary which is called the House of Repose that (PVN: contained) it is good and the land [P + of Israel] that its fruits are fat; and he bent his shoulders to labor in the Law and all his brothers brought (him) tribute."

[yy] Nfmg: "bring up a redeemer" (*prwq*).

[zz] P: "a redeemer."

[a] P: "together the whole assembly of the tribes of the sons of Israel."

[b] CTg Z: "all the heads of the tribes. . . ."

[c] Or: "Dan shall be the redeemer"; VN: "This shall be the redeemer."

[d] VN: "above all kingdoms."

[e] VN: "that lies in the way"; P, Nfmg: "Dan was (P: will be) like a serpent, a venemous serpent (*hrmny'*) that lies in wait at the cross roads, (that bites the horses) in the heels and makes him sick and from fear of him his rider turns about and falls backward. (He is Samson bar Manoah, the dread of whom is upon his enemies. He goes out to war against those who hate him and kills kings together with rulers)." (*Text within parentheses not in Nfmg.*)

Notes, Chapter 49

[29]The Great Sea," i.e., the Mediterranean. HT: "the Sea."

[30]"he shall rule over ports"; HT: "he shall be a haven for ships." According to Josh 19:11, Zebulun's territory did not reach the sea. This geographical reference may represent a later situation, e.g., the conquests of Alexander Jannaeus. See note 35 to Gen 49 in Grossfeld, *Neofiti*; Grossfeld, 1988, 166; also Aberbach and Grossfeld, 1982, 292f.; Aberbach and Grossfeld, 1976, 13, note 2.

[31]"(Issachar) a strong tribe"; HT: "a bony (or: strong) ass," lit. "an ass of bone," i.e., of substance. The Pal. Tg. probably considers this particular animal reference pejorative and omits it out of reverence for the ancestors.

[32]"(He saw) from the beginning (*mn šyrwy'*) . . . tribute"; HT: "He saw that a resting place (*mnḥh*) was good and that the land was pleasant." Nf here renders *mnḥh* of the HT as "from the beginning" (*mn šyrwy'*, from root *šr'*, "to begin"), a phrase used rather frequently in Nf. However, since Nf, the Pal. Tgs., and the Tgs. in general render HT *mnḥh* and the root *nwḥ* through the root *šr'*, "rest," "to dwell," (*mšrwy*, "resting place," "dwelling place") and since the translation of Nf as given in the text leaves the important word *mnḥh* of the HT untranslated, we should probably regard *mn* ("from") as an intrusion and render as: "(He saw) a (or: the) resting place. . . ." Thus Grossfeld, *Neofiti*, note 37 to Gen 49. Issachar's zeal for the Torah is also a feature of rabbinic tradition; see Syrén, 132f.

[33]"From those of the house of Dan . . . with rulers"; HT: "Dan shall judge his people as one of the tribes of Israel." The Pal. Tg. paraphrase of these verses concentrates on the judge, Samson, the expected redeemer from the tribe of Dan. The tradition found in *Gen. R.* 98, 14 does likewise: "*Dan shall be a serpent on the way* (49:17) . . . so was Samson."

who hate him.[f] He goes out to war against those that hate him and kills kings together with rulers." 18. *Our father Jacob[g] said: "Not to the redemption of Gideon[h][34] bar Joash does my soul look, which is the redemption of an hour; and not to the redemption of Samson bar Manoah does my soul look, which is a transient[i] redemption.[j] Rather to the redemption of him[k] does my soul look that you have said to bring your people, the house of Israel.[m] To you, to* your redemption,[n] *do I look, O Lord.[o]* 19. *From those of the house of Gad[p][35] there shall come forth camps[q] equipped and armed.* They shall make the people of Israel[r] *pass over the Jordan, and they shall subdue the land before them. And afterward they shall return to their place*

Apparatus, Chapter 49

[f] VN: "the fear of him is upon those who hate him and he slays kings together with rulers."

[g] Nfmg: "(our father Jacob said) when he saw Gideon bar Joash and Samson bar Manoah: <...> I do not look for, since his redemption is a transient redemption (lit.: the redemption of an hour) and I do not yearn for (*mwdy*[*q*]) since the redemption is the redemption of a moment; for your redemption have I looked and yearned, Lord of all ages, since your redemption is an eternal redemption."

[h] Nfi: "of Samson."

[i] Correcting '*bwr* of text to '*byr*, see CTg X.

[j] CTg X (a Tosefta): "for your redemption I await (O Lord). Our father Jacob said: Not for the redemption of Gideon bar Joash, which is a passing ('*br*) redemption, and not for the redemption of Samson bar Manoah, which is a transient redemption (lit.: "the redemption of an hour"); but rather for the redemption of the Messiah son (*bn*) of David who is eventually to come (?; *l'yt'h*; or: "which he will eventually bring") to the children of Israel—to his redemption does my soil look."

[k] P: "to the redemption which you have said" (VN +: "in your Memra").

[m] CTg FF (Tosefta) (a fragmentary text): "their father said to them: Not for the redemption of Gideon bar Joash do I wait, for it is a transient redemption (lit.: "the redemption of an hour") and not for the redemption of Samson bar Manoah, which is a transient redemption (lit.: "r. of an hour"), but for the redemption of the King Messiah, which is the eternal redemption which you have promised (lit.: "said") in your Memra to br(ing)."

[n] Nfmg: "to him, to his redemption"; P: "to him to the redemption"; VN: "to him, to your redemption does my soul look."

[o] Nfmg: "who is (*dhw*) the Lord."

[p] PVN: "from those of the house of Gad there shall come forth camps, equipped, armed. And they shall make Israel cross the Jordan and bring them into possession of the land of Canaan, and after this they shall return in peace to their tents."

[q] Nfi: "seeds (or: "descendants") equipped armed"; Nfmg: "armed equipped."

[r] or: "they shall pass over the Jordan with Israel."

Notes, Chapter 49

[34]"Not to the redemption of Gideon ... O Lord"; HT: "I wait for your redemption, O Lord." Nf's paraphrase is very close to the understanding of the verse in *Gen. R.* 98,14: "Our ancestor Jacob saw him (i.e., Samson prophetically) and thought that he was the Messiah. But when he saw him dead he exclaimed: He too is dead." As noted earlier, the nature of the relationship between the Pal. Tg. and rabbinic tradition in the interpretation of the Patriarchal Blessings is uncertain. The tradition of *Gen. R.* may well depend on the Pal. Tg. For other rabbinic parallels of Nf Gen 49:18, see notes 45, 46 to the chapter in Grossfeld, *Neofiti*.

[35]"From those of the house of Gad ... plentiful wealth"; HT (RSV): "Raiders shall raid Gad, but he shall raid at their heels." Nf, like the Pal. Tgs., interprets the entire verse of the role played by Gad in the conquest of the land (cf. Num 32:16-32; Deut 3:18ff.; Josh 1:22ff.; 4:12f.). We find this same reference in the interpretation of the verse in *Gen. R.* 98,15.

with plentiful wealth.^s 20. *Blessed are you of the house of* Asher!^{t 36} *How fat are the fruits of your land!*^u *And behold, it will bring forth produce*^w *(which will be)* the delicacies of the kings *of the sons of Israel.* 21. Naphtali is a *swift runner,*³⁷ *announcing good tidings. It was he who announced to our father Jacob from the beginning that Joseph was still alive. And he girded himself and went down*^x *to Egypt in a short time and brought the title deed of possession of the field*^y *from the palace of Joseph. And when his mouth used to bear (good) tidings in the assemblies of Israel, milk and honey went forth from his lips.* 22. *My son Joseph, how you have grown! My son, you who have grown and become mighty!*³⁸ *and again you are destined to become mighty. I compare you,*³⁹ *my son Joseph, to a vine planted* by springs *of water that sends its roots into the ground,*^z *and breaks the teeth of all*^{aa} *the rocks, and sends its branches high and overshadows all the trees. Thus did you, Joseph my son, conquer*^{bb} *in your wisdom all the magicians*^{cc} *of the Egyptians and all their wise men,*^{dd} *when they mounted you on the second chariot of Pharaoh*^{ee} *and acclaimed before you: 'Long live the father of the king, who is a master in wisdom and young*^{ff} *in years.'*

Apparatus, Chapter 49

^s Nfmg: "the Jordan and they shall bring them into possession...," etc., as in PVN.

^t PVN: "Blessed is Asher. How rich is his land. His land will supply the delicacies of kings of the children of Israel"; Nfmg: "Blessed is Asher; how"; = PVN.

^u Nfi: "the fruits (of your land are) fat."

^w Nfmg: "and the land will supply"; cf. PVN.

^x PVN: "that Joseph was still alive; he went down to Egypt."

^y PVN, Nfmg: "(of) the field of Kephela; (and) when he opened his mouth in the congregation of Jacob (P:

"of Israel") his tongue was sweet as honey" (P: "his lips flowed milk and honey"; = Nf).

^z PVN: "to the abyss and splits."

^{aa} Nfmg: "and splits the teeth of all"; = PVN.

^{bb} Nfmg: "you teach."

^{cc} P: "all the wise men of the Egyptians and all their magicians."

^{dd} Nfmg: "and all their magicians"; = P.

^{ee} Nfmg: "which Pharaoh has"; = P; VN: "which Pharaoh had."

^{ff} Nfmg: "and tender."

Notes, Chapter 49

³⁶"... house of Asher ... sons of Israel"; HT: "Asher's food shall be rich, and he shall yield royal dainties."

³⁷"Naphtali is a swift runner ... from his lips"; HT: "Naphtali is a hind let loose, that bears comely fawns." The Hebrew *'mry špr*, rendered above as "comely fawns," is interpreted in the Pal. Tg. paraphrase as "words of beauty." The end of the paraphrase gives examples of Naphtali's good tidings. The midrash on the bearing of the good tidings that Joseph was still alive is also found in an anonymous midrash cited by M. Kasher, *Torah Shelemah* VI, note 289, p. 1838 (cf. Grossfeld, *Neofiti*, note 50 to Gen 49). The midrash on the fetching of the deed of possession is found in a number of rabbinic texts (noted by Grossfeld, loc. cit.), e.g., *Gen. R.* 98,17: "you find that when they went up to inter our ancestor Jacob, the children of Heth came to dispute their right to bury him (in the cave of Machpelah). Whereupon Naphtali ran like a hind and brought the title deeds from Egypt and confirmed (*špr*) their rights." The concluding sentence of the blessing is also paralleled in rabbinic texts, e.g., *Gen. R.* 97 (supplement) and 71,8 (on Gen 30:8, citing Ps 19:11).

³⁸"My son Joseph ... to become mighty"; HT (RSV): "Joseph is a fruitful (*prt*) bough, a fruitful (*prt*) bough by a spring." The Pal. Tg. paraphrase interprets *prt* as "grow (up)." So also does *Gen. R.* 98,18 (on Gen 49:22) and 78,10 (on Gen 33:5): "You have waxed great"; likewise the Vulgate: *filius accrescens Ioseph, filius accrescens.* On the Pal. Tg. paraphrase of Gen 49:22-24 and its relationship to Jewish tradition, see Syrén, 141-144.

³⁹"I compare you ... in years." This paraphrase is built on the HT (RSV): "a fruitful bough by a spring." The "bough" is understood as "vine," "spring" is taken literally, and the image of the growing vine developed: it put down roots and sent up branches. The text goes on to spell out from the biblical record and some non-biblical sources how Joseph prospered in Egypt, conquering its magicians and wise men, honored by the second chariot (Gen 41:37-45), the salutation *Abrek* (compare with Nf paraphrase as in 41:43).

And the daughters *of the kings*[40] *and the rulers*[gg] *gazed at you by the windows,*[hh] *and listened to you from the lattices, and cast before you chains, rings and necklaces*[ii] *and breast pendants and all kinds of gold, hoping you would raise your eyes and look at one of them. Far from you, Joseph, my son! You did not raise your eyes nor look*[jj] *at one of them.*[kk] *And the daughters of the kings and of the rulers said one to the other: 'This is Joseph, the pious man, who has not gone after the appearances of his eyes nor the imaginations of his heart.'*[mm] *Those are they that destroy the son of man from the world.*[nn] *Because of this there will arise from him two tribes: Manasseh and Ephraim who will receive a portion and an inheritance with his brothers in the division of the land.* 23. *They spoke against him,*[oo][41] *but all the magicians of Egypt and their wise men*[pp] were no match for him. They spoke evil before their master, and they informed against him *before Pharaoh, the king of Egypt, in order to bring him down from his dignity*[qq] *and to remove him from his royal throne.*[rr] *They spoke calumnious language against him in the palace of Pharaoh, which was more*

Apparatus, Chapter 49

[gg] VN: "the daughters of rulers gazed"; P: "the daughters of kings and of rulers."

[hh] Nfmg + P: "and from the windows they looked on you from the beginning and cast upon you chains, (P +: rings), necklaces (*catella*; Greek or Latin loan word), and breast pendants (*correcting* P) to see if you would raise your countenance and look at one of them."

[ii] *catella*; Greek or Latin (*catena*) loan word.

[jj] Nfmg: "you did not raise your face and did not look"; cf. P.

[kk] Nfmg: "(one) of them, so that you would not be a partner with her in Gehenna in the world to come and the daughters of"; cf. P: "one of them, lest you be a partner with her in Gehenna, and the daughters of. . . ."

[mm] text lit.: "his hearts."

[nn] Nfmg 1°: "since these cast out man from this world; hence"; Nfmg 2°: "these destroy the son of man from the midst of the world"; cf. PVN: "since the appear-

ance of the eyes and the imaginations of the heart destroy the son of man (VN: "of men") from the midst of the world."

[oo] P: "They spoke to him and rose up against him and informed against him before Pharaoh the king of Egypt in order to bring him down from his royal throne; and they spoke evil against (or: concerning) him in calumnious language (lit.: "third" or "threefold, tongue") in the palace (*palation*, Greek loan word) of Pharaoh, which was harsher on him than arrows"; Nfmg: "and they spoke to him and rose against him and they ate before"; cf. P. VN in v. 23 as Nf, with variants as below.

[pp] Nfi: "and all the wise men."

[qq] Nfmg: "to bring him down from his dignity (they spoke)"; VN: "from his glory, they spoke."

[rr] Nfmg: "his royal throne, and they spoke evil against (or: concerning) him in a third tongue"; =P.

Notes, Chapter 49

[40]". . . daughters of kings . . . imaginations of the heart." The paraphrase is based on the HT: *bnwt ṣ'dh 'ly šwr*, lit. "the daughters (=the branches) have run (=grown) over the wall." The paraphrase of Nf (and Pal. Tg.) is found also in Jewish sources, e.g., *Gen. R.* 98,18: "*The daughters run over the wall.* You find that when Joseph went forth to rule over Egypt, daughters of kings used to look at him over the lattices and throw bracelets, necklets, ear-rings, and finger-rings to him, so that he might lift up his eyes and look at them. Said the Holy One, blessed be He, to him: You did not lift up your eyes and look at them. By your life, I will give your daughters an ornament in the Torah." Other texts in Hebrew in Grossfeld, op. cit., note 55.

[41]"They spoke against him . . . arrows: HT (RSV): "The archers fiercely attacked him, shot at him and harassed him sorely." Archers with their arrows are understood as slanderers with their slanderous tongues. There is a similar understanding of the text in rabbinic sources, e.g., *Gen. R.* 98,19, where slander is compared to an arrow: both kill from afar. "Slander is spoken in Rome and kills in Syria." In Nf (and Pal. Tg.) Joseph's enemies are again identified as the Egyptian magicians and wise men. The same identification in the Jewish midrash *Sekh Tob*, in loc. (p. 318). Text in Grossfeld, *Neofiti*, note 56.

harassing[ss] for him than arrows. 24. But he placed[tt] *his confidence* in the Strong One.[42] *He stretched out* his hand[43] *and* his arms *to beseech mercy from* the Strong One of *his father* Jacob, *with the strength of whose arm*[uu] *all the tribes* of *Israel are sustained.*[44] 25. May *the Memra of* the God of your father *be at your aid,*[45] *and may the God of the heavens*[46] bless you *with the best of the dew*[47] *and the rain that descend* from the heavens from above and with the blessing *of the springs*[48] of the abyss *that come up*[ww] *from the earth,* from beneath. *Blessed are* the breasts[49] *from which you sucked* and the womb *within which you lay.*[xx] 26. May the blessings of your father[50] *be added for you,*[yy] to the blessings *with which my fathers Abraham*

Apparatus, Chapter 49

[ss] Nfmg: "(more) cutting."

[tt] P: "and he put."

[uu] VN: "under whose strong arm the tribes of Israel are guided and come"; P: "since it is from under whose strong arm, since it is from there, that all the tribes of the sons of Israel sing" (corr. to "are guided").

[ww] P: "that gush forth and come up from the earth below, and by the blessings of your father and your mother"; Nfmg: "that gush forth and come up"; = P.

[xx] Also in VN: "Blessed are the breasts from which you sucked and the womb in which you lay"; cf. Luke 11:27.

[yy] PVN: "May the blessings of your father be added to the blessings with which (VN +: my fathers) Abraham and Isaac blessed me (P: you) who are comparable to the mountains, and to (PVN: from) the blessings of the four mothers Sarah, Rebekah, Rachel, and Leah, who are comparable to the hills. May all these blessings come, and let them become a crown of majesty on the head of Joseph, and on the brow of the (P + pious) man who was king (VN: lord) and ruler over the land of Egypt, and who was concerned about the glory of his father, (P +: and did not change the crown of majesty of his brothers)."

Notes, Chapter 49

[42]"He placed in the Strong One his confidence"; HT: "But his bow remained firm" (lit. "in strength"). The paraphrase understands Jacob's bow of HT as his confidence, and "strength" of HT as God, "the Strong One." In *Gen. R.* 98,20 the HT is understood of Joseph's sexual passion. In *Gen. R.* 89, 2 (on Gen 41:5, with an exposition of Ps 40:5), however, Joseph is praised for having placed his trust in the Lord.

[43]"He stretched out his hand . . . Jacob"; HT (RSV): "his arms were made agile, by the hands of the mighty One of Jacob."

[44]"with the strength of whose arm . . . sustained"; HT (RSV): "by the name of (*mšm*; or: from there) the Shepherd, the Rock of Israel." Nf takes *m-šm* to refer to the preceding "Strong One" (i.e., God) and to the "arm" of God (v. 24a). It also paraphrases "Shepherd" as "the One who sustains" (cf. Tg. Ps 80:2).

[45]"Memra . . . at your aid"; HT (RSV): "by the God of your father, may he help you." "At your aid" is a good Targumic expression, often rendering "God (the Lord) is (or: be) with you" (though less so in Nf; cf. Nf 28:20; 31:5; 35:3; see Introduction, p. 28).

[46]"God of the heavens"; Nf's invariable translation of HT: "El Shaddai"; see Introduction, p. 35.

[47]"the best of the dew . . . from above"; HT: "with the blessings of the heavens above." For Nf's paraphrase see Deut 33:13; Gen 27:28, 39.

[48]"blessings of the springs . . . from beneath"; HT: "blessings of the deep that couches beneath."

[49]"Blessed are the breasts from which you sucked and the womb within which you lay"; HT: "blessings of the breasts and of the womb." An almost identical Aramaic paraphrase of the HT is found in *Gen. R.* 98,20: "*Blessings of the breasts and of the womb,* which means: Blessed be the breasts that suckled such a one and the womb which brought forth such a one." This is almost identical with Luke 11:27. On the possible relationship between the two see R. Le Déaut, 1962, 51; idem, *Targumic Literature and New Testament Interpretation* (Rome, 1974) 246; McNamara, 1966A, 131; Syrén, 151f.

[50]This verse is a paraphrase of HT: "The blessings of your fathers are mighty beyond the blessings of my progenitors," *hwry 'd,* generally corrected to *hrry 'd,* "(eternal) mountains." In the Pal. Tg. paraphrase HT *hwry* (whatever of the possible corruption of the primitive text) is understood as designating Jacob's progenitors, Abraham and Isaac, to which the Pal. Tg. of the marginal gloss (see Apparatus) adds the four matriarchs Sarah, Rebekah, Rachel and Leah. A similar interpretation is found in rabbinic sources; texts in Syrén, 135f.; and Grossfeld, *Neofiti,* note 66 to Gen 49.

and Isaac[zz] *blessed me, which the lords of the world Ishmael and Esau longed for from the beginning.*[51] *Let all these blessings come; let them become a crown of dignity* on the head[52] of Joseph, and on the brow of the *pious* man *who was master and ruler over the land of Egypt, and paid attention to the honor of his father and the honor of his brothers.*[a] 27. Benjamin[b] *is a strong tribe.*[53] *In his territory will the sanctuary be built and in his possessions will the Glory of the Shekinah of the Lord dwell.* In the morning *the priests will offer the perpetual lamb with the minhah,* and in the evening[c] they will divide *what remains of the offerings of the sons of Israel."* 28. All these are twelve tribes of Israel and this is *the blessing* with which he blessed them; each[d] according to his own blessing he blessed them. 29. And he commanded them and said to them: "*Behold,* I am being gathered to my people. Bury me with my fathers in the cave which is in the field of Ephron, the Hittite, 30. in the cave that is in the field of Kephela which is opposite Mamre of Canaan, the field which Abraham bought from Ephron the Hittite as a burial-possession. 31. There they buried Abraham and Sarah his wife. There they buried Isaac and Rebekah his wife, and there I buried Leah. 32. The purchase of the field and the cave in it was from the sons of Heth." 33. And Israel completed giving command to his sons and gathered his feet within the bed and ended (his days) and *died* and was gathered to his people.

Apparatus, Chapter 49

[zz] Nfmg: "who are comparable to mountains and to (text: from) the blessings of the four mothers, Sarah, Rebekah, Rachel, and Leah, who are comparable to hills: let them all come"; = PVN.

[a] Nfmg: "and did not change any of this majesty of his brothers"; cf. P., in note *yy* above.

[b] PVN: "(P: Benjamin is a) strong (tribe), likened to a violent bear. In his territory the sanctuary will be built and the Glory of the Shekinah of the Lord will

dwell in his possessions. . . .," etc., as in Nf, with some variants; Nfmg: "likened to a violent bear and in (his) territory"; cf. PVN.

[c] P: ("and at twilight they shall offer the lamb of the whole burnt offering and (its) libations" and in the evening . . ." Nfmg: "(the lamb) of the whole burnt and its libations and between."

[d] Nfmg: "(which) their father spoke with them and he blessed them each."

Notes, Chapter 49

[51] "which the Lord of the world . . . from the beginning," probably reading the HT as "to the (utmost) longing (*'d t'wt*) of the everlasting hills." In Nf the everlasting hills are identified with Ishmael and Esau. In rabbinic literature this same biblical text is interpreted with reference to the yearning of the patriarchs ("fathers of the world"), e.g., *Gen. R.* 98,20. See further Grossfeld, *Neofiti,* note 68 to Gen 49.

[52] "On the head . . . of his brothers." Nf is a paraphrase of the HT (RSV): "May they be on the head of Joseph, on the brow of him who was separate from his brothers.

[53] "Benjamin . . . sons of Israel." The Nf (and Pal. Tg.) paraphrase is on HT: "Benjamin is a ravenous wolf, in the morning devouring the prey and at even dividing the spoils." *Gen. R.* 99,1 records a discussion between R. Jose the Galilean and R. Akiba on the meaning of this verse. For the former it referred to the mountains; for the latter to the tribes, with explicit mention of the Temple being in the territory of Benjamin. The same belief on the location of the Temple, or at least part of it, in Benjamin is found in other rabbinic texts (e.g., *Gen. R.* 93,12) and already in the *Testament of Benjamin* 9,2 (in the *Testament of the Twelve Patriarchs*: "the Temple of God shall be your portion"). In the Targumic paraphrase all the pejorative references to Benjamin are removed (ravenous wolf, war references). The Pal. Tg. paraphrase concentrates on just one point: the Temple and its daily sacrifices. The HT terms "prey" and "spoils" are understood as the daily sacrifices, as they also are in some rabbinic sources, e.g., *Gen. R.* 99,3: "R. Phinehas applied the verse to the altar. As a wolf seizes, so does the altar seize the sacrifices. *In the morning,* etc. *The one lamb you shall offer in the morning* (Num 28:4), *And at the even,* etc. *And the other you shall offer at dusk* (Num 28:4)." For some reason which is not quite clear, the Temple altar was also compared in Jewish tradition to a ravenous wolf (cf. 1 Kgs 8:5; Josephus, *Ant.* 15,11,6, 421; other texts noted in Grossfeld, *Neofiti,* note 71 to Gen 49). See also B. Barry Levy, 1, 1986, 304f.

CHAPTER 50

1. And Joseph fell upon the face of his father and wept over him and kissed him. *And Joseph laid his father* [1] *on a bed of ivory, overlaid with gold,* [a] *inlaid with pearls, filled and reinforced with precious (?) stone,* [b] *linen and purple. Precious wines and precious aromatic spices were poured out there. Precious perfumes* [c] *were burnt there. Kingdoms and rulers from the sons of Ishmael stood there. Rulers from the sons of Esau stood there. Rulers from the sons of Keturah stood there. There stood Judah, the lion, the warrior of his brothers.* [c bis] *Judah answered and said to his brothers: "Come, let us plant* [d] *for our father a tall cedar,* [2] *its top reaching to the heavens and its roots* [e] *reaching to the generations of the world. For from him there have gone forth the twelve tribes of the sons of Israel. For from him have gone forth priests with their trumpets and Levites with their harps."* Then Joseph *bent down* [f] *over the neck of his father and* Joseph *wept over him and kissed him.* 2. And Joseph commanded

Apparatus, Chapter 50

[a] VN for entire v. 1 almost verbatim as Nf; variants of VN and P given below. Both begin: "and Joseph laid his father on an ivory bed."

[b] PVN: "strengthened with byssus (=linen) material."

[c] PVN: "there stood there men from the sons of Esau; there stood there rulers from the sons of Ishmael; there stood there Judah the lion . . ."; P continues: "and he said to his brothers: Come, let us weep . . ."; Nfmg 1°: "fine (gold), and set with precious stones and jewels and reinforced with stones (*b'bn[yn]*); correct to: "material" *bm'nyn*?; or to *b'tny'*, "cords") of linen and purple. There were poured out, poured out, wines (correcting text) perfumes. There stood warriors from those of the house of Esau; there stood rulers from those of the house of Jacob, there stood the lion"; Nfmg 2°: "there were poured out heated dates (*tmryn*; corr. to *ḥmryn*, "wines"), there were burned <. . .> and there stood thick (*'byn*: corr. to:

ṭbyn, "good") aromas; there stood those of the house of Esau; there stood warriors from those of the house of Jacob; from those of the house of Ishmael they were standing (there); the lion."

[c bis] Nf text: *gwbryn d'hwy*, "men of his brothers"; correct to (?): *gbrhwn*, "warrior of (his brothers)"; cf. VN *gw(?)bryhwn d'hwy*; CTg FF (Tosefta), [*gyb*]*ryhwn*.

[d] Nfmg 1°: "and they built upon (or: to) our father"; Nfmg 2°: "and let us build upon (or: to)"; PVN: "let us weep to (or: or) our father, the tall cedar."

[e] Nfmg: "(let) its branches reach to all the dwellers of the earth and its roots reach the lower part of the abyss. From him there arose in Israel twelve tribes. From him, <priests> to offer sacrifice, and from him there arose Levites in their divisions to make music. Behold, therefore, he bowed down."

[f] Nfi: "and then he trembled"; or probably to be read as: "and then he bowed down."

Notes, Chapter 50

[1] "And Joseph laid his father . . . and kissed him." This long midrash on the events surrounding Jacob's death is found in the various Pal. Tg. texts (Nf, PVN), in Ps.-J. and the Targumic Tosefta CTg X, "but has no apparent parallel in rabbinic literature"—Grossfeld, *Neofiti*, note 1 to Gen 50. Note that the Aramaic text of Nf rendered "filled . . . precious perfumes" has a number of rare words and is probably in part corrupt. Thus: "precious (?) stones linen," *b'bn' bw'h bwṣ*. The term *bw'h* ("unclear"—Sokoloff, 1990, 87) does not occur elsewhere. VNL has *bm'ny bwṣ'*, "with linen material," of which Nf may be a corruption. Likewise the term rendered "precious wines," *ḥmdnyn* (=? "desirous things"—Sokoloff, 1990, 204), also a hapax legomenon, is possibly a corruption of *ḥmryn*, "wines," found in PVNL. CTg FF (a Tosefta), however, has *ḥmrnyyn* ("wines"—Klein, 1986, I, 170).

[2] "Come let us plant (*nbn*, lit. "build") for our father a tall cedar (*'rz'*)." Since the use of *nbny* (generally used in the sense of "build") for planting a tree is quite unusual, B. Barry Levy (1, 1986, 309f.) is of the opinion that it seems that Judah wanted to build an *'rz'*, i.e., "a chest for collecting bones, a sarcophagus," possibly a pyramid. Thus, at least, with regard to the original form of the paraphrase, which would have been elaborated later when *'rz'* was believed to have denoted to a cedar.

his servants, the physicians, to embalm [g] his father. And the physicians embalmed Israel. 3. And forty days were completed for him, for thus are completed the days of embalming. [h] And the Egyptians wept for him seventy days. 4. And the days of weeping passed, and Joseph spoke with *the men of* [3] the house of Pharaoh, saying: "If [i] I have found grace *and favor* [4] in your sight, speak, I pray, in the hearing of [j] Pharaoh saying: 5. 'My father made me swear saying: Behold I am dying. In my grave that I dug [k] for myself in the land Canaan, there you [m] will bury me. And now, I will go up, I pray, to bury my father and return." 6. And Pharaoh said: "Go up and bury your father as he has made you swear." 7. And Joseph went up to bury his father. And there went up with him all the *rulers* [n][5] of Pharaoh and all the *administrators* [6] *of* the land of Egypt, 8. and all *the men of* [3] the house of Joseph, his brothers and the house of his father. Only their little ones and their sheep and their oxen they left in the land of Goshen. 9. And there went up with him both chariots and horsemen and the host was very great. [o] 10. And they arrived [p] at the threshing-place of Atadaḥ, which is beyond the Jordan, and they made there a very big and bitter lamentation. And he *observed* [q][7] for his father a mourning of seven days. 11. And the inhabitants of the land *of Canaan* [r] saw [8] the mourning in the threshing-place of Atadaḥ and they said: "This is a bitter mourning for the Egyptians." Because of this its name was called Ebel-misraim, which is beyond the Jordan. 12. And his sons did for him according as he had commanded them. 13. And his sons carried him to the land of Canaan and buried him in the cave of the field *of Kephela*, which field Abraham bought as a burial-possession from Ephron the Hittite, in front of Mamre. [s] 14. And after he had buried his father, Joseph returned to Egypt, he and his brothers and all that came up with him, to bury his father. 15. And the brothers of Joseph saw that their father was dead and said: "Perchance Joseph will bear a

Apparatus, Chapter 50

[g] Nfmg: "the physicians to embalm" (different word and forms).

[h] Nfmg: "embalming" (different word).

[i] Nfmg +: "I pray."

[j] Nfmg: "before him."

[k] Nfmg: "was acquired."

[m] In text "you" sing.; Nfmg: "you (plur.) shall bury."

[n] Nfmg: "sages."

[o] Nfmg: "strong."

[p] Nfmg: "they came."

[q] Nfmg: "and he made for his father."

[r] Nfmg: "the land of the Canaanites."

[s] Nfmg: "which is opposite Mamre."

Notes, Chapter 50

[3] "the men of"; an addition to the usual style of Nf.

[4] "grace and favor"; *ḥn wḥsd*; HT: *ḥn*; usual Nf paraphrase of HT *ḥn*; see note to 6:8 and 32:6.

[5] "rulers (of Pharaoh)"; HT: "servants."

[6] "administrators of Pharaoh," *epitropos*, Greek loan word; HT: "the elders of his house and all the elders of the land of Egypt." Nf leaves portion of the HT untranslated.

[7] "he observed"; HT: "he made."

[8] "the inhabitants of the land of Canaan saw"; HT: "the Canaanite inhabitants of the land saw."

grudge against us and repay[t] us all the evil that we have heaped on him." 16. And *the tribes*[u] commanded *Bilhah*, Joseph's *foster-mother,*[9] to say *to him*: "Your father[w] commanded before he died[x] saying: 17. 'Thus shall you say to Joseph: We beseech, *forgive* now, *and pardon* the offenses[10] of your brothers[y] and their sins because they have heaped evil on you. And now *forgive*, we pray, and pardon *the rebelliousness* of the servants of the God[z] of your father.'" And Joseph wept as he spoke[aa] *with her.*[11] 18. And his brothers also went and fell before him and said: "Behold, we are your servants." 19. And Joseph said to them:[bb] "Do not be afraid, *because far from me to* repay *you the evil that you did to me.*[cc] *Are not the thoughts of the sons of man manifest before the Lord?*[12] 20. And you planned evil against me; *before the Lord it was reckoned*[13] *as good*[dd] so as to *preserve alive*[14] this day a numerous people.*[ee] 21. And now do not fear:[ff] I will provide[gg] for you and your little ones." *Joseph answered and said to them:*[hh] *"Ten stars*[15] *tried to destroy one star,*

Apparatus, Chapter 50

[t] Nfmg 1°: "hates us and he repays"; Nfmg 2°: "that (Joseph) retains for us."

[u] PVB (Bomberg 1517): "and the tribes commanded Bilhah, Rachel's maid, to say to Joseph: Your father commanded before he died (lit.: "was gathered") saying."

[w] Nfmg 1°: "Rachel's maid to say to Joseph: Your father"; = VB; Nfmg 2°: "to Bilhah to say to Joseph: Your father."

[x] Nfmg: "was gathered" (= PVB).

[y] Nfmg: "pardon the sins (lit.: "debts") of the servants of."

[z] Nfmg: "the sins (lit.: "debts") of the servants of the God."

[aa] Nfmg: "as they spoke."

[bb] PVB: "And Joseph said to them: Fear not, because for me the evil you have done me is over. Are not the thoughts of the sons of man (manifest) before the Lord?"

[cc] Nfmg: "because from me the evil you have done is over"; cf. PVB.

[dd] Nfmg: "evil, the Memra of the Lord beckoned it as from before."

[ee] Nfmg: "to preserve alive as the time of this day an assembly of many multitudes" (Greek loan word: *ochlos*).

[ff] P: "Now do not fear. I will sustain you and your little ones, and comfort them. And he said to them: Eleven stars sought to destroy one star and were not able; and one star—how could it destroy eleven stars? For this reason he spoke consolations to their heart."

[gg] Nfmg: "Joseph answered <...> I will sustain"; cf. P.

[hh] Nfmg: "Joseph said to them: Ten stars <...> and how could one star be able to destroy."

Notes, Chapter 50

[9]"the tribes . . . commanded Bilhah, Joseph's foster-mother." The same insertions into HT: "they commanded Joseph saying" also in Frg. Tgs. and Ps.-J. This haggadic addition is also found in rabbinic literature, e.g., *Tanh*. B. *ṣw*; X; *Leq. Tob*, ad loc. *Sekh. Tob*, ad loc. (texts in Grossfeld, *Neofiti*, note 8 to Gen 50).

[10]"forgive now and pardon the offenses"; HT: "forgive the transgression."

[11]"with her"; HT: "to him"; change due to introduction of Joseph's foster-mother into the paraphrase.

[12]"far from me . . . before the Lord"; HT: "am I in the place of God?"

[13]"before the Lord it was reckoned"; HT: "God reckoned it."

[14]"in order to preserve alive"; HT: "in order to do . . . ," etc.; Nf omits translation of "to do," possibly by error, as it is found in Ps.-J. and Pesh.

[15]"Joseph answered and said . . . ten stars." This midrash, found also in P, is likewise attested in rabbinic texts, e.g., *Gen. R.* 100,9: ". . . you have been likened to the stars. Ten stars wished to destroy one star, but could not prevail against it. Can I then change the natural order of the world (that one star should destroy) twelve stars?"

and they were not able to destroy it. And how will it be possible that one star could destroy ten stars?" And he consoled them and spoke to[^ii] their hearts *words of peace.*[16] 22. And Joseph dwelt in Egypt, he and *the men of* his father's house. And Joseph lived a hundred and ten years. 23. And Joseph saw the sons of Ephraim, the third *generation;*[17] also the sons of Machir, the son of Manasseh; they were born upon the knees of Joseph. 24. And Joseph said to his brothers: "Behold, I am about to die,[^jj] but *the Lord*[^kk] *will remember* you *in his good mercies*[18] and bring you up from this land to the land he swore to Abraham, to Isaac and to Jacob." 25. And Joseph adjured the sons of Israel, saying: "When *the Lord* shall *remember you in his good mercies,*[18] you will bring up[^mm] my bones from here." 26. And Joseph died at the age of a hundred and ten years; and they embalmed *him,*[19] and put him in the coffin in Egypt.[^nn]

Apparatus, Chapter 50

[^ii] Nfmg: "with."
[^jj] Nfmg: "be gathered" (i.e., die).
[^kk] Nfmg: "the Memra of the Lord."
[^mm] Nfmg +: "with you."

[^nn] VB: "and they embalmed him and put him in a sarcophagus (Greek loan word: *glôssokomos* or *glôssokomon*, "casket") in the land of Egypt"; Nfmg P: "in a casket" (*glôssokomon*).

Notes, Chapter 50

[16]"words of peace"; an addition to HT.
[17]"generation"; addition in HT.
[18]". . . remember in his good mercies"; HT: "God will surely visit you." Nf's paraphrase here is in keeping with the translation's overall principle on the rendering of HT texts with reference to God's remembering or visiting: on which see note to 8:1 (with "remember" in HT) and 21:1 ("visit").
[19]"him": in addition in Nf to HT.

SELECT BIBLIOGRAPHY

Manuscripts of the Palestinian Targums

Neofiti

Biblioteca Apostolica Vaticana, Codex Neofiti 1.

Fragment Targums

Paris, Bibliothèque Nationale, MS Hébr. 110, fol. 1–16 (=P);

Biblioteca Apostolica Vaticana, Ebr. 440, fol. 198–227 (=V);

Nürnberg, Stadtbibliothek Solger 2.2°, fol. 119–147 (=N);

Leipzig, Universitätsbibliothek B.H., fol. 1 (=L);

New York, Jewish Theological Seminary (Lutzki) 605, (E.N. Adler 2587), fol. 6, 7 (=J);

London, British Library Oriental 10794, fol. 8 (=Br.);

Moscow, Günzberg 3 (copied from MS Nürnberg);

Sassoon Private Collection 264, fol. 225–267 (copied from 2nd *Biblia Rabbinica*).

Cairo Genizah Manuscripts of the Palestinian Targums

Principally in libraries in:
      Cambridge, University Library (Taylor-Schechter Collection);
      Oxford, Bodleian Library;
      Leningrad, Saltykov-Schedrin Library (Antonin Collection);
      New York, Jewish Theological Seminary (Adler Collection).

Pseudo-Jonathan

London, British Library, Additional 27031.

EDITIONS OF TEXTS

Neofiti I

Díez Macho, A. *Neophyti* I. Targum Palestinense. MS de la Biblioteca Vaticana. Vols.
    1–5. Madrid-Barcelona: Consejo Superior de Investigaciones Científicas;
    1 *Génesis*, 1968; 2 *Exodo*; 3 *Levitico*, 1971; 4 *Numeros*, 1974; 5 *Deuteronomio*,
    1978.

Genizah Fragments

Kahle, P. *Masoreten des Westens II*. Stuttgart: Kohlhammer, 1930.

Klein, M. L. *Genizah Manuscripts of Palestinian Targum to the Pentateuch*. 2 vols. Cincinnati: Hebrew Union College, 1986.

Fragment Targums

Ginsburger, M. *Das Fragmententhargum*. Berlin: Calvary, 1899; reprint, Jerusalem: Makor, 1969.

Klein, M. L. *The Fragment-Targums of the Pentateuch According to Their Extant Sources*. 2 vols. Analecta Biblica 76. Rome: Biblical Institute Press, 1980.

Pseudo-Jonathan

Clarke, E. G., with Aufrecht, W. E.; Hurd, J. C.; Spitzer, F. *Targum Pseudo-Jonathan of the Pentateuch: Text and Concordance*. Hoboken, N.J.: Ktav, 1984.

Díez Macho, A. *Biblia Polyglotta Matritensia*. Series IV. *Targum Palaestinense in Pentateuchum*. Additur Targum Pseudojonathan ejusque hispanica versio. Editio critica curante A. Díez Macho, adjuvantibus L. Díez Merino, E. Martínez Borobio, T. Martínez Saiz. Pseudojonathan hispanica versio: T. Martínez Saiz. Targum Palaestinensis testimonia ex variis fontibus: R. Griño., Madrid: Consejo Superior de Investigaciones Científicas. L. 2, *Exodus*, 1980; L. 3, *Leviticus*, 1980; L. 4, *Numeri*, 1977; L. 5, *Deuteronomium*, 1980; L. 1, *Genesis*, 1989.

Ginsburger, M. *Pseudo-Jonathan*. (Thargum-Jonathan ben Usiël zum Pentateuch). Nach der Londoner Handschrift (Brit. Mus. Add. 27031). Berlin: Calvary, 1903.

Rieder, D. *Pseudo-Jonathan*: Targum Jonathan ben Uziel on the Pentateuch copied from the London MS. (British Museum Add. 27031). Jerusalem: Salomon's, 1974. Reprinted with Hebrew translation and notes; 2 vols. Jerusalem, 1984–85.

Onqelos

Berliner, A. *Targum Onkelos*. Herausgegeben und erläutert von A. Berliner. Berlin: Gorzelanczyk, 1884.

Sperber, A. *The Bible in Aramaic*. Vol. 1, *The Pentateuch according to Targum Onkelos*. Leiden: Brill, 1959.

Other Targum Texts

Díez Macho, A. "Nueva Fuente para el Targum Palestino del día séptimo de Pascua y Primero de Pentecostés," in *Escritos de Biblia y Oriente*. Miscelánea conmemorativa del 25° aniversario del Instituto Español Bíblico y Arqueológico (Casa de Santiago) de Jerusalén. Bibliotheca Salmanticensis, Estudios 38; ed., R. Aguirre, F. García López. Salamanca-Jerusalem: Universidad Pontificia, 1981, 233–257.

idem: "Nuevos Fragmentos de Tosefta Targúmica," *Sefarad* 16 (1956) 313–324.

idem: "Deux nouveaux fragments du Targum Palestinien à New York," in *Studi sull'
Oriente e la Bibbia offerti a P. G. Rinaldi*. Genoa: Studio e Vita, 1967, 175–178.

Hurwitz, S. *Machsor Vitry*, nach der Handschrift im British Museum (Cod. Add. No.
27200 u. 27201). Leipzig, 1899; 2nd edition Nürnberg: Bulka, 1923; reprint
Jerusalem: Aleph, 1963, 305–344.

Kasher, R. "A Targumic Tosefta to Genesis 2:1-3," *Sinay* 78 (1976–77) 9–17.

Klein, M. "The Targumic Tosefta to Exodus 15:2," *JJS* 26 (1975) 61–67.

Komlosh, Y. "The Targum Version of the Crossing of the Red Sea," *Sinay* 45 (1959)
223–238.

Translations of the Palestinian Targums of the Pentateuch

Etheridge, J. W., *The Targums of Onkelos and Jonathan ben Uzziel on the Pentateuch,
with Fragments of the Jerusalem Targum from the Chaldee*. 2 vols. London:
Longman, Green, Longman, 1862, 1865. Reprint in one volume, New York:
Ktav, 1968.

Le Déaut, R. with J. Robert. *Targum du Pentateuque. Traduction des deux Recensions
Palestiniennes complètes*. 4 vols. Trans. R. Le Déaut with J. Robert. Sources
Chrétiennes 245, 256, 261, 271. Paris: Cerf. Vol. 1, *Genèse*, 1978; vol. 2, *Exode
et Lévitique*, 1979; vol. 3, *Nombres*, 1979; vol. 4, *Deutéronome*, 1980.

Codex Neofiti 1: Spanish translation by A. Díez Macho; French translation by R. Le
Déaut; English translation by M. McNamara and M. Maher in the *editio
princeps*, ed. A. Díez Macho.

Pseudo-Jonathan: Spanish translation by T. Martínez Saiz in the Díez Macho edition in
Biblia Polyglotta Matritensia. See above. French translation in Le Déaut-Robert;
see above. Hebrew translation in Rieder, 1984–85; see above.

Rabbinic Sources

Mekilta de-Rabbi Ishmael. 3 vols.; edited and translated by J. Z. Lauterbach. Philadelphia: JPS, 1933–35; reprint 1949.

Mekilta de-Rabbi Shimon bar Yohai, eds. J. N. Epstein and E. Z. Melamed. Jerusalem:
Hillel Press, (no date).

Midrash Bereshit Rabbah. Critical edition with notes and commentary. 3 vols., eds. J.
Theodor and Ch. Albeck. Jerusalem: Wahrmann, 1965.

Midrash Tanhuma. Wilna, 1833; reprint Israel, no date. (Referred to as *Tanh. A*).

Midrash Tanhuma. 2 vols., ed. S. Buber. Wilna, 1885; reprint Jerusalem, 1964. (Referred to as *Tanh. B.*).

Pesikta de Rab Kahana. 2 vols., ed. B. Mandelbaum. New York: Jewish Theological
Seminary, 1962.

Pirke de Rabbi Eliezer, ed. D. Luria. Warsaw, 1852.

Sifre on Deuteronomy, ed. L. Finkelstein. Berlin, 1939; reprint New York: JPS, 1969.

Sifre on Numbers, ed. H. S. Horovitz. Leipzig: Fock, 1917; reprint Jerusalem: Wahrmann, 1966.

Talmud Yerushalmi. Krotoschin, 1866; reprint Jerusalem, 1960.

Tosefta, ed. M. S. Zuckermandel. Jerusalem: Wahrmann, 1963.

Translations of Rabbinic Works

The Babylonian Talmud. Translated into English with notes, glossary and indices. Ed. I. Epstein. 18-vol. edition. London: Soncino, 1978.

Los Capítulos de Rabbí Eliezer. Versión crítica, introducción y notas por M. Pérez Fernández. Biblioteca Midrásica 1. Valencia: Institución S. Jerónimo para la Investigación Bíblica, 1984.

The Fathers According to Rabbi Nathan. Trans. J. Goldin. Yale Judaica Series 10. New Haven: Yale University Press, 1955. (Referred to as *ARN* A).

The Fathers According to Rabbi Nathan (Abot de Rabbi Nathan), Version B. Trans. A. J. Saldarini. Studies in Judaism in Late Antiquity 11. Leiden: Brill, 1957. (Referred to as *ARN* B).

The Midrash on Psalms. Translated from the Hebrew and Aramaic by W. G. Braude. 2 vols. Yale Judaica Series XIII. New Haven: Yale University Press, 1958–59.

The Midrash Rabbah. Ed. H. Freedman and M. Simon. New Compact Edition in 5 vols. London: Soncino, 1977. (Referred to as *Gen. R., Exod. R.*, etc.).

The Mishnah. Trans. H. Danby. Oxford: University Press, 1939.

Pesikta de-Rab Kahana. Trans. W. G. Braude and I. J. Kapstein. Philadelphia: JPS, 1975.

Pesikta Rabbati. 2 vols. Trans. W. G. Braude. Yale Judaica Series XVIII. New Haven-London, 1968.

Pirke de Rabbi Eliezer. The Chapters of Rabbi Elizier the Great. Translated and Annotated by G. Friedlander. New York: Sepher-Hermon, 4th ed. 1981.

Sefer ha-Yashar, or *The Book of Yasher. Referred to in Joshua and Samuel.* Trans. M. M. Noah. New York: Noah and Gould, 1840.

Tanna debe Eliyyahu—The Lore of the School of Elijah. Translated from the Hebrew by W. G. Braude and I. J. Kapstein. Philadelphia: JPS, 1981.

General

Aberbach, M.: 1969, "Patriotic Tendencies in Targum Onkelos," *The Journal of Hebraic Studies* 1, 13–24.

Aberbach, M., and Grossfeld, B.: 1976, *Targum Onkelos on Genesis 49.* SBL Aramaic Studies 1. Missoula, Mont.: Scholars Press.

Aberbach, M., and Grossfeld, B.: 1982, *Targum Onkelos to Genesis.* New York: Ktav.

Alexander, P. S.: 1972, "The Targumim and Early Exegesis of 'Sons of God' in Genesis 6," *JJS* 23, 60–71.

idem: 1974, *The Toponomy of the Targumim with Special Reference to the Table of Nations and the Boundaries of the Holy Land.* Dissertation, Oxford University.

idem: 1976, "The Rabbinic Lists of Forbidden Targumim," *JJS* 27, 178–191.

idem: 1985, "The Targumim and the Rabbinic Rules for the Delivery of the Targum," *VTSupp* 36, 14–28.

Allony, N.: 1975, "The Jerusalem Targum Pseudo-Jonathan. Rieder's edition" (in Hebrew), *Beth Miqra* 62, 423–425.

Aptowitzer, A.: 1930–31, "The Heavenly Temple According to the Haggadah" (Hebrew), *Tarbiz* 2, 137–153, 257–287.

Aptowitzer, V.: 1924, "Asenath, the Wife of Joseph. A Haggadic Literary-Historical Study," *HUCA* 1, 239–306.

Aruch Completum sive Lexicon vocabula et res quae in Libris Targumicis, Talmudicis, et Midraschicis continentur, explicans. N. b. Jechielis. Ed. A. Kohut. Vienna: Bróg, 1878–92.

Bacher, W.: 1874, "Das gegenseitige Verhältniss der pentateuchischen Targumim," *ZDMG* 28, 59–72.

idem: 1884, 1890, *Die Agada der Tannaiten.* 2 vols. Strasbourg: Tübner.

idem: 1899, 1905, 1965, *Die exegetische Terminologie der jüdischen Traditionsliteratur.* 2 vols. Leipzig, 1899, 1905. 2 vols. in one. Darmstadt: Wissenschaftliche Buchgesellschaft, 1965.

idem: 1906, "Targum," *JE* 12, 57–63.

Bamberger, B. J.: 1975, "Halakic Elements in the Neofiti Targum: A Preliminary Statement," *JQR* 66, 27–38.

Barnstein, H.: 1899, "A Noteworthy Targum MS. in the British Museum," *JQR* 11, 167–171.

Barry Levy, B.: see under Levy, Barry B.

Bascom, R.: 1985, "The Targums: Ancient Reader's Helps?" *The Bible Translator* 36, 301–316.

Beer, B.: 1859, *Leben Abraham's nach Auffassung der jüdischen Sage.* Leipzig: Leeiner.

Bernstein, M. J.: 1986, "A New Manuscript of Tosefta Targum," *Proceedings of the Ninth World Congress of Jewish Studies.* Jerusalem, August 4–12, 1985. Jerusalem: World Union of Jewish Studies, 151–157. The toseftas dealt with are located at Gen 44:18 and 45:4.

Beyer, K.: 1983, *Die aramäischen Texte vom Toten Meer.* Göttingen: Vandenhoeck und Ruprecht.

Black, M.: 1967, *An Aramaic Approach to the Gospel and Acts*, 3rd ed. Oxford: Clarendon, 1967.

Bloch, R.: 1955A, 1978, "Note méthodologique pour l'étude de la littérature Rabbinique," *Recherches de Science Religieuse* 43, 194–227. Also published in English as "Methodological Note for the Study of Rabbinic Literature," trans. W. S. Green and W. J. Sullivan, in *Approaches to Ancient Judaism: Theory and Practice*. Ed. W. S. Green. Brown Judaic Studies I. Missoula, Mont.: Scholars Press, 1978, 51–75.

idem: 1955B, "Note sur l'utilisation des fragments de la Geniza du Caire pour l'étude du Targum Palestinien," *REJ* n.s. 14, 5–35.

idem: 1957, "Juda engendra Pharès et Zarah de Thamar (Mt 1:3)," in *Mélanges bibliques rédigé en l'honneur de André Robert*. Travaux de L'Institut Catholique de Paris, no. 4. Paris, pp. 381–389.

Böhl, F.: "Die Metaphorisierung (Metila) in den Targumim zum Pentateuch," *Frankfurter Judaistische Beiträge* 15 (1987) 111–149.

Bowker, J.: 1969, *The Targums and Rabbinic Literature*. Cambridge: University Press.

Bowker, J. W.: 1967, "Haggadah in the Targum Onqelos," *JSS* 12, 51–65.

Brayer, M. M.: 1950, *Studies in the Pseudo Jonathan of the Bible. Book of Genesis*. Unpublished doctoral dissertation. New York: Yeshiva University.

idem: 1963, "The Aramaic Pentateuch Targums and the Question of Avoiding Anthropomorphisms" (in Hebrew), *Talpiyot* 8, 513–525.

idem: 1964, "The Pentateuchal Targum Attributed to Jonathan ben Uzziel—A Source for Unknown Midrashim" (in Hebrew), in *The Abraham Weiss Jubilee Volume*. Ed. M. S. Feldbaum. New York, 201–231.

idem: 1971, "The Debate Between a Sadducee and a Pharisee in the Mouths of Cain and Abel" (in Hebrew), *Beth Miqra* 44, 583–585.

Brock, S.: 1979, "Jewish Traditions in Syriac Sources," *JJS* 30, 212–232.

Burchard, C.: 1970, "Zum Text von 'Joseph und Aseneth'" *JStJud* 1, 3–34.

Caquot, A.: 1976, "La parole sur Juda dans le testament lyrique de Jacob (Gen 49, 8-12)," *Semitica* 26, 5–32.

Cashdan, E.: 1967, "Names and the Interpretation of Names in the Pseudo-Jonathan Targum to the Book of Genesis," in *Essays Presented to Chief Rabbi Israel Brodie on the Occasion of His Seventieth Birthday." Ed.* H.J. Zimmels, J. Rabbinowitz, and L. Finestein. London: Soncino, pp. 31–39.

Cathcart, K.J., and Gordon, R.P.: *The Targum of the Minor Prophets*. The Aramaic Bible 14. Wilmington, Del.: Michael Glazier, 1989.

Charlesworth, J. H., ed.: 1983, 1985, *The Old Testament Pseudepigrapha*. 2 vols. London: Darton, Longman and Todd.

Chester, A.: 1986, *Divine Revelation and Divine Titles in the Pentateuchal Targumim.* Texte und Studien zum Antiken Judentum 14. Tübingen: Mohr (Siebeck).

Chiesa, B.: 1977, "Contrasti ideologici del tempo degli Asmonei nella Aggádáh e nelle versioni di Genesi 49, 3," *Annali del Istituto Orientale di Napoli* 37, 417–440.

Churgin, P.: 1933–34, "The Targum and the Septuagint," *AJSL* 50, 40–65.

idem: 1943, "On the Origin of Targumic Formulas" (in Hebrew), *Horeb* 7, 103–109.

idem: 1946, "The Halakah in Targum Onkelos" (in Hebrew), *Horeb* 9, 79–93.

Clarke, E.G.: 1974–75, "Jacob's Dream at Bethel as Interpreted in the Targums and the New Testament," *SR* 4, 367–377.

idem: 1984, *Targum Pseudo-Jonathan of the Pentateuch: Text and Concordance.* See above under "Editions of Texts: Pseudo-Jonathan."

idem: 1986, "Noah: *gbr ṣdyq* or *gbr zky?*" in *Salvacion en la Palabra*, 337–345. See under Muñoz León.

Cook, E.M.: 1986, *Rewriting the Bible: The Text and Language of the Pseudo-Jonathan Targum.* Ph.D. dissertation, University of California, Los Angeles.

Cook, J.: 1983, "Anti-Heretical Traditions in Targum Pseudo-Jonathan," *JNSL* 11, 47–57.

Cowling, G. J.: 1968, *The Palestinian Targum: Textual and Linguistic Investigations in Codex Neofiti I and Allied Manuscripts. Unpublished doctoral thesis. Aberdeen.*

Dalman, G.H.: 1897, "Die Handschrift zum Jonathantargum des Pentateuch, Add. 27031 des Britischen Museum," *MGWJ* 41, 454–456.

idem: 1927, 1960, *Grammatik des Jüdisch-Palästinischen Aramäisch. Aramäische Dialektproben.* 2nd ed. Leipzig, 1927; reprint, Darmstadt: Wissenschaftliche Buchgesellschaft, 1960.

Delcor, M.: 1970, "La portée chronologique de quelques interprétations du Targoum Néophyti contenues dans le cycle d'Abraham," *JStJ* 1, 105–119.

Díez Macho, A.: 1956, "Nuevos Fragmentos de Tosefta Targumica," *Sefarad* 15, 313–324.

idem: "The Recently Discovered Palestinian Targum: Its Antiquity and Relationship with the Other Targums," *VTSupp* 7, 222–245.

idem: 1963, "El Logos y el Espíritu Santo," *Atlántida* 1, 381–396.

idem: 1972, *El Targum Introducción a las Traducciones Aramaicas de la Biblia.* Barcelona: Consejo Superior de Investigaciones Científicas.

idem: *Neophyti 1.* Targum Palestinense. MS de la Biblioteca Vaticana. Vols. 1–5. Madrid-Barcelona: Consejo Superior de Investigaciones Científicas:
1 *Génesis,* 1968;
2 *Exodo*; 3 *Levitico,* 1971;
4 *Numeros,* 1974;
5 *Deuteronomio,* 1978.

idem: 1981, "L'Usage de la troisième personne au lieu de la première dans le Targum," in *Mélanges Dominique Barthélemy.* Études Bibliques offertes à l'occasion de son 60ᵉ Anniversaire. Ed. P. Casetti, O. Kiel, and A. Schenker. Orbis Biblicus et Orientalis 38. Fribourg: Éditions Universitaires; Göttingen: Vandenhoeck und Ruprecht, 61–89.

idem: 1986, *(In memoriam), Salvacion en la Palabra*; see under Muñoz León.

Díez Merino, L.: 1976, "El Suplicio de la Cruz en la Literatura Judia Interestamental," *Liber Annuus Studi Biblici Franciscani* 26, 31–120.

idem: 1984, "El Sintagma *ns' 'ynym* en la tradición aramea," *Aula Orientalis* 2 (1984) 23–41.

Doubles, M.C.: 1968, "Indications of Antiquity in the Orthography and Morphology of the Fragment Targum," in *In Memoriam Paul Kahle*. Ed. M. Black and G. Fohrer. Beihefte zur Zeitschrift für die alttestamentliche Wissenschaft 103. Berlin: Töpelmann, 79–89.

Elbogen, L.: 1931, *Der jüdische Gottesdienst in seiner geschichtlichen Entwicklung.* 3rd ed. Frankfurt am Main, 1931; reprint Hildesheim: Olms, 1962.

Epstein, A.: 1892, "Les Chamites de la Table Ethnographique selon le Pseudo-Jonathan," *REJ* 24, 82–98.

idem: 1895, "Tosefta du Targoum Yerouschalmi," *REJ* 30, 44–51.

Eskhult, M.: 1981, "Hebrew and Aramaic *'älôqîm*," *Orientalia Suecana* 30, 137–139.

Esterlich, P.: 1967, "El Targum Pseudojonathán o Jerosolimitano," in *Studi sull' Oriente e la Bibbia offerti a P.G. Rinaldi*. Genoa: Studio e vita, 191–195.

Faur, J.: 1975, "The Targumim and Halakha," *JQR* 66, 19–26.

Finkelstein, L., see above (under "Rabbinic Sources") *Sifre on Deuteronomy.*

Fitzmyer, J. A.: 1971, *The Genesis Apocryphon of Qumran Cave 1. A Commentary.* 2nd, rev. ed. Biblica et Orientalia 18a. Rome: Biblical Institute.

Foster, J. A.: 1969, *The Language and Text of Codex Neofiti in the Light of Other Palestinian Sources.* Ph.D. dissertation. Boston University Graduate School.

Geiger, A.: 1928, *Urschrift und Übersetzungen der Bibel.* 2nd ed. Frankfurt am Main: Madda.

Ginzberg, L.: 1900, *Die Haggada bei den Kirchenvätern und in der apokryphischen Literatur*, Berlin: Calvary.

idem: 1909–46, *The Legends of the Jews.* 7 vols. Philadelphia: JPS (referred to as *Legends*).

Ginsburger, M.: 1900, "Verbotene Thargumim," *MGWJ* 44, 1–7.

idem: 1903, *Pseudo-Jonathan.* (See above under "Pseudo-Jonathan").

Goldberg, A. M.: 1963, "Die spezifische Verwendung des Terminus Schekhinah im Targum Onkelos als Kriterium einer relativen Datierung," *Judaica* 19, 43–61.

idem: 1969, *Untersuchungen über die Vorstellung von der Schekhinah in der frühen rabbinischen Literatur.* Studia Judaica V. Berlin: De Gruyter.

Golomb, D. M.: 1983, "Nominal Syntax in the Language of Codex Neofiti I: Sentences Containing a Predicate Adjective," *JNES* 42, 181–194.

Gordon, R.P.: See above, Cathcart, K.J., and Gordon, R.P.

idem: 1985, *A Grammar of Targum Neofiti.* Harvard Semitic Monographs 34. Chico, Calif.: Scholars Press.

Gottlieb, W.: 1944, "Targum Jonathan ben Uzziel to the Torah" (in Hebrew), *Melilah* 1, 26–34.

Grelot, P.: 1959, "Les Targum du Pentateuque. Étude comparative d'après Genèse IV, 3-16," *Semitica* 9, 59–88.

idem: 1963, "L'exégèse messianique d'Isaïe LXIII, 1-6," *RB* 70, 371–380.

idem: 1972, Review of R. Le Déaut-J. Robert, *Targum des Chroniques*, in *Biblica* 53, 132–137.

Gronemann, S.: 1879, *Die Jonathan'sche Pentateuch-Uebersetzung in ihrem Verhältnisse zur Halacha.* Leipzig: Friese.

Grossfeld, B.: 1973, "Targum Onkelos and Rabbinic Interpretation to Genesis 2:1, 2," *JJS* 24, 176–178.

idem: 1979, "The Relationship Between Biblical Hebrew *brh* and *nws* and Their Corresponding Aramaic Equivalents in the Targum—*'rq, 'pk, 'zl*: A Preliminary Study in Aramaic-Hebrew Lexicography," *ZAW* 91, 107–123.

idem: 1988, *The Targum Onqelos to Genesis.* The Aramaic Bible 6. Wilmington, Del.: Michael Glazier.

idem: 1992, *An Analytic Commentary of the Targum Neofiti to Genesis: Including Full Rabbinic Parallels.* New York: Ktav. Cited as Grossfeld, *Neofiti*.

Grossfeld, B., and Aberbach, M.: 1976, *Targum Onqelos on Genesis 49.* SBL Aramaic Studies I. Missoula, Mont.: Scholars Press.

Grossfeld, B., and Aberbach, M.: 1982, *Targum Onqelos to Genesis.* New York: Ktav.

Havazelet, M.: 1976, "Parallel References to the Haggadah in the Targum Jonathan Ben 'Uziel and Neofiti: Genesis, Exodus and Leviticus," *JJS* 27, 412–418.

Hayward, C.T.R.: 1974, "The Memra of *YHWH* and the Development of its use in Targum Neofiti I," *JJS* 25, 412–418.

idem: 1980, "Memra and Shekhina: A Short Note," *JJS* 31, 210–213.

idem: 1981, *Divine Name and Presence: The Memra.* Totowa, N.J.: Allanheld, Osmun.

idem: 1987, *The Targum of Jeremiah.* The Aramaic Bible 12. Wilmington, Del.: Michael Glazier.

idem: 1989, "The Date of Targum Pseudo-Jonathan: Some Comments," *JJS* 40, 7–30.

Heinemann, J., *Aggadah and Its Development* (in Hebrew). Jerusalem: Keter, 1974.

Heller, B., "Muhammedanisches und Antimuhammedanisches in den Pirke Rabbi Eliezer," *MGWJ* 69 (1925) 47–54.

Herr, M.D., "Pirkei de-Rabbi Eliezer," *EJ* 13, 558–560.

Isenberg, S.: 1970, "An Anti-Sadducee Polemic in the Palestinian Targum Tradition," *Harvard Theological Review* 63, 433–444.

Isenberg, S. R.: 1968, *Studies in the Jewish Aramaic Translations of the Pentateuch.* Unpublished Ph.D. dissertation. Harvard University.

idem: 1971, "On the Jewish-Palestinian Origins of the Peshitta to the Pentateuch," *JBL* 90, 69–81.

Itzchaky, E.: 1982, *The Halakah in Targum Jerushalmi I.* Pseudo-Jonathan b. Uzziel and Its Exegetic Methods (in Hebrew). Unpublished Ph.D. dissertation. Ramat-Gan: Bar-Ilan University.

idem: 1985, "Targum Yerushalmi I and the School of R. Ishmael" (in Hebrew). *Sidra* 1, 45–57.

Jastrow, M.: 1950 (etc.; reprints; preface 1903), *A Dictionary of the Targumim, the Talmud Babli and Yerushalmi, and the Midrashic Literature.* 2 vols. New York: Pardes.

Jaubert, A.: 1963, L'image de la colonne (1 Timothée 3, 15)," in *Studiorum Paulinorum Congressus Internationalis Catholicus 1961.* Analecta Biblica 17–18. 2 vols. Rome: Pontifical Biblical Institute, vol. 2, 101–108.

Jerome, *Hebraicae quaestiones in Libro Geneseos.* Ed. P. De Lagarde (in CCL 72, 1–56, Turnhout: Brepols, 1959).

Kadari, M.Z.: 1963, "The Use of *d*-clauses in the language of Targum Onkelos," *Textus* 3, 36–59.

Kahle, P.: 1930, *Masoreten des Westens* II. Stuttgart: Kohlhammer.

idem: 1959, *The Cairo Geniza.* 2nd ed. Oxford: Blackwell.

Kasher, M.: 1974, *Torah Shelemah.* Vol. 24. *Targumey ha-Torah. Aramaic Versions of the Bible. A Comprehensive Study of Onkelos, Jonathan, Jerusalem Targums and the Full Jerusalem Targum of Vatican Neofiti 1.* Jerusalem.

Kasher, R.: 1976–77, "A Targumic Tosephta to Gen 2:1-3" (in Hebrew), *Sinay* 78, 9–17.

idem: 1986, "Targumic Conflations in the MS Neofiti I" (in Hebrew). *HUCA* 57, Hebrew section 1–19.

Kasowski, Ch.J: 1940, *Osar Leshon ha-Onkelos. Concordance to Targum Onkelos.* 2 vols. Jerusalem.

Kaufman, S. A.: 1973, review of J.P.M. van der Ploeg *et al., The Job Targum from Qumran, JAOS,* 93, 317–327.

idem: 1976 review of G. J. Kuiper, *The Pseudo-Jonathan Targum and Its Relationship to Targum Onkelos, JNES* 35, 61–62.

Klein, M. L.: 1974, "Notes on the Printed Edition of MS Neofiti I," *JSS* 19, 216–230.

idem: 1975, "A New Edition of Pseudo-Jonathan," *JBL* 94, 277–279.

idem: 1976, "Converse Translation: A Targumic Technique," *Biblica* 57, 515–537.

idem: 1979, "The Preposition *qdm* ('before'), a Pseudo-Anti-Anthropomorphism in the Targum," *JTS* n.s. 30, 502–507.

idem: 1980, *The Fragment-Targums of the Pentateuch.* 2 vols. Rome: Biblical Institute Press.

idem: 1981, "The Translation of Anthropomorphisms and Anthropopathisms in the Targumim," *VTSupp* 32, 162–177.

idem: 1982, *Anthropomorphisms and Anthropopathisms in the Targumim of the Pentateuch*, with parallel citations from the Septuagint (in Hebrew). Jerusalem: Makor.

idem, 1982A, "Associative and Complementary Translation in the Targumim," *Eretzisrael*, 16 (H. M. Orlinsky volume), 134*–140*.

idem: 1986, *Genizah Manuscripts of Palestinian Targum to the Pentateuch.* Cincinnati: Hebrew Union College Press.

idem: 1988, "Not to be Translated in Public—*l' mtrgm bṣybwr*." *JJS* 39, 80–91.

Komlosh, Y.: 1963, "The Aggadah in the Targums of Jacob's Blessing" (in Hebrew), *Bar Ilan* 1, (= P. Churgin memorial volume), 195–206.

idem: 1968, "Characteristic Tendencies in Targum Onqelos" (in Hebrew), *Bar Ilan* 6, 181–190.

idem: 1973, *The Bible in the Light of the Aramaic Translations* (in Hebrew). Bar-Ilan University: Dvir.

idem: 1977, "Characteristics of Targum Neophyti of Exodus" (in Hebrew), in *Proceedings of the Sixth World Congress of Jewish Studies.* Jerusalem: Academic Press, 1, 183–189.

Kosmala, H.: 1979, 1963, "At the End of Days," in *Messianism in the Talmudic Era.* Ed. L. Landman. New York: Ktav, 1979, 302–312. This essay was originally published in the *Annual of the Swedish Theological Institute* 2 (1963) 23–37.

Krauss, S., "Die biblische Völkertafel im Talmud, Midrasch und Targum," *MGWJ* 39 (1895), 1–11; 49–63.

Kuiper, G. J.: 1968, "A Study of the Relationship Between *A Genesis Apocryphon* and the Pentateuchal Targumim in Genesis 14, 1-12," in *In Memoriam Paul Kahle.* Beihefte zur Zeitschrift für die alttestamentliche Wissenschaft 103. Eds. M. Black and G. Fohrer, Berlin: Töpelmann.

idem: 1972, *The Pseudo-Jonathan Targum and Its Relationship to Targum Onkelos.* Studia Ephemeridis "Augustinianum" 9. Rome: Institutum Patristicum "Augustinianum."

Kutscher, E. Y.: 1957, 1965, "The Language of 'Genesis Apocryphon,'" in *Scripta Hierosolymitana* IV. Eds. Ch. Rabin and Y. Yadin. 2nd ed. Jerusalem: Magnes, 1965, 1–35.

idem: 1976, *Studies in Galilean Aramaic*. Bar Ilan Studies in Near Eastern Languages and Culture. Trans. from Hebrew and annotated with additional notes by M. Sokoloff. Jerusalem: Ahva.

Lazry, G.: 1968, "Some Remarks on the Jewish Dialectical Aramaic of Palestine During the First Centuries of the Christian Era," *Augustinianum* 8, 468–476.

Le Déaut, R.: 1963, *La Nuit pascale. Essai sur la signification de la Paque juive à partir du Targum d'Exode XII, 42*. Rome: Pontifical Biblical Institute.

idem: 1966, *Introduction à la littérature Targumique*. Première partie. Rome: Pontifical Biblical Institute.

idem: 1968, "Lévitique 22:26–23:34 dans le Targum Palestinien. De l'importance des gloses du Codex Neofiti I," *VT* 18, 458–471.

idem: 1970, "Aspects de l'intercession dans le Judaïsme ancien," *JStJ* 1, 35–57.

idem: 1974, "The Current State of Targumic Studies," *Biblical Theology Bulletin* 4, 3–32.

idem: with J. Robert: 1978, 1979, 1980, *Targum du Pentateuque. Traduction des deux recensions Palestiniennes complètes*. 4 vols. Trans. R. Le Déaut with J. Robert. Sources Chrétiennes 245, 256, 261, 271. Paris: Cerf. Vol. 1, *Genèse*, 1978; vol. 2, *Exode et Lévitique*, 1979; vol. 3, *Nombres*, 1979; vol. 4, *Deutéronome*, 1980.

idem: 1987, "Quelques usages de la racine *ZMN* das les Targums du Pentateuque," in *La vie de la Parole. De l'Ancien au Nouveau Testament*. Études . . . offertes à P. Grelot. Paris: Desclée, 1987, 71–78.

Le Déaut, R., and Robert, J.: 1971, *Targum des Chroniques*. 2 vols. Analecta Biblica 51. Rome: Biblical Institute Press.

Lehmann, M. R.: "1QGenesis Apocryphon in the Light of the Targumim and Midrashim," *Revue de Qumran*, 1 (1958–59) 249–263.

Lentzen-Deis, F.: 1970, *Die Taufe Jesu nach den Synoptikern*. Frankfurt am Main: Knecht.

Levey, S. H.: 1974, *The Messiah: An Aramaic Interpretation*. The Messianic Exegesis of the Targum. Monographs of the Hebrew Union College 2. Cincinnati/New York: Hebrew Union College-Jewish Institute of Religion.

Levine, E.: 1968, "Contradictory Sources in Targum Jonathan ben Uzziel" (in Hebrew). *Sinay* 64, 36–38.

idem: 1970, "The Aggadah in Targum Jonathan ben 'Uzziel and Neofiti 1 to Genesis: Parallel References," in *Neophyti I*. Ed. A. Díez Macho (see above under "Neofiti"). Vol. 2, *Exodo*, 537–578.

idem: 1971A, "Some Characteristics of Pseudo-Jonathan Targum to Genesis," *Augustinianum* 11, 89–103.

idem: 1971B, "A Study of Targum Pseudo-Jonathan to Exodus," *Sefarad* 31, 27–48.

idem: 1972, "British Museum Aramaic Additional MS 27031," *Manuscripta* 16, 3–13.

Levine, E. B.: 1969, "Internal Contradictions in Targum Jonathan ben Uzziel to Genesis," *Augustinianum* 9, 118–119.

Levy, Barry B.: 1986, 1987, *Targum Neophyti 1. A Textual Study.* Vol. 1, Introduction, Genesis, Exodus; vol. 2, Leviticus, Numbers, Deuteronomy. Lanham, New York, London: University Press of America.

Levy, J., 1881, 1966, *Chaldäisches Wörterbuch über die Targumim und einen grossen Theil des rabbinischen Schriftthums.* Leipzig; reprint Köln: Melzer, 1966.

idem: 1924, *Wörterbuch über die Talmudim und Midraschim.* 4 vols. Reprint of 2nd ed. (Berlin-Vienna). Darmstadt: Wissenschaftliche Buchgesellschaft, 1963.

Liebermann, S.: 1962, *Hellenism in Jewish Palestine* 2. New York: Jewish Theological Seminary, 2nd ed.

Loader, J. A.: 1978, "Onqelos Genesis 1 and the Structure of the Hebrew Text," *JStJ* 9, 198–204.

Lund, S., and Foster, J.: 1977, *Variant Versions of Targumic Traditions Within Codex Neofiti I. SBL*, Aramaic Studies 2. Missoula: Scholars Press.

Luzarraga, J.: 1973, *Las tradiciones de la nube en la Biblia y en el judaísmo primitivo.* Analecta Biblica 54. Rome: Pontifical Biblical Institute.

McCarthy, C.: 1981, *The Tiqqune Sopherim and other Theological Corrections in the Masoretic Text of the Old Testament.* Freiburg (Schweiz) and Göttingen.

idem: 1989, "The Treatment of Biblical Anthropomorphisms in the Pentateuchal Targums," *Back to the Sources.* Biblical and Near Eastern Studies in Honour of Dermot Ryan. Ed. K. Cathcart and J. F. Healey. Dublin, 1989.

McNamara, M.: 1966A, *The New Testament and the Palestinian Targum to the Pentateuch.* Analecta Biblica 27. Rome: Pontifical Biblical Institute, 1966; reprint 1978.

idem: 1966B, "Some Early Rabbinic Citations and the Palestinian Targum to the Pentateuch," *Rivista degli studi orientali* 41, 1–15.

idem: 1972, *Targum and Testament.* Aramaic Paraphrases of the Hebrew Bible: A Light on the New Testament. Shannon: Irish University Press.

idem: 1977, "The Spoken Aramaic of First Century Palestine," in *Church Ministry.* Ed. A. Mayes. Proceedings of the Irish Biblical Association 2. Dublin: Dominican Publications.

idem: 1983A, *Palestinian Judaism and the New Testament.* Wilmington, Del.: Michael Glazier.

idem: 1983B, *Intertestamental Literature.* Wilmington, Del.: Michael Glazier.

idem: 1986, "On Englishing the Targums," in *Salvación en la Palabra*, ed. D. Muñoz León, 447–461.

Maher, M.: 1971, "Some Aspects of Torah in Judaism," *Irish Theological Quarterly* 38, 310–325.

idem: 1988, *Targum Pseudo-Jonathan of Exodus 1–4*. Ph.D. dissertation, National University of Ireland (University College Dublin).

Mann, J.: 1940, *The Bible as Read and Preached in the Old Synagogue*. Vol I. The Palestinian Triennial Cycle: Genesis and Exodus. Cincinnati, 1940. Reprint with Prolegomenon by B. Z. Wacholder. New York: Ktav, 1971.

Maori, Y.: 1975, *The Peshitta Version of the Pentateuch in Its Relation to the Sources of Jewish Exegesis* (in Hebrew). Unpublished Ph.D. dissertation. Hebrew University, Jerusalem.

idem: 1983, "The Relationship of Targum Pseudo-Jonathan to Halakhic Sources" (in Hebrew). *Te'uda* 3, 235–250.

Marmorstein, A.: 1905, *Studien zum Pseudo-Jonathan Targum*. Pozsony: Alkalay.

Martínez Borobio, E.: 1976, "El Uso de *qdm* y *mn qdm* ante YHWH en la literatura Targumica y las Frases o 'Formulas de Respeto' que se originan," *Miscelánea de Estudios Arabes y Hebräicos* 25, 109–137.

idem: 1975, *Estudios linguisticos sobre el Arameo de MS. Neofiti I*. Madrid: Universidad Complutense.

Maybaum, S.: 1870, *Die Anthropomorphien und Anthropopathien bei Onkelos und den spätern Targumim*. Breslau: Schletter.

Moore, G. F.: 1922, "Intermediaries in Jewish Theology: Memra, Shekinah, Metatron," *Harvard Theological Review* 15, 41–85.

idem: 1927–30, *Judaism in the First Centuries of the Christian Era*. 3 vols. Cambridge, Mass.: Harvard University Press.

Muñoz León, D.: 1974A, *Dios-Palabra. Memra en los Targumim del Pentateuco*. Institución S. Jeronimo 4. Granada.

idem: 1974B, "El 4o de Esdras y el Targum Palestinense," *Estudios Biblicos* 33 (1974) 323–355; 35 (1975) 49–82.

idem: 1977, *Gloria de la Shekina en los Targumim del Pentateuco*. Madrid: Consejo Superior de Investigaciones Científicas. Instituto "Francisco Suarez."

idem (ed.): 1986, *Salvación en la Palabra, Targum. Derash. Berith*. En memoria del profesor Alejandro Díez Macho, Madrid: Ediciones Cristiandad.

Neubauer, A.: 1868, *La Géographie du Talmud*, Paris: Frères.

Neumark, M.: 1905, *Lexikalische Untersuchungen zur Sprache der jerusalemischen Pentateuch-Targume*. Heft I. Berlin: Poppelauer.

Nickelsburg, G. W. E.: 1984, "The Bible Rewritten and Expanded," in *Jewish Writings of the Second Temple Period*. Ed. M. E. Stone. Assen: Van Gorcum; Philadelphia: Fortress.

Niehoff, M.: 1988, "The Figure of Joseph in the Targums," *JJS* 39, 234–250.

Noah, M. M. (trans.). *Sefer ha-Yashar or The Book of Jasher.* See above under "Translations."

Odeberg, H.: 1939, *The Aramaic Portions of Bereshit Rabba.* With Grammar of Galilean Aramaic. Lunds Universitets Årsskrift. N.F. Avd. 1 Bd. 36. Nr. 4. 2 vols. Lund: Gleerup; Leipzig: Harrassowitz.

Ohana, M.: 1972, *Le Targum Palestinien et la Halaka.* Unpublished doctoral thesis. University of Barcelona.

idem: 1973, "Agneau pascal et circoncision: Le problème de la Halakha Prémishnaïque dans le Targum palestinien," *VT* 23, 385–399.

idem: 1974, "Prosélytisme et Targum palestinien: Données nouvelles pour la datation de Néofiti 1," *Biblica* 55, 317–332.

idem: 1975, "La polémique judéo-islamique et l'image d'Ismaël dans Targum Pseudo-Jonathan et dans Pirke de Rabbi Éliezer," *Augustinianum* 15, 367–387.

Pérez-Fernández, M.: 1981, *Tradiciones Mesiánicas en el Targum Palestinense.* Estudios exegéticos. Institución San Jerónimo 12. Valencia-Jerusalem: Institución San Jerónimo-Casa de Santiago.

idem: 1984, "Versiones targúmicas de Génesis 3,22-24," in *Simposio Biblico Español* (Salamanca, 1982). Eds. N. Fernández Marcos, J. Trebolle Barrera, J. Fernández Vallina. Madrid: Universidad Complutense, pp. 457–475.

Petermann, I. H., *De duabus Pentateuchi paraphrasibus chaldaicis.* Part I. *De indole paraphraseos, quae Ionathanis esse dicitur.* Berlin: Academic Press, 1829.

Peters, C.: 1934, "Targum und Praevulgata des Pentateuchs," *Oriens Christianus* 31, 49–54.

idem: 1935, "Peschittha und Targumim des Pentateuchs," *Le Muséon* 48, 1–54.

Philo. *Philo with an English Translation.* Ed. and trans. F. H. Colson, and G. H. Whitaker. 10 vols. and 2 supplementary vols. Loeb Classical Library. London: Heinemann; Cambridge, Mass.: Harvard University Press, 1929–41. Reprint 1956–62.

Prigent, P.: 1974, "*In Principio.* A propos d'un livre récent," *RHPR* 54, 391–397.

Pseudo-Philo. *Pseudo-Philo's Liber Antiquitatum Biblicarum.* Ed. G. Kish. Publications in Mediaeval Studies. Notre Dame, Ind.: University of Notre Dame, 1949.

Rappaport, S.: 1930, *Agada und Exegese bei Flavius Josephus.* Vienna: Alexander Kohut Memorial Foundation.

Rashi, *Pentateuch with Targum Onkelos, Haphtaroth and Rashi's Commentary.* Hebrew text with trans. by M. Rosenbaum and A. M. Silbermann with A. Blashki and L. Joseph. 5 vols. Jerusalem: Silbermann Family, 1973.

Revel, D.: 1924–25, "Targum Jonathan to the Torah" (in Hebrew). *Ner Ma'aravi* 2, 17–122.

Ribera, J.: 1983, "La expreción aramaica *mn qdm* y su traducción," *Aula Orientalis* 1, 114–115.

Ribera i Florit, J.: 1983B, "Evolución morfológica y semantica de las particulas *k'n* y *'ry* en los diversos estadios del arameo," *Aula Orientalis*, 227–233.

idem: 1984, "Elementos comunes del Targum a los Profetas y del Targum Palestinense," in *Simposio Biblico Español*. Salamanca, 1982. Ed. N. Fernández Marcos, J. Trebolle Barreta, J. Fernández Vallina. Madrid: Universidad Complutense, pp. 487–493.

Rieder, D.: 1965, "Comments and Clarifications on Targum Jonathan ben Uzziel" (in Hebrew), *Sinay* 56, 116–119.

idem: 1968, "On the Ginsburger Edition of the 'Pseudo-Jonathan' Targum of the Torah" (in Hebrew), *Leshônenu* 32, 298–303.

idem: 1974, 1984–1985, *Pseudo-Jonathan*; see above under "Editions of Texts," p. 232.

idem: 1975, "Comments on the Aggadot in Targum Jonathan b. Uzziel to the Torah" (in Hebrew), *Beth Miqra* 20, 428–431.

Rodríguez Carmona, A.: 1978, *Targum y resurrección. Estudio de los textos del Targum Palestinense sobre la resurrección*. Granada.

idem: 1980, "Nota sobre el vocabulario sacerdotal en el Targum Palestinense," *Cuadernos Biblicos* 4, 71–74.

Sandmel, S.: 1955, "Philo's Place in Judaism: A Study of Conceptions of Abraham in Jewish Literature, II," *HVCA* 26, 151–332.

Schäfer, J. P.: 1970, "Die Termini 'Heiliger Geist' und 'Geist der Prophetie' in den Targumim und das Verhältnis der Targumim zueinander," *VT* 20, 304–314.

Schäfer, P.: 1971, "Berešit Bara' 'Elohim. Zur Interpretation von Genesis 1,1 in der rabbinischen Literatur," *JStJ* 2, 161–166.

idem: 1971–72, "Der Grundtext von Targum Pseudo-Jonathan. Eine synoptische Studie zu Gen 1." Das Institutum Judaicum der Universität Tübingen, 8–29.

idem: 1972, *Die Vorstellung vom Heiligen Geist in der Rabbinischen Literatur*. Munich: Kösel.

idem: 1975, *Rivalität zwischen Engeln und Menschen*. Untersuchungen zur rabbinischen Engelvorstellung. Berlin-New York: de Gruyter.

Schmerler, B.: 1932, *Sefer Ahavat Yehonathan. Genesis* (in Hebrew). Bilgary.

Schulthess, F.: 1924, *Grammatik des Christlich-Palästinischen Aramäisch*. Tübingen: Mohr (Siebeck).

Schürer, E.: 1973, 1979, 1980, *The History of the Jewish People in the Age of Jesus Christ (175 B.C.–A.D. 135)*. A new English version revised and edited by G. Vermes, F. Millar, M. Black. Literary editor P. Vermes. 3 vols. Edinburgh: T & T Clark, 1973, 1979, 1987.

Seligsohn, H.: 1858, *De duabus Hierosolymitanis Pentateuchi paraphasibus*. Particula 1: De origine hierosolymitanae utriusque paraphasis ex onkelosiana Pentateuchi versione ducenda. Bratislava.

Seligsohn, H., and Traub, J.: 1857, "Ueber den Geist der Uebersetzung des Jonathan ben Usiel zum Pentateuch und die Abfassung des in den Editionen dieser Uebersetzung beigedruckten Targum jeruschalmi," *MGWJ* 6, 96–114, 138–149.

Shinan, A.: 1975, "'Their Prayers and Petitions.' The Prayers of the Ancients in the Light of the Pentateuchal Targums" (in Hebrew), *Sinay* 78, 89–92.

idem: 1975–76, "*lyšn byt qwdš'* in the Aramaic Targums of the Torah" (in Hebrew), *Beth Miqra* 21, 472–474.

idem: 1976, "'And the Lord put a Mark on Cain.' On Targum Pseudo-Jonathan to Gen 4:15" (in Hebrew), *Tarbiz* 45, 148–150.

idem: 1977A, "Midrashic Parallels to Targumic Traditions," *JStJ* 8, 185–191.

idem: 1977B, "The Aramaic Targums of the Creation Story and Ps 104" (in Hebrew), *Shnaton* 2, 228–232.

idem: 1979, *The Aggadah in the Aramaic Targums to the Pentateuch* (in Hebrew). 2 vols. Jerusalem: Makor.

idem: 1982, "A Word to the Wise Is Sufficient" (in Hebrew), *Criticism and Interpretation* 18, 69–77.

idem: 1982–83, "The Theoretical Principles of the Meturgemanim" (in Hebrew), *Jerusalem Studies in Jewish Thought* 2, 7–32.

idem: 1983A, "Folk Elements in the Aramaic Targum Pseudo-Jonathan" (in Hebrew), in *Studies in Aggadah and Jewish Folklore*. Presented to Dov Noy on his 60th Birthday. Ed. I. Ben-Ami and J. Dan. Jerusalem: Magnes, 139–155.

idem: 1983B, "Miracles, Wonders and Magic in the Aramaic Targums of the Pentateuch" (in Hebrew), in *Essays on the Bible and the Ancient Near East*. Festschrift I. L. Seeligman. 2 vols. Ed. A. Rofé and Y. Zakovitch. Jerusalem: Rubinstein, 2, 419–426.

idem: 1983C, "The Angelology of the 'Palestinian' Targums on the Pentateuch," *Sefarad* 43, 181–198.

idem: 1985, "The 'Palestinian' Targums—Repetitions, Internal Unity, Contradictions," *JJS* 36, 72–87.

idem: 1986, "On the Characteristics of Targum Pseudo-Jonathan to the Torah" (in Hebrew), in *Proceedings of the Ninth World Congress of Jewish Studies*. Jerusalem: World Union of Jewish Studies, 109–116.

idem: 1990, "Dating Targum Pseudo-Jonathan: Some More Comments," *JJS* 41, 57–61.

Silverstone, A. E.: 1931, *Aquila and Onkelos*. Manchester: University Press.

Skinner, J.: 1912, *Genesis*. The International Critical Commentary. Edinburgh: T & T Clark.

Sokoloff, M.: 1980, "Notes on the Vocabulary of Galilean Aramaic" (in Hebrew), in *Studies in Hebrew and Semitic Languages*. Dedicated to the Memory of E. Y.

Kutscher. Ed. G. B. Safratti, P. Artzi, J. C. Greenfield, and M. Kadarri. Ramat-Gan: Bar-Ilan University, 166–173.

idem: 1990, *A Dictionary of Jewish Palestinian Aramaic of the Byzantine Period.* Ramat-Gan, Israel: Bar-Ilan University.

Speier, S.: 1966–67, 1969–70, "The Relationship Between the 'Arukh' and 'Targum Neofiti I'" (in Hebrew), *Leshonenu* 31 (1966–67) 23–32; 34 (1969–70) 172–179.

Speiser, E. A.: 1964, *Genesis.* The Anchor Bible. New York: Doubleday.

Sperber, A.: 1934–35, "The Targum Onkelos," *PAAJR* 6 (1934–35) 309–351.

idem: 1959. See above under "Editions of Texts: Onqelos."

Spiegel, S.: 1967, *The Last Trial.* New York: Random House.

Splansky, D. M.: 1981, *Targum Pseudo-Jonathan: Its Relationship to Other Targumim, Use of Midrashim and Date.* Unpublished Ph.D. dissertation, Hebrew Union College, Cincinnati.

Stemberger, G.: 1974, "Die Patriarchenbilder der Katakombe in der Via Latina," *Kairos* 16, 50–76.

Strack, H. L. and Billerbeck, P.: 1922–69, *Kommentar zum Neuen Testament aus Talmud und Midrasch.* 4 vols. Munich: Beck.

Strack, H. L., and Stemberger, G.: 1982, *Einleitung in Talmud und Midrasch.* 7th ed. Beck'sche Elementarbücher. Munich: Beck. Eng. trans. by M. Bockmuehl, *Introduction to the Talmud and Midrash,* Edinburgh: T & T Clark, 1991.

Syrén, R.: 1986, *The Blessings in the Targums. A Study on the Targumic Interpretations of Genesis 49 and Deuteronomy 33.* Acta Academiae Abonensis, ser. A., vol. 64, nr. 1. Åbo: Åbo Akademi.

Tal (Rosenthal), A.: 1974, "MS Neophyti I: The Palestinian Targum to the Pentateuch. Observations on the Artistry of a Scribe," *Israel Oriental Studies* 4, 31–43.

idem: 1975, *The Language of the Targum of the Former Prophets and Its Position Within the Aramaic Dialects* (in Hebrew). Texts and Studies in the Hebrew Language and Related Subjects 1. Tel-Aviv: Tel-Aviv University.

idem (Tal, A.): 1979–80, "Studies in Palestinian Aramaic," *Leshonenu* 44, 43–65.

Towner, W. S.: 1973, *The Rabbinic Enumeration of Scriptural Examples.* Leiden: Brill.

Urbach, E. E.: 1975, *The Sages. Their Concepts and Beliefs.* 2 vols. English trans. Jerusalem: Magnes.

Vermes, G.: 1961, *Scripture and Tradition in Judaism.* Studia Post-Biblica 4. Leiden: Brill; 2nd rev. ed. 1973.

idem: 1963A, "The Targumic Versions of Genesis IV 3-16," *Annual of Leeds University Oriental Society* 3 (1961–62) 81–114.

idem: 1963B, 1975, "Haggadah in the Onkelos Targum," *JJS* 8 (1963) 159–169. Reprint in G. Vermes, *Post-Biblical Jewish Studies.* Studies in Judaism in Late Antiquity. Leiden: Brill, 1975, 127–138.

idem: 1978, "The Impact of the Dead Sea Scrolls on Jewish Studies During the Last Twenty-Five Years," in *Approaches to Ancient Judaism: Theory and Practice.* Ed. W. G. Scott. Brown Judaic Studies I. Missoula: Scholars Press, 201–214.

Vorster, W. S.: 1971, "The Use of the Prepositional Phrase *bmymr'* in the Neofiti I Version of Genesis," in *De Fructu Oris Sui.* Essays in Honour of Adrianus van Selms. Pretoria Oriental Series. Ed. J. H. Eybers, F. C. Fensham, et al., Leiden: Brill.

Wieder, A. A.: 1974, "Three Philological Notes," *Bulletin of the Institute of Jewish Studies* 2, 103–109.

York, A. D.: 1974, "The Dating of Targumic Literature," *JStJ* 5, 49–62.

idem: 1979, "The Targum in the Synagogue and in the School," *JStJ* 10, 74–86.

Zunz, L.: 1892, *Die gottesdienstlichen Vorträge der Juden, historisch entwickelt.* 2nd ed. Frankfurt am Main: Kaufmann; this work, supplemented by H. Albeck, has been republished in Hebrew, Jerusalem, 1942.

INDEXES

BIBLICAL

SAMARITAN PENTATEUCH

TARGUMIM
Targum Onqelos

Pseudo-Jonathan

Palestinian Targum (General)

Neofiti 1

Neofiti Margins

Fragment Targums (General)

Manuscript P

Manuscript V

Genesis	
1:27	18
3:7	21
3:20	18
4:7	62
4:10	20
6:8	73
6:14	19
10:2	18, 22, 23
10:3	22
10:4	18, 22
10:10	22
10:11	20
10:13	22
10:14	22
10:17	22, 23
10:18	18, 20, 22
11:22	23
12:15	20
14:9	23
14:14	22
15:1	19
19:1	21, 103
19:2	20
19:31	20
21:13	21
22:10	21, 39
22:14	17
24:2	122
24:10	18
25:16	19
25:19	56
25:25	21
26:16	20
27:40	61
27:45	21
28:10	38
28:12	18
31:29	20
32:16	19
34:12	21
35:9	18
37:3, 33	20
37:25	23
37:36	21
38:25	17, 20, 39
38:26	64
39:4	18
39:13	19
40:12	20
40:16	19
41:43	19

43:30	19
44:18	18
44:19	20
47:11	22
47:21	20
49:19	21
49:21	20, 21
49:22	19
50:1	20

Exodus	
1:1	23
1:8	20
1:11	22
2:12	38
8:5	21
12:42	23
14:24, 25	20
17:11	36
19:3	38
19:21	20
22:15	21
24:10	21
26:32	17
27:4	19
27:9	18
28:18	19
28:19	21
28:20	20, 21
28:42	18
32:5, 18	19
32:6	36
34:33	21
35:11	20

Leviticus	
1:1	38
5:15	32
10:20	19
19:9	20
22:27	27
23:29	76
24:20	27
25:34	20

Numbers	
4:7	21
7:13	21, 32
11:12	20

11:18	19
12:7	19
12:16	19
17:3	21
20:17	21
21:6	20, 39
21:29	19
23:9	20
24:19	23
24:24	19, 20, 22
24:29	19
31:22, 50	19
32:52	18
33:3	22
34:5	22
34:6	20, 22
34:7, 8	22
34:9	23
34:11	22
34:15	22, 23
35:2, 4	20

Deuteronomy	
1:1	21
1:44	22
2:8	22
3:11	18
3:14	22
6:3	31
17:8	105
19:5	21
20:11	21
22:3	21
22:20, 21	27
24:13	21
25:15	31
27:3	31
27:18	20
28:68	19
32:4	20
32:10	21
32:14	22
32:29	19
32:42	20
32:43	19
33:2	22
33:10	21
33:21	20
33:23	22
33:29	20
34:1	22

Manuscript N

Genesis	
4:7	62
6:8	73
10:2, 3, 14	22
10:18	18
12:15	20

19:1	103
22:10	39
24:2	122
25:19	56
27:40	61
28:10	38

36:6 (7)	20
38:25	39
38:26	64
39:4	18
40:16	19
49:22	19

Manuscript L

Cairo Genizah Pal. Tg. Fragments

Targum Nebi'im

Targum Ketubim

ANCIENT VERSIONS

RABBINIC

I. Tosefta, Mishnah, Talmud

II. Midrash

POST-BIBLICAL
Qumran

Apocrypha and Pseudepigrapha

Early Jewish Writers

Early Christian Writers

AUTHORS